PSYCHOLOGY
APPLIED
TO TEACHING

SECOND EDITION

Psychology Applied to Teaching

SECOND EDITION

ROBERT F. BIEHLER
California State University, Chico

HOUGHTON MIFFLIN COMPANY • BOSTON
Atlanta   Dallas   Geneva, Ill.   Hopewell, N.J.   Palo Alto   London

Material reprinted by permission of the publisher from Millie Almy, *Young Children's Thinking*. (New York: Teachers College Press, copyright 1966 by Teachers College, Columbia University), pp. vi, 42, 48, 129–130.

Material from *Teaching: A Course in Applied Psychology* by Wesley C. Becker, Siegfried Engelmann, and Don R. Thomas. © 1971, Science Research Associates, Inc. Reprinted by permission of the publisher.

Material abridged from the books *Taxonomy of Educational Objectives, Handbook I: Cognitive Domain*, edited by Benjamin S. Bloom, copyright 1956 by David McKay Company, Inc., and *Taxonomy of Educational Objectives, Handbook II: Affective Domain* by David R. Krathwohl, Benjamin S. Bloom, and Bertram B. Masia, copyright © 1964 by David McKay Company, Inc. Reprinted by permission of the publisher.

Material from *The Process of Education* by Jerome S. Bruner is reprinted by permission of Harvard University Press. Copyright © 1960 Harvard University Press.

Material from *Toward a Theory of Instruction* by Jerome S. Bruner is reprinted by permission of Harvard University Press. Copyright © 1966 The Belknap Press of Harvard University Press.

Material from *The Lives of Children*, by George Dennison. Copyright © 1969 by George Dennison. Reprinted by permission of Random House, Inc. and Penguin Books Ltd./Allen Lane The Penguin Press.

Material from "Experience and Education," by John Dewey, The Kappa Delta Pi Lecture Series, Copyright, 1938 by Kappa Delta Pi, by permission of Kappa Delta Pi, An Honor Society in Education.

Material from *The Transfer of Learning* by Henry C. Ellis reprinted with permission of Macmillan Publishing Co., Inc. Copyright © 1965 by Henry C. Ellis.

Material from Herbert Ginsburg and Sylvia Opper, *Piaget's Theory of Intellectual Development: An Intro-* duction, © 1969, pages 176, 204–205, 221. By permission of Prentice-Hall, Inc., Englewood Cliffs, New Jersey.

Material from *How to Survive in Your Native Land* by James Herndon. Copyright © 1971, by James Herndon. Reprinted by permission of Simon and Schuster and Barthold Fles, Literary Agent.

Material from *The Way It Spozed to Be* by James Herndon. Copyright © 1965, 1968, by James Herndon. Reprinted by permission of Simon and Schuster and Barthold Fles, Literary Agent.

Material from *Toward a Psychology of Being*, 2nd ed. by Abraham H. Maslow © 1968 by Litton Educational Publishing, Inc. Reprinted by permission of Van Nostrand Reinhold Company.

Material from *The Greening of America*, by Charles A. Reich. Copyright © 1970 by Charles A. Reich. Reprinted by permission of Random House, Inc. A portion of the book originally appeared in *The New Yorker* in somewhat different form.

Material from *Beyond Freedom and Dignity*, by B. F. Skinner. Copyright © 1971 by B. F. Skinner. Reprinted by permission of Alfred A. Knopf, Inc.

Material quoted from page 235, *The Technology of Teaching* by B. F. Skinner is reprinted by permission of Appleton-Century-Crofts. Copyright © 1968 by Meredith Corporation. Material quoted from Chapter 3 of *The Technology of Teaching* was originally published in "Teaching Machines," by B. F. Skinner in *Science*, Vol. 128, pp. 969–977, 24 October 1958, and is reprinted by permission of the publisher and the author. Material quoted from Chapter 5 of *The Technology of Teaching* was originally published in "Why Teachers Fail" by B. F. Skinner in *Saturday Review*, October 16, 1965. Copyright 1965 by Saturday Review Co. First appeared in *Saturday Review*, October 16, 1965. Used with permission.

Printed in the U.S.A.

Library of Congress Catalog Card Number: 73-9190

ISBN: 0-395-17168-7

PREFACE

A TEXT IN A FIELD SUCH AS EDUCATIONAL PSYCHOLOGY MUST ALWAYS be in a continual process of development. An author who feels he has done an up-to-date job summarizing current knowledge sends off a manuscript one day only to receive the next a book or journal that calls attention to new information. An experiment that seemed destined to have a profound impact on education loses significance when replications fail to corroborate initial conclusions. An educational technique that led to dramatic increases in measured learning when practiced by those who developed it turns out to have a negligible or even negative effect when others try it out under carefully controlled conditions. Letters are received calling attention to sections of the first edition of a text that are seen as incomplete or misleading. The author's own interpretations change as he tries to fit new information from books and journals and reactions from students and colleagues into his conception of the structure of the field. When the manuscript for a revision has been completely edited and sent to the printer, the author discovers—even as he reads the proofs—that he is already thinking about ways to improve the next revision. All of these factors—and more—have contributed to the desire to make available a second edition of *Psychology Applied to Teaching*.

The changes that have been made are based on experiences using the first edition with over four hundred students. Thirty-six professors who used the first edition have provided feedback, either on their own initiative or at my request. The manuscript for the second edition was read in whole or in part by ten reviewers. Thus, this revision is based not only on my own experiences in using *Psychology Applied to Teaching* but also on the reactions of many students and colleagues.

Features of the first edition that have been retained because they were well received include the general format and design, wide margins, lists of Key Points, and "functional" illustrations. Since not all students made use of the write-in spaces, these have been reduced. The major change in format is the replacement of the brief end-of-chapter bibliographies with updated and expanded versions of the "Suggestions for Further Reading, Writing, Thinking, and Discussion" that were included in the Study Guide for the first edition. This shift has been made because it appeared that merely listing a few books at the end of a chapter rarely led to further reading. The Study Guide "Suggestions," on the other hand, seemed to provide sufficient direction to stimulate supplementary reading, observation, or experimentation. Unfortunately, only students who were asked to obtain the Study Guide were aware of these "Suggestions." To make them available to all readers of the text, and to increase the likelihood that interest aroused by a point made in a chapter might be sustained or increased by suggestions made in the same section of the text, they have been placed at the end of each chapter. Also to be found at the ends of several chapters are lists of recommended readings in *Psychology Applied to Teaching: Selected Readings* (1972), which provide extended commentaries on points noted in the chapters or mentioned in the "Suggestions."

The questions on the Key Points in the revised Study Guide for this edition are intended to help the student master the ideas about educational psychology presented in the text to the point of being able to apply them to teaching. The sixty-five projects for research, observation, and analysis in Part 2 of the Guide may be either formally assigned or used for independent study. Their purpose is to help the student function as a teacher-theorist by acquainting him with scientific methods and giving him experience in observing and recording behavior. The Guide has been punched and its pages perforated to make it possible both to keep it as a handy supplement in a binder with class notes and to allow individual study projects given as supplementary assignments to be handed in.

Changes in content can be summarized most succinctly chapter by chapter:

Chapter 1, Prologue — The discussion of empirical-inductive and theoretical-deductive approaches to science has been replaced by an analysis of current developments in education and psychology including performance contracting, accountability, free schools, and open education, and by analyses of the inequality of educational opportunity. Different aspects of the teacher-theorist concept noted in Chapters 1 and 2 of the first edition have been shortened and consolidated. In keeping with the interest in educational objectives stemming from the emergence of accountability and related developments, basic purposes of education are analyzed with reference to goals described by Virginia Voeks.

Chapter 2, Background for a Teacher-Theorist — Jerome Bruner's classic statement on the nature and importance of transfer (which appeared in Chapter 1 of the first edition) is placed at the beginning of this chapter to explain the rationale of the text. The brief outline of associationism and field theory intended to serve as an advance organizer has been retained, but the discussion of positions on development and the outline of the nature-nurture controversy have been dropped. These latter topics have been replaced by an analysis of the historical development and current status of "controlled" and "free" education. Since many students of educational psychology are confused because they fail to comprehend that different theorists have basically different conceptions of psychology as a science, Maslow's description of humanistic psychology has been moved from Chapter 9 to Chapter 2 to emphasize differences between this conception and the behaviorist-associationist view. Statements by John Dewey are used to summarize points covered in the first two chapters and to establish the theme that a teacher should seek a balance between controlled and free approaches to education.

Chapter 3, Development: Principles and Theories — Discussions of the work of Gesell and his associates have been replaced by a presentation of Erik H. Erikson's theory of development. The section on Piaget has been revised, expanded, and clarified, and his influence on the open education movement is explained. Differences between the views of Piaget and Bruner have been made more explicit.

Chapter 4, Age-Level Characteristics — Lists of Havighurst's developmental tasks for each age level have been replaced by Erikson's stages, the implications of which are treated in sections after each set of grade levels. The implications of the theories of Piaget and Bruner have been revised and expanded to tie in with the revisions in Chapter 3. Erikson's stage of identity vs. role confusion is used as the main theme in the "implications" section on high school, and this is related to an analysis of Kenneth Keniston's views on adolescence, which in turn leads to a discussion of drug use and abuse.

Chapter 5, Two Views of the Learning Process — Sections on behavior modification and computer assisted instruction and an example of a branching program have been added to the discussion of programmed learning. Techniques of open education are described, and the importance of the gradual, orderly implementation of such methods is stressed. The chapter concludes with a section relating what has been discussed to material in preceding chapters, and with an analysis of some basic differences in underlying assumptions. Gordon Allport's comparison of the views of Locke and Leibnitz is used for this purpose.

Chapter 6, Teaching Different Types of Learning — This chapter opens with an analysis of instructional objectives, including observations by Mager, Gronlund, Ebel, and Ojemann. The section on Gagné's conditions of learning has been revised, clarified, and expanded.

Chapter 7, Minimizing Forgetting, Maximizing Transfer — A brief section on short-term and long-term memory has been added, and Mager's views on how to teach to increase the likelihood of approach tendencies appear at the end of the chapter.

Chapter 8, Teaching Skills and Attitudes — The discussion of the Jacob study has been dropped; a new section describes the development of methods for encouraging attitudes proposed by Kohlberg, Raths and his colleagues, and Bronfenbrenner.

Chapter 9, Motivation: Theory and Applications — Substantial changes have been made. The treatment of some aspects of Maslow's theory has been shortened since a general description of it now appears in Chapter 2. The section on Maslow's conception of a choice situation involving safety and growth, which appeared in Chapter 14 of the first edition, has been shifted to this chapter. The work of McClelland and Atkinson and others on achievement motivation has been incorporated into the discussion of level of aspiration. As background for the analysis of goals to strive for in arranging motivational experiences, controlled and free approaches to motivation are contrasted. The "Suggestions for Arousing and Sustaining Interest in Learning" have been reorganized, expanded, and clarified, and related to new material in early chapters.

Chapter 10, Teaching the Disadvantaged — This chapter has been almost completely rewritten. The views of Coleman, Jencks, and others on inequality of educational opportunity are summarized and a brief description of factors typical of the disadvantaged is provided. The bulk of the chapter is organized in terms of descriptions of programmed and discovery approaches to teaching the disadvantaged, which are then summarized in the form of "Suggestions for Teaching the Disadvantaged" arranged to parallel those offered in the preceding chapter on motivation.

Chapter 11, Evaluating Classroom Learning — Much of the material first presented in this chapter has been reorganized to encourage the reader to engage in a critical examination of the purposes of tests and grades. A section on National Assessment has been added. A major addition is a comprehensive description of how a mastery learning approach might be instituted.

Chapter 12, Evaluating Achievement and Learning Ability — The descriptions of classic experiments relating to the relative impact of heredity and environment on intelligence have been dropped, since it is difficult to select and present data on this controversial topic without favoring a particular point of view. Instead, the nature-nurture debate is presented with reference to the views of Skinner, Huxley, Jensen, Herrnstein, and Hunt. The section on group tests has been revised and expanded; the discussion of creativity and intelligence has been dropped.

Chapter 13, Teaching Exceptional Students — The section on teaching techniques for use with slow learners has been completely revised. The section on the Doman and Delacato technique has been dropped.

Chapter 14, Teaching to Encourage Need Gratification — Various sections of this chapter that impressed some readers as ambiguous or misleading have been clarified.

Chapter 15, Establishing a Favorable Classroom Environment — A section on the use of behavior modification techniques has been added.

Chapter 16, Teaching for Your Own Self-Actualization, and 17, Epilogue — Only minor changes have been made.

A major goal of the first edition was to provide analyses of what were perceived to be strengths and weaknesses of different points of view so that the reader could make up his own mind. Student reactions and communications from professors have been taken as evidence that this goal was reasonably well achieved. For example, a half dozen professors criticized the book because it was so heavily slanted in favor of programmed instruction and so critical of the discovery approach. An equal number criticized it because it was so heavily slanted in favor of the discovery approach and so critical of programmed instruction. These reactions — plus statements of appreciation for the way in which different points of view were given *equal* treatment — have led to the conclusion that the analyses of the strengths and weaknesses of different approaches should be retained essentially as they were presented in the first edition.

I would like to express my appreciation to Marjorie Roberts for converting rough drafts and revision after revision into a final, beautifully prepared manuscript; and to the following psychologists for offering comprehensive or detailed suggestions for making this second edition of *Psychology Applied to Teaching* an improvement over the first: James A. Adams, John S. Baird, Michael Bradley, Richard Brozovich, William Carse, Alice T. Clark, Donald L. Clark, Ruth E. Cook, W. A. Downie, James E. Dunning, Dale S. Farland, Robert W. Fernie, Shirley H. Grossman, Mary Frances Holman, Jesse Lair, Russell G. Langton, Mary T. Littlejohn, Marianne Lynch, Phelon J. Malouf, Douglas McClennen, J. Michael O'Malley, Ellis B. Page, Sister Loretta Petit, Neal T. Pinckney, Daniel Reschly, Orlando A. Rivera, R. G. Rossmiller, John G. Safarik, Mary Schilling, Frank J. Sparzo, Bert Speece, Paul L. Ward, Dennis A. Warner, Nina Westcott, Ben F. Williams, Roger Wood, and Donald D. Young.

Robert F. Biehler

EXPLANATION OF LISTS OF OBJECTIVES

BENJAMIN BLOOM HAS DONE MUCH TO MAKE EDUCATORS MORE AWARE of the importance of formulating objectives as a basis for organizing learning experiences and for making evaluation more logical and effective. He has taken the lead by developing a taxonomy of educational objectives (described in Chapter 6, pp. 297ff., and Chapter 8, pp. 390ff.), which serves as a focus for listing goals, and he has also stressed the value of *learning for mastery* (discussed in Chapter 1, pp. 11–13, and in Chapter 11, pp. 548–563). According to the latter concept, a student should be evaluated on the basis of objectives he has achieved, or mastered, rather than his performance as compared with that of fellow students; the reason for this is that a relative-performance approach to evaluation assumes that only a minority of students are capable of high quality work.

This book presents two kinds of objectives, both of them in terms of an organizational frame of reference derived from the taxonomy of educational objectives developed by Bloom and his associates. One group of objectives consists of the lists of Key Points that appear at the beginning of each chapter to help you grasp the highlights and organization of the presentation, to focus your attention on ideas considered especially important, and to serve the instructor (if he so desires) as the basis for assignments and for examinations to evaluate mastery.

The second group of objectives is made up of more general goals: skills, attitudes, and general cognitive abilities. The attempt to enable you to achieve these goals is made in terms of the overall presentation, not just in specific chapters or sections of chapters, so this list is provided only at the beginning of the book — in the section after this one.

Regarding the development of instructional objectives, it has been argued that there are many advantages to formulating and stating *explicit* goals that are based on *observable performance*, for example, "The student is able to count to 100," as opposed to vague generalizations, for example, "The student appreciates the concept of number." This point of view has been emphasized by Robert Mager (1962), Ralph Tyler (1964), and John DeCecco (1968). They argue that when a teacher provides a list of specific instructional goals, not only is he better able to take steps to see that the objectives are achieved but also the goals themselves guide the students directly toward mastery. Furthermore, specific objectives readily serve as the basis for test items, and evaluation is an important, if not indispensable, part of education.

Although these advantages are impressive, there are potential pitfalls in listing explicit objectives. Robert Ebel observes:

Defining educational objectives in terms of desired behavior . . . appears to assume that despite the highly complex and rapidly changing world in which we live, a teacher can know ahead of time how the scholar ought to behave in a given set of circumstances. It also seems to assume that the teacher is entitled to prescribe his behavior for him. . . . It seems important to suggest strongly that the proper starting point of educational planning in a democracy is not the kind of behaviors present adults desire future adults to exhibit, but rather the kind of equipment that will enable them to choose their own behaviors intelligently. (1972, pp. 62–64)

In a sense, these observations by Ebel reflect the complaint of students who resent having to "memorize and regurgitate" what the teacher says is important. It is possible that a student who is told in advance exactly what he should learn and then specifically asked to demonstrate that he is temporarily able to supply the preselected answer on demand will feel that he is being manipulated and that he is performing at a simple-minded and perhaps ignominious level. It also seems possible that overemphasis of points selected by the instructor will limit the depth and variety of reading and thinking that students would do if allowed more freedom to react in terms of their own interests and inclinations.

In an effort to balance the advantages and shortcomings of listing goals, the Key Points in this book are offered simply as the points that one psychologist feels are desirable for you at least to think about as you prepare for a career as a teacher. The points have been organized under the following headings: Facts, Trends and Sequences, Classifications, Criteria, Experiments, (or Experiments and Studies), Concepts, Principles, Theories, and Methodology. Although the basic classification scheme is derived from Bloom's taxonomy of educational objectives, many of his categories have been omitted and a few new ones added.

The rationale for this sequence is that facts, trends, classifications, criteria, and experiments serve as the foundation for concepts, principles, and theories, and these in turn should serve — as much as possible — as the basis for pedagogic methods. If you are asked to explain what you have read in the text by answering questions based on the Key Points, you will have the opportunity to test your ability to apply and interrelate information learned. (To help you do this, Key Points are printed in color in the margin.)

The basic premise of this book is that understanding selected facts, concepts, and principles in psychology will help you solve problems of pedagogy. Even though you may not be able to anticipate at this time the potential value of some of the information presented, you are asked to accept the probability that mastering the basic points in this text will enhance your resources for functioning as a creative, innovative, versatile educator later on. Teaching is an art, and each person who practices an art should be allowed maximum freedom to function in a way that expresses his unique personality. But any artist is more likely to make the most of his unique abilities if he is provided with "equipment that will enable him to choose his own behaviors intelligently." If you adopt this standpoint in viewing examinations and lists of key ideas to be emphasized on examinations, you will not look upon them as threats to individuality. Especially keep in mind that once you begin teaching you will be free to use all concepts as you please, whether you mastered them because they were emphasized by your teacher or simply for your own benefit.

In view of the observations just noted, you are urged to follow this procedure in using the lists of Key Points at the beginning of each chapter:

1. Before reading a chapter, look over the list in order to preview what are considered the most important ideas.

2. Read the chapter in its entirety to gain an overall impression of what is discussed, to react generally to it, and to select particular ideas that have personal relevance. (Extra-wide margins are provided so that you can add notes.)

3. Refer back to the list of Key Points as a guide for rereading the chapter, particularly if the list is to be used as the basis for examinations. Testing yourself *before* exams by attempting to explain each point should prove an efficient and well-organized method of study.)

(Note: A Study Guide has been prepared to help you master material presented in the text and also to encourage you to engage in reading and involvement with points mentioned. For each chapter of the text two kinds of study aids are presented in the Guide: questions designed to help you test and improve your mastery of Key Points [particularly in preparation for examinations] and suggested topics for further reading and research.)

GENERAL OBJECTIVES

This book has been written to help you achieve the following general goals:

COGNITIVE DOMAIN

Translation
Translate discussions of psychology and teaching into proper and consistent classroom applications.

Interpretation
Interpret books and articles about new developments in psychology and education and know their limitations and implications.

Extrapolation
Theorize about the possible impact of various approaches to teaching.

Draw conclusions from articles, books, and sets of data.

Application
Apply principles of psychology to classroom practice.

Analysis
Make critical analyses of studies, theories, and practices in psychology and education.

Synthesis
Integrate separate ideas and principles into more or less consistent approaches to teaching.

Relate new concepts to already existing theories and practices.

Evaluation
Evaluate the effectiveness of various theories and techniques of teaching.

AFFECTIVE DOMAIN

Awareness
Be aware of the possible impact of a Zeitgeist on the conceptions of a theorist.

Be aware of the impact of personal involvement and cognitive dissonance on the way individuals conduct research and interpret data.

Develop awareness of the interrelationships between different approaches and conceptualizations, for example, science and the humanities.

Willingness to receive
Develop a tolerance for different points of view.

Feel free to develop a personal style of teaching, selecting ideas from a variety of sources.

Controlled or selected attention
Keep well informed about new developments in psychology and education.

Be sensitive to the way an experiment or theory may be influenced by the beliefs of those who develop and interpret it.

Function as a dispassionate, objective teacher-theorist when appropriate (to minimize the impact of emotional involvement).

Acquiescence in responding
Function as a responsible professional — one who keeps informed on new developments and who understands and upholds codes of professional ethics.

Willingness to respond
Develop the habit of applying the principles of psychology to classroom practice.

Develop the habit of interpreting ideas from a wide variety of sources in terms of the principles of psychology.

Acceptance and commitment to values
Find pleasure in teaching and in reading and speculating about teaching, learning, and human behavior.

Organization of a value system
Try to develop a consistent value system and a coherent philosophy of teaching.

CONTENTS

PART 3   LEARNING

PART 4   MOTIVATION

PART 5   EVALUATION

PART 6   INDIVIDUAL DIFFERENCES AND ADJUSTMENT

PART

BACKGROUND

1 PROLOGUE

KEY POINTS

Trends and Sequences
Education seen as "great equalizer" in 1830s
"Cult of efficiency" in education due to demands for economy
Performance contracting and accountability emerge in 1960s
Free schools develop as alternatives to public education

Classifications
Goals of education (Voeks)

Reports
Social class only characteristic related to school achievement (Coleman Report)
Research on impact of teacher expectancy

Concepts
Meritocracy
Teacher-practitioner, teacher-theorist
Cognitive dissonance, experimenter bias effect, Hawthorne effect
Self-fulfilling prophecy (Pygmalion effect)

Theories
Spontaneous schooling (Stephens)

Methodology
Open education
Learning for mastery
Using scientific methods to avoid false generalizations

CHAPTER CONTENTS

THIS IS PROBABLY THE MOST PERPLEXING BUT ALSO THE MOST ADVAN-tageous time in history for a person to think about becoming a teacher. It is perplexing because many people are questioning whether schools and teachers serve any useful purpose at all. Some speak of completely "deschooling" society (Illich, 1971). Others go to elaborate lengths to form and finance "alternative" schools independent of public educational systems; in some of these schools little or no attempt is made to provide formal instruction of any kind on the grounds that it does more harm than good. Even those who feel that public education has some redeeming features talk of a "crisis" in the classroom (Silberman, 1970). Parents who continue to send their children to public schools may not feel that the situation is critical, but they are voicing concern about the apparent ineffectiveness of the education their children are receiving. At a time when inflation and higher taxes are causing an escalating financial burden, they are more concerned than ever about getting their money's worth. In many cases, a solution is sought by reasoning that since competitive free enterprise has made America the most powerful and productive nation in history, we should therefore apply business methods to education. It is argued—among other things—that schooling will improve if teachers are evaluated in terms of the amount of learning they produce, just as workers are paid according to their productivity.

A teacher confronted with a demand to be more productive may turn for help to those who apply scientific methods to the study of education—only to discover that some theorists interpret available evidence to indicate that students seem to learn the same amount at about the same rate regardless of the type of school and school program (Jencks, 1972a, 1972b). Furthermore, comparisons frequently demonstrate that quite different techniques produce about the same results (Stephens, 1967).

This situation has led many teachers and parents—and even more students—to question previously accepted ideas about the purposes, techniques, and values of education. This is why you have a special advantage as you think about a teaching career. Never before have so many thought and written so much about education; never before have so many experiments with different approaches to schooling taken place at one time. As a result, you have an unparalleled opportunity to examine basic questions about education, weigh the values of different theories—some of which are diametrically opposed—and actually observe widely varying types of schooling.

The fact that you are reading these opening pages suggests that you are thinking about becoming a teacher. As you start to read this book, you are probably asking yourself many questions: Does it make sense to try to *become* a teacher? Even if you are sure you want to become a teacher, is there any point in studying *how* to teach? Does anyone know enough to help? How can you be sure techniques advocated by one person are any better than those proposed by someone else? Even if you become convinced that some people know something of value about teaching, can they communicate this to others, or are teachers born rather than made? Even if you are sure you want to teach and find someone who seems able to give you what appears to be potentially valuable information, will you be able to find a satisfying job once you have learned about teaching? If you obtain a job in a public school and achieve the security of tenure, a steady though modest salary, and fringe benefits, must you inevitably lose your sense of integrity or find yourself compelled to teach in such a way that you destroy your pupils' individuality and creativity? If you take a position in an "alternative" school, will you have any sense of permanence or security, or earn enough to live in reasonable comfort?

You will have to do considerable soul-searching and probably make more than a few trials and errors before you find answers to these questions. The purpose of this book is to help you come to some tentative conclusions. By way of introduction, and to provide some perspective, this chapter will trace current trends in American education to historical developments and relate them to questions about teacher preparation and to the purposes and potential values of education.

Early Developments in American Education

In the early 1800s, schooling beyond the elementary grades was restricted for the most part to a privileged minority. Then, with the arrival of large numbers of immigrants, compulsory education was extended through high school. The schools were to provide *all* children—regardless of their background—with equivalent skills. Horace Mann, a lawyer and secretary of the Massachusetts Board of Education and one of the most influential spokesmen on education in the 1830s and 1840s, wrote that education would become "the great equalizer of the conditions of men—the balance wheel of the social machinery" (Cremin, 1957, p. 87). Those who endorsed this policy did not at first realize that a system that provides opportunities for individuals to achieve success through their own efforts also is a competitive system. The number of jobs that offer high prestige and remuneration is always limited, and many of the most desired occupations usually require higher education. As efforts to provide educational opportunities for all American youth continued, places in colleges and universities that previously had been reserved for young people from families of wealth and social position gradually were offered to anyone who could prove his worth as a scholar. In order to select the best students, however, it was necessary to compare students. As a result, instead of functioning as a "great equalizer," the schools became more and more concerned with sorting students out.

Education seen as "great equalizer" in 1830s

The attempt to provide education for all children also caused problems because of the sheer numbers of students and teachers involved. Schools inevitably reflect the culture in which they exist, and at the beginning of this century—when mass-production methods were being perfected—solutions to problems of education were sought through the application of practices that had proven successful in business and industry. Raymond E. Callahan (1962) has described how equating the school with the factory led to a conception of pupils as raw material to be converted into finished products. In time, attempts were made to "produce" different types of graduates by placing some students in college preparatory programs and others in vocational programs, further accentuating the sorting-out function of the schools.

"Cult of efficiency"

Because a democratic form of government stresses involvement of citizens, schools were organized to permit parents to exert considerable control. Economy became a major concern of voters, leading to what Callahan refers to as a "cult of efficiency" in American education.

These three factors—the competitive nature of our society, the application

6

Some observers see similarities in the assembly-line methods used to produce automobiles—and college graduates.

COURTESY OF EDUCATIONAL AFFAIRS DEPARTMENT, FORD MOTOR COMPANY

PHOTO BY BRUCE DAVIDSON/MAGNUM PHOTOS, INC.

of business methods to education, and the pressure exerted by citizens concerned with efficiency—have contributed to the development of schools in which students are sorted out as they progress through what is essentially an academic assembly line and in which there is considerable emphasis on productivity in education.

Recent Developments in American Education

Recent developments in American education illustrate how the factors just noted continue to influence schooling.

Performance Contracting

Within the last few years *performance contracting*—a technique that epitomizes American business methods—has emerged on the educational scene. A school district that has many students who are deficient in some skill, such as reading or arithmetic, hires an independent company (typically, created for the specific task at hand) to produce an agreed-upon amount of improvement within a given period of time. If the students do not achieve the established level, and the company fails to meet the terms of the contract, it is not paid. If the students exceed that level, the company receives a bonus. The approach most performance contractors follow is to break down what is to be learned into a series of steps (just as a job in industry is arranged for assembly-line production) and reward the student for each correct response (just as workers are paid for what they produce). In most cases, simply discovering that an answer is correct is the reward, but many companies use tangible rewards. For supplying a correct answer (or completing a program), a student may be given candy or money, or tokens that can be traded in for prizes. In some cases, teachers are rewarded (with a bonus of several hundred dollars) if they are especially successful in inducing their students to learn. And in an experiment financed by the Office of Economic Opportunity, *parents* of children who did well in certain programs were paid bonuses.

Performance contracting

Accountability

A second current development illustrating the impact of historical trends in American education is *accountability*. This refers to the demand (noted earlier) by many parents and school board members that teachers should be held accountable for the amount of learning they produce. The emergence of this concept can be traced to many influences in addition to the general factors already noted: reports that many American students are deficient in basic skills; general dissatisfaction with education; the suspicion held by some parents that new developments featuring greater student initiative mean that teachers no longer do their jobs conscientiously; and a job market in which many applicants

Accountability

8

are competing for a limited number of jobs, leading to a conviction among school boards that only the best (most productive) teachers should be retained.

Many parents want to make sure their children have productive teachers because they are convinced that doing well in school is a necessary first step to becoming successful in America. They endorse the idea that school *should* be competitive and want proof—in the form of high grades, above-average achievement test scores, and admission to prestigious colleges—that their children have learned the necessary information and skills to do well. However, more and more parents are questioning this conception of education. Arguments that the traditional American approach to education is destructive are being endorsed by an increasing number of people.

Paul Goodman maintains in *Compulsory Mis-Education* that the primary goal of our schools is "regimentation and brainwashing" (1964, p. 13). In *Coming of Age in America,* Edgar Z. Friedenberg observes that the fundamental pattern, even in the better schools of America, is one of "control, distrust, and punishment" (1965, p. 37). In *How Children Fail,* John Holt asserts that most children attending public schools in America fail "because they are afraid, bored, and confused. They are afraid, above all else, of failing, of disappointing or displeasing the many anxious adults around them, whose limitless hopes and expectations for them hang over their heads like a cloud" (1964, p. 16). In *The Greening of America,* Charles Reich indicts American schools as being "intensely concerned with training students to stop thinking and start obeying" (1970, p. 143), adding that "one of the great purposes of the school is to indoctrinate the inmates" (p. 145). He says, "In school ... the object is not simply to train each child to function in the State, but to begin the process of arranging everyone in a hierarchy of statuses" (p. 146).

The Free School Point of View

Rejecting school systems that promote such regimentation, control, and failure, many people are turning to schools based on the philosophy of A. S. Neill, founder of Summerhill, the famous progressive school in England: "My view is that a child is innately wise and realistic. If left to himself without adult suggestion of any kind, he will develop as far as he is capable of developing" (1960, p. 4). Many endorse the views of Herbert Kohl, who advocates a free approach to education in *The Open Classroom* (1969), or those of George

Many American parents and school board members believe that students —and in some cases, teachers—should compete against each other. The competitive nature of our society was satirized by Jules Feiffer in his interpretation of our reaction to the launching of Russia's Sputnik, the first man-made earth satellite, in 1957. Up to the time Neil Armstrong stepped off the ladder of Apollo II in 1969, the United States spent $35,595,000,000—or approximately $700 for every family—to make sure we would be *first* to land a man on the moon.

Dennison, who notes in *The Lives of Children,* "When the conventional routines of a school are abolished (the military discipline, the schedules, the punishments and rewards, the standardization), what arises is neither a vacuum or chaos, but rather a new order, based first on relationships between adults and children . . ." (1969, p. 9), or those of Carl Rogers, who in *Freedom to Learn* (1969) advocates self-directed experiential learning.

Free schools as alternatives to public education

Parents who agree with some or all of these observations are sending their children to independent *alternative* or *free, schools.* Many of them are discovering, however, that such schools are not free of problems. A basic difficulty is that parents must pay taxes to support the public school system and also pay tuition to finance the free school. Consequently, most free schools operate on a budget that usually results in a less than satisfactory school building, inadequate materials, and low salaries. In addition, the expectation that free schools will automatically bring about the "new order" of congenial relationships described by Dennison seems to be realized in only a few instances. As Jonathan Kozol has put it, "Free schools in all sections of the nation often prove to be of almost irresistible attraction to some of the most unhappy and essentially aggressive people on the face of the wide world" (1972, p. 65). A related point is the fact that those who are drawn to the free schools are, naturally enough, inclined to express freedom in the way they live. Because they covet personal freedom, they often find it difficult to make compromises or come to agreement with others. They also are highly mobile. Consequently, many free schools disband after only a few months, either because of philosophical differences or because the founders move elsewhere. Differences over school policy are such a common problem that Kozol, in *Free Schools,* recommends that the preferred organizational arrangement for such a school be that of a benevolent dictatorship, with one person making all the major decisions. A teacher in a *public* school, therefore, might have more freedom than one in a free school who must do exactly what the director says or risk being fired. (Few free schools have tenure regulations to protect teachers from sudden dismissal.)

Open Education

Other parents who are bothered by the regimented, competitive aspects of the traditional public school, are showing interest in what is frequently referred to as *open education.*[1] This form of schooling has been most completely developed

[1] In this book, the term *traditional public school* refers to a tax-supported school in which teachers are responsible for presenting a prescribed standard curriculum and students are evaluated according to a scale of relative performance, for example, from A to F. The terms *free schools* and *alternative schools* are used interchangeably; they refer to schools set up outside the public educational system that stress a student-centered approach and noncomparative grading. *Open education* refers to the type of schooling being developed in Great Britain and North Dakota. You should remain aware, however, that some educators use these terms in different and not always consistent ways; for example, "free" and "open" may be used as synonyms or to refer to *either* a Summerhill *or* British-North Dakota approach, and "alternative school" may be used to refer to a public school with an innovative curriculum.

by British educators who have come under the influence of the Swiss psychologist Jean Piaget. Piaget has demonstrated that children do not think the ways adults do and that they have their own ways of experimenting, absorbing, and analyzing experiences. Many primary-grade teachers in Britain have taken account of Piaget's observations and arrange their classrooms and curricula so that children *Open education* can learn from direct personal experience and from each other. In the United States, this approach to education is being developed in a highly systematic way in the entire school system of North Dakota and less comprehensively by many teachers who divide their classrooms into learning centers, allow considerable freedom of choice, and encourage their pupils to interact in self-selected groups.

Learning for Mastery

Another development designed to minimize the competitive pursuit of grades and test scores is the *learning for mastery* approach proposed by Benjamin Bloom (1969). Bloom points out that the traditional comparative grading system has evolved in such a way that we have lost sight of the degree to which it limits learning. Grading "on the curve" is probably as much a product of the concern of American psychologists for objectivity and measurement as it is of competitiveness. Most American psychologists, in studying behavior, stress accurate observation, precise measurement, and statistical analysis of results. As a consequence, all kinds of evaluation techniques have been perfected. In most cases, these have been used primarily to differentiate among groups and individuals—partly because this is what the school system has been expected to do, partly because psychologists are usually interested in observing differences among groups that have been exposed to different conditions. Bloom has called attention to the fact that this preoccupation with measuring differences among students and assigning grades on an A-to-F scale has led to a situation where only students in the top third of any class are likely to feel that they have been successful. As a result, the majority of students come to think of themselves as incapable of learning, and their teachers may think the same way.

To correct for this fatalistic and defeatist viewpoint, Bloom recommends that we assume, first, that all students can learn and, second, that the basic differences among students—if *any* differences are recognized—should be measured not by how much and how well they learn in a fixed period of time, but rather by how long it takes them to learn a fixed amount of material. He also recommends that tests be used to diagnose and instruct, not to discriminate. In a mastery approach, educational objectives are specified, materials are developed to assist *Learning for mastery* students to achieve them, and those who have difficulty in gaining mastery are given additional opportunities and remedial instruction. Under ideal circumstances almost all students eventually achieve mastery, and competitiveness is reduced considerably.

FRANK SITEMAN

RON BENVENISTI/MAGNUM PHOTOS, INC.

The learning centers and emphases on individual study, in open classrooms contrast markedly with the traditional approach to curricula and teaching methods.

Learning for mastery holds promise as a means for improving schooling, but the difficulties of providing education in a competitive society are complex. In *Excellence,* John Gardner points out that competition causes aspirations to soar and ambition to be stirred but that it also leads to anxiety and frustration. He notes that when competition becomes too extreme, the strong and capable thrive, but the less able feel defeated and incompetent. This often frustrates the less able into attempts to hold back the more competent. However, in such an equalitarian society, few people achieve their potential, and the level of functioning of the society as a whole is determined by the lowest common denominator. America is still primarily a competitive society that uses its educational system to perform a preliminary sorting out of those most likely to succeed—in terms of jobs that carry with them influence, responsibility, and high pay. As Gardner notes, "The schools are the golden avenue of opportunity for able youngsters, but by the same token they are the arena in which less able youngsters discover their limitations" (1961, p. 66). Awareness of this has led to some of the criticisms of the traditional public school.

Inequality of Educational Opportunity

Although some parents and educators reject competitive education, many people still defend the basic belief that America *should* be a *meritocracy,* which appropriately rewards those who are able to demonstrate their merit. They also believe that the educational system should funnel the most promising students into the "best" colleges and thence into the most important jobs; a basic argument in support of this policy is that it is the essence of democracy to give all children an equal chance to prove their worth. Evidence has accumulated, however, suggesting that the system falls far short of giving all children an equal chance. Jerome Karabel has said: "Higher education is inextricably linked to the transmission of inequality from generation to generation. . . . The entire process helps insure that the already affluent receive an education which enables them to retain their privilege and position" (1972, p. 39). Karabel suggests that one way to equalize educational opportunity is to establish an open admissions policy in all institutions of higher learning—particularly the most selective colleges, which produce a disproportionately large number of graduates who "succeed." Students who attend these colleges do well, Karabel maintains, because only those who show exceptional promise are accepted; the business and professional communities—cognizant of the screening that the educational system has carried out for them—compete for graduates of these schools. Thus those with the most favored backgrounds are given the best education and the greatest opportunities for advancement. Some people feel this is as it should be, but Karabel argues that we should think of education in different terms. He notes: "The higher education system should concern itself with maximizing the educational growth of the student, whatever his level at entrance. The critical variable is the 'value

Meritocracy

added' by college attendance; a truly successful institution would change a student's performance level rather than insure its own prestige by 'picking winners' through a stringent selection process" (p. 40). The same point could be applied to education at other levels.

The Coleman Report and Its Implications

The key to this solution lies in finding ways to maximize educational growth. Educators and governmental officials have for years been searching for techniques that will produce "value added" schooling. They have been concerned particularly about those who do not do well in school. Among other things, the Civil Rights Act of 1964 directed the United States Office of Education to undertake a survey to determine "the lack of availability of equal educational opportunities for individuals by reason of race, color, religion, or national origin in public education institutions." James S. Coleman of Johns Hopkins University was selected to head a team of researchers that over a two-year period obtained data from over 4,000 schools, 60,000 teachers, and 570,000 students. The results were presented in 1966 in *Equality of Educational Opportunity*, often called the Coleman Report. Instead of finding evidence—as expected—of identifiable inequalities in educational opportunity and that more successful students were being exposed to "better" forms of instruction, Coleman and his colleagues discovered that no particular school characteristic had a measurable positive impact on student achievement. The only characteristic that showed a consistent relationship to academic performance was the social class of the student body. Children from middle- and upper-class homes did better than those from disadvantaged backgrounds.

Coleman Report

Significance of social class

The Coleman Report aroused considerable controversy and was scrutinized by dozens of critics. One comprehensive analysis was undertaken by Frederick Mosteller and Daniel P. Moynihan, who spent three years collecting critiques of the report. They published their conclusions in *On Equality of Educational Opportunity*, and the general consensus of the contributors was that the Coleman study was an accurate reflection of the situation.

Among the articles in the Mosteller and Moynihan book is an essay (Chapter 4) by Coleman in which he notes that one of the most significant contributions of *Equality of Educational Opportunity* was that it changed the definition of equality of educational opportunity from equality of resources (inputs) to equality of achievement (output). The result is that educators are now more concerned with finding inputs that will bring about positive changes in academic achievement. This accords with Karabel's point that schools should be primarily

> "Coleman and his colleagues discovered that . . . the only characteristic which showed a consistent relationship to academic performance was the social class of the student body."

Is Socialism the Only Way to "Equalize" America?*

Jencks has written a more complete analysis of points noted in his article in the Mosteller and Moynihan book under the title *Inequality: A Reassessment of the Effect of Family and Schooling in America.* He interprets the evidence in the Coleman Report and related analyses as indicating that most attempts to bring about equality through the educational system have failed, including desegregation, busing, providing extra funds for educational programs, and Head Start and other forms of compensatory education. He observes, "There is no evidence that school reform can substantially reduce the extent of cognitive inequality, as measured by tests of verbal fluency, reading comprehension, or mathematical skill. Neither school resources nor segregation has an appreciable effect on either test scores or educational attainment" (1972a, p. 8). He explains the ineffectiveness of educational reform by suggesting that children are influenced much more by what happens outside of school than by what happens in the classroom. (Some observers maintain that the superior school performance of upper- and middle-class students is due not to better forms of education but to the "hidden curriculum" of the home.) He also believes that the relationship between teacher and pupil is more important than the curriculum or methods of instruction.

Jencks maintains that the schools have been asked to do too much and that inequality of opportunity in the society as a whole will remain until inequalities in income and environmental conditions are reduced. In order to accomplish this, he says, "We will have to establish political control over the economic institutions that shape our society. This is what other countries usually call socialism. Anything less will end in the same disappointment as the reforms of the 1960s" (p. 265).

Inequality is sure to arouse considerable controversy, and you are urged, in reading this book, to make your own interpretations as background for evaluating the interpretations of others. Even though substantial reduction of inequality in American life may require political action, it would seem desirable for teachers to continue doing what they can to assist disadvantaged students in developing the skills and attitudes with which they can compete for better jobs. It does not seem likely, given the present political situation, that socialism will be established in the near future. Nor does it seem likely that compulsory school laws will be changed. Since children will continue to attend schools, it makes sense to do everything possible to make the most of educational opportunities that do exist.

* This is the first of many boxes that appear throughout this book. They serve as parenthetical amplifications of points made in the text and frequently take the form of questions for you to consider. It is felt that you are more likely to react to such questions by considering them in the relevant section of the text rather than by reading them at the end of the chapter. If you prefer to read through a section, however, without making even such slight digressions, you can skip these supplementary notes and read them after you have reached the end of the section. But if you like to tangle with ideas as they crop up, you may wish to stop and read the boxes en route.

concerned with a "value added" view of education. Still unanswered, however, is the question of which pedagogical techniques show the greatest promise for bringing about positive changes in academic achievement. The possibility of finding simple or clear-cut answers seems remote.

Christopher Jencks (1972b) analyzed many variables in the Coleman Report data and found none that had any clearly identifiable relationship to academic achievement. Among the variables were physical facilities, length of school day or school year, whether pupils had attended kindergarten, pupil turnover, teachers' salaries, the kind of college the teachers attended, whether teachers held advanced degrees or not, and whether teachers were black or white. J. M. Stephens (1967) carried out a similar analysis by comparing reviews of research on the relative effectiveness of different factors, methods, and procedures in teaching (including size of class and school, individualized instruction, ways of selecting and training teachers, ability grouping, discussion versus lecture, group-centered versus teacher-centered approaches, the use of television, and programmed instruction). He reached the same general conclusion as Jencks: essentially the same results were obtained regardless of the approach.

The Teacher-Practitioner and Teacher-Theorist

These findings may lead you to wonder if there is any point in preparing yourself to become a teacher. It might appear that no matter what you do, the results will be the same—and that you should therefore simply do what comes naturally. Up to a point this is probably a good policy, one that Stephens suggests as a general guideline. After discovering that most techniques produce the same results, he proposed a theory of *spontaneous schooling,* which urges teachers to feel free to select teaching methods that fit their styles and personalities—or those of different groups of pupils—since various methods seem to lead to the same amount of learning. Thus the "spontaneous" element recommended by Stephens stresses freedom of choice; it is not the same as a totally "intuitive" or unplanned approach to teaching. Some educators have argued that teaching is an art that cannot be practiced—or even studied—in an objective or scientific manner. For example, Gilbert Highet, a distinguished professor of literature, explains the title of his *The Art of Teaching* as follows:

Theory of spontaneous schooling (Stephens)

[This book] is called *The Art of Teaching* because I believe that teaching is an art, not a science. It seems to me very dangerous to apply the aims and methods of science to human beings as individuals, although a statistical principle can often be used to explain their behavior in large groups and a scientific diagnosis of their physical structure is always valuable. But a "scientific" relationship between human beings is bound to be inadequate and perhaps distorted. Of course it is necessary for any teacher to be orderly in planning his work and precise in his dealing with facts. But that does not make his teaching "scientific." Teaching involves emotions, which cannot be systematically appraised and employed, and human values, which are quite outside the grasp of science. A "scientifically" brought-up child would be a pitiable monster. A "scientific" marriage would be only a thin and crippled version of a true marriage. A "scientific" friendship would be as cold as a chess problem. "Scientific" teaching, even of scientific subjects, will be inadequate as long as both teachers and pupils are human beings. Teaching is not like inducing a chemical reaction: it is much more like painting a picture or making a piece of music, . . . like planting a garden or writing a friendly letter. You must throw your heart into it, you must realize that it cannot all be done by formulas, or you will spoil your work, and your pupils, and yourself. (1957, pp. vii–viii)

As a reaction to Highet's statement, you might find this comment by Paul Woodring (*A Fourth of a Nation*) interesting:

> The fact that teaching is held to be an art rather than a science does not mean . . . that methodology cannot be taught. Every artist learns his methods from another artist who acts as teacher. The genius will develop his own methods, but it cannot be expected that all of the more than a million American teachers will be geniuses.
>
> The fact that Highet has taken time out from a busy life to write an excellent book on *The Art of Teaching* would seem to indicate that he agrees that this art can, at least in some small part, be learned from books. (1957, p. 52)

It seems difficult to argue with Woodring's observation. Even an artist with tremendous creative potential is almost certain to learn some basic techniques at the beginning of his career from an experienced artist who serves as teacher. And the most fervent advocates of a free school approach must believe that the followers of "artistic" or "intuitive" methods of education can learn from others, judging by the number of books they publish. The question remains, however; Is it possible to study the art of teaching scientifically? Or, to be more specific, can the study of educational psychology be of value to future teachers? Stephens suggests that you think of yourself as two prospective teachers within the same individual—a *teacher-practitioner* and a *teacher-theorist*. He explains the reasons for this dual point of view in this way:

Teacher-practitioner
teacher-theorist

> The requirements of the teacher-practitioner and of the teacher-theorist are both very real and very important. They are, however, somewhat different, and the differences in these requirements are nowhere more striking than in the matter of caution versus confidence. There are times, unquestionably, when the teacher-practitioner should not be assailed by doubts or qualifications, when he should carry out with confidence and with decision any course of action that he has undertaken. At these times, any large measure of doubt, uncertainty, or hesitation may seriously reduce his effectiveness.
>
> The hesitation or uncertainty which might work against the practitioner presents no handicap to the theorist. On the contrary, caution, admission of uncertainty, willingness to withhold judgment are of the utmost importance when the teacher-theorist is forming his opinions about the nature of the educational process. The

teacher-theorist, therefore, must receive training in this very necessary practice of entertaining doubts and qualifications. (1956, pp. v–vi)

This volume attempts to keep in mind both the theoretical *and* the practical aspects of teaching. Recognizing the fact that you will need to function as a teacher-practitioner, specific techniques are offered and definite recommendations made. But you will also find frequent speculations about theory that take into account your need to function as a teacher-theorist.

Stephens makes the following additional remarks[2] regarding the theme of the theorist-practitioner:

"Education is a very familiar process . . . . It is a process, moreover, that has been managed at times by rather ordinary people . . . . We can hardly declare educational ideas to be out of bounds for amateurs . . . . Without for a moment ignoring the familiar and common-sense nature of education, we nevertheless must realize that there are few fields in which it is easier to go astray and which are so permeated by misconceptions."

One pitfall is that of wishful thinking. "The professional educator must have considerable faith in the educational process . . . . He must hope and believe that it will accomplish great things . . . . Teaching is often such a warm, emotional, enthusiastic process. It calls for devotion and commitment to a given course of action. It is possible that a cold, analytic attitude of suspended judgment would prevent the teacher from stimulating students and would make for poor rapport. [Compare these views with Highet's.]

"These convictions and emotional commitments which may be so necessary in the practice of education are obvious handicaps in the careful and precise study of education. Enthusiastic feelings or warm hopes should not influence our decisions as to what is so. . . .

"To understand a process, we must try to put our feelings and wishes in cold storage for a time, and having done so, we must try to face the facts with an open mind. But although we must face facts, we need not become the slaves of facts. . . ."

While we are seeking to *understand* a process, we should adopt the scientific attitude. Science can help us understand a process and form trustworthy opinions by calling our attention to common pitfalls in evaluating observations in education and by supplying techniques for avoiding these. Listed below are some of these pitfalls and techniques:

1. Generalizing from one or a few cases. "The scientist tries to have enough cases to rule out mere chance."

2. Generalizing from unusual or outstanding cases. "The tendency to remember and utilize the dramatic incident is always with us. . . ." The scientist tries to avoid this pitfall by selecting cases at random and by making systematic, objective records of behavior.

3. Failure to use a definite control, or comparison, group. Unless one uses such a group, it may be difficult to justify a conclusion.

Using scientific methods to avoid false generalizations

[2] For the sake of brevity, part of this quotation has been paraphrased. Exact quotations are enclosed in quotation marks.

4. Lack of precision in observing, measuring, and describing data. The casual observer seldom uses precise methods in making observations or measurements. The scientist tries to use consistent measuring devices and formal criteria, and makes a precise statement of his results.
5. Uncritical acceptance of a hypothesis. In interpreting relationships, the casual observer may uncritically accept the first plausible hypothesis that presents itself. The scientist tries to list all plausible hypotheses and then tests each one as systematically as possible. (1956, pp. 20–33)

From these comments you can draw an excellent set of precepts for teaching: Have faith in yourself, and keep in mind that teaching should be a warm, emotional, enthusiastic process. But when you *theorize* about education, put your feelings in cold storage for a time, and try to face facts with an open mind. Remain alert to the pitfalls as you gain understanding of a process or relationship, for such alertness may protect you from drawing erroneous conclusions.

Teaching as Testing-of-Hypothesis Behavior

Arthur P. Coladarci has suggested a conception of teaching that amplifies Stephens's notion of the teacher as a theorist and a practitioner. Coladarci feels that the teacher's role is to help the learner change his behavior in specified directions.

> The educator's decisions about methods, materials, and curricular procedures should be thought of as hypotheses regarding the way in which the desired behavior changes can be brought about. These hypotheses must be *tested* continuously by inquiring into the degree to which the predicted behavior actually occurred. [This view is referred to by Coladarci as "teaching behavior defined as testing-of-hypothesis behavior."] The crucial element is *tentativeness;* ideas and decisions about method and curriculum are to be held hypothetically, continuously tested and continuously revised if necessary. (1956, p. 490)

Coladarci argues that an intelligent hypothesizer thinks along the lines of the following model: "On the basis of the best information now available to me, I hypothesize that this procedure will bring about this result." He suggests that educational psychology provides some of the information on which teachers may base hypotheses and also assists them to acquire the attitudes and skills necessary to intelligent hypothesizing and testing of hypotheses (e.g., how to interpret data, how to observe accurately, how to avoid common fallacies in logic).

The bulk of this book provides information for you to use in making hypotheses regarding which techniques of teaching are most promising for a given situation. But emphasis is also placed on the attitudes and skills you will need to acquire to develop and test hypotheses. As you teach, it will be desirable for you to engage in testing-of-hypothesis behavior. Take all the information available, decide which approach to teaching seems most promising, put that approach into operation with enthusiasm and confidence—but be tentative and objective in assessing the results. To benefit from your "experiment," you will need to play the role of an objective theorist in evaluating your efforts as a practitioner.

It is important to theorize about education, to avoid not only the pitfalls described by Stephens but also a disorganized, haphazard approach to teaching. Charles E. Silberman was asked by the Carnegie Corporation to study the education of educators. He published his conclusions in *Crisis in the Classroom*. In the opening chapter he observes that perhaps the primary cause of the ineffectiveness of American education is *mindlessness*. He notes:

> By and large, teachers, principals, and superintendents are decent, intelligent, and caring people who try to do their best by their lights. If they make a botch of it, and an uncomfortably large number do, it is because it simply never occurs to more than a handful to ask *why* they are doing what they are doing—to think seriously or deeply about the purposes or consequences of education. . . . We must find ways of stimulating educators . . . to think about what they are doing and why they are doing it. (1970, p. 11)

Psychological Mechanisms That Complicate Theorizing

This book hopes to encourage you to follow your natural inclinations but also to think about what you will do when you teach and why you will do it. It also hopes to assist you to begin functioning as a teacher-theorist in preparation for becoming an effective teacher-practitioner. To function as a teacher-theorist you will need to keep in mind the scientific attitude as described by Stephens. You should be willing to withhold judgment until you have considered different opinions and examined available lines of evidence. As you theorize, you are asked to be open-minded about all sorts of approaches to teaching. If you commit yourself too wholeheartedly to one particular point of view, you may be unable to function as an objective appraiser because of the tendency to ignore or reject ideas that don't fit the view you espouse. This is called *cognitive dissonance*, and it has been studied intensively by Leon Festinger (1957). Festinger has demonstrated that the weighing of alternatives is more realistic *before* a decision has been made than it is *afterwards*. Once someone has made up his mind about something, he resists "dissonant" ideas, even though the evidence may be consistent and impressive; for example, a confirmed smoker will disbelieve studies that link smoking and cancer. *Cognitive dissonance*

Compounding this already substantial problem of theorizing is the possible influence of two other factors; the *experimenter bias effect* (Rosenthal, 1966) and the *Hawthorne effect* (Roethlisberger and Dickson, 1934). The experimenter bias effect, sometimes referred to as EBE, is the subtle and unintentional transmission of an expectancy of the experimenter to the subjects of a study. *Experimenter bias effect* The Hawthorne effect—so called because the term was first coined in a study made at the Hawthorne (Illinois) plant of Western Electric—is the tendency of subjects in some experiments to respond to almost *any* change, apparently *Hawthorne effect* because of their appreciation that someone is paying attention to them.

The ramifications of the experimenter bias effect and the Hawthorne effect can be illustrated by the following hypothetical situation: An educator who has developed a new teaching technique sets up an experiment to determine if the method is effective. In describing his new approach to the teachers who are to try it, he unintentionally infuses them with his enthusiasm. The teachers, impressed with the new method—and the feeling that they are "pioneers"—approach their classes with verve. The excitement of the teacher is communicated to the pupils, who are also intrigued by the newness of the technique and appreciate the fact that the teacher has taken the trouble to try something different. Consequently, the students put out more effort, and the results of the experiment are positive. But the truth of the matter may well be that the pupils reacted more to the teacher's attitude and the change in procedure than they did to the new technique itself.

The Roethlisberger and Dickson study setting forth the Hawthorne effect found, quite understandably, that factory production went up when work conditions were improved. However, when the conditions were deliberately made worse, production went up even higher—apparently just because of the change. If this phenomenon applies to school situations, a technically "inferior" technique of teaching might bring about improvement just because it is different.

The interaction of these subtle psychological mechanisms—cognitive dissonance, the experimenter bias effect, and the Hawthorne effect—can become rather complex when you try to apply psychology to teaching. For one thing, these various "effects" help explain why different researchers come up with different results. It is usually prudent to wait until an initial study has been repeated several times before assuming that a principle has been clearly established. Frequently, an experiment repeated by a different person will not yield the results obtained by the pioneer researcher. An example of this is provided by research that, appropriately and also paradoxically, was derived from the experimenter bias effect.

As an outgrowth of his work on the EBE, Rosenthal, along with Lenore F. Jacobson, performed an experiment that has received a great deal of publicity, particularly in newspapers and magazines. In May 1964, all the pupils in an elementary school took a general ability test with the impressive but fictitious title "Test of Inflected Acquisition." The following September the teachers were informed of the "results" of the test. They were told that the superior scores of five pupils in each class indicated that they were "likely to show unusual intellectual gains in the year ahead." But there was no actual difference between the test performances of these "superior" pupils, who had simply been selected at random, and those of the other children. Rosenthal and Jacobson reported in *Pygmalion in the Classroom* that the students who were labeled potential achievers showed significant gains in IQ and that the reason for these gains was the fact that their teachers expected more from them. They explain this

phenomenon by what is called a *self-fulfilling prophecy*[3]: One person's predic-   *Self-fulfilling prophecy*
tion of another's behavior somehow comes to be realized. They suggest that
this phenomenon operates by the teacher's communicating her enthusiasm and
faith to the pupil—just as an experimenter sometimes communicates certain
expectations to subjects, thereby biasing the results of the study.

Although newspaper and magazine reporters have uncritically accepted the
conclusions of Rosenthal and Jacobson as a well-established discovery of revolu-
tionary significance, scientists have not. In a review of *Pygmalion in the
Classroom*, Robert L. Thorndike pointed out some methodological errors and
concluded, "The indications are that the basic data upon which this structure
[the Pygmalion effect] has been raised are so untrustworthy that any conclusions
based on them must be suspect" (1968, p. 711). In another review Richard
E. Snow summed up his evaluation by saying, "Pygmalion, inadequately and
prematurely reported in book and magazine form, has performed a disservice
to teachers and schools, to users and developers of mental tests, and perhaps
worst of all, to parents and children whose newly gained expectations may
not prove quite so self-fulfilling" (1969, p. 199).

Even more damaging to Rosenthal's emphasis on the impact of expectation
is evidence provided by Theodore X. Barber and M. J. Silver (1968), who analyzed
a large number of studies on the EBE and concluded that the majority of them
failed to show the effect. Barber, with five colleagues (1968), made five attempts
to replicate the EBE and failed. In addition, William L. Claiborn (1969), Jean
José and John J. Cody (1971), and Elyse S. Fleming and Ralph G. Anttonen
(1971) reported that they attempted to replicate the study described in *Pygmalion
in the Classroom* and failed. However, Rosenthal (1969) has argued that the
Barber studies were not exact replications of his work. Furthermore, Eleanor
Burke Leacock (1969), Alfred L. Shaw (1969), D. H. Meichenbaum, K. S. Bower,   *Research on impact of*
and R. R. Ross (1969), and Myron Rothbart, Susan Dalfen, and Robert Barrett   *teacher expectancy*
(1971), found evidence that confirmed some aspects of the Pygmalion study.
These conflicting reports prompted the publication of *Pygmalion Reconsidered*
(1971) edited by Janet D. Elashoff and Richard E. Snow, which consists of
a lengthy critique by the editors, a review of studies on teacher expectancy,
six reviews of *Pygmalion in the Classroom* (including that of Thorndike), a reply
to the Elashoff and Snow critique by Rosenthal entitled "Pygmalion Reaffirmed,"
and a reply by Elashoff and Snow to Rosenthal's reply. Leon H. Levy (1969)
has offered some explanations for discrepancies in the evidence provided by
Rosenthal and Barber, as have Pamela Rubovits and Martin L. Maehr (1971).
All of this suggests that neither the experimenter bias effect nor the Pygmalion

[3] The term *Pygmalion effect* is frequently used as an alternative to *self-fulfilling prophecy*. Pygmalion   *Pygmalion effect*
was a mythical Greek sculptor who carved a statue that was so beautiful he fell in love with
it. This legend prompted George Bernard Shaw to choose *Pygmalion* for the title of his play (which
later became the musical *My Fair Lady*) because when Eliza Doolittle, the lowly flower girl, came
to seem such a lady—upon being treated as one—Professor Higgins fell in love with her.

The heroine of Shaw's *Pygmalion,* the cockney flower girl Eliza Doolittle (Audrey Hepburn, in the movie version, *My Fair Lady*) makes a grand entrance as a "lady" at a ball. The self-fulfilling prophecy is sometimes called the Pygmalion effect; as Eliza explains to her admirer, Colonel Pickering, "The difference between a lady and a flower girl is the way she is treated. I shall always be a flower girl to Professor Higgins, because he always treats me as a flower girl, and always will; but I know I can be a lady to you, because you always treat me as a lady, and always will."

effect are yet clearly established—illustrating at the same time the risks of generalizing from a single investigation.

(Even though there is reason to question some of the current data upon which the Pygmalion effect is based, it seems likely that expectation and the self-fulfilling prophecy have a significant effect on some pupils. J. Philip Baker and Janet Crist, who did the review of research included in *Pygmalion Reconsidered,* concluded, "The question for future research is not whether there are expectancy effects, but how they operate in school situations" (1971, p. 64). Until further research delineates the exact nature of the hypothesis, perhaps the most prudent course is to remain aware that a low—or high—expectation implanted by test scores, grades, or stereotypes about certain pupils may lead to a self-fulfilling prophecy if a child is treated as if he is less—or more—capable of learning than his classmates.)

In addition to assisting you to interpret discrepancies in research reports, understanding such psychological mechanisms as the experimenter bias effect may help make you aware of the ways students respond to the attitudes of their teachers and that, therefore, you should have a strong commitment to the teaching techniques you use. You need to show your pupils that you really believe in what you are doing. Your enthusiasm and confidence will likely have much to do with your success as a teacher. But overcommitment to a given idea or method, as earlier noted, may cause you to refuse to acknowledge dissonant evidence—evidence that a different theory or a variation in method is called for. And the Hawthorne effect suggests that occasional changes in teaching approach may have advantages over complete consistency.

One way to try to reconcile these somewhat conflicting factors is to be committed but flexible. And this is pretty much what Stephens's theory of spontaneous schooling encourages you to do. You should be enthusiastic about the techniques and theories you apply in the classroom, but be open-minded and objective when you later evaluate the results.

Theory of spontaneous schooling (Stephens)

In keeping with the spontaneous schooling approach, contrasting points of view will be described throughout this book. An attempt has been made to provide you with sufficient background information to enable you to relate the specific principles discussed to their appropriate theoretical framework; observations on the strengths and weaknesses of different approaches will be offered for your consideration. This should permit you to avoid the "mindless" approach to teaching that Silberman suggests is the basic reason for the ineffectiveness of American education.

At this point, a summary of what has been covered so far is offered to provide a framework for further analysis.

It has been assumed that America is, theoretically, a meritocracy: success depends on individual merit, ability, and willingness to work.

The schools of America have attempted to provide education that will equip children from a wide variety of backgrounds with roughly equivalent skills so that all will have essentially equal opportunities for success.

In order to provide such an education for millions of pupils, and because educational institutions reflect the surrounding culture, schools have used an assembly-line approach to education.

Citizens have expected the right—within a democratic form of government—to exert control over what takes place in the schools, and they have demanded efficiency and economy in education. Although the schools were originally intended to serve as a "great equalizer," evidence has accumulated indicating that the schools do not provide equal opportunities for children. Those who come from favored backgrounds do well in school and get the best jobs; those who come from disadvantaged backgrounds are able to succeed only through extraordinary effort.

Efforts have been made to discover if the schools attended by students who are successful have any specific qualities that lead to more effective education. It appears that no particular school characteristic has been identified as likely to increase school achievement.

While no specific characteristic seems to be the key to improving education, it has been argued that many features of the traditional approach to schooling have a *negative* impact. In many public schools, education takes place in an atmosphere of regimentation, control, and distrust. Evaluating students by comparing them leads to a situation where learning becomes a means to an end, pressure and tension are intense, cheating is common, and most students are made to feel unsuccessful.

Attempts are being made to alleviate the negative aspects of education, including the formation of alternative free schools, open education, and learning for mastery.

Although free schools are becoming more popular, the overwhelming majority of American children will continue to attend public schools. Many parents prefer the traditional public school to free schools; few can afford to pay "double tuition." Because of their size and bureaucratic complexity, public school systems tend to be monolithic and resistant to change. Consequently, most attempts to improve education will have to be carried out by individual public school teachers in their own classrooms.

It has been suggested that a basic reason most public school teachers have been unsuccessful in improving education is because they have not been systematic enough in thinking about what they are doing and why they are doing it. Teaching is an art, and it is important for a teacher-practitioner to follow his or her natural inclinations and teach with enthusiasm, emotional commitment, and confidence. However, in order to benefit from personal experience and the experiences of others in efforts to improve instruction, it is important that the teacher also function as a theorist—to be cautious and objective and adopt a scientific attitude when analyzing his or her own efforts or reports of observations by others. This is necessary in order to guard against being misled by wishful thinking and by such psychological mechanisms as cognitive dissonance, the experimenter bias effect, and the Hawthorne effect.

In addition to objective analysis of classroom reactions, the teacher-theorist might also develop a philosophy of the basic purposes of education—or at least learn enough about the theoretical background of various viewpoints in American education and psychology to understand the evolution and intent of common school practices and to teach with a degree of consistency.

The rest of this chapter will deal with the basic purposes of education. The next chapter presents background for a teacher-theorist by analyzing two major positions on learning and two basic conceptions of education.

Considering Basic Purposes of Education

Attempting to describe purposes of education may seem too abstract and idealistic to be of value, but if you are to formulate ideas about what you will do in your classroom and why you will do it, the effort is worthwhile. The "mindlessness" noted by Silberman can be overcome only by thinking about basic goals. A conception of "a highly educated person" described by Virginia Voeks in *On Becoming an Educated Person* is presented here as a framework for thinking since it states goals in a form which permits analysis of your feelings about your own education as you theorize about general purposes. Voeks suggests that you ask yourself, "To what ends am I attending college?" and then lists several possibilities:

> You could become better fitted for a particular vocation. . . .
> You could develop deeper comprehension of this world of which you are a part, and an eagerness to go on learning. . . .
> You could increase your ability to see interrelationships of all kinds and make new, more meaningful integrations. . . .
> You could build wider, deeper interests and develop the habit of continually extending your interests. . . .
> You could develop an increasing appreciation and love for the arts—including skillful compositions of all sorts. . . .
> You could develop a deeper compassion and understanding of all other people.
> You could gain a new appreciation of individual differences. . . .
> You could acquire skills in thinking—as contrasted with memorizing or blindly accepting "authority". . . .
> You could acquire a growing ability to assume responsibility for your own life.
> You could earn a good life, as well as a good living. (1970, pp. 5–26)

Goals of education (Voeks)

Even though the frame of reference for these possibilities is college education, they may be used as a basis for thinking about ways to improve education at all levels. Consider the following questions with reference to the goals Voeks lists.

Improving Education: Some Questions

Education should fit students for a particular vocation.

What is the best way to prepare students for vocations in a technological society whose jobs require greater skills than ever before and whose job requirements are likely to change rapidly? In *Future Shock*, Alvin Toffler

Speculating About Inadequacies of Higher Education

All the goals listed by Voeks are presented in the form of possibilities—things that *could* happen. Many students, yourself included, perhaps, seem to feel that few if any of these goals are achieved to a really satisfying extent simply by completing their degree requirements. In thinking about ways to improve education, you might begin by noting which aspects of your college experience have been most satisfying and which have been most disappointing. Take into account that some requirements may have been well-intentioned, even if the results were unsatisfactory. For example, most colleges establish minimum course requirements in general education, a major, and a minor. The intent of such requirements is to encourage the development of "deeper comprehension of the world," "increase your ability to see interrelationships and make integrations," "help you build wider and deeper interests," and "increase your appreciation of the arts." It is reasoned that a set of courses carefully preselected by professional educators is more likely to assist a student to achieve these goals than a curriculum chosen by an inexperienced young person with few specific goals in mind.

It appears that few general education sequences achieve their goals, and this has led some colleges to drop all such requirements. However, unless students

---

recommends that "nothing should be included in a required curriculum unless it can be strongly justified in terms of the future" (1970, p. 409). The best way to do this is to equip students to cope with change by stressing how to "learn, unlearn and relearn" (p. 414).

John Gardner agrees with Toffler, saying that a technological society "demands talent, particularly that which can adapt to innovation and change" (1961, p. 34), and that "only high ability and sound education equip a man for the continuous seeking of new solutions" (p. 37). Gardner further observes, "The traditional democratic invitation to each individual to achieve the best that is in him requires that we provide each youngster with the particular kind of education which will benefit *him*. That is the only sense in which equality of opportunity can mean anything. The good society is not one that ignores individual differences, but one that deals with them wisely and humanely" (p. 75). He suggests that we encourage individuals at all levels of ability to strive for excellence, saying that "all excellence involves discipline and tenacity of purpose" (p. 92). He adds, "High performance, particularly where children are concerned, takes place in a framework of expectation" (p. 101).

By contrast, Charles Reich maintains in *The Greening of America* that the young person who has reached the state of Consciousness III "rejects the whole concept of excellence and comparative merit. . . . and refuses to evaluate people by general standards" (1970, p. 243). He argues that the current world "demands a different personality than the old world, which asked for aggressive, disciplined,

at such institutions select courses to achieve goals such as those listed by Voeks, they may benefit less than they would have from a planned series of courses. Perhaps the basic fault is not with suggested programs of courses but with how they are taught. Unfortunately, many instructors of required courses in a general education sequence (or of any college course for that matter) have been guilty of "mindlessness" and have given little thought to how they might help students achieve their goals. Furthermore, few college professors have had formal (or even informal) preparation in the art of teaching—it is assumed that knowledge of a subject is all that is needed. Consequently, not all college teachers make efforts to analyze and perfect pedagogical techniques. Quite often they teach the way they were last taught, which was in graduate school. Graduate education places great emphasis on the mastery of technical information and on the screening of candidates; exams stress details and comparative grading practices are used to eliminate less promising candidates for advanced degrees. These practices have advantages in selecting Ph.D. candidates and training them in specific subjects, but they do not contribute to the development of the well-educated person described by Voeks. If you feel that your college education has been less successful than you had hoped it would be, you might analyze these and other possible causes for its lack of effectiveness; this might also help you to avoid making similar mistakes in the future.

competitive pursuit of definite goals" (p. 258). James M. O'Kane (1972) has suggested that the Reich philosophy is most appealing to students who come from well-to-do homes. Some children from affluent backgrounds, realizing that they will find it extraordinarily difficult to equal or surpass their parents, may favor a view that minimizes material achievement. O'Kane suggests that attempts by such young people to convert others to the same philosophy are unlikely to succeed, however, because the children of white- and blue-collar workers, eager to make the most of their opportunities to improve their lot, will take over the technocratic and professional positions left vacant by the offspring of those presently occupying them. (As O'Kane puts it, there is a "blueing" rather than a "greening" of American society.)

Most students eventually will earn a living, whether by choice or necessity. Examining the Help Wanted advertisements or the lists of interviews at college placement offices will reveal that most wage earners still work for large corporations or their subsidiaries. There are more people seeking jobs than there are jobs available. Competition for jobs of high skill, satisfaction, responsibility, and pay will continue—if some young people choose not to strive for such jobs, others will. Almost all jobs not involving manual labor will require some education, and, generally speaking, those with more education will secure the most interesting and remunerative positions.

Assuming the statements in the preceding paragraph are accurate, what then is the best kind of education "to fit students for a particular vocation"? What

In recent years especially, jobs have been difficult to find. In one instance, typical of many, seven hundred people applied for four openings.

might you do to prepare a larger proportion of your students to compete for rewarding jobs while minimizing excessive competition, pressure, and failure? How might you assist students to acquire the kind of background that will give them a wide variety of vocational choices and equip them to adapt to rapid change? How can you avoid perpetuating the differences that exist before pupils enter school and, at the same time, assist disadvantaged students to enhance their chances to obtain desirable jobs?

Education should assist students to develop deep comprehension of this world, and equip them with eagerness to go on learning.

What can be done to make learning less of a means (high grades, admission to prestigious colleges, qualifying for jobs) and more of an end in itself? How can teachers arrange instruction so that students leave their classrooms not with a sigh of relief—and with the prospect of forgetting all they have learned—but with eagerness to learn more?

Education should increase the abilities of students to see interrelationships and to make integrations.

What can be done to get away from compartmentalized education in which each subject—or isolated aspect of a subject—is analyzed without reference to anything else? How can teachers make the most of the values of structured materials or teach specialized courses and at the same time assist students to fit what they learn into a more comprehensive conception of the world?

Education should encourage students to express themselves and become more appreciative of how others do the same.

What can be done to eliminate practices that squelch creativity in the early grades and instead encourage students to express themselves freely in personal and innovative ways? How can teachers encourage students to share ideas and learn from each other, rather than keep ideas to themselves so as not to jeopardize their chances of doing better than others? What can be done to reduce the competitiveness that tends to produce jealousy and envy toward those who learn easily or hatred and intolerance toward those who do not. How can teachers encourage cooperation, mutual understanding, sympathy, and compassion?

The Values of Teacher Preparation—
Even if You Never Teach

Perhaps the question that enters your thoughts more than any other as you progress through a teacher preparation program is: Will I be able to get a job when I get my credential? There is no point in ignoring the fact that there are presently more teachers than jobs. If you are fortunate, you will find a position as soon as you graduate. If the fates are less kind to you, you may find yourself seeking a nonteaching job and brooding about "wasted" college years. If you are apprehensive about such a possibility, consider first of all that your credential will remain in force a year or more after you graduate. Furthermore, the courses you take in a credential program provide a "general purpose" kind of education that make you attractive to many employers. In addition, the knowledge you acquire should assist you to be better able than most graduates to fill Toffler's prescription for coping with rapid occupational change by making you well-informed about how to "learn, unlearn, and relearn." Finally, the courses you are taking have value not only in preparing you for a variety of careers but also in assisting you to become a better educated person as described by Voeks.

Education should encourage skills in thinking, not blind acceptance of "authority."

What can be done to reduce the extent to which students are forced to "memorize and regurgitate" and feel compelled to give teachers only what they demand? How can teachers encourage critical, independent thinking?

Education should assist students to assume responsibility for their own lives.

What can be done to eliminate a school environment characterized by distrust and control? How can teachers assist students to gradually assume greater responsibility for their own actions?

Education should permit students to earn a good life as well as a good living.

What can be done to reduce the degree to which so many Americans find themselves engaged in a compulsive, unfulfilling pursuit of status symbols? How can teachers provide the kind of education that will permit a greater enjoyment of life?

Assumptions Regarding Your Career as a Teacher

In thinking about how you might achieve some of these goals, you should probably assume that you will be teaching for most of your career in a public school. Whatever their merits, free schools do not appear a realistic solution to improving education for more than a very few students. If at this stage of your career you feel that you prefer an alternative school, read *Free Schools* and learn about the immense effort that Kozol insists is necessary to finance, equip, and run such a school. In his opinion, it is impossible to provide a satisfactory education in a public school; but the fact remains that for every child from the Boston ghetto who attends Kozol's school (or its equivalent), there are countless thousands of equally disadvantaged children who have no choice but to attend public schools. If the teachers of these children do not find ways to help them learn within the framework of a public school system, the inequalities of educational opportunity will persist.

As noted previously, many alternative schools lead precarious existences. You might find it interesting and rewarding to teach in such a school briefly, but for security, a decent living, and retirement benefits, a public school position is the more realistic option. There is a possibility that a variety of alternative schools will spring up if the *voucher system* is instituted. Under this system, parents are provided with a voucher equivalent to the money expended per pupil in public schools and allowed to use it to pay tuition at any school they choose. At the present time, this seems only a remote possibility, and even if parents were provided with vouchers, most would probably continue to choose public schools. The great majority of parents want their children to have an education that will make it possible for them to succeed. Some interpretations of "success" in America are hollow, superficial, and unrewarding, but it is only natural for parents to hope their children eventually will find interesting, well-paid jobs. An established, accredited, public school whose graduates are consistently accepted by institutions of higher learning is the most logical choice for parents who have such hopes for their children. And though expectations sometimes lead to the fear of failure described by Holt, Gardner notes that "high performance takes place in a framework of expectation."

Realistically, you also should think in terms of finding ways to improve education by adjusting to the conditions of public school education even as you try to improve it. A number of young teachers have challenged school regulations, had their contracts terminated, and written books about their experiences. We have now reached the point where such books have achieved the purpose of calling attention to some of the weaknesses of public education. There is no longer much logic in defying the system to the point of being fired or to be so dedicated a teacher that you cannot sustain the pace for more than a year or two. Public school education can be improved only by teachers who continue to teach in public schools. (Herbert Kohl was able to teach in the manner he describes in *36 Children* for two years. He then moved to Spain to recuperate before reentering education—but in a less strenuous situation. George Dennison is honest enough to explain why he gave up running the First Street School: "It was not merely lack of money that closed the school. We ourselves were not strongly enough motivated to make the sacrifices that would have been necessary to sustain it" [1969, p. 273]. He notes that he returned to a full-time career as a writer after the school closed.)

Attempting to Improve Education

The purpose of this book, along with the supplementary and the evaluation materials, is not only to help prepare you to become a teacher but also to show you some ways you might attempt to correct the negative aspects of American public education in a manner that should be acceptable to almost any school administrator, school board member, or parent. Following is an outline of what are considered to be undesirable practices and how this book attempts to correct for them while achieving some of Voeks's educational goals.

In many traditional public schools, students are exposed to a standard curriculum where the only variation allowed is in quantity and rate of learning. While you will be asked to learn certain prescribed information in this book, you also will be urged to make your own choices and to do further reading, thinking, and analysis of related ideas that strike you as having personal value.

The assembly-line aspects of traditional education often lead to prearranged, overly structured learning and excessive specialization and compartmentalization. This book is designed to make the most of organization and structure but in ways that permit individual flexibility. To avoid compartmentalization (and also to achieve a deeper comprehension of the world and the development of interrelationships and integrations), the topics in the book include developments in a variety of disciplines; the views of humanists, novelists, laymen, and scientists other than psychologists are noted. Furthermore, analyses of theories and the factors that led to their development are presented so that you can relate the material to what you already know.

The open education approach has called attention to the value of encouraging students to learn from their own experience and from each other. It is hoped that as you read, you will engage in considerable self-directed learning, and several suggestions are offered to encourage interaction with classmates.

In acquiring information to prepare you to become a teacher, you will be asked to learn certain information to serve as a basis for becoming a teacher-practitioner. Even if you consider teaching an art, you can benefit from learning about what others have learned. But in order to interpret what you read about teaching now and in the future, and also to evaluate the effectiveness of the techniques you use, you also will need to function as a teacher-theorist. This book will help you achieve what Voeks describes as "acquisition of skills in thinking"—as contrasted with blind acceptance of authority. You are urged to become a teacher-theorist not only to make the most of a scientific attitude—with which you can avoid the pitfalls of wishful thinking—but also to approach teaching with a habit of thinking about what you are doing and why you are doing it.

While this book attempts to get away from regimentation, a rigidly prearranged curriculum, an assembly-line aura, and overconcern with memorization and blind acceptance of authority, it is nonetheless more of a structured than a free approach. Structure is stressed because in order to master concepts and principles that will equip you to deal with a wide variety of unpredictable situations, you must first thoroughly learn and understand considerable background information presented in an organized way.

It is for these reasons that you may be asked to memorize some of the information presented in this book and to demonstrate (on exams, or the equivalent) that you understand it. Some things you will be asked to learn may strike you as practical and worthwhile; others may appear worthless or arbitrary. You are asked to accept on faith that every bit of information you are asked to learn from this book has been selected because it has high potential pay-off value—because it will assist you to grasp principles and because it has proved valuable to a significant number of experienced teachers.

John Holt has argued that any form of education that involves examinations makes students become "producers" rather than "thinkers" (1964, pp. 23, 48) and forces them to become "answer-centered" rather than "problem-centered" (p. 118). He also maintains that asking questions is the primary reason so many pupils fear school and think of themselves as failures, and that any type of teacher direction is a form of "coercion" (p. 221). You have doubtless had teachers who dominated their classes, asked pointless questions, and accepted only answers that fit their own conceptions. But this does not mean that every form of education that asks students to explain what they know is inevitably destructive. Requesting students to provide answers can lead to positive results—as in a mastery approach. In order to put this system into practice it is first necessary to describe goals. Following a "mindless" approach with no clear idea of what you hope to accomplish forces you to proceed by trial and error. By taking the trouble to note and organize goals, on the other hand, you and your students can take specific steps to achieve them. To discover how successful each student is, you need feedback—you can get it by asking questions. If the answers reveal some lack of understanding of a particular point, you can take steps to assist the student to comprehend what he has missed. The questions (and answers) also provide students with specific incentives to learn and make it possible to evaluate them—not in comparison to other students but with reference to established standards. By meeting the standards, the student gains a sense of satisfaction and esteem. A crucial factor in learning for mastery centers around the question: What sort of goals should you establish and how do you discover if they have been achieved?

For reasons noted in the section "Explanation of Lists of Objectives" (pp. x–xii), goals for this book are stated in the form of general objectives and Key Points. They are stated briefly so that you will not feel you must concentrate only on completely circumscribed information. They are, though, called to your attention so that you can concentrate on the points selected to build your own conception of ideas in psychology. In this sense the information chosen for special emphasis is designed to enhance your ability to make individual applications and not to reduce it.

Depending on your instructor's approach, you may be asked to memorize information relating to the Key Points as a means of mastering the material. This need not be *rote* memorization if you bear in mind the meaning of what you are learning. Nor does answering questions need to be mindless parroting. As much as possible, you will be asked on exams and other assignments to *apply* what you have learned. In too many courses, the learning comes to an abrupt end as soon as the final exam has been completed. If the course has been a disagreeable experience, the ultimate result may be that anything to do with the subject will be avoided in the future. In this case, education is destructive—it inhibits further learning.

Robert F. Mager has observed that your primary goal as a teacher should be to "[send] students away from your instruction anxious to use what you have taught them—and eager to learn more" (1968, p. 3). He found this most likely to happen if students did well and felt comfortable in the presence of the subject or activity. This book takes full account of Mager's findings. The intent is to assist everyone to learn at a respectable level and thereby experience the feeling of doing well. But, in order for this to happen, you must *demonstrate* that you have learned, which means you must first of all master the subject. Learning the principles of any subject requires some memorization—at the very least a thorough understanding of basic ideas. Being "comfortable" in the presence of a subject does not mean lack of exertion. A person who makes little effort to master a subject or activity will probably feel *un*comfortable around it because he realizes his ineptitude. An individual is more likely to feel satisfied when engaged in an activity he can do well, and doing well requires effort. The text and *Study Guide* have been designed to make your efforts as interesting as possible and to equip you with information you will be able to use.

If studying this book leads you to feel you have done well in learning educational psychology, you will be inclined to remember and use what you have learned and want to learn more after the course is finished. And speculating about what you will do when you teach brings us back to the questions noted at the beginning of this chapter. To conclude it, a few responses to those questions are offered.

Does it make sense to try to *become* a teacher? The answer, of course, will depend primarily on your own background, interests, and plans for the future. But in terms of the need for teachers who can improve American education, it is essential that eager and willing young people become teachers.

Is there any point in studying how to teach? If you hope to avoid the mindlessness that plagues American education and benefit from what others have learned, it seems essential to read, think, and discuss how the systematic study of education and psychology can be applied to improving education.

Are teachers born rather than made? While it is probably true that some people who have had no formal courses in teaching do a better job in the classroom than some who have had dozens of courses, it seems almost inevitable that even outstanding natural teachers could benefit from the experiences and observations of others. The teacher-practitioner can learn about techniques perfected by fellow practitioners; the teacher-theorist can learn to relate techniques to underlying theories, apply principles in a wide variety of situations, and use the scientific attitude to avoid being misled by wishful thinking.

Will you be able to find a satisfying job in teaching? This depends on a great many factors including your personality and just plain luck. A basic assumption of this book is that it is possible to do an excellent job of teaching in a public school and to find ways to minimize the negative aspects of the educational establishment. Being successful at bringing about even minor improvements with a small number of children is likely to be quite satisfying; encouraging learning in a classroom environment that eliminates intimidation, reduces fear, and assists almost all students to experience success should be more than a bit fulfilling.

Summary

In this chapter, current trends in American education have been traced to the competitiveness of our society, the application of business methods to education, and the concern about efficiency. Two current outgrowths of these developments are performance contracting and accountability, both of which stress that teachers should *produce* learning. As a reaction against what some consider undesirable aspects of education, various forms of free and open education are becoming more popular. In addition, techniques such as learning for mastery are being adopted to reduce competitiveness.

Interest in less competitive forms of schooling derives from increasing awareness that our present school system not only fails to provide equality of educational opportunity but instead perpetuates differences that existed before children enter school. Attempts to find specific techniques to make education more effective as an equalizing force have been unsuccessful to date, which some observers interpret as an indication that teachers should think of teaching as an art and do what comes naturally in the classroom. However, all artists can learn skills from others, and such psychological mechanisms as cognitive dissonance, the experimenter bias effect, and the Hawthorne effect distort our observations and perceptions. To guard against being misled in assessing the effect of different approaches to teaching, it will be desirable for you to make an effort to be objective, cautious, and tentative and to function as a teacher-theorist. At the same time, you will want to be confident, enthusiastic, and committed in the classroom, which requires you to act as a teacher-practitioner. J. M. Stephens' theory of spontaneous schooling emphasizes such a conception of instruction, stressing that many different approaches to teaching can be equally effective and that you should feel free to choose from alternatives.

While it will be desirable for you to follow your own spontaneous inclinations up to a point, you will want to avoid a "mindless" approach to teaching by considering basic purposes of education. Goals described by Voeks can serve as a starting point for such an analysis. By taking account of goals, it will be possible to make a reasonably systematic effort to improve education.

Suggestions for Further Reading, Writing, Thinking, and Discussion

1-1 *Examining a Journal Consisting of Reports of Experiments in Psychology and Education*

In order to gain some direct experience with the raw material of psychology—the building blocks that are eventually combined to establish a principle or theory—you might examine one or more of the professional journals in psychology, which consist primarily of reports of experiments. Listed below are titles of such journals likely to be found in a typical college library.

American Educational Research Journal
Behavioral Science
Child Development
Developmental Psychology

Educational and Psychological
    Measurement
Exceptional Child
Genetic Psychology Monographs

Harvard Educational Review	Journal of Teacher Education
Journal of Abnormal and Social Psychology	Merrill-Palmer Quarterly of Behavior and
Journal of Applied Behavior Analysis	Development
Journal of Educational Psychology	Mental Hygiene
Journal of Educational Research	Psychological Monographs
Journal of Educational Sociology	Psychological Review
Journal of Experimental Child Psychology	Psychology in the Schools
Journal of Experimental Education	Society for Research in Child Development
Journal of Experimental Psychology	Monographs

To develop awareness of the nature of research in psychology, examine recent issues of some of these journals. To gain some experience as a teacher-theorist, you might select an article describing an experiment that intrigues you or appears relevant to your own interests, grade level, and subject. Then write an abstract of the article following the outline below:

Author of article

Title of article

Journal in which article appears (including date, volume number, and page numbers)

Purpose (or description of problem)

Subjects

Procedure (or methods)

Treatment of data

Results

Conclusions

Are there any criticisms that you can make of the procedure or of the conclusions?

What inferences for your own teaching can you draw from this experiment (if any)?

Would you be willing to change your methods of teaching on the strength of this one article?

1-2 *Examining a Journal of Abstracts and Reviews*

Unless you are familiar with research in a particular aspect of educational psychology, you may find it difficult to fit an individual study reported in a journal into a general framework or relate it to other similar research. In most cases, it is prudent to find out what other experiments of a similar type have revealed about a particular point before making generalizations from the results of a single study. A variety of journals and reference works exists to assist you to do this. The journals listed below consist of abstracts (brief summaries of results) of articles that appear in the type of journal listed in the preceding section.

Child Development Abstracts and Bibliography	Exceptional Child Education Abstracts Psychological Abstracts

The following encyclopedias contain reviews and analyses of research reported in the journals listed in this and the preceding section:

The Encyclopedia of Education (1971) edited by Lee C. Deighton

Encyclopedia of Educational Research (1969) edited by Robert L. Ebel

Handbook of Research on Teaching (2nd ed., 1972) edited by R. M. W. Travers

Review of Research in Education (1973) edited by Fred N. Kerlinger

The Teacher's Handbook (1971) edited by Dwight W. Allen and Eli Seifman

The journal *Contemporary Psychology* provides reviews of new books in psychology, and the *Annual Review of Psychology* provides information reflected by the title—a specialist in each of several areas of psychology reviews significant studies that have appeared during a given year.

The *Review of Educational Research* features articles that describe, relate, and analyze reports of studies on a particular theme.

To discover the nature of these journals and reference works, examine some of them and perhaps prepare a brief description of the most promising titles to save for future reference. Or select a topic of interest, search for reports of experiments and summarize the conclusions you reach.

1-3 *Reading a "Discussion" Article in a Professional Journal*

In addition to descriptions of actual experiments, "discussion" articles are published in some professional journals and in many teachers' magazines. Listed below are journals of this type.

JOURNALS CONSISTING OF GENERAL DISCUSSIONS OF TRENDS AND DEVELOPMENTS

The following journals consist of descriptions of trends, developments, and techniques as well as interpretations of research data. In some articles, research studies are cited, in others interpretations of approaches to teaching are offered without reference to specific data. Many of these journals also feature sections on "tricks of the trade," and most provide book reviews.

Change (Higher Education)

Clearing House (Junior and Senior High School Teaching)

Elementary School Journal

Exceptional Children

Journal of General Education

Journal of Higher Education (College and University Teaching)

Junior College Journal

Phi Delta Kappan

Teachers College Journal

Teachers College Record

Theory Into Practice

JOURNALS CONSISTING OF BRIEF COMMENTARIES ON TRENDS AND DEVELOPMENTS

The following journals consist of short (usually less than five pages) articles on trends, developments, and techniques in education.

Childhood Education	*Educational Technology* (Programmed instruction, behavior modification, etc.)
Education	
Educational Forum	*High School Journal*
Educational Leadership	*Journal of Education*
Educational Record (College and University Teaching)	*School Review*

Note: *Education Digest* is made up of condensations of articles selected from the types of journals listed in this and the preceding section.

MAGAZINES FOR TEACHERS

The following publications provide articles, usually in magazine format, with emphasis on journalistic style, abundant illustrations, and colorful graphic design:

Grade Teacher	*Psychology Today*
Instructor	*Saturday Review of Education*
Learning	*Today's Education*

If you look through some recent issues of several of these journals, you will discover the nature of typical discussion articles on psychology and education. For future reference, you might read an article that you feel is relevant to your own interests, grade level, and subject and then write a synopsis of the author's arguments. If any of these arguments are pertinent to your own theorizing about teaching, briefly analyze your thoughts, perhaps by following an outline such as this one:

Author of article

Name of article

Journal in which article appeared (including date, volume number, and page numbers)

Synopsis of arguments presented

Your reaction to the arguments

1-4 *Discovering the Nature of Journals for Teachers of Specific Grade Levels and Subject Areas*

Almost every field of study in education has one or more journals devoted to reports of research, reviews of related experimental studies, discussions of teaching techniques, descriptions of "tricks of the trade," and analyses of subject matter. The following list of journals may help you discover what is available in your area or areas of interest:

African Studies Bulletin	*American Music Teacher*
Agricultural Education Magazine	*American Speech*
American Biology Teacher	*American String Teacher*
American Business Education	*American Vocational Journal*

Arithmetic Teacher

Art Education

Athletic Journal

Audiovisual Instructor

Business Education World

Coach and Athlete

Coaching Clinic

Education and Training of the Mentally Retarded

Educational Theatre Journal

Elementary English

Elementary School Guidance and Counseling

English Language Teaching

English Studies

Forecast for Home Economics

French Review

Geographical Teacher

German Review

Gifted Child Quarterly

Hearing and Speech News

History Today

Improving College and University Teaching

Industrial Arts and Vocational Education

Industrial Arts Teacher

Instrumentalist

Journal of Industrial Teacher Education

Journal of Negro Education

Journal of Nursing

Journal of Reading

Journal of Research on Science Teaching

Journal of School Health

Journal of Secondary Education

Journal of Special Education

Reading Specialist

Marriage and Family Living

Mathematics Teacher

Music Education Journal

Music in Education

Music Journal

National Business Education Quarterly

National Elementary Principal

Physical Educator

Physics Teacher

Recreation

Safety Education

Scholastic Coach

School Arts

School Counselor

School Musician

School Musician Director and Teacher

School Science and Mathematics

School Shop

Science Educator

Science Teacher

Swimming Technique

Teaching Exceptional Children

Tennis

Theatre Arts

Theatre World

Today's Speech

Track Technique

To discover what is available, check titles in the above list that sound promising, spend some time in the periodicals section of your college library, and examine some recent issues. You might select an article you find of interest and write an abstract of it, together with your own interpretation. Or prepare a brief description of journals that impress you as worthy of attention. This list could serve as a source of information on what journals to consult after you begin your teaching career.

1-5 Becoming Acquainted with ERIC

As the number of journals listed on the preceding pages indicates, thousands of articles are published each year on every conceivable aspect of educational psychology and education. To assist psychologists and educators to discover what has been published on a specific topic, the Educational Resources Information Center (ERIC) has been established by the U. S. Office of Education. ERIC publishes three sources of information:

Current Index to Journals in Education—Annual Cumulation, which contains an index of articles in over 300 education and education-oriented journals published in a given year. There are four sections in each volume: Subject Index (which lists titles of articles organized under hundreds of subject headings) Author Index, Journal Contents Index (which lists the tables of contents for each issue of journals published that year), and Main Entry Section (which provides the title, author, journal reference, and a brief abstract of articles published in journals covered by the *Index*).

Research in Education, which lists curriculum guides, catalogs, and the like; and papers, reports, and monographs not published in journals. The Document Resume section presents descriptions of the documents arranged according to the ERIC classification scheme, together with information about where each can be obtained. There is also a Subject Index (titles of documents listed according to the ERIC classification), an Author Index, and an Institution Index (titles of articles listed with reference to source).

ERIC Educational Documents Index, which lists titles of documents noted and abstracted in *Research in Education* and also in *Office of Education Research Reports.* Each document is classified under up to five "Major Descriptors" (general categories) and perhaps also under "Minor Descriptors" (more specific categories).

As these descriptions indicate, for information on what is available in journals, you should refer to *Current Index to Journals in Education—Annual Cumulation.* For information about curriculum guides, pamphlets, and reports not published in journals, consult the *ERIC Educational Documents Index* for titles, and *Research in Education* for descriptions and information about how to obtain such documents.

You are urged to examine a recent issue of these publications to discover what is available in the ERIC network and how you might obtain information.

1-6 *Reading a Critique of American Education*

As background for taking steps to improve American education, you might read one or more critical analyses of traditional public schools. One of the most recent and highly regarded critiques is *Crisis in the Classroom* (1970) by Charles E. Silberman. In Part II, Silberman gives his views on "What's Wrong with the Schools," and in Part III he describes "How the Schools Should Be Changed."

Two other recent books that provide provocative critiques are *Deschooling Society* (1971) by Ivan Illich and *The Greening of America* (1970) by Charles A. Reich (see Chapter V, "The Lost Self," for an analysis of what is wrong, Chapter XII, "The Greening of America," for a prescription for reform). If you read one of these books—or another critique of your own choice—summarize the criticisms of the author and then evaluate these in terms of your own observations and opinions.

1-7 *Sampling the Views of Paul Goodman*

Paul Goodman was a prolific and provocative commentator on our society in general and its educational system in particular. In college, he majored in philosophy, but after graduation turned to literature and wrote several novels. He underwent psychotherapy at this time, which prompted him to co-author a book on Gestalt therapy and to study and practice this form of analysis. After a period of relative obscurity and indifferent professional success, Goodman achieved considerable notoriety with the publication of *Growing Up Absurd* (1956) in which he described the plight of the young person in American society and criticized the American approach to education. He became the patron saint of the free speech movement of the 1960s and his reputation was further enhanced when he wrote *Compulsory Miseducation* (1962) and *The Community of Scholars* (1964) (now available in paperback form in one volume), in which he presented many of the arguments which are now championed by advocates of free and open education. A later defense of humanistic approaches to education appeared as *Like a Conquered Province* (1969). The relationship of mutual admiration between Goodman and young people cooled in the late 1960s for reasons noted in the Preface to *New Reformation* (1969): "In 1958, I called them my 'crazy young allies' and now I am saying that, when the chips are down, they're just like their fathers." The possibility of a reconciliation with his former "young allies" was eliminated by a fatal heart attack in 1972. If you would like to sample Goodman's style and opinions, perhaps the best book to peruse would be *Compulsory Miseducation*. If you are favorably impressed, you might read sections of the other books.

1-8 *Assessing the Impact of "Efficiency" on American Education*

Many schools in this country emphasize efficiency and economy. This emphasis sometimes leads to educational practices that are improvements from one point of view, but their undesirable by-products may make life difficult for teachers. The impact of citizens' demands for efficiency and economy in education is discussed in *Education and the Cult of Efficiency* (1962) by Raymond E. Callahan. In the last chapter Callahan sums up his views on the current situation and remarks on factors that tend to cause difficulties and misunderstandings. If you read any sections of this book, you might give a general analysis of your reactions or offer your own comments on the pros and cons of making education "efficient."

In *The Organization Man* (1956), William H. Whyte, Jr., describes the effect of American business methods on our way of life. Part I, "The Ideology of Organization Man," gives a general overview of his analysis. Chapters 7 and 8 concentrate on the impact of business on education, and Part 5, "The

Organization Scientist," tells how an organization approach to science and technology tends to limit creativity. The last chapter sums up the case against the organization. If you have ever brooded about the influence of the establishment on the American way of life—and education—you will find sections of *The Organization Man* highly provocative.

1-9 *Finding Out About the Background of Present Developments in Education*

Callahan and Whyte give their interpretations of the impact of business on American education. For a more comprehensive analysis of earlier trends that influenced current educational practice, see *The Transformation of the School* (1961) by Lawrence A. Cremin or one of these books by Paul Woodring: *Let's Talk Sense About Our Schools* (1953), *A Fourth of a Nation* (1957), or *Introduction to American Education* (1966).

1-10 *Finding Out More About Accountability, Performance Contracting, and the Voucher System*

Three current developments that might be traced to the impact of American business on education are accountability, performance contracting, and the voucher system. If you would like to find out more about these developments, consult these books: *Accountability for Educational Results* (1973) edited by R. W. Hostrop, J. A. Mecklenburger, and J. A. Wilson; *Learning C.O.D.—Can the Schools Buy Success?* (1972) edited by J. A. Mecklenburger, J. A. Wilson, and R. W. Hostrop; and *Educational Vouchers: Concepts and Controversies* (1972) edited by George R. LaNoue.

1-11 *Sampling Varying Views of the Art of Teaching*

Whereas psychologists are primarily interested in ways to encourage a scientific approach to teaching—even as they seek ways to allow for artistic elements—those outside of science may do the opposite. A comprehensive presentation of the view that teaching is an art that may be spoiled by overemphasis on science is to be found in Gilbert Highet's *The Art of Teaching* (1957). Highet explains why he considers teaching to be an art, describes what he believes are the qualities of a good teacher, discusses basic methods of instruction, and provides a brief account of some of the great teachers of history and the methods they used.

A more complete account of teaching techniques used by famous teachers of history is provided in *The Master Teachers and the Art of Teaching* (1967) by John E. Colman. In the first chapter, Colman outlines "The General Approach" and then devotes a chapter to each of nineteen different approaches to teaching—including the Socratic method, the Jesuit method, and Communist methods. The last chapter is titled "Be an Artist!" and concludes with this statement: "Teaching is nothing less than the vibrant contact of one mind with another mind. And that is an art. Be an artist . . . And so teach!"

Original discourses on the art of teaching by many of the famous teachers described by Highet and Colman may be found in *Three Thousand Years of Educational Wisdom* (1954) by Robert S. Ulich.

1-12 *Tuning in on Some of William James's "Talks to Teachers"*

William James, considered by many to be the "father" of American psychology, commented on the relationships between the art of teaching and the science of psychology in a series of lectures he gave to groups of teachers. These were eventually published in 1899 in *Talks to Teachers*. In his introduction to the paperback reprint of this book (1958), Paul Woodring says, "No writer before or since his time has quite equalled James' gift for making psychology interesting and understandable." This is high praise indeed, and you are likely to enjoy dipping into *Talks to Teachers*. If you obtain the paperback edition, read Woodring's introduction, which gives some enlightening background about James and how his ideas relate to present-day education. You are also urged to read Chapter 1, "Psychology and the Teaching Art." In addition, the Talks to Students at the end of the book are fascinating. There are three of these talks: "The Gospel of Relaxation" (offering "gay nineties" readers advice on how to cope with the breakneck pace of American life), "On a Certain Blindness in Human Beings" (which contains excerpts from the writings of Stevenson, Wordsworth, Whitman, and Tolstoy), and "What Makes Life Significant."

As you read James, you might note your reactions in a general way—picking and choosing and commenting on ideas that impress you. You will probably gain more from doing this if you make allowance for the fact that James wrote the book more than seventy years ago. It might be interesting to compare the observations of a "free-thinking" educator of 1900 vintage with the opinions of current educators. Keep in mind, too, that if many of James's statements on principles of psychology and pedagogy seem naive or puzzling, it is because psychology was an extremely new science when *Talks to Teachers* was written.

1-13 *Learning More about Stephens's Theory of Spontaneous Schooling*

J. M. Stephens has devoted his long professional life to the study of educational psychology. His concern with the science *and* art aspects of teaching was first expressed when he discussed the distinctions between the teacher-theorist and the teacher-practitioner in *Educational Psychology* (1951). Sixteen years later the same concern was put differently when he proposed his theory of spontaneous schooling, described in *The Process of Schooling* (1967). This short paperback is both interesting and thought-provoking. If you are unable to read the entire book, you might read Chapter 1, "The Argument in Brief"; Chapter 3, "The

Origins and Social Role of the School"; Chapter 6, "Spontaneous Tendencies and Scholastic Achievement"; Chapter 8, "The Effective Teacher: His Characteristics and Place in Society"; or Chapter 11, "Prescription for Relaxation".

1-14 *Testing a Hypothesis*

To get into the habit of functioning as a teacher-theorist, you might make an effort to follow the suggestion of Arthur Coladarci and think of teaching as testing-of-hypothesis behavior. If you have the opportunity to act as a teacher aide or the equivalent during the time you are taking the course for which this text is assigned, you might pick out an idea, set up a hypothesis, and test it.

For example, a teacher aide in a first grade was impressed by the concept of individual differences. She got to thinking about the standard wide-lined paper traditionally used in teaching lettering in the primary grades. Hypothesizing that not all children would be inclined to print letters of exactly the same size, she obtained paper with lines of varying widths and permitted the students to take their choice. Some children preferred relatively narrow lines as opposed to the standard wide lines. She then tried to determine whether the use of narrow lines actually improved printing skill. Although unable to do a completely scientific job, she got enough feedback to convince her that some children benefit from the opportunity to print on a smaller scale than others.

Another example: Think of a new unit or approach to teaching as a hypothesis by saying to yourself, "If I ask them to respond to this material in class discussion, I ought to get a better response than I did when I used a lecture approach."

You should be aware, however, of the limitations of functioning as a teacher-theorist. J. M. Stephens has pointed out that the scientist tries to avoid pitfalls in establishing relationships by using sufficient unselected cases, by using a control group, by being precise in observing, and by exploring all possible hypotheses. You may not be able to meet the first of these conditions in setting up an experimental approach to teaching since you will have no choice about the pupils in your classes. It may also be impossible to have a control group. Furthermore, you may find it impractical to apply the results of a teaching experiment with one group to a future group because no two classes are alike. (As a matter of fact, the same class may not react the same way the second time around.) Nevertheless, you can attempt to be precise and objective in observing, and keep in mind the importance of considering alternative explanations to be tested by further experimentation.

If you are intrigued by this concept, write down a hypothesis about teaching and outline how you might test it in at least a somewhat scientific manner. If you can, test it out on a class of public school pupils. If this is not possible, you might try to function vicariously as a teacher by identifying with one of your college instructors as he presents a lecture or guides a discussion. If the presentation goes over well, think about it and analyze why it worked. If one approach doesn't work as well as another, dream up some alternate hypotheses you might test if *you* were the teacher.

1-15 *Becoming Aware That There Are Almost Always At Least Two Sides to Arguments in Education and Psychology*

Because of the impact of personal involvement and the nature of cognitive dissonance, the Hawthorne effect, and the experimenter bias effect, a new development in education is often presented as the best way to solve a particular problem of teaching, and criticisms or alternate techniques are ignored or minimized. A man who has devoted several years to perfecting a novel technique naturally begins to think of it as a "cause" and to defend it against criticism and reject counterproposals made by others. This tendency to favor a certain point of view often leads to a polarization of arguments. Throughout the text, an effort has been made to give both sides of key issues so that you can make up your own mind. (It must be noted, however, that the author is not immune to the human frailties that lead to personal affinities for certain ideas in education, so some points of view are favored over others in the way the discussion in the text is presented.)

As you read about new developments in education, remain aware of the polarizing or dichotomizing tendencies that stem from the psychological mechanisms mentioned above. If a theorist argues in favor of one approach, keep an eye out for counterarguments. (In the text and in these Suggestions, you are referred to many articles or books setting forth a point of view different from that emphasized.) *Today's Education* often presents one or more educators arguing for a position and also one or more arguing against it. And quite often, critical observations from the "other side" in the form either of letters to the editor or articles giving follow-up critiques follow an original article. To get experience with this aspect of theorizing about education and psychology, you might read one of the differences-of-opinion articles in *Today's Education* or browse through a bound set of some other teachers' journal for a given year looking for letters or articles that summarize counterarguments to ideas presented earlier. If you make such a comparison, list the arguments for and against and then record your own position on the subject being debated.

1-16 *Examining Varying Interpretations of the Self-Fulfilling Prophecy*

The publication of *Pygmalion in the Classroom* (1968) by Robert Rosenthal and Lenore Jacobson stimulated several psychologists to attempt replications of the original experiment, others to write critical analyses of the book, others to analyze the nature of the experimenter bias effect from which the Pygmalion effect was derived, still others to write articles attempting to explain discrepancies between studies and interpretations. If you would like to sample a variety of views on the Pygmalion effect, refer to the list of studies noted on page 23 of this chapter. Or examine the Appendix ("The Nature of Behavioral Science") of *Psychology Applied to Teaching: Selected Readings.* It contains a series of articles from the *Journal of Consulting and Clinical Psychology* that present evidence and analyses for and against the experimenter bias effect, a condensed version of *Pygmalion in the Classroom,* and a critical review of the Rosenthal and Jacobson book. If you follow either of these suggestions, you might summarize the information you examine, draw your own conclusions, and comment on the implications of these conclusions.

1-17 *Finding Out About Free Schools*

If you have only vague awareness of what the free school movement is about, you may wish to read one or more books or articles on this approach to education. An excellent comprehensive description is provided by Jonathan Kozol in *Free Schools* (1972). For an account of the history of a free school, read *The Lives of Children* (1969) by George Dennison. *Free the Children* (1972) by Allen Graubard has been praised by many advocates of free schools. *This Book Is About Schools* (1970) edited by Satu Repo is a collection of articles from the "journal" of free education, *This Magazine Is About Schools.* For a down-to-earth description of how to set up and run one type of free school, look for *Rasberry Exercises* (1970) by Salli Rasberry and Robert Greenway.

You might also look for other books on free education or be on the alert for articles in magazines and newspapers. If you read one or more accounts of the free education approach, you may clarify your thoughts by describing the type of school and noting your reactions. What do you see as advantages and disadvantages? Would you like to teach in such a school? Why or why not?

1-18 *Considering the Possibility of Integrated Separatism*

Up until recently, one of the basic goals of American education has been to facilitate the "melting pot" aspect of life in the United States. Emphasis has been placed on "Americanizing" individuals from a wide variety of ethnic backgrounds to the point that all races, religions, and nationalities share common attributes. Within the last few years, many minority groups have begun to actively resist this trend and have sought to proclaim and maintain their identity. (The "Black is Beautiful" movement and schools of Black Studies are examples.) Although such trends have been of value to many members of minority groups in providing a sense of identity, they have also created problems in that success in American society frequently depends on joining the mainstream.

In recognition of this situation, a *Multi-Culture Institute* has been established in San Francisco. The Institute is a private school for 3- to 9-year-olds, and it deliberately stresses the fact that people from varying backgrounds are different while maintaining awareness that all Americans have similarities. This is done by dividing the curriculum into two separate parts. In the morning, all children are placed in integrated classrooms where they study a standard curriculum of reading, writing, and arithmetic. In the afternoon, each ethnic group meets in its own separate classroom with a teacher of the same background to study its own culture. At frequent intervals, the separate classes meet and tell each other about aspects of their art, music, beliefs, etc. For example, a special holiday might be commemorated by inviting every pupil in the school to eat foods prepared by a particular group and to find out about and participate in the celebration. What are your reactions to this approach to education? What do you consider to be advantages and disadvantages? You might also speculate about how you might introduce a simplified form of this approach in your own classroom.

1-19 *Sampling Views on Equality and Inequality of Educational Opportunity*

In some ways, the team of investigators headed by James S. Coleman was asked to discover if the goal stated by Horace Mann in the 1830s was being achieved in the 1960s. Mann asserted that the schools would be the "great equalizer," and Coleman and his colleagues were asked by the government to discover if there was a "lack of availability of equal educational opportunities for individuals by reason of race, color, religion, or national origin." They published their conclusions in *Equality of Educational Opportunity* (the Coleman Report) and touched off a debate that still continues. The Coleman Report itself is difficult to analyze because of its size and complexity, but if you would like to gain background information to draw your own conclusions, an excellent single source is *On Equality of Educational Opportunity* (1972) edited by Frederick Mosteller and Daniel P. Moynihan. The first part consists of ten interpretations of the Coleman Report by eminent psychologists, sociologists, and educators, including Coleman and Christopher S. Jencks. The second part discusses "Implications for the Future." If possible, you might also sample sections of *Inequality: A Reassessment of the Effect of Family and Schooling in America* (1972) by Jencks and several associates, which consists of a detailed analysis of the Coleman Report plus reports of the research conducted by the Center for Educational Policy Research. To increase your understanding of the nature of inequality, you might read sections of either or both of these books, summarize the points made, and comment on your own interpretations.

Recommended Reading in *Psychology Applied to Teaching: Selected Readings*

If you would like to do further reading in books or articles mentioned in this chapter (and in the preceding "Suggestions for Further Reading, Writing, Thinking, and Discussion") without having to track down several separate volumes, you might peruse *Psychology Applied to Teaching: Selected Readings* (Boston: Houghton Mifflin, 1972). This is a collection of excerpts from books and articles from journals in psychology. The following selections provide extended commentaries on points noted in this chapter or mentioned in the "Suggestions."

Learning for Mastery: excerpt from *Mastery Learning: Theory and Practice* by James H. Block, Selection 28, p. 420. (See also Suggestion 1–3.)

The Nature of Structure: "The Importance of Structure" by Jerome S. Bruner, Selection 1, p. 1. (See also Suggestion 1–4.)

Theory of Spontaneous Schooling: "The Argument in Brief" by J. M. Stephens, Selection 3, p. 18. (See also Suggestion 1–5.)

Teaching as an Art: "Psychology and the Teaching Art" by William James, Selection 2, p. 12. (See also Suggestion 1–12.)

Self-Fulfilling Prophecy: "Teachers' Expectancies—Determinants of Pupils' IQ Gains" by Robert Rosenthal and Lenore Jacobson, Selection 38, p. 552; Review of *Pygmalion in the Classroom* by Robert L. Thorndike, Selection 39, p. 557; four articles from the *Journal of Consulting and Clinical Psychology,* Selection 34, p. 519; "On Not So Replicated Experiments and Not So Null Results," by Robert Rosenthal, Selection 35, p. 532; "Reflections on Replications and the Experimenter Bias Effect" by Leon H. Levy, Selection 37, p. 546. (See also Suggestion 1–16.)

 BACKGROUND FOR A

TEACHER-THEORIST

KEY POINTS

Trends
Free education approach of Rousseau and Tolstoy again popular in 1970s
Controlled education becomes ultrasystematic under influence of Skinner
Open education develops as compromise between free and controlled approaches

Experiments
Conditioning of dog to salivate when bell rings (Pavlov)
Shaping of rat and pigeon behavior by reinforcement (Skinner)
Solving of stick problem by ape through insight (Kohler)

Concepts
Specific transfer of skills, general transfer of principles, structure (Bruner)
Zeitgeist
Gestalt

Theories
Behaviorism (Watson)
Associationism (Stress on objectivity, research, analysis)
Cognitive-field theory (thought, fields of forces)
Skinner's version of S-R associationism culminating in programmed instruction
Bruner's form of cognitive-field theory leading to his type of discovery approach
Maslow's conception of humanistic psychology
Perceptual view of behavior (Combs and Snygg)

Methodology
Themes of open education (Walberg and Thomas)

CHAPTER CONTENTS

THE OPENING CHAPTER EMPHASIZED THAT THIS BOOK, ALONG WITH THE supplementary and evaluation materials, is devised to assist you to learn an organized set of ideas about psychology. The aim is to encourage you to learn the material well enough to be able—and eager—to apply it when the course is finished and to continue to fit new perceptions into your view of psychology. If you develop a clear enough set of ideas, you will be able to apply what you have learned consistently and logically, thus avoiding a mindless approach to teaching.

The Nature and Importance of Transfer

Jerome Bruner has given a succinct and exceptionally clear description of what teachers try to accomplish. The following passage, which has achieved the status of a classic statement, sums up many of the points made in the first chapter:

> The first object of any act of learning, over and beyond the pleasure it may give, is that it should serve us in the future. Learning should not only take us somewhere; it should allow us later to go further more easily. There are two ways in which learning serves the future. One is through its specific applicability to tasks that are highly similar to those we originally learned to perform. Psychologists refer to this phenomenon as specific transfer of training; perhaps it should be called the extension of habits or associations. Its utility appears to be limited in the main to what we usually speak of as skills. A second way in which earlier learning renders later performance more efficient is through what is conveniently called nonspecific transfer or, more accurately, the transfer of principles and attitudes. In essence, it consists of learning initially not a skill but a general idea, which can then be used as a basis for recognizing subsequent problems as special cases of the idea originally mastered. This type of transfer is at the heart of the educational process—the continual broadening and deepening of knowledge in terms of basic and general ideas.
>
> The continuity of learning that is produced by the second type of transfer, transfer of principles, is dependent upon mastery of the structure of the subject matter.... It is simple enough to proclaim, of course, that school curricula and methods of teaching should be geared to the teaching of fundamental ideas in whatever subject is being taught. But as soon as one makes such a statement a host of problems arises.... The first and most obvious problem is how to construct curricula that can be taught by ordinary teachers to ordinary students and that at the same time reflect clearly the basic or underlying principles of various fields of inquiry. The problem is twofold: first, how to have the basic subjects rewritten and their teaching materials revamped in such a way that the pervading and powerful ideas and attitudes relating to them are given a central role; second, how to match the levels of these materials to the capacities of students....
>
> ... Mastery of the fundamental ideas of a field involves not only the grasping of general principles, but also the development of an attitude toward learning and inquiry, toward guessing and hunches, toward the possibility of solving problems on one's own.... To instill such attitudes by teaching requires something more than the mere presentation of fundamental ideas. Just what it takes to bring off such teaching is something on which a great deal of research is needed, but it would seem that an important ingredient is a sense of excitement about discovery—discovery of regularities of previously unrecognized relations and similarities between ideas, with a resulting sense of self-confidence in one's abilities. (1960b, pp. 17–20)

Specific transfer

Transfer of principles

Importance of structure

The Rationale of This Book

This book attempts to rewrite the basic subject matter and revamp the teaching materials of educational psychology to match them to your capacities as students with limited experience in teaching. Considerable emphasis is placed on skills, specific techniques, and applications. This amounts to teaching for specific transfer of training, which seems justified since many aspects of teaching *are* techniques. At the same time, this book hopes to encourage general transfer as much as possible, since transfer of principles and attitudes is at the heart of the educational process. And by stressing applications and urging you to think of your own, the book attempts to introduce the excitement of discovery mentioned by Bruner. If you can relate what is recorded in these pages to the classroom and discover previously unrecognized relationships and similarities between ideas, you may experience that elusive sense of excitement, as well as increased self-confidence in your own abilities.

The use of the word "applied" in the title of this book reflects the hope that you not only read and react to this book now but also use it in the future as a reference in developing your ideas on teaching. Because you probably have had little if any experience with behind-the-scenes aspects of teaching, you may find it difficult at this stage of your career to relate general principles of psychology to classroom problems. Therefore, you may see no reason—other than general interest or exam requirements—for learning what is discussed. By the time you *have* accumulated enough teaching experience to make practical use of the concepts, you may have forgotten them. To prevent this, principles will be presented as they relate to actual classroom practice whenever possible.

However, for this approach to work you will need to develop ideas and applications of your own. To encourage you to do so, the text will present many questions for you to consider and provide write-in spaces for your responses to these questions; the margins are wide enough for you to make notes. As you read each section and chapter, it will be to your advantage to think of past teachers and classes and recollect efficient and not-so-efficient techniques. When you observe or assist in the public schools, record the actions and interactions of both pupils and teachers—and your own reactions to them. During or after your Methods course, use this book as a frame of reference for organizing suggestions that strike you as noteworthy. During or after your student teaching, record techniques that impress you as worthwhile. Then during your first months and years of teaching, jot down new techniques and revise earlier ones that fail to live up to expectations.

Following some or all of these suggestions should give you a head start toward feeling prepared when you first step in front of a class of your own. In a sense you will have at hand a custom-designed reference work. When a problem develops, you may be able to search out a relevant suggestion—or find an idea you previously thought through—that will point to a promising solution. And as you theorize about teaching, you may be able to arrange your ideas into a more or less systematic pattern.

To take advantage of the continuity of learning produced by transfer of principles, you will need to master the structure of educational psychology. To accomplish that goal you will need to understand and attempt to reconcile

BROWN BROTHERS

John B. Watson (1878–1958)   Wolfgang Köhler (1887–1967)

some of the differing opinions held by psychologists. These differences are illustrated most clearly by two major schools of learning theory that have developed in American psychology. They will be fully discussed at length in Chapter 5, but at this juncture a brief overview is presented to serve as an organizational frame of reference.

Two Major Positions on Learning

To understand how learning theory developed, you need to know a bit about the history of psychology. Psychology is generally considered to have been established as a science when a German named Wilhelm Wundt founded a psychological laboratory in Leipzig in 1879. Wundt was primarily interested in sensation and perception, and he placed heavy reliance on the method of *introspection*. Introspection in this sense meant the describing of the way one perceives certain events or objects. For example, Wundt would confront a subject with various visual patterns and ask him to describe what he saw.

The field of psychology was originally thought of as an outgrowth of philosophy. Yet Wundt and his followers had backgrounds in medicine and physiology. The philosophy-physiology conflict led to considerable debate on the nature of psychology as a science. The question was raised—and continues to be debated—as to whether it is possible to deal scientifically with nonobservable

BROWN BROTHERS

THE BETTMANN ARCHIVE

Edward L. Thorndike (1874–1949)   Ivan Pavlov (1849–1936)

phenomena (such as thoughts and feelings). The personal decision a psychologist makes about this basic question will tend to influence his ideas about psychology and its application to the educational process.

Most early psychologists followed Wundt's lead until disagreements and offshoots from his original ideas developed. Many of the disagreements were crystallized explicitly in the work of John B. Watson (1925). Watson argued that if psychologists were to be really scientific, they should not trust subjective data (the introspective reactions of subjects) but should concern themselves only with overt, observable behavior. This emphasis on overt behavior led to the label *behaviorism* to describe Watson's approach. In developing his theory of behaviorism, Watson was strongly influenced by the work of Ivan Pavlov, and mention of Pavlov brings us to learning theory.

Theory of behaviorism

Pavlov, you probably are aware, described the learning behavior he observed as the formation of associations between stimuli and responses. He would ring a bell and then put food out for a dog, which made the dog salivate. After repeating the process several times the dog, having associated the sound with the food, would salivate upon simply hearing the bell. Pavlov explained this by saying the dog had been *conditioned* to respond. Watson, the champion of objectivity, endorsed Pavlov's theory enthusiastically and applied it to a theory of child development and child rearing based on conditioning (Watson, 1928). His passion for objectivity led him to suggest, among other things, that parents should suppress tendencies to show affection for their children.

Pavlov experiment: dog conditioned to salivate

Although Watson is acknowledged as the founder of behaviorism, he did not develop a behavioristic learning theory. The first American learning theorist was Edward L. Thorndike (1932), who spent his long and prolific professional life searching for laws of learning patterned after the laws of physics. Thorndike may be more familiar as the man who conducted experiments in which cats learned to release themselves from cages by trial-and-error discovery of how to operate a latch mechanism. He published over 500 books and articles on many aspects of educational psychology, specializing in learning, evaluation, and transfer. Watson, Thorndike, and their followers were instrumental in initiating three important themes that have dominated learning theory in America: associations between stimuli and responses, objective observation of overt behavior, and the establishment of laws of learning.

Nature of associationism

At the same time that stimulus-response (S-R) theories were being formulated, a group of German psychologists were performing experiments to show that man and higher-order primates learn also through the development of *insight.* Instead of seeing learning as the formation of associations between stimuli and responses, they viewed it as the rearrangement of previous ideas and experiences leading to new patterns of thought, or insight. They chose the German word *Gestalt* ("configuration") to signify their belief in the importance of patterns; but they also spoke of *cognitive-field theory, cognitive* emphasizing thought and

Gestalt

Historical Background of Psychology

The comments made in this chapter on the philosophical and historical background of modern psychology are necessarily oversimplified, but *A History of Experimental Psychology* by Edwin G. Boring analyzes the subject in detail. If you are intrigued by the history and philosophy of science, you will enjoy sampling this volume since Boring combines great erudition with literary style. His general approach is revealed in the following excerpt:

Impact of Zeitgeist

> The progress of science is the work of creative minds. Every creative mind that contributes to scientific advance works, however, within two limitations. It is limited, first, by ignorance, for one discovery waits upon that other which opens the way to it. Discovery and its acceptance are, however, limited also by the habits of thought that pertain to the culture of any region and period, that is to say, by the *Zeitgeist:* an idea too strange or preposterous to be thought in one period of western civilization may be readily accepted as true only a century or two later. Slow change is the rule—at least for the basic ideas. On the other hand, the more superficial fashions as to what is important, what is worth doing and talking about, change much more rapidly, depending partly on discovery and partly on the social interaction of the wise men most concerned with the particular matter in hand—the cross-stimulation of leaders and their followers, of protagonists and their antagonists. A psychologist's history of psychology is, therefore, at least in aspiration, a dynamic or social

field theory stressing the conception of a "field of forces" in behavior, that is, the interaction of factors influencing a person's behavior at a given moment. (The psychological field of forces is analogous to the gravitational or electromagnetic fields described by physicists.)

Two clusters of ideas regarding the nature of psychology and how it can be applied to teaching and learning have emerged from these early theories—one stressing S-R associations, the other patterns of thought. The associationist position is exemplified most clearly by the work of B. F. Skinner, whose theory of learning derives from Pavlov and Thorndike. Skinner has proposed a variation on the S-R idea. The best-known illustration of Skinner's concept is programmed learning. Students are presented with a series of questions (stimuli) and encouraged to compare their answers (responses) to those provided in the program. When they supply correct answers, they are *reinforced;* responses that are reinforced are strengthened and likely to be retained.

Many American educational psychologists sympathize with some or all of Skinner's beliefs; that is, they agree that learning consists mainly of the development of associations between stimuli and responses, and they endorse related ideas that more or less emerge from this conviction. Others, however, accept principles derived from the work of the German Gestalt psychologists. The current leading spokesman for this point of view is Jerome Bruner, whose

---

psychology, trying to see not only what men did and what they did not do, but also why they did it or why, at the time, they could not do it. (1950, p.3)

As this statement suggests, *A History of Experimental Psychology* relates the development of famous psychologists to the prevailing Zeitgeist. It points out the influence of particular individuals, developments, and events on psychology. Boring describes, for example, how René Descartes contributed to the start of modern psychology when he developed the idea that the body of man is a machine but that his mind is free and separate; how John Locke also contributed when he proposed the *tabula rasa* (the mind of an infant is a "blank slate") concept and suggested that ideas come from experience; how empiricism (learning through the senses) developed in Germany, leading eventually to the establishment of Wundt's laboratory; how Darwin's *The Origin of Species* led to interest in comparative psychology (the study of animal as well as human behavior) and genetics; how the American ethos influenced Thorndike, John Dewey, Watson, and Skinner; and how the German Zeitgeist influenced the Gestalt psychologists and Sigmund Freud. If you would like to get a clearer picture of all these men, their theories, and their times, Boring has provided it. Incidentally, if you smiled a bit at his name, a reading of his *History* will show you that the name is certainly not descriptive of the man.

analysis of structure was quoted at the beginning of this chapter. The concept of structure, involving as it does arrangements and patterns of ideas, is one of the best illustrations of the Gestalt approach.

In this book frequent contrast will be made between the Skinner and Bruner theories. To give you some background for making meaningful comparisons, here is a brief survey of the main points, first in Skinner's version of S-R associationism and then in Bruner's interpretation of cognitive-field theory.

S-R Associationism: Skinner

Skinner endorses the behaviorist belief that only overt behavior—that is, behavior that can be observed by others (or *measurable* manifestations of overt behavior such as brain waves)—is appropriate to scientific study. Because of this preoccupation with strictly scientific observation, he restricts his highly controlled experiments to the lower animal forms. The following Skinner-box experiment is typical of his approach. A hungry rat is placed in a closed box containing only a lever and a food tray. When the rat presses the lever under conditions chosen by the experimenter, it is rewarded with a food pellet. After providing a sufficient number of reinforcing experiences, the experimenter can shape the rat's behavior at will.

Skinner-box experiment

Success in influencing the behavior of rats (and pigeons) has led Skinner and other S-R psychologists to generalize that teachers or schoolbooks should function in much the same way—they should shape the behavior of pupils by presenting sequences of stimuli and responses and reinforcing responses that lead the pupil to the desired outcome. In programmed learning, which is the clearest illustration of the S-R concept applied to education, a *program* of stimuli replaces or supplements the conventional text or teacher in presenting subject matter.

Skinner's interpretation of S-R associationism

From the discussion above it should be obvious that teaching consistent with the S-R approach would require considerable control by the teacher. Your role would be much like that of a programmer, shaping the responses of your pupils to produce a predetermined end result.

Cognitive-Field Theory: Bruner

Jerome Bruner and his fellow cognitive-field theorists endorse a quite different —and in some respects opposing—set of beliefs. Field theorists start out with the assumption that psychologists should be concerned not only with overt behavior but also with the underlying mental processes that cause behavior. They view learning as either the gaining of new insights or the changing of old ideas and perceptions leading to new insights. Because the field theorist's conception of what is appropriate for scientific study differs from the S-R associationist's, the field theorist is more inclined to experiment on higher-order animals and on human beings. And he is likely to study these organisms in more or less natural situations. Some field theorists argue that Skinner's experiments may be somewhat misleading since the rat's environment is so completely controlled that only the type of contrived and artificial behavior permitted by the experimenter can occur. They say that while the Skinner box does permit almost complete experimental control and thus is thoroughly scientific, this very control may distort the results.

The field theorist *encourages* learning by the way he arranges the environment, but he does not *control* learning as the S-R theorist does. In a typical Gestalt experiment, learning occurs by the subject's perception of relationships, or, in other words, by his gaining insight into the solution of a problem. One famous field theory experiment conducted by Wolfgang Köhler involved an ape named Sultan, who solved a problem by perceiving the relationship between two sticks (which could be used as rakes) and a banana placed outside his cage. (This experiment is described in detail in Chapter 5.)

Köhler experiment: insight gained by ape

Whereas the teaching machine is the preeminent S-R educational method, the *discovery approach* is perhaps the best example of the field theorist's pedagogic technique. If, as a teacher, you were to become an advocate of the

Skinner's Reply to Field Theory Critics

To acquaint you with both sides of key arguments in psychology—so that you can make up your own mind on these questions—an "equal space" policy is followed in this book. Here are some of Skinner's answers to field theory critics as given in *The Technology of Teaching* (1968):

> Some objections to the use of [teaching machines] in the classroom can easily be foreseen. The cry will be raised that the child is being treated as a mere animal and that an essentially human intellectual achievement is being analyzed in unduly mechanistic terms. . . . It is true that the techniques which are emerging from the experimental study of learning are not designed to "develop the mind" or to further some vague "understanding" of . . . relationships. They are designed, on the contrary, to establish the very behaviors which are taken to be the evidences of such mental states or processes. (P. 26)
>
> A common objection [to programmed learning] is that most of the early work responsible for the basic formulation of behavior was done on so-called lower animals. It has been argued that the procedures are therefore appropriate only to animals and that to use them in education is to treat the student like an animal. So far as I know, no one argues that because something is true of a pigeon, it is therefore true of a man. . . . Relatively simple organisms have many advantages in early stages of research, but they impose no limit on that research. Complex processes are met and dealt with as the analysis proceeds. Experiments on pigeons may not throw much light on the "nature" of man, but they are extraordinarily helpful in enabling us to analyze man's environment more effectively. What is common to pigeon and man is a world in which certain contingencies of reinforcement prevail. The schedule of reinforcement which makes a pigeon a pathological gambler is to be found at racetrack and roulette table, where it has a comparable effect. (P. 84)

Bruner's interpretation of field theory

discovery approach, you would try to provide situations that would encourage insight so that your pupils could discover ideas on their own. You would supply subtle assistance but would not try to manipulate or shape behavior.

Two Basic Conceptions of Education

Programmed learning and the discovery approach are current examples of psychological theory applied in the classroom. Although the degree to which they are based on scientific observation, experimentation, and analysis is a recent development, the basic educational concepts they rest on are not new. For hundreds of years educators have argued the advantages and disadvantages of teacher-guided instruction and self-directed learning. In nearly all periods in history most people have assumed that learning experiences in school settings should be organized by a teacher. At frequent intervals, however, educational leaders have emerged who have been repelled by the common abuses of authority that occur in controlled education and by the degree to which imposed learning snuffs out curiosity, creativity, and interest in further learning. In 1762, for example, Jean Jacques Rousseau published *Émile*, in which he criticized all aspects of formal learning and proposed that education should be completely natural and spontaneous. A hundred years later, Leo Tolstoy advocated the same basic point of view. He wrote:

Free education of 1970s similar to that of Rousseau and Tolstoy

> Education is a compulsory, forcible action of one person upon another for the purpose of forming a man such as will appear (to society) to be good. . . . Education is the tendency toward moral despotism raised to a principle. . . . I am convinced that the educator undertakes with such zeal the education of a child because at the base of this tendency lies his envy of the child's purity, and his desire to make him like himself, that is, to spoil him. (1967, pp. 110–111)

Tolstoy spent almost ten years attempting to institute a form of schooling which would not be a "compulsory, forcible action of one person on another."

Early in this century, John Dewey observed; "The history of educational theory is marked by opposition between the idea that education is development from within and that it is formation from without" (1938, p. 1). He went on to say, "At present [the 1930s] the opposition . . . tends to take the form of contrast between traditional and progressive education" (p. 2). He described traditional education as the transmission of bodies of information, skills, standards, and rules of conduct that had been worked out in the past. Progressive education, on the other hand, stressed learning not through teacher-led instruction but through personal experience, with emphasis on the immediate present.

Descriptions of the free-school approach by Neill (1960), Holt (1964), Kohl (1967, Kozol (1972), Dennison (1969), and others present many of the arguments and suggestions made by Dewey sixty years ago. Many of these discussions present free (or progressive) education as an alternative to controlled (or traditional) education, which gives the impression that a teacher must make

Jean Jacques Rousseau (1712–1778)

Leo Tolstoy (1828–1910)

A. S. Neill (1883–1973)

John Holt (1923–   )

a choice between extremes. In the Preface to *Experience and Education,* Dewey suggested a more constructive point of view: "It is the business of an intelligent theory of education to ascertain the causes for the conflicts that exist and then, instead of taking one side or the other, to indicate a plan of operations proceeding from a level deeper and more inclusive than is represented by the practices and ideas of the contending parties" (1963, p. v). Even if it may not be possible to be completely successful in developing an "overall plan which is deeper and more inclusive," analysis of the differences may assist you in making decisions as to when a controlled or free approach is appropriate and how you might use techniques derived from both in a manner consistent with underlying theory.

Assumptions of Controlled Education

Advocates of controlled instruction have operated on the assumption that it is the responsibility of knowledgable adults to help children learn. One of the most carefully worked out defenses of this point of view is that of B. F. Skinner in *Beyond Freedom and Dignity.* Skinner sums up his basic argument in favor of a controlled over a permissive approach in this way: "Permissiveness is not . . . a policy; it is the abandonment of policy, and its apparent advantages are illusory. To refuse to control is to leave control not to the person himself, but to other parts of the social and non-social environments" (1971, p. 84).

To understand his reasoning, you should take into account Skinner's assumption that virtually all behavior results from environmental experiences. If this view is accepted, then the key to understanding behavior is to analyze the kinds of experiences a person has had. If we hope to solve personal, social, and educational problems, Skinner maintains, we should decide in advance what the most desirable kind of behavior is, then carefully arrange the proper chain of experiences to produce it. He has had the courage to write a novel, *Walden Two* (1948), in which he describes how he would create a complete society based on this assumption. This is a book you ought to read since it not only illustrates the techniques Skinner advocates but is also a fascinating and entertaining story. In *The Technology of Teaching* (1968) Skinner presents in an even more systematic way many of the ideas described in *Walden Two,* emphasizing their relevance to teaching.

Controlled education becomes ultrasystematic under influence of Skinner

Skinner views conventional education as extremely inefficient. To improve it, he feels we must make teaching more scientific, mainly through programmed instruction. Skinner suggests that the first step in putting programmed instruction into practice is for the teacher to define explicitly what she wants her students to learn. Next she should make up a program of questions and answers, organizing the material to be learned into a logical series of small steps, then encourage each pupil to proceed through the sequence at his own rate. (Suggestions on how to write and use programs are offered in Chapter 5.) But Skinner believes that subject matter is not all that should be taught through programmed

Skinner's programmed approach to education

THE NEW YORK TIMES

B. F. Skinner   Born in 1904 into a professional family in Susquehanna, Pennsylvania, Skinner early showed the inventiveness that later produced the Skinner box and teaching machines. One of his numerous boyhood inventions was a steam cannon he used to shoot plugs cut from potatoes and carrots over the roofs of neighborhood houses. As an English major at Hamilton College, he was elected to Phi Beta Kappa, and after graduation he spent two years attempting to establish himself as a writer. Dissatisfied with his efforts, he entered Harvard to do graduate study in psychology and earned his Ph.D. in 1931. Except for a few years of teaching at the University of Minnesota and Indiana University, Skinner has spent his entire professional career at Harvard. When psychology department chairmen were asked in 1970 to nominate the man who had produced the greatest impact on American psychology, Skinner was the overwhelming first choice. With the publication of *Beyond Freedom and Dignity* in 1971, Skinner achieved considerable notoriety. He was the subject of a cover story in *Time* magazine (September 20, 1971) and appeared on numerous television talk shows. A brief biography by T. George Harris appeared in the August 1971 issue of *Psychology Today,* pp. 33–35.

instruction. He argues that students can be taught how to think and encouraged to develop perseverance and even originality and creativity. He suggests that the famous creators in history—artists, composers, and scientists—were simply the result of accidental patterns of reinforcement, that is, events that strengthened particular forms of behavior. He regards the great individual as having contributed quite little to his greatness, which he sees as largely the result of a favorable chain of experiences. He concludes, therefore, that by judicious reinforcement we should be able to systematically produce what nature has created by accident.

Criticisms of Controlled Education

Although Skinner's suggestion that we be more systematic and scientific in our efforts to encourage desirable behavior makes sense from his point of view, it appears to have disadvantages—if not dangers—when it is seen from another angle. The major criticism is summed up by Arthur Combs and Donald Snygg in this way: "The environmental approach to behavior has led us to believe that almost anything can be accomplished in dealing with people if we are

---

Some Views on Determinism

The conflict regarding determinism is not new. Around the turn of the century Herbert Spencer argued, "The great man must be classed with all other phenomena in the society that gave him birth, as a product of its antecedents." He goes on to say that although the great man may seem to be the initiator of changes, "if there is to be anything like a real explanation of these changes, it must be sought in that aggregate of conditions out of which both he and they have risen." (Notice the similarity of this argument to Boring's theory of the importance of the Zeitgeist.) William James replied to Spencer in this way:

> If anything is humanly certain, it is that the great man's society, properly so called, does not make him before he can remake it. . . . Can it be that Mr. Spencer holds the convergence of sociological pressures to have so impinged upon Stratford-upon-Avon about the twenty-sixth of April, 1564, that a W. Shakespeare, with all his mental peculiarities, had to be born there? . . . And does he mean to say that if the aforesaid W. Shakespeare had died of cholera infantum, another mother at Stratford-upon-Avon would need have engendered a duplicate copy of him, to restore the sociologic equilibrium? (Both the Spencer and James quotations are from Huxley, 1958, pp. 121–22.)

What are your reactions? Was Shakespeare the product of Elizabethan England, of accidental contingencies of reinforcement, as Skinner puts it? If he had died as an infant, would his equal have been produced if the same contingencies of reinforcement had been applied to any other infant in Stratford-upon-Avon? Or was there something special about Shakespeare, something determined by his inheritance and his unique personality?

---

sufficiently skillful in the manipulation of the proper forces at the proper time.... [This approach] requires that someone must know what the 'right' goal is in order effectively to manipulate the required forces" (1959, p. 311). Skinner and other environmentalists believe that a more mature, experienced person can determine "right" behavior better than a child. However, Combs and Snygg and other advocates of free instruction question this premise. They believe that since each child is unique, only he can determine what is "right" for him; therefore, education should be largely self-directed. Skinner argues that such an approach assumes "that the balance of control is left to the individual, when in fact it is left to other conditions" (1971, p. 99). He maintains that a controlled environment does not necessarily lead to uniformity and regimentation. If properly planned, he says, it can lead to greater diversification and variety than "accidental" environments in which development is left largely to chance.

The key to this argument is: How can controlled education be "properly planned" to encourage diversity rather than uniformity? Some forms of structured education now in existence, for example, the traditional public school, appear to lead to regimentation and to minimize diversity. Instead of preparing students to willingly engage in self-directed learning after they leave the classroom, they seem to do the opposite. And many applications of the principles of associationism, such as programmed learning and performance contracting, have featured exactly the kind of preplanned environment Skinner maintains should lead to improved learning, but they have not been conspicuously successful in doing so. (Research on this point will be discussed in Chapter 5.)

The common abuses of controlled learning have led advocates of free learning to reject *any* form of structured learning. John Dewey, however, observes:

> When external authority is rejected, it does not follow that all authority should be rejected, but rather that there is need to search for a more effective source of authority. Because [traditional] education imposes the knowledge, methods, and the rules of conduct of the mature person upon the young, it does not follow ... that the knowledge and skill of the mature person has no directive value for the experience of the immature. On the contrary, basing education upon personal experience may mean more multiplied and intimate contacts between the mature and the immature than ever existed in the traditional school, and consequently more, rather than less, guidance by others. The problem, then, is: how these contacts can be established without violating the principle of learning through personal experience. (1938, pp. 8–9)

These following remarks, made by Dewey in 1938, apply as much now as they did then:

> Many of the newer schools tend to make little or nothing of organized subject-matter of study; to proceed as if any form of direction and guidance by adults were an invasion of individual freedom, and as if the idea that education should be concerned with the present and future meant that acquaintance with the past

has little or no role to play in education. [This illustrates] . . . a theory and practice of education which proceeds negatively or by reaction against what has been current in education rather than by a positive and constructive development of purposes, methods, and subject matter on the foundation of a theory of experience and its educational potentialities. (Pp. 9–10)

The open-education movement is a current example of what Dewey meant by "a positive and constructive development of purposes, methods, and subject-matter on the foundation of a theory of experience and its educational potentialities."

Themes of Open Education

Herbert J. Walberg and Susan Christie Thomas (1972) feel that while enthusiasm for open education is increasing rapidly, so is confusion about exactly what is involved. They therefore reviewed all available literature on open education, broke it down into components, and then sought to verify their description with prominent open educators. They eventually evolved a list of eight "open education themes" to be used in evaluating this form of instruction.[1] Following is a list of the eight themes of what takes place in a typical open classroom, as described by Walberg and Thomas:

Themes of open education

1. *Provisioning* for Learning:
   Manipulative materials are supplied in great diversity and range with little replication, i.e., not class sets. Children move freely about the room without asking permission. Talking among children is encouraged. The teacher does group children by ability according to tests or norms. Children generally group and re-group themselves through their own choices.
2. *Humaneness*, Respect, Openness and Warmth:
   Children use "books" written by their classmates as part of their reading and reference materials. The environment includes materials developed or supplied by the children. Teacher takes care of dealing with conflicts and disruptive behavior without involving the group. Children's activities, products, and ideas are reflected abundantly about the classroom.
3. *Diagnosis* of Learning Events:
   Teacher uses test results to group children for reading and/or math. Children expect the teacher to correct all their work. Teacher gives children tests to find out what they know. To obtain diagnostic information, the teacher closely observes the specific work or concern of a child and asks immediate, experience-based questions.
4. *Instruction*, Guidance, and Extension of Learning:
   Teacher bases her instruction on each individual child and his interaction with materials and equipment. The work children do is divided into subject matter areas. The teacher's lessons and assignments are given to the class as a whole. Teacher bases her instruction on curriculum guides or text

[1]Although most advocates of open education probably endorse most of the points on this list, some undoubtedly disagree with specific sections. Thus the list is not "official"; it is simply a composite interpretation indicating general trends.

books for the grade level she teaches. Before suggesting any extension
or redirection of activity, teacher gives diagnostic attention to the particular child and his particular activity.

5. *Evaluation* of Diagnostic Information:
   Teacher keeps notes and writes individual histories of each child's intellectual, emotional, physical development. Teacher has children for a period
   of just one year. Teacher uses tests to evaluate children and rate them
   in comparison to their peers. Teacher keeps a collection of each child's
   work for use in evaluating his development. Teacher views evaluation
   as information to guide her instruction and provisioning for the classroom.

6. *Seeking* Opportunities for Professional Growth:
   Teacher uses the assistance of someone in a supportive, advisory capacity.
   Teacher has helpful colleagues with whom she discusses teaching.

7. *Self-Perception* of Teacher:
   Teacher tries to keep all children within her sight so that she can make
   sure they are doing what they are supposed to do.

8. *Assumptions* about Children and Learning Process:
   The emotional climate is warm and accepting. The class operates within
   clear guidelines made explicit. Academic achievement is the teacher's
   top priority for the children. Children are deeply involved in what they
   are doing. (1972, pp. 200–201)

As this description indicates, open education (as practiced by the leading
proponents surveyed by Walberg and Thomas) involves considerable adult
guidance. It is an eclectic approach, allowing freedom but also supplying
direction. Walberg and Thomas sum up the basic philosophy this way: "Open
educators hold that the teacher and the child, in complementary roles, should
together fashion the child's school experience. Thus, open education differs from
teacher-centered, child-centered, programmed, textbook, or other materials-cen-
tered approaches in that it combines all three, with both the teacher and the
child determining learning goals, materials, and activities" (p. 198).

Open education as a compromise between control and freedom

Open education appears to have many advantages, and you may already
be convinced that you would like to pattern your teaching on it. Regardless
of your feelings about open education techniques, you can take advantage of
Dewey's suggestion that you try to combine the best aspects of different
approaches to teaching—rather than just react negatively to aspects of current
education you do not like. Analysis of some features of contemporary education
leads to the conclusions stressed by the most outspoken critics—there is undeniably too much regimentation, control, rote memorization, parroting back only
what the teacher says, competitiveness, and mindlessness. But eliminating all
control by the teacher appears to be what Dewey called a "reaction against
what is current in education rather than . . . a positive and constructive development." If associationism is understood, its techniques can be used constructively.
Similarly, a firm grasp of field theory will permit an effective use of the discovery
approach. To this end, brief outlines of the background and assumptions of
associationism and discovery learning will now be offered.

Learning More About Open Education

Walberg and Thomas developed their description of open education themes because "there has been very little research on Open Education, aside from testimonials by exponents and reporters" (1972, p. 197). By providing their summary, they have made it possible to identify teaching techniques that reflect an open approach and also to evaluate their effectiveness. The eight themes represent one of the most carefully derived descriptions of open education available. Among other, more detailed accounts of this approach are the following:

The most comprehensive description is *Children and Their Primary Schools* (1967) (usually called the Plowden Report, after Lady Plowden, who headed it). Accounts of the British approach written by teachers who have practiced it include *Inside the Primary School* (1971) by John Blackie, *Primary Education in Britain Today* (1970) edited by Geoffrey Howson, and a series of twenty-three booklets being issued by Citadel Press under the title *Informal Schools in Britain Today*. Descriptions of open education by American educators include *Schools Are for Children: An American Approach to the Open Classroom* (1971) by Alvin Hertzberg and Edward Stone, *Homework: Required Reading for Teachers and Parents* (1971) by Gloria Channon, *The English Infant School and Informal Education* (1971) by Lillian Weber, *Children Come First* (1971) by Casey and Liza Murrow, *Open Education: Promise and Problems* (1972) by Vito Perrone (dean of the Center for Teaching and Learning

Background and Nature of Associationism

Associationism developed as American psychologists applied the methods of the natural and physical sciences to human behavior. As noted in the earlier description of behaviorism, most American psychologists felt that it was not possible to study thinking and feeling in an objective manner. So they concentrated on overt behavior and performed highly controlled experiments featuring precise measurements and the analysis of specific variables. Although behaviorism did much to establish trends in research and theorizing, American psychology also was influenced by the fact that scientists who teach in American universities place primary emphasis on research and the preparation of future researchers. Furthermore, in order to be as precise and objective as possible, most scientists concentrate on specific variables when they perform experiments. This leads to the accumulation of numerous brief studies on related aspects of a given point, which in turn predisposes the researcher to specialize.

Many psychologists are influenced by these factors, in both their approach to teaching and their conception of education: Relationships with students are often deliberately detached and objective, courses frequently consist of technical analyses of specific points, and subject matter is usually divided into specialized areas of study. Objectivity, emphasis on research, and concentrating on analysis of specific variables are necessary and valuable in appropriate situations, but they can lead to complications if applied too literally to undergraduate education.

at the University of North Dakota, center of the open education movement in the United States), *The School Without Walls* (1971) by John Bremer and Michael von Maschzisker (which describes the Philadelphia Parkway program), and *Open Education: A Sourcebook for Parents and Teachers* (1972) edited by Ewald B. Nyquist and Gene R. Hawes. Two books by reporters are *Schools Where Children Learn* (1971) by Joseph Featherstone and *Crisis in the Classroom* (1970) by Charles E. Silberman.

When reading any of these books, particularly those by Featherstone and Silberman, it would be prudent to assume the role of teacher-theorist and guard against wishful thinking. Silberman, for example, uses an "item" technique to back up his arguments in favor of open education, that is, his descriptions of classroom incidents are favorable to the open method and unfavorable to structured forms of teaching. Unfortunately, this is unsatisfactory evidence since unsystematic and unverifiable bits of information could be used to prove any point. Open education has tremendous appeal, it has aroused great enthusiasm, and it may be the basic technique you hope to use in your classroom. But you are more likely to make the most of the method if you evaluate it critically—by putting your feelings in cold storage, as Stephens suggests, and by applying the scientific method to avoid false generalizations. Open education is still in an early process of development, and any new technique always has limitations or inconsistencies that pioneer enthusiasts are likely to overlook.

The attitudes associationists recommend are somewhat dehumanized, and the teaching techniques they have developed seem mechanistic to many observers. It sometimes appears that psychologists committed to the behaviorist-associationist position have not considered the point made by Stephens (noted in Chapter 1): "It is possible that a cold, analytic attitude . . . would prevent the teacher from stimulating students and would make for poor rapport." As Stephens notes, the goals stressed by behaviorist-associationists are appropriate for a teacher-theorist but not always for a teacher-practitioner. Admiration for the order and rigor of scientific methods has also made it difficult for many psychologists to accept the proposition noted by Combs and Snygg that attempts by some human beings to control others are fundamentally different from attempts to control things or animals.

Some who have read Skinner's *Beyond Freedom and Dignity* (1971), for example, have been bothered by his precise, ultrascientific manner of expression, or by what appears to be a cold-blooded conception of human behavior.[2] A few American political leaders were sufficiently outraged to demand that Federal grants for Skinner's research be withdrawn. The *APA Monitor* for January-February 1972 (p. 6) reported that Representative Cornelius Gallagher made the following remarks in the House: "I certainly believe that Dr. Skinner has every

---

[2] In an interview with Elizabeth Hall in the November 1972 issue of *Psychology Today*, Skinner comments on and answers many of the criticisms of *Beyond Freedom and Dignity*.

right, both as a citizen and as a distinguished academic, to publish his ideas and to speak for them in any way he can. But what I question is whether he should be subsidized by the Federal Government especially since, in my judgment, he is advancing ideas which threaten the future of our system of

---

Excerpts from *Beyond Freedom and Dignity*

The following excerpts sum up Skinner's major arguments in *Beyond Freedom and Dignity.* As you read them, you will understand why literal interpretation of these statements has led to attacks by governmental figures and others.

Almost all our major problems involve human behavior, and they cannot be solved by physical and biological technology alone. What is needed is a technology of behavior, but we have been slow to develop the science from which such a technology might be drawn. One difficulty is that almost all of what is called behavioral science continues to trace behavior to states of mind, feelings, traits of character, human nature, and so on. Physics and biology once followed similar practices and advanced only when they discarded them. . . . As the interaction between organism and environment has come to be understood . . . effects once assigned to states of mind, feelings, and traits are beginning to be traced to accessible conditions, and a technology of behavior may therefore become available. It will not solve our problems, however, until it replaces traditional prescientific views, and these are strongly entrenched. (1971, pp. 24–25)

In what we may call the prescientific view (and the word is not necessarily pejorative) a person's behavior is at least to some extent his own achievement. He is free to deliberate, decide, and act, possibly in original ways, and he is to be given credit for his successes and blamed for his failures. In the scientific view (and the word is not necessarily honorific) a person's behavior is determined by a genetic endowment traceable to the evolutionary history of the species and by the environmental circumstances to which as an individual he has been exposed. Neither view can be proved, but it is in the nature of scientific inquiry that the evidence should shift in favor of the second. As we learn more about the effects of the environment, we have less reason to attribute any part of human behavior to an autonomous controlling agent. And the second view shows a marked advantage when we begin to do something about behavior. Autonomous man is not easily changed; in fact, to the extent that he is autonomous, he is by definition not changeable at all. But the environment can be changed, and we are learning how to change it. The measures we use are those of physical and biological technology, but we use them in special ways to affect behavior. (Pp. 101–102)

Science has probably never demanded a more sweeping change in a traditional way of thinking about a subject, nor has there ever been a more important subject. In the traditional picture a person perceives the world around him, selects features to be perceived, discriminates among them, judges them good or bad, changes them to make them better (or, if he is careless, worse), and may be held responsible for his action and justly rewarded or punished for its consequences. In the scientific picture a person is a member of a species shaped by evolutionary contingencies of survival, displaying behavioral processes which bring him under the control of the environment in which he lives, and largely under the control of a social environment which he and millions of others like him have constructed and maintained during the evolution of a culture. The direction of the controlling relation is reversed: a person does not act upon the world, the world acts upon him. (P. 211)

government by denigrating the American tradition of in   dignity, and self-reliance." If account is taken of why associa   on observable behavior and the manipulation of environme   control behavior, it becomes apparent that there is nothin   Skinner's intentions. He is simply arguing that we should try to be   in arranging factors that cause behavior. Associationists believe tha   are properly manipulated, we should be able to produce more "i   human dignity, and self-reliance" than occur by accident.

Even so, many people, including an increasing number of psychologi   that scientific methods could be used to improve the human condi   not the methods used in the natural and physical sciences. They f   overemphasizing an approach that applies to human methods perfecte   studying objects could lead to treating humans as objects. Though not inevi   this is enough of a possibility to have led to the development of *human*   *psychology.* This movement in American psychology is also referred to as *th*   *force psychology,* the *perceptual view, holistic-dynamic psychology, organism*   *psychology,* or *self-psychology.* As some of these designations suggest, the   principles of field theory are congruent with the assumptions of humanistic   psychology. The man most responsible for the development of this point of   view was Abraham H. Maslow.

Maslow's Principles of Humanistic Psychology

In the Preface to *Motivation and Personality*, Maslow describes the Zeitgeist   that affected his development as a psychologist. He explains how being in New   York City, "the center of the psychological universe" of the late thirties, led   to contact with Max Wertheimer and Kurt Koffka, two of the founders of Gestalt   psychology; how he studied psychoanalysis in preparation for a career as a   psychotherapist; and how he became fascinated by anthropology. These and   other influences led him to try to "synthesize holistic, dynamic and cultural   emphases" into a systematic theory of psychology that would also "enable me   to serve better my humanistic aims" (1954, p. ix). Thus, unlike Skinner and   most other American psychologists, who were influenced primarily by beha-   viorism, Maslow approached psychology from a Gestalt point of view—with   heightened awareness of Freudian doctrine, with interest in the impact of culture,   and as a scientist-humanist.

In *Motivation and Personality* and *Toward a Psychology of Being* (1968), Mas-   low combines ideas from all these diverse influences into a systematic theory.   Both are highly recommended as a permanent addition to your professional   library. Maslow describes *Toward a Psychology of Being* as "a clear confrontation   of one basic set of orthodox values by another newer system of values which   claims to be not only more efficient but also more true" (p. 222). The older   set of values is represented by behaviorism, the newer system by humanistic psychology. Maslow felt that too much stress on objectivity is limiting. Here is the way he put it:

> We must help the "scientific" psychologists to realize that they are working on the basis of *a* philosophy of science, not *the* philosophy of science, and that *any* philosophy of science which serves primarily an excluding function is a set of blinders, a handicap rather than a help. *All* the world, *all* of experience must be open to study. *Nothing,* not even the "personal" problems, need be closed off from human investigation. . . .
>
> I know that these remarks may be easily misunderstood as an attack upon science. They are not. Rather I am suggesting that we enlarge the jurisdiction of science so as to include within its realm the problems and the data of personal and experiential psychology. Many scientists have abdicated from these problems, considering them "unscientific." Leaving them to non-scientists, however, supports that separation of the world of science from the world of the "humanities" which is now crippling them both. (P. 218)

Since you are being asked to consider a variety of ideas as you theorize about teaching, Maslow's remarks are especially appropriate. In the first chapter of *Motivation and Personality,* Maslow argues:

> A psychological interpretation of science begins with the acute realization that science is a human creation, rather than an autonomous, non-human, or *per se* "thing" with intrinsic rules of its own. Its origins are in human motives, its goals are human goals, and it is created, renewed, and maintained by human beings. . . . The psychologist, especially if he has had any clinical experience, will quite naturally and spontaneously approach any subject matter in a personal way by studying people, rather than the abstractions they produce, scientists as well as science. (1954, p. 1)

These comments reveal the importance of considering the Zeitgeist that influences theorists.

Basic Assumptions of Maslow's View of Behavior and Development

Maslow sums up his conception of behavior and development in the last chapter of *Toward a Psychology of Being,* called "Basic Propositions of a Growth and Self-Actualization Psychology," of which there are forty-three. The following statement represents the most systematic attempt of any theorist to describe a coherent philosophy upon which to base free education:

Maslow's conception of humanistic psychology

> We have, each one of us, an essential inner nature which is instinctoid, intrinsic, given, "natural," i.e., with an appreciable hereditary determinant, and which tends strongly to persist. . . .
>
> These are potentialities, not final actualizations. Therefore, they have a life history and must be seen developmentally. They are actualized, shaped or stifled mostly

Abraham H. Maslow   Born in Brooklyn, New York, in 1908, Maslow earned B.A., M.A., and Ph.D. degrees in comparative and experimental psychology at the University of Wisconsin and promptly began there his long teaching career. In the years that followed he studied with leading figures in Gestalt psychology and psychoanalysis, and at a time when he was trying to merge ideas from these various sources into humanistic psychology, he met the arch-behaviorist Edward L. Thorndike. Maslow writes, "Although disapproving of everything I was trying to do, [Thorndike] made me his research assistant, promised to support me as long as necessary, and encouraged me to disagree with him" (Maslow, 1954). At the peak of his career, Maslow was chairman of the Department of Psychology at Brandeis University and in 1967 served as president of the American Psychological Association. Author of *Motivation of Personality* and *Toward a Psychology of Being,* this leading educator and founder of humanistic psychology had just finished a revision of the first book in June 1970 when he suffered a fatal heart attack.

The Perceptual View of Behavior

In keeping with the "equal-space" policy, here are some excerpts from *Individual Behavior* by Arthur Combs and Donald Snygg in which they present a *perceptual view* of behavior basically similar to Maslow's observations; it is offered as an alternative to Skinner's environmentalist view as outlined in *Beyond Freedom and Dignity:*

> [A] concept commonly held . . . sees man as the *victim* of his environment. He is what he is because of what has happened to him. Unfortunately, this point of view, while making possible great strides in some aspects of human living, has, at the same time, made it difficult for us to understand some of our most pressing problems. It has given rise to a mechanistic conception of human beings as physical objects whose behavior is the result of forces acting upon them. It has largely dehumanized psychology, making of human beings little more than objects to be manipulated at will. . . .
>
> Such a view of behavior places the responsibility quite outside the individual himself. The implications of this view are widespread throughout all phases of our society. (1959, pp. 309–310)

As an alternative to this conception, Combs and Snygg propose this view:

> [Man] is part controlled by and in part controlling of his destiny. [This view] provides

(but not altogether) by extra-psychic determinants (culture, family, environment, learning, etc.). . . .

This inner core, even though it is biologically based and "instinctoid," is weak in certain senses rather than strong. It is easily overcome, suppressed or repressed. . . .

It is possible to study this inner nature scientifically and objectively (that is, with the right kind of "science") and to discover what it is like (*discover*—not invent or construct). It is also possible to do this subjectively, by inner search and by psychotherapy, and the two enterprises supplement and support each other. An expanded humanistic philosophy of science must include these experimental techniques. . . .

However, this inner core, or self, grows into adulthood only partly by (objective or subjective) discovery, uncovering and acceptance of what is "there" beforehand. Partly it is also a creation of the person himself. Life is a continual series of choices for the individual in which a main determinant of choice is the person as he already is (including his goals for himself, his courage or fear, his feeling of responsibility, his ego-strength or "will-power," etc.) We can no longer think of the person as "fully determined" where this phrase implies "determined only by forces external to the person." The person, insofar as he *is* a real person, is his own main determinant. Every person is, in part, "his own project" and makes himself.

If this essential core (inner nature) of the person is frustrated, denied or suppressed, sickness results, sometimes in obvious forms, sometimes in subtle and devious forms, sometimes immediately, sometimes later. . . .

This inner nature, as much as we know of it so far, is definitely not primarily

us with an understanding of man deeply and intimately affected by his environment but capable also of molding and shaping his destiny in important ways. . . .

If the [perceptual] view of human behavior . . . is accurate, it calls for a very different approach to human problems [from the environmental view]. How people perceive themselves and the world in which they live is an internal, personal matter. What people believe about themselves and their environment is not directly open to manipulation. A man's perceptions arise within himself. We cannot *make* people perceive. Effective, satisfying human relationships can only be developed through helping ourselves and others to perceive more freely and accurately. Man is not a puppet bandied about at the mercy of the forces exerted upon him. On the contrary, he is a creature of discretion who selects his perceptions from the world he lives in. He is not the victim of events but is capable of perceiving, interpreting, even creating events.

The perceptual view sees man as a growing, dynamic, creative being continuously in search of adequacy. Instead of an object at the mercy of environment, he is, himself, a purposive agent engaged in a never-ending business of becoming. People in this sense are processes rather than objects, growing rather than static, and call for the same kind of treatment we accord other growing things. . . . The perceptual view leads to methods of dealing with people which recognize the internal character of perception and seek to affect behavior through processes of facilitation, helping, assisting, or aiding the normal growth strivings of the organism itself. (1959, pp. 309–312)

*Perceptual view
of behavior*

"evil," but is rather what we adults in our culture call "good," or else it is neutral. . . .

No psychological health is possible unless this essential core of the person is fundamentally accepted, loved and respected by others and by himself. . . .

For all these reasons, it is at this time best to bring out and encourage, or at the very least, to recognize this inner nature, rather than to suppress or repress it. Pure spontaneity consists of free, uninhibited, uncontrolled, trusting, unpremeditated expression of the self, i.e., of the psychic forces, with minimal interference by consciousness. Control, will, caution, self-criticism, measure, deliberateness are the brakes upon this expression made intrinsically necessary by the laws of the social and natural worlds outside the psychic world. . . .

In the normal development of the healthy child, it is now believed that, much of the time, if he is given a really free choice, he will choose what is good for his growth. . . . This implies that *he* "knows" better than anyone else what is good for him. A permissive regime means not that adults gratify his needs directly but make it possible for *him* to gratify his needs, and make his own choices, i.e., let him *be*. It is necessary in order for children to grow well that adults have enough trust in them and in the natural processes of growth, i.e., not interfere too much, not *make* them grow, or force them into predetermined designs, but rather *let* them grow and *help* them grow in a Taoistic rather than an authoritarian way. (1968, pp. 190–199)

The discovery approach first advocated by field theorists—and many free school approaches as well—is based explicitly or implicitly on this set of propositions. It is assumed that as much as possible children should be allowed to learn in their own way so that their inner nature will not be suppressed. However, since the inner nature of children is weak, and since discipline is necessary to assist them in dealing with frustration and deprivation and, eventually, in achieving ego-strength, teachers should supply assistance by arranging the environment to promote learning.

John Dewey's Suggestions for Balancing Control and Freedom

The fundamental problem that will face you as a teacher is: How can you supply children with necessary support and guidance without suppressing their inner nature? John Dewey devoted his professional life to this question, and some of his observations may help clarify your own thinking as you prepare for a career in teaching. Here are some excerpts from *Experience and Education,* in which Dewey sums up his philosophy of education, together with parenthetical notes relating his observations to points made on the preceding pages:

> The belief that all genuine education comes about through experience does not mean that all experiences are genuinely or equally educative. Experience and education cannot be directly equated to each other. (P. 13)

> It is not enough to insist upon the necessity of experience, nor even of activity in experience. Everything depends upon the *quality* of the experience which is had. The quality of any experience has two aspects. There is an immediate aspect of agreeableness or disagreeableness, and there is its influence upon later experiences. The first is obvious and easy to judge. The *effect* of an experience is not borne on its face. It sets a problem to the educator. It is his business to arrange for the kind of experiences which, while they do not repel the student, but rather engage his activities are, nevertheless, more than immediately enjoyable since they promote having desirable future experiences. (P. 16)

(Compare these comments to Bruner's analysis of transfer and structure presented

John Dewey   John Dewey was born on a farm near Burlington, Vermont, in 1859. He later described the Vermont in which he was reared as being at that time the most democratic area of the United States, and he believed that this atmosphere was a primary cause of his later concern for democracy in education. After graduating from the University of Vermont, Dewey taught high school for two years in Pennsylvania and spent a year as a teacher in a rural school in Vermont. He then entered Johns Hopkins University and earned a Ph.D., writing his dissertation on psychological aspects of the theories of Immanuel Kant, the German philosopher who emphasized individual freedom. For a number of years, Dewey taught philosophy at the University of Michigan and the University of Minnesota, but he focused his attention on education when he joined the faculty at the University of Chicago in 1894. At Chicago, he developed techniques of instruction and wrote on many aspects of educational philosophy and method. From Chicago he went to Columbia University, where he continued to develop his views of education until his retirement in 1929. Dewey remained in New York City until his death in 1952, at the age of 93.

at the beginning of this chapter. Both stress the importance of *arranging* experiences so that they serve the student in the future.)

> Because the kind of advance planning heretofore engaged in has been so routine as to leave little room for the free play of individual thinking or for contributions due to distinctive individual experience, it does not follow that all planning must be rejected. On the contrary, there is incumbent upon the educator the duty of instituting a much more intelligent, and consequently more difficult, kind of planning. He must survey the capacities and needs of the particular set of individuals with whom he is dealing and must at the same time arrange the conditions which provide the subject-matter or content for experiences that satisfy these needs and develop these capacities. The planning must be flexible enough to permit free play for individuality of experience and yet firm enough to give direction towards continuous development of power. (Pp. 64–65)

(Compare this point to the eight open-education themes outlined earlier. Both stress careful teacher direction of individual students and the arrangement of conditions likely to facilitate learning.)

> The principle that development of experience comes about through interaction means that education is essentially a social process. This quality is realized in the degree in which individuals form a community group. It is absurd to exclude the teacher from membership in the group. As the most mature member of the group he has a peculiar responsibility for the conduct of the interactions and intercommunications which are the very life of the group as a community. That children are individuals whose freedom should be respected while the more mature person should have no freedom as an individual is an idea too absurd to require refutation. (P. 66)

(Compare this point of view to the philosophies of almost total child-direction advocated by Tolstoy, Neill, and Holt.

> The ideal aim of education is creation of power of self-control. But the mere removal of external control is no guarantee for the production of self-control. . . . It may be a loss rather than a gain to escape from the control of another person only to find one's conduct dictated by immediate whim and caprice; that is, at the mercy of impulses into whose formation intelligent judgment has not entered. A person whose conduct is controlled in this way has at most only the illusion of freedom. Actually he is directed by forces over which he has no command. (Pp. 75–76)

(Compare the last point to Skinner's observation that "to refuse to control is to leave control not to the person himself, but to other parts of the social and non-social environments.")

> It is . . . a sound instinct which identifies freedom with power to frame purposes and to execute or carry into effect purposes so framed. Such freedom is in turn identical with self-control; for the formation of purposes and the organization of means to execute them are the work of intelligence. (P. 77)

(Compare this observation to the associationist suggestion that teachers first describe what they want students to learn, then arrange learning experiences to lead to achievement of these goals.)

> Traditional education tended to ignore the importance of personal impulse and desire as moving springs. But this is no reason why progressive education should identify impulse and desire with purpose and thereby pass lightly over the need for careful observation, for wide range of information, and for judgment if students are to share in the formation of the purposes which activate them. In an *educational* scheme, the occurrence of a desire and impulse is not the final end. It is an occasion and a demand for the formation of a plan and method of activity. Such a plan . . . can be formed only by study of conditions and by securing all relevant information. (Pp. 83–84)

(Compare this to Bruner's observations that mastery of an organized body of information is necessary to permit wide application of general principles.)

> The teacher's business is to see that the occasion is taken advantage of. Since freedom resides in the operations of intelligent observation and judgment by which a purpose is developed, guidance given by the teacher to the exercise of the pupils' intelligence is an aid to freedom, not a restriction upon it. . . . I have heard of cases in which children are surrounded with objects and materials and then left entirely to themselves, the teacher being loath to suggest even what might be done with the materials lest freedom be infringed upon. Why, then, even supply materials, since they are a source of some suggestion or other? . . . It is impossible to understand why a suggestion from one who has a larger experience and a wider horizon should not be at least as valid as a suggestion arising from some more or less accidental source. (Pp. 84–85)

(Compare this point to Skinner's observations on the values of programmed instruction.)

> It is possible of course to abuse the office, and to force the activity of the young into channels which express the teacher's purpose rather than that of the pupils. But the way to avoid this danger is not for the adult to withdraw entirely. The way is, first, for the teacher to be intelligently aware of the capacities, needs, and past experiences of those under instruction, and, secondly, to allow the suggestion made to develop into a plan and project by means of the further suggestions contributed and organized into a whole by the members of the group. (P. 85)

(Compare this observation to the eight themes of open education.)

Summary

In this chapter, two major positions on learning—associationism and cognitive-field theory—have been described, and two basic conceptions of education—guided-structured-traditional and free-open-progressive—have been outlined. The views of leading exponents of these two positions have been summarized, and the observations of John Dewey (which were made after he had devoted a lifetime of thought to seeking an optimum balance between freedom and control) have been quoted.

Suggestions for Further Reading, Writing, Thinking, and Discussion

2-1 *Reacting to a Section of Bruner's "The Process of Education"*

In *The Process of Education* (1960b) (available as a Vintage paperback), Jerome Bruner discusses four major themes: (1) "the role of structure in learning and how it may be made central in teaching," (2) readiness, (3) the nature of intuition, and (4) "the desire to learn and how it may be stimulated." Each theme is discussed in a separate (short) chapter. If you read one of these chapters, write a brief résumé of Bruner's arguments. You might discuss such things as points that impressed you, points you disagree with, ideas that seemed vague or unrealistic or inconsistent, ideas you think you might be able to use in your own teaching. An example of one of the statements you might find provocative is found in Chapter 3: "We begin with the hypothesis that any subject can be taught effectively in some intellectually honest form to any child at any stage of development." If this seems hard to accept, read what Bruner has to say—and see if he is able to win you over.

2-2 *Reading a Capsule History of Learning in American Psychology*

As an aid to understanding current developments in psychology and education, you may find it interesting and helpful to read a capsule history of learning in American psychology. An excellent, concise overview is provided in the first chapter of *The Conditions of Learning* (1970) by Robert Gagné, in the section headed "Learning in American Psychology" (pp. 7–19). If you examine Gagné's account, you might find it helpful to write a brief outline to use as a reference when you read about specific experiments, theories, and techniques.

2-3 *Reading an Autobiographical Sketch by a Famous Psychologist*

Edwin G. Boring has variously expressed his interest in the impact of the Zeitgeist of the times on a theorist. In addition to his book *A History of Experimental Psychology* (1950), he established and helped edit a series of volumes (five so far) consisting of brief autobiographical sketches of famous psychologists. For a description of his own life by one or more of the psychologists mentioned in the text, search for the appropriate volume of *A History of Psychology in Autobiography*. Here is a list of the men already mentioned in the text with the volume number of the series in which each one's autobiography appears. (Note: Volumes II and III were edited by Carl Murchison; Volumes IV and V by Boring and others.)

Edward L. Thorndike, Volume III (1936)
John B. Watson, Volume III (1936)
Edwin G. Boring, Volume IV (1952)
B.F. Skinner, Volume V (1967)

(At appropriate places later in this text your attention will be called to the autobiographies of other psychologists not yet noted.)

Since B. F. Skinner is mentioned more frequently in the text than any other man, his autobiography may be of special interest. This is how it begins:

> My Grandmother Skinner was an uneducated farmer's daughter who put on airs. She was naturally attracted to a young Englishman who came to America in the early 1870's looking for work, and she married him. (He had not found just the work he wanted when he died at the age of ninety.) (Vol. V, p. 387)

If you read any of the sketches, try to relate the background and experiences described to what you know of the man's theories or specialty within psychology. Is the impact of the Zeitgeist apparent?

2-4 *Discovering the Nature of Earlier Versions of Free Schools*

The free school movement of today is a modern version of a basic approach to education that has often been advocated in the past. Two ardent champions of a natural form of education were Jean Jacques Rousseau and Leo Tolstoy. In *Émile,* Rousseau described what he considered the ideal education of an imaginary French boy of that name. Although Rousseau's proposals remained essentially imaginary, partly because they conflicted with religious views of that period, many of his basic arguments were endorsed by the Swiss educator Heinrich Pestalozzi and by the German Friedrich Froebel, founder of the Kindergarten and author of *The Education of Man* (1887). Perhaps the most famous advocate of free education was Leo Tolstoy, who spent almost ten years attempting to establish a free school in Russia. As one might expect of a novelist, he wrote about his views at some length, and a comprehensive selection of his observations can be found in *Tolstoy on Education* (1967). If you are intrigued by the free school movement or enjoy reading books of historical interest, you might sample sections of *Émile, The Education of Man,* or *Tolstoy on Education.* Summarize the arguments presented and add your own observations.

2-5 *Reading a Concise Statement of John Dewey's Views of Education*

John Dewey is generally considered the preeminent American educational theorist. Although many of his ideas have been misinterpreted and his approach to schooling has often been in conflict with trends in American culture, aspects of the open school movement of today are derived from or similar to his conception of education. Dewey's most comprehensive book on education was *Democracy and Education* (1916), but *Experience and Education* (1938), which was written toward the end of his career, is considered to be the clearest and most concise presentation of his views. If you would like to find out why Dewey had and continues to have such an impact on American schooling, you are urged to read this short book and note sections that impress you as particularly valuable.

2-6 *Analyzing the Behavioristic View of Determinism*

The publication of *Beyond Freedom and Dignity* (1971) by B. F. Skinner brought the behavioristic view of determinism to the attention of many Americans who had previously been unaware of this position. The book was offered in condensed form in the August 1971 issue of *Psychology Today;* it was widely advertised and offered as a selection by several book clubs. Critical reviews aroused considerable controversy, which was intensified by numerous television appearances by Skinner. If you would like to discover for yourself what caused the furor, you are urged to read either the *Psychology Today* condensation or the book itself. An alternate way to sample the views of Skinner is to read excerpts (particularly the first and last chapters) of *Science and Human Behavior* (1953), his earlier book outlining the behavioristic view. The same basic arguments are presented in both books, but some students have reported that the earlier analysis is easier to understand than *Beyond Freedom and Dignity*. If you read either, you might summarize your interpretation of Skinner's position and note your reactions.

2-7 *Analyzing the Perceptual Psychologist's View of Behavior*

Not all psychologists endorse the behaviorist position. Arthur Combs and Donald Snygg assert, for example, that "the facts of human behavior . . . are not the facts that exist for others, but the facts that exist for the behaver. . . . The data with which we must deal in understanding and changing human relation-ships, then, are feelings, attitudes, beliefs, and values." For more about the perceptual—as opposed to the behavioristic—view of psychology, browse through Chapters 14 and 15 of *Individual Behavior* (1959) by Combs and Snygg or examine *The Professional Education of Teachers: A Perceptual View of Teacher Preparation* (1965) by Combs.

2-8 *Evaluating a Utopia Based on the Principles of Science*

In *Walden Two* (1948), Skinner describes a fictional utopia based on the principles of his approach to a science of human behavior. It is a fascinating story, and you might read it to see whether you think you would like to live in the sort of world he imagines. What aspects of *Walden Two* strike you as most appealing? What aspects would you find difficult to accept? Do you think real people would react to the utopia as the characters in the novel do? Can you come up with an improved utopia of your own? (If you would like to compare your hypotheses regarding *Walden Two* to a description of actual experiences with such a community, read *A Walden Two Experiment: The First*

Five Years of Twin Oaks Community (1973) by Kathleen Kinkade or excerpts from it that appear in the January 1973 and February 1973 issues of *Psychology Today*.)

2-9 *Reacting to Descriptions of Overcontrolled Negative Utopias*

Aldous Huxley was an eloquent champion of individuality and freedom and a critic of any sort of control over human behavior. He first expressed his view on the dangers of control in his novel *Brave New World* (1932). Twenty-six years later came a collection of essays entitled *Brave New World Revisited* (1958); still later is the novel *Island* (1962), his conception of a utopia in which the freedom of the individual would be preserved.

George Orwell provided two interpretations of the dangers of too much control in *Animal Farm* (1946) and *1984* (1949), and Ray Bradbury described his conception of an oppressively controlled society in *Fahrenheit 451* (1967).

If you have ever speculated about the possible dangers of too much control over behavior, you will enjoy reading one of these books. If you do, you might attempt to relate aspects of the imaginary societies described to life in contemporary America.

2-10 *Sampling Abraham H. Maslow's Views on Humanistic Psychology*

Abraham H. Maslow is generally acknowledged as the leading spokesman for humanistic psychology. He explains his reasons for preferring this view of psychology in *Toward a Psychology of Being* (2nd ed., 1968), *Motivation and Personality* (2nd ed., 1970), and *The Farther Reaches of Human Nature* (1972). If you would like to gain a reasonably complete grasp of his observations, read Chapters 1, 2, 3, 4, and 14 of *Toward a Psychology of Being* or the Preface, Chapter 1, Chapter 2, and the Appendixes of *Motivation and Personality*. If you sample any of Maslow's descriptions of his view of humanistic psychology, you could clarify your understanding by writing an interpretation of it in your own words.

2-11 *Reading Critical Analyses of Free and Open Education*

A substantial number of books on free and open education have been called to your attention in the first two chapters, and others will be noted later. If you would like to read some critical analyses of these approaches—particularly if you are so enthusiastic about them you see few if any weaknesses—examine *Radical School Reform: Critique and Alternatives* (1973) edited by Cornelius J. Troost. In Part 1 a number of observers offer critiques of books by such leading advocates of free and open education as John Holt, Neil Postman and Charles Weingartner, George Leonard, George Dennison, Charles Silberman, and Ivan Illich. Part 2 is devoted to discussions of the values of a structured curriculum, Part 3 to arguments that the teaching of values cannot be successfully carried out in a free school environment, and Part 4 to examinations of elements of the open school approach which seem most likely to have lasting value. If you feel positively disposed toward free or open education, you might jot down the reasons you favor it and also note what you consider to be possible disadvantages. Then, do your best to remain aware of the possible impact of cognitive dissonance and read sections of *Radical School Reform: Critique and Alternatives*. As you examine arguments noted in this book, relate them to the points you listed before you started.

Recommended Reading in *Psychology Applied to Teaching: Selected Readings*

If you would like to do further reading in books or articles mentioned in this chapter (and in the preceding "Suggestions for Further Reading, Writing, Thinking, and Discussion") without having to track down several separate volumes, you might peruse *Psychology Applied to Teaching: Selected Readings* (Boston: Houghton Mifflin, 1972). This is a collection of excerpts from books and articles from journals in psychology. The following selections provide extended commentaries on points noted in this chapter or mentioned in the "Suggestions."

The Nature and Importance of Transfer: "The Importance of Structure" by Jerome S. Bruner, Selection 1, p. 2. (See also Suggestion 2–1.)

Two Major Positions on Learning: section on "Learning in American Psychology" from *The Conditions of Learning* by Robert M. Gagné, Selection 17, p. 267. (See also Suggestion 2–2.)

The Nature of Associationism: section on "Operant Conditioning" from "The Technology of Teaching" by B. F. Skinner, Selection 15, p. 212.

Cognitive Field Theory: "How Does Cognitive Field Theory Deal with Learning and Teaching?" by Morris L. Bigge, Selection 16, p. 237.

Assumptions of Controlled Education: excerpt from *Science and Human Behavior* by B. F. Skinner, Selection 5, p. 42. (See also Suggestion 2–6.) Excerpt from *Walden Two* by B. F. Skinner, Selection 7, p. 73; "The Technology of Teaching" by B. F. Skinner, Selection 15, p. 210. (See also Suggestion 2–6.)

Criticisms of Controlled Education: excerpt from *Individual Behavior* by Arthur Combs and Donald Snygg, Selection 6, p. 61.

Maslow's Principles of Humanistic Psychology: excerpt from *Toward a Psychology of Being* by Abraham H. Maslow, Selection 30, p. 452. (See also Suggestion 2–10.)

The Perceptual View of Behavior: excerpt from *Individual Behavior* by Arthur Combs and Donald Snygg, Selection 6, p. 61. (See also Suggestion 2–7.)

The Behavioristic View of Determinism: excerpt from *Science and Human Behavior* by B. F. Skinner, Selection 5, p. 42. (See also Suggestion 2–6.)

Evaluating a Utopia Based on the Principles of Science: excerpt from *Walden Two* by B. F. Skinner, Selection 7, p. 73. (See also Suggestion 2–8.)

Reacting to a Description of an Overcontrolled Negative Utopia: excerpt from *Brave New World* by Aldous Huxley, Selection 8, p. 90. (See also Suggestion 2–9.)

PART

DEVELOPMENT

DEVELOPMENT:

PRINCIPLES AND THEORIES

KEY POINTS

Sequences and Trends
Eight ages of man (Erikson)
Egocentric speech, socialized speech (Piaget)
Moral realism, moral relativism (Piaget)
*Intellectual development: sensorimotor, preoperational, concrete operations,
  formal operations (Piaget)*
Enactive, iconic, and symbolic thought (Bruner)

Experiments and Studies
Walking by cradleboard babies at same age as others (Dennis and Dennis)
Faster skill learning by older preschoolers (Hilgard)
Imprinting of any moving object by newborn goslings (Lorenz)
50 percent of intelligence by age 4—speculative hypothesis (Bloom)

Concepts
Standardization groups and their limitations
Overlap
Prehension
Group, or actuarial, prediction
Critical periods
Operation (Piaget)

Principles
Development as a product of maturation and learning
Less predictable behavior in older children
Progression from general to specific responses
Irregular nature of short-term growth
Variance in rates of development
Organization, adaptation, conservation, decentration, equilibration (Piaget)

Theories
Intellectual development (Piaget)
Development (Erikson)

CHAPTER CONTENTS

A LOGICAL PLACE TO BEGIN DISCUSSING ASPECTS OF PSYCHOLOGY that are of possible value to a teacher is the pupils—the reason teachers are needed in the first place. The first fact to recognize is that the children in the first grade are very different from the young adults in senior high school. Most of the ideas and principles presented in this book will not be of much value to you unless you can adjust the applications of these principles to the particular grade level you will teach. A principle may be relevant at all grade levels, but the specific way of applying it will vary. This chapter discusses the theoretical matters you will need to take into account in analyzing the developmental trends described in Chapter 4. These trends are presented in the form of age-level characteristics and include suggestions on how you might use this information in your teaching.

The Age-Level Approach and Its Limitations

A brief digression to explain the age-level approach and its limitations is necessary at this point. In developmental psychology the subjects are evolving individuals, and in studying them two approaches are commonly used. One is to select a particular kind of behavior—social behavior, for example—and analyze changes that occur as the child develops. The other approach is to use a progressive series of age spans as the point of reference, studying preschool children by considering all phases of their behavior, then primary-grade children, and so on.

In this book the age-level approach has been used because owing to the organization of schools into grades, a teacher deals with *all* the characteristics of a certain age level at one time. However, for a comprehensive study of development, the behavior approach is probably more satisfactory because certain limitations are inherent in the age-level approach. Two of them will now be discussed.

Weaknesses of the Standardization Group

Standardization groups and their limitations

Age-level characteristics are norms, which means they suggest what is "normal" for a "typical" child of a certain age. When a psychologist sets out to establish these norms, he obviously can't measure all children, so he selects a *sample.* If he is conscientious, he tries to insure that this small sample is representative of all children in the country. Actually, it is impossible to do this even under ideal circumstances, but some researchers achieve a greater degree of success than others. Quite a few, especially those who labor under pressures of various sorts, don't even come close. You should keep this in mind when you consider the norms presented in the next chapter. Some age-level characteristics, such as features of physical growth, may be based on an excellent sample of several thousand children from all parts of the country, all economic levels, and almost all races, nationalities, and religions. Other characteristics, such as aspects of friendship and popularity, may be based on a sample of twenty or thirty children attending an experimental school, with every one of these the son or daughter of an upper-middle-class, white, Protestant college professor.

One way a textbook writer can call the reader's attention to this problem is to describe the sample on which each age-level characteristic is based and hope the reader will exercise proper restraint in generalizing from the results. An alternate method is to omit the information on the sample but emphasize tentativeness and caution in interpreting age-level descriptions. To save space and avoid tedium, the latter approach is used in this book. Thus you are urged to keep constantly in mind the fact that some of the age-level studies described herein were based on small, possibly atypical samples of children and therefore may not yield characteristics typical of all children.

Group Prediction, Not Individual Prediction

Age-level characteristics always refer to a nonexistent, typical child—even when the sample of children studied is sufficiently large and varied. In determining the characteristics of a particular age level, observers "average" the behavioral traits of many (or a few) children, and in the process many subtle variations of behavior are canceled out.

The kind of prediction about behavior one can make on the basis of such group averages is sometimes called *actuarial* prediction. You are probably familiar with this word in relation to insurance: actuaries prepare the figures on which insurance rates are based. These figures indicate the likelihood that a certain incident will occur so many times out of every hundred or thousand cases. When the actuary predicts, for example, that a specific number of drivers of a certain age, vocation, and residential area will have accidents in a particular time period, all such drivers will pay the same insurance rates because it is not possible to predict which individuals will actually be involved in accidents. Descriptions of groups of children function the same way. They may tell with some accuracy how a few hundred children out of a thousand will behave, but they do not enable one to predict how a *particular* child will behave or how small groups of children will behave.

Group or actuarial prediction

This point leads to a very important concept in psychology—that of individual differences. One of the few unchallenged statements a psychologist can make is that individuals are different. Whatever the behavior characteristic being studied, some children will have more of it than the norm for that age level and some will have less. In addition, the degree of variation often increases with age. A major problem every teacher is constantly trying to solve is how to allow for individual differences—in maturation, learning ability, and personality. When you read the next chapter, in order to maintain a degree of perspective keep in mind that the various age levels overlap.

Study of a simplified diagram (Figure 3–1) will help to clarify this phenomenon of *overlap*. Many age-level traits are distributed according to the bell-shaped curve illustrated. This means that when a particular characteristic (e.g., height) is measured in an age-level group and the results are plotted on a frequency distribution, most children are clustered around the middle with some trailing out toward the extremes above and below. When children at different age levels are compared on some trait, some younger children are found to surpass some older children. Figure 3–1 shows a hypothetical distribution of height in seven- and eight-year-olds. As you can see, some of the seven-year-olds are taller than some of the eight-year-olds, even though the *average* eight-year-old is taller

Concept of overlap

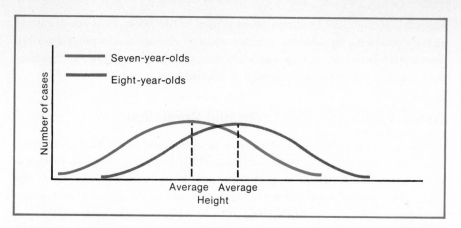

Figure 3–1 Hypothetical Distributions of Height in Seven- and Eight-Year-Olds

than the *average* seven-year-old. Since age-level characteristics indicate only averages, they cannot possibly show such subtle variations as these.

Although some standardization groups may be inadequate and the factor of overlap is a complication, knowledge of age-level characteristics can be extremely helpful to you as a teacher—provided you exercise judgment in interpreting them.

An additional safeguard against a too literal interpretation of age-level characteristics is provided in the following section, which analyzes some general principles of development. Awareness of such principles should help you introduce a degree of continuity into your speculations about development.

General Principles of Development

The following principles are accepted by almost all developmental theorists. However, the conversion of them into actual school programs has resulted in conflicting sets of practices in dealing with preschool children. These practices are derived from conceptions discussed in the first two chapters. At one extreme are the views of Rousseau, Tolstoy, Neill, Maslow, and Combs and Snygg, which emphasize "natural" development; at the other are the guided experience views of Skinner and his fellow behaviorist-associationists. Before this conflict is discussed, however, the principles endorsed by advocates of both positions will be described.

Development as a Product of Maturation and Learning

Development a product of maturation and learning

Age-level characteristics are the product of the interaction between two major forces: maturation and learning. Put in the simplest terms, *maturation* means changes that are primarily the result of growth and relatively independent of exercise and training; *learning* means changes that are primarily the result of experience.

At conception the human organism is a single cell about the size of a pinpoint. Within this cell are thousands of genes, which determine many characteristics of the child and the sequence of their appearance. But for maturation to take place, the organism must be nourished by an environment. The kind of environment determines in part how and when maturation takes place. The experiences of the child within his environment, together with the traits he inherits, mold his personality.

The identical elements in these biological and environmental forces cause all children to be similar to each other in some respects. But the fact that each individual has a unique combination of genes and is exposed to a unique set of experiences makes each one different from every other. In the discussion that follows, it should not be forgotten that although all children tend to follow essentially the same pattern of growth, differences in heredity and environment cause each one to pass through this sequence in his own individual way.

Less Predictable Pattern of Development with Increasing Age

Even though each child passes through the sequence of development in a unique way, the sequence itself followed by most children is very similar. This orderly sequence, or pattern, is most apparent in the very young child, whose developing behavior is dominated by maturational factors. As the child grows older, he is caught up in an increasingly tangled web of experiences and is exposed to an increasingly varied environment. As a result, his behavior becomes less predictable.

Less predictable behavior in older children

The orderly pattern of behavior found in very young children apears to be controlled by a built-in timetable. A dramatic illustration of this is provided by a study made of two Hopi Indian tribes (Dennis and Dennis, 1940). One tribe used the traditional cradleboard; the other did not. The babies bound to the cradleboard were prevented from exercising their legs for more than an hour or so a day. Babies in the other tribe were given twenty-four-hour freedom to exercise, to try to stand and walk. Yet the cradleboard babies walked, on the average, at the same age as the noncradleboard babies. The implication is that early maturation of the nerves and muscles is controlled by factors within the organism. The environment appears to have relatively little effect on the pattern and rate of growth of the young child unless physical or emotional deprivation, or both, is extreme.

Dennis and Dennis study: exercise not necessary

In the high school senior, by contrast, environment displaces maturation as the primary determinant of behavior, or development. The seventeen-year-old roams over an extensive physical environment, especially if he has a car, and interacts with hundreds of people every day. He also brings with him a complex

VAN BUCHER/PHOTO RESEARCHERS, INC.

"... although all children tend to follow essentially the same pattern of growth, differences in heredity and environment cause each one to pass through this sequence in his own individual way."

HELEN BARSKY/PHOTO RESEARCHERS, INC.

pattern of memories, feelings, and attitudes. What's more, his sequence of physical growth is nearing completion so that maturational factors have relatively little influence. Because his environment is so complex and ever changing and because the genetically determined timetable no longer has much effect, the behavior of adolescents tends to be more variable and less predictable than the maturation-dominated behavior of the young child.

The greater variability in the behavior of older students results also from the greater variability in their growth rate. Consider, for example, two aspects of growth that appear to be largely dependent on built-in factors: walking, a skill that develops about the end of the first year, and sexual maturity, which occurs at adolescence. The difference between the ages at which a fast and a slow maturer walk is about four or five months. The difference between the ages at which a fast and a slow maturer attain puberty is about four or five *years*. This widening gap between fast and slow maturers applies to many other aspects of growth as well and points up the fact that it is often more important to take overlap into account when evaluating statements about the "typical" behavior of older pupils than when assessing such statements about younger ones.

From General to Specific Responses

The impact of built-in, maturational factors upon younger children is apparent not only in the uniformity and predictability of their behavior but also in the forms of their behavior. The responses of the infant are generalized; more specific and differentiated reactions appear later. If you stimulate a baby almost anywhere on his body, he will respond with uncoordinated movements of the arms and legs and head. In time, the child eliminates the superfluous movements and responds in a more specific, coordinated way. This phenomenon is largely the result of the development of the nervous system. Nerve networks emanate from the brain and spinal cord, and the child gains control of the nerves and muscles closest to these first.

From general to specific responses

Prehension illustrates this aspect of maturation. It is the ability of a baby to pick up a small object between his thumb and forefinger. Most babies acquire this skill at about nine months. Before that time they have control only over the muscles of the arm and hand, picking up an object by "palming" it. If they are unable to palm it, they can't pick it up. If you have the opportunity, observe the inability of a six-month-old baby to pick up a pea-sized object; or watch a four-year-old try to tie his shoelaces; or note the exasperation a six-year-old suffers when he can't make his hand print letters as neatly as you can. Then you will appreciate how essential maturation is in enabling a child to perform certain skills and will take it into account in your teaching.

Nature of prehension

Continuous Long-Term Development but Irregular Short-Term Growth

Irregular nature of short-term growth

Over a period of years the progress in the development of a child is apparent. For a limited period such as a school year, however, his development may appear to be irregular. He may achieve a certain form of behavior and then inexplicably backslide to the former level. You should not be surprised at such regressions. They seem to be an almost inevitable part of growing up. Finding the reasons for these reverses may not be possible in many cases. If you can't arrive at a ready explanation (e.g., illness, fatigue, overexcitement), perhaps your best course is to accept the situation and make subtle attempts to encourage redevelopment.

Variance in Rates of Development

Variance in rates of development

Not only do some children mature faster than others, and not only do some characteristics in the same child mature faster than others, but even different aspects of the same characteristic in the same child mature at different rates. There is increasing evidence, for example, that the various factors comprising intelligence develop at different speeds. Add to this the influence of each child's daily experiences, which tend to divert his behavior in certain directions, and you begin to understand why children vary to such an amazing degree. Their infinite variety is what makes them so interesting, exasperating, and difficult to teach.

Two Current Views of Readiness

For you as a future teacher, perhaps the most complicating consequence of these developmental principles has to do with *readiness*—the concept that moments occur in the sequence of development when a child is optimally ready to learn certain skills. Theorists disagree on the way educational programs should be structured to allow for readiness, and their differences of opinion have led to one of the major educational controversies of this decade. As mentioned in Chapter 2, Maslow, Combs and Snygg, Neill, and Holt feel that children should be allowed considerable freedom to learn at their own pace and in their own way. Skinner and his fellow environmentalists, on the other hand, argue that early development is too important to be left to chance. Some advocates of this view are trying to speed up sense development in infants; others have developed methods to teach two-year-olds to read and three-year-olds to do "algebra"; and some legislators and school administrators insist that the education of all children should begin at the age of four. The reasoning behind these practices is that waiting for a child to become ready on his own is wasteful and inefficient. The proponents of guided development argue that we should, instead, note what appear to be typical trends, or stages, of development and systematically lead all children through them. They feel that this is more scientific and efficient, enabling children to advance more rapidly. What follows is a brief history of the research that led to these two opposing points of view.

Origin of Concept of "Natural" Readiness

In the 1930s a series of studies demonstrated that older, more mature children were able to learn more rapidly and easily than younger children. In one of the most frequently mentioned experiments (Hilgard, 1932), a group of two- and three-year-old children was given training for twelve weeks in buttoning, ladder climbing, and the use of scissors. A matched control group was given no specific training. At the end of the twelve-week period, the trained group did better at the skills. The control group, then three months older than the experimental group had been at the onset of its training, was given just *one* week of instruction. At the end of this week the control group was as proficient as the experimental group, which had received *three months* of training at an earlier age. The conclusion was that general physiological maturation, plus experiences other than the specific training, had contributed to the faster development of the skills in the control group.

Hilgard study: older children learn faster

This experiment, and many others like it, led to the belief that adults should allow a child to become ready for school by permitting him to mature and to absorb experiences from his environment at his own pace and in his own way. Advocates of this theory reasoned that the postponement of formal instruction until a child reaches a certain level of development is efficient because a sufficiently mature child is more likely to start his school career with confidence, is less apt to fail in his efforts at learning, and is able to learn more in a shorter time. It was tacitly assumed, however, that in the normal process of growing up practically all children would develop the general skills needed for readiness. It is now apparent that this is an erroneous assumption.

Origin of Concept of Critical Periods

During the years when these ideas of "natural" readiness were being put into practice, an almost opposite view began to evolve from several different kinds of studies.

One group of scientists performed experiments on animals to demonstrate the existence of *critical periods* in development. An early, trend-setting study was done by Konrad Lorenz (1957), who described *imprinting*—a type of learning that occurs within a limited period of time early in life and is relatively unmodifiable thereafter.[1] He showed that newborn goslings will adopt as their

Lorenz on imprinting

[1] Lorenz has recorded many other observations of animals in *King Solomon's Ring* (1952) and *On Aggression* (1966). If you have an interest in natural science, you are likely to find both these books delightful and provocative. The latter volume offers some fascinating hypotheses on why human beings are so violent and aggressive.

mother any moving object they meet in the first few hours after they are hatched. This tendency to imprint an attachment to a mother-object occurs during a very short span of time—hence the term *critical period*. Other investigators (Hebb, 1947; Riesen, 1958; Thompson and Heron, 1954) discovered that if animals were kept under conditions of sensory deprivation (e.g., total darkness) when young, either they were permanently retarded in their development or they took longer to learn than animals reared under normal conditions.

Nature of critical periods

These experiments led to renewed interest in the possibility originally suggested by Sigmund Freud that there are critical periods in the development of human infants and young children. The experiments also raise the related question of whether a deprived environment leads to permanent retardation, an enriched environment to permanent increments of growth. Evidence described by the Austrian physician René Spitz (1946) suggests that there is a critical period in infants. Spitz, after observing babies cared for in hospital nurseries during wartime, theorized that an infant given insufficient attention during the first months of its life may fail to respond to stimulation and, in extreme cases, waste away and die. This theory was popularized by Margaret Ribble in her book *The Rights of Infants* (1943), in which she maintained that mother love is a prerequisite to satisfactory development. Other evidence of the effect of neglect on human infants was provided by observations of children reared in orphanages (Dennis, 1960; Skeels et al., 1938). It was discovered that children who receive less than normal amounts of adult attention are retarded in many areas.[2]

These observations were brought into sharper focus by the work of Martin Deutsch (1964), who described the limiting conditions under which children from deprived environments are reared. Deutsch discovered that such youngsters may show improvement in their behavior if they are provided with intensive, preschool experiences. The best-publicized outgrowth of these experiments is the Head Start program, which tries to give children from deprived environments extra stimulation to counteract their lack of the experiences a middle-class child has as a matter of course.

It has been discovered, for example, that many children from poor environments have never been exposed to objects that teachers and curriculum planners take for granted they are familiar with. Furthermore, these children lack an entire cluster of motivational factors: the interest of their parents in interacting,

[2] However, in still other studies (Dennis and Dennis, 1941; Dennis and Najarian, 1957; Rheingold, 1956; Rheingold and Bayley, 1959) little or no evidence of retardation due to restricted experience was found. For some explanations of these conflicting reports, see Yarrow (1961).

Konrad Lorenz was the first moving object seen by these goslings after they were hatched. As a result, they adopted him as their "mother."

Evaluating Readiness in Terms of Developmental Tasks

The nature and importance of readiness and of critical periods are emphasized by what Robert J. Havighurst has referred to as *developmental tasks,* which he defines this way: ''A developmental task is a task which arises at or about a certain period in the life of the individual, successful achievement of which leads to his happiness and to success with later tasks, while failure leads to unhappiness in the individual, disapproval by the society, and difficulty with later tasks'' (1952, p. 2). Havighurst feels that the concept of developmental tasks can be useful to teachers in delineating purposes of education and in curriculum planning. He observes, ''When the body is ripe, and society requires, and the self is ready to achieve a certain task, the teachable moment has come. Efforts at teaching which would have been largely wasted if they had come earlier, give gratifying results when they come at the *teachable moment,* when the task should be learned'' (p. 5).

In *Developmental Tasks and Education* (1952), Havighurst lists and describes developmental tasks from infancy through adulthood. Here are some of the tasks for the school years:

Elementary Grades

Learning physical skills necessary for ordinary games (p. 15).

Learning to get along with age mates (p. 17).

Learning an appropriate masculine or feminine social role (p. 19).

Developing fundamental skills in reading, writing, and calculating (p. 20).

Developing conscience, morality, and a scale of values (p. 23).

Secondary Grades

Achieving new and more mature relations with age-mates of both sexes (p. 33).

Achieving a masculine or feminine social role (p. 37).

Achieving emotional independence of parents and other adults (p. 42).

Selecting and preparing for an occupation (p. 47).

Preparing for marriage and family life (p. 52).

Developing intellectual skills and concepts necessary for civic competence (p. 54).

Acquiring a set of values and an ethical system as a guide to behavior (p. 62).

If you find that this list of tasks clarifies your thinking about how to allow for readiness and critical periods, you might read Havighurst's complete description in *Developmental Tasks and Education*.

especially verbally, with them; the enthusiasm of their parents over their development; the encouragement from their parents to do well in school. These differences between the environment of a slum child and that of a middle-class child were overlooked by the early advocates of readiness. It is now apparent that the maturation of a child from a deprived environment cannot be left entirely to "natural" forces. Readiness involves more than physiological maturation; it also is based on the quality of experiences.

Critical Period Theory: Speculation That Enriched Early Experience Boosts IQ

When the various experiments on critical periods just described were being conducted, other psychologists were analyzing the relationship between such periods and intellectual development. Some significant breakthroughs in this area of study led to speculation that since lack of environmental stimulation leads to retardation, systematically *enriched* stimulation during the critical period of the first six years or so will produce a significant *advance*. J. McV. Hunt, who has presented the most comprehensive argument for this critical period theory in his book *Intelligence and Experience,* writes:

> With a sound scientific educational psychology of early experience, it might become feasible to raise the average level of intelligence as now measured, by a substantial degree. In order to be explicit, it is conceivable that this "substantial degree" might be of the order of 30 points of I.Q. (1961, p. 267)

Hunt bases his argument on the neurological theory of D. O. Hebb (1949) and the developmental theory of Jean Piaget (1952). Hebb has suggested that an enriched, early, sensorimotor experience can serve as a foundation for later intellectual development, and Hunt argues that early experience might therefore function as an IQ booster. He suggests that we build learning experiences for the child by taking into account a hierarchy of stages in the development of intelligence—a hierarchy that has been mapped by Jean Piaget.

Jerome Bruner has made a similar proposal. In a famous statement he even puts forth the hypothesis that "any subject can be taught effectively in some intellectually honest form to any child at any stage of development" (1960b, p. 33). He proposes that we do this by noting the stage of intellectual development a child has reached and arranging the curriculum accordingly. Although Bruner uses different terms to describe the stages of intellectual development, his hierarchy is very similar to Piaget's.

Further support for the critical period theory that we should provide all children with an enriched and "scientifically sound" early experience is given by Benjamin Bloom in his book *Stability and Change in Human Characteristics.* In it Bloom reviews research data on the height, weight, IQ scores, and personality measures of individuals studied over a period of time. His general conclusions are that changes in these measurements are closely related to environmental conditions and that "variations in the environment have the greatest quantitative effect on a characteristic at its most rapid period of change" (1964, p. vii).

To define the period during which intelligence changes most rapidly, Bloom relies on an analysis of IQ scores obtained from the same individuals over a period of years. On the basis of this data he formulates his own version of the critical period theory. He states that 50 percent of adult intelligence is achieved by age four, 80 percent by age eight. He then asserts that if a child lives in an impoverished environment for the first four years of his life, he may lose as many as 2.5 IQ points per year and that this loss will be irreversible—the child will never be able to make it up.[3]

Bloom: 50 percent of intelligence by age four

In Bloom's opinion, therefore, a child's preschool and primary-grade education are the most important experiences of his life. His theory implies that a child who is exposed to a rich and carefully planned environment for his first eight years, during which he will have achieved 80 percent of his ultimate intellectual potential, can more or less "coast" after that, whereas a child who does not receive a rich and balanced education during these first eight years will never be able to offset the handicap.

However, there is evidence contradicting Bloom's theory. First of all, Bloom maintains that lack of *physical* as well as mental growth early in life is a permanent loss, but Tanner (1963) found evidence that even when physical growth is seriously stunted for a time by malnutrition or illness, the organism has a "target-seeking" tendency to return to its natural growth curve. In a similar analysis Krogman (1962) presented evidence that heredity is the "great master" in determining physical growth. Both these studies indicate that the child will zero in on his genetically determined height even though he may suffer environmental deprivation early in life. In addition, Arthur Jensen (1969) has pointed out some flaws in the extrapolations made by Bloom. Jensen claims that when Bloom's method of estimating mental growth is applied to physical growth, the resulting prediction is that the average four-year-old will achieve a height of six feet, seven inches, by the age of seventeen.

At the 1973 convention of the American Association for the Advancement of Science, Jerome Kagan presented evidence that leads to questions regarding the Bloom hypothesis. Kagan reported on research in which children in America and Guatemala were compared over a period of years. The American children were reared in normal environments, the Guatemalan children in impoverished environments in which they were confined to dirt-floor huts the first year. During their early years of life, the Guatemalan children were so far behind their American counterparts they were considered severely retarded. But by the age of eleven, the two groups were equal in intellectual skills.

---

[3] In recent publications Bloom has placed less emphasis on the idea of irreversible losses. In a paper published in 1968 he argues that experiences during the preschool and elementary school years are likely to be of special significance but adds, "Undoubtedly, however, some changes can take place at later points in the individual's career."

The early-experience theory of Hunt, Bloom, and Bruner has led to a valuable new interest in preschool education. However, the view that early losses in intellectual development are irreversible tends to put great pressure on parents and teachers. If the Bloom hypothesis is accepted literally, parents as well as preschool and primary-grade teachers may feel driven to produce what they consider to be the ideal environment for the child. Yet many psychologists believe that a relaxed, free atmosphere is most conducive to learning.

In sorting out your thoughts on readiness—as well as development and education in general—the theories of two leading child psychologists may help you gain some perspective. The distinguished psychoanalyst Erik H. Erikson

---

A Different View of the Impact of Early Experience

John E. Anderson, director of the Institute of Child Development at the University of Minnesota, observed toward the end of his distinguished career:

> Many discussions of child personality . . . [give the impression] that the young child is passive, delicate, unusually subject to shock and trauma and responsive to all possible stimuli. . . . This is also the purport of much of the psychoanalytic teaching about children. The adult is what he is, not because of inadequacy in his makeup or training, but because of a traumatic experience. Since this experience cannot be found in the present it is pushed back into an earlier period. When it cannot be found there, it is pushed still further back. Thus, the trauma of adolescence moves back into late childhood, then into early childhood, then into infancy, then to birth, and then into the fetal period. The only place left for trauma is conception. (1948, pp. 404–410)

Anderson presents considerable evidence to support a less dramatic but more reassuring picture of the child. He argues that the child is active not passive, remarkably resilient and not delicate, and more a product of *repeated* experiences than of one or two traumatic experiences at a critical period. Furthermore, he suggests that the child exerts substantial influence on his own behavior and does much to create his own world.

Anderson's view seems especially appropriate for a teacher. If you endorse the critical-period concept too literally, you are almost forced into fatalism. If one of your pupils was not breast-fed properly or another was given overly rigid toilet training, you would have to assume that only psychoanalysis could help. You might also stay awake nights brooding about the possibility that you had traumatized one or more of your pupils. On the other hand, if you think of children as being in a continuous process of development and conceive of their personalities as the product of hundreds of thousands of episodes occurring over a long period of time, you will be able to approach teaching in a more optimistic and relaxed manner. This is not to say that single episodes *never* have an impact on a child; it is simply an attempt to help you avoid making teaching any more complicated and nerve-wracking than it already is.

has developed a theory of personality development derived from the work of Sigmund Freud. His description of stages of development is useful background for speculating about the advantages and disadvantages of guided experience as opposed to natural development. Jean Piaget has provided the description of stages of intellectual development that Hunt proposes be used in attempts to increase intelligence, but he has also provided the theory that has made a major contribution to an almost opposite conception of education—the British free school movement. In addition, many school practices not directly related to either of these movements are based on Piaget's observations.

Erikson's Theory of Development

Erikson's extension of Freudian theory emphasizes that in addition to the stages of psychosexual development proposed by Freud, psycho*social* stages of ego development take place. Whereas Freud believed that the experiences of a child during the earliest years of life were of supreme importance—thus stressing the concept of critical periods—Erikson believes that personality development takes place throughout the entire life cycle.

Erikson's Background

As a young man, Erikson served as a tutor and later became interested enough in education to accept a position at a school in Vienna. His desire to understand the behavior of his pupils—together with an interest in the theories of Freud—led to psychoanalytic training and eventually a career as a child psychiatrist. When he joined the faculty of Harvard shortly after he came to this country in 1933, he became acquainted with several leading anthropologists. They aroused his interest sufficiently for him to conclude that his understanding of child behavior might be clarified by studying child rearing in simpler societies. Soon after, he began making field studies of the Sioux and Yurok Indians. Erikson was struck by the extent to which their emotional problems seemed a consequence of lack of continuity between their tribal history and customs and their existence in twentieth-century America. He hypothesized that the Indians found it difficult to *identify* with the white culture. Unable to explain this conflict in terms of the stress on sexual drives of psychoanalytic theory, he began to formulate a view of development that centered around the ego of the individual and the culture in which he lived.

This conception of development was given impetus when Erikson served on the staff of a veterans' rehabilitation center during World War II. As he interviewed patients, he came to the conclusion that many of them were experiencing difficulties reconciling their activities and attitudes as soldiers with the activities and attitudes of their prewar civilian life. He used the term *identity*

CLEMENS KALISCHER

Erik H. Erikson Erikson was born in Frankfurt, Germany, in 1902. His parents were Danish, but shortly after his birth his father died. Erik's mother later married the pediatrician who had cured her son of a childhood illness and the family remained in Germany. As a young man, Erikson became an artist specializing in portraits. (He describes his first career in these terms, "I was an artist then, which in Europe is a euphemism for a young man with some talent and nowhere to go.") He settled in Vienna, and a position as a tutor with a family on friendly terms with Freud eventually led to interest in psychoanalysis which culminated in psychiatric training. Erikson came to America in 1933 to become the first child analyst in the Boston area. In the following years he taught at Harvard, Yale, and the University of California at Berkeley. From 1951 to 1961 he was on the staff of the Austen Riggs Center, a private residential treatment center for disturbed young people. At the present time he is Professor of Human Development and Lecturer on Psychiatry at Harvard.

confusion to describe this condition, to emphasize the same sort of problem faced by the Indians—lack of a consistent conception of ego, or self.

The hypotheses formulated to explain the behavior of Indians and servicemen were corroborated and reinforced during subsequent years of clinical practice with disturbed children. Eventually Erikson worked out a complete, consistent conception of development that he described in *Childhood and Society*. He proposed that in addition to the psycho*sexual* stages described by Freud, there are psycho*social* stages of ego development in which the child establishes a series of orientations to himself and his social world. In contrast to Freud, who stressed the impact of early experiences, Erikson proposed that personality development continues throughout the entire life span. The stages are described as dichotomies of positive and negative factors—desirable traits likely to encourage the development of a person who enjoys a rich, full life, and dangers likely to lead to various forms of mental illness. Each stage is influenced by those preceding it, but each adds a new dimension in a person's interaction with himself and his environment. The way these stages parallel—and differ from—those of Freud is indicated in Table 3-1.

Erikson's theory of development

Erikson's Eight Ages of Man

The designations, age ranges, and essential characteristics of Erikson's eight ages of man are:

Trust vs. Mistrust (Birth to 1 Year)

Eight ages of man (Erikson)

Trust is fostered by "consistency, continuity, and sameness of experience" [4] in the satisfaction of the infant's basic needs by the parents. The "quality of the maternal relationship" is more important than "absolute quantities of food or demonstrations of love." If the needs of the infant are met as they arise and if the parents communicate genuine affection, the child will think of his world as safe and dependable. If the care is inadequate, inconsistent, or negative, the child will think of his world with fear and suspicion.

Autonomy vs. Doubt (2 to 3 Years)

"Muscular maturation sets the stage for experimentation . . . outer control [of which] must be firmly reassuring" and must also strike a balance between overprotection and lack of support. If the child is permitted and encouraged to try to do what he is capable of doing at his own pace and in his own way, he will develop a sense of autonomy. If the parents are impatient and do too many things for the child, he will doubt his ability to deal with the environment.

---

[4] All material in quotes is from Chapter 7 of *Childhood and Society*, 2nd ed.

Table 3-1 Developmental Stages of Erikson and Freud

Erikson's psychosocial stages	Age range	Freud's psychosexual stages*
Trust vs. Mistrust. Adequate care and genuine affection lead to view of world as safe and dependable. Inadequate care and rejection lead to fear and suspicion.	Birth to 1 year	*Oral Stage.* Mouth region provides greatest sensual satisfaction. Unfortunate experiences causing a fixation at this level may lead to greed and possessiveness or verbal aggressiveness.
Autonomy vs. Doubt. Opportunities for child to try out skills at own pace and in own way lead to autonomy. Overprotection or lack of support may lead to doubt about ability to control self or environment.	2–3 years	*Anal Stage.* Anal and urethral areas provide greatest sensual satisfaction. Unfortunate experiences causing a fixation at this level may lead to messiness, extreme cleanliness, or frugality.
	3–4 years	*Phallic Stage.* Genital region provides greatest sensual satisfaction. Unfortunate experiences causing a fixation at this level may lead to inappropriate sex roles.
Initiative vs. Guilt. Freedom to engage in activities and patient answering of questions lead to initiative. Restriction of activities and treating questions as a nuisance lead to guilt.	4–5 years	*Oedipal Stage.* Parent of opposite sex is taken as object of sensual satisfaction—which leads to tendency to regard same-sexed parent as a rival. Unfortunate experiences causing a fixation at this level may lead to competitiveness.
Industry vs. Inferiority. Being permitted to make and do things and being praised for accomplishments lead to industry. Limitation on activities and criticisms of what is done lead to inferiority.	6–11 years	*Latency Period.* Resolution of Oedipus complex by identifying with parent of opposite sex and satisfying sensual needs vicariously.
	11–14 years	*Puberty.* Integration of sensual tendencies from previous stages into unitary and overriding genital sexuality.
Identity vs. Role Confusion. Recognition of continuity and sameness in one's personality, even when in different situations and when reacted to by different individuals, leads to identity. Inability to establish stable traits in perception of self leads to role confusion.	12–18 years	

*The description of Freudian stages in this table is derived from Elkind, 1970, p. 108.

Initiative vs. Guilt (4 to 5 Years)

The ability to participate in many physical activities and to use language sets the stage for initiative, which "adds to autonomy the quality of undertaking, planning, and 'attacking' a task for the sake of being active and on the move." The danger of this stage is a sense of guilt over the goals contemplated and the acts initiated in one's exuberant enjoyment of new locomotor and mental power." If the child is given freedom to initiate activities and if the parents take time to answer questions, his tendencies toward exploration will be encouraged. If the child is restricted and made to feel his activities and questions are pointless or a nuisance, he will feel guilty about doing things on his own.

Industry vs. Inferiority (6 to 11 Years)

"The child must forget past hopes and wishes, while his exuberant imagination is tamed and harnessed to the laws of impersonal things—even the three R's." "He now learns to win recognition by producing things . . . he develops a sense of industry." "The child's danger at this stage lies in a sense of inadequacy and inferiority." If the child is encouraged to make and do things, is allowed to finish what he starts, and is praised for his efforts, industry results. If what the child attempts is treated as bothersome and if his efforts are derided, inferiority results.

Identity vs. Role Confusion (12 to 18 Years)

"The growing and developing youths, faced with (a) physiological revolution within them, and with tangible adult tasks ahead of them are now primarily concerned with what they appear to be in the eyes of others as compared with what they feel they are. . . . In their search for a new sense of continuity and sameness, adolescents have to refight many of the battles of earlier years." The goal is development of ego identity, "the accrued confidence of sameness and continuity." "The danger of this stage is role confusion," particularly doubt about sexual and occupational identity. If the adolescent succeeds in integrating roles (as reflected by the reactions of others) in different situations to the point of experiencing continuity in his perception of self, identity develops. If he is unable to establish a sense of stability in various aspects of his life, role confusion results.

Intimacy vs. Isolation (Young Adulthood)

"The young adult, emerging from the search for and insistence on identity, is eager and willing to fuse his identity with others. . . . He is ready for intimacy." "The danger of this stage is that intimate, competitive, and combative relations are experienced with and against the selfsame people," which may lead to isolation.

Generativity vs. Self-Absorption (Middle Age)

"Generativity . . . is primarily the concern of establishing and guiding the next generation." Those unable to do this become victims of self-absorption.

Integrity vs. Despair (Old Age)

Integrity "is the acceptance of one's one and only life cycle as something that had to be and that, by necessity, permitted of no substitutions." "Despair expresses the feeling that the time is now short, too short for the attempt to start another life and to try out alternate roads to integrity."

Freud believed that the developing individual derives sensual pleasure from different zones of the body at different ages, culminating in adult sexuality. Under normal circumstances, earlier stages are outgrown, but if extreme experiences occur, development may become *fixated* at that point and a permanent trait of personality may be formed. Erikson stresses the interaction between ego and society; he proposes that although earlier stages pave the way for later development, it is possible for a person to overcome the aftereffects of unfortunate prior experiences if favorable experiences take place at advanced stages. For example, a child who has been overprotected by his parents and enters school with a sense of guilt rather than initiative (regarding his ability to do things on his own) might acquire a sense of industry rather than inferiority if his first-grade teacher permits him to try things on his own and praises him for his accomplishments. On the other hand, negative experiences at a particular

---

Harry Stack Sullivan's Emphasis on the Self-Concept

Erikson believes the child's perceptions of himself and the culture in which he is reared are just as important as the sexual drives stressed by Freud. The importance of *interpersonal relationships* on the development of the self-concept was stressed by the American psychiatrist Harry Stack Sullivan (1953). Sullivan maintained that a person's conception of himself emerged from *reflected appraisals* of other persons. The self-concept of the infant is influenced by the treatment he receives from those who care for him. If the parents are loving and comforting, the child will develop positive feelings about himself; if the parents are anxious, tense, and rejecting, negative feelings about the self may be implanted. Positive feelings are communicated most effectively through the process of *empathy*—the subtle but deep comprehension of common thoughts and feelings. When the child masters language, verbal appraisals of approval and disapproval influence his self-concept; and when he enters school, the reactions of his teachers and peers become important.

If a negative self-concept is implanted by negative appraisals at any stage of development, the child will tend to see in others what he sees in himself in an effort to convince himself that others are as bad as he perceives himself to be. If, however, such a child develops a close enough relationship with another person (e.g., a friend, a teacher, or a psychotherapist), he may be able to accept negative thoughts and neutralize his negative self-evaluation.

Sullivan emphasizes that an atmosphere of acceptance, approval, and support is most likely to encourage a positive self-concept. He says that those who work with children should strive to be *participant-observers;* that is, they should make an effort to empathize with a child and try to understand how he feels in a given situation in order to become aware of the impact of reflected appraisals. (This point of view, which urges you to concentrate on how the child *feels,* is also stressed by Combs and Snygg, and stands in contrast to the behaviorist view, which emphasizes objectivity and analysis of overt behavior.)

---

stage may cancel out positive traits that had been previously established. A first-grade teacher who severely limits independent activity on the part of her students and criticizes and belittles almost everything they attempt, may cause a sense of inferiority to develop even in children who previously had been encouraged to achieve a sense of initiative.

Characteristics of Erikson's Eight Ages of Man appropriate to different grade levels will be discussed in the next chapter. At this point you may wish to make your own inferences about approaches to education most likely to encourage a child to achieve the positive attributes of each stage while avoiding the dangers noted.

Erikson stresses the importance of the development of identity through interaction between the individual's ego and the society in which he lives. Jean Piaget has concentrated on the development of intelligence, and his contributions to education and psychology will now be analyzed.

Theories of Piaget

Jean Piaget has achieved a unique status as an authority on the general intellectual development of children. He has published several dozen books and articles, and his hierarchy of stages of intellectual development has been endorsed and applied by many psychologists and educators. A general overview of his theories will be examined at this point; more specific analyses of each of his stages of development will be presented in the next chapter. Piaget's theories are producing such a wide-ranging impact on current educational practice that you are urged to read a comprehensive analysis of his work. Some suggestions for further reading are noted at the end of this chapter.

Piaget's Background

Bärbel Inhelder, Piaget's chief collaborator, has described him as a "zoologist by training, an epistemologist by vocation, and a logician by method" [1953, p. 75]. His training as a zoologist came as a result of an early interest in biology that led him to earn undergraduate and graduate degrees in that field. His vocation as an epistemologist derived from the influence of an uncle who urged the adolescent Piaget to widen his horizons and consider philosophical as well as scientific matters. In his analysis of philosophy, Piaget found he was most attracted by epistemology and questions about the nature and origin of knowledge. His logical methods would seem to stem from the tendencies toward order and precise observation that appeared so early in life, as well as from his training in science and epistemology. The direction of his interests and his methods was influenced by his early work in developing intelligence tests, a consequence of his first job—a position at the Binet Laboratory in Paris. As

Jean Piaget Piaget was born in Neuchâtel, Switzerland in 1896. His father was a professor of medieval literature whose scholarly pursuits had an early impact on the young Jean—when he was 11 years old he wrote a description of an albino sparrow he had seen which was published in a natural history magazine; a paper published at 15 so impressed a museum official that he offered Piaget a job as curator of one collection. Following up on this early scientific interest, Piaget earned undergraduate and graduate degrees in biology at Neuchâtel University. (The Ph.D. was granted when he was 21.) After some postgraduate study and work in Paris, Piaget was appointed director of research at the Jean Jacques Rousseau Institute in Geneva. He eventually became codirector of the Institute, which was later affiliated with Geneva University. Although he has been a visiting scholar at many European and American universities, Piaget spends most of his time in Geneva or in his Alpine farmhouse where he does much of his writing.

he listened to children respond to test questions, Piaget found that he was fascinated more by wrong answers than correct ones. He became convinced that children think in ways substantially different from adults and concluded that a comprehensive analysis of the nature and development of thinking in children would permit him to combine his basic interests in biology and epistemology. He has engaged in this analysis for over fifty years and has produced a comprehensive description of every aspect of children's thinking. No other person has observed, analyzed, and described child behavior and thought more comprehensively or incisively.

Basic Principles of Piaget's Theory

The conception of intellectual development that Piaget has arrived at after a lifetime of study reflects his basic interests in biology and epistemology. He

Organization
postulates that human beings inherit two basic tendencies: *organization* (the tendency to systematize and organize processes into coherent systems) and

Adaptation
adaptation (the tendency to adapt or adjust to the environment). Just as the biological process of digestion transforms food into a form that the body can use, Piaget believes intellectual processes transform experiences into a form the child can use in dealing with new situations. And just as the biological processes must be kept in a state of balance, Piaget believes intellectual processes seek a balance through the process of *equilibration*. Equilibration is a form

Equilibration
of self-regulation that permits the child to bring coherence and stability to his conception of the world and to make inconsistencies in experience comprehensible.

The two basic tendencies of organization and adaptation combine to produce cognitive *structures,* or *schemata,* that permit the child to differentiate between experiences and generalize from one experience to another. *Organization* is

Organization
illustrated by a child combining two separate skills, such as looking and grasping, into a more advanced skill—picking up something he is looking at. *Adaptation*

Adaptation
occurs through two complementary processes: *accommodation* to the external environment, which takes place as a result of interacting with objects in a variety of ways, and *assimilation* of these new experiences, either by incorporating them into existing schemata or by developing new ones.

These various principles can be illustrated by the example of a young child encountering a ball for the first time. From experiences with objects he has encountered previously, the child will have *organized* the separate skills of looking and grasping. He is therefore benefiting from past experience when he reaches for and tries to pick up the ball. His first efforts may be unsuccessful if he has never before tried to pick up an object that rolls, so he will *adapt* by *accommodating* to the new object—altering grasping techniques already mastered—and by *assimilating* this new feature into his *structure* or *scheme* of objects-to-be-picked-up. If the first ball he encounters is small and red, he will think of it as typical of all balls until he encounters other balls of different sizes and colors. At that point, his need to maintain *equilibration* will cause him to fit the inconsistency between his original and later experiences with balls into his conception of *ball* by further processes of accommodation and assimilation. In time, the child's understanding of *ball* will permit him to recognize all types of balls and to understand their common qualities.

As the child develops, the way he organizes and adapts to environmental experiences is reflected by a succession of stages of thought and behavior. Each stage involves a period of formation and attainment; each is an attainment in itself but also serves as the starting point for the next, and preceding stages become a part of stages that follow. The rate at which a particular child proceeds through these stages varies to some extent, but Piaget believes the sequence is the same in all children.

The infant and young child up to two years old is preoccupied with his senses and his motor activities, and so Piaget calls this the *sensorimotor* stage. By the end of this stage, the child has organized his experiences to the point where he can attempt new ways to deal with unique situations, rather than using only schemes that worked on roughly equivalent earlier situations.

The thinking of the preschool child centers around mastery of symbols, which permits him to benefit more from past experiences and to mentally manipulate things he previously manipulated physically. Piaget believes that symbols are derived from mental imitation and that they involve both visual images and bodily sensations. Because symbols are based on the child's own experiences, they have qualities unique to each child. Rather than standing for things in a direct way, they represent one person's knowledge of things. All children probably have some similarities in their conception of what a bicycle is, for example, but each child will also have a unique idea of a bicycle. This will be so because personal experiences with bicycles will have been different. When children learn to use words as symbols, the same reservation applies—a word will have a personal meaning for each child. Piaget believes that one of the most distinctive features of the speech and thought of young children is that it is primarily *egocentric*; that is, the child is unable to take into account another person's point of view. He interprets words and uses them in terms of his own experience, not yet grasping the possibility that other children and adults who have had different experiences may have different conceptions. The ability to take into account the views of others—called *socialized* speech and thought—does not develop until the age of seven or eight years. Thus the way younger children use words is different from the way older children and adults use them.

Egocentric speech

Socialized speech

The egocentric speech and thought of the preschooler results not only from his personal interpretation of words but also from his inability to think about more than one thing at a time. This quality also influences the way he reasons about things. This is illustrated most clearly by Piaget's experiments to determine the degree of understanding of the principle of *conservation*—the idea that mass, or substance, does not change when the shape or appearance of an object is transformed. In a typical conservation experiment a child is presented with a situation in which water (or juice, or beans, or whatever) is poured from one of two identical beakers into a tall, thin beaker; water from the other is poured into a short, squat beaker. The preschool child, who can think of only one quality at a time, will maintain that the tall beaker contains more water because he concentrates solely on height. It is not until the child has organized and adapted to experiences over the next two or three years that he becomes capable of *decentration*—the ability to keep from centering his attention on only one quality. When the child can take into account both height and volume, he is able to understand that the amount of water remains the same even when its shape is altered. However, being able to understand the conservation of quantity does not permit the six-year-old to immediately understand and apply a general principle. Children typically do not completely grasp the conservation of weight until they are nine, or of volume until they are twelve. This illustrates that the child must organize and adapt to still more experiences before he can generalize.

Conservation

Decentration

Operation

Piaget uses the concept of *operation* to explain the way in which conservation is mastered. He defines an operation as "an interiorized action which modifies the object of knowledge" (1964, p. 8). The most distinctive feature of an operation is its *reversibility*—awareness that conditions can be reversed or returned to their original state. In the case of the beaker experiment, the interiorized action permits the child to mentally reverse the pouring of water from one beaker to another (when the beakers are actually in front of him). Before that time, the child is *preoperational,* and he cannot make mental modifications such as reversals. The kind of operation engaged in by the elementary-grade child is limited to objects actually present or with which he has had direct, concrete experience, as illustrated by the inability of the child to generalize. For this reason, Piaget describes this stage as that of *concrete operations*. It is not until further maturation, organization, and adaptation that the child—typically around the end of elementary school—becomes capable of *formal* operations that permit him to deal with abstractions. (The term "formal" reflects the development of *form* or structure of thinking. It also might be thought of as emphasizing the ability of the adolescent to *form* hypotheses.)

Comprehension of abstractions leads to a tremendous widening of intellectual horizons—the adolescent can form ideals, speculate about contrary-to-fact propositions, and develop hypotheses. As the adolescent gains more experience with formal operations, he may become more involved with possibilities and less concerned with reality. This sometimes leads to difficulties if the theorizing is not related to practical difficulties (as in solutions to social and political problems, for example). And although mastery of formal operations makes it

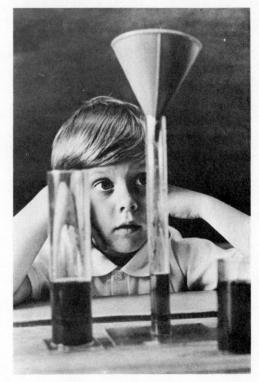

Piaget conservation problem. (PHOTO BY THE NEW YORK TIMES)

Moral Realism and Relativism

In addition to studying language, thought, reasoning, and intelligence, Piaget has analyzed moral development and judgment. Just as the preoperational child is egocentric in speech and limited in his thinking by his inability to decenter, the judgment of the young child is also influenced by the fact that he cannot take into account the point of view of others and that he can think only of one thing at a time.

This leads to what Piaget calls *moral realism.* He studies and illustrates it with situations in which a child is asked to assess the guilt of two children: one wants to help his father by filling his pen but makes a big blot on the table cloth when he opens the bottle; another decides to play with his father's pen and makes a small blot. The younger child concentrates on the amount of damage, not the motives, and argues that the child who made the bigger blot is more guilty, even though

possible for the adolescent to adapt to a great variety of problems and to be flexible in his thinking, it also leads to complications because the young person can now mentally explore the pros and cons of various future possibilities—for example, the choice of a career, which can be a source of considerable anxiety.

Table 3-2 is a highly simplified representation of Piaget's conception of the stages of intellectual development.

Table 3-2 Stages (or Periods) of Intellectual Development as Described by Piaget

Name of stage and age range	Description
Sensorimotor (birth to 2 years)	Learning about properties of things through senses and motor activity. Eventual development of new ways of dealing with situations.
Preoperational (2–7 years)	Mastery of symbols permits mental manipulation of symbols and objects. Acquisition of language that is *egocentric*—words have a unique meaning to each child, which limits ability to consider others' points of view. Gradual acquisition of ability to *decenter* (think of more than one quality at a time) and understand *conservation.*
Concrete operational (7–11 years)	Ability to conserve, decenter, and reverse but only with reference to concrete objects. Capacity to mentally manipulate concrete experiences that previously had to be physically manipulated. Ability to deal with *operations*—interiorized actions involving reversibility—but no ability to generalize beyond actual experience.
Formal operational (11 years and above)	Ability to deal with things not present and with abstractions. More interested in possibilities than realities, capable of imagining various future alternatives and of developing hypotheses.

Stages of intellectual development (Piaget)

his intentions were praiseworthy. This is called moral realism because the child focuses on the "realistic," or material, side of things. Moral realism is also reflected in the literal interpretation of rules. Because his egocentrism prevents him from understanding that other people have different points of view, the primary grade child tends to think of rules as "sacred" judgments. (He may break rules in some cases, however, because he does not completely understand them.)

Moral realism

At around the age of eleven or twelve years, children become capable of *moral relativism.* They are now able to decenter and think of several qualities at once, and they have overcome their egocentrism by becoming aware that other people may have different points of view. Consequently they take into account motives and circumstances in making moral judgments. And they are more flexible about rules since they realize that rules are simply agreements among individuals as to forms of conduct appropriate to given situations.

Moral relativism

Applications of Piaget's Theory

Piaget's description of the stages of intellectual development has been shown (by Piaget and many other investigators whose work is reported in Almy et al., 1968, Ginsburg and Opper, 1969, and Elkind, 1970) to be quite accurate and valid. Children *do* go through the stages he has described. This has led to considerable speculation about how we should use this information. In this country, there has been a tendency for applications of Piaget's theories to center around how the information he has provided might be used to speed up intellectual development. This undoubtedly reflects our American preoccupation with efficiency and the associationist-environmentalist tradition in American psychology. As discussed previously, Hunt has suggested that awareness of Piaget's stages and other information about development should permit us to increase intelligence by 30 points. Piaget, however, and some of his most devoted followers in this country—for example, David Elkind, Herbert Ginsburg, and Sylvia Opper—are disturbed by too much emphasis on acceleration of learning. Piaget believes attempts to speed up the process of intellectual development are not only unlikely to be successful but *may* cause difficulties. Elkind (1968) reports that in an interview Piaget commented on what he called the "American question," which he said is asked every time he comes to this country and only here: "If there are stages that children reach at given norms of ages, can we accelerate stages ... How far can we speed things up?" Piaget's answer is summed up in these statements:

In the realm of education ... students should be allowed a *maximum* of activity on their own, directed by means of materials which permit their activities to be cognitively useful. In the area of logico-mathematical structures, children have real understanding only of that which they invent themselves, and each time that we try to teach them something too quickly, we keep them from reinventing it themselves. Thus, there is no good reason to try to accelerate this development too much; the time which seems to be wasted in personal investigation is really gained in the construction of methods [in Almy, 1966, p. vi].

> It is a great mistake to suppose that a child acquires the notion of number and other mathematical concepts just from teaching ... When adults try to impose mathematical concepts on a child prematurely, his learning is merely verbal; true understanding of them comes only with his own mental growth. (1953, p. 76) [5]

Piaget's background and views of development help explain these answers. Consider his belief in the inherited tendencies of organization and adaptation (reflecting his interest in biology), his conviction that children think in fundamentally different ways than adults, his emphasis on the need for the child to develop his own conception of the world. Piaget distinguishes between "merely verbal learning" and "true" learning, which involves the acquisition of a new structure of mental operations that permits the child to assimilate new experiences and to generalize from novel situations. The second type of learning can occur only after the child has developed the necessary mental equipment. Ginsburg and Opper describe what might occur if the child is pushed too fast:

> If there is too great a disparity between the type of experience presented to the child and his current level of cognitive structure, one of two things is likely to happen. Either the child transforms the experience into a form which he can readily assimilate and consequently does not learn what is intended, or else he merely learns a specific response which has no strength or stability, cannot be generalized, and will probably disappear soon. It is for this reason that the child's learning, in school or out, cannot be accelerated indefinitely. There are some things he is not ready to learn because the necessary cognitive structure is not yet present. If forced to deal with such material, the child does not achieve genuine learning. (1969, p. 176)

J. Smedslund (1961) conducted experiments to determine if it is possible to accelerate understanding of the principle of conservation. His results corroborate the views of Piaget and Ginsburg and Opper—superficial learning may occur, but even the child who has been given instruction or training is unable to generalize. Studies by P. Greco (1959) and J. F. Wohlwill (1959) have led to the same conclusion. And David Elkind (1970) has suggested that if young children are exposed to too much formal instruction—which prevents them from becoming totally involved in their own explorations—we may produce "intellectually burned" children who later shun intellectual activities just as a burned child shuns fire.

Instead of attempting to accelerate learning with the hope that it will improve a child's capacity to learn, Piaget, Elkind, and Ginsburg and Opper advise

---

[5] Piaget makes a book-length analysis of the points summarized in these brief excerpts in *Science of Education and the Psychology of the Child* (1970).

Some Speculations on the "American Question"

Piaget reports that educators and psychologists in the United States seem overly concerned about accelerating the intellectual development of children. Perhaps this is, at least in part, a reflection of the "cult of efficiency" in American education. It may also be partly due to competition with Russia. To clarify this last statement a bit of background is needed.

The Russian psychologist L. Vygotsky (1959, English translation, 1962) has theorized that it is possible and desirable to teach children how to form concepts. Although he agrees with Piaget that the child forms certain concepts through his own experience, Vygotsky argues that other concepts *can* be taught. At the Institute for Preschool Education in Moscow, a carefully designed program of systematic stimulation has been developed, and Russian parents and preschool teachers are urged to do everything possible to facilitate the intellectual development of children. Thus our own emphasis on acceleration may be due in part to the feeling that *they* know something we don't know and that future generations of Russians may be smarter than future generations of Americans unless we accelerate faster than they do.

Perhaps the most logical explanation of the "American question" has been supplied by Millie Almy, who specializes in research on the acceleration of preschool learning:

> Piaget is said to have remarked that whenever you tell Americans about some process of development their immediate question is, "How can you accelerate it?" In fairness, strategy that attempts to unravel a developmental process by providing training prior to the time when a concept would "normally" appear, does not necessarily imply the judgment that the concept *ought* to be taught earlier. On the other hand, the incredulous expression of the experimental psychologist who discovers that his own otherwise intelligent five-year-old does not conserve, and the sometimes grim determination with which he sets about correcting this condition bear witness to the fact that some American psychologists do have some interest in speeding up the process of cognitive development. (1966, p. 42)

Almy adds these perceptive remarks:

> We detect in some of the reports of experimentation, and in some of the discussions of the possibilities for advancing the child's understanding by matching or pacing his intellectual development, a degree of impatience with the playful, imaginative, highly personalized thought of the young child. We infer that the sooner childish thoughts are put away, the more surely and the more insightfully the person enters into the intellectual kingdom set up for him by the great thinkers in the various disciplines. . . . Viewed from another direction, the playful and, to the adult, unsystematized thought of the young child may serve to integrate the patterns of action . . . that make up the intellectual repertoire of the infant and toddler. . . . There is no guarantee that instruction in specific concepts will necessarily hasten the transition from one level of thinking to the next. But even if evidence accrues that it does, the question of whether such acceleration, from a long-term view, enhances or stultifies the individual's abilities for speculative, imaginative, even creative thinking still needs investigation. (Pp. 129–30)

teachers to operate on the assumption that capacity determines learning and that the most important ideas of a child are not taught but spontaneously acquired. They urge teachers to take into account the stage of development achieved by the pupils in their classes and to arrange class activities so that they assist and encourage learning by children themselves. British educators have used this basic interpretation of Piaget's theory in developing their form of open education. In British elementary schools it is assumed that children need to engage in a variety of self-selected activities, in order to organize and adapt their own experiences and that since children learn differently from adults, they should be encouraged to learn from each other.

Some advocates of free education, for example, Neill and Holt, argue that the same basic philosophy should be followed at all levels of schooling; that is, students should learn almost everything on their own and/or by interacting with their peers. Any attempt on the part of an older, more knowledgable adult to explain something he has learned is considered a hindrance rather than an aid.

There are many reasons for suggesting that teachers permit their students to engage in self-instruction and to avoid too much imposed learning, including the possibilities that much teacher-directed learning may be pointless busywork and that it often leads to regimentation and limits creativity. In light of Piaget's stages, however, it is apparent that avoiding teacher direction because of the belief that children should learn from direct experience and from their peers does not take into account the possibility that teachers can *arrange* the classroom environment to facilitate learning. This is especially true when students reach the stage of formal operations. When the junior or senior high school student becomes capable of dealing with abstractions, he can benefit to a considerable degree from the observations of others who have evolved systematic patterns of ideas on given subjects. Both the student and the teacher think in the same way at the same level, and abstract thought usually becomes more powerful when structure is made apparent. It makes little sense for a teacher of older students to withhold information on the grounds that it will be more meaningful if each student discovers it himself, since much knowledge is the product of the collective efforts of thousands of thinkers over a period of years. This is not to say that students at the level of formal operations should never engage in independent study or group discussion with classmates, since such activities are excellent forms of learning. But it does not appear that teachers who deal with more mature students should feel hesitant about presenting organized subject matter. Students who are capable of formal operational thought will probably welcome and benefit from information presented by teachers who have given considerable thought to the arrangement of information likely to enhance learning by others. (As Dewey put it in the excerpts presented in Chapter 2, "As the most mature member of the group [the teacher] has a peculiar responsibility for the conduct of the interactions and intercommunications which are the very life of the group as a community. . . . Since freedom resides in the operations of intelligent observation and judgment by which a purpose is developed, guidance given by the teacher to the exercise of the pupils' intelligence is an aid to freedom, not a restriction upon it. (1938, p. 66)

(As noted at the beginning of this section on Piaget, specific educational implications of his theory will be discussed in each section of the next chapter, which deals with age-level characteristics.)

Bruner's Theory of Instruction

Although Hunt has emphasized the preschool, acceleration-of-learning possibilities inherent in Piaget's theory and has served as a consultant to the Head Start program, the man who has developed what is perhaps the most comprehensive educational program based on a hierarchy of stages similar to that of Piaget is Jerome Bruner. In *Toward a Theory of Instruction*, Bruner offers principles for shaping the intellectual growth of children according to a preconceived "grand plan." This long-range view emphasizing structure reflects Bruner's position as a leading field theorist. His concern for structure is seen also in the following observation: "There is an absence of theory of instruction as a guide to pedagogy. A theory of development must be linked both to a theory of knowledge and to a theory of instruction, or be doomed to triviality" (1966, p. 21).

In his own theory of instruction, Bruner suggests that intellectual development runs the course of three successive systems of representation. He calls the first *enactive* representation because the young child defines events and objects in terms of the actions he takes toward them. By the age of three or so, what he terms *iconic* representation appears. This system of thought depends on visual or other sensory organization, with the child using highly concrete visual imagery. The most advanced form of representation Bruner refers to as *symbolic*. At this point the child is able to develop images that have an autonomous status. This he does by translating experience into language and by using language as an instrument of thinking. These systems, you will note, parallel Piaget's sensorimotor, concrete operations, and formal operations stages.

Stages of intellectual development (Bruner)

Bruner's general description of stages parallels that of Piaget, but he differs from Piaget in his interpretation of the role of language in the development of thought. Piaget theorizes that thought and language are closely related—but different—systems. He believes the thinking of the child is based on a system of inner logic that evolves as a child organizes and adapts to experiences. He also believes the symbols of the younger child are based on visual images and imitation. This hypothesis is based primarily on observations that two-year-old children are able to engage in accurate imitations of complex behavior at a time when their language skills are quite primitive. Bruner, however, maintains that thought is internalized language, and that syntactical rules of language rather than logic can be used to explain mastery of conservation and other principles. He bases his hypothesis on experiments carried out by his students and colleagues, which are reported in Chapters 9 and 10 of *Studies in Cognitive Growth.*

Bruner modified the beaker experiment devised by Piaget, having the water poured behind a cardboard screen that permitted the child to see only the tops of the beakers and not the amount of water. When children were asked if there would be the same amount of water in tall and short beakers, most were able to give the correct answer, although many of the same children were unable to conserve when the screen was removed and they could actually watch the beakers being filled. Bruner explains that the child who sees the water being poured is impelled by the visual presence of the pouring to concentrate on visual cues, whereas the child who is asked to describe what has happened without seeing it uses symbolic representation, which "frees" him from the concrete.

Bruner sums up his views, as compared with Piaget's, in this way:

> At the Institute in Geneva, cognitive development is seen as almost purely a matter of maturation, maturation that takes place by a process of internalization of logical forms; logic, first expressed motorically, is gradually internalized until it can be used symbolically—at which time physical action becomes no longer necessary for thought. . . . At the Cognitive Center at Harvard, cognitive development is conceived more in terms of the internalization of technologies from the culture, language being the most effective technology available. . . . Harvard also stresses the differences in the ways the world can be represented: enactively, ikonically,[6] and symbolically. Although there is a developmental sequence in terms of which—or more properly, how many—of these modes are available to a person, all three remain "in the system" throughout life, and there is always interaction among them. By recognizing the ikonic mode of representing reality and thus bringing into cognition the role of imagery—a factor which Piaget tends to ignore—Harvard casts a somewhat different light on the conservation problem. It becomes possible to view the lack of conservation as a misleading ikonic representation, rather than as merely the absence of the appropriate logical forms (as Piaget leads us to believe). Hence the value of a screening procedure to knock out the ikonic mode and allow for other more appropriate ones that may also be available. (1966, p. 214)

It should be noted that some aspects of Bruner's view of Piaget differ from the interpretations of other American psychologists. Descriptions by Elkind, Ginsburg and Opper, and Almy note that Piaget takes pains to emphasize that maturation is not the only factor in mental development—he lists and describes

---

[6] In *Studies in Cognitive Growth,* Bruner spells it *ikon,* in *Toward a Theory of Instruction* he spells it *icon.*

those other influential categories: experience, social transmission, and equilibration (the process of self-regulation). And although Piaget does not stress the use of words as symbols, he certainly does not—as Bruner maintains—"ignore" imagery. Furthermore, Piaget believes that all the types of thinking he has described remain "in the system" for life even after a person is capable of formal operational thought, he will sometimes revert to lower levels of thought. Bruner suggests that symbolic thought is "available" to the child at an early age; Piaget is convinced that formal operational thought can be used only by those who have organized and adapted experiences—first in preoperational terms and then in the form of concrete operations. Bruner thus implies that the most advanced kind of thinking a child can be assisted to engage in is the most appropriate. Piaget maintains that whatever kind of thinking a child uses on his own is the most appropriate kind and that attempts to impose more sophisticated kinds of thoughts are ill-advised.

Bruner also differs from Piaget in his estimate of the degree to which some environments can slow or stop the sequence of development. He believes that spurts are touched off when certain capacities begin to develop, and he describes the overall sequence as basically the development of a series of prerequisites. As he puts it, "Some capacities must be matured and nurtured before they can be called into being (1966, p. 27)." This view is similar to Piaget's to the extent that it stresses a hierarchical sequence, but Bruner does not share Piaget's views on "the American question." He writes:

> ". . . the idea of "readiness" is a mischievous half-truth. It is a half-truth largely because it turns out that one *teaches* readiness or provides opportunities for its nurture; one does not simply wait for it. Readiness, in these terms, consists of mastery of those simple skills that permit one to reach higher skills" (p. 29).

Bruner engaged in research on infants in an effort to determine the nature of the simplest skills that serve as a basis for further learning, and reported some of his conclusions (as well as observations on other matters) in *The Relevance of Education* (1971).

Recap of the Development Debate

Although Bruner labels the theory of "natural" readiness as "a mischievous half-truth," in some situations *lack* of allowance for readiness may be just as "mischievous." For example, two kindergarten teachers discovered that they shared a concern about some of their pupils. Each teacher had about half a dozen boys who were among the youngest children in the class and who appeared to be slow maturers. These boys were unable to do many simple tasks that their classmates accomplished with ease, and they also seemed a bit intimidated by the greater maturity and confidence of their older classmates. The teachers were apprehensive that if the boys were promoted to the first grade, they might be doomed to a tortuous academic career. But when the teachers suggested that the boys repeat kindergarten so that they would be the most mature rather than the least mature pupils in the class, the parents were almost unanimously opposed. They were afraid that the slower start would permanently handicap their children. Many of them had read or heard about Bloom's version of the critical period theory—that the first six years are crucial and that irreparable harm will be done if a child fails to be stimulated properly during these early years.

In this particular situation, allowing for natural development in the absence of concern about "making" these boys ready would seem to be a desirable course of action. Although Bruner's argument that we should *teach* readiness rather than wait for it has merit, differences in rate of development cannot be ignored. Moreover, the idea that children should be *made* ready tends to make parents and teachers apprehensive about those who don't progress as rapidly as others; this fear often leads, in turn, to unintentional pressure on the child, causing him to feel even more insecure and tense. His teacher and parents may feel obligated to overwhelm him with experiences he is unable to assimilate. In such cases a readiness test might alert the teacher and parents to the possibility that the child should be allowed to find himself at his own pace and in his own way. All this suggests that "a mischievous half-truth" may be implicit in *both* sides of the readiness argument.

Perhaps the central question in the development debate is this: Is it better to surround children with stimuli and partly structured experiences and allow them considerable freedom to choose *what* they find meaningful *when* they find it meaningful? Or is it better to note what appear to be characteristic, progressive patterns, or stages, in child development and then systematically lead all children through this sequence?

Following are some specific questions well worth considering. Say you decide to lead your pupils through a systematic program of experiences. How can you be sure that the children who were observed in order to establish the sequence were typical? How can you be certain that the people who developed the theory were not influenced by preconceptions? It may be, for example, that Piaget's beautifully logical hierarchy of stages is as much a product of his orderly mind as of actual child behavior.[7] Also, if you choose a systematic program, do you run the risk of disrupting maturation by inflicting a contrived pattern on children? And even if the children observed in the sample were typical and the patterns accurate, is there danger in providing extra stimulation for a child from an environment that is already culturally rich?

---

[7] J. H. Flavell, who has written a definitive analysis of Piaget's theories, notes that Piaget has "a penchant for symmetry and neatness of classifications" (1963, p. 38).

Is It Unwise to Be Too Concerned
about Early Experience?

Barbara Merrill (1946) conducted an experiment in which thirty mothers and their preschool children were observed interacting in a standardized playroom. After an initial observation, fifteen of the mothers were taken aside individually and told that their children's play performance in the previous session had not been an altogether satisfactory sample of his potentialities. As Merrill notes, this was done to increase the motivation of the mothers to have their children do well. The other fifteen mothers were not told anything. Then all thirty mothers were again closely observed as they interacted with their children while they played in the standardized playroom.

The researchers found that the "experimental" mothers showed significant increases in directing, interfering, criticizing, and structuring changes in activities. Thus the information that their children were not working up to capacity led to more authoritarian control on their part. Other studies (Read, 1945; Radke, 1946) have indicated that authoritarian parental attitudes cause children to be submissive, lacking in security and independence, and also emotionally unstable.

Emphasis on critical periods and the argument that preschool experience is essential to adequate development might be thought of as a similar kind of warning to parents that they should make sure their children work up to capacity. It seems likely that pressure to do the "right" thing before it is too late predisposes parents to direct and structure their children's play. It also appears likely that if a child did not perform "properly", he would be interfered with and criticized. Thus parents (and teachers) who are overly concerned about arranging precisely the right sequence of experiences for their children might inadvertently produce youngsters who are submissive, insecure, and unstable. On the basis of the Read and Radke experiments it appears that parents who are relaxed about child rearing and permit their children considerable freedom to develop in their own way will actually produce "better" children than those who try too hard.

You might speculate about the implications these studies have for teaching. It will obviously be to your advantage—and that of your pupils—to encourage all of them to make the most of their abilities. But if your attempts to do this involve too much directing, interfering, criticizing, and structuring of activities, you may defeat your purpose.

Even if you are able to demonstrate in an experiment that, as Bruner claims, it is possible to teach anything in some meaningful fashion to any child at any stage of development, all pertinent factors in the study must be taken into account. In experiments frequently cited as proof that the I.Q. can be improved (Kirk, 1948; Deutsch, 1962, Engelmann, 1971), *tutoring* was the basic teaching technique used. Bruner also has used tutorial or very-small-group techniques with a selected assortment of above-average students in attempting to prove his anything-can-be-taught-to-anybody thesis. Is it defensible to apply the findings of such studies to situations in which the teacher must deal with thirty to forty unselected pupils?

Are Bloom's arguments—that the early years are the most crucial and that if a child does not learn at this time the handicap will be irreversible—valid? If they are, we should probably devote more of the school budget to the primary grades and concentrate on perfecting their curricula. Or are the original readiness advocates correct in saying that a school system will get more for its money by waiting for children to mature before instruction begins? In three surveys of research on the effectiveness of early versus late instruction (Baer, 1958; Hall, 1963; Tyler, 1964), the general conclusion was that a given amount of instruction is more effective when administered to an older child than when given to a younger one.

The final question and perhaps the most important: Have the accelerated learning advocates overlooked the possibility that a child may experience failure if he is asked to learn before he has reached the point at which he is likely to respond? And have they considered that if he *does* fail, this may produce in him a poor attitude toward learning, which will be difficult to overcome?

When you look over the age-level characteristics described in the following chapter, you are urged to think back to these questions and ponder them further.

Summary

This chapter has analyzed the theoretical questions you will need to take into account in interpreting the age-level characteristics described in the next chapter. You have been acquainted with some of the problems inherent in using the age-level approach, notably the difficulty of finding truly representative standardization groups and the fact that group norms will not enable you to predict the behavior of individual children. Since the age-level approach focuses on specific characteristics for specific age levels, you will find it helpful to offset this somewhat arbitrary division of growth into discrete groups of qualities by keeping in mind general principles of development and the overall continuity of development.

A basic question that faces any educator who theorizes about development is readiness. You have considered some of the experiments that led to the concept of critical periods in development and the theory that children should be provided with guided experience at what are considered to be crucial stages of their lives. Piaget's mapping of the stages of intellectual development has opened up the possibility of assisting children through these stages at a faster-than-normal rate by means of special training. Piaget himself has some misgivings about doing this, but Bruner feels that readiness can and should be taught.

Erik H. Erikson's ages of man serve as background for making decisions about readiness and for speculations about relationships between development and education.

Suggestions for Further Reading, Writing, Thinking, and Discussion

3-1 *Looking for Literal Examples of Overlap*

A factor that complicates the prediction of student behavior on the basis of age-level characteristics is *overlap*. To become aware of how and why this is so, consider making this simple study: Station yourself outside a public school toward the end of the day and observe students as they emerge from their classrooms. Those who come out of each room will usually be the same chronological age. First, note the range of sizes and shapes within a given group. Then as the children begin to mix in the hall or school grounds, see if you can clearly identify those who belong to the same age group. If you make such a survey, report your results and comment on their implications.

3-2 *Becoming Aware of the Complications of Actuarial Prediction*

Scientists try to predict behavior so that it will be possible to control behavior. Knowing age-level characteristics permits teachers to forecast and thus control (or allow for) the behavior of their students. The predictions may, however, have only limited value as the basis for uniformly successful pedagogical techniques because of the nature of *group* or *actuarial* prediction. Individuals vary tremendously, and there are exceptions to any rule. To get an idea of the range of individual differences to be found in practically any classroom, obtain permission to observe in a class at the grade level you expect to teach. Pick out two students who strike you as being at opposite extremes with regard to one or more qualities you select (e.g., energy, self-confidence, physical size, attractiveness). Observe each one for five or ten minutes (more, if you can) and write a brief personality sketch of each student. Then compare your two sketches. Do they seem to be describing students who are essentially the same or noticeably different? Comment on the implications of your findings.

3-3 *Checking on the Predictability and Uniformity of Behavior at Different Age Levels*

One of the principles mentioned in this chapter is that the pattern of development becomes less predictable with increasing age. To test the applicability of this principle, make arrangements to observe a nursery school (with children of approximately the same chronological age) and a high school class. Note behavior that seems typical of each group. You might concentrate on such things as coordination, size, or impression of general maturity. Do you detect greater variability in the younger or the older students? Write your reactions and comment on the implications of your observations.

3-4 *Observing Development from General to Specific Responses*

Another principle noted in this chapter is that development proceeds from general to specific responses. To test the applicability of this principle, make arrangements to observe in an elementary school. Start in the kindergarten, paying special attention to how well the children are able to manipulate small objects such as pencils and scissors. Then go to a third grade and finally a sixth grade. (If this is not possible, observe children from different grade levels at play during recess.) Do the older students seem to have greater control over their fine muscles? Note your reactions and comment on the implication of your observations.

3-5 *Checking on Irregularities in Growth*

Still another principle mentioned is that although long-term growth is continuous, short-term growth may be irregular. To test the applicability of this principle, obtain permission to interview an elementary school teacher and ask her whether she notices occasional backsliding in her pupils. Write down any specific examples she gives, and then comment on the implications of such regressions in behavior.

3-6 *Relating the Observations of Lorenz to Human Behavior*

No less an authority than Julian Huxley has called Konrad Lorenz "one of the outstanding naturalists of our day." In *King Solomon's Ring* (1952) Lorenz describes many of his early observations and experiments with animals, including his first observations of *imprinting*. (You will find it at the beginning of Chapter 5, "Laughing at Animals.") Almost any part of this book is enjoyable and instructive, but Chapter 8 ("The Language of Animals") and Chapter 11 ("Morals and Weapons") are especially interesting. The latter chapter examines a theme that is developed more completely in *On Aggression* (1966)—the nature of aggression in animal and man. Sample Chapter 3 ("What Aggression Is Good For"), Chapter 13 ("Ecce Homo!"), or Chapter 14 ("Avowal of Optimism"). If you read any sections of either of these books, briefly record your reactions—perhaps with emphasis on how they relate to education and our society.

3-7 *Sampling Hunt's Views on "Intelligence and Experience"*

James McVicker Hunt is perhaps the leading advocate of the hypothesis that enriched stimulation during critical periods produces sizable increments in intelligence. For Hunt's defense of the hypothesis, look for *Intelligence and Experience* (1961). Many parts of this book are quite technical, but you will find a summary in Chapter 9. (Chapter 8 presents "Some Reinterpretations" of studies relating to the impact of heredity and environment on intelligence—from the viewpoint of the current leading spokesman for environmentalists.) A less comprehensive but more up-to-date presentation of Hunt's case for the environmental point of view can be found in Chapter 15 of *Intelligence: Genetic and Environmental Influences* (1971) edited by Robert Cancro. The title of the chapter is "Social Aspects of Intelligence: Evidence and Issues," which was written by Hunt in collaboration with Girvin E. Kirk. If you read any of these chapters, you might summarize the arguments presented and note your reactions.

3-8 *Learning More About Preschool Education*

Evidence pointing to the importance of critical periods and arguments about the importance of earlier experience on development has led to considerable interest in preschool education. For an analysis of the causes and nature of the preschool education boom of the 1960s, examine *Preschool Education Today* (1966) edited by Fred M. Hechinger. This brief paperback includes chapters by many of the leading advocates of preschool education, including Martin Deutsch and J. McVicker Hunt.

If you would like information on teaching techniques, look for *Teachers of Young Children* (1972) by Robert D. Hess and Doreen J. Croft.

3-9 *Sampling Bloom's Observations on Stability and Change in Human Characteristics*

The "bible" of many advocates of early-childhood education is Benjamin Bloom's *Stability and Change in Human Characteristics* (1964). If you are curious as to how Bloom arrived at his estimate that 50 percent of adult intelligence is achieved by the age of four and 80 percent by the age of eight, examine his arguments in Chapters 1, 3, 6, and 7. Are you convinced that these estimates are reasonable, well established, and valid? Speculate too about Bloom's hypothesis that IQ "losses" early in life are irreversible. For example, do you think a child who has had a relatively unstimulating preschool environment will fail to respond if he encounters an enthusiastic and effective first-grade teacher? Mentally compare a child who goes to nursery school not with a child who is *deprived* of almost all stimulation but with one who stays home and plays with toys in the backyard. If you follow up on either or both of these suggestions, you might write a brief summary of your reactions.

3-10 *Reading about the Education of the Wild Boy of Aveyron*

Jean Marc Itard (1775–1838) was a physician who became intrigued with the possibility of "humanizing" a feral child discovered in the company of a pack of wolves in a forest in the Aveyron region of France. He spent five years attempting to convert the wolf-child into a young man. His efforts were hampered by the fact that the boy's sight and hearing were severely impaired, but Itard's experiences, reported in *The Wild Boy of Aveyron,* make a fascinating study. If you would like to gain some insight into how Itard set about his task, browse through this book and summarize your reactions. Keep in mind that Itard based his methods on only limited data about behavior and learning. In the 170 years since he worked with Victor (the wolf-boy), a great deal of information that was not available to Itard has been discovered and tested. In later chapters of this text, different educators' techniques for working with deprived and retarded children will be discussed. At this point you might describe how *you* would approach the job if you were asked to educate a nine-year-old boy found leading a pack of wolves in Yellowstone Park. (Note: Francois Truffaut's film "Wild Child" is a somewhat fictionalized interpretation of *The Wild Boy of Aveyron.*)

3-11 *Discovering More About the Theory of Erik H. Erikson*

Erik H. Erikson's books are of considerable significance in speculating about development and education. In the first six chapters of *Childhood and Society* (2nd ed., 1963), he describes how studying American Indians and observing patients referred to him for treatment led to the development of his Eight Ages of Man (described in Chapter 7). In the final chapters of this book, Erikson analyzes the lives of Hitler and Maxim Gorky with reference to his conception of development. For a concise biography of Erikson and a capsule description of his stages of development, read "Erik Erikson's Eight Ages of Man" by David Elkind, which appeared in the April 5, 1970 issue of *The New York Times Magazine.* For a comprehensive analysis of Erikson, his theory and its significance, examine *Erik H. Erikson: The Growth of His Work* (1970) by Robert Coles. If you read sections of any of these books by or about Erikson, you might summarize the points that impress you and note their significance for teachers.

3-12 *Gaining Further Understanding of Piaget's Theory*

Since Jean Piaget has probably had a greater impact on theoretical discussions of development and the emergence of educational practices such as open education than any living psychologist, you may wish to find out more about him. Of his own books, you might consult *The Language and Thought of the Child* (1952), *The Origins of Intelligence in Children* (1952), and *The Psychology of the Child* (1969), which was written in collaboration with Bärbel Inhelder. An inexpensive paperback that provides a biography of Piaget and an analysis of his work with emphasis on classroom applications is *Piaget's Theory of Intellectual Development: An Introduction* (1969) by Herbert Ginsburg and Sylvia Opper. Other highly regarded books about Piaget are *The Origins of Intellect: Piaget's Theory* (1969) by John L. Phillips, *Piaget for Teachers* (1970) by Hans Furth, and *Understanding Piaget* (1971) by Mary Pulaski. A brief, highly readable account of Piaget and his theories is David Elkind's "Giant in the Nursery: Jean Piaget," which originally appeared in the May 26, 1968 *New York Times*

Magazine and is reprinted in Elkind's book *Children and Adolescence: Interpretive Essays on Jean Piaget* (1970). If you read sections of any of these books, write a summary with emphasis on the educational implications of Piaget's theory.

3-13 *Tuning in on "Sesame Street" and "The Electric Company"*

One of the most effective applications of the theories of Piaget (and of related descriptions of intellectual development) is "Sesame Street," the television program designed to provide preschool children with enriched learning experiences to foster readiness. (This program also puts into practice Bruner's suggestion that everything possible be done to *teach* readiness.) To gain some ideas for applying Piagetian (and other) principles in your own classroom, watch several "Sesame Street" programs and note techniques you feel you might adapt for your own use. If you will be teaching in the primary grades and would like some leads for assisting slow readers to improve, watch episodes of "The Electric Company," which is specifically aimed at second-grade slow readers.

Recommended Reading in *Psychology Applied to Teaching: Selected Readings*

If you would like to do further reading in books or articles mentioned in this chapter (and in the preceding "Suggestions for Further Reading, Writing, Thinking, and Discussion") without having to track down several separate volumes, you might peruse *Psychology Applied to Teaching: Selected Readings* (Boston: Houghton Mifflin, 1972). This is a collection of excerpts from books and articles from journals in psychology. The following selections provide extended commentaries on points noted in this chapter or mentioned in the "Suggestions."

Views of Preschool Education: excerpt from *Preschool Education Today* by Fred N. Hechinger, Selection 11, p. 138. (See also Suggestion 3–8.)

Erikson's Theory of Development: "Erik Erikson's Eight Ages of Man" by David Elkind, Selection 10, p. 120. (See also Suggestion 3–11.)

Piaget's Theory of Development: "Giant in the Nursery—Jean Piaget" by David Elkind, Selection 12, p. 147. (See also Suggestion 3–12.)

Bruner's Theory of Development: "Patterns of Growth" by Jerome S. Bruner, Selection 13, p. 170.

4 AGE-LEVEL CHARACTERISTICS

CHAPTER CONTENTS

Preschool and Kindergarten: 3 to 6 Years
Physical, Social, Emotional, and Mental Characteristics
Developmental Trends and Their Implications, as Seen by Erikson, Piaget,
* and Bruner*

Primary Grades (1, 2, and 3): 6 to 9 Years
Physical, Social, Emotional, and Mental Characteristics
Developmental Trends and Their Implications, as Seen by Erikson, Piaget,
* and Bruner*

Elementary Grades (4, 5, and 6): 9 to 12 Years
Physical, Social, Emotional, and Mental Characteristics
Developmental Trends and Their Implications, as Seen by Erikson, Piaget,
* and Bruner*

Junior High (7, 8, and 9): 12 to 15 Years
Physical, Social, Emotional, and Mental Characteristics
Developmental Trends and Their Implications, as Seen by Erikson, Piaget,
* and Bruner*

Senior High (10, 11, and 12): 15 to 18 Years
Physical, Social, Emotional, and Mental Characteristics
Developmental Trends and Their Implications, as Seen by Erikson

ON THE FOLLOWING PAGES YOU WILL FIND AN OUTLINE OF AGE-LEVEL characteristics, as well as suggestions on how to use this information in your teaching. The developmental span is divided into five levels, corresponding to the common grade divisions in school: preschool and kindergarten, primary, elementary, junior high, and senior high. Under each level are described the various physical, social, emotional, and mental characteristics for that level.

Even though many school districts have different types of grade-level organization—such as an ungraded system, a grouping of kindergarten through eighth grade followed by four years of high school, or the new *middle school* arrangement—the five-level arrangement used here seems the most workable. If you find yourself observing or teaching in a school with a different organization, it should be a simple matter to adapt the following outline by regrouping the characteristics according to the age spans in your particular system.

Space has been provided after certain sections for you to note down related characteristics and further applications. You may not feel that doing this is relevant at the moment, but in an actual teaching situation, you may find that recorded ideas are well worth the trouble. If you don't make a note of techniques for handling different problems as their solutions occur to you, you may forget them. One of the purposes of this book is to provide you with a framework for noting your ideas in a reasonably systematic way.

Although you may be tempted to read only the characteristics for the grade you have decided to teach, it will be unfortunate for several reasons if you skip over the rest of the chapter. First of all, a characteristic discussed at one level may be apparent at many or all other levels, and reading about it elsewhere may provide you with further insight. Second, even if a characteristic is described at only one level, remember that this placement is somewhat arbitrary, that growth is not so uniform, smooth, and continuous that a generalization applies only within a three-year span. Many traits will overlap into adjacent levels because of the wide range of individual differences. Finally, both you and your students will benefit if you try to understand the overall process of growth.

Preschool and Kindergarten: 3 to 6 Years
Physical Characteristics

1. *Preschool children are extremely active. They have good control of their bodies and enjoy activity for its own sake.*

Provide plenty of opportunities for the children to run, climb, and jump. Arrange things so that this takes place as much as possible under your control. If you follow a policy of complete freedom, you may discover that thirty improvising three- to five-year-olds can be a frightening thing. In the space below you might note some specific games and activities you could use to achieve semicontrolled play.

_____

_____

_____

2. *Because of their inclination toward bursts of activity, kindergartners need frequent rest periods. They themselves often don't recognize the need to slow down.*

Schedule quiet activities after strenuous ones. Have rest time. Be alert to the possibility that excitement may build up to a riot level if the attention of "catalytic agents" and their followers is not diverted. Below you might list some signals for calling a halt to a melee (e.g., playing the opening chords of Beethoven's Fifth Symphony on the piano) or for diverting wild action into more or less controlled activity (e.g., marching around the room to a brisk rendition of "The Stars and Stripes Forever").

---

3. *The children's large muscles are more developed than those that control fingers and hands. Therefore, they may be quite clumsy at, or physically incapable of, such skills as tying shoes, buttoning coats, etc.*

Slower development of fine muscle control

Avoid too many finicky activities such as pasting paper chains. Provide big brushes, crayons, and tools. In the space below you might note other activities or items of king-size equipment that would be appropriate in view of the children's level of muscular development.

---

4. *Kindergartners find it difficult to focus their eyes on small objects; therefore, their eye-hand coordination may be imperfect.*

If possible, minimize the necessity for the children to look at small things. (Incomplete eye development is the reason for large print in children's books.) Again, avoid too many finicky activities.

5. *Although the children's bodies are flexible and resilient, the bones that protect the brain are still soft.*

Soft skull bones

Be extremely wary of blows to the head in fights between children. If you notice a fight involving such a blow, intervene immediately; warn the class that this is dangerous and explain why.

6. *Although boys are bigger, girls are ahead of boys in practically all other areas of development, especially in fine motor skills, so don't be surprised if boys are clumsier at manipulating small objects.*

It may be desirable to avoid boy-girl comparisons or competitions involving such skills.

Should Girls Start School Earlier Than Boys?

From time to time it has been suggested that girls enter first grade at the age of six years and boys at seven or even eight years. The main argument is that girls mature faster than boys so that boys have an initial disadvantage in terms of readiness, a disadvantage they may never overcome. (It is well established that girls do better than boys in most subjects and in overall grade point average throughout their school careers.)

What are some arguments for and against this proposal? If you don't approve of it, how do you feel about segregating classes by sex so that boys aren't left at the starting gate because of their relative immaturity? What do you think of separating boys from girls only for certain activities, for example those involving fine motor skills?

7. Handedness is established in most children, and 90 percent are right-handed.

It is probably unwise to attempt to force a lefty to change. Being right-handed may be more convenient, but it is usually not that important. Compelling a child to switch may make him feel queer, guilty, nervous, and upset. The possibility of causing various adjustment problems, such as stuttering, does not justify the attempt.

Social Characteristics

1. Most children have one or two best friends, but these friendships may change rapidly. Preschoolers tend to be quite flexible socially; they are usually willing and able to play with most of the other children in the class. Favorite friends tend to be of the same sex, but many friendships between boys and girls develop.

You might make it a habit to notice whether some children seem to lack the ability or confidence to join others. In some cases a child may prefer to be a loner or an observer rather than a participant. But if you sense that a child really *wants* to get to know others, you might provide some assistance. Sociograms are often used to reveal which playmates a shy child would like to get to know.

2. Play groups tend to be small and not too highly organized; hence they change rapidly.

You should not be concerned if children flit constantly from one activity to another. Such behavior is normal for this age group, although it may drive

Suggestions for Using Sociometric Techniques

Sociometric techniques have been developed to help teachers obtain information about companion preferences. The simplest approach is to ask each student to write down (or report verbally) the name of the classmate he likes best. In some cases you may want to phrase the question more subtly; for example, "Write the name of someone you have fun with" or "Write the name of someone you would like to sit next to." In other cases you could request more than one choice and even negative choices. For most purposes, however, simply asking for the name of the best liked classmate is most satisfactory since the teacher's task of recording several choices can be a complicated one. Perhaps the simplest and best way to record responses is the *target diagram* (Northway, 1940), illustrated in Figure 4–1.

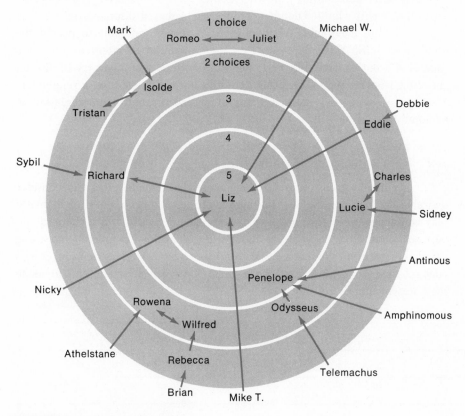

FIGURE 4–1 Target Diagram

This diagram is largely self-explanatory. As you can see, it focuses attention on the *stars* in the center and the *isolates* outside the circle. If an isolate seems content to be a nonentity, a loner, perhaps you should respect his preference. But in the case of the child who appears eager to join others yet unable to take the first step, you might subtly help by pairing him on some activity with the classmate he chooses.

If you would like more information about how to obtain, interpret, and use sociometric techniques, consult *Sociometry in the Classroom* by Norman E. Gronlund or issues of the journal *Sociometry*.

you wild, especially on certain days. You might do some thinking about how much control you will want to exert over your pupils. At what point does insistence on perseverence become an unnatural demand that may interfere with constructive behavior and even lead to destructive behavior?

3. Quarrels are frequent, but they tend to be of short duration and quickly forgotten.

When thirty children are thrown together for the first time in a restricted environment with a limited number of objects to be shared, disputes over property rights, etc., are inevitable. When possible, it seems preferable to permit the children to settle these differences on their own and to intervene only if a quarrel gets out of hand. If you do have to interfere, you might try to distract the antagonists by suggesting other activities instead of acting as a referee and forcing a showdown. (Other methods of classroom control are discussed in Chapter 15.)

4. Preschoolers enjoy dramatic play; most of the plots they invent stem from their own experiences or TV shows.

Provide simple props, ones that encourage the kinds of plots you consider desirable. In the space below you might note some specific types of dramatic play you will want to encourage—and *dis*courage if you think that there should be restrictions. How do you feel about war games, for example? Some argue that games featuring aggression are desirable because they release tension. Others contend that such games predispose children to violence and tend to make them unsympathetic to suffering.

5. Awareness of sex roles begins.

By the time they enter kindergarten, most children have at least a rudimentary understanding of behavior that is considered appropriate for males and females in our society. Until recently it was assumed that this was desirable and should be encouraged, but the policy is now being questioned. Florence Howe (1971)

SIGH!

I DON'T THINK I'D MIND SCHOOL AT ALL IF IT WEREN'T FOR THESE LUNCH HOURS...I GUESS I'LL SIT ON THIS BENCH...

I HAVE TO SIT BY MYSELF BECAUSE NOBODY ELSE EVER INVITES ME TO SIT WITH THEM...

PEANUT BUTTER AGAIN! OH, WELL, MOM DOES HER BEST...

THOSE KIDS LOOK LIKE THEY'RE HAVING A LOT OF FUN...I WISH THEY LIKED ME... NOBODY LIKES ME...

THE PTA DID A GOOD JOB PAINTING THESE BENCHES...

I'D GIVE ANYTHING IN THE WORLD IF THAT LITTLE GIRL WITH THE RED HAIR WOULD COME OVER, AND SIT WITH ME...

I GET TIRED OF ALWAYS BEING ALONE...I WISH THE BELL WOULD RING...

A BANANA...RATS! MOM ALWAYS...STILL, I GUESS SHE MEANS WELL...

I BET I COULD RUN JUST AS FAST AS THOSE KIDS... THAT'S A GOOD GAME THEY'RE PLAYING...

THAT LITTLE GIRL WITH THE RED HAIR IS A GOOD RUNNER...

AH, THERE'S THE BELL! ONE MORE LUNCH HOUR OUT OF THE WAY...

TWO-THOUSAND, ONE-HUNDRED AND TWENTY TO GO!

analyzed teaching materials and activities used in elementary schools and concluded that boys are depicted as active, adventurous, self-confident, and ambitious, whereas girls are represented primarily as homemakers. She argues that starting in kindergarten, girls are conditioned to accept homemaking as their only role and by the end of elementary school the stereotype is so strong it is difficult to overcome. As a result, girls dutifully prepare for a role as housewife, only to discover in their twenties that they want something beyond it. Betty Friedan, in *The Feminine Mystique,* suggests, "A massive attempt must be made by educators and parents . . . to stop girls from growing up wanting to be 'just a housewife' . . . by insisting, with the same attention from childhood on that [is given] to boys, that girls develop the resources of self, goals that will permit them to find their own identity" (1963, p. 351). If you agree with this philosophy, you may want to plan how such a feminine role might be encouraged as soon as children enter school.

Emotional Characteristics

1. *Kindergarten children tend to express their emotions freely and openly. Anger outbursts are frequent.*

Some psychologists have suggested that many people are so concerned about concealing their emotions, they suppress feelings that they should express. It is probably desirable to let children at this age level express their feelings openly, at least within broad limits, so that they can recognize and face their emotions. Some kindergarten teachers even urge children to analyze unacceptable bits of behavior. They may say to a child, for example, "Why do you think you just hit Debbie with the shovel?" You might do some thinking ahead as to whether you will feel comfortable using this approach. In his *Between Parent and Child* (1965) and *Teacher and Child* (1971), Haim Ginott offers some specific suggestions on how a parent or teacher can help a child develop awareness of his feelings. This book may help you work out your own philosophy and techniques for dealing with emotional outbursts.

Anger outbursts are more likely to occur when children are tired, hungry, and/or exposed to too much adult interference (Goodenough, 1931). If you take such conditions into account and try to alleviate them (e.g., by providing a nap or a snack), temper tantrums may be minimized. However, by the time a child enters the grades, he should have made a start at learning to control his anger himself. In the space below you might jot down any techniques you have observed or can think of that will help children accomplish this goal. If some of the techniques described by Ginott strike you as especially promising guidelines, note these also.

2. Because they are exposed to many new and strange situations and because they possess vivid imaginations, preschool children may have many fears, including some highly irrational ones.

Suppressed and only partly recognized fears may cause considerable difficulty later in life in the form of specific phobias or general feelings of anxiety. For this reason, it is extremely unwise to tease a child who shows fear, to force him into the feared situation, or simply to ignore his fear. A better approach is to show the child that you accept him *and* the fear and that he can feel secure in the school situation.

Some specific techniques that have been found effective (Holmes, 1935) include permitting the child to approach things at his own pace and in his own way; letting him observe—on his own, not with elaborate "assistance" from others—that other children are not afraid; and explaining why an apparently threatening situation or object is actually innocuous. It is also important to remember that children are very much influenced by adult example. Whether they become afraid or accept something as a matter of course may depend on what you do. If you have any idiosyncratic fears (e.g., of snakes, bugs, or mice), you might practice putting up a front of masterful composure.

3. Jealousy among classmates is likely to be fairly common at this age since kindergarten children have much affection for the teacher and actively seek approval. When there are thirty individuals competing for the affection and attention of just one person, some jealousy is inevitable.

It will be desirable for you to spread your attention around as equitably as possible; and when you praise particular children, do it in a private or casual way. If a child is given lavish public recognition, it is only natural for the other children to feel resentful. Think back to how you felt about teachers' pets during your own school years. If you have observed or can think of other techniques for minimizing jealousy, jot them down in the space below.

Mental Characteristics

1. Kindergartners are quite skillful with language. Most of them like to talk, especially in front of a group.

Providing a "sharing time" gives children a natural opportunity for talking, but many will need help in becoming good listeners. Some sort of rotation scheme is usually necessary to divide talking opportunities between the gabby and silent extremes. For less confident children, you might provide activities or experiences for them to talk about, a field trip, a book, a film, etc. In the

---

The "Magic Circle" and the Human Development Program

In the January 1968 issue of *Psychology Today,* psychotherapist Harold Bessell describes the *Human Development Program* he has devised for kindergarten pupils. It consists of a series of daily, twenty-minute "share and tell" periods. The teacher invites ten children at a time to form a "Magic Circle" and asks them questions such as, "What did you do that somebody liked? What did you do that somebody did not like?" The children also explore their positive and negative feelings, thoughts, and behavior by reacting to pictures; and a series of physical activities, some of which resemble Montessori school projects, are engaged in to improve motor coordination. The aim of the program is to develop greater self-confidence, self-awareness, and understanding of social interaction.

If you are intrigued by the description of this program, you might pick up some interesting ideas for "guided sharing" by referring to the article in *Psychology Today.*

---

space below you might note down some comments to use if a pupil starts to share the wrong thing (e.g., a vivid account of a fight between his parents) or if he tries to "one-up" a classmate (e.g., "Your cat may have had five kittens, but *our* cat had a *hundred* kittens.")

---

2. Imagination and inventiveness are at a peak at this level.

Since most people tend to lose this precious gift as they grow older, you should encourage it in your pupils as much as possible—in play, storytelling, and painting. However, some children may be so imaginative that they fail to distinguish between reality and make-believe, which can lead to adjustment problems. One way to handle this without squelching a child's imagination completely is to encourage him to tell stories during special story times but not during the rest of the day and to stress that although it is wonderful to be able to make up stories, sometimes it is necessary to describe *exactly* what happened.

Developmental Trends as Seen by Erikson

Preschoolers at the age of three years are at Erikson's stage of *Autonomy vs. Doubt.* Those four and five years of age are at the *Initiative vs. Guilt* level.

Characteristics of both levels provide background for theorizing about preschool education.

Erikson: importance of autonomy

Autonomy develops when a child is permitted and encouraged to do what he is capable of doing. As Erikson notes, "Muscular maturation sets the stage for experimentation . . . outer control [of which] must be firmly reassuring" (1963, pp. 251–252). Doubt may develop if the child attempts to do too much, which may cause him to lack confidence in his ability to deal with the environment.

The older preschool child and the kindergartner are at the age of Initiative vs. Guilt. Initiative Erikson describes in these terms:

Erikson: importance of initiative

> [The child is] in free possession of a surplus of energy which permits him to forget failures quickly and to approach what seems desirable (even if it also seems uncertain and even dangerous) with undiminished and more accurate direction. Initiative adds to autonomy the quality of undertaking, planning, and "attacking" a task for the sake of being active and on the move. . . . The child at no time is more ready to learn quickly and avidly, to become bigger in the sense of sharing obligation and performance than during this period of development. He is eager and able to make things cooperatively, to combine with other children for the purpose of constructing and planning, and he is willing to profit from teachers and to emulate ideal prototypes. (Pp. 255–258)

The danger of this age is that guilt may occur if the surplus of energy leading to initiative results in "acts of aggressive manipulation and coercion" (p. 255), for example, jealous rage.

Implications of Erikson's Observations

Encouraging autonomy

It would seem that teachers at the preschool level should permit pupils to engage in considerable free experimentation to encourage the development of autonomy but provide some guidance to reduce the possibility of the establishment of doubt. More specifically, teachers might subtly direct a child who is attempting something beyond his capabilities toward activities he is likely to be able to accomplish. As Erikson puts it:

> "Firmness must protect [the child] against the potential anarchy of his as yet untrained sense of discrimination. . . . As his environment encourages him to 'stand on his own feet,' it must protect him against meaningless and arbitrary experiences of shame and of early doubt. . . . From a sense of self-control without loss of self-esteem comes a lasting sense of goodwill and pride; from a sense of loss of self-control and of foreign over-control comes a lasting propensity for doubt and shame" (pp. 252–254).

Encouraging initiative

Teachers at the kindergarten level, it would appear, should permit considerable self-initiated activity and perhaps intervene only when a child infringes on the rights of others. In terms of Erikson's theory, too much of a prescribed curriculum at the preschool level (as advocated by educators who hope to speed up mental development) might limit the development of autonomy and initiative and perhaps produce doubt and guilt. However, organized and structured activities might be presented in a manner designed to permit considerable self-direction on the part of the child.

Developmental Trends as Seen by Piaget

Preschool and kindergarten children (and most first and some second graders as well) are at the *preoperational* level. This means they will be capable of using symbols to stand for objects, which makes mental manipulation possible. Their use of language will be egocentric, however. Words will have different meanings for different children, and most kindergartners will not be able to take into account the fact that other people have different points of view. During the preoperational period, the child gradually becomes capable of *decentration* and eventually can think of more than one quality at a time.

Piaget: preoperational thought

Piaget: egocentric speech and thought

In order to grasp the fact that the language and thought of the preoperational child is qualitatively different from your own, you might ask kindergarten pupils to explain more fully what they mean by certain words—particularly if you are a bit baffled by their statements. To gain insight into the impact of lack of ability to decenter, try some of Piaget's simple experiments with individual pupils. As background for your experiments, you should bear in mind that children typically go through a three-stage process in their understanding of any aspect of conservation: at first, they simply do not grasp the concept; then they pass through a transition period in which they can understand it only in some situations; finally, they grasp the idea completely enough to supply correct answers in all situations involving a particular kind of conservation.

Dealing with preoperational and egocentric thought

The child's earliest awareness of conservation is of mass or substance. If you try the beaker experiment (described in the preceding chapter on p. 116) or show a four-year-old two clay balls of the same size and then flatten one of them as he watches, he is likely to say that the taller beaker or the flattened piece of clay contains more. By age five most children comprehend that the mass is the same regardless of the shape, but they may reveal incomplete comprehension by even a slight change of procedure—such as pouring water from the tall beaker into a vase, then asking if the amount is the same or if there is more water in the vase. Awareness of conservation of weight typically takes place between the ages of seven and ten, complete understanding of volume between ten and twelve. The fact that a child can understand one type of conservation but is unable to generalize to other types illustrates the difference between concrete operations and formal operations.

To demonstrate the nature of the development of conservation to yourself, you might conduct a series of Piaget experiments. First, place two clay balls of equal size on a scale to show that they are the same weight and then flatten one ball. Only an older kindergarten pupil is likely to predict that they will still balance. Next, drop the two clay balls into equal amounts of water in graduated cylinders and then flatten one. Probably not even the oldest child in kindergarten will be able to predict that the water level will be raised the same amount by both the round and elongated bits of clay. Other experiments involve matching rows of objects. Place before the child a row of seven pennies, buttons, blocks, or the like. Then ask the child to pick out from a collection of similar objects the "same number" or "as many" as there are in the row. After the child has arranged his row of objects, ask him if the two rows are the same. Take the objects in the original row and spread them out so that they extend over a wider area. Then ask if the two rows are the same. Most five-year-olds are likely to maintain that the longer row now has more. Even though they may be capable of matching objects on a one-to-one basis (putting one directly underneath another), their inability to decenter leads them to concentrate on the single dimension of length. The slightly older child, capable of concrete operational thought, will be able to mentally spread out the objects in the compact row (or mentally reverse the action when you widen the gap

---

An Early Childhood Curriculum Based on Piaget's Theory

The experiments conducted by Piaget and described by Ginsburg and Opper and Almy are intended primarily to help you understand how children think at different age levels so that you can arrange appropriate learning experiences and comprehend what your students say. As noted in Chapter 3, many American psychologists believe such understanding should be used to speed up development. Celia Stendler Lavatelli has developed a curriculum and sets of materials based on the Piaget experiments that are to be used to foster intellectual development. In the Introduction to *Piaget's Theory Applied to an Early Childhood Curriculum* she explains her approach in this way:

> This book describes an application of [Piaget's] theories to early childhood curriculum. It reviews relevant aspects of Piaget's theory, describing and explaining how the child acquires classification, number, measurement, space and seriation concepts. It also describes how the theory may be applied to instructional processes for four, five and six-year-old children. The program is designed to help children acquire logical ways of thinking; it provides children with concrete materials upon which to carry out certain actions, and it supplies to the teacher the key questions or problems to ask of children. (1970, p. 2)

A Materials Kit, *Early Childhood Education Curriculum—A Piaget Program,* and an accompanying Teacher's Guide—have been prepared to supplement the text. If you are interested in attempting to arrange learning experiences to promote intellectual development in preschool and kindergarten children, you might examine these books and the materials kit.

---

between the objects in the row you altered) and realize that the number has not been changed.

Piaget feels that a child must grasp the principle of conservation before he can comprehend the concept of number, since the understanding of number is based on the awareness that cardinal numbers are invariant, regardless of other factors. And understanding the concept of number requires more than the ability to count. To demonstrate this for yourself, take six caramels and four lemon drops (or the equivalent) and ask children to count them. Then make sure they understand that both caramels and lemon drops are called candy. At this point ask, "Which are more, the caramels or the candy?" Chances are that most kindergarten children will answer, "Caramels." You might find it enjoyable and instructive to try these experiments.

For more complete information about conducting Piaget experiments, consult *Piaget's Theory of Intellectual Development* (1969) by Ginsburg and Opper or *Young Children's Thinking* (1966) by Almy, Chittenden, and Miller.

Developmental Trends as Seen by Bruner

According to Bruner, the kindergarten child is likely to be functioning at the level of *iconic* representation, that is, learning primarily through actions and through visual and sensory experience and organization. Bruner also points out that the child at this stage finds it difficult to delay gratification once he has completed a task.

Bruner: iconic mode of representation

In addition, Bruner is also convinced that emotional overtones toward learning are established at this age level; therefore, he favors a playful, relaxed approach on the teacher's part. He suggests that a child will be more willing to try things and less upset by failure if he learns that "the outcomes of various activities are not as extreme as he either hoped or feared" (1966, p. 134).

Implications of the Piaget-Bruner Observations

Herbert Ginsburg and Sylvia Opper offer this general conclusion regarding the teaching implications of Piaget's theory: "Perhaps the most important single proposition that the educator can derive from Piaget's work and thus use in the classroom, is that children, especially young ones, learn best from concrete activities" (1969, p. 221). This seems straightforward enough. However, the way you set about encouraging such concrete activities will depend in large part on how you feel about guided experience as opposed to "natural" development. If you share the desire of many psychologists and educators in the United States to accelerate learning as much as possible, you might take steps to help kindergarten children grasp the concept of conservation. If, on the other hand, you endorse Piaget's opinion that it is better to permit the child to absorb experiences in his own way and at his own rate, you might provide a rich environment to permit a maximum amount of concrete activity while minimizing attempts to *show* your pupils how to structure those experiences. This opinion is seconded by Ginsburg and Opper, who put it this way:

> A good school should encourage the child's activity, and his manipulation and exploration of objects. When the teacher tries to bypass this process by imparting knowledge in a verbal manner, the result is often superficial learning. But by promoting activity in the classroom, the teacher can exploit the child's potential for learning, and permit him to evolve an understanding of the world around him. . . . The teacher's major task is to provide for the child a wide variety of potentially interesting materials on which he may act. The teacher should not teach, but should encourage the child to learn by manipulating things. (1969, p. 221)

Bruner, on the other hand, believes—on the basis of the Harvard experiments using a screen to prevent the child from seeing the pouring of water in the beaker experiment—that training might assist children to grasp conservation at an earlier level. He argues that language can serve as a prop to assist the child to more rapidly overcome his dependence on visual perception. Piaget, stressing visual imagery and imitation rather than language, disagrees. If you do consider attempting to assist children to grasp conservation earlier by using the screening technique, you might ask yourself if it is worth the time and trouble. The question pretty much boils down to this: Will time spent in training be better spent in free exploration?

Almy: age best predictor of ability to conserve

Millie Almy (1966), who has carried out comprehensive experimental analyses of Piaget's theories, found that chronological age is the best predictor of a child's ability to conserve, which corroborates Piaget's emphasis on the importance of "natural" development. However, she also discovered that children from disadvantaged backgrounds progressed through the Piaget stages in sequence but at a slower pace than children from richer environments. She hypothesizes that the major reason for their retardation was perhaps a lack of sufficient vocabulary to identify properties and objects such as size, shape, color, and texture. For children who have not yet learned to describe such qualities, she recommends training in language development. "Sesame Street," as you may be aware, emphasizes this kind of language instruction; you might use similar techniques if you have children from disadvantaged backgrounds in your classes. Almy stresses, however, that further language training is probably of little value to children who already have a large vocabulary. In fact, it may be necessary to keep in mind that children with considerable verbal facility may mislead you if you assume that they thoroughly understand all the things they say so glibly.

Almy: disadvantaged children lag in intellectual development

Bruner's observations regarding emotional overtones toward learning suggest that you should recognize the kindergartner's need for immediate gratification and encourage a relaxed, give-it-a-try atmosphere in your classroom. Formal instruction regarding the concept of conservation may cause children to fear giving wrong answers even though they do not grasp the questions as rapidly as others, which could result in a tense rather than a relaxed atmosphere.

Primary Grades: 6 to 9 Years

Physical Characteristics

1. *These children are still extremely active. Because they are required to participate for the first time in largely sedentary pursuits, energy is released in the form of nervous habits, for example, pencil chewing, fingernail biting, hair twirling, general fidgeting.*

You will have to decide what noise and activity level should prevail during work periods. A few teachers insist on absolute quiet, but this can cause the children to work so hard at remaining quiet to avoid the wrath of the teacher that they cannot devote much effort to their lessons. The majority of teachers allow a certain amount of moving about and talking. Whatever you decide, be on the alert for the point of diminishing returns because of too much or too little restriction.

You may be able to minimize the amount of desultory activity if you avoid situations in which your pupils must stay glued to their desks for long periods. Have frequent breaks, and try to work activity into the lessons themselves (e.g., have children go up to the board, bring papers to your desk, and occasionally write in the air rather than on paper). In the space below you might jot down other techniques for encouraging your pupils to be active while doing classwork.

---

2. *Children at these grade levels still need rest periods; they become fatigued easily as a result of physical and mental exertion.*

Schedule quiet activities after strenuous ones (e.g., story time after recess or lunch), relaxing activities after periods of mental concentration (e.g., art after reading or spelling).

3. *Large-muscle control is still superior to fine coordination. It is difficult for many children, especially boys, to manipulate a pencil.*

Avoid requiring much writing at one time. If drill periods are too long, skill may deteriorate and the children may develop a negative attitude toward writing or toward school in general.

4. *The eyes don't fully accommodate until most children are about eight years old. Consequently, as noted, many primary-grade pupils may have*

Full accommodation of eyes at age eight

difficulty focusing on small print or objects. Quite a few children may be farsighted because of the shallow shape of the eye.

Avoid requiring too much reading at one stretch. Be on the alert for signs of eye fatigue (e.g., rubbing the eyes, blinking). Encourage the children to read books with large print.

5. The common illnesses of childhood are most apt to occur during this age period.

Don't be surprised if your beautifully organized lesson plans are disrupted by frequent absences. Be on the alert for pupils who seem to be coming down with something. If they can be isolated or sent home, the number of other children infected will be held to a minimum. If you remember any specific techniques for controlling infection that were mentioned in a health or biology class, you might note them as reminders in the space below.

_____

_____

_____

6. At this age children tend to be extreme in their physical activities. They have excellent control of their bodies and develop considerable confidence in their skills, with the result that they often underestimate the danger involved in their more daring exploits. The accident rate is at a peak in the third grade.

You might keep a first-aid book handy, but also try to prevent reckless play. For example, during recess encourage class participation in "wild" but essentially safe games (e.g., relay races involving stunts) to help the children get devil-may-care tendencies out of their systems. In the space below you might list some other games to use for this purpose.

_____

_____

_____

Social Characteristics

1. At this level children become somewhat more selective in their choice of friends. They are likely to have a more or less permanent best friend and may also pick out a semipermanent "enemy."

In the primary grades, as in kindergarten, you might use sociograms to gain some insight into friendships and then give tentative assistance to children who have difficulty in attracting friends. Also, be on the alert for feuds, which can develop beyond good-natured quarreling.

2. Children in the latter part of this age span like organized games in small groups, but they may be overly concerned with rules.

Keep in mind that, according to Piaget, children at this age are still *moral realists:* they find it difficult to understand how and why rules should be adjusted to special situations.

Continuance of moral realism in children

3. Quarrels are still frequent. Words are used more often than physical aggression, but many boys still indulge in punching, wrestling, and shoving.

Occasional fights are to be expected, but if certain children, especially the same pair, seem to be involved in one long battle, you should probably try to effect a truce. If you can discover the reason for the animosity, so much the better.

If you have observed or can think of some effective techniques for breaking up a fight or for arranging things so that a fight can have a reasonably satisfactory—noninjurious—conclusion, you might jot them down. Consider, for example, how you feel about having two boys settle their differences via a formal, private boxing match complete with overstuffed gloves.

_____

_____

_____

4. Competition becomes noticeable. Boasting may be common.

Competition is an inevitable part of both school and life, and up to a point it is a desirable form of motivation. However, competition has many negative consequences, so do your best to limit public comparisons and encourage the children to compete with *themselves* instead of with others. If a child feels he is competing successfully against himself, he may not need to resort to bragging to convince himself and others that he is superior. But if you still encounter boasting—in games, for example—encourage the children (taking special care not to sound syrupy) to be gracious winners as well as good losers.

5. Boys and girls begin to show different interests, both in schoolwork and in play. The degree of this sex cleavage, *as it is sometimes called, varies considerably. In some classes, when the children clearly recognize that different roles have been assigned to boys and girls in our society, a battle of the sexes results.*

To discourage such antagonism, play down comparisons between boys and girls. Eliminate unwelcome boy-girl combinations when possible, for example, by permitting children to choose their own desks.

Is the Early Environment of Boys Too Feminine?

In the United States boys, as compared with girls, do not do as well in school, develop many more behavior problems, and have a higher suicide rate. There are obviously many reasons for such problems of learning and adjustment, but the primary cause according to one theory is the advantage girls have in learning their sex role. The American child associates almost exclusively with women during the first ten years. The mother takes primary responsibility for early rearing, and later most primary-grade teachers are women. The argument goes that this works out perfectly for girls since they are understood by and find it easy to understand members of the same sex. The boy, on the other hand, has no empathy with older females, has no appropriate model to pattern his behavior after, and begins to show confusion and insecurity.

What do you think of this explanation? What can be done to minimize the influence of a predominantly feminine early environment? For some comprehensive—and provocative—theorizing on this question, read *The Feminized Male* by Patricia Sexton. (Excerpts from this book are presented in an article in the January 1970 issue of *Psychology Today*.) An even more provocative analysis of male-female interaction is provided by Esther Vilar in *The Manipulated Man* (1973).

Emotional Characteristics

1. *Children of this age are becoming alert to the feelings of others. Unfortunately, this permits them to hurt others deeply by attacking a sensitive spot without realizing how devastating their attack is.*

It sometimes happens that teasing a particular child who has reacted to a gibe becomes a group pastime. Be on the alert for such situations. If you are able to make a private and personal appeal to the ringleaders you may be able to prevent an escalation of teasing, which may make a tremendous difference in the way the victim feels about school. You might also do some thinking ahead regarding what tack to take with a pupil who uses verbal aggression to get rid of feelings of hostility. Note any ideas in the space below.

2. *Primary-grade pupils are sensitive to criticism and ridicule and may have difficulty adjusting to failure. They need frequent praise and recognition.*

Because they tend to worship their teachers, young children may be crushed by criticism. Provide positive reinforcement as frequently as possible, and reserve

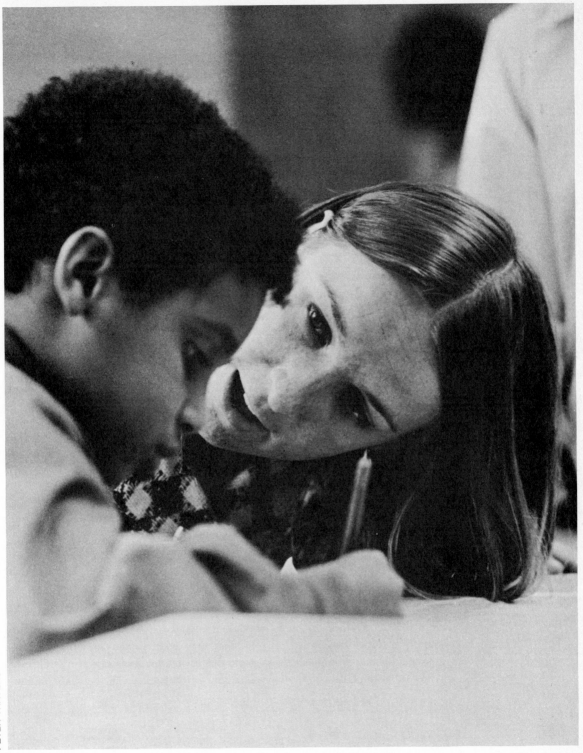

your negative reactions for nonacademic misbehavior. It is important to avoid ridicule and sarcasm *scrupulously*.

3. At this level children are eager to please the teacher. They like to help, enjoy responsibility, and want to do well in their schoolwork.

The time-honored technique for satisfying the urge to "help" is to assign jobs (e.g., eraser cleaner, wastebasket emptier, paper distributor) on a rotating basis. In the space below you might note other techniques for equally distributing helping opportunities. (Do you remember, for example, any particular chores you enjoyed as a pupil?)

_____

_____

_____

Or do you, along with some critics of this practice, feel that any task done to earn the approval of an adult is undesirable in the sense that the adult is using "love" as a bargaining agent? If you don't use some signs of affection (e.g., a smile, a pat on the back, a kind word), what sort of reinforcement *should* you use?

Mental Characteristics

1. Generally speaking, primary-grade pupils are extremely eager to learn.

One of the best things about teaching in the primary grades is the built-in motivation of pupils. The teacher's problem is how to make the most of it. (Some suggestions for doing this are offered in Chapter 9.)

2. They like to talk and have much more facility in speech than in writing. They are eager to recite—whether they know the right answer or not.

The high school teacher may have difficulty in stimulating voluntary class participation—not the primary-grade teacher. The problem here is more likely to be one of controlling participation so that children speak up only when called on. Frequent reminders to take turns and be good listeners are necessary. And even if you are successful in this area, you may feel a bit unsettled to find that a child, after wildly waving his hand to be recognized, will often supply a hopelessly wrong answer. You may want to develop some phrases that gently and/or humorously indicate that an answer is erroneous or irrelevant. If you can think of some now, you might jot them down in the space below.

_____

_____

_____

Some Characteristics of Classroom Recitation

H. V. Baker (1942) took notes on class discussions in second, fourth, and sixth grades and classified each recitation into one of three categories. Here are his results:

Contribution	Grade 2	Grade 4	Grade 6
New topic not obviously related to what any earlier speaker had said	87%	33%	23%
New topic but apparently suggested by something said by a previous contributor	8%	24%	33%
Logical continuation of a topic previously introduced	5%	43%	44%

Source: Table form adapted from Arthur Jersild, *Child Psychology*, 6th ed., 1968, Prentice-Hall, Inc., with permission. Data adapted by Jersild from H. V. Baker, *Children's Contributions in Elementary School Discussion*, Child Development Monographs, No. 29 (New York: Teachers College, Columbia University, 1942) with permission.

These results might be offered as support for Piaget's contention that a child moves from egocentric to socialized speech at around the age of seven or eight.

An additional reason for the apparently unrelated contributions of the second graders is their intense desire to recite. Saying something unrelated to what the preceding reciter said *might* mean that the child wasn't taking into account the topic of the moment. It might also mean that he had put up his hand five minutes before, when what he wanted to say was relevant, but that several other contributors had been recognized first and had nudged the discussion away from the original point. Such an occurrence leaves the reciter with three choices: (1) He can say, "Never mind." (2) He can forget about what he was going to say and make a lame effort to say something that *is* related to what the preceding speaker said. (3) He can go right ahead and say what he has spent the last five minutes preparing to say.

Ramifications of egocentric recitation

The results of the Baker study suggest that older pupils are more likely to resort to the first and second alternatives. But it might be argued that the third also has considerable merit. If you insist that everything said in class recitation be a logical continuation of what was said before, will you be helping or hindering intellectual exploration? As you think over how you might handle "irrelevant" remarks, consider the implications of the three alternatives open to the child.

3. Upon discovering the power of words, many children experiment with vulgar language. They know that they get a reaction, although they don't understand exactly why.

Probably, your first response to vulgar language should be to ignore it in the hope that it will be dropped from lack of reinforcement. If this doesn't work, a short talk with the ringleaders should do the trick. One effective approach is simply to state that such words are not pleasant to listen to and are *not* to be used. This neatly sidesteps the problem of explaining *why* they are disagreeable—which might get you into trouble. For example, consider where the following exchange leaves you. You tell a child that such words are naughty and that people who use them are not nice, and then the child announces that Daddy and Mommy use them. If you can think of other ways to handle vulgar language, note them in the space below.

_____

_____

_____

4. Concepts of right and wrong begin to develop. Usually these are concerned with specific acts at first and only gradually become generalized. The idea of fairness looms large, and "It's a gyp" is a frequent complaint. The tendency to tattle on others may be part of this whole concern for rules.

Studies of the development of ethical concepts (Hartshorne and May, 1928) suggest that the best way to help children at this level gain a broader understanding of ethics is to discuss specific acts as they occur, encouraging the pupils to think about *why* an act is good or bad. Reciting "commandments" or the equivalent seems to have little effect, since young children can't apply abstract concepts and often don't even understand the words.

How Should You Handle Tattling?

The tendency of primary-school children to tattle is fairly common. One explanation is that the tattler wants attention. Another is that he has a newly discovered concern for rules; *he* obeys them and he wants to make sure others do the same.

How do you think you should handle a tattler? One teacher made the rule-breaker stay after school and write an appropriate "apology" ten times; the one who informed on him had to write, "I will not be a tattletale" 100 times. Another teacher made the informant wear a large badge bearing the legend "I am a tattletale." Still another teacher organized her class into what she called "The Secret Spies." Each child was encouraged to watch his classmates, and for every referral he made, he got so many points. What do you think of these methods? What other techniques could you use for handling tattling?

_____

_____

_____

_____

It is extremely important to be consistent in dealing with rule violations. The reason for this is Piaget's finding that children at this age level are still moral realists, having difficulty comprehending the subtleties involved in various situations. If some students seem upset about what appears to be an inconsistency, you might try to point out the circumstance which made necessary an adjustment in rules.

Developmental Trends as Seen by Erikson

The primary-grade child is at Erikson's stage of *Industry vs. Inferiority*. Erikson describes industry in these terms.

> The child must forget past hopes and wishes, while his exuberant imagination is tamed and harnessed to laws of impersonal things—even the three R's. . . . for the child must begin to be a worker and potential provider . . . [and] win recognition by producing things. . . . To bring a productive situation to completion is an aim which gradually supersedes the whims and wishes of play. His ego boundaries include his tools and skills; the work principle . . . teaches him the pleasure of work completion by steady attention and persevering diligence. (Pp. 258–259).

Erikson: importance of industry

The danger of this stage "lies in a sense of inadequacy and inferiority. If [the child] despairs of his tools and his skills or of his status among his tool partners, he may be discouraged from identification with them and with a section of the tool world" (p. 260).

Implications of Erikson's Observations

Erikson's comments on inferiority highlight the desirability of avoiding comparative grading practices. If the primary-grade student is forced to compete against his classmates and is publicly compared with others, it is inevitable that only a small proportion of children will feel successful. Most pupils will experience a sense of inadequacy and inferiority (and low status with peers) at the beginning of their school careers, which is likely to create a self-fulfilling prophecy reaction that will perpetuate a sense of inadequacy. Perhaps the best way to avoid this situation—and at the same time provide positive experiences in completing assigned work—is to use some form of a mastery approach and assist almost all pupils to achieve a performance level likely to produce satisfaction in a job well done.

Encouraging industry

Developmental Trends as Seen by Piaget

According to Piaget, the switchover from *egocentric* to *socialized* speech takes place at about the second grade; hence the older primary-grade child is more likely to consider the viewpoints of others. In terms of intellectual development,

Switch from egocentric to socialized speech and thought

the primary-grade child is at the stage of *concrete operations*. Toward the end of the first grade, children reach the extremely important pivotal point when comprehension of the principle of *conservation* permits them to grasp the concept of number. This enables them to use both cardinal numbers (1, 2, 3, etc.) as invariants—regardless of whether they apply to caramels, gum, or candy—and ordinal numbers (first, second, third, etc.). Understanding of the concepts of ordinal numbers permits the child to classify objects according to their qualities, such as size and weight. This ability to order objects—to arrange them in various series according to different criteria—is a clear illustration of *decentration*; that is, the child centers his thinking not on just one aspect of a subject or object but on two or more dimensions at once. It explains why an older child can solve conservation problems: he can take into account both size and weight or size and volume simultaneously. Decentration also permits the child to grasp the concept of *reversibility*—to comprehend that pouring water from the tall and short beakers back into the original containers restores the original condition and that addition reverses subtraction. However, the primary-grade pupil still lacks the capacity to deal with objects abstractly; hence the use of the term *concrete* to describe his operations, or mental acts. Because he is limited to dealing with actual experiences, he is unable to generalize or deal with hypothetical situations or weigh possibilities.

Piaget: concrete operations

Developmental Trends as Seen by Bruner

Bruner: iconic mode of representation

According to Bruner, primary-grade children still use the iconic mode of representation; that is, they make use of visual or sensory images. As noted earlier, Bruner differs from Piaget in stressing that language is the key factor in intellectual development. On the basis of the results of the screen experiment—in which children were able to conserve at an earlier age when they were not concentrating on the water actually being poured—he maintains that language frees a child from immediate appearances. Bruner also differs from Piaget in the degree of structure he believes should be supplied by the teacher. He argues that readiness should be taught: "If you wish to teach the calculus in the eighth grade, then begin it in the first grade by teaching the kinds of ideas and skills necessary for its mastery later" (1966, p. 29). Thus he argues for careful anticipation and preparation for what will come later.

Bruner believes that the child at this level is still likely to be so tied to the immediate environment that he will need prompt gratification for the things he does. And he again stresses the importance of a relaxed classroom atmosphere.

Implications of the Piaget-Bruner Observations

The fact that an understanding of the conservation principle is a vital step in intellectual development has led to considerable speculation about what primary-grade teachers should do—if anything—to encourage mastery of it.

Various views on the effectiveness of teaching conservation have been presented earlier. Almy, who reviewed Piaget's own writings and all previous studies on this question, came to the conclusion that much further study is necessary. She says that Piaget's emphasis on "natural" development is "at once provocative and frustrating" for the educator. It is provocative because Piaget delineates the hierarchy of stages that lead to conservation, frustrating because he suggests that teachers should not use this information to attempt to "teach" conservation. The "American question" is perhaps a reflection of the frustration so many educational theorists experience because of their eagerness to take maximum advantage of Piaget's theory. On the basis of her own analysis, Almy concludes:

> Despite the current spate of experimentation related to conservation, it seems unlikely that either psychology or education is prepared to launch any large-scale attempt at acceleration. But better understanding of the ways the child does acquire the concept of conservation offers considerable promise for more effective instruction of children during the early childhood years. (1966, p. 48)

Almy and her associates carried out several studies to discover how instruction can be made more effective. On the basis of the results of research, Almy offers primary-grade teachers suggestions regarding the kinds of classroom techniques and experiences that will make instruction more effective. (These suggestions are based on points made in Chapter 7 of *Young Children's Thinking* (1966) by Almy, Chittenden, and Miller.) To paraphrase Almy:

1. Try to become thoroughly familiar with Piaget's theory so that you will be aware of how your students organize and synthesize ideas. You may gain extra insight if you analyze your own thinking, since you are likely to discover that in some situations you operate at a concrete rather than an abstract level.

   Guidelines for teaching suggested by Almy

2. If possible, assess the level and the type of thinking of each child in your class. Ask individual children to perform some of the Piaget experiments and spend most of your time listening to each child explain his reactions. You might conduct some of the experiments described earlier, or read about other experiments in Chapter 3 in *Young Children's Thinking* by Almy et al., especially pp. 52–53, or *Piaget's Theory of Intellectual Development* by Ginsburg and Opper.

3. Remember that learning through activity and direct experience is essential. Provide plenty of materials and opportunities for children to learn on their own.

4. Arrange situations to permit social interaction so that children can learn from each other. To facilitate this, placing some advanced thinkers with less mature thinkers seems preferable to using homogeneous grouping.

5. Plan learning experiences so that they take into account the level of thinking attained by an individual or group; that is, encourage children to classify

things on the basis of a single attribute before you expose them to problems that involve relationships between two or more attributes. Ask many questions and give your students many opportunities to explain their interpretations of experiences so that you remain aware of their level of thinking.

6. Keep in mind the close association between language and thinking. Make sure students, particularly those with disadvantaged backgrounds, understand such terms as *more* and *less, most* and *least*. (Encourage pupils to watch "Sesame Street.")

Bruner's emphasis on language suggests that you encourage verbal interchange of ideas so that students get into the habit of using symbolic forms of communication. His emphasis on teaching readiness implies that you attempt to anticipate skills students will need later and prepare them in systematic fashion. Perhaps the most significant implication of Bruner's theory is the importance of maintaining a relaxed, open atmosphere so that your pupils will feel free to respond and hypothesize without fear of negative consequences.

Elementary Grades: 9 to 12 Years

Physical Characteristics

Growth spurt in most girls, some boys

1. *A growth spurt occurs in most girls and starts in early-maturing boys (Shuttleworth, 1939). On the average, girls between the ages of eleven and fourteen are taller and heavier than boys of the same age. (Olson and Hughes, 1950)*

Because of this period of accelerated growth in many children at the late elementary-grade level, notably in early-maturing girls, the children in a single sixth-grade class vary considerably in height and weight—especially boys and girls. If a fast-maturing girl thinks that the ideal female is demure and petite, she may be upset about her size. Your explanation that most of the boys will catch up in a year or two may make it easier for her to accept the fact that she is tall.

2. *Many girls reach puberty. Secondary sex characteristics begin to appear. Concern and curiosity about sex are almost universal, especially among girls.*

Average age of puberty: girls—12.5, boys—14

The average age of puberty for girls in the United States is between twelve and thirteen (Tanner, 1968); the range is from nine to sixteen years. For boys the average age of puberty is fourteen years; the range is from eleven to eighteen years. Since sexual maturation involves drastic biological and psychological adjustments, children are concerned and curious. It seems obvious that giving accurate, unemotional answers to questions about sex is desirable. However, for your own protection you should find out about the sex-education policy at your school. Some school districts forbid discussion of sex in class even on an informal basis. If no restrictions exist but you yourself feel uncomfortable about the thought of leading a discussion, you might make use of one of the many excellent films or pamphlets available. You might also consider asking the school nurse to lead a class discussion.

3. *Fine motor coordination is quite good, and therefore the manipulation of small objects is easy and enjoyable for most children. As a result, arts and crafts and music activities are popular.*

Encouraging active participation in drawing, painting, model making, ceramics, etc., is an excellent way to make the most of the children's newly developed manipulative skills. Ideally, such activities center on originality and creativity rather than on copying or assembling prefabricated kits. You might encourage the playing of musical instruments by holding amateur hours or concerts, or by inviting individual pupils to perform during music periods. In the space below note other activities that would encourage your pupils to use their new motor skills in creative ways.

_____

_____

_____

_____

_____

4. *Bone growth is not yet complete; therefore bones and ligaments can't stand heavy pressure.*

If you notice boys indulging in strenuous tests of strength (e.g., punching each other on the arm until one of them can't retaliate), you might suggest that they switch to competition involving coordinated *skills*. Also, in team games encourage rotation of especially tiring positions, for example, the pitching position in baseball.

5. *Boys forge ahead in strength and endurance and enjoy rough play so much that they often injure themselves.*

It is probably best to ignore a moderate amount of roughhouse play, punching, and shoving unless two boys get overexcited and lose control or unless the play disrupts the class. However, the desire to demonstrate "manliness" may lead boys to more dangerous activities such as glue sniffing and attempts to "black themselves out" by holding their breath. If you simply tell boys not to do these things, they are likely to indulge in them outside of school. Therefore,

MARK SILBER, DIMENSION

it is best to explain *why* such actions are dangerous and foolish—that they may cause permanent injury, including brain damage—and to encourage boys to demonstrate their virility in the usual sports and games.

Social Characteristics

1. *The peer group becomes powerful and begins to replace adults as the major source of behavior standards and recognition of achievement.*

During the early school years, parents and teachers set standards of conduct and most children try to live up to them. By the end of elementary school, however, children may be more eager to impress their friends than to please the teacher. Unfortunately, some children, especially boys, may try to impress their classmates by defying or ignoring the teacher.

As peer groups become more important, children sometimes organize themselves into more or less exclusive, all-boy and all-girl cliques. Generally speaking, these groups operate most actively outside of school. However, occasionally a battle between two groups may lead to trench warfare in class, for example, exchanging venomous notes. If this occurs, a sometimes effective device is to place members of opposing factions on cooperative committees. Such committees will need close supervision, especially during the first few days, but this strategem may enforce a truce.

Another aspect of group behavior at the elementary level is the tendency to devise what amount to initiation rituals, for example, demonstrations of nerve, such as shoplifting. In some cases, however, such illegal activities simply stem from a child's desire to get back at authority for placing so many restrictions on him just when he wants to be most independent. If you encounter thefts in class or a chip-on-the-shoulder attitude, keep in mind the growing independence of the child at this grade level and his need for understanding rather than simple punishment.

2. *The interests of boys and girls become more divergent. There may be a battle of the sexes in the form of exchange of insults, competition in schoolwork and games, etc.*

Such antagonism probably results from the children's developing recognition of the different roles assigned to boys and girls in our society. Boys tend to be critical of girls for a longer period of time, perhaps because girls have the best of it physically and scholastically. Public comparisons and out-and-out competition between boys and girls probably should be avoided.

3. *Team games become more popular, and class spirit grows stronger.*

Since Little League activities and similar highly organized pursuits may dominate your pupils' free time, you might encourage informal sandlot games with rotating team members. However, you may discover that the team spirit of your pupils will almost force you to organize games with fixed team membership. In the space below you might note some team games or activities you could use with this age group, especially games that minimize the possibility of antagonism between contestants.

_____

_____

_____

_____

4. *Crushes and hero worship are common. Sometimes the teacher is the idol; more frequently baseball, TV, records, and movie stars are the subjects of adulation.*

It may be necessary for you to gently cool the ardor of an adoring pupil. A simple but effective technique is to reveal that you are already spoken for by mentioning a husband or wife, boyfriend, or girlfriend. But whatever you decide to do, remember that the child may be completely serious about his or her infatuation and that therefore ridicule or even humorous treatment of the situation is unwise.

Emotional Characteristics

1. *Conflict between the group code and adult rules may cause difficulty, including juvenile delinquency.*

If you establish classroom control in a fair, consistent manner, head-on collisions between conflicting standards of behavior usually can be avoided. Encouraging children to make suggestions on rules of deportment for the class is one way to achieve a compromise. (Chapter 15 is devoted to a comprehensive analysis of constructive classroom control.)

If severe problems develop despite your efforts, it may help you to know that case histories reveal that "career delinquents" often commit their first serious offense at this age and that a common motive is to gain the approval of the peer group. Theoretically, providing recognition in class for such a child would eliminate his need to take matters into his own hands. Although nipping delinquency in the bud is not usually so simple, you might at least try this technique.

2. *Children at this level are able to take into account extenuating circumstances and to accept the idea that rules and codes are suggested courses of action rather than absolute dictums. To use Piaget's terminology, they are becoming moral relativists.*

"Class Standards—As Proposed by Sixth Graders

Although upper elementary-grade pupils are sometimes capable of moral relativism, they still frequently think as moral realists. An example of this is provided by their interpretation of rules. One fifth-grade teacher who asked his pupils to suggest class rules had to call a halt when the list reached sixty—with no end in sight. (One reason for the length of the list was that specific rather than general rules were suggested, for example, "Don't run in the hall," "Don't run in the classroom," "Don't run on the way to lunch," "Don't run on the way back from lunch," etc.)

Mrs. Ann Bliss, a sixth-grade teacher in Reseda, California, asked her pupils to propose "class standards." The following list—which illustrates how budding moral relativists still think in literal, specific terms—was reprinted in the February 27 1971 issue of *Saturday Review*.

Listen to the teacher when she is talking or yelling.
Keep your shoes on in school.
Don't say shut up if the teacher doesn't like it.
Don't stay in the restroom all day.
Don't go to the bathroom all the time.
The bathroom isn't a meeting place and classes aren't held there.
Don't hide in the bathroom on hot days.
Don't play with thing.
Leave your treshures at home.
Stand when you walk into class.
Be ploite to all the teachers, not just yours.
Don't be a taital tail.
Don't lend back of your chair.
Don't scrap your chair.
Stay in your set.
Stay in your sit.
Try not to hit your classmates.
Be good to the little people.
Don't ride on another girl's back, you could get hurt.
No pooping bags at lunch.
Don't spit on the playground.
If the teacher says something funny, don't pound on your desk.
Don't bother the Princeble.
Youse are time wisley.
Four people don't have to take one hurt person to the office.
Don't fall out of your chairs.
Don't crew gum or candy.
Don't crawl on floors.
Witch your mouth.
Wash your language.

As mentioned, the most effective way to help children develop a healthy moral sense is not to lead them in mechanical recitation of platitudes but to discuss with them specific acts as they occur. For example, you could have a class talk about why a child who finds a lost purse should return it—instead of having everyone chant in unison, "Honesty is the best policy." In addition, you might read stories or describe situations to stimulate discussion of common ethical problems children face. Finally, when you are teaching pupils to be considerate and sympathetic as well as honest and fair, always keep in mind the powerful effect of your own example. (More complete suggestions for encouraging moral development are offered in Chapter 8, "Teaching Skills and Attitudes.")

Mental Characteristics

1. *At the elementary level, children are curious about almost everything. Collections of things abound, and a child may suddenly drop one to start another.*

Obviously, curiosity is an asset and should be capitalized on. Encourage children to find answers themselves rather than always supplying them, but remember that this can be overdone: A coy "Why don't you find that out for yourself?" will sometimes kill interest.

If a child asks a question you are unable to answer, remember that bluffing is dangerous and foolish. Your pupils will not expect you to know everything, but they will lose faith in you if you attempt to cover up ignorance. And if a child obviously knows more about a given topic (e.g., rocket fuels) than you do, the smart thing to do is to encourage his contributions and let the class benefit from his knowledge.

If a child flits from one interest to another, this does not necessarily mean he lacks mental discipline and should be forced to persevere. At this age a child should sample many different activities so that later he can specialize in the ones he likes best. If he is forced to stick to something that no longer intrigues him, he may develop such a distaste for it that he will later resist exposing himself to other hobbies and pursuits. Nevertheless, it is obviously an advantage—if not an actual necessity—for a pupil to learn *some* perseverance. The trick seems to be to encourage a pupil to keep at a job until he does it well without causing him to dislike it by feeling he is being badgered. If you can think of specific ways to do this, note them in the space provided.

_____

_____

_____

_____

_____

2. *Many elementary-grade children set unrealistically high standards for themselves and tend to be perfectionists. Frequently, the inability to live up to such standards leads to feelings of frustration and guilt.*

It is desirable, of course, to encourage each child to do his best, and his best is often better than either he or the teacher expects. But when a child sets an impossibly high standard, he is doomed to fail. A good way to teach a pupil to develop realistic levels of aspiration is to have him start out with simple tasks and work up to difficult ones. In doing so, he not only tests his capabilities but also has some experience with success, and the latter makes it easier for him to accept failure when he reaches his limits. If you suspect that pressure from home (e.g., in the form of a bribe) is the cause of outlandishly high goals, you, the principal, or the school psychologist might try to reason with the parents.

3. *Children at the elementary-grade level want to become more independent, but at the same time they both want and need adult guidance and support. This ambivalence may cause disorganized, unpredictable, or inappropriate behavior that defies rational analysis.*

About the only thing you can do is be as patient and understanding as possible toward erratic behavior.

Developmental Trends and Their Implications as Seen by Erikson

The elementary-grade child is still in Erikson's stage of Industry vs. Inferiority. The observations made with reference to primary-grade children thus apply as well at this level. Teachers should attempt to provide tasks involving meaningful work, encourage and assist all students to achieve these, and minimize comparative and competitive learning situations.

Developmental Trends as Seen by Piaget

According to Piaget's descriptions, the child at this age should be capable of considering the ideas of others and communicating with them since he is well into the socialized speech phase of language development.

Piaget also observes that during this period—more specifically, during the fifth and sixth grades—the child shifts from the level of *concrete operations* to the stage of *formal operations*. Concrete operations are logical and systematic, as exemplified in the solving of conservation problems, but the child's thinking at this stage is still tied to direct experience. Even though he may not have to manipulate objects in order to understand their relationships as he did at

Concrete operations to formal operations

the preoperational stage, his thinking is limited to actual experiences. In areas about which he has acquired no direct knowledge, he reasons by analogy to something he *has* experienced.

When he reaches the stage of formal operations, however, the student can construct theories and make logical deductions about their consequences without having had previous direct experience on the subject. He can deal with abstractions and mentally explore similarities and differences because he has mastered reversibility and decentration. He can think his way through new problems, moving forward and backward and taking into account as many or as few qualities as seem relevant to him. As Flavell puts it, the older child has at his command "a coherent and integrated cognitive *system* with which he organizes and manipulates the world around him" (1963, p. 165).

Developmental Trends as Seen by Bruner

Bruner: symbolic mode of representation

In the language of Bruner, the elementary-grade child moves from *iconic* to *symbolic* representation. Bruner emphasizes the same general shift as Piaget but in different terms:

> Intellectual development is marked by increasing capacity to deal with several alternatives simultaneously, to tend to several sequences during the same period of time, and to allocate time and attention in a manner appropriate to these multiple demands. (1966, p. 6)

Implications of the Piaget-Bruner Observations

If you will be teaching at any grade from fourth through eighth, you should keep in mind the differences between concrete and formal operations. It is likely that your students will sometimes function one way, sometimes another. Consequently, it would be well to give *all* your students plenty of opportunities to explain their thoughts, particularly with regard to abstractions, so that you can discern and take into account the level of awareness they have reached on various ideas.

As for the question of accelerating students' switchover to the level of formal operations, the same differences of opinion that were noted earlier are found at this level.

Piaget, Elkind, and Ginsburg and Opper argue that it is better to permit the student to absorb experiences at his own rate and in his own way and that efforts to speed up abstract thinking may be a waste of time—or even cause confusion and anxiety.

However, Bruner and others insist that vigorous efforts should be made to help upper-elementary-grade students function at the level of symbolic thought by introducing them to strategies of inquiry. Bruner suggests that teachers arrange situations in which children are encouraged to ask questions about phenomena (perhaps the game Twenty Questions) and to hypothesize about why certain things happen. (This is the basic technique of the *discovery approach*, and it will be fully discussed in the next chapter.)

Junior High Grades: 12 to 15 Years

Physical Characteristics

1. *Most girls complete their growth spurt at the beginning of this period. The boys' growth spurt, however, usually is not completed before the eighth or ninth grade, and it may be precipitous. Some boys add as much as six inches and twenty-five pounds in a single year.*

The accelerated period of growth that begins for some children in the late elementary grades involves almost all pupils in junior high. The variation between individual students is tremendous. Some early-maturing, ninth-grade girls look as if they could almost be the mothers of some late-maturing, seventh-grade boys. Generally speaking, late-maturing boys have the most difficult time of all in adjusting to this situation, especially because of the premium put on athletics as *the* royal road to masculinity. You might encourage such boys to seek status through other forms of endeavor (e.g., schoolwork, music, student government).

2. *Puberty is reached by practically all girls and by many boys, so secondary sex characteristics become increasingly apparent. These include breast and hip development in girls and voice change and shoulder development in boys. Concern about the physical and psychological changes associated with puberty is almost universal.*

The remarks previously made about sex education in the elementary grades apply even more directly to this age group. You should check on school policy and act accordingly. Girls, particularly, need accurate information, since the changes associated with menstruation may produce fear if the process is not understood.

3. *There is likely to be a certain amount of adolescent awkwardness—probably due as much to self-consciousness as to sudden growth—and a great deal of concern about appearance. Both boys and girls take pains with their grooming; and what they may lack in finesse, they more than make up for in imagination and verve.*

To maintain a reasonable degree of decorum, as well as interest in scholarship, you may have to explain gently but firmly that your class is not the place for applied cosmetology—unless, of course, you see nothing wrong with this.

4. Although this age period is marked by generally good health, the diet and sleeping habits of many junior high students are poor. In a television interview one dietitian estimated that only 10 percent of all pupils at this age have an adequate diet.

Take advantage of every opportunity to stress the desirability of good health habits, emphasizing the extent to which diet influences one's appearance—a major concern of adolescents. Although coke, fries, and greasy burgers are too permanent a fixture of the adolescent ethos to eliminate with mere words, your comments might slightly reduce the intake of such unnutritious foods.

5. Physical and mental endurance are limited at this time, probably as a result of several factors: the diet and sleeping habits just mentioned, the draining of energy by the process of growth, and the disproportionately small size of the heart. Although there is no clear-cut agreement on this last point, many authorities stress that heart development does not spurt as the rest of the body does.

Junior high pupils are likely to show a certain amount of listlessness and lassitude. Frequent changes of pace and breaks for relaxation may alleviate ennui to a certain extent. The new rotating-schedule plans represent an attempt to spread "dead" periods around. Under this scheme pupils take each subject at a different hour every day. This keeps classes from always getting stuck with the same teacher and subject (and vice versa) at the time of day when the doldrums are most likely to have set in.

Social Characteristics

1. The peer group becomes the source of general rules of behavior. There is frequently a conflict between the peer code and the adult code, owing partly to the drastic cultural changes that have taken place over the last twenty-five years.

Some parents adjust the rules more than others, which leads to the "Mary's mother says *she* can go" sort of argument. And since many parents are influenced by such arguments more than they are willing to admit and tend to give in a bit here and there, the ultimate result is that adolescents themselves establish many of the ground rules.

In a sense, developing a code of behavior is a groping toward adult independence and therefore is to be desired. You might try to make the most of this

JULIE O'NEIL

movement toward independence by encouraging your students to help develop a set of class rules and by making clear that the test of their readiness for such a privilege is whether they are responsible enough to abide by their decisions.

2. Junior high school students feel a need to conform because they want to be part of the crowd; cliques are common.

Adolescents often find it reassuring to dress and behave like everyone else because they lack confidence and need tangible evidence that they "belong." To counteract this tendency, try to encourage individuality and creative non-conformity in class. You might give open-ended assignments, for example, or merely show a willingness to accept offbeat approaches to problems. The difficulty here is to distinguish between something that is different merely for the sake of being different and a genuine expression of individuality. Although giving the student the benefit of the doubt is probably a good idea, you might want to point out that *sometimes* it is necessary to be predictable.

3. Students are greatly concerned about what others think of them. Therefore, both friendships and quarrels become more intense, and best friends may replace parents as confidants.

As a result of their preoccupation with what the group thinks and their desire to belong, junior high students may circulate some form of Slam Book, that is, a notebook in which each person writes down exactly what he thinks of particular individuals. Girls occasionally organize Lemon Parties, in which character assassinations are delivered personally. If you become aware of either of these activities, you might emphasize the desirability of *constructive* criticism.

4. Girls are more advanced socially than boys of the same age and therefore tend to date older boys who are at about the same point of maturation. In reaction to this, many younger boys may try to cover up their immaturity and lack of confidence by teasing and being obstreperously critical of girls.

Since dating is a desirable prelude to courtship, activities that permit relaxed boy-girl relationships are to be encouraged.

Emotional Characteristics

1. At this age a student is likely to be moody and unpredictable—partly because of biological changes associated with sexual maturation and partly because of his own confusion about whether he is a child or an adult.

Perhaps the only thing a teacher can do is to be consistent in handling the class and to treat students as responsible young adults whenever possible. The latter usually involves a certain amount of trial and error—in offering privileges and having them misused—before a satisfactory compromise is reached.

2. Students may behave boisterously to conceal their lack of self-confidence.

Helping the loudest and brassiest students to be successful in schoolwork may make life a lot quieter and easier for everyone concerned. A basic way to do this is to encourage self-competition.

3. Anger outbursts may be common. These often result from a combination of psychological tension, biological imbalance, and fatigue, the latter caused by overexertion, lack of proper diet, or insufficient sleep.

It is probably best to minimize sporadic outbursts of anger when they occur. The light touch, changing the subject, and beginning a new activity are techniques that may avert a showdown. If a student's anger becomes chronic, however, you may have to seek help from the counseling office. (This problem will be discussed more completely in Chapter 14.)

4. Adolescents tend to be intolerant and opinionated, probably because of lack of self-confidence. It is reassuring for them to think that there are absolute answers—and that they know them.

In class discussion, stress the importance of considering another person's point of view in order to improve your own ideas—and practice this yourself. Be on the alert for the very pushy, opinionated student who intimidates his classmates so that no one dares to disagree with him. If you can think of graceful ways to convince such a student that allowing others to express their ideas doesn't mean that he has capitulated, you might note them in the space below.

_____

_____

_____

_____

5. In junior high school, students begin to look at parents and teachers more objectively and may be angry that they have been deluded into attributing omniscience to mere mortals.

A frequent reaction of adolescents to their discovery that adults are fallible is defiance of adult authority. The junior high teacher is caught in a trap by the newfound ability of the student to detect and expose adult weaknesses. The growing independence of the adolescent adds fuel to the fire, since many of his wishes are directly blocked by teachers and parents. One way to handle this is to have pupils discuss or write about their negative feelings. Remember that although it is important for the teacher to try to understand the reasons for rebellion, it is equally important for the adolescent to learn to control himself, because living in society involves honoring some restrictions on individual freedom.

Mental Characteristics

1. *Students at this age can comprehend abstract concepts to an increasing degree and therefore are better able to understand moral and ethical principles.*

Since some students may not understand the true meanings of such concepts as democracy and capitalism until the eighth grade or so, you might give short quizzes to determine the degree of understanding of key ideas before embarking on an intensive study or discussion. And when you do encounter twisted interpretations of abstract concepts (e.g., in class discussions), remember that ideas are more likely to be clarified by a patient, sympathetic, open-minded teacher than by one who ridicules or categorically rejects student errors.

2. *Although the attention span of junior high students can be quite lengthy, there may be a tendency to daydream. Detours into fantasy and "dreams of glory" probably take place because the students lack the real thing and also because their opportunities for excursions into fantasy are limited.*

Try to give assignments that challenge the imagination in as many ways as possible. You might present intriguing puzzles or problems as opposed to tedious drill. Or assign a theme on "The Kind of Animal I'd Like to Be If Reincarnated" rather than on "My Pet." You might also encourage "useful" dreams about the future—involving, for example, the kind of job the student might like, what is involved in getting such a job, etc. If you can think of any specific assignments to foster the creative use of imagination, note them in the space below.

_____

_____

_____

_____

_____

Developmental Trends and Their Implications as Seen by Erikson

Junior high school students are approaching Erikson's stage of Identity vs. Role Confusion. However, since the impact of this stage is felt most directly in senior high school, it will be discussed at that level. (Postponing the analysis of Erikson's observations does not imply that junior high students are less involved than slightly older peers in their search for identity; it is done to avoid repetition.)

Developmental Trends as Seen by Piaget

Because the final phase of intellectual development is reached at the junior high level, this discussion applies to all grades from the seventh through the twelfth.

Piaget suggests that during the early adolescent years, intellectual development consists largely of growing sophistication in handling formal operations. Since he places the crucial period of switchover from concrete to formal operations at about the sixth grade, he believes that some children in the lower junior high grades may still function only at the concrete operations level. However, he thinks that most junior high school students are capable of grasping abstract concepts to a certain extent.

Piaget has developed two logical models to describe the stages in the formal operations period: the sixteen Binary operations and the INRC group. (The initials INRC stand for *identity, negation, reciprocity,* and *correlativity.*) These models are extremely complex, but the general trends they represent can be illustrated by one of Piaget's experiments with adolescents. To carry out this experiment on your own, either obtain or assemble a simple pendulum. Then change the length of the string several times, releasing the weight from different heights, and ask students to explain why the pendulum swings at different rates.

The way junior high school students explain such phenomena reveals that they are not bound to the actual situation as is true of students still in the period of concrete operations. Junior high pupils can imagine what occurs in this situation and to consider all kinds of hypothetical alternatives. The adolescent is also able to think in terms of combinations of factors, for example, the length of the string and the force of the swing. His thinking is flexible and versatile, and he is not likely to be confused by unusual results since he is capable of anticipating all sorts of possibilities.

Aspects of period of formal operations

Piaget does not restrict his analysis of intellectual development to scientific problem solving. He maintains that the newfound ability of the adolescent to function at the level of formal operations may predispose him to become involved in all kinds of abstract and theoretical matters, including those in the social and political arena. As Ginsburg and Opper put it:

> [The adolescent] constructs elaborate political theories or invents complex philo-
> sophical doctrines. He may develop plans for the complete reorganization of society
> or indulge in metaphysical speculation. Having just discovered capabilities for
> abstract thought, he then proceeds to exercise them without restraint. Indeed,
> in the process of exploring his new abilities, the adolescent sometimes loses touch

with reality, and feels that he can accomplish everything by thought alone. (1969, pp. 204–205)

Developmental Trends as Seen by Bruner

According to Bruner, the student at this age learns to use the *symbolic* form of representation in increasingly sophisticated ways. The teacher can help him do this, Bruner suggests, by continuing to use the discovery approach and by emphasizing mastery of concepts and abstractions.

Implications of the Piaget-Bruner Observations

When the junior high school student becomes capable of formal operational thought, there is no longer a qualitative difference between his thinking and that of adults—including the teacher's. (There *is* a difference in the sophistication of the thinking between adolescents and adults.) This brings up the question of how logical it is to use Piaget's theory as a basis for an open school approach with older students. At the primary and elementary levels, techniques that involve having children learn through their own activities and from each other are in harmony with Piaget's ideas, since he has demonstrated that the thought of children is different from that of adults and has argued that early learning takes place through the development of each child's own internalized logic. However, as the older student becomes capable of formal operations, these arguments no longer apply. There are many reasons other than Piaget's theory for advocating that older students be active, engage in self-directed learning, and learn by interacting with their peers, but the fact that they can interact with adults at their own level suggests that they should be given opportunities to do so. As soon as a student is asked to deal with complex, organized subject matter, it would seem desirable for those who have devoted years if not a lifetime to the study of a given topic to share what they have learned with him. If this is done properly, the student is assisted to take off on his own. Knowledge in most subject areas is cumulative, and not acquainting students with what others have learned puts them in the position of having to learn by themselves everything that earlier thinkers already have learned.

Since students at the junior and senior high school levels are still perfecting their grasp of the more sophisticated types of reasoning, you should not take it for granted that they are thinking the same way you do. Try to keep well informed on how your students interpret ideas that come up in class by encouraging free discussion and by assigning papers that are not to be graded.

Also watch for the tendency of the adolescent (starting at about the ninth grade) to indulge in unrestrained and unrealistic political theorizing. Perhaps the best way to handle such immature forms of thinking is to help students realize that they have overlooked certain considerations. But when the issues are complex and charged with emotion, this may not be a simple task.

One other point to consider is the fact that the ability to consider alternatives can be a source of considerable anxiety to young people, particularly at a time when sex-role confusion and the imminent choice of a career may be causing identity confusion.

Senior High Grades: 15 to 18 Years
Physical Characteristics

1. *Most students reach physical maturity, and virtually all attain puberty. Although almost all girls reach their ultimate height, some boys may continue to grow even after graduation. Tremendous variation exists in height and weight and in rate of maturation.*

Late-maturing boys seem to have considerable difficulty adjusting to their slower rate of growth, especially since physical coordination also tends to lag. Encouraging such boys to find nonathletic ways to satisfy their need for recognition is recommended just as it was for students at the junior high level.

2. *The physical changes associated with puberty cause the older adolescent to have the appearance of an adult. His realization that there will be no further physical changes because of growth may add to an already extreme self-consciousness.*

Because high school students are very concerned about their appearance, preoccupation with grooming might easily disrupt your class unless you ask that it be limited to certain times and places. (Some teachers permit hair combing, etc., during the last three minutes or so of each class period.) In some cases a particular feature (e.g., protruding ears) may even drive an individual to paranoid delusions that everyone is staring or laughing at him. If you become aware of a student who seems preoccupied over a correctable physical feature, a tip to the school nurse might help him explore the possibility of having the defect remedied.

3. *Sexual maturity is established, leading to glandular changes and imbalance. According to Kinsey (1948), the male sex drive is at a peak at the ages of sixteen and seventeen.*

A strong sex drive and severely limited opportunities to satisfy it are sources of much concern to many young people. On the one hand, the two most common forms of direct satisfaction, masturbation and premarital intercourse, often involve disapproval. On the other hand, biological urges are intensified by curiosity and the feeling that one must indulge in sexual activity to be adequate and "normal."

Glandular changes often lead to physical symptoms such as acne, which frequently can be alleviated by improved diet and special medical treatment. The school nurse can probably recommend a dermatologist for a student who seems extremely self-conscious about his condition.

Social Characteristics

1. *The peer group dominates the lives of students, and the conflict between the peer and adult codes increases. Pressures to conform are extreme, the most obvious sign of this being fads in dress.*

In his book *The American People* (1948), the British anthropologist Geoffrey Gorer suggests that the American adolescent, rather than his parents, establishes the rules that govern his behavior. Gorer maintains that because of the "melting pot" character of the American culture, there is no single, accepted set of rules for child rearing as there is, in his view, in "purer" cultures. Therefore, to check on the rightness of their child-rearing practices, American parents constantly compare their own families with others. The astute adolescent realizes this and skillfully exploits it by forcing his parents to let him do what Johnny is allegedly doing. And since many parents apparently feel that they would reveal a lack of self-confidence if they came right out and asked Johnny's parents about the truth of such reports, the teen-ager is in control. Gorer's views may not be completely accurate, but *The American People* is highly recommended supplementary reading as a provocative, sometimes infuriating book containing many hypotheses about our culture.

2. *The most pervasive preoccupation for many students is the opposite sex. Dating, going steady, and marriage dominate their thoughts and conversation during this period.*

Although learning social skills is a necessary prelude to courtship and marriage, you may find it difficult to compete with boy-girl interaction as you try to teach subject matter.

3. *Girls are still more mature socially than boys of the same age and continue to date older boys. Girls tend to have a small number of close girl friends, boys a wider circle of male friends on a more casual basis. But because of the competitive nature of both dating and schoolwork, neither boys nor girls may feel that they can completely trust these friends.*

In class you can minimize vicious competition between members of the same sex by playing down public comparisons.

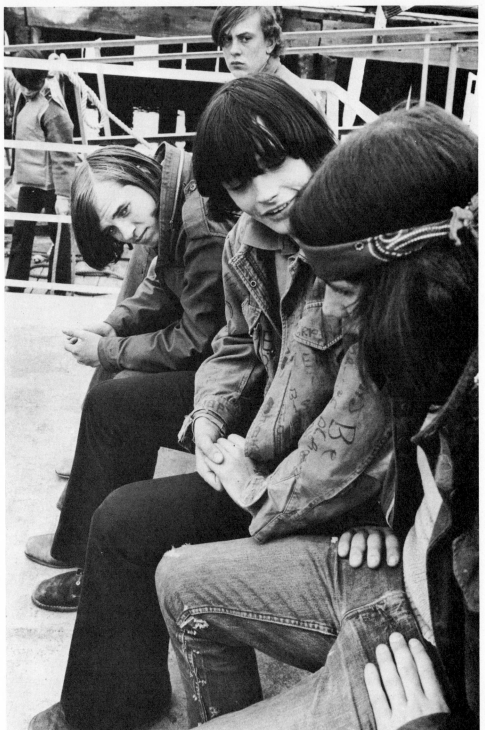

How Should You Handle a Crush?

Being the object of a crush at the elementary level may be rather enjoyable. At the secondary level it may be something quite different. Imagine yourself in this situation (it actually happened). It is your first year of teaching high school. You are in your room alone after school. It is quite late, and the building is more or less deserted. A student of the opposite sex suddenly materializes, undulates up to your desk, grabs your shoulder, and says (with considerable fervor), "You really turn me on!" What would you do? After you decide, read *Up the Down Staircase* (1964) by Bel Kaufman for a description of how some mishandled crushes led to complications. See whether the situation you come up with resembles those used by the characters in the novel.

Emotional Characteristics

1. *The adolescent revolt is an expression of the universal changeover from childhood to adulthood. In our society we lack clearly prescribed forms of behavior for making this difficult change. As a result, the adolescent must take matters into his own hands.*

In various primitive societies a boy is considered a man when he has passed certain tests and performed certain feats. But since we have no such clearly defined standards, adolescents must indulge in a chaotic process of trial and error to try to prove to their peers, their parents, and themselves that they are grown up. For example, it used to be virtually *de rigueur* for every American boy to drink at least part of a six-pack of beer before he graduated from high school; now drugs have replaced alcohol. And to demonstrate their maturity in other unmistakable ways, adolescents—boys in particular—frequently feel impelled to defy adult authority. As a high school teacher, you will be in a position of authority, and you may therefore be the target of a certain amount of rebellion and hostility.

Perhaps the best way to handle the adolescent revolt is first to try to understand it and second to do everything you can to help your students become competent in the subject you teach. An important way to prove adulthood is to become skilled in doing something. If you are recognized as a person dedicated to developing such skill in students, even in a limited way, rebellion and hostility might be considerably lessened in your classroom. (For a more detailed discussion of the key role that competence plays in adolescent adjustment, see *The Vanishing Adolescent* by Edgar Z. Friedenberg.)

2. *Because of their increasing independence, many adolescents are in frequent conflict with their parents. They may turn to you for sympathy and advice.*

The adolescent is in a perplexing predicament. In most cases he is dependent upon his parents for physical necessities and feels obligated to them because of the care they have always provided. Yet he must break away from his parents in order to become an independent adult, so a certain amount of family conflict is inevitable. When such friction occurs, the adolescent may feel guilty, which in turn widens the gap between him and his parents.

A student who is upset by such a chain of events may feel the need to confide in another adult, and therefore you may be asked to act as a sympathetic listener. (Some general suggestions on how to play this role are given in Chapter 14.)

Mental Characteristics

1. *At this age young people have close to maximum intellectual efficiency, but lack of experience limits both their knowledge and their ability to use what they know.*

Since many things can be learned only through experience, students may continue to have difficulty grasping abstract concepts and may be incapable of fully understanding the emotions depicted in novels, drama, and poetry. Just as at the junior high school level, discussion and informal quizzing to determine the depth of students' understanding may be necessary to show you how to communicate with them.

2. *Students' realization that they need to develop their own "philosophies of life" in regard to ethical, political, and religious matters may be threatening to them, but it offers an excellent opportunity for guided discussion.*

Teachers, particularly those in the social sciences, can do much to clarify confused thoughts about "life." At the same time keep in mind the fact that some groups in the community may react negatively to discussions of explosive subjects such as politics and religion. This brings up the question of whether parents have the right to insist that the primary responsibility for developing a moral code in their children is theirs. You should not be afraid to hold discussions on these subjects, but remember that to use class time or class assignments to emphasize a personal point of view is an infringement of academic freedom, especially since you have an unfair advantage in the form of your grade book. If you speak out against a certain political party or religion, for example, you are inflicting your biases on a captive audience.

Developmental Trends as Seen by Erikson

High school students are at Erikson's stage of *Identity vs. Role Confusion*. which Erikson describes this way: "The growing and developing youths, faced with . . . tangible adult tasks ahead of them are now primarily concerned with what they appear to be in the eyes of others as compared with what they feel they are" (1968, p. 261). The goal at this stage is development of *ego*

BY PERMISSION OF JOHN HART AND FIELD ENTERPRISES, INC.

Erikson: importance of identity

identity, "the accrued confidence that the inner sameness and continuity prepared in the past are matched by the sameness and continuity of one's meaning for others" (p. 261).

At the present time, achieving a sense of personal identity is probably more difficult than it has ever been. A primary reason is that the danger of this stage is role confusion, particularly about sexual and occupational identity. In our contemporary society there is considerable uncertainty about sex roles, as exemplified by the Women's Liberation Movement and campaigns to increase tolerance of homosexuality. There is also great uncertainty about occupational identity because of rapid technological change.

Erikson points out that in some cases, young people who are unable to cope with sex-role and occupational confusion choose a *negative identity* "perversely based on all those identifications and roles which, at critical stages of development, had been presented to them as most undesirable or dangerous and yet also as most real" (p. 174). He notes that in some instances "the negative identity is dictated by the necessity of finding and defending a niche of one's own against the excessive ideals either demanded by morbidly ambitious parents or indeed actualized by superior ones. In both cases the parents' weaknesses and unexpressed wishes are recognized by the child with catastrophic clarity" (p. 175). Thus a high school student who is unable to establish a sense of positive identity may concentrate on building a negative identity featuring characteristics that his parents have indicated they dread or abhor. If the parents of a student who is unable to make a clear sex-role or occupational choice have continually stressed that they fear or are repelled by drug addiction, for example, he may engage in exaggerated abuse of drugs.

Implications of Erikson's Observations

Although recent developments blurring differences in sex roles may reduce the importance of developing sexual identity, there is also the possibility that they may increase it. For teachers this poses the problem noted in the discussion of social behavior in kindergarten: Is it a good policy to encourage boys and girls to learn "appropriate" sex roles in school as a means of encouraging sexual identity, or will doing so perpetuate the abuses objected to by Women's Liberationists? It is difficult to decide what is "appropriate" for each sex and at the same time avoid the kind of stereotyping that leads to a conception of males as leaders, moneymakers, and controllers of power and females as homemakers, "servants" of men, or love objects, whose primary purpose is insuring male comfort. If all traditional conceptions of masculine and feminine pursuits are abandoned, perhaps sexual identity will become unimportant. On the other hand, since some sex-role characteristics appear to be biologically based (e.g., the male physical aggressiveness expressed in sports), the problems of finding sexual identity might be magnified if no differences were recognized. In making up your mind about what you might do to encourage sex role identification in your classes, consider both the disadvantages and advantages. It would seem that there should be ways to encourage girls to be feminine—if they desire it—without inevitably placing them in an inferior position. (Betty Friedan offers a thoughtful discussion of this question in the last two chapters of *The Feminine Mystique* (1963). *Encouraging identity*

Although sex role confusion is one problem the adolescent faces, Erikson believes the inability to center on an occupational identity is more disturbing since, more than any other factor, a career will determine the identity of the young adult. In *Identity: Youth and Crisis* (1968), he points out that in technological societies in which preparation for a career is a lengthy process, a *psychosocial moratorium* is desirable (pp. 128, 157, 242) to give the young person an opportunity to integrate elements from previous stages. This process is made more difficult because the young adult has reached Piaget's stage of formal operations which makes it possible for him to anticipate the future and weigh many possibilities. Erikson notes that the choice of a career is easiest for the youth who "is able to identify with new roles of competency and invention" (1968, p. 130), that is to say, the one who feels reasonably comfortable in a technological society. An adolescent will resist a society that prevents him from developing his sense of identity.

The most difficult problem you are likely to face regarding identity will be dealing with students who are leaning toward or committed to a negative identity. Erikson observes, "The escape of many gifted if unstable young individuals into a private utopia might not be necessary were it not for a general development to which they feel unable to submit, namely, the increasing demand for conformity, uniformity, and standardization which characterizes the present stage of this, our 'individualistic' civilization" (p. 195). The "private utopia" Erikson refers to is a negative identity. He explains why dealing with students who choose a negative rather than a positive identity is so difficult:

Teachers, judges, and psychiatrists who deal with youth come to be significant representatives of that strategic act of "recognition," the act through which society "identifies" and "confirms" its young members and thus contributes to their developing identity. . . . If, for simplicity's sake or in order to accommodate ingrown habits of law or psychiatry, they diagnose and treat as a criminal, as a constitutional misfit, as a derelict doomed by his upbringing, or indeed as a deranged patient a young person who, for reasons of personal or social marginality, is close to choosing a negative identity, that young person may well put his energy into becoming exactly what the careless and fearful community expects him to be—and make a total job of it. (P. 196)

This is another example of the self-fulfilling prophecy: If you treat a student as a "negative" person, he will think of himself as such and act that way. On the other hand, you may find it next to impossible not to "confirm" some aspects of a student's negative identity if he has chosen to express himself in ways that totally disrupt your classroom. Perhaps the best solution to this dilemma is to be aware of the nature of negative identity and try to understand why many young people feel impelled toward it.

In *Identity: Youth and Crisis*, Erikson offers observations on factors in our society that push students in a negative direction. Kenneth Keniston has provided a more comprehensive analysis in *The Uncommitted* (1965). This book is based on in-depth analyses of a small group of Harvard undergraduates selected for study because of extreme alienation, that is, an unwillingness to accept the values of our technological society. If you wish to examine your own feelings about teaching in an American public school, as well as make efforts to understand and assist high school students to select a career and form an identity in contemporary America, you are urged to read Keniston's book, since it expands the study of alienated students to serve as an analysis of our entire society.

Many of Keniston's observations were later stressed by Alvin Toffler in *Future Shock* (1970) and Charles Reich in *The Greening of America* (1970). Although the Keniston work is not as superficially titillating as the other two, it discusses the same subjects on a much deeper and thought-provoking level. He points out that chronic social change (treated at length in *Future Shock*) has led to a generational discontinuity whereby identification with parents is replaced by partial identification with other groups and that many young people thus commit themselves to change itself—a major theme of *The Greening of America*. In commenting on the difficulty of making an occupational decision (as stressed by Erikson), Keniston maintains that the development of our technological society has led to a fragmentation of tasks that forces individuals to become specialists and also to subordinate feelings. Awareness that parents and other adults find it difficult to become involved in such work—which they see as primarily a means for earning money to spend while not working—causes many young people to either postpone occupational decisions as long as possible or to try to avoid them entirely. Those who plan on a career may expect little personal fulfillment; those who avoid one try to postpone binding commitments and seek identity in private experience. Here is the way Keniston sums up many of the points made in *The Uncommitted:*

We allow our society to divide our lives and ourselves into two compartments, one for cognition, work, instrumental values, and ego skills, the other for all the rest of life; and we further insist of ourselves that the first compartment will take consistent precedence over the second. This creates a variety of human problems. The psyche resists compartmentalization; men strive toward integration. To maintain a divided life takes a heavy toll of energy; and even when it succeeds it exhausts us and leads to a sense of inner division. . . . Furthermore, the supremacy of technological values means that our society has no honored place for those who do not possess the virtues of its values. . . . What our society lacks, then, is a vision of itself and of man that transcends technology. It exacts a heavy human toll not because technology exists, but because we allow technology to reign. It alienates so many not simply because they do not share its wealth, but because its wealth includes few deeply human purposes. It is a society that too often discourages human wholeness and integrity, too frequently divides men from the best parts of themselves, too rarely provides objects worthy of commitment. In all these ways, it exacts a heavy human toll. (1965, p. 366)

To attempt to overcome this situation, Keniston suggests we consider the goals of the alienated. "Though their goals are often confused and inarticulate, they converge on a passionate yearning for openness and immediacy of experience, on an intense desire to create, on a longing to express their conception of the world, and, above all, on a quest for values and commitments that will give their lives coherence" (p. 386). This description is basically similar to what Erikson means by identity. It is also an extremely difficult set of goals to achieve, particularly for students—and teachers. It appears that many of the aspects of contemporary education that are seen as major contributing influences to the technology trap make matters worse. In observations (1970) made after the publication of *The Uncommitted*, Keniston offered the hypothesis that academic pursuits have been unsuccessful in assisting students to achieve the kind of meaning sought by the alienated and that many have sought it on their own—often through drugs. He points out that academic pressure to get high grades that serve as passports to careers has made it difficult for young people to consider or explore existential and ultimate questions. In addition, *stimulus flooding* and *psychological numbing* (as described in detail in *Future Shock*) have caused students to pursue experience for its own sake. Many young people have turned to drugs in the hope of finding meaning and opening up experience. Keniston suggests that teachers and others who work with young people should try to understand the motives of those who use drugs and also try to provide alternate ways for young people to find meaning and satisfying experience. He notes: "[We] must demonstrate to our students that there are better and more lasting ways to experience the fullness, the depth, the variety and the richness of life than that of ingesting psychoactive chemicals. It would be a pity, for example, to allow the advocates of LSD to take exclusive possession of the term 'consciousness expansion.' Consciousness expansion seems to me not the sole prerogative of psychoactive compounds, but of education in its fullest sense" (1970, p. 128).

Providing such education is obviously an extremely difficult goal to achieve, but while making the effort you might become aware of some starting points, perhaps by considering some of the goals of education noted by Voeks—deeper comprehension of the world, increased ability to see interrelationships and make meaningful integrations, deeper interests, appreciation of the arts, deeper compassion. If you assist your students to achieve some of these goals, they may not feel quite so driven to drugs.

Even as you try to teach in a mind-expanding way, however, you should take into account that young people experiment with drugs for a great variety of reasons, so your efforts to displace marijuana or LSD with learning may not be completely successful. Keniston emphasizes the search for meaning and experience as basic reasons for drug use, Beatrice and Edwin Lipinski (1970) list four peer-group factors that may motivate a young person to use drugs: being able to talk to others about drug experiences may be a passport to acceptance or heroic elevation, challenge or dare, proof of flexibility, and proof of emotional maturity and intellectual depth. They also list seven individual factors: curiosity, experimentation, personal challenge; a feeling of being left behind or missing something; individual proof of emotional maturity and intellectual depth; seeking meaning; seeking answers to philosophical or personal questions; solving personal problems and feelings of inadequacy; and closeness to other people. Obviously, some of these motives will be so powerful in some students that they will almost be compelled to try drugs, regardless of your attempts to interest them in other forms of mind expansion.

Because of laws governing the sale and use of drugs, and the fact that many parents feel that they alone of all adults have the right to make direct suggestions to their children about drug use, it is usually unwise for a teacher to offer specific advice on the matter, even if directly asked. Most physicians, health officers, and others who specialize in dealing with drug use and abuse seem to feel that the best single policy is to supply information and permit each young person to make up his own mind. Hundreds of articles, pamphlets, and books on the subject have been published and continue to appear. You might purchase and make available to students who ask for information books that strike you as meeting the criteria for evaluating drug education materials noted by Allan N. Fox and Richard E. Horman (1970): Don't talk down to students, do not exaggerate claims pro or con, communicate a sympathetic attitude, give the impression that the material comes from credible sources, and mention alternatives. An inexpensive paperback that meets these criteria and presents such a variety of views that even the most rigid parent would find it difficult to complain of one-sidedness is *Drug Awareness* (1970) edited by Horman and Fox. A comprehensive, highly regarded source of information on drugs is *Licit*

Do Schools Train for Alienation?

In *The Greening of America* (1970), Charles Reich maintains that our school system is set up to deliberately train students for alienation. He notes:

Training toward alienation, from elementary school onward, reaches its climax when the student is forced to make his choice, first of a college major, then of a career. Surrounding these moments is a gradually built-up picture of man as a creature who has one single "right" vocation in life, the vocation for which he is "best fitted," and for which he can be aptitude tested and trained. The choice is surrounded by great anxiety and doubt, particularly because the student may find that his own nature fails to conform to the expected norm. He may find that he is seriously interested in music, surfing, and astronomy, that no career can encompass these interests, and that consequently he is faced with having to give up a part of himself. Often he has an "identity crisis" at this point, and it would only seem fair to say that the crisis is really not of his making at all, but one forced upon him by society's demand that he give up a portion of the identity which he has already formed. This sort of "choice" can only be a sad and desperate moment. For a young person is not only asked to give up a large portion of the "identity" he already has in favor of something unknown and perhaps far less satisfying; he must also give up all the as yet undiscovered possibilities within him, and thus commit a part of himself to death before it can be born and tried out. When a college student decides on medicine, he puts out of his mind the chance that he might learn about literature and discover a special affinity there; he will never give that potential in him a chance, but for a long time he will wonder about it. (1970, pp. 151–152)

This is a more extreme view of points made by Keniston. If you succeed in assisting your students to meet some of Voeks's goals of education, it might be argued that the schools can prevent alienation. Apparently, Reich does not feel that it is possible for a person to pursue a career as an astronomer during working hours, play the piano evenings, and surf on weekends; or to become a doctor who practices medicine but also reads, and perhaps even writes. The basic purpose of courses in general education has always been to encourage the development of a "well-rounded man" capable of pursuing a variety of interests. Reich (and, to some extent, Keniston) feels that a technological society makes it difficult for a person to do this. Jacques-Yves Cousteau ventures a different opinion: "The fascinating thing on this planet is that despite all talk about over-specialization, to a person who is interested, it's much easier to know everything going on in the world today than it was for Leonardo da Vinci. This is a time of super-Leonardos" (in Davidson, 1972, p. 89). The key phrase in this statement is "a person who is interested." Many aspects of education undoubtedly tend to squelch interest, but perhaps those who are unable to benefit from the opportunities for varied interests provided by a technological society also have themselves to blame because they devote too much time to self-pity. If a college student chooses a major and later discovers that it is not as appealing as he has hoped, he can choose from dozens of others. If a person feels trapped in his first career choice because he later discovers that he does not enjoy that form of work, it would seem more sensible to prepare for a different job than to blame "society" for what is really one's own doing.

and Illicit Drugs (1973) by Edward M. Brecher and the Editors of *Consumer Reports*.

(Note: The National Coordinating Council on Drug Education evaluated over 200 films on drugs and concluded that only 16 percent were "scientifically and conceptually acceptable" and that over half of them were ineffective or potentially harmful. If you would like information regarding ratings of films on drugs, the report may be obtained from the National Coordinating Council on Drug Education, 1211 Connecticut Avenue, Washington, D.C., 20036. The price is $5.00)

Developmental Trends and Their Implications, as Seen by Piaget and Bruner

For a description of these trends and their implications for teaching, see the latter portion of the section on junior high school students. Piaget and Bruner perceive no qualitative developmental changes at the senior high school level, just a growing sophistication with formal operations and with symbolic representation.

To help you evolve an overall picture of development, Figure 4–2 (on the facing page) briefly summarizes the age-level characteristics described in this chapter.

Now that you are familiar with age-level characteristics, you might attempt to fit them into a more comprehensive framework by thinking back to the material of the preceding chapter. It may be helpful, for example, to connect the characteristics with the five general principles of development discussed there: (1) Development is the product of maturation and learning. (2) The pattern of growth becomes less predictable as the child grows older. (3) Growth usually proceeds from general to specific responses. (4) The continuity of growth is usually more apparent over a long period than a short one. (5) Various aspects of growth progress at different rates in different children.

As you think back over the outline of age-level characteristics you have just read and as you observe and interact with pupils at a particular grade level, you might also begin to develop your own personal theory of readiness. Would you let pupils "develop" readiness by giving them considerable freedom to choose how and when they will respond? Or would you arrange a systematic series of learning tasks to be followed by all children in the same manner?

In arriving at an answer, you might ask yourself two further questions: How uniform is development? In view of the atypical nature of standardization groups, the limitations of actuarial prediction, the tendency for individual differences to be obliterated by average trends, and the nature of overlap, are age-level descriptions accurate enough to serve as a basis for a highly systematic and controlled curriculum?

Figure 4-2 Summary of Age-level Characteristics

	Physical	Social	Emotional	Mental	Trends described by Erikson, Piaget, and Bruner
Kindergarten	Active; large-muscle control; bones soft; boys bigger, girls more mature.	Flexible friendships; small, loosely organized play groups; quarrels frequent; dramatic play; little sex-role awareness.	Free emotional expression; frequent anger outbursts; fears and jealousy common.	Like to talk, vivid imagination.	Autonomy vs. Doubt Initiative vs. Guilt Egocentric speech Moral realism Preoperational thought Iconic representation
Primary Grades	Active; large-muscle control; eye development incomplete; susceptible to illnesses; accident rate at peak.	More selective friendships; small-group activities; quarrels frequent; competition emerges.	Sensitive to feelings and to criticism and ridicule; need praise; eager to please.	Eager to learn; like to talk; concepts of right and wrong emerge.	Industry vs. Inferiority Socialized speech Moral realism Concrete operations Iconic representation (Some ability to use formal and symbolic thought
Elementary Grades	Growth spurt; puberty occurs in some girls; fine motor coordination; poor posture; bones and ligaments soft; boys like rough play.	"Gang" age; sex cleavage; team games; hero worship.	Peer code-adult code conflict; "character" traits emerge.	Curious; wide interests; may be perfectionists; want independence but with support and guidance.	Industry vs. Inferiority Socialized speech Moral relativism Formal operations Symbolic representation
Junior High	Growth spurt and puberty; concern about appearance; adolescent awkwardness; limited physical and mental endurance.	Peer group takes over; need for conformity; friendships and quarrels more intense; girls more advanced socially.	Moody, unpredictable; temperamental; may be opinionated and intolerant; critical of adults.	Able to deal with some concepts; tendency to daydream.	Identity vs. Role Confusion Socialized speech Moral relativism Formal operations Symbolic representation
High School	Physical maturity reached; impact of puberty; self-conscious.	Peer group dominant; concern about opposite sex; need for conformity.	Adolescent revolt; conflict with parents; moody and preoccupied.	Close to maximum mental efficiency but inexperienced; search for a philosophy of life and sense of identity. Conflicts over sex role and occupational identity.	Same as for junior high school level

Summary

In this chapter you have been acquainted with the characteristics of students at different age levels. In addition to the clusters of physical, social, emotional, and mental qualities represented for each age group, the stages of development described by Erik H. Erikson, as well as the stages of intellectual development described by Jean Piaget and Jerome Bruner, have been highlighted. Throughout the discussion you have been encouraged to think in terms of how you as a practicing teacher might use the information offered.

Suggestions for Further Reading, Writing, Thinking, and Discussion

4-1 *Comparing Real Students with Hypothetical Students*

For the various reasons given in analyzing potential weaknesses of age-level characteristic descriptions, no discussion of developmental trends can be wholly accurate. Consequently, you might find it of interest to observe students at the grade level you propose to teach and compare what you see with the descriptions that have been provided. If possible, observe students in and out of class and then reread the appropriate set of descriptions for that grade level. What bits of behavior fit the descriptions, and what episodes or characteristics are contradictory? Pick out the *single* characteristic that impresses you the most and speculate about what you might do—if anything—to allow for it when you begin to teach.

4-2 *Trying Out a Piaget Experiment*

One of the best ways to assess a student's level of intellectual development (and to learn a great deal about the theories of Jean Piaget) is to perform one of the experiments of Piaget (or his followers). At the primary level, you might use the beaker or clay experiments or at the upper elementary or junior high school level, the pendulum problem. Detailed descriptions of these and many other experiments performed by Piaget appear in Chapters 3 and 4 of *Piaget's Theory of Intellectual Development* (1969) by Herbert Ginsburg and Sylvia Opper. If you will be teaching at the primary-grade level, you might also consult *Young Children's Thinking* (1966) by Millie Almy, E. Chittenden, and P. Miller. In case you do try out a Piaget experiment, note the results and your own reactions, including any insight you gained into how the mind of a child or an adolescent works. (It would be interesting to compare your own results with those of classmates who tried the experiment on other children.)

4-3 *Checking on Understanding of Abstract Concepts*

If you do not have time to perform one of Piaget's experiments, you might use a simpler technique to get insight into the thought processes of a child.

Ask a teacher at almost any level beyond the primary grades to have the students write out the Pledge of Allegiance to the flag and then *explain* it; e.g., what is the meaning of *allegiance, republic, indivisible, liberty, justice?* Analyze the results, write an evaluation of how well the students really understand what they are saying, compare your evaluation to Piaget's outline of the stages of intellectual development, and comment on the implications. (For example, how many students seem to have reached the stage of *formal* operations?)

4-4 *Checking on Moral Realism and Moral Relativism*

Piaget has suggested that children tend to be *moral realists* until about the end of the elementary school years, when they become *moral relativists.* For insight into this distinction, obtain permission to ask pupils at lower and upper grades in an elementary school to explain how they would react to these situations:

a. Suppose your mother had bought a new dress. She was very proud of it, but you thought it looked terrible. If she asked you what you thought about it, what would you say?

b. Suppose two boys had stolen candy bars in a supermarket. One boy had plenty of money to pay for them, and the other came from a poor family, had no money, and was very hungry. Should both boys be punished in the same way if they are caught?

c. Suppose John was playing ball on the playground and accidentally hit Mary and gave her a bloody nose. During the same recess period David got mad at Jane and hit her. It hurt, but it wasn't nearly as bad as Mary's bloody nose. John caused greater injury to Mary than David did to Jane. Does this mean John should be punished more severely than David?

According to Piaget, younger children are more likely to apply the letter of the law (*never* tell a lie) than the spirit of the law (it is all right to tell a "white lie"); they are less likely to take into account circumstances (such as hunger and poverty); and they are more likely to judge the seriousness of an act by its practical consequences rather than by the intent of the individual (a child who causes a more serious injury should be more severely punished even if he did it accidentally). Did the responses from younger and older students fit these predictions? Summarize and comment on your results.

4-5 *Looking for Examples of Egocentric Recitation*

According to Piaget, a child's speech is primarily egocentric, or self-centered, until he reaches the age of seven or eight. Controlled observations of this hypothesis have led to the conclusion that the differentiation between egocentric and socialized speech is not as clear-cut as Piaget originally suggested. However, younger children do seem to have more difficulty taking into account the views expressed by their fellow students during class recitation. If you have the opportunity to observe in an elementary school classroom during a discussion period, replicate the observational study conducted by H. V. Baker—that is, classify the contributions made by different students under the following headings:

New topic not obviously related to what an earlier speaker said

New topic but apparently suggested by something said by a previous contributor

Logical continuation of a topic previously introduced

Describe your results and comment on their implications. (Note: You might try a similar analysis in a high school or college class to discover whether more mature students are always able to continue logically a topic previously introduced. If quite a few students do not do this, what are some possible explanations for "disorganized" recitation? What techniques might you use to make discussions flow more smoothly? Would you be inclined to either gently criticize or ignore irrelevant contributions, for example?)

4-6 *Recording the Activities of an "Inactive" Student*

When children enter school, they are required to learn to live with the inevitable restrictions imposed by the demands of group interaction. For example, they must learn that thirty-five children cannot speak at once, that they have to remain relatively quiet at certain times, that they must sit more or less in one place during formal or semiformal presentations or study periods. Many elementary students have a hard time controlling their natural inclinations to move about. To check on this problem—and at the same time gain insight into why the noise and activity level is high in elementary classrooms—obtain permission to observe in an elementary school. Pick out two or three pupils, observe each one for three to five minutes, and try to write down everything they do at a time when they are ostensibly "inactive," e.g., working on a written assignment, watching the teacher. (Record your observations as unobtrusively as possible. Some college students got carried away by this project and found themselves being mimicked by half a roomful of elementary pupils—all of them taking notes on the college student taking notes on them.) If you perform this assignment, summarize and comment on your findings.

4-7 *Analyzing the Hypotheses that American Males Are Feminized and Manipulated*

A number of observers have suggested that one reason males in the United States have a higher suicide rate, a lower life expectancy, and more problems of many kinds than females is feminization early in life. Patricia Sexton has written at length about this hypothesis in *The Feminized Male* (1969). (An abridged version of her arguments can be found in an article in the January 1970 issue of *Psychology Today*.) In *The Manipulated Man* (1973), Esther Vilar argues that men in America are controlled by women all their lives and that the belief that women are being persecuted by men is a delusion perpetuated by women's liberationists. If you have ever speculated about the male-female relationship in our society, you might read either or both of these books and note your reactions.

4-8 *Analyzing the Role of Women in Contemporary American Society*

The Women's Liberation movement has called attention to the nature and extent of discrimination against females in our society, but considering Erikson's views on identity vs. role confusion, it has also led to new difficulties. If you would like to examine a comprehensive analysis of the difficulties facing American women, the following books and articles are recommended: *The Feminine Mystique* (1963) by Betty Friedan; "Equality Between the Sexes: An Immodest Proposal" by Alice S. Rossi, in *Life Cycle and Achievement in America* edited by Rose Laub Coser (1964); *Occupation: Housewife* (1971) by Helena Z. Lopata; *Woman's Place* (1970) by Cynthia Fuchs Epstein; "A Woman Anthropologist Offers a Solution to the Woman Problem" by Sheila K. Johnson, which appeared in the August 27, 1972 *New York Times Magazine*, pp. 7–39; *Psychology of Women: A Study of Bio-Cultural Conflicts* (1971) by Judith M. Bardwick; *Readings on the Psychology of Women* (1972) edited by Judith M. Bardwick. If you read any of these books or articles—or others of your own choice—you might note the disadvantages as well as advantages of women's liberation.

4-9 *Discovering How Education Crosses the Wires of the Sexes*

Sexton and Vilar emphasize the problems of American males, the women's liberationists those of females; in *The Imperial Animal* (1971), Lionel Tiger and Robin Fox argue that *both* males and females suffer in contemporary America because of inappropriate techniques of education. This is so because our schools fail to take into account the way the sexes are "wired." In the course of evolution, Tiger and Fox maintain, males and females became "wired" to engage in different activities: "Female learning is especially relevant to childbearing and domestic roles, male learning to the groups in which they will one day find themselves as politicians, defenders, monitors, hunters, thinkers, etc." (p. 171). They go on to say, "Being male means essentially doing male things. If males are prevented from doing those things—some of which are deep in the wiring system—there remains the grim possibility that they will be unable to perform effectively their functions of protection, provision and even procreation" (p. 175). In their opinion, coeducation, the use of females to teach young males, and the tendency for higher education to persuade females to engage in male pursuits all cause problems: "It would be too simple, but not untrue, to say that the boy loses early in the game because he is expected to behave like a girl, while the girl loses later in the game because she is expected to behave like a boy" (p. 172). Tiger and Fox also argue that other aspects of American schooling such as large schools and busing are harmful because they fail to take into account the way children are "wired." If you would like to become acquainted with their complete analysis of weaknesses in American education, read Chapter 6 of *The Imperial Animal*.

If you are intrigued by the idea that the sexes are "wired" in different ways but prefer the medical to the anthropological interpretation, see *Man and Woman, Boy and Girl* (1973) by John Money and Anke A. Ehrhardt. This book provides reports of twenty years of research on individuals who in one way or another experienced an imbalance in hormones associated with sex characteristics. Considerable evidence is presented to back up the conclusion that men and women—if left to themselves—would behave in different ways. This leads to the question of what happens when "wired" tendencies are subjected to cultural influences that may conflict with them. Tiger and Fox offer one answer; you might examine either or both of these books to discover if you come up with a different answer.

4-10 *Obtaining and Analyzing Sociometric Data*

If you have the opportunity to observe or work with an elementary class for a period of several weeks, ask the teacher for permission to obtain some sociometric responses from the pupils. At the end of a written assignment, have students write down the name of the person they most like to work with. Before recording the responses on a target diagram, make your own estimate as to who the stars and isolates will be and request the teacher to do the same. (If you know the children well, you might even try to guess the choices each pupil will make.) Then compare your guesses with the actual results. Time permitting, repeat the request for sociometric responses a month later and check on the consistency of choices. Comment on your findings and speculate on what you might do with the sociometric information that you have obtained.

4-11 *Reading and Reacting to a Book on Adolescence*

In many respects, the most difficult and complex stage of development is adolescence. Countless books have been written on the problems young people face (and create) in our society, and every high school teacher should find it of interest to read one or more analyses of this phase of development. Paul Goodman has written two provocative books on the subject. In *Growing Up Absurd* (1956), he argues that growing up in America is literally an "absurdity." In Part 2 of *Compulsory Miseducation* (1964) he presents a critique of high school education and in Part 3 an evaluation of college education. In Chapter 10 he puts forward "Two Simple Proposals" for reforming the systems.

Edgar Z. Friedenberg has also written two books on adolescence. In *The Vanishing Adolescent* (1959) he asserts that adolescence *is* conflict, that conflict is necessary for the young person to discover self-definition, and that lack of conflict in the lives of American youth means that adolescence has "vanished." (If you read this book, ask yourself whether there is more conflict now than there was in 1959 when the book was published.) In *Coming of Age in America* (1965), Friedenberg compares adolescents in the United States to those in colonial African countries (Chapter 1), describes his perceptions of a "typical" American high school (Chapter 2), gives a description of student values (Chapter 3), and analyzes the shortcomings of educational practice (Chapter 4). In the concluding section of Chapter 6 he offers some prescriptions. (Among other things he suggests that most young teachers enter the field because they see teaching as "the easiest of professions" and that the selection of credential candidates must be upgraded.)

Peter Blos presents a psychoanalytic interpretation in *On Adolescence* (1962). In Chapter 1 he discusses "Puberty and Adolescence," in Chapter 2 "Phases of Adolescence," and in Chapter 5 "The Ego in Adolescence." Two case histories are presented in Chapter 7.

Understanding Adolescence (2nd ed., 1973) edited by James F. Adams includes chapters on physiological, cognitive, and emotional aspects of adolescence; sex education, activism, the counterculture, and drug use. (Chapter 12, "The Need for Involved Youth," is by Senator George S. McGovern.)

In *The Uncommitted: Alienated Youth in American Society* (1965) Kenneth Keniston provides case histories and a general analysis of the nature of alienation in American college students of the 1960s. To gain a general impression of this book, read Chapter 1, "The New Alienation," and Chapter 13, "Alienation and American Society." In *Young Radicals: Notes on Committed Youth* (1968), Keniston compares the background and characteristics of students who engage in active dissent, with those inclined toward the withdrawal and detachment that was typical of many of the young adults described in *The Uncommitted*. For a general impression of Keniston's analysis of young radicals, you might read Chapter 2, "Personal Roots: Struggle and Specialness," Chapter 3, "Personal Roots: Turmoil, Success, and the End of the Line," and Chapter 4, "Becoming a Radical."

If you examine any of these books on adolescence and young adulthood, you might summarize the points made by the author(s) and analyze them with reference to your own experiences and observations.

4-12 *Sampling Erikson's Views on Identity*

Erik H. Erikson gives a detailed analysis of the problems facing adolescents in *Identity: Youth and Crisis* (1968). If you will be teaching in high school, or if you have ever been troubled in your own search for identity, you may find this book thought-provoking. Be warned, however, that Erikson addresses his remarks primarily to fellow clinicians and professionals of the older generation. The person under thirty may have to curb a tendency to be defensive over descriptions of youthful foibles that happen to coincide with aspects of his own behavior. Although Erikson does not ridicule the behavior of young people, he does have an incisive way of describing it. To discover whether you are able to weigh his observations without feeling that you are being attacked, read Chapter 1, which is an excellent summary of his views on identity.

Erikson has also written two biographies analyzing (among other things) the identity crisis of his subjects with reference to the Zeitgeist of the times. (These are in-depth variations of what Edwin G. Boring has done in his *History of Experimental Psychology*.) The biographies are of two extremely different individuals: Martin Luther and Mahatma Gandhi. If you enjoy biographies or have ever wondered about the lives and times of Luther or Gandhi, look for *Young Man Luther* (1958) or *Gandhi's Truth* (1969). If you sample any of Erikson's works, you might summarize his views and add your own observations.

4-13 *Discovering More About William Glasser's Views on Failure and Identity*

William Glasser is a psychiatrist who has developed views of childhood and adolescence that parallel those of Erikson in many respects. Just as Erikson stresses the importance of encouraging a sense of industry rather than inferiority, Glasser calls attention to the impact of failure on the self-concept of students in *Schools Without Failure* (1969). And just as Erikson has called attention to the need of the adolescent to develop a sense of identity, Glasser emphasizes the same general idea in *The Identity Society* (1971). He argues that young people can develop positive identities if they become involved and achieve success. Many teachers and parents report that they have gained considerable insight from reading Glasser's books. If you would like to learn more about his views, you might read Chapter 1, "The Problem of Failure," Chapter 3, "The Impact of School," and Chapters 7 and 8, "Preventing Failure," all in *Schools Without Failure*, or sample sections of *The Identity Society*. If you read any of these books by Glasser, write a résumé of his arguments and note your own reactions.

4-14 *Assisting Teen-Agers to Understand Their Rights and Responsibilities*

One of the most obvious trends in American education is the interest in establishing (and recognizing) the rights of students. Many college and high school students have expressed dissatisfaction with the way they are treated and have resorted to a variety of techniques to bring about improvement. In recognition of this—and in an effort to help teen-agers learn about both their rights and responsibilities—a special program was introduced in the fall of 1971 in four junior high schools in Prince Georges County, Maryland. Its aim is to assist teen-agers in understanding how laws are made and also make them aware of their rights and how they can deal with social and legal problems through established channels. If you will be teaching social studies at the junior or senior high school level, you may want to read a complete description of the program. Look for an article by Barnard Law Collier starting on page 64 of the May 22, 1971 issue of *Saturday Review*. (The title is "Learning to Cope in Prince Georges County.") If you do read more about the program, summarize the points made and add your own reactions, perhaps in the form of ideas to try out in your classroom.

4-15 *Reading a Comprehensive Description of Age-Level Characteristics*

If you would like to read a more complete description of development than that provided in this and the preceding chapter, look for a text in developmental psychology. You are sure to find several of these in any college library. Two widely used books of this type are *Child Development and Personality* (3rd ed., 1969) by P. H. Mussen, J. J. Conger, and J. Kagan and *Childhood and Adolescence* (3rd ed., 1972) by L. Joseph Stone and Joseph Church. For books that concentrate primarily on age-level characteristics, look for *The Gesell Institute's Child Behavior* (1955) by Frances Ilg and Louise Bates Ames; *Growing from Infancy to Adulthood* (1958) by Edward Britton and J. Merritt Winans; or *These Are Your Children* (3rd ed., 1966) by Gladys Gardner Jenkins, Helen S. Schacter, and William W. Bauer.

Recommended Reading in *Psychology Applied to Teaching: Selected Readings*

If you would like to do further reading in books or articles mentioned in this chapter (and in the preceding "Suggestions for Further Reading, Writing, Thinking, and Discussion") without having to track down several separate volumes, you might peruse *Psychology Applied to Teaching: Selected Readings* (Boston: Houghton Mifflin, 1972). This is a collection of excerpts from books and articles from journals in psychology. The following selections provide extended commentaries on points noted in this chapter or mentioned in the "Suggestions."

Piaget's Theory of Development: "Giant in the Nursery—Jean Piaget" by David Elkind, Selection 12, p. 147.

Bruner's Theory of Development: "Patterns of Growth" by Jerome S. Bruner, Selection 13, p. 170.

Erikson's Theory of Development: "Erik Erikson's Eight Ages of Man" by David Elkind, Selection 10, p. 120.

Erikson's Views on Identity: Prologue from *Identity: Youth and Crisis* by Erik H. Erikson, Selection 14, p. 185. (See also Suggestion 4–12.)

PART

LEARNING

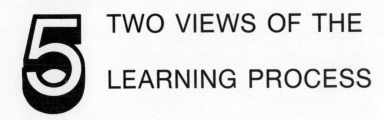

TWO VIEWS OF THE LEARNING PROCESS

KEY POINTS

Classifications
Impulsive and reflective thinkers, analytic and thematic thinkers (Kagan)

Experiments
Conditioning of dog to salivate when bell rings (Pavlov)
Opening of latch by cat through trial and error (Thorndike)
Shaping of behavior of rat and pigeon by reinforcement (Skinner)
Solving of stick problem by ape through insight (Köhler)

Concepts
Emitted behavior, elicited behavior
Classical conditioning, operant conditioning
Terminal behavior
Life space (Lewin)

Principles
Reinforcement, extinction, generalization, discrimination
Closure

Theories
Skinner's version of S-R associationism
Bruner's version of cognitive-field theory

Methodology
*Using programmed techniques: shaping behavior, vanishing prompts, using
  linear and branching programs, considering lowest-common-denominator
  effect, using behavior modification*
*Using the discovery approach: emphasizing contrast, stimulating informed
  guessing, introducing disturbing data, permitting mistakes*
Using techniques of open education

CHAPTER CONTENTS

NOW THAT YOU HAVE SOME FAMILIARITY WITH WHAT PUPILS TEND TO be like at different age levels, it's time to turn to a discussion of how you can help them learn. This chapter will give you a more complete description of the two contemporary approaches to learning contrasted in Chapter 2—the first based on S-R associationism and the second on cognitive-field theory. Although thousands of experiments on learning have been performed and dozens of theories have resulted, this book describes only a few of these experiments and emphasizes only the views of B. F. Skinner and Jerome Bruner. An explanation for such a circumscribed approach is in order.

For the most part, psychologists interested in learning theory have leaned toward the pure rather than the applied side of things. Because of their concern for theory, they have tried to develop laws of learning at the highest possible level of abstraction. The consequence has been that, until recently, most learning theorists haven't been too concerned with what goes on in the classroom. In addition, many learning theories are quite technical and derived from somewhat esoteric experimental data. So in order to benefit from a comprehensive survey of several learning theories, you would have to become thoroughly familiar with the subtle differences between them before you could make consistent applications. In a course devoted exclusively to learning, you might find you could do this. In an educational psychology course, however, learning is one of many topics, and therefore it has been necessary to focus on those learning theories that are regarded as having the greatest potential value for teachers.

Both Skinner and Bruner have developed teaching programs, they have functioned as spokesmen for their respective points of view, their observations touch upon so many aspects of education that their contrasting opinions are noted in almost every chapter of this book, and each has written a concise explanation of his views that is available in inexpensive paperback form. For all these reasons, this chapter is organized in terms of the observations of Skinner and Bruner.

The analysis of their views will include five elements: (1) a brief history of the classic experiments that provided the basis for each approach, (2) a summary of what are believed to be the advantages of each approach, (3) a description of the teaching methods designed to make the most of these advantages, (4) a critical analysis of these methods, and (5) a list of suggestions for putting each of these methods into practice in your own classroom.

S-R Associationism and Programmed Learning

To understand Skinner's interpretation and implementation of S-R associationism, it is necessary to consider some of the original experiments that led to the development of programmed learning. A brief review of these experiments was presented in Chapter 2. Here is a more detailed analysis.

Experiments of Pavlov

The first man to study learning under highly controlled experimental conditions was the famous Russian, Ivan Pavlov. Originally a physiologist, in 1904 he won the Nobel Prize in medicine for his studies of the digestive process. In these studies he measured the amount of saliva a dog produced when it was fed. One day as he approached a dog with a tray of food, he noticed saliva start to flow, and he realized that the mere *sight* of the food had produced the

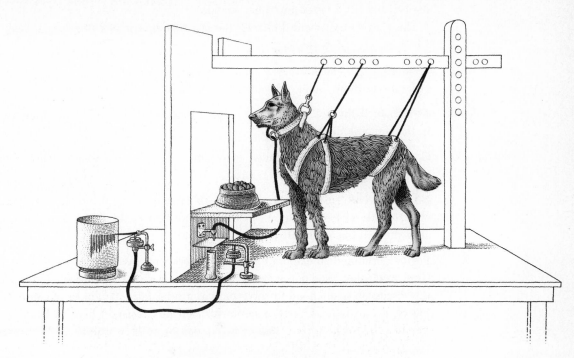

Figure 5–1   Pavlov's Apparatus for Studying Conditioning.

response that had originally been stimulated by the dog's actually *chewing* the food. Pavlov devoted the rest of his life to experiments aimed at investigating and understanding this phenomenon.[1] (This is a classic example of how a scientist often stumbles onto something extremely important as a by-product of his original research.)

As noted in Chapter 2, one of Pavlov's earliest experiments was the one in which he set up a carefully controlled situation to condition a dog to salivate when a bell was rung. A bell would be rung, and two or three seconds later a dish of powdered food would be presented to the dog. After repeating this process ten or twenty times, the sound of the bell alone was sufficient to cause the dog to salivate. However, if the bell was sounded too many times without food being presented, the response would tend to disappear. Pavlov noticed that after a dog had been conditioned to salivate to a bell, it would tend to react similarly to almost *any* sound, such as a whistle. To prevent indiscriminate

Pavlov: conditioning of dog to salivate when bell rings

[1] Pavlov's complete treatise on conditioning, *Conditioned Reflexes*, is available in an inexpensive paperback published by Dover Press in 1960.

salivating, he found it necessary repeatedly to reward the dog with food after the bell but never after any other sounds.

This classic experiment illustrates the four key principles found in practically all variations of S-R theory:

Reinforcement

Reinforcement. The salivary response to the bell was strengthened as a result of food repeatedly being presented immediately after the bell was rung.

Extinction

Extinction. If the bell was rung too many times without the food to reinforce it, the response disappeared.

Generalization

Generalization.[2] The dog tended to respond to any sound roughly similar to the ringing of the bell.

Discrimination

Discrimination. To teach the dog to distinguish between the right sound and other sounds, *selective reinforcement* was used; that is, the dog was given food after the bell but never after any other sound.

Pavlov performed an elaborate series of experiments involving aspects of these basic principles, as did psychologists in other parts of the world. But since this discussion is intended to serve only as a brief introduction to modern S-R theory, no analysis of these experiments will be presented here. Instead, we turn directly to the work of the man who did the most to popularize Pavlovian theory in the United States, John B. Watson.

Influence of Watson

As noted in Chapter 2, Watson was not a learning theorist in the strict sense. He did, however, conduct some famous experiments that demonstrated the power of Pavlovian conditioning on human behavior. He also established the tradition of objectivity in psychological studies—a tradition represented by the associationist's definition of psychology as the science of observable behavior. As you will recall, Watson is the acknowledged founder of behaviorism.

Watson based one of his most famous experiments (Watson and Rayner, 1920) on the observation that young children have a "natural" fear of sudden loud sounds. He set up a situation in which a two-year-old boy named Albert was encouraged to play with a white rat. After a preliminary period, Watson suddenly hit a steel bar with a hammer just as Albert reached for the rat, and the noise frightened the child so much that he came to respond to the rat with fear. He had been conditioned to associate the rat with the loud sound.

---

[2] Strictly speaking, this should be referred to as *stimulus* generalization to distinguish it from *response* generalization, which occurs when the response is altered. Salivation does not allow for any variation in response, but in other situations, the organism may vary its reactions to a stimulus. The significance of the general principle, though, is the same in either case.

The success of this experiment led Watson to believe that he could control behavior in almost limitless ways by arranging sequences of conditioned responses. He trumpeted his claim in this famous statement:

> Give me a dozen healthy infants, well formed, and my own special world to bring them up in, and I'll guarantee to take any one at random and train him to become any type of specialist I might select—doctor, lawyer, artist, merchant-chief and, yes, even beggarman and thief, regardless of his talents, penchants, tendencies, abilities, vocations, and race of his ancestry. (1925, p. 82)

Watson never made good on his boast, partly because it soon became apparent that Pavlovian conditioning[3] provided only some of the clues to the nature of learning and partly because he left academic life and turned to business, where he applied the principles of Pavlovian conditioning to advertising. If you think of a certain image when you see a particular brand of cigarettes, you are proving that Pavlovian conditioning does work, even though it is not possible to "train" children to become "specialists."

Experiments and Laws of Thorndike

Although Watson publicized conditioning theory and established the concern for objectivity that has dominated American psychology ever since, the first American learning theorist was Edward L. Thorndike. Thorndike was a protégé of William James, the father of American psychology, and himself became the father of educational psychology.

In one of his earliest experiments (Thorndike, 1898) a hungry cat was put into a "problem box," that is, a cage with a door that would open if the cat properly manipulated a release mechanism. A dish of food was placed outside the cage to motivate the cat to try to get out. In its initial efforts the cat would jump around in an agitated manner and eventually hit the release mechanism by chance. After repeated trials, it learned to confine its efforts to one part of the cage. Eventually it made the correct response almost immediately. Thus the cat discovered how to open the door by a trial-and-error learning process. (See Figure 5-2, p. 208.)

Thorndike: opening of latch by cat through trial and error

Thorndike emphasized that learning consists of connections between stimuli and responses and that repetition is essential to learning—observations that established trends for almost all subsequent learning theories developed in

[3] What is referred to as *Pavlovian conditioning* in this paragraph is also called *classical conditioning* or *respondent conditioning*. These terms differentiate between the type of S-R learning described by Pavlov and the type described by B. F. Skinner, which will be analyzed following the discussion of Thorndike. The word *classical* is used in recognition of the fact that Pavlov's work was based on an original "classic" experiment; *respondent* is used to emphasize the fact that the reaction to the stimulus is originally an automatic response.

Classical conditioning

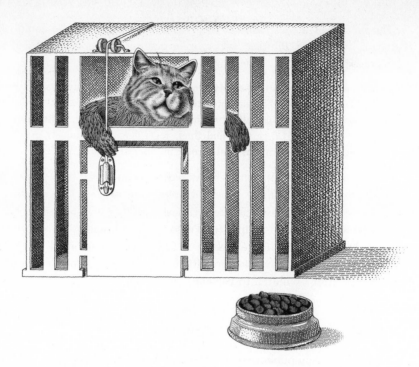

Figure 5–2 Cat in Thorndike Puzzle Box.   The hungry cat learns to release the cage door and reach food through trial-and-error learning.

America. The man who has done the most to develop and *apply* the ideas originally proposed by Thorndike is B. F. Skinner.

Experiments and Theory of Skinner

Skinner: shaping of behavior of rat by reinforcement

After being immersed in behaviorism during graduate study at Harvard, Skinner began experimenting with rats.[4] He constructed a box—later called a *Skinner box* (Figure 5-3)—that was equipped with a bar that could be depressed and a food tray. He would put a hungry rat into the box, and for want of anything better to do, the rat would occasionally wander over and push the bar down. After a while, Skinner would reinforce this action by having a food pellet fall into the tray whenever the bar was depressed. Then food pellets would be supplied under some conditions when the bar was pushed down (e.g., when a tone was sounded) but not under others. The rat would learn this, and the rate of pressing would drop noticeably when the tone was not sounded.

[4] Skinner's own account of his experiments appears in Section II of *Science and Human Behavior.*

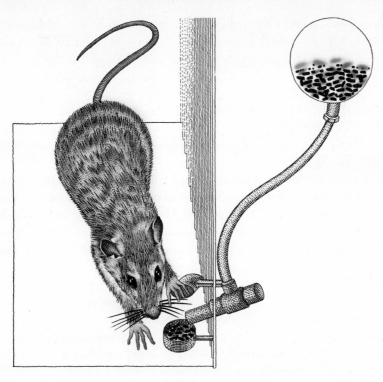

Figure 5–3   Rat in Skinner Box.   The hungry rat is reinforced with a food pellet when it presses the bar under conditions selected by the experimenter.

All the basic principles of Pavlovian conditioning are found in this experiment. The rat learned to press the bar more frequently when this behavior was *reinforced* by a food pellet. If it was not reinforced, *extinction* occurred. For a while the rat *generalized* and pushed the bar down at the same rate whether a tone was sounded or not. Eventually, after selective reinforcement had been repeated often enough, it *discriminated* and pushed the bar more frequently when the tone was sounded.

Although this experiment seems similar to Pavlov's work with dogs, Skinner has pointed out important differences, notably in regard to the source of the behavior. In Pavlov's experiment the dog was essentially passive, and its response (salivation) had to be *elicited* by the experimenter. Skinner's rats (like Thorndike's cats) *emitted* behavior in an essentially spontaneous way. And since the rats "operated" the bar, Skinner's kind of conditioning is called *operant*. (Some psychologists use the term *instrumental* since the behavior is instrumental in bringing about the reinforcement.)

One of the best examples of emitted behavior and operant conditioning is the way a child learns to talk. Parents don't have to stimulate a baby to make sounds; he does it on his own from the moment he is born. At about the age

Distinction: elicited and emitted behavior

Operant conditioning

of six or seven months the typical child spontaneously repeats sounds, such as "Da-da." If the parents overhear this, they are likely to lavish all sorts of reinforcement on him, especially when he emits "Da-da" in the presence of Daddy. The child knows a good thing when he sees it, and after a few weeks or months he says "Da-da" whenever he encounters any object that remotely resembles Daddy. This generalization is considered cute until the day the mother has the bridge club over and the baby greets the mailman with an exuberant cry of "Da-da." At this point selective reinforcement is applied, and the baby learns to discriminate.

Further experiments by Skinner and his followers illustrate other aspects of learning. In some studies, one rat is rewarded every time it presses the bar, whereas another is rewarded at unpredictable intervals (the latter is called a *variable reinforcement schedule*). The rat that is rewarded every time it presses the bar is quite vulnerable to lack of reinforcement and stops pressing the bar very soon after the food supply is cut off. The rat that is rewarded at unpredictable intervals is very resistant to extinction, however, and will keep pressing the bar long after the food supply is cut off—just as people keep feeding coins into slot machines time after time after time.

In other experiments, a rat is punished by an electric shock *until* it presses the bar. In this situation, learning occurs to avoid punishment rather than to earn a reward. The results of such experiments reveal that a rat learns faster under punishment than rewards, but it also forgets rapidly when the punishment is removed and tends to become fearful about being put back in the box. Rewarding the rat may be a slower process, but it produces learning that is more resistant to extinction and is also free of negative by-products.

Skinner: shaping of behavior of pigeon by reinforcement

Skinner eventually switched from rats to pigeons. In early experiments a pigeon was rewarded with a food pellet—at first when it approached a disk, then only when it nodded toward it, and eventually only when it actually pecked it. After the pigeon had been conditioned in this way, food pellets were flipped into the cage at the whim of the experimenter. The pigeon thereupon repeated whatever it had been doing just before each pellet arrived, apparently believing that these actions were the key to the reinforcement. This shows that reinforcement may strengthen *any* act that precedes it, even if the act is meaningless.

Furthermore, it was discovered that such meaningless acts may be highly resistant to extinction. For example, one persistent pigeon was rewarded—only once—at a moment when it happened to be performing a sort of dance step, and the bird repeated the step ten thousand times before stopping for as long as fifteen minutes. This is similar to the way in which human beings develop superstitions. A baseball player on a hitting streak may insist on sitting next to the water cooler just because he happened to be sitting there the day the streak began.

By judiciously rewarding the spontaneous action of birds, Skinner has shaped behavior in ways that Watson never came close to duplicating. Some pigeons have been taught, for example, to peck out tunes on a xylophone and to play table tennis. (If you would like to attempt roughly similar feats with a pet dog or cat, read Skinner's article "How to Teach Animals" in the December 1951 issue of *Scientific American,* pp. 26–29.)

On the basis of such simple experiments with rats and pigeons, Skinner developed both a general approach to teaching and the specific technique of programmed instruction. For a concise overview of his work see his book *The Technology of Teaching,* an inexpensive paperback of less than three hundred pages that you might seriously consider purchasing for your private professional library. Many of Skinner's basic points are summarized in the following pages.

Skinner on the Shortcomings of Current Educational Practice

Skinner feels that current educational practice is not only inefficient but frequently harmful. He further asserts that "the most widely publicized efforts to improve education show an extraordinary neglect of method" (1968, p. 93). He places part of the blame on educational psychologists, who, he says, "spent half a century measuring the results of teaching while neglecting teaching itself" (p. 94). As Skinner puts it, "What is taught often tends to be simply what can be measured by tests and examinations" (p. 235). He describes the standard-assign-and-test situation, designed for ease of measurement, as follows:

> The teacher does not teach; he simply holds the student responsible for learning. The student must read books, study texts, perform experiments, and attend lectures, and he is responsible for doing so in the sense that, if he does not correctly report what he has seen, heard, or read, he will suffer aversive consequences. Questions and answers are so staple a feature of education that their connection with teaching almost never occasions surprise, yet as a demand for a response which will meet certain specifications, a question is almost always slightly aversive. An examination, as a collection of questions, characteristically generates the anxiety and panic appropriate to avoidance and escape. Reading a student's paper is still likely to be called correcting it. Examinations are designed to show principally what the student does *not* know. (1968, pp. 99–100)

In this passage Skinner emphasizes one particular shortcoming of current educational practice—the *aversive* nature of educational control. Elsewhere in *The Technology of Teaching* he elaborates:

> The child at his desk, filling in his workbook, is behaving primarily to escape from the threat of a series of minor aversive events—the teacher's displeasure, the criticism or ridicule of his classmates, an ignominious showing in a competition, low marks, a trip to the office "to be talked to" by the principal, or a word to the parent who may still resort to the birch rod. (P. 15)

But Skinner also stresses three other shortcomings of traditional teaching methods:

1. The lapse of time between an act and reinforcement. For example, a teacher wandering up and down an aisle checking problems may provide reinforcement several minutes after a problem is finished; an exam may not be handed back until days after it is written.
2. Lack of a well-organized presentation of stages in teaching complex skills. For example, a math workbook may group together problems that have little relation to each other, or it may present blocks of material that are too large for the student to assimilate at one time.
3. The relative infrequency of reinforcement. Large classes and split sessions severely limit the reinforcement a teacher can supply to individual pupils. It is inadequate even in a small, all-day class. Skinner maintains that in teaching math to elementary school pupils, even under excellent conditions a teacher may be able to provide only a few thousand reinforcements, though perhaps *fifty* thousand such reinforcements are required to do the job properly.

Skinner on the Advantages of Programmed Learning

In Skinner's opinion the experimental analysis of behavior has now provided enough understanding of the learning process so that a truly effective educational system can be set up. Experiments in which the behavior of a pigeon is shaped by reinforcing the pigeon's movements in the right direction illustrate the key idea behind Skinner's technological approach; that is, the learning of students in school should be *shaped* by a series of reinforcements. The basic technique is described by Skinner in these terms:

Skinner's version of S-R associationism leading to programmed learning

> [The two basic considerations of programmed learning are] the gradual elaboration of extremely complex patterns of behavior and the maintenance of the behavior in strength at each stage. The whole process of becoming competent in any field must be divided into a very large number of very small steps, and reinforcement must be contingent upon the accomplishment of each step. . . . By making each successive step as small as possible, the frequency of reinforcement can be raised to a maximum, while the possibly aversive consequences of being wrong are reduced to a minimum.

These requirements are not excessive, but they are probably incompatible with the current realities of the classroom. In the experimental study of learning it has been found that the contingencies of reinforcement [5] which are most efficient

---

[5] *Contingencies of reinforcement* is a phrase that appears frequently in discussions of operant conditioning. It reflects the fact that reinforcement is *contingent* (or dependent) on the organism responding in a certain way.

Some applications of programmed learning involve the use of elaborate teaching machines hooked up to a computer.

in controlling the organism cannot be arranged through the personal mediation of the experimenter. An organism is affected by subtle details of contingencies which are beyond the capacity of the human organism to arrange. Mechanical and electrical devices must be used. Mechanical help is also demanded by the sheer number of contingencies which may be used efficiently in a single experimental session. We have recorded many millions of responses from a single organism during thousands of experimental hours. Personal arrangement of the contingencies and personal observation of the results are quite unthinkable. . . . The simple fact is that, as a mere reinforcing mechanism, the teacher is out of date. (1968, pp. 21–22)

Teaching Machines

Teaching machines have been developed to supply the kind of mechanical help needed by the out-of-date teacher. Although such machines vary considerably in size, style, and sophistication, almost all of them have certain features in common. Skinner comments:

> The important features of the device are these: reinforcement for the right answer is immediate. The mere manipulation of the device will probably be reinforcing enough to keep the average pupil at work for a suitable period each day, provided traces of earlier aversive control can be wiped out. A teacher may supervise an entire class at work on such devices at the same time, yet each child may progress at his own rate, completing as many problems as possible within the class period. If forced to be away from school, he may return to pick up where he left off. . . .
>
> The device makes it possible to present carefully designed material in which one problem can depend upon the answer to the preceding problem and where, therefore, the most efficient progress to an eventually complex repertoire can be made. (1968, p. 24)

Programs

Though the machine is the mechanical means used to provide reinforcement, the crucial factor in programmed learning is the program that is fed into the machine. The creation of truly successful programs is not easy, and only a handful of people seem to be capable of originating them. The director of Harvard's Center for Programmed Instruction once expressed the opinion in an interview that there are only two dozen competent programmers in the country. Skinner himself has said, "It must be admitted that a considerable measure of art is needed in composing a successful program" (1968, p. 49). To get an idea of what a program looks like, glance at Figure 5-4, a set of frames from a program designed to teach spelling to third- and fourth-grade pupils.

After the pupil has printed his answer to the first question, he moves a knob on the teaching machine, which pulls a transparent cover over what he has written (so he can't erase) and at the same time uncovers information that

1. **Manufacture** means to make or build. *Chair factories manufacture chairs.* Copy the word here:

☐ ☐ ☐ ☐ ☐ ☐ ☐ ☐ ☐ ☐ ☐

2. Part of the word is like part of the word **factory.** Both parts come from an old word meaning *make* or *build.*

m a n u ☐ ☐ ☐ ☐ **u r e**

3. Part of the word is like part of the word **manual.** Both parts come from an old word for *hand.* Many things used to be made by hand.

☐ ☐ ☐ ☐ **f a c t u r e**

4. The same letter goes in both spaces.

m ☐ **n u f** ☐ **c t u r e**

5. The same letter goes in both spaces:

m a n ☐ **f a c t** ☐ **r e**

6. **Chair factories** ☐ ☐ ☐ ☐ ☐ ☐ ☐ ☐ ☐ ☐ ☐ **chairs.**

Source: B. F. Skinner, "Teaching Machines," *Science,* Vol. 128 (October 24, 1958), p. 972. Reprinted by permission.

Figure 5-4 Part of a Program in Elementary-Grade Spelling

reveals whether or not his response is correct. If necessary, he writes a second response. He moves the knob again, pulling the transparent cover over this second response and revealing the correct answer. At that point he turns another knob, which uncovers a new frame—and so it goes.

A section of a more elaborate program designed for a high school physics course is reproduced in Figure 5-5 (p. 216). To "take" the course, cover the words in the right-hand column, and check your responses after you mentally fill in the blanks. (For additional frames in this course see *The Technology of Teaching,* pages 45–47.)

In developing such a program, the first step is to define the *terminal behavior,* that is, what is to be learned. Then terms, facts, and laws, or principles, must be arranged in a sequence designed to lead the student to the desired terminal behavior. This requires first making the steps small enough that the frequency of reinforcement will be maximized, then putting them in the proper order and arranging them so that the student will be adequately prepared for each frame, or numbered problem, when he reaches it.

In arranging the sequence of steps, a programmer may use a *linear* program, which tries to insure that every response will be correct. Or he may use a

Terminal behavior

Distinction: linear and branching programs

Sentence to be completed	Word to be supplied
1. The important parts of a flashlight are the battery and the bulb. When we ''turn on'' a flashlight, we close a switch which connects the battery with the _____.	bulb
2. When we turn on a flashlight, an electric current flows through the fine wire in the _____ and causes it to grow hot.	bulb
3. When the hot wire glows brightly, we say that it gives off or sends out heat and _____.	light
4. The fine wire in the bulb is called a filament. The bulb ''lights up'' when the filament is heated by the passage of a(n) _____ current.	electric
5. When a weak battery produces little current, the fine wire, or _____, does not get very hot.	filament
6. A filament which is *less* hot sends out or gives off _____ light.	less
7. ''Emit'' means ''send out.'' The amount of light sent out, or ''emitted,'' by a filament depends on how _____ the filament is.	hot

Source: B. F. Skinner, ''Teaching Machines,'' *Science*, Vol. 128 (October 24, 1958), p. 973. Reprinted by permission.

Figure 5-5   Part of a Program in High School Physics

branching program, in which there is less concern that all responses be right; if a wrong answer is supplied, the student is provided with a branching set of questions to enable him to master the troublesome point. Since it would be impossible to provide supplementary frames for all the wrong answers that might be written in by a student, branching programs are often multiple-choice. The student thus selects his answer from a small number of alternatives, and a branch is supplied to correct wrong responses. Another type of branching program provides the student with a more complete explanation of the misunderstood material and then urges him to go back and study the original explanation more carefully. The latter type of branching program is illustrated in Figure 5-6.

Skinner prefers the linear approach, which was used in writing the frames reproduced in Figures 5-3 and 5-4, because it requires the student to supply

Page 6: A course *description* tells you something about the content and procedures of a course; a course *objective* describes a desired outcome of a course.

Whereas an objective tells what the learner is to be like as a result of some learning experiences, the course description tells only what the course is about.

The distinction is quite important, because a course description does not explain what will be accepted as adequate achievement; it does not confide to the learner the rules of the game. Though a course description might tell the learner which field he will be playing on, it doesn't tell him where the foul lines are, where the goalposts are located, or how he will know when he has scored.

It is useful to be able to recognize the difference between an objective and a description, so try an example.

Which of the statements below looks most like an *objective?*

To be able to explain the principles for developing reading readiness in the primary grades . . . . turn to page 7.

Discusses principles, techniques, and procedures in developing reading readiness in the primary grades . . . . turn to page 8.

Page 7: You said "To be able to explain the principles of reading readiness in the primary grades" was a statement of an objective.

You are correct! The statement describes an *aim* rather than a course. It doesn't do a very good job of it, but at least it does attempt to describe a goal rather than a process.

Now let us move on. TURN TO PAGE 10

Page 8: Oh, come on now! The collection of words that led you to this page is a piece of a course description, and not a very good description at that. I hope you are not being misled by the fact that college catalogs are composed of such phrases. They are *not* statements of intended learning outcomes and they are *not* what we are concerned with here.

Let me try to explain the difference this way. A course description describes various aspects of a PROCESS known as a "course." A course objective, on the other hand, is a description of a PRODUCT, of what the learner is supposed to be like as a *result* of the process.

Return to page 6 and read the material again.

Source: Adapted from *Preparing Instructional Objectives* by Robert F. Mager, Copyright © 1962, pp. 6–8. Reprinted by permission of Fearon Publishers.

Figure 5-6 Part of a Branching Program on Instructional Objectives

his own responses and because it maximizes reinforcement. Other psychologists, notably N. A. Crowder (1963), favor branching programs because the student is able to advance in larger steps and because the machine can "talk back" to the student and thus come closer to approximating a human tutor.

Vanishing prompts

In composing a program, the writer strives to progressively reduce the degree of *prompt,* or the number of cues necessary to elicit the correct answer. In the parlance of programming, the prompt is "vanished." But in reducing cues, it is important not to go too far too fast; as Skinner puts it, "Don't lose your pigeon." In the program for teaching spelling (Figure 5-3), notice how the degree of prompt is gradually reduced. This type of prompt is called *formal* because it hints at the physical *form* of the response. In the physics unit (Figure 5-4), however, *thematic* prompts are used; answers are deduced from themes or associations previously learned.

Applications of Operant Conditioning Developed by Skinner and His Associates

Although the kinds of programs just described are the basic tool of a technology of teaching, other programs or techniques derived from operant conditioning have been developed by Skinner and his associates (see Chapter 4 of *The Technology of Teaching.*) One such technique (described in *Handwriting with Write and See* by Skinner and Sue Ann Krakower) is used to teach handwriting to primary-grade pupils. The various letter shapes are printed on a chemically treated paper, and the child traces over them with a special pen. When he traces accurately, the pen produces a gray line. When he strays off the letters, the pen produces a yellow line. At first the printed prompt consists of the entire letter shapes. As the child progresses, parts of the letters are gradually vanished until only a few dots and dashes provide the prompt.

Sophisticated devices resembling jukeboxes have been used to develop a musical sense in children. The child tries to match beats and sounds produced by the machines; his correct responses are reinforced by candy or tokens or simply by his own recognition that he is in tune. Other machines have been developed to help preschool children learn to discriminate between shapes and patterns by looking at a sample reproduced in one window and selecting an equivalent shape from other windows. More elaborate machines, developed to establish reading readiness, present auditory as well as visual patterns, which are often followed by a programmed reading series.

Still other programs have been designed to aid memorization of poetry and vocabulary words. At first, students are exposed to a poem or to a word, which is accompanied by a picture and a definition (as in an illustrated dictionary). Then the material is gradually vanished so that control of the response shifts from the machine to the student. Skinner believes that operant conditioning can even be used to teach thinking (by conditioning the student to develop techniques of self-management, e.g., paying attention and studying efficiently), to foster creativity (by inducing greater amounts of behavior and reinforcing what is original), and to encourage perseverance and dedication (by systematically widening the ratios of reinforcement).

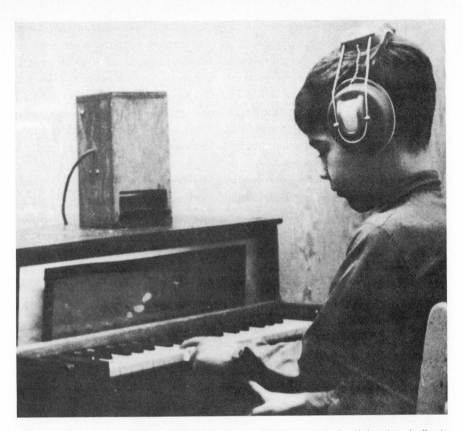

A machine used to teach "musical thinking." The keys may be lighted to indicate a set from which choices are to be made to match the notes, intervals, melodies, etc. played by the machine. Incorrect keys are silent. Correct matches may be reinforced through the dispenser on the top of the machine, which delivers candy or tokens.

Source: *The Technology of Teaching* by B. F. Skinner. Copyright © 1968 by Meredith Corporation. Reproduced by permission of Appleton-Century-Crofts, Educational Division, Meredith Corporation.

Other Applications of Operant Conditioning

Though Skinner, his students, and his followers have developed the specific techniques just described, principles of operant conditioning have been applied in a variety of ways by other psychologists. Behavior modification, use of instructional objectives, performance contracting, and accountability all are derived—at least in part—from Skinner's experimentation and theory.

Behavior modification is a term used in many ways, but basically it refers to the use of operant conditioning techniques to—as the phrase indicates—modify behavior. In some cases, the behavior change is brought about by a literal application of the techniques Skinner uses on rats and pigeons. In one case (Wolf, Mees, and Risley, 1964) an autistic child who had been born with cataracts and who frequently exploded into violent temper tantrums could not be induced to wear corrective glasses even though he was doomed to permanent blindness without them. First of all, therapists extinguished his temper tantrums by making sure that they were never followed by reinforcing circumstances. Then the child was deprived of food and put in a room with several sets of empty eyeglass frames scattered about. Every time he picked up a frame, he was given something to eat. In time, his behavior was shaped so that he put the frames on his face in the proper position. At that point the frames were given lenses, and his sight was saved. Literal applications of Skinner's methods in controlling the behavior of hungry pigeons have been used by Lindsley (1960) and by Ayollon and Azrin (1965) in dealing with psychotic patients.

Techniques of behavior modification

More frequently, behavior modification does not involve inducing hunger to increase the impact of food as a reinforcer, but rather it consists primarily of reinforcing desirable responses while ignoring undesirable ones. In classroom settings, reinforcement may consist of praise, opportunities to engage in desired activities, candy or money, or tokens that can be traded in for prizes. Kinds of classroom behavior modified through such techniques vary from overall academic performance (Evans and Oswalt, 1967) to reducing classroom noise (Schmidt and Ulrich, 1969) and eliminating disruptive behavior (Thomas, Becker, and Armstrong, 1968). The term *educational engineering* is frequently used to refer to behavior modification applied to learning; a description of a comprehensive program for teaching emotionally disturbed students through consistent application of operant conditioning principles will be presented in Chapter 14.

Skinner's basic technique of deciding terminal behavior and then shaping behavior has been used by some theorists as a starting point for the development of *instructional objectives* that are used to structure learning experiences. (Instructional objectives will be analyzed in the next chapter.) Use of instructional objectives has in turn led to the development of the *learning for mastery* approach and to *performance contracting*. Both techniques consist of stating what is to be accomplished, arranging learning experiences to assist students to meet the stated goals, and evaluating student performance to determine if the objectives have been met. In a mastery approach, the student may achieve the objectives through learning procedures that may or may not be explicitly programmed. Almost all performance contracting approaches, however, use operant conditioning techniques. Materials are presented in step-by-step fashion, correct responses are reinforced with praise, candy, tokens, or money.

The concept of stressing terminal behavior and the idea of performance contracting have contributed to the development of *accountability*. When teachers specify detailed objectives for their students to achieve, and when companies are paid (or not paid) on the basis of the degree to which they produce previously agreed upon amounts of learning, a logical next step is

"Computerized" Systems of Instruction
Based on Operant Conditioning

Several systems of instruction combine two products of a technological society—computers and operant conditioning. In *Computer Managed Instruction* (CMI), the computer takes over functions a teacher may find it difficult to handle efficiently. These include storing information about students, teaching materials, test scores, etc., and analyzing the relationships of these various factors to suggest activities appropriate for individual students. An example of this use of computers is the *Program for Learning in Accordance with Needs* (PLAN) developed by J. C. Flanagan (1968). Under PLAN, units of instruction are arranged in two-week modules, and for each unit there are several alternate sets of materials and procedures. Considerable stress is placed on having the student select from among alternatives and direct his own learning. The computer handles test-scoring, record-keeping, scheduling, and analysis of student progress. In *Individually Prescribed Instruction* (IPI), developed by W. W. Cooley and Robert Glaser (1969), the entire curriculum in a subject is broken down into units. (A math curriculum, for example, features 430 specific objectives and 88 units of study.) The student in IPI takes a placement test that identifies his initial level of understanding and is then provided with a unit of appropriate difficulty. He works his way through the unit until he meets the objectives, then he goes on to the next unit.

In *Computer Assisted Instruction* (CAI), the computer functions essentially as a tutor. In some cases, students push buttons in responding to multiple-choice questions, in others the student responds by touching a cathode ray tube with a special light pen, in still others questions and messages appear on a TV-like screen. (For more complete information, see *Computer Assisted Instruction: A Book of Readings* edited by R. C. Atkinson and H. A. Wilson.)

(An approach that combines a form of computer with human manipulation of visual and auditory devices is the "talking typewriter" developed by Omar Khayyam Moore (1966). A child is seated in a booth containing an elaborate electric typewriter. The controller remains outside and observes through a one-way window. In Phase I, Free Exploration, the child manipulates the machine on his own. The controller sets it so that a recorded voice pronounces each letter as its key is struck. In Phase 2, Search and Match, a letter appears on a screen, and all keys except the correct one are locked. The child searches until he matches the projected letter. In Phase 3, Word Construction, a word is projected—for example, *barn*, along with a picture of a barn. The recorded voice gives instructions: "Space, b-a-r-n, barn." In Phase 4, Reading and Writing, sentences or brief stories are presented together with illustrations. Moore has taught preschoolers to read with his elaborate machine. Obviously, the cost of such a device limits its use, but one might employ some of the same techniques to teach slow-learning children to read by using an ordinary typewriter and substituting one's own voice and hands for the auditory and visual cues.)

to argue that teachers should be judged on the same general basis—in terms of their productivity.

This brief survey of educational innovations derived directly or indirectly from operant conditioning techniques should make it clear that the theories of Skinner have had wide-ranging influence on education. (The November 1972 issue of *Psychology Today* devotes several articles to analyses of how the work of Skinner has led to applications of operant conditioning principles in an astonishingly wide variety of situations.)

Skinner and His Critics

Chapters 1 and 2 introduced you to the differences of opinion between S-R associationists and cognitive-field theorists and also to criticisms of the associationist-environmentalist position by humanists (such as Highet) and governmental figures, so you are aware that programmed instruction has been attacked on several fronts. Here is a summary of some of the most frequent charges, together with Skinner's replies.

One criticism is that the theory is based on experiments performed on lower animals and that the student working on a program is being treated like an animal. Briefly, Skinner's answer to this criticism, noted in Chapter 2 (pp. 60–61), is that in early stages of research the study of relatively simple organisms has many advantages because it allows one to observe behavior in a simple, clear-cut form; he also contends that the results of such research are often valid for human beings as well. The fact that techniques developed with rats and pigeons have been successfully applied to human behavior is proof of this point.

Another charge is that programmed learning produces regimentation and limits creativity. Skinner replies, "In principle, nothing could be more regimented than education as it now stands" (1968, p. 90). He maintains, in fact, that programmed instruction actually *furthers* freedom in the sense that it reduces the aversive features of the learning environment and at the same time teaches techniques of self-management and self-reliance. Although a student completing a subject-matter program may not be allowed a great deal of freedom to be creative or to engage in original thought, Skinner argues that creativity can be taught separately through other programs. Crutchfield (1966) has developed such techniques, which will be described in the next chapter.

Critics also object to the fact that many programs are designed so that the student will answer almost every response correctly. They feel that easy material will be forgotten quickly and that the student will fail to develop perseverance and hence be unable to cope with difficult problems later on. Skinner responds:

> The standard defense of "hard" material is that we want to teach more than subject matter. The student is to be challenged and taught to "think." The argument is sometimes little more than a rationalization for a confusing presentation, but it is doubtless true that lectures and texts are often inadequate and misleading

by design. But to what end? What sort of thinking does the student learn in struggling through difficult material? It is true that those who learn under difficult conditions are better students, but are they better because they have surmounted difficulties, or do they surmount them because they are better? In the guise of teaching thinking we set difficult and confusing situations and claim credit for the students who deal with them successfully. (1968, p. 51)

Skinner acknowledges that a student may come to depend on a teaching machine, but he argues that a student may also come to depend on a teacher. He claims that machines, like human beings, can wean pupils away from dependence by use of appropriate techniques.

Still another charge is that programmed learning is just a glorified version of animal-training techniques that have been practiced for centuries and that such methods are so obvious everyone already knows the basic techniques of programmed instruction. Skinner does not deny this outright, but he argues that present-day programming is so refined and advanced that the original methods derived from animal training have been left far behind. When you finish this section, you might ask yourself whether before reading it you had already known everything Skinner has described or whether you developed some new thoughts about learning.

Finally, critics have protested that machines will eventually replace teachers. Skinner says, in rebuttal, that machines will actually *improve* the teacher's financial position by making it possible for him to teach more material to more students. And "in return for his greater productivity, he can ask society to improve his economic condition" (1968, p. 258). Skinner then refers to what Beardsley Ruml pointed out many years ago—the fact that teachers' salaries have not kept pace with those in other professions largely because their productivity has not increased at the same rate, that many teachers today are no more productive than teachers a hundred years ago. Notice how this emphasis on productivity ties in with the "cult of efficiency" in American education.

A key problem in Skinner's position is, of course, how do we measure productivity. By the number of students taught? By the percentage of students who pass multiple-choice tests based on programs? By the percentage of students who continue to study a given subject on their own? With so many conflicting criteria, a machine-aided teacher might find it extremely difficult to convince others that he deserves an increase in pay.

Unanswered Criticisms of Skinner

Even if you are reasonably satisfied with Skinner's defense of programmed instruction, it is important to recognize that some questions remain unanswered. Because Skinner has devoted his professional life to the study of operant conditioning and programmed instruction, he tends to regard it as the *only* way to teach. He seems to find it difficult to admit that other methods have advantages or that teaching machines have limitations.

Skinner's description of the shortcomings of current educational practice is a case in point. No one would deny that many aversive factors are involved in traditional teaching, but to imply that in a traditional school most children learn only to escape punishment is misleading. Nor does it seem fair to say that "the customary procedure [in the classroom] has been to maintain the necessary anxiety by inducing errors" (1968, p. 51). Machines do not have a monopoly on positive reinforcement. They may dispense it more consistently and efficiently than teachers, but it might be argued that these very qualities could render mechanical reinforcement less effective in the long run.

Furthermore, some of the aversive factors that Skinner criticizes in traditional schooling are also present in programmed instruction. Having pupils work on programs will not eliminate competition, for example—unless pupils are completely isolated from one another, which is impossible. Even if you *could* do away with competition in school, you wouldn't be able to prevent out-of-school comparisons. It is easy to picture the brightest girl in the class carrying on thus: "How far did *you* get today? *I* got to frame 79, and I've finished the whole program for spelling, and I . . ." Nor will programmed instruction eliminate grades and the negative pressure they generate. Skinner suggests that with programmed instruction any student who completes a program should get an A. But what happens when one child gets his A after two days of effort and his neighbor gets his after two *weeks*? Will such discrepancies reduce or magnify the aversive consequences of differences in performance?

An even more striking example of Skinner's enthusiasm for programmed learning is his claim that the manipulation of the teaching machine should alone be "reinforcing enough to keep a pupil at work for suitable periods every day" (p. 24). This overestimation of the inherent appeal of twirling knobs or pushing buttons may be due simply to wishful thinking. However, it could also reflect generalization from animal research. A pigeon that spends all its nonexperimental time in a diskless cage is understandably delighted when placed in a "rich" environment, for example, a cage with a disk and a food tray. The environment of a child, on the other hand, is far from sterile. In actual practice, teachers report that even primary-grade children rapidly lose interest in the purely manipulative aspects of machine instruction.

Apparently, Skinner's enthusiasm has prevented his seeing some of the deficiencies of programmed instruction. Many critics are especially dissatisfied with his attempt to refute the charge that programs limit creativity. Clearly, when the person composing a program decides in advance what is to be learned and how it is to be learned, a student has no opportunity to develop in his own way. He is limited by what the programmer knows and values and by how the programmer learned.

It is true that the student might use the material in an original way *after* he has finished the program, but there is the possibility that programmed instruction interferes with this process. For example, some students who have completed programs report that although they have progressed quickly and satisfactorily and feel that they have learned something, they aren't sure where to go from there. Typically, the next step is to take an exam, usually the multiple-choice type, which is highly similar to the program in that stimuli are presented and responses are chosen. But what happens *after* the exam? If the student cannot respond unless he is stimulated in the same way he was in the program or exam, he will rarely be able to apply what he has learned to real life situations.

What we are dealing with here is the subject of transfer, discussed in Chapter 2, which is basic to education. Ellis has pointed out (1965, pp. 69–70) that little research has been done on the transferability of programmed learning; in almost all studies the experimenter determines the degree of learning solely on the basis of each child's performance on a test given immediately after the completion of the program. Skinner maintains that the student can be taught to transfer ideas through separate programs designed for this purpose and that a properly written program will wean the student from the machine, but there is little evidence to back up this contention. On logical grounds alone, it seems reasonable to question the transfer value of programmed instruction. (Transfer will be discussed further in Chapter 7.)

Programmed Instruction and the Classroom Teacher

A brief historical sketch may help you to clarify your thoughts about the controversies that have just been described. When programmed instruction became popular in the 1950s, it was hailed by some educators as the answer to all school problems. Schools were envisioned in which each pupil would be assigned to a cubicle and spend most of his time manipulating teaching machines, watching televised lectures and demonstrations, and doing independent study. America's leading electronics manufacturers vied with each other to produce elaborate teaching machines, some of them capable of reinforcing the student with recorded vocal responses that approximated the effect of a warm, friendly teacher. Foundation grants and state and federal pilot programs multiplied at a rapid rate. School superintendents, already attuned to the business approach to education and eager to show that they were abreast of current developments, competed with one another to acquire both machines and grants.

Initial enthusiasm was followed by disappointment in many circles as some of the limitations of a primarily technological approach to education became apparent. For one thing, many publishers had issued hurriedly written materials in an effort to beat their competitors, and many of these "crash programs" (the pun was irresistible) proved ineffective. For another, the cost of the more elaborate computerized machines was so great that school systems were unable to buy them without some sort of subsidy, and most foundation and government grants were reserved for short-term pilot studies.

When performance contracting developed, however, uncertainty about programming was replaced by new enthusiasm. Educational technologists headed most of the companies that won contracts; thoroughly convinced of the values of operant conditioning in education, they set up learning situations that maximized applications of Skinner's teaching techniques. Materials were programmed in the most scientific manner possible, and traditional reinforcement in the form of the student's satisfaction in having provided correct answers and being given praise was supplemented, as noted, with tangible rewards such as candy and money.

By their very nature, performance contracts supply direct information about their effectiveness—if a majority of students exceed the agreed-upon criterion, the contracting company makes money; if most fail, the company is not paid. The first comprehensive report on the results of performance contracting appeared in 1972 in a pamphlet published by the Office of Economic Opportunity, *An Experiment in Performance Contracting: Summary of Preliminary Results.* Despite the care and consistency in planning and the use of rewards as reinforcement, the OEO report reveals that almost all of the performance contracts funded by the government failed to produce the agreed-upon amount of learning. Several companies went out of business. Thus operant conditioning techniques, tried out under close to optimum conditions and evaluated with great objectivity and sophistication, were proved less successful than had been hoped. The disappointing results might be explained in a number of ways: the performance contractors tried to do too much, or they did not take into account the extent of the lack of readiness of the pupils they worked with, or they were not given enough time to bring about improvement, or techniques for applying operant conditioning principles to school problems had not been completely perfected; or behavior modification methods may assist students to master specific responses (e.g., answers to workbook problems) but not basic skills that permit them to answer similar but different problems (e.g., questions on standardized tests).

Even though comprehensive applications of operant conditioning principles have not been completely successful, it is nonetheless clear that the technique is highly effective in *some* situations and with *some* pupils. If you are favorably impressed with Skinner's arguments—if you like the emphasis on reinforcement, the flexibility in adjusting to different rates of learning, and the efficiency of programmed instruction—you may well want to use it in your teaching. In that case, three avenues are open: You can write your own program, you can use someone else's programs, or you can try to apply behavior theory in the framework of the traditional classroom without actually using formal programs.

Writing Your Own Program

Composing a program from scratch requires considerable time, care, and expertise. If you feel inclined to try, you will need to consult one or more books written for novice programmers. Three of the best are *A Guide to Programmed Instruction* by Jerome P. Lysaught and Clarence M. Williams, *Good Frames and Bad: A Grammar of Frame Writing* by Susan Meyer Markle, and *Practical Programming* by Peter Pipe.

But even with the aid of these books, be prepared for some frustrations. For one thing, initial attempts to write a program are usually unsuccessful because of the difficulty of anticipating the different ways in which children will react. Remember, it is essential that almost all questions be answered correctly (Skinner sets the minimum at about 95 percent) in order to make the most of rein-forcement, avoid aversive consequences, and maintain continuity. Almost in-variably, original programs will "lose" many students because the programmer cannot anticipate how all children will respond and so he will fail to ask the right questions in exactly the right sequence.

Since programmed instruction provides detailed and permanent feedback in the form of answers supplied by the pupils, it would seem that a teacher could easily correct a program by examining these answers. One problem here is time. Obviously, only a painstaking analysis of all responses can reveal every programming error. Moreover, such an analysis sometimes has to be repeated several times, and this often produces subsidiary problems: The children may become bored when they are presented with the same program again, or their responses may not be valid because of their previous exposure to the questions.

In addition to the sheer amount of work involved in writing and testing programs, there is the problem of allowing for individual differences in ability. Skinner argues that programs do allow for differences because each child proceeds at his own rate, but this is not a complete answer. Every teacher, even one who deals with homogeneously grouped students, must pace a presentation so that it is not too fast for the slow learners and not too simple for the fast ones. The most common solution is an almost automatic tendency to concentrate on the slow students. When a teacher does this, she can be reasonably sure that she is getting through to the less able students even though the brighter ones may be bored.

Program writers have the same problem and usually arrive at the same solution. Markle (1963) notes that in order to insure that approximately 95 percent of the answers will be correct, as Skinner suggests, programmers are forced to keep revising programs for the *lowest common denominator*—the slowest students in the group. This eventually leads to programs that most students can complete fairly easily, but it also leads to programs that are oversimplified and repetitious. A slow student won't be bothered by this, but a bright pupil may become

Lowest-common-denominator effect

bored and absentminded, just as he would if he were listening to an overly simple lecture. If he can supply answers automatically, he may gain only superficial understanding or slide over a key point. And if he is irritated by the simplicity of the program, he may not even be willing to backtrack to find errors he has made. Of course, you could cope with the problem of ability differences by writing two sets of programs, but this would be possible only if you had an unlimited amount of time, which you will not have.

In view of all these problems, it is probably more realistic to assume that you will have to depend on using published materials if you wish to give programmed instruction a try.

Using Published Programs

Hundreds of programs have been published. They cover all sorts of subjects, and they vary considerably in quality. You can consult several journals to discover what is available: *The Journal of Programed Instruction, Programed Instruction* (the bulletin of the Center for Programed Instruction), and *Programed Instructional Materials* edited by Kenneth Komoski. If you have complete freedom to choose a program, in order to make sure you pick out a fairly decent one consult the book *A Guide to Evaluating Self-Instructional Programs* by Paul Jacobs, Milton Maier, and Laurence Stolurow.

You should realize, however, that even if you find a program that seems appropriate for your curriculum, that is rated as adequate, and that your school district can afford, you still face complications. It has been found, for example, that programs perfected on one group of children may not succeed with another group. This sometimes occurs because the curriculum in the standardization school was atypical in subtle ways and prepared the children for some of the questions. Children who are products of a different curriculum may be unable to answer these questions, and if they get off the track just once or twice, the entire program may be ineffective.

As mentioned earlier, you will also be faced with the task of holding down competition so that pupils don't race to see who can finish first. It seems logical to assume that a child who skims through a program is less likely to absorb it thoroughly than one who takes his time. You may want to disguise, as much as possible, the rates at which individual students are learning.

The fact that pupils finish the program at different times—which Skinner sees as an *advantage* of machine instruction—creates still another problem. Unless you are able to assign individual students one program after another, which is unlikely, you will be faced with the task of organizing activities for an ever-increasing number of pupils. Finding ways to occupy the time of rapid learners who complete an assignment early is not a problem unique to programmed learning, but the nature of machine instruction may require you to be especially ingenious in devising supplementary exercises until the entire class is ready to go on to another assignment.

Suggestions for Applying Operant Conditioning in the Classroom

Taking all these points into account, you may decide that the most realistic approach is to use selected aspects of programmed learning within the framework of the traditional classroom. In this section you will find some suggestions on how to do this—how to apply the principles and techniques of operant conditioning in your own classes. These suggestions are derived from the experiments described at the beginning of this section, and they have been developed in an attempt to make the most of the advantages and to minimize the disadvantages of programmed learning just described. A summary of the suggestions is given below to assist you to grasp the overall structure of this section in advance and to provide you with a concise list for future reference. The same practice is followed in the next section of this chapter and in succeeding chapters.

1. Remain aware of the extent and disadvantages of aversive control.
2. Provide as much reinforcement as possible—in most cases, immediately after a pupil responds.
3. If students generalize erroneously, use selective reinforcement to teach them to discriminate.
4. If you are teaching a subject that has clearly specified terminal behavior, organize the work into units, or steps, and present them in sequence.
5. If you are attempting to shape behavior by leading your students through a progressive sequence of stages, vanish your prompts properly.
6. Keep in mind the impact of different reinforcement schedules on the rate of extinction.
7. Be sure to consider the potential value of programmed instruction when working with the disadvantaged, with slow learners, or with pupils who lack self-confidence.
8. When appropriate, apply operant conditioning principles in shaping desirable forms of behavior and establishing and maintaining classroom control.

1. Remain aware of the extent and disadvantages of aversive control.

Many of the types of aversive control described by Skinner as typical of traditional educational practice will probably become almost automatic unless you do your best to remain aware of them. As you teach, you might ask yourself at frequent intervals if your students are learning primarily to avoid the unpleasant consequences of not knowing. You should also consider the wide-ranging impact of punishment, as demonstrated by Skinner's experiments in which rats were shocked until they learned: the rats learned rapidly, but they also forgot quickly and became afraid of the entire environment associated with the punishment. The punishment of sarcasm, ridicule, or severe criticism may produce similar results—rapid forgetting and a fearful or negative attitude toward school, which may block further learning.

2. Provide as much reinforcement as possible—in most cases, immediately after a pupil responds.

Although the teaching machine dispenses reinforcement more efficiently than a teacher, you can do many things to increase your effectiveness as a reinforcing agent.

As much as possible, set up learning situations that let you supply reinforcement immediately; for example, make it possible for students to check their answers as soon as they finish a unit. When you introduce a new subject of study, reinforce as many correct responses as possible. After students have developed a degree of mastery, the frequency of reinforcement may be reduced, but in most cases it should still be immediate. There may be times when students resent immediate feedback, particularly if they are eager to find answers on their own; but in general, the more immediate your reinforcement, the better.

Examples

Ask questions you are sure at least some of your students can answer.

Have some pupils work at the board while the others work at their desks.

After giving a problem go over the correct answer immediately afterwards.

When you assign reading or give a lecture or demonstration, have a short, self-corrected quiz or an informal question-and-answer session immediately afterward to check on how much the pupils really learned.

Hand back and discuss all exams. Even though your students may have written their answers a week earlier, they will still be getting "immediate" reinforcement by looking at the answer as you discuss it.

Have pupils team up with each other and engage in "programmed" question-and-answer sessions.

In the space below you might note other techniques you could use to get immediate feedback and give immediate reinforcement in your classes.

_____

_____

_____

_____

How Do You Feel About Tangible Rewards?

As noted, a feature of most performance contracting approaches is the use of tangible rewards. This technique can be traced partly to Skinner's experiments with rats and pigeons, in which food is used as the reinforcer. However, since performance contractors are engaged in the *business* of producing learning—or else no pay—it is unsurprising that they have made literal application of business methods to education. Since they are managers who are paid according to how much their "workers" produce, they pay those who come through for them. If you are ever held accountable for the exact amount of learning you produce in your students, you may find yourself thinking in the same terms. But many advocates of educational engineering (and some teachers who are not held strictly accountable for their productivity) use tangible rewards in their classes, even if they have no pressure on them to have students learn an agreed-upon amount of material.

What are the advantages and disadvantages of using tangible rewards to stimulate continued learning? Some who criticize them maintain that the tendency of Americans to think of life mainly in terms of acquiring material goods is too extreme already and that it should not be encouraged further in the schools. Some who favor tangible rewards argue that money is a more direct and honest reward than praise or gold stars. They point out that high grades will eventually be cashed in for jobs that provide higher salaries and argue that through proper management of reinforcement, social reinforcers such as praise can be programmed to gradually replace material rewards. What are your reactions to these views—and to the entire question of tangible rewards?

---

3. If students generalize erroneously, use selective reinforcement to teach them to discriminate.

Your students' generalizations will seldom be as obvious as those of Pavlov's dogs or Skinner's rats, but many pupils will be unable to discriminate between similar things. A first-grader may write the letter *p* when he means *q*, a fifth-grader learning a foreign language may confuse irregular verb forms, an art student in high school may find it difficult to distinguish between Manet and Monet. One way to combat this tendency is to be alert for it and provide opportunities for your students to indicate whether their understanding is clear or confused.

Once you become aware of confusion, you can counter it with selective reinforcement. When a student prints the letter in the correct way, for example, reinforce it by saying something like, "That's right. The *p* has the line on the left." If he uses the wrong form, withhold reinforcement.

4. If you are teaching a subject that has clearly specified terminal behavior, organize the work into units, or steps, and present them in sequence.

Even if you don't actually write a program, you might use the same basic approach to prepare a lecture or arrange a demonstration; a study by Roe (1960) found that a programmed lecture is just as effective as a machine program. In the space provided you might note aspects of the subject matter you will be teaching that strike you as suited to a programmed approach. You might also try to sketch out a frame or two just to get the feel of it.

During your first year of teaching, you might also try to write an entire program, even if you can't perfect it. Skinner maintains that you can learn a lot about conventional teaching by doing this: "The programmer will usually find that he has been accustomed to leave much to the student—that he has frequently omitted essential steps and neglected to invoke relevant points" (1968, p. 50).

Subjects or units you might try to program:

_____

_____

_____

_____

First attempt at writing a frame for a unit in a future class:

_____

_____

_____

_____

_____

_____

_____

_____

_____

_____

_____

5. *If you are attempting to shape behavior by leading your students through a progressive sequence of stages, vanish your prompts properly.*

You might take a cue from the program depicted in Figure 5–4 and the description on p. 218 of how pupils are taught poems and vocabulary words.

Start out with complete information and progressively reduce the amount of prompt.

Examples

Using the overhead projector, print a spelling word; then cover up parts of the word and ask your pupils to supply the missing letters. Gradually work up to a completely verbal presentation with no visual cues. (Use Figure 5–4 as a guide.)

To teach your students the parts of a microscope, power tool, sewing machine, etc., use a labeled drawing or projected picture—or even the actual device with labels attached—and gradually vanish the cues.

In the space below you might note some other vanishing exercises to try in your classes:

_____

_____

_____

_____

_____

_____

_____

_____

6. Keep in mind the impact of different schedules of reinforcement on the rate of extinction.

Think back to the experiments described earlier, and you may recall that rats on variable reinforcement schedules are more persevering than those who are rewarded consistently. You might try to apply these findings to the classroom, although providing and evaluating variable reinforcement in classes will certainly not be as simple as it is in the laboratory. For example, there is a film on operant conditioning; it shows first some pigeon experiments depicting various schedules of reinforcement, then a classroom situation in which a boy is called on several times in a row when he raises his hand. Calling upon the boy reinforces his eagerness to recite, but the response is rapidly extinguished when the teacher abruptly stops calling on him. However, several experienced teachers who saw this film tried to duplicate the experiment in their own classrooms. They reported that as far as they could tell, varying the reinforcement schedule applied to hand-raising in actual classrooms made no difference. The same pupils put up their hands at the same rate regardless of the reinforcement supplied. The moral of this experience is obvious but worth noting: Children are not pigeons.

An animal that has no life outside a Skinner box and only a limited repertoire inside it may have its behavior shaped by a specific change in its environment precisely because its environment is so restricted. If all a pigeon sees are food pellets, sudden failure of the pellets to appear is a cage-shaking experience. But children are infinitely complex, and their behavior at any given moment may be influenced by countless stimuli within their environment and countless others outside it. If a pupil happens to be paying attention and wants more than anything in the world to please his teacher, he might be upset if he is not reinforced when he raises his hand. But if he is engrossed in examining the beautiful blond hair of the girl in front of him or in dreaming about the Little League game that evening, he won't care at all about not being reinforced. In fact, he won't even *realize* that he isn't being reinforced.

Some criticisms of delayed reinforcement can also be questioned on the same grounds; that is, responses produced in sterile environments may be not at all characteristic of those in rich environments. If a pigeon does not receive its food pellet immediately, it fails to see a connection between the act it performed and the reward. But human beings are fully capable of responding to delayed reward. Suppose a teacher says to a child, "By the way, I didn't have the chance to say anything last week because the bell rang, but I thought your report was excellent." This may be just as reinforcing as an immediate response. And most students seem to be reinforced by positive statements on a term paper that is read carefully and handed back even a month after it was "emitted."

Nevertheless, you might bear in mind that if responses aren't reinforced occasionally, they may be extinguished and that immediate reinforcement is normally most desirable. It is also possible that an occasional absence of reinforcement will help your pupils develop perseverance, although you may find it difficult to "manipulate" such behavior.

7. *Be sure to consider the potential value of programmed instruction when working with the disadvantaged, with slow learners, or with pupils who lack self-confidence.*

By providing feedback for every response and by arranging the questions so that almost all responses will be correct, programmed instruction furnishes constant positive reinforcement and also allows the student actually to *see* that he is learning. These advantages may be won at the cost of simplification and repetition, but for some pupils these two attributes are assets rather than liabilities. There are wide differences in the way individual pupils react to programs, but you may find teaching machines especially appropriate for children who come from disadvantaged homes, those who are slow learners, and those who are anxious about their ability to learn and therefore need signs of progress. All these children will probably thrive on the right reinforcement diet and the simple repetitive approach of a program. On the other hand, a bright, self-confident student who enjoys straying off on intriguing tangents may detest programmed instruction. This type of student may derive greater benefit from less structured forms of learning.

8. *When appropriate, apply operant conditioning principles in shaping desirable forms of behavior and establishing and maintaining classroom control.*

Behavior modification techniques can be used to hold down undesirable classroom behavior and shape positive and desired action. The basic technique is to be *consistent* in the way you strengthen desired behavior with positive reinforcement and to weaken undesirable behavior with punishment—if ignoring undesirable behavior does not lead to extinction. Many teachers make life difficult for themselves because they inadvertently strengthen behavior they want to weaken. This can occur if children get attention only when they are criticized; such criticism may be reinforcing. Or a teacher may think she is punishing when she is actually supplying reinforcement; for example, sending a wisecracking boy out of the room may be just what he wants and will increase rather than decrease his tendency to wisecrack. To avoid these situations, be alert to the way students react to reinforcement or punishment. You might also analyze your efficiency as a reinforcing agent. Wesley C. Becker, Siegfried Engelmann, and Don R. Thomas (1971) suggest using a wristband golf score counter or a grocery-shopping hand calculator to tally the number of times students are praised or criticized. They also suggest that teachers remind themselves to praise by giving out tokens or candy whenever they dispense positive reinforcement. They suggest that through such techniques teachers can shape their praising behavior by becoming more aware of it.[6] In addition, they recommend that activities such as going out to recess and passing out paper be used as rewards for desired behavior and not "given" away. This suggestion is based on a principle stated by David Premack (1965), who demonstrated how preferred activities can be used to reinforce less preferred ones. Another psychologist, Lloyd Homme (1966), converted this principle into what he calls "Grandma's Rule," variations of which are stated by Becker, Engelmann, and Thomas, in these terms:

Techniques of behavior modification

You do what I want you to do before you get to do what you want to do.

First you work, then you play.[7]

___

[6] If you ever want to make a *comprehensive* analysis of your teaching behavior, examine one or more of the observation scales that have been developed for that purpose: The Flanders Interaction Analyses technique (Amidon and Flanders, 1963), the Verbal Interaction Category System (Amidon and Hunter, 1967), the Observational System for Instructional Analyses (Hough, 1967), or the Observation Schedule and Record (Medley and Mitzel, 1963).

[7] "We allow our society to divide our lives and ourselves into two compartments, one for cognition, work, instrumental values, and ego skills, the other for all the rest of life; and we further insist of ourselves that the first compartment will take consistent precedence over the second. This creates a variety of human problems." (Keniston, 1970, p. 366)

To teach a child to carry out his responsibilities, require a less preferred activity to come before a more preferred activity (fun).

Activities the child likes to do can be used to reinforce things he cares less about.

Activities can be used as reinforcers. (1971, p. 28)

As with all applications of operant conditioning principles, you might establish classroom control by first deciding the terminal behavior you wish to achieve and then arrange circumstances to shape behavior by reinforcing steps in the desired direction. (More detailed suggestions for using operant conditioning techniques in establishing and maintaining classroom control are presented in Chapter 15.)

The book by Becker, Engelmann, and Thomas is a comprehensive manual for applying operant conditioning techniques. Many teachers who have taken courses in behavior modification report very favorable results in using it to control their students. If you react favorably to "Grandma's Rule" and the other suggestions just given, you may wish to read a book or take a course on behavior modification. Before you do, however, you might consider these points.

Some critics of controlled education argue that the primary reason teachers of such classes need to devote so much time to managing student behavior is because the pupils are being forced to engage in contrived learning. Advocates of free education argue that discipline problems are rare in free classrooms because the students are engaged in self-selected learning activities. Another point has to do with some of the possible disadvantages of reinforcement. When techniques such as those described by Becker, Engelmann, and Thomas are used too much, students may develop a "what will I get if I do this?" attitude or spend much of their time figuring out how to please the teacher—who is seen primarily as a dispenser of rewards. The basic principle of "Grandma's Rule" is described by Becker, Engelmann, and Thomas in this way: "If the child performs in the desired way, he gets the pay-off; if not, he does not." They offer the following examples as models of how "Grandma's Rule" might be applied: "Jeannie, you raised your hand, so I'm going to call on you to answer . . . Alice is all finished, so she can help me hand out these corrected papers . . . Jeffrey has been working hard. He can clean erasers for me today" (p. 28).

If such statements are used too frequently as reinforcers, competition for earning a prized activity as a reward could lead to anxiety, resentment, jealousy, and constant conniving. Advocates of "Grandma's Rule" claim that when one pupil gets reinforced for certain behavior, it rubs off on other pupils and causes them to behave in the same manner. It might also rub them the wrong way.

Still another difficulty is satiation. Pupils may at first respond to reinforcement in the form of praise or desired activity. But extensive use of premeditated reinforcement can make the school day appear to consist primarily of variations on a single theme—earning a pay-off. (It seems possible that this is one of the reasons performance contracting has failed.) Furthermore, it is likely that even quite young pupils eventually will catch on to the technique and realize how they are being manipulated. And if older pupils have heard about behavior modification, your efforts to apply operant conditioning principles may be immediately recognized and lead to countermeasures. For each of your attempts to shape the behavior of your students, they might carry out an experiment to shape *your* behavior; if you move to one side of the room, they may smile and act interested; if you move to the other side, they may frown and yawn. If they are successful, you will gravitate to the desired side of the room—which might provide more satisfaction than any reinforcement you could supply.

There may well be times when you want to use behavior modification techniques to improve your teaching or your control of the class, and you may find that an awareness of reinforcement will help you avoid *creating* problems, but occasional use would seem to be preferable to full-time application. If you devote too much time to shaping behavior, you may become so preoccupied with control and the dispensation of reinforcements that you will lose all spontaneity and naturalness. Instead of a place where students learn by satisfying their own needs, you may create an environment where students are trained to believe that learning takes place only to satisfy others.

At this point, you may be asking yourself how well equipped you are to teach now that you have read about programmed instruction. If you will be teaching subjects that possess clearly defined terminal behavior, you may have found much to your liking. If, on the other hand, you will be teaching less systematic and specific material, you may feel that Skinner's approach has little you can sink your teeth into. If that's the case, you will be especially eager to learn more about cognitive-field theory, the *other* main approach to learning, which is discussed in the remaining pages of this chapter.

Cognitive-Field Theory and the Discovery Approach

Experiments of Köhler

In the 1920s, at about the same time that Thorndike was propounding and revising his laws, a group of German psychologists began experimenting with chimpanzees. The man who eventually emerged as the leading spokesman for this group was Wolfgang Köhler.

Köhler's most famous experiment, which was mentioned in Chapter 2, involved

Figure 5–7 Köhler's Most Famous Experiment. Sultan first raked in the long stick with a shorter one and then used the long stick to rake in the banana. He solved the problem by perceiving the relationship among the three objects.

Köhler: stick problem solved by ape through insight

a chimpanzee named Sultan.[8] Sultan was put in a large cage with a variety of objects including some short sticks (see Figure 5-7). He discovered that he could use a stick to rake things toward him when he was feeling lazy. One day Köhler put a banana and a very long stick outside the cage; both objects were too far for Sultan to reach with his arm, but the stick was closer than the banana. Sultan first picked up one of the short sticks in the cage and tried to rake in the banana. The stick wasn't quite long enough, and he threw it down and stomped off to another part of the cage in a fit of pique. As he sat brooding, his eyes suddenly focused on the two sticks and the banana, all arranged in a row. He jumped up, ran over to the small stick, used it to rake in the larger stick, and triumphantly raked in the banana. Köhler showed that the learning experience involved a rearrangement of Sultan's *pattern* of thought. The ape had previously raked things, but the idea of using one stick to rake another and then the banana involved a new application of his prior activity.

This experiment illustrates the essence of learning as viewed by a field theorist:

[8] For Köhler's own account of this experiment, see his *The Mentality of Apes* (1925).

the perception of new relationships. Sultan did not solve the problem by being conditioned or by trial and error; he solved it by gaining insight into the relationship between the two sticks and the banana. Some theorists argue Sultan may have been conditioned to rake things in the first place and that his insight consisted of mental trial and error, but the nature of his solution seems sufficiently different from these forms of learning to merit designation as a distinct kind of reaction.

Field theorists usually concede, however, that Sultan's previous experience with the essentials of the problem had been necessary in order for insight to take place and that insight had been facilitated by the arrangement of the environment. Sultan had previously raked things, and the sticks and banana were placed fairly close to each other. Other apes that had not had any raking experience or happened to face away from the sticks and banana, failed to solve the problem.

Influence of Lewin

Köhler's experiments stimulated other Gestalt psychologists to perform related experiments and to develop comprehensive theories, almost all of which emphasized the importance of insight. In this book Jerome Bruner has been chosen to represent contemporary psychologists who endorse the Gestalt point of view, with Arthur Combs and Donald Snygg as supplementary spokesmen. Also, in order to give credit where it is due, the work of Kurt Lewin (1951) will now be mentioned as an important step in the transformation of Gestalt psychology into cognitive-field theory.

Lewin was born and educated in Germany, and it seems likely that the prevailing German Zeitgeist influenced his development. His special interests in psychology centered around perception—perhaps because Wilhelm Wundt's interest in the field led to a "traditional" German concern for this topic—and motivation. (Perception, motivation, and the theoretical-deductive approach, also traditionally German, are the basic ingredients of Gestalt psychology.) Although a psychologist by profession, Lewin must have been something of a mathematician and physicist at heart because he applied concepts from these sciences to human behavior. More specifically, he devised a system of diagramming behavioral situations that reflected his familiarity with the *field of forces* concept of physics and that led to the use of the term *field theory.* Perhaps his single most influential contribution to psychology, however, was the concept of the *life space.*[9] As Lewin defined it, the life space of an individual consists of everything one needs to know about that individual in order to understand his behavior in a specific psychological environment at a specific time.

Lewin's concept of the life space

[9] For Lewin's own account of the life space concept and some of his diagrams of behavior, consult Chapter 15 in *Manual of Child Psychology*, 2nd ed., 1954, edited by Leonard Carmichael.

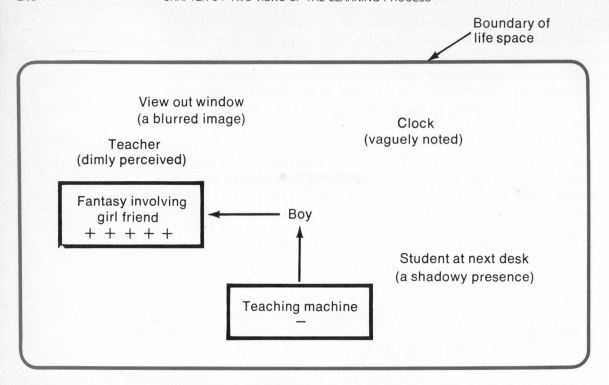

Figure 5–8 Life space of a Daydreaming Boy. This Lewinian diagram, together with an artist's conceptualization of it, depicts the life space of a high school boy seemingly at work on a teaching machine but actually thinking of other matters. The pluses and minuses indicate the degree of the boy's attraction being given to each activity, and the arrows show the direction of his attention.

In developing this concept, Lewin focused attention on one of the central ideas that separates S-R associationists from cognitive-field theorists, which was described in the statements by Combs and Snygg quoted in Chapter 2. To understand behavior, one should observe people not as they seem to others but as they seem to themselves. As Combs and Snygg put it, "People do not behave solely because of the external forces to which they are exposed. People behave as they do as a consequence of how things seem to them" (1959, p. 11). Figure 5–8 illustrates this perceptual point of view, the life space concept, and a Lewinian diagram all at the same time. It depicts the life space of a teenager who is supposedly working on his teaching machine but is actually thinking about what will happen when he has parked his car in a secluded spot after taking his girl to a drive-in movie.

Lewin was an inspiring teacher, and when he died in 1947, he left behind a devoted band of followers to carry on his work.[10] These followers proposed theories of learning based on the original insight experiments of Köhler and on the concepts of the life space and of fields of forces developed by Lewin. To illustrate the kind of teaching that has derived from these theories of learning, we shall now turn to some of Bruner's observations about the discovery approach and its underlying principles.

Bruner on Structure and Intuition

Since field theorists regard learning as a rearrangement of thought patterns, they stress the importance of structure and of providing opportunities for intuitive thinking in the classroom. In *The Process of Education,* Bruner lists four advantages of emphasizing structure in teaching:

> [1] Understanding the fundamentals makes a subject more comprehensible. . . . [2] Unless detail is organized into a structured pattern, it is rapidly forgotten. Detailed material is conserved in memory by representing it in simplified ways. . . . [3] An understanding of fundamental principles and ideas appears to be the main road to adequate transfer. . . . [4] Structure permits a person to narrow the gap between elementary and advanced knowledge. (1960b, pp. 23–26)

In view of the Gestalt emphasis on insight, it is not surprising that Bruner also stresses the importance of intuition in learning. Here are some of his observations on intuitive, as opposed to analytic, thinking:

> The emphasis in much of school learning and student examining is on explicit formulations, upon the ability of the student to reproduce verbal or numerical formulae. It is not clear, in the absence of research, whether this emphasis is inimical to the later development of good intuitive understanding—indeed, it is

---

[10] One of Lewin's pupils, Alfred J. Marrow, has written a highly regarded biography of him titled *The Practical Theorist* (1969).

242

even unclear what constitutes intuitive understanding. Yet we can distinguish between inarticulate genius and articulate idiocy—the first represented by a student who, by his operations and conclusions, reveals a deep grasp of a subject but not much ability to "say how it goes," in contrast to the student who is full of seemingly appropriate words but has no matching ability to use the ideas for which the words presumably stand.

In contrast to analytic thinking, intuitive thinking characteristically does not advance in careful, well-defined steps. . . . Usually intuitive thinking rests on familiarity with the domain of knowledge involved and with its structure, which makes it possible for the thinker to leap about, skipping steps and employing shortcuts in a manner that requires a later rechecking of conclusions by more analytic means, whether deductive or inductive.

It seems unlikely that a student would develop or have confidence in his intuitive methods of thinking if he never saw them used effectively by his elders. The teacher who is willing to guess at answers to questions asked by the class and then subject his guesses to critical analysis may be more apt to build those habits into his students than would a teacher who analyzes everything for the class in advance. (Pp. 55–62.)

A Unit Taught by the Discovery Method

To illustrate how Bruner converts these various ideas about structure and intuition into classroom practice, here is a social studies unit for fifth-grade pupils as briefly described in *Toward a Theory of Instruction*, Chapter 4: "The content of the course is man: his nature as a species, the forces that shaped and continue to shape his humanity. Three questions recur throughout: What

Jerome S. Bruner   Bruner was born in New York City in 1915. His family expected him to go into law, but he did not take enthusiastically to that discipline—or any other—during his undergraduate years at Duke University until an incident diverted him to an interest in psychology. He was threatened with expulsion from the university for cutting chapel when his psychology teacher, William McDougall, successfully intervened in his behalf. Impressed by this act, Bruner did some work in McDougall's psychology lab that led him to move on to Harvard and earn a Ph.D. in psychology. He remained at Harvard, where he became Director of the Center for Cognitive Studies, except for a year at the Institute for Advanced Studies at Princeton and for occasional lectureships here and abroad. Bruner is currently a member of the Department of Experimental Psychology at Oxford University. He served as president of the American Psychological Association in 1964, and in 1962 the APA honored him with its Distinguished Scientific Contribution Award.

is human about human beings? How did they get that way? How can they be made more so?" (1966, p. 74).

In seeking answers to these questions, the pupils study five subjects considered to be significant humanizing forces: toolmaking, language, social organization, the management of man's prolonged childhood, and man's urge to explain his world.[11] To give you an idea of how these subjects are studied, here is a brief account of the subunit on language:

Opening discussions are on the question of what communication is. One topic is the contrast between the ways in which human beings and animals send and receive messages. Each section of the subunit features a presentation by the teacher (e.g., a demonstration of how bees communicate by dancing) to provide structure. And there are class activities that demonstrate how pictures, diagrams, charades, and words refer to things; and games in which columns of words are arranged into a variety of sentences. Eventually, the topic of how language is acquired by children is explored, with a culminating section on the origins and functions of human language and the role of language in shaping human characteristics.

The four specific techniques used in presenting these topics are:

Bruner's techniques for encouraging discovery

Emphasizing contrast (e.g., contrasting man with animals, modern man with prehistoric man, man with child)

Stimulating informed guessing (e.g., asking the students to hypothesize how an Eskimo decides which breathing holes to stalk in hunting seals and then showing a film to illustrate how he actually *does* decide)

Encouraging participation (e.g., using games such as charades to illustrate concepts in language)

Stimulating awareness (e.g., having students analyze comic book detective stories to make them conscious of how they attempt to solve mysteries)

Bruner's approach to teaching—implicit in this description of a unit on man—is summarized in the following statement:

Bruner's version of field theory leading to the discovery approach

To instruct someone in [a] discipline is not a matter of getting him to commit results to mind. Rather, it is to teach him to participate in the process that makes possible the establishment of knowledge. We teach a subject not to produce little living libraries on the subject, but rather to get a student to think mathematically for himself, to consider matters as an historian does, to take part in the process of knowledge-getting. Knowing is a process, not a product. (1966, p. 72)

---

[11] The Curriculum Materials for *Man: A Course of Study* may be obtained from Curriculum Development Associates, Inc., 1211 Connecticut Ave., N.W., Washington, D.C., 20036.

If you are in sympathy with aspects of this approach, you are urged to get a copy of *Toward a Theory of Instruction* as a companion volume to Skinner's *The Technology of Teaching.* Having both books in your professional library will provide you with a comprehensive set of observations on learning. (At this point, you might think a bit about how you would program a course in the study of man. What sort of program would you write? Would you enjoy writing such a program more than leading Bruner-style discussions?)

Variations of *Man: A Course of Study*

Bruner's *Man: A Course of Study* has prompted others to develop their own variations of this approach. If you feel that you would like to institute such a unit in your classes, you might find it valuable to read about the adaptations made by others.

In *Fantasy and Feeling in Education*, Richard M. Jones argues that Bruner's technique is too sterile and suggests that discovery sessions should be arranged to stimulate pupils' "emotional and imaginal responses" (1960, p. 9). He describes class sessions in which the Bruner materials were tried out and says that the most meaningful learning took place in a situation of "controlled emotion" (p. 25). He describes the values—as well as the dangers—of an approach that stresses emotion and imagination, and in Chapters 7, 8, and 9 of his book offers suggestions as to how it might be put into practice.

In an article in the June 1971 issue of *Theory into Practice*, Peter B. Dow analyzes the social implications of the Bruner curriculum with reference to Jones's *Fantasy and Feeling in Education* and Paolo Freire's *Pedagogy of the Oppressed.*

In *The Lives of Children* George Dennison asserts that Bruner is too concerned with "control, social engineering, manipulation" (1969, p. 253). He suggests that the discovery approach is more effective when it is arranged so that students can interact with the teacher and each other in situations in which they are free to reveal themselves. He presents his critique and describes ways to improve on the Bruner approach (as well as education in general) in Chapter 12 of his book.

In Chapters 5, 6, and 7 of *Teaching Strategies for the Culturally Disadvantaged*, Hilda Taba and Deborah Elkins describe units that are similar to those in Bruner's *Man*, although they were developed independently. The chapters, which comprise a unit called "The Family of Man," are titled "Human Hands," "Walls in Our Life," and "Aspirations." Although the techniques described were developed for use with disadvantaged junior high school pupils, they can be adapted for use at almost any grade level and with all types of students. The suggestions for arranging class sessions and developing specific topics are more detailed and concrete than Bruner's and should prove especially valuable if you are not quite sure how to institute a discovery approach on *Man.*

Teaching for Memory, Understanding, and Reflection

Although Bruner, and Combs and Snygg, provide excellent accounts of learning from a cognitive-field theory point of view, perhaps the most comprehensive and scholarly analysis of the cognitive-field theory approach to teaching is found in *Learning Theories for Teachers* by Morris L. Bigge. (Most of this book is incorporated in *Psychological Foundations of Education,* 2nd ed., by Bigge and Maurice P. Hunt.) Bigge offers a more systematic and detailed treatment of essentially the same ground covered by Bruner and by Combs and Snygg. In the last chapter of *Learning Theories for Teachers*, he distinguishes three levels of learning and teaching that merit mention:

Bigge assigns the name *memory level* learning and teaching to the committing of facts to memory by students. He argues that although facts learned this way may eventually be used to solve problems, pure memorization is ineffective because in the absence of meaning, facts are quickly forgotten.

Understanding level learning and teaching, in Bigge's terminology, involve the perception of relationships. Instead of memorizing an assortment of facts, the student gains an understanding of a smaller number of principles that he can use in solving future problems. As Bigge defines it, understanding level learning and teaching involve control by the teacher—students are essentially passive and are told what the principles are and how they might be used.

Bigge argues that although the understanding level is to be preferred to the memory level, *reflection level* learning and teaching are even better. In this approach, students are required to participate actively in developing insight by attacking a problem posed by the teacher. Bigge suggests three general techniques for producing especially effective discussion:

Bigge's techniques for encouraging discovery

Switch the subject matter (e.g., try to convince students in a political science class that the federal government should not interfere with the economy, and when they have accepted the idea, ask them whether they favor protective tariffs for specific products).

Introduce disturbing data (e.g., show a movie that depicts ideas contrary to those the students take for granted).

Permit students to make mistakes (e.g., allow something to go wrong in a problem or experiment, and then ask the students why it happened).

Bigge admits that the reflective level approach requires free discussion and lots of time and therefore is inappropriate to a rigid schedule. But he maintains that if the proper conditions can be met, the approach is usable in most subject areas, at most grade levels, and with children of all levels of ability. He also offers evidence that students who successfully use the reflective method are highly motivated, tend to score higher than others on standardized achievement tests, show a gain in critical insight, and use their learning outside of class. It should be noted that these results are from studies done by people who *believed* in the reflective approach, so contagious enthusiasm may have affected student performance in a type of Hawthorne effect.

In reflection level teaching, students participate actively in developing insight.

Summary of Arguments for the Discovery Approach

Most of the arguments of those who advocate the discovery approach have already been mentioned, but they will be summarized here to provide a concise case for the field theory conception of teaching.

Bruner claims that teaching that emphasizes structure (a basic feature of his version of the discovery approach) makes subject matter more comprehensible, minimizes forgetting, is more likely to lead to transfer, and makes it easier for the student to progress from elementary to advanced knowledge. He also argues that it is an ideal way to encourage the most mature mode of thought—the symbolic mode. Finally, he maintains that it leads to intuitive understanding, a type of understanding he regards as not only exciting to students but also very likely to increase their self-confidence and self-reliance.

In *Individual Behavior*, Combs and Snygg argue that a student taught by the discovery method is more likely to acquire favorable attitudes toward a particular subject and toward learning in general, with the result that he will probably continue to learn; he will sense that the teacher has made an effort to consider how pupils feel about what they are learning. In addition, Combs and Snygg share Bruner's belief that a pupil who learns by discovery is more likely to acquire a sense of adequacy. They maintain that too much exposure to lectures, texts, or programs tends to make a student dependent on others and minimizes the likelihood of his seeking answers or solving problems on his own.

As just now mentioned, Bigge offers evidence to substantiate many of these claims. He reports that when taught by the reflective approach (his version of the discovery method), students are highly motivated, score higher on all types of tests, gain in critical insight, and are more likely to participate in out-of-class study. An advocate of the discovery approach would attribute these positive results to the fact that such students are actively involved in learning, which leads to deeper understanding and better memory, and that they expend intellectual effort in discovering ideas on their own, which causes them to place a higher value on what they have learned.

Criticisms of the Discovery Approach

S-R associationists counter these arguments by focusing on the disadvantages and weaknesses of the discovery method. In *The Technology of Teaching*, for example, Skinner levels the following criticisms at the discovery approach:

> [The method of discovery] is designed to absolve the teacher from a sense of failure by making instruction unnecessary. The teacher arranges the environment in which discovery is to take place, he suggests lines of inquiry, he keeps the student within bounds. The important thing is that he should tell him nothing.
>
> The human organism does, of course, learn without being taught. It is a good thing that this is so, and it would no doubt be a good thing if more could be learned in that way. Students are naturally interested in what they learn by themselves because they would not learn if they were not, and for the same reason they are more likely to remember what they learn in that way. There are reinforcing elements of surprise and accomplishment in personal discovery which are welcome alternatives to traditional aversive consequences. But discovery is no solution to the problems of education. A culture is no stronger than its capacity to transmit itself. It must impart an accumulation of skills, knowledge, and social and ethical practices to its new members. The institution of education is designed to serve this purpose. It is quite impossible for the student to discover for himself any substantial part of the wisdom of his culture, and no philosophy of education really proposes that he should. Great thinkers build upon the past, they do not waste time in rediscovering it. It is dangerous to suggest to the student that it is beneath his dignity to learn what others already know, that there is something ignoble (and even destructive of "rational powers") in memorizing facts, codes, formulae, or passages from literary works, and that to be admired he must think in original ways. It is equally dangerous to forego teaching important facts and principles in order to give the student a chance to discover them for himself. Only a teacher who is unaware of his effects on his students can believe that

children actually discover mathematics, that (as one teacher has written) in group discussions they "can and do figure out all the relationships, facts, and procedures that comprise a full program in math."

There are other difficulties. The position of the teacher who encourages discovery is ambiguous. Is he to pretend that he himself does not know. . . . Or, for the sake of encouraging a joint venture in discovery, is the teacher to choose to teach only those things which he himself has not yet learned? Or is he frankly to say, "I know, but you must find out" and accept the consequences for his relations with his students?

Still another difficulty arises when it is necessary to teach a whole class. How are a few good students to be prevented from making all the discoveries? (1968, pp. 109–111)

All these criticisms may be true in certain situations. A generally ineffective and incompetent teacher (or even a generally effective teacher on an off day) might resort to generalizing about the marvelous by-products of discovery to cover up his own inadequacy. In point of fact, those who back discovery to the hilt sometimes carry on about the virtues of *any* kind of experience. John Holt is an excellent example. In *How Children Fail* and *How Children Learn*, he comments on the deep educational significance of trivial activities (e.g., repeatedly picking up a magazine dropped by a two-year-old, engaging in a "spanking" game with preschoolers), and he writes fondly about essentially pointless exercises (e.g., inscribing numbers on rolls of paper). Many people share Holt's belief that there is too much concern for measurable learning in American schools, but it seems a bit absurd to claim that *everything* a child does on his own has deep—and immeasurable—educational value. A teacher who does this often may well be simply trying to absolve himself and his students from a sense of failure.

Even for a teacher who is outstandingly effective and competent in using the discovery method, occasional failure is inevitable simply because not all discovery sessions are likely to be productive. Skinner has pointed out the undeniable truth that genuine discovery is rare inside *or* outside the classroom. The most ardent believers admit that discovery is so inefficient and time-consuming that learning frequently proceeds fitfully. And since mastery of minimum amounts of material is a prerequisite for higher education in the United States, students who are exposed only to the discovery approach may not learn enough to qualify for admission to most colleges and universities. Even when this somewhat arbitrary requirement imposed by our educational system is disregarded, it seems reasonable to question whether students would learn much through exclusive use of the discovery method. And is there really anything wrong with having an enthusiastic person tell others what he has learned?

It must be acknowledged that many interpersonal problems arise when the discovery method is used. For one thing, students may become frustrated if the teacher refuses to tell them what he obviously knows, especially on days when discussion has been disorganized and unproductive. For another, it is

Some Reactions to Summerhill

In *Walden Two*, Skinner describes a fictional Utopia based entirely on the principles of operant conditioning.* In *Summerhill,* A. S. Neill describes that school, where the discovery approach is essentially a way of life. Unlike Skinner's imaginary society, Summerhill has been in existence for more than forty years. How does such an all-out, consistent experiment in teaching by discovery work out in practice? Neill provides selected evidence in *Summerhill* to back up his contention that a self-demand approach to education is highly successful. A more objective and systematic evaluation of the school has been presented by Emmanuel Bernstein (1968).

Bernstein went to England, visited Neill at Summerhill, bought a motor scooter, and then called on fifty graduates of the school. In his interview with Neill, Bernstein was told that most of the graduates went into "the arts." He found, however, that the occupations of the fifty graduates he talked with were typical of the general population and did not include a great many artists.

He also found wide differences in personal reactions to the school. Ten of the fifty graduates had nothing but praise for Summerhill. They felt that their experience at the school "had given them confidence, maturity, and had enabled them to find a fulfilling way of life" (p. 38). On the other hand, seven of the fifty felt Summerhill had been harmful to them. Most of these felt that their experience at the school had "led them to find more difficulty in life than they might have otherwise experienced" (p. 40). An interesting point that emerged from the interviews was that those who had stayed at Summerhill for the *fewest* number of years tended to feel that they had benefited the most; those who had attended the longest "appeared most likely to have difficulty and tenacious adjustment problems" (p. 40).

Perhaps the most significant point of all was the finding that "the majority of Summerhillians had only one major complaint against the school: the lack of academic opportunity and inspiration, coupled with a dearth of inspired teachers" (p. 41). Few of the graduates who had children of their own sent them to Summerhill. Some who did not have children at the time they were interviewed indicated that they might send their offspring to the school but only for a few years before the age of ten or so.

---

* In "Commune: A Walden-Two Experiment," an article that begins on page 35 of the January 1973 issue of *Psychology Today*, Kathleen Kinkade describes life at Twin Oaks, a commune near Richmond, Virginia, that has existed for five years. The article is an excerpt from her book *A Walden Two Experiment: The First Five Years of Twin Oaks Community.*

A Saturday-night General Meeting at Summerhill, which is attended by everyone at the school and led by one of the older students. At these meetings, both teachers and students vote on the rules that govern their community and on the sanctions imposed against those who break them.

highly likely that, as Skinner suggests, one or two pupils will tend to monopolize the discoveries since a whole class will rarely experience insight at the same moment. And it seems probable that this situation will create jealousy, resentment, or feelings of inferiority in students who never come up with a discovery of their own. When a *teacher* presents a perceptive explanation, this problem doesn't exist.

Another interpersonal difficulty arises from the fact that only one person can speak at a time. There are techniques, such as buzz sessions, that the teacher can use to distribute recitation opportunities, but no matter what he does, one pupil will inevitably function as a lecturer, and the rest of the group will be forced at least temporarily into the role of listeners. As listeners, they may be less involved—and enlightened—than they would be if they were working on a teaching machine, especially if the speaker is inarticulate and long-winded or given to prefacing every phrase with "I mean . . . you know." (Some college students complain about discussion courses because they say that they can listen to and argue with their classmates any time. In the classroom they prefer to hear what the teacher has to offer.)

Suggestions for Applying Cognitive-Field Theory in the Classroom

Even taking account of these limitations of the discovery approach, there are many ways you might use field theory ideas in your classroom. Here are some suggestions on how to do so.

1. The first step is to establish a relaxed atmosphere.
2. Next, structure the discussion by presenting a provocative issue or question that will encourage the development of insight.
3. Once the discussion is under way, do your best to keep it on the track. Redirect digressions back to the original subject. Question and analyze points made.
4. Keep in mind the importance of structure in promoting comprehension of new relationships.
5. Consider the possibility that the discovery method is most appropriate for bright, confident, highly motivated pupils and for topics that lack clear terminal behavior.
6. Make use of the techniques of open education.
7. Consider the possibility that attitudes are more important than subject matter, that how you teach is more important than what you teach.

1. *The first step is to establish a relaxed atmosphere.*

For the discovery method to work properly, pupils must feel free to express ideas without fear of ridicule or failure. Combs and Snygg describe the ideal atmosphere for learning as free from threat. They also point out that in order for the learning of information to affect behavior, the individual must perceive the relationship of the information to himself and that the discovery of such personal meaning proceeds best in an unhurried, unharried atmosphere. They further argue that "making mistakes is an essential part of learning, and where errors are not permitted there is likely to be little learning" (1959, p. 396). Skinner, of course, flatly disagrees and does his best to eliminate mistakes so that there will be as much positive reinforcement as possible. (Ask yourself this question: Is making a mistake in a relaxed conversation and being corrected by someone else always an aversive experience?)

Even if you feel personally able to create a relaxed atmosphere, some practical matters still must be considered. First of all, the current emphasis on providing an individualized schedule for each pupil may make it difficult for you to keep the same group of pupils together for very long. Team teaching also complicates things for an advocate of the discovery approach. And perhaps most important, requirements established by state or local education departments and hierarchical curricula within a school system may restrict your freedom. Given the "cult of efficiency" in American education, school boards and administrators are seldom sympathetic to teaching techniques that don't produce immediate and tangible results. Consequently, you may be required to make sure that your students master quite specific tasks (e.g., that they complete a program or pass a particular test). All these factors indicate that you may need to do some ingenious arranging to use the discovery approach in an unhurried way.

2. *Next, structure the discussion by presenting a provocative issue or question that will encourage the development of insight.*

This is the crux of the discovery approach. The basic idea is to *arrange* things so that insight will take place, just as Köhler arranged the sticks and banana so that Sultan would perceive the relationship between them. You can present a question that emphasizes just one point, or you can try to encourage understanding of several related ideas. Topics will, of course, vary with grade level and subject area. In deciding how to use the discovery approach in your own classes, you may want to consider the techniques described by Bruner—and also those discussed by Bigge in the next-to-last supplementary note. Here is a combined list of these techniques, together with a specific application of each one. In the spaces provided you might describe similar applications you could use when you begin to teach. In thinking about possibilities, keep in mind that the gaining of insight depends on appropriate previous experience.

Emphasize contrast (e.g., contrast animal behavior with human behavior).

_____

_____

_____

_____

Stimulate informed guessing (e.g., ask students to speculate on how an Eskimo stalks seals, then show a movie on the subject).

_____

_____

_____

_____

Encourage participation (e.g., have students engage in games like charades).

_____

_____

_____

Stimulate awareness (e.g., have students analyze detective stories to make them conscious of how they attempt to solve mysteries).

_____

_____

_____

Switch the subject matter (e.g., convince students that the government shouldn't interfere with private enterprise, then ask them how they feel about specific tariffs).

_____

_____

_____

Introduce disturbing data (e.g., show a movie that depicts ideas contrary to those that students take for granted).

_____

_____

_____

_____

Permit students to make mistakes (e.g., allow an experiment to be set up the wrong way, and after things go wrong, ask the students to speculate on the reasons).

_____

_____

_____

_____

If you can think of any other applications that seem appropriate for discovery sessions but do not fit into any of these categories, jot them down here.

_____

_____

_____

_____

_____

3. *Once the discussion is under way, do your best to keep it on the track. Redirect digressions back to the original subject. Question and analyze points made.*

Some advocates of the discovery method assert that *any* discussion has value and thereby strengthen Skinner's argument that the method is set up to make instruction unnecessary. If you are going to function as a leader, you should exert some control. It is usually best, for example, to steer a discussion back to a central theme if digressions develop. Nevertheless, you may sometimes find it better to let the class pursue an irrelevant but important topic; in any case your control should always be subtle and indirect to maintain an unharried atmosphere.

In dealing with tangential remarks, remember the opinion by Combs and Snygg that "making mistakes is an essential part of learning" and Bruner's statement that "intuitive thinking characteristically does not advance in careful, well-defined steps." And you might keep in mind this additional point made by Bruner: "It seems unlikely that a student would develop or have confidence in his intuitive methods of thinking if he never saw them used effectively by his elders" (1960, p. 62).

4. *Keep in mind the importance of structure in promoting comprehension of new relationships.*

The aim of the discovery approach is to produce some relatively specific insight in the minds of most, if not all, class members—in other words, to impel

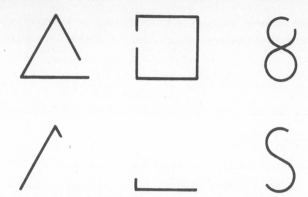

Figure 5–9 Closure. After looking at the top three figures briefly, one sees them as complete. This perceptual tendency illustrates the Gestalt principle called *closure*. The bottom figures, however, are too incomplete for closure to take place.

students to reorganize their perceptions in some fairly definite way so that they grasp new relationships. Therefore, completely open-ended discussions that trail off without any kind of conclusion are usually undesirable—unless, of course, the students are dealing with personal opinions and have been exposed to a variety of stimulating ideas.

The Gestalt principle of *closure* emphasizes this idea. In Figure 5–9 you will find the type of designs used in experiments conducted by field theorists. When subjects are shown the bottom set of figures for a few seconds and asked to reproduce them from memory, they depict the designs quite accurately. But most subjects do not produce faithful copies of the upper figures; they tend to close the gaps and depict *complete* designs. The principle behind this

*Gestalt principle of
closure*

perceptual tendency also applies to behavior. People tend to want to close discussions and activities, to find solutions to problems. Therefore, if discovery sessions repeatedly fail to provide any closure at all, your students may become frustrated and develop a distaste for the technique. In a sense programmed learning is effective in providing closure, for even if a student does not finish a program, the completion of even a few frames gives him a sense of accomplishment. However, this aspect of programmed learning may also be *un*desirable because of a phenomenon related to closure.

B. Zeigarnik (1927) demonstrated the tendency for students to recall unfinished tasks and to forget completed ones. The explanation she offered was that a "tension system" builds up within an individual until a task is finished. Thus the feeling of accomplishment engendered by filling in separate frames on a program may lead to forgetting when the task is finished, whereas a sense of dissatisfaction induced by an incomplete discovery session may predispose students to remember and want to return to the subject. In fact, some advocates of the discovery approach (Postman and Weingartner, 1969) urge teachers to deliberately cut off discussions before closure is achieved on the assumption that the participants will be more likely to remember what has been analyzed and more inclined to complete the learning experience on their own.

Bruner (1966, p. 119), however, suggests that the Zeigarnik effect holds only if a task has structure, that is, a specific beginning, a recognizable sequence, and a clear-cut end result. You should keep this in mind if you attempt to take advantage of the Zeigarnik effect; do not expect your students to remember a discussion or feel impelled to seek answers out of class simply because you end a disorganized discovery session at some arbitrary point. It will be necessary for you to establish structure and help students make considerable progress toward finding a solution before you cut off discussion.

The suggestion that you structure discovery sessions implies that you should have a specific idea of what you want your students to learn before you start. However, you need to be flexible enough to allow your students to take a somewhat different tack or go beyond what you figured out by yourself. This is what Bigge means by reflection-level teaching. If you give your students a chance, you may be amazed at how much you can learn from them. This is, in fact, an important advantage of the discovery approach as opposed to programmed learning.

5. Consider the possibility that the discovery method is most appropriate for bright, confident, highly motivated pupils and for topics that lack clear terminal behavior.

Although many advocates of the discovery method maintain that it can be used at all grade levels, with pupils of all levels of ability, and with all subjects of study, it is clearly more appropriate in some situations than in others. There is a strong possibility, for example, that very young children do not derive full benefits from the method. This is suggested by Piaget's observation that such children may still be at the egocentric level of speech and also by the Baker study (summarized in Chapter 4), which indicated that primary-grade children find it difficult to stay on the track in class discussion. In addition, it seems reasonable to conclude that although bright, confident pupils who are excited about school and learning might thrive on a steady diet of discovery, slow pupils—after repeatedly observing their classmates beaming with satisfaction at the moment of insight—might become discouraged. Furthermore, pupils who aren't particularly interested in school, for whatever reason, and those who have a strong need to feel that they have accomplished something might be better off working on teaching machines than napping through class discussions.

As for subject matter, some topics, such as man or personal reactions to literary works, are tailor-made for discussion. Other topics, such as how to operate a power saw or a theory in chemistry, are simply not suitable. It seems absurd

Different Styles of Conceptualization

Impulsive and reflective thinkers

Jerome Kagan (1964a, 1964b) has done a series of studies on the styles of conceptualization manifested by different children. He has concluded that some children seem to be characteristically *impulsive*, whereas others are characteristically *reflective*. He notes that impulsive children have a fast conceptual tempo; they tend to come forth with the first answer they can think of and are concerned about giving quick responses. Reflective children, on the other hand, take time before they speak; they seem to prefer to evaluate alternative answers and to give correct responses rather than quick ones. Kagan discovered that when tests of reading and of inductive reasoning were administered in the first and second grades, impulsive pupils made more errors than reflective pupils. He also found that impulsiveness is a general trait; it appears early in a person's life and is consistently revealed in a great variety of situations.

Analytic and thematic thinkers

Kagan has also described *analytic* and *thematic* styles of conceptualization. He reports that analytic students tend to note details when exposed to a complex stimulus, whereas thematic students respond to the pattern as a whole. Kagan found that these styles are just as permanent and generalized as impulsiveness and reflectivity.

Awareness of these varying styles of conceptualization may help you understand (in part, at any rate) the wide individual differences in the way your pupils will react to different approaches to teaching. An impulsive student, for example, may ruin class discussion by blurting out the first thing that pops into his head, upstaging the reflective types who are still in the process of formulating more searching answers. To minimize this possibility, you may want to have an informal rotation scheme for recitation or sometimes require that everyone sit and think about a question for two or three minutes before answering.

Thematic students may thrive on the global aspects of the discovery approach but be frustrated by the step-by-step detail of a program. Analytic students, on the other hand, may feel uncomfortable with open-ended discussions but delight in proceeding frame by frame.

These characteristics seem to be somewhat independent of intelligence. Therefore, in deciding whether programmed learning or the discovery approach is appropriate for certain students, consider not only their intellectual ability but also their conceptual styles. Even if you can't accurately classify a child as one type or another, you will at least be aware of some of the reasons why one technique does not appear to work equally well with all types of pupils.

to deliberately avoid telling pupils something others have already learned or figured out merely for the sake of letting them try to discover it on their own. And, as noted earlier, students may prefer the teacher's insight to that of a classmate. Most important of all, you may find that by disclosing information in an efficient way, you can produce many more experiences of insight than the pupils could if left to themselves.

6. *Make use of the techniques of open education.*

Many techniques of open education are congruent with the discovery approach. The themes of open education described by Walberg and Thomas provide a general description: Allow for involvement and activity, encourage and permit students to learn from each other, structure and organize materials, use tests to diagnose and aid learning, establish a warm and accepting classroom climate. In *Open Education: Promise and Problems*, Vito Perrone gives more detailed information about specific practices. He points out that there are many interpretations of this approach but that most open classes feature the following common attributes:

Activity.   Typically, many activities are going on at one time, and children are free to move from one activity to another. The classroom atmosphere is relaxed and students are encouraged to talk to each other.

Learning areas.   Open classrooms usually are divided into separate learning areas by screens, bookcases, and planters. At the elementary level, it is common to find special areas for art, reading, language arts, science, math, drama, woodworking, etc.

Cooperative planning.   At the beginning of the day in an elementary level open class, students commonly are permitted to engage in free, self-selected examination of materials in the various learning areas. After an hour or so, the class will be called together for a planning session. The teacher may describe some activity or call attention to additions to learning centers, and students are invited to describe books or activities they have found especially interesting. Then, each student draws up a personal plan for the day. These plans may include designated times when selected students will meet with the teacher in small groups for instruction in specific skills, for example, using reference materials, taking advantage of context in reading. At the end of the day, the students come together again and describe the activities they have found especially interesting or instructive.

Individualized planning.   The teacher attempts to concentrate on the learning of individual pupils. She observes individuals, converses with them, keeps records of their progress (to the point of writing something about each child every day), and collects records that pupils keep of their own activities, as well as actual exercises or reports they have prepared. (This description emphasizes an important point about open schooling: it usually requires more effort than

Techniques of open education

traditional teaching. However, many teachers who have switched from traditional to open education seem to agree that the effort is worth it.)

To date, most open education methods have been developed for the elementary level. As noted in the discussion of Piaget's theory in Chapters 3 and 4, an approach that stresses direct experience and interaction with peers is especially appropriate for students who are functioning at the stage of concrete operations. For students who are capable of formal operations, using such assumptions as a basis for an open approach is no longer completely consistent. However, you may wish to use the same basic techniques at the secondary level as a means of permitting greater student initiative and avoiding some of the disadvantages of controlled education.

If you will be teaching at the secondary level, you might provide for more student activity and interaction by structuring discovery sessions through use of the techniques described a few pages earlier, by organizing small group discussions, or by inviting pairs or small groups of students to exchange views on text materials or outside reading. You might experiment with activity areas if you are teaching a subject that lends itself to such an approach. For example, in a science class it would be possible to set up different demonstrations and apparatus, arrange displays, and establish a library corner. Cooperative, individualized planning could be instituted by using a *contract approach* whereby each student meets with you at the beginning of a report period to agree on a project that might consist of a term paper, several book reports, an experiment, or the like. Such projects might be presented to the rest of the class either in small group, round-robin fashion, or as more formal presentations.

You might select or devise organized sets of materials so that students can work individually at their own pace, using tests primarily to discover weaknesses or misinterpretations. Then, you might meet with small groups of students who are experiencing a common difficulty (e.g., understanding a particular concept, finding references in the library) and help them overcome it.

To individualize instruction, you might set aside certain class periods for tutorial sessions. Instead of requiring written reports, invite students to sign up for ten-minute blocks of time on designated days to give you an oral report. This will not only save the student the trouble of writing or typing a report and you the trouble of reading it, it will give you the opportunity to interact with each of your students on a person-to-person basis and to probe more deeply into interpretations.

To increase the amount of information about individuals, encourage students to keep their own records to supplement those you maintain.

Although most of these open education techniques are derived from principles of cognitive-field theory, a programmed approach developed by Fred S. Keller (1968) might also be used to permit individual learning and encourage student interaction. (Keller's method is sometimes called the *Personalized System of Instruction*.) Keller first wrote a series of thirty units for a course in psychology that consisted of sections of the required text supplemented by a programmed version of the material. Students were provided with the first unit and told to study until they felt they thoroughly understood it, at which point they were asked to take a short quiz of ten fill-in questions and one short-answer essay on the material. Immediately after writing the answers, the student took the test to a proctor (a student who had earned an A in the course the previous semester) to be corrected. For marginal answers, the proctor asked for further clarification. If the student met a predetermined criterion with or without any clarifying comments, his success was indicated on a wall chart and he was given the next unit. If he failed the exam by only one or two answers, the proctor called attention to sections of the text that should be read over and the student was told to study for another thirty minutes. Then he was given another chance at the test. If he missed four or more questions, he was told he was not ready and to study the material more intensively. Students who passed the first three units by a certain date were told they would have the privilege of attending a lecture or demonstration, a procedure that was followed for subsequent units. Thus all the presentations by the instructor served as vehicles of motivation and reinforcement. At the end of the semester, a final examination consisting of questions based on the quizzes was given.

If you have been impressed by descriptions of learning for mastery that have been noted in preceding chapters, you will recognize this as a variation of the mastery approach. Also, it is clearly a direct application of principles of operant conditioning (state the terminal behavior, arrange instruction in step-by-step stages, provide immediate reinforcement). At the same time, this method fits many aspects of open education: it makes it possible for students to study independently and learn at their own pace, it makes provision for them to learn from each other, it presents material in a structured and organized fashion, and it uses tests to diagnose and aid learning.

Variations of the Keller technique have been developed by S. N. Postlethwait (1967), who uses independent study sessions featuring tapes and films and has student proctors give oral quizzes and tutorial assistance; by Harry C. Mahan (1967), who favors Socratic-type programming involving tape-recorded interchanges between instructor and students, and by C. B. Ferster and M. C. Perrott (1968), who use an interview technique in which students are asked to explain sections of the text.

If you will be dealing with subject matter that lends itself to a unit approach, you might use the Keller technique (or one of these variations) in an open class situation by either having students who have completed certain units act as proctors or by grading all exams (or listening to oral interviews) yourself. In either case, students are likely to respond favorably to the freedom of moving at their own pace, to the interaction with others, and to the efforts made to help them master the material.

As this brief list of suggestions indicates, there are many ways you might adapt to the secondary level open-education techniques developed at the primary level. If you examine the themes of open education described by Walburg and Thomas or the brief outline of techniques noted by Perrone, or if you read one or more of the books on open education noted in Chapter 2, and come up with other techniques for using an open education approach, note them in the space below.

_____

_____

_____

_____

The Desirability of Gradual and Orderly Introduction of Open Education

Descriptions of the theory and techniques of open education which are presented in this book are intended to arouse your interest in this form of education. You should keep in mind, however, that such techniques are most likely to be successful if they are introduced in a deliberate, orderly way. The reasons for this have been described by Roland S. Barth in *Open Education and the American School* (1972). In Chapter 3, "Romance and Reality: A Case Study," Barth describes what happened when seven enthusiastic but inexperienced young teachers made an all-out effort to use an open education approach in two elementary schools. They encountered so much resistance from students, parents, and administrators, the following year only two of them were still teaching—one in an independent school, the other in a university laboratory school.

In analyzing what went wrong Barth concludes:

> The central message of (this) case study (and of many other attempts as well) is plain: the forms, the intensity, and the extent of resistance to change of public schools in the direction of open education are educational constants. The fact of the matter is that *most* parents' concepts of quality education are along the lines of the traditional, rigorous, transmission-of-knowledge model. *Most* parents care deeply about their children and rely heavily upon "school" to bring them success, wealth, and satisfaction. (1972, p. 205)

He goes on to say:

> The most dramatic attempts to move from traditional to informal classrooms have led invariably to the most dramatic failures. . . . It is for this reason that I believe the most successful informal classroom teachers will be those who have been trained in traditional ways, who have taught several years in traditional ways, and who are beginning to question the validity and effectiveness of traditional ways. Teachers who have found traditional education wanting and who are looking for something better will move slowly, without the impatience of youth. And they will always have in reserve their competence with the traditional model and the

security it provides for teacher and student alike. Therefore, they will probably make fewer mistakes. (P. 216)

If you have reacted favorably to the descriptions of open education in this book (and to those you have read elsewhere), you are urged—for reasons noted by Barth—to experiment with such techniques in a gradual, orderly way. Read about open education until you feel you thoroughly understand it, and then introduce promising techniques in step-by-step fashion. For information, refer to the books noted on pages 70–71. Perhaps the best single source, though, is *Open Education and the American School.* The description of what went wrong with Barth's attempt at open education (Chapter 3), and an analysis of conditions associated with successful experiences (Chapter 5), should help you avoid making many mistakes. You can check on the extent to which you endorse underlying assumptions by reading Chapter 1, and learn about the various roles played by an open classroom teacher in Chapter 2. As an added bonus, there is an extensive annotated bibliography describing books and pamphlets, articles, materials, films, and periodicals dealing with open education.

To sum up: If you hope to enhance the likelihood of enjoying success if and when you attempt open education, prepare yourself and introduce techniques in a gradual way.

7. *Consider the possibility that attitudes are more important than subject matter, that how you teach is more important than what you teach.*

The field theorist emphasizes that how students *feel* about what they learn is of great importance. From this point of view, even though you may not get as much measurable learning from a half dozen discovery sessions as you would get from an equal number of lecture or programmed learning sessions, the end result might be more desirable and significant, depending on the criteria that are applied. Combs and Snygg have expressed this view in the following terms:

> Since the purpose of the schools is to develop each child to maximum capacity as a productive and happy member of society, the real test of their success is not the degree to which the pupils can talk about desirable techniques or even the degree to which they are able to use them in school at the command of the teacher but the degree to which they voluntarily use them in their daily life outside of school. In other words, the attitudes which are acquired along with subject matter may be even more important than the subject matter itself.
>
> The learning of any skill or item of subject matter is accompanied by the formation of attitudes by the pupil toward the subject, toward school, toward his teacher, toward teachers in general, toward adults, toward society, and toward himself which may be desirable or undesirable. As a result, how subject matter is taught may be even more important than what is taught. (1959, p. 382)

These observations serve as an introduction to some concluding remarks about associationism and field theory and how they may be applied in the classroom.

A Subject Matter Switch

To illustrate some of the strengths and weaknesses of each basic approach, here is a description of a discovery unit and a programmed unit, together with some speculations about what might happen if the same subject were taught by the opposite method.

Robert B. Davis (1966) has used the discovery approach in teaching math to culturally deprived junior high school pupils with low I.Q.'s. In one of his exercises, students are asked to solve quadratic equations such as:

$$(\square \times \square) - (5 \times \square) + 6 = 0.$$

Davis points out that the only method available to these students is trial and error, and he puts forth many claims for this method. First of all, he argues that in making their trials and errors, "pupils get a great deal of experience using variables and signed numbers, and in a situation they do not regard as drill" (p.116). Second, he says that when students eventually discover the rules for solving such equations, they are so excited about uncovering a secret their friends do not yet share, they feel sufficiently rewarded for their efforts. Finally, he says that his method "brings history into the classroom" in the sense that students come to understand why modern math is the product of a long series of trials and errors. To help them understand this process even more clearly, he advocates *torpedoing*, that is, providing a challenge by presenting slightly different equations that cannot be solved by the original rule.

Now suppose that Skinner created a program to teach the same thing. In it the students would be shaped systematically to achieve awareness of the rule. Like Davis's pupils, they would get "a great deal of experience using variables and signed numbers" in a situation they would "not regard as drill," but their trials would rarely result in errors. Furthermore, all pupils would be more or less guaranteed success. (Davis gives the impression that most of his pupils were highly enthusiastic. He does not speculate about how a student might feel if he hadn't yet discovered the correct rule and his classmates were chortling with delight about their "secret." Nor does he mention what happened when his slower students were torpedoed.) Which technique is better? Or do they both have strengths and weaknesses?

To look at this question from the other side, consider the physics program reproduced earlier in this chapter (Figure 5–5). Suppose Bruner wanted to create a discovery unit on the same subject—the relationship between heat and light. He might encourage his students to talk about matches, candles, campfires, and light bulbs. Then he might wave around a flashlight and ask them to guess why the bulb lights, what part the filament plays, why it glows, etc. In this case the students would learn about heat and light by carrying on a lively class discussion instead of by writing responses and moving knobs on a machine. Which teaching technique is better, do you think? Or do they both have strengths and weaknesses?

Relating Programmed Instruction and the Discovery Approach to Preceding Chapters

In speculating about the relative merits of programmed instruction and the discovery approach, and in making decisions about when each might be used, it will be helpful to take into account points made in preceding chapters.

In Chapter 1, common criticisms of American education were noted: regimentation, control, mechanization, competition, and mindlessness. As a framework for seeking ways to overcome these limitations, goals of education were listed: preparation for a career, deeper comprehension of the world, discovery of interrelationships, development of wider and deeper interests, appreciation of individual differences, acquisition of skills in thinking, and assuming responsibility for one's own life.

In Chapter 2, John Dewey's views of education were summarized: the desirability of avoiding an overreaction against disliked aspects of education, seeking to understand the causes of differences of opinion about education, not choosing sides but making the most of different points of view. Themes of open education were listed: allowing for activity and involvement, encouraging students to learn from each other, providing teacher direction to make possible individualized learning, using structured and organized materials to facilitate learning and using tests to diagnose weaknesses to be corrected by remedial instruction, and establishing a warm and accepting climate. Abraham Maslow's conception of the positive—but weak—inner nature of human beings was noted, and Dewey's views of education based on assumptions similar to those of Maslow were summarized, including his suggestion that teachers try to arrange learning experiences to promote future desirable experiences and eventual self-control.

Chapter 3 included Erikson's theory of development, which stresses stages of Initiative vs. Doubt, Industry vs. Inferiority, and Identity vs. Role Confusion. All these emphasize the child's need to gain a feeling of control over his own destiny and to develop a sense of continuity and sameness. Kenneth Keniston's views parallel those of Erikson in their emphasis on the need for young adults to find meaning, make integrations, and experience education as consciousness expansion.

In Chapters 3 and 4 Piaget's theory of intellectual development was outlined. Applications of his theory vary from attempts to accelerate development to the British open-school approach, which assumes that children are different from adults and that they should learn through their own experiences and by interacting with their peers. Bruner's suggestion that we *teach* readiness is a variation on the former theme.

In this chapter, you have been acquainted with the background, research, principles, and theories of programmed learning and of the discovery approach.

On the basis of his experiments with rats and pigeons, Skinner suggests that you first explicitly state terminal behavior and then arrange learning experiences so that your students are led to achieve it—step by step. The early experiments by Gestalt psychologists led to Bruner's suggestion that teachers *arrange* learning situations so that students will make their own discoveries.

If account is taken of these points, an outline of goals you might strive for as you consider using programmed and discovery approaches can be noted.

Goals to Strive for in Arranging Learning Experiences

Minimize regimentation, control, mechanization, and mindlessness.

Maximize deeper comprehension, widening of interests, discovery of interrelationships; encourage acquisition of skills of thinking.

Use understanding of causes of differences of opinion in education to make the most of different points of view.

Allow for activity and involvement, encourage students to learn from each other, individualize instruction, structure and organize materials, use tests to diagnose and aid learning, establish a warm and accepting classroom climate.

Attempt to encourage students to develop initiative, industry, and a sense of identity.

Particularly with older students, stress meaning and integration of ideas.

Take into account the stage of intellectual development achieved by your students.

Consider the advantages of stating terminal behavior and arranging learning experiences to assist students to achieve it (particularly in a mastery approach).

Take into account the values of learning that come into play when students are assisted to make discoveries of their own.

It is apparent that exclusive use of either programmed learning or the discovery approach will not permit you to achieve all these goals. Consequently, you will probably want to make use of techniques derived from both.

If you feel at a loss as to how to begin combining ideas from both views of learning into a reasonably coherent scheme, you might use the themes of open education described by Walberg and Thomas as a frame of reference. The open education approach represents an attempt to overcome negative aspects of traditional public education. It strives to achieve many of the goals of education described by Voeks. It takes into account Piaget's theory of intellectual development. In many respects, it is similar to the approach to education advocated by Dewey. It makes use of principles and techniques from both programmed learning and the discovery approach in a way that combines active, personal, individualized, self-directed learning; it promotes interaction with classmates; and it encourages systematic guidance by the teacher. When the time comes for you to make specific plans for what you will do when you first step into the classroom, you may find it helpful to write your own interpretation of the themes of open education listed on pages 68–69 as a first step.

Using the Views of Locke and Leibnitz to Understand Differences in Approach

In making decisions about how you might combine programmed and discovery techniques, you are urged to keep in mind Dewey's observation that "it is the business of an intelligent theory of education to ascertain the causes for the conflicts that exist." Gordon Allport, a distinguished psychologist who agreed with this reasoning, made an effort to explain and reconcile opposing points of view in psychology. In *Becoming*, he traces the sources of many of the basic differences of opinion that have been described in this book by contrasting the views of two philosophers, John Locke and Gottfried Leibnitz. Locke argued that the mind of a newborn child is a *tabula rasa*, or blank slate, and that sensations, experiences, and associations make their mark on the slate. He saw human beings as essentially passive organisms that react only when stimulated. Allport suggests that the behaviorist-associationist-environmentalist position that is endorsed by most American psychologists is based on Locke's point of view. He lists five presuppositions that emerge from endorsing the basic conception of the newborn infant as a *tabula rasa:* what is external and visible is more fundamental than what is not—that is, what happens to the organism from the outside is of primary importance; learning is regarded as the substitution of one effective stimulus for another or of one response for another; what is small and molecular is more important than what is large and molar; all animals, from lower forms to human beings, are basically equivalent (which leads to the conviction that the results of experiments on animals such as rats and pigeons can be applied directly to humans); and what is earlier is more fundamental than what is later in development, since first impressions will have the most profound influence.

By contrast, Leibnitz argued that the intellect is not a passive, blank slate but is self-propelled and perpetually active in manipulating what it senses and

John Locke (1632–1704)   Gottfried Leibnitz (1646–1716)

experiences according to its own inherent nature. Thus the person is seen not as a collection of acts but as the *source* of acts, and activity is seen not as the result of stimulation but as purposive. This point of view is the foundation of Gestalt psychology and cognitive-field theory. It is the basis of the theories of Piaget, Combs and Snygg, and Maslow and the practices of Neill, Holt, Kohl, Kozol, and other advocates of open education. In Leibnitz's view, Locke's five presuppositions are reversed: what happens to the organism on the *inside* (not the outside) is of primary importance; learning is regarded as the perception of new relationships (not the accumulation of associations); understanding of *structure* is essential (not what is small and molecular); higher-order animals and humans are different from lower-order animals (species are *not* equivalent); present experiences are of primary concern (not past experiences).

Many of the differences of opinion discussed in this book can be understood by taking account of the basic differences between the Lockeian and Leibnitzian

Empiricism, Innate Ideas, and
Transformational Grammar

To contrast points of view on basic assumptions, Allport refers to the conceptions of Locke and Leibnitz. For the same purpose, he might have used the views of David Hume and René Descartes (among others). Hume developed Locke's observations into a doctrine of *cause and effect* that stressed many of the basic ideas of S-R associationism. Descartes proposed a *dualism,* emphasizing that although the body is a machine, the mind has a free soul. As opposed to Locke and Hume, who espoused *empiricism*—the conviction that things are learned almost exclusively through experience—Descartes maintained there are *innate ideas* that are not traceable to experience.

With the development of behaviorism and associationism, Descartes' theory was pushed into relative obscurity. However, the work of linguist Noam Chomsky (1968) has renewed interest in the possibility of innate ideas. Chomsky maintains that all languages rest on the same basic principles, and analysis of how children in different countries learn to use their native language led him to postulate that these principles are innate. The behaviorist-associationist explanation of language acquisition (Skinner, 1957) stresses the building up of S-R associations through imitation and reinforcement. Chomsky argues that this does not account for the creative and innovative aspects of language; that is, a child can use and understand combinations of words he has never previously associated or has had reinforced. In addition, children from widely varying backgrounds seem to learn to speak at about the same age and to use the same grammar, even though the depth and variety of their experiences differ to a substantial extent. Chomsky suggests that language is based on *invariant properties,* or *linguistic universals,* that are genetically determined. Thus, he argues, the mind of the newborn child is *not* a blank slate.

Chomsky bases his *transformational grammar* on the principles of language he has described, and if you will be teaching in either the elementary grades or in junior or senior high school English classes, you are almost certain to encounter this conception of language. Chomsky makes a distinction between the *underlying* (or deep) structure and *surface* structure of a sentence and emphasizes the importance of analyzing how one is transformed into the other. For example, the sentence with the surface structure "They are eating apples" could be interpreted in different ways, depending on the underlying structure; for example, two or more people are eating apples, the apples in a store are for eating rather than cooking, the apples in a fairy tale eat children. In the Chomsky approach to grammar, the relationship between underlying and surface structure is analyzed to clarify meaning.

Even if you are not directly involved in teaching English, you are likely to come across discussions of language centering around the possibility of "innate ideas" as an alternative to the "blank slate" view, and the implications of these views for approaches to education.

René Descartes (1596–1650)   David Hume (1711–1776)

points of view. B. F. Skinner and others of the behaviorist-associationist-environmentalist school base their experiments and theories on the five presuppositions listed by Allport. They are also influenced by the Zeitgeist of a technological society. They concentrate on overt behavior not only because they believe that what happens to the organism from the outside is of fundamental importance but also because they are eager to use the methods of physical and natural science in order to be as objective as possible. They conceive of learning as the accumulation of associations between stimuli and responses not only because this view reduces the necessity for speculating about mental processes but perhaps also because it reflects the keystone of American technology—the assembly line. They concentrate on what is small and molecular not only because this is compatible with an analysis of associations between stimuli and responses but also because the requirements of objective and precise research and the desire to function as productive scholars lead to the publication of large numbers of specific research studies. They endorse the idea of equivalence of species not only because of belief in the *tabula rasa* concept and the desirability of concentrating on molecular units but also because animals can be experimented on with greater ease and fewer restrictions than is possible with human subjects. And they stress the importance of early experience not only because first impressions on the blank slate of intellect and personality are considered most fundamental but also because of the conviction that it is a mistake to allow behavior to be influenced by accidental or chance contingencies of reinforcement.

An understanding of these factors makes it possible to understand why Skinner has conducted his rat and pigeon experiments and developed programmed learning; why he wrote *Walden Two*, *The Technology of Teaching*, and *Beyond Freedom and Dignity*; why performance contracting approaches usually make use of operant conditioning techniques; why Becker, Engelmann, Thomas, and other advocates of behavior modification urge teachers to shape behavior; why Hunt, Bloom, and others who stress the importance of critical periods insist that enriched early experiences will lead to increases in intelligence; and why Piaget is asked "the American question."

Understanding these causes not only makes clear why many of these developments and viewpoints have emerged but also raises questions about the basic assumptions upon which they rest. Before you make any decisions about applying operant conditioning techniques in your classroom, you should ask yourself if you endorse the *tabula rasa* concept and the presuppositions based on it. You should also explore the possibility that there may be important differences between theory and practice. The five assumptions described by Allport were adopted for purposes of scientific rigor and to facilitate the development of theories of learning. If these assumptions are applied too literally to the practice of teaching, however, they lead to a conception of instruction that stresses overt behavior at the expense of feelings and attitudes, that concentrates on learning as the presentation of a series of specific stimuli to which students are expected to supply preselected responses, that tends to exclude exploration of more global ideas and of individual interpretations, and that features manipulation of student behavior by dispensation of rewards. Perhaps because they have been so concerned with scientific method and so involved in developing a consistent theory, Skinner and others who take the behaviorist-associationist-environmentalist position have found it difficult to acknowledge the possibility that direct application of their point of view to education may intensify some of the most threatening and negative aspects of our society: overcompartmentalization, overspecialization, fragmentation, mechanization, regimentation, standardization, materialism, conformity, control, and repression of feeling and emotion. Perhaps it is a mistake to leave many experiences to accidental contingencies or chance, but it may be just as much if not more of a mistake for a teacher to attempt total control over aspects of student development.

A teacher who becomes too concerned about manipulating the classroom environment and student behavior risks practicing control for the sake of control.

This point can be clarified by considering Skinner's experiments with animals. Many operant conditioning enthusiasts follow the practice of taking to a psychology class a hungry rat or pigeon in a Skinner box and asking students to specify what they would like the animal to do, for example, walk a figure-eight pattern. They supply food pellets when the animal moves in the desired direction and shape the desired behavior in a matter of minutes. It is an impressive demonstration, and both psychologist and students are reinforced by the extent to which the behavior of the animal has been controlled. Teachers who take a course in behavior modification and find that their first attempts to shape student behavior are successful are often equally impressed as well as excited about the possibilities of further control. It seems possible, however, that teachers who make substantial use of operant conditioning techniques might—without realizing it—tend to use such methods not only to produce behavior they have carefully preselected as likely to benefit students but also to make life easier for themselves and perhaps because they are reinforced by the degree to which they can control others. In such cases, learning may be limited rather than enhanced. In analyzing this possibility, consider some differences between animal and human behavior.

The pigeon whose behavior is shaped by an experimenter does not really benefit by being induced to walk in a figure-eight pattern. All it needs is food, and it could obtain this with less effort by not walking in circles. However, neither does it suffer, because even its spontaneous behavior would consist of random movements of various kinds. In a sense, then, only the experimenter benefits, because he has demonstrated his ability to produce such behavior; and even if the pigeon is manipulated, it makes no difference. Those who make use of operant conditioning techniques with human beings do so because they believe they can produce behavior that will benefit those who are controlled. Unlike pigeons, though, human beings are capable of engaging in self-directed behavior that *might* be more beneficial to them than what is selected by others. This means that manipulation of one human being by another might make a difference, since the question arises: Who is to decide what will be beneficial—the controller or the individual? This is the point raised by Combs and Snygg in Chapter 2; such an approach "requires that someone must know what the 'right' goal is in order effectively to manipulate the required forces" (1959, p. 311). In deciding on "right" goals, the teacher might inadvertently choose those that will benefit her more than her students, perhaps because of a desire to establish a class routine that will simplify instruction, perhaps because shaping the behavior of others gives her a sense of power. (If, because all rewards are dispensed by a teacher, students seldom feel that their own behavior is reinforcing, it is difficult for a teacher *not* to feel a sense of importance and power.)

In *Beyond Freedom and Dignity* Skinner observes: "In the prescientific view . . . a person's behavior is at least to some extent his own achievement.

He is free to deliberate, decide, and act, possibly in original ways, and he is to be given credit for his successes and blamed for his failures. In the scientific view . . . a person's behavior is determined by a genetic endowment . . . and by the environmental experiences to which as an individual he has been exposed" (1971, p. 101). He sums up by saying, ". . . A person does not act upon the world, the world acts on him" (p. 211). When Skinner maintains that the "world" acts on the individual, he speaks of "environmental experiences." However, he does not make explicit the fact that in the operant conditioning view, it is not an amorphous "world," but those who *arrange* experiences who are actually responsible for the behavior of the individuals they manipulate. In this sense, the experimenter or teacher deserves the credit for success that the prescientific view attributes to the individual. (The teacher, in this view, is also blamed for failure, which may be one explanation for current interest in accountability.)

Skinner deserves full credit for what he induces his rats and pigeons to do, since they would never be able to perform on their own the feats he has conditioned them to perform. But, do teachers deserve similar credit when their students learn? With considerable effort a child may be trained to score fifteen points higher on an intelligence test, or master aspects of conservation a month ahead of schedule, or finish a program on some subject, or line up for recess with precision. If the child accomplishes these things, it is the individual who provided the training or wrote the program or supplied reinforcement that is responsible and deserves the credit, not the "world" or "experiences." Even though he might not say it, the teacher in such situations may think, "*I* made this child intelligent," or "*I* taught this child how to think," or "Wow! Look at 'em jump into line when I give the signal."

But, unlike the rat or pigeon, the child can use language and thought to enhance exploration of ideas on his own and organize and adapt to experiences that make him potentially capable of even more impressive and personally valuable accomplishments if left to his own devices.[12] Skinner notes, "To refuse to control (as in permissiveness) is to leave control not to the person, but to other parts of the social and non-social environments" (p. 84). He implies that the "other parts" of the environment will influence the individual in the same way and to the same extent as those that are deliberately arranged. Those who favor the view of Leibnitz, however, believe that the individual will have greater freedom to *choose* from nonarranged "other parts" than from experiences that are highly structured by others. This notion is expressed by Maslow in these terms: "It is necessary in order for children to grow well that adults have enough trust in them and in the natural processes of growth, i.e., not interfere too much, not *make* them grow, or force them into predetermined designs, but rather *let* them grow and *help* them grow" (1968, p. 199).

---

[12] As Skinner himself has observed, "The human organism does, of course, learn without being taught." (1968, p. 110).

These observations have been provided to stimulate you to analyze the basic reasons why Skinner and other advocates of operant conditioning developed and recommend the practices that have been discussed—and will continue to be discussed—in this book. You are urged to think about the possibility that there may be differences between assumptions adopted for purposes of developing a consistent and respectable theory and assumptions underlying teacher-pupil relationships. At the same time, keep in mind that rejecting all applications of principles of operant conditioning may limit your effectiveness as a teacher. If no guidance whatever is provided, students *will* be entirely at the mercy of chance. If the instructor refuses to acknowledge that he is the most mature member of the group and that he therefore has the responsibility to provide some direction, the result may be a disorganized "sharing of ignorance" that might just as well take place outside of the classroom. You are urged to reread the observations of Dewey that were presented at the end of Chapter 2 for a philosophy of education that represents a constructive compromise of guided and free points of view. You are also urged to use the list of goals of education presented a few pages earlier as a set of guidelines in deciding how to combine techniques from operant conditioning and the discovery approach in making the most of both approaches. Using programmed methods in such a way that they set the stage for personal discovery (which is the technique used in this book) would seem to be the most promising and potentially valuable way to do this.

Critics of programmed instruction and behavior modification sometimes refer to those who seem preoccupied with control and manipulation as Machiavellian. Critics of extreme interpretations of the Leibnitzian point of view, on the other hand, see those who agree with Neill that if a child is "left to himself without adult suggestion of any kind [he] will develop as far as he is capable of developing" as romantics. Obviously, you do not have to totally endorse one view or the other in order to make use of techniques practiced by Skinner or Neill. However, as you select and apply methods based on operant conditioning and the discovery approach, keep in mind the basic assumptions underlying each point of view. In that sense, you might strive to function as a Machiavellian romantic—or, if you prefer, a romantic Machiavelli.

Summary

In this chapter you have examined two contemporary views of the learning process: S-R associationism as interpreted by B. F. Skinner and cognitive-field theory as interpreted by Jerome Bruner. Classic studies by Ivan Pavlov, Edward L. Thorndike, and Skinner provided the research evidence that ultimately led to the development of programmed instruction. This type of learning has its advantages and disadvantages, and you have been given some suggestions for writing programs of your own, for using programs developed by others, and for using aspects of programmed instruction in dealing with everyday classroom problems and activities.

The experiments of Wolfgang Köhler, the theorizing of Kurt Lewin, and the views of Jerome Bruner set the stage for the development of the discovery approach to learning. There are arguments for and against this type of learning, and you have been provided with some suggestions for applying cognitive-field theory in the classroom.

In line with the ideas stressed in the opening chapters, you have been urged in this chapter to make judicious use of the techniques of *both* general approaches as opposed to making an attempt to be completely faithful to just one approach.

Suggestions for Further Reading, Writing, Thinking, and Discussion

5-1 *Sampling a Section of Skinner's "The Technology of Teaching"*

The Technology of Teaching (1968) is B. F. Skinner's most concise and application-oriented discussion of operant conditioning techniques related to pedagogy. There are several sections of this book you might want to sample with the idea of eventually purchasing a copy for future reference. For an overview of programmed learning and teaching machines, see Chapter 3. In Chapter 5, "Why Teachers Fail," Skinner describes what he perceives to be common mistakes made by many teachers. See if you agree with his critique. In Chapter 8, "The Creative Student," he discusses determinism and the issue of personal freedom. If you read of these chapters, or another of your choice, you might record your reactions to general or specific arguments made in the book.

5-2 *Reacting to Some Dialogues with Skinner*

B. F. Skinner: The Man and His Ideas (1968) is a series of dialogues with Skinner (originally filmed for educational television) recorded by Richard I. Evans. In Chapter 1 you will find "Reactions to Various Psychological Concepts," including the theories of Pavlov and Freud. Chapter 2, "Aversive Versus Positive Control of Behavior," deals with the incentive system in the Soviet Union and gives Skinner's reactions to criticisms of his Utopian novel *Walden Two*. Chapter 3, "The Formal Educational System," includes some of Skinner's observations on overconformity and the changing role of the American woman. If you are intrigued by Skinner and his theories, you may find it enjoyable to read and react to one or more of the dialogues recorded in this book.

(Note: Even though the books by Skinner and Huxley described below in 5-3 and 5-4 were mentioned in the "Suggestions for Further Reading, Thinking,

Writing, and Discussion" for Chapter 2, they are again called to your attention on the assumption that information presented in Chapter 5 might have aroused more interest in applying learning theory to create a utopia [either a positive or negative one].)

5-3 *Speculating about Skinner's Utopia*

In *Walden Two* (1948), B. F. Skinner describes his conception of a utopia based on the application of science to human behavior. To get the full impact of the novel and of Skinner's ideas, you should read the entire book. (As a matter of fact, it may be hard to put down once you begin it.) However, if you cannot read the whole thing at this time, Chapters 12 through 17—in which the approach to child rearing and education at Walden Two is described—may be of special interest to you as a future teacher. Starting at page 95 and continuing to at least page 148 will give you a good sample of life in Skinner's utopia. Then record your reactions, including perhaps an opinion as to whether you might like to join a society based on the ideas of Walden Two. You might also take a stab at sketching out a utopia of your own—perhaps you will be able to improve on Skinner's version.

5-4 *Considering Views of Negative Utopias*

In *Brave New World* (1932), *Animal Farm* (1946), *1984* (1949), and *Fahrenheit 451* (1967), Aldous Huxley, George Orwell, and Ray Bradbury present conceptions of what might be characterized as negative utopias. *Brave New World,* in particular, is founded on the principles of conditioning. Whereas Skinner describes how such principles could be used to set man free, Huxley shows how they could be used to enslave man. If you read *Brave New World,* ask yourself whether any of the predictions Huxley made in 1932 have come true. (For example, is our behavior conditioned by TV commercials? How many people make habitual use of pain relievers or tranquilizers?) Or if you read the accounts of Orwell or Bradbury, you might note techniques they describe that are in use today and that might be abused.

5-5 *Making a First Effort at Writing a Program*

In writing a program, you should start by getting some initial feedback from a sample of students. If you feel inclined toward programmed learning, select a concept from this course, or from a subject you will eventually teach, then write a ten-frame program, try it out on four or five classmates, and note their reactions. Even if the frames and reactions are not exactly the same as those you might eventually use with younger students, the feedback you get could help you sort out your thoughts regarding programmed instruction. For suggestions on how to write the program, look over a few actual programs or glance through *Good Frames and Bad: A Grammar of Frame Writing* (1964) by Susan

Meyer Markle, *A Guide to Programmed Instruction* (1963) by Jerome Lysaught and Clarence Williams, or *Practical Programming* (1966) by Peter Pipe.

5-6 *Trying a Program Yourself and Recording Your Reactions*

A good way to find out about a pedagogical technique is to try it yourself—from the *student* point of view. To clarify your thoughts about programmed instruction, record your reactions to any programmed books, units, or courses you have taken, or—if you have never been exposed to this technique—seek out a programmed unit and work through it. To find a suitable program, ask your instructor for assistance, check with classmates who have used one in the past, browse through a college bookstore, or consult with the person in charge of a curriculum and materials section of a library.

5-7 *Devising Your Own List of Suggestions for Using Behavior Modification*

If the possibilities of behavior modification seem attractive, you may wish to examine issues of the journal *Educational Technology* or read one or more books on the systematic application of principles of operant conditioning to classroom problems, perhaps for the purpose of drawing up your own list of guidelines for future use. If you browse through the education and psychology sections of your college bookstore, you are likely to find a number of books on behavior modification. Or you might look for these titles in the library: *Instructional Product Development* (1971) edited by Robert L. Baker and Richard E. Schutz, *An Empirical Basis for Change in Education* (1971) edited by Wesley C. Becker, *Teaching: A Course in Applied Psychology* (1971) by Wesley C. Becker, Siegfried Engelmann, and Don R. Thomas, *Classroom Behavior* (1972) by Donald G. Bushell, Jr., *A New Learning Environment* (1971) by Harold L. Cohen and James Filipczak, *Analysis and Modification of Classroom Behavior* (1972) by Norris G. Haring and E. Larkin Phillips, *Classroom Uses of Behavior Modification* (1972) edited by Mary B. Harris, *Behavior Technology: Motivation and Contingency Management* (1971) edited by Lloyd Homme and Donald Tosti, *Behavior Modification in Education* (1973) by Donald L. Macmillan, *Changing Classroom Behavior: A Manual for Precision Teaching* (1969) by Merle E. Meacham and Allen E. Wiesen, *Operant Conditioning in the Classroom* (1971) edited by Carl E. Pitts, *Reinforcing Productive Classroom Behavior: A Teacher's Guide to Behavior Modification* (1971) edited by Irwin G. Sarason and others, *Learning is Getting Easier* (1972) by S. R. Wilson and D. T. Tosti.

5-8 *Sampling Bruner's "Toward a Theory of Instruction"*

Toward a Theory of Instruction (1966) is Jerome Bruner's most concise and application-oriented book on teaching. Sampling a few sections of this book will help you decide whether to purchase a copy for future reference. Chapter 1, "Patterns of Growth," and Chapter 3, "Notes on a Theory of Instruction," provide general descriptions of Bruner's views on teaching and learning. Chapter 4 describes a course of study (of man) taught through the use of the discovery approach. You might read these chapters or another section of your own choice, and record your reactions.

5-9 *Pondering the Place of Fantasy and Feeling in Education*

Richard M. Jones participated in the development of the discovery approach to teaching social studies that Bruner describes in *Toward a Theory of Instruction*. As Jones observed the experimental teaching sessions, he decided that Bruner had made an excellent start toward a theory of instruction but had not carried the technique to its logical conclusions. In *Fantasy and Feeling in Education* (1968), Jones suggests that teachers do everything possible to enlist the "emotional and imaginal responses" of the child as he learns. He describes class sessions in which the Bruner materials were tried out and argues that the most meaningful learning took place when a situation of "controlled emotion" existed. If you will be teaching at the upper elementary level and are attracted by Bruner's approach to teaching the unit on *Man* (or if you hope to make learning a highly personal experience, regardless of grade level and subject matter), you will find *Fantasy and Feeling in Education* of interest. In Chapter 2 Jones explains the importance of controlled emotion, in Chapter 3 he develops the theme that affect and imagery are the skills most needed to teach social studies, and in Chapter 4 he makes contrasts between insight and *outsight*. Chapter 6 is devoted to a theoretical frame for considering emotional growth that is based on Erik H. Erikson's interpretation of Freudian theory, and in the remaining three chapters Jones presents his version of a more complete theory of instruction than that offered by Bruner and a description of how he feels "Man: A Course of Study" should be taught. If you read any of these chapters, you might note the points you feel will be of value when you begin to teach.

5-10 *Writing a Description of a Discovery Unit*

If the discovery approach strikes you as promising, briefly describe a unit you might eventually use in a class that features one or more of the specific discovery techniques proposed by Bruner (emphasize contrast, stimulate informed guessing, encourage participation, stimulate awareness), Bigge (switch subject matter, introduce disturbing data, permit mistakes), or Davis (torpedoing). To get feedback, write a short description of a discovery unit and show the outline to some classmates for their reactions. Summarize their responses and add comments of your own.

5-11 *Speculating about the Perceptual View of Behavior*

In *Individual Behavior* (1959), Arthur Combs and Donald Snygg discourse extensively on their version of cognitive-field theory, which they call "the perceptual approach to behavior." Part I of this book provides theoretical background; Part II consists of a discussion of implications and applications.

As a future teacher, you will find chapters in the latter section particularly interesting. Chapter 15, "The Individual and His Society," presents a series of principles pertaining to individuals and their relationships in society. In Chapter 17 "The Goals and Purposes of Education" are discussed. Chapter 18 is devoted to "The Teaching Relationship." Combs provides "A Perceptual View of Teacher Preparation" in *The Professional Education of Teachers* (1965) and, in the process, offers many suggestions applicable to all forms of education.

5-12 *Describing the Way Two Fanatics Might Approach the Teaching of Square Dancing*

To point up the differences between programmed learning and the discovery approach, you might find it enjoyable to write a description of how square-dancing, for example, could be taught by two extremists. First, tell how a person fanatically committed to S-R theory would set about the task. Then turn your imagination to how a true believer in the discovery approach might arrange things if he were asked to teach square-dancing. (Any other idea or activity could be substituted for square-dancing. The important thing is to let yourself go—write a wildly exaggerated account of how S-R principles and field theory might be used to the point of becoming ridiculous. In the process you may learn about both the strengths and the weaknesses of each approach to learning.)

5-13 *Reading and Reacting to Neill's "Summerhill"*

If you have never read any of A. S. Neill's books on education and child rearing, you might want to do so before embarking on a teaching career. In *Summerhill* (1960), probably the most straightforward account of the school of that name, Neill sets forth the philosophy he has put into practice for over forty years; you are urged to first read the Foreword by Erich Fromm. In the opening section of the book, Neill gives a complete, although somewhat disorganized, exposition of what the school is like. For a more complete and specific idea as to what actually takes place at Summerhill, browse through *Living at Summerhill* (1968) by Herb Snitzer. For opinions of some Summerhill graduates that will provide a frame of reference for sorting out your reactions, read "What Does a Summerhill Old School Tie Look Like?" by Emmanuel Bernstein in the January 1968 issue of *Psychology Today*. Neill comments on a variety of aspects of child rearing and education in *Freedom—Not License!* (1966); he recounts how he was influenced to found Summerhill in his autobiography, *Neill! Neill! Orange Peel!* (1972). If you read any of these accounts of Neill's philosophy and methods, you might summarize the points made and comment on which ones you endorse or find hard to accept.

5-14 *Reacting to Holt's Criticisms of American Education*

John Holt has been one of the most outspoken critics of American education during the past decade, notably in *How Children Fail* (1964), *How Children Learn* (1967), *The Underachieving School* (1969), *What Do I Do Monday?* (1970)

and *Freedom and Beyond* (1972). Holt is a sensitive and perceptive observer, and you may endorse many of the points he makes regarding the shortcomings of traditional educational practice. As you read his prescriptions for reform, however, ask yourself about the feasibility and practicality of the alternatives he suggests. In Parts I and II of *How Children Fail*, Holt discusses the strategies children use to avoid a sense of failure and why they fear failure to such an extent. What might you do in your own classes to avoid the sorts of situations he describes? Part III takes up "real learning" and offers some suggestions on the proper way to teach—ideas that are developed more completely in *How Children Learn*. If you feel somewhat bitter about your own school experiences, you may find yourself in sympathy with Holt's proposals for reform. But, in assessing them, try to come up with ideas of your own that are not as extreme (and perhaps more realistic).

5-15 *Reading an Autobiographical Sketch of a Learning Theorist*

Now that you have read about learning theory, you may be inclined to read an autobiographical sketch of one of the theorists selected for inclusion in *A History of Psychology in Autobiography*. Sketches by Edward L. Thorndike and John B. Watson appear in Volume III (1936) edited by Carl Murchison. The sketch by B. F. Skinner appears in Volume V (1967) edited by Edwin G. Boring and Gardner Lindzey. If you read one of these autobiographies, speculate about how the impact of the Zeitgeist of the times and the background and experiences of the individual might have influenced his theory. (Note: Skinner describes his own perceptions of how he was operant-conditioned to perform in certain ways as he studied the experiments he was conducting on rats and pigeons in "A Case History in Scientific Method," which you will find in Volume II of *Psychology: A Study of Science, General Systematic Formulations, Learning and Special Processes*, edited by Sigmund Koch, pages 359–379.)

5-16 *Reading Other Analyses of the Psychology of Learning*

The description of learning in this chapter is one person's interpretation of selected aspects from a complex and extensive area of psychology. If you would like to read more complete analyses by those with different points of view, you might examine chapters on learning on other texts in educational psychology. Most of these are written from an associationist point of view, a reflection of the fact that most American psychologists stress an S-R approach. Two highly regarded works of this type are *The Psychology of Learning and Instruction* (1968) by John P. DeCecco, and *Learning and Human Abilities* (3rd ed., 1971) by Herbert Klausmeier and Richard Ripple. For a text written from the field theory point of view, look for *Psychological Foundations of Education* (2nd ed., 1968) by Morris L. Bigge and Maurice P. Hunt. (Part of this book has been published in a slightly revised form as *Learning Theories for Teachers* [2nd ed., 1971] by Bigge.) Another such text is *Educational Psychology: A*

Cognitive View (1968) by David P. Ausubel. Of books devoted exclusively to learning, *Learning: A Survey of Psychological Interpretations* (rev. ed., 1971) by Winfred F. Hill, and *The Psychology of Learning Applied to Teaching* (2nd ed., 1971) by B. R. Bugelski are especially recommended.

Recommended Reading in
Psychology Applied to Teaching: Selected Readings

If you would like to do further reading in books or articles mentioned in this chapter (and in the preceding "Suggestions for Further Reading, Writing, Thinking, and Discussion") without having to track down several separate volumes, you might peruse *Psychology Applied to Teaching: Selected Readings* (Boston: Houghton Mifflin, 1972). This is a collection of excerpts from books and articles from journals in psychology. The following selections provide extended commentaries on points noted in this chapter or mentioned in the "Suggestions."

Experiments That Led to Programmed Learning: "Learning in American Psychology," section of excerpt from *The Conditions of Learning* by Robert M. Gagné, Selection 17, p. 267.

The Nature of Operant Conditioning: "Operant Conditioning," section of "The Technology of Teaching" by B. F. Skinner, Selection 15, p. 212.

Applications of Operant Conditioning: "The Technology of Teaching" by B. F. Skinner, Selection 15, p. 210. (See also Suggestion 5–1.)

The Nature and Significance of Structure: "The Importance of Structure" by Jerome S. Bruner, Selection 1, p. 2.

Teaching for Memory, Understanding, and Reflection: "How Does Cognitive Field Psychology Deal with Learning and Teaching?" by Morris L. Bigge, Selection 16, p. 237.

The Nature of a Programmed Utopia: Excerpt from *Walden Two* by B. F. Skinner, Selection 7, p. 73. (See also Suggestion 5–3.)

Views of a Negative Utopia: Excerpt from *Brave New World* by Aldous Huxley, Selection 8, p. 90. (See also Suggestion 5–4.)

The Perceptual View of Behavior: Excerpt from *Individual Behavior* by Arthur Combs and Donald Snygg, Selection 6, p. 61. (See also Suggestion 5–11.)

Using the Views of Locke and Leibnitz to Understand Differences in Approach: Excerpt from *Becoming* by Gordon W. Allport, Selection 9, p. 106.

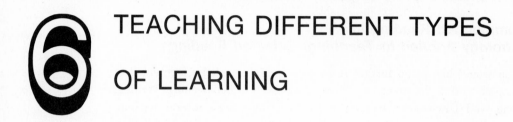

TEACHING DIFFERENT TYPES OF LEARNING

KEY POINTS

Sequences
Discovery stages: preparation, incubation, illumination, verification (Wallas)

Classifications
Types of learning: signal, stimulus-response, chaining, verbal association, discrimination, concept, rule, problem solving (Gagné)
Taxonomy of educational objectives, cognitive domain (Bloom)

Concepts
Habitual set, functional fixedness

Methodology
Using instructional objectives
Teaching verbal associations by using chaining, mediating links (mnemonic devices, advance organizers)
Teaching concepts and principles by describing terminal behavior and then guiding learning step by step
Teaching problem solving by using techniques of Crutchfield, Suchman, and Bruner and by employing heuristics
Encouraging creativity by following the suggestions of Torrance

CHAPTER CONTENTS

YOU HAVE JUST BEEN ACQUAINTED WITH TWO BASIC APPROACHES TO instruction and urged to make use of techniques derived from both. The themes of open education described by Walberg and Thomas have been suggested as a frame of reference for doing this. Three of these themes are: diagnosis of learning events; instruction, guidance, and extension of learning; and evaluation of diagnostic information. The basic technique for arranging learning experiences in accordance with these themes is provided by the programmed instruction procedure of stating terminal behavior and then assisting students to move toward the specified goal.

Robert Glaser (1962) has taken the simple method used by Skinner in shaping the behavior of rats or pigeons and derived from it a basic teaching model that divides instruction into the following four components: instructional objectives, entering behavior, instructional procedures, and performance assessment. All are self-explanatory, with the possible exception of *entering behavior,* which is similar to *readiness* in that it refers to the student's level of understanding before instruction begins. Glaser has expanded his teaching model into *Individually Prescribed Instruction,* which was mentioned in the preceding chapter as an example of a comprehensive system of instruction based on principles of operant conditioning. (The components of IPI are: state the objectives as observable student behaviors, assess each student's capabilities, offer alternative modes of instruction, monitor and continually assess each student's performance, use performance data and other data to monitor and improve the entire system.)

The first step in Glaser's teaching model and in IPI is to state the terminal behavior in the form of instructional objectives. In keeping with the behaviorist emphasis on overt behavior, educational technologists who favor variations of Glaser's model of teaching stress that objectives should describe what the student actually will *do* at the completion of the learning experience.

Using Instructional Objectives

A particularly effective explanation of why it is desirable to focus on behavioral objectives is presented by Robert F. Mager in *Preparing Instructional Objectives.* (Excerpts from this book were presented in Fig. 5-6, p. 217, to illustrate a branching program.) Mager summarizes the basic message in the opening paragraph of his book:

> Once an instructor decides he will teach his students something, several kinds of activity are necessary on his part if he is to succeed. He must first decide upon the goals he intends to reach at the end of his course or program. He must then select procedures, content, and methods that are relevant to the objectives; cause the student to interact with appropriate subject matter in accordance with principles of learning; and, finally, measure or *evaluate* the student's performance *according to the objectives or goals* originally selected. (1962, p. 1)

Mager sums up the techniques for accomplishing this instructional sequence:

1. A statement of instructional objectives is a collection of words or symbols describing one of your educational *intents.*
2. An objective will communicate your intent to the degree you have described what the learner will be DOING when demonstrating his achievement and how you will know when he is doing it.
3. To describe terminal behavior (what the learner will be DOING):
   (a) Identify and name the over-all behavior act.
   (b) Define the important conditions under which the behavior is to occur (givens or restrictions, or both).
   (c) Define the criterion of acceptable performance.

4. Write a separate statement for each objective; the more statements you have, the better chance you have of making clear your intent.

5. If you give each learner a copy of your objectives, you may not have to do much else. (P. 53)

In *Stating Behavioral Objectives for Classroom Instruction,* Norman E. Gronlund points out that Mager's objectives are most appropriate for teaching simple skills and specific items of information, since each objective is an end in itself. For more advanced types of instruction, Gronlund recommends stating a general objective first and then clarifying it by noting *samples* of the type of performance that indicates understanding. He notes that using sampling types of objectives leads to emphasizing more general principles and that mastering principles is more likely to lead to learning that involves understanding rather than simple recall.

Gronlund recommends the following procedure for stating objectives:

1. State the general instructional objectives as *expected learning outcomes.*

2. Place under each general instructional objective a list of specific learning outcomes that describes the *terminal behavior* students are to demonstrate when they have achieved the objective.

   (a) Begin each specific learning outcome with a *verb* that specifies definite, *observable behavior.*

   (b) List a sufficient number of specific learning outcomes under each objective to describe adequately the behavior of students who have achieved the objective.

   (c) Be certain that the behavior in each specific learning outcome is relevant to the objective it describes.

3. When defining the general instructional objectives in terms of specific learning outcomes, revise and refine the original list of objectives as needed.

4. Be careful not to omit complex objectives (e.g., critical thinking, appreciation) simply because they are difficult to define in specific behavioral terms.

5. Consult reference materials for help in identifying the specific types of behavior that are most appropriate for defining the complex objectives. (1970, p. 17)

When you begin to teach, you are urged to consider the use of instructional objectives. In some subject areas and at some grade levels, you may find that a detailed list of all objectives you want your students to achieve will be ideal. Such a list will permit you to be highly systematic in your approach to instruction, it will lend itself to precise identification of weak areas, it will give your students specific goals to strive for and information about how they are doing, and it will simplify arranging your instruction for accountability—if you are required to prove your productivity. If you follow Mager's suggestions, you might state objectives in terms of a *time limit* (e.g., correctly solve at least seven addition problems consisting of three two-digit numbers within a period of three minutes), a *minimum number of correct responses* (e.g., given a collection of twenty rock

Using instructional objectives

specimens, correctly identify by labeling at least fifteen), or a *proportion of correct answers* (e.g., correctly spell 90 percent of the words included in the spelling exercises presented during the preceding four days).

If you follow Gronlund's suggestions, you might devise objectives such as this list a teacher developed to use in a literature course:

> Appreciates good literature.
> 1. Describes the differences between good and poor literature.
> 2. Distinguishes between selections of good and poor literature.
> 3. Gives critical reasons for classifying a selection as good or poor.
> 4. Selects and reads good literature during free reading period.
> 5. Explains why he likes the particular selections of good literature that he reads.
>   (1970, p. 16)

Or, you might use this description of objectives to reflect understanding of scientific principles as a model to follow:

> Understands scientific principles.
> 1. States the principle in his own words.
> 2. Gives an example of the principle.
> 3. Identifies predictions that are in harmony with the principle.
> 4. Distinguishes between correct and incorrect applications of the principle. (1970, p. 34)

Another technique for stating instructional objectives, which is described and illustrated by John P. DeCecco in *The Psychology of Learning and Instruction,* is to describe them in this form:

> When you have finished reading this section on instructional objectives, you should be able to meet these objectives:
> 1. List the four components of Glaser's teaching model.
> 2. Describe terminal behavior in terms of the three components noted by Mager.
> 3. Distinguish between the types of instructional objective recommended by Mager and Gronlund.
> 4. Write two instructional objectives that illustrate Mager's suggestions and two which illustrate Gronlund's suggestions.

(Mager, Gronlund, and DeCecco present logical arguments in defense of using behavioral objectives but supply no data to substantiate their claims. Many other psychologists, however, have studied the impact of objectives, and Phillipe C. Duchastel and Paul F. Merrill, 1973, reviewed over fifty of these. They concluded, "A number of studies have shown facilitative effects. However, an equal number of studies have failed to demonstrate any significant difference" (1973, p. 54). They point out that one interpretation of this conclusion is that, since "objectives sometimes help and are almost never harmful . . . one might as well make them available to students" (p. 63). They also note that while they were concerned in their review only with research relating to facilitation of learning, behavioral objectives also give direction to teaching and curriculum development, and provide guidance for evaluation.)

In thinking about how you might use instructional objectives, you may wish to consider points made at the beginning of this book in the "Explanation of Lists of Objectives" (pp. x-xii). In some subject areas and at some grade levels, a list of explicit instructional objectives may be appropriate. In other situations, however, less specific objectives (such as those stated as key points or the equivalent) may pave the way for wider applications by your students. As Robert Ebel pointed out in the statement quoted earlier, "The proper starting point of educational planning ... is not the kind of behaviors present adults desire future adults to exhibit, but rather the kind of equipment that will enable them to choose their own behaviors intelligently." This point of view accords with observations made at the end of the last chapter regarding the degree to which a teacher should attempt to control the learning environment. In some cases it may be desirable to list all learning outcomes in the form of specific objectives stated in behavioral terms; in other cases it may be preferable to set the stage for more student-directed learning by offering objectives in a form that allows room for individual interpretation.

Ralph H. Ojemann (1968) amplifies Ebel's observations, stating that the behaviorist emphasis on overt behavior has been helpful in making descriptions of objectives more useful in many ways but that it has also contributed to neglect of a different type of objective. First he depicts a *school* or *laboratory* situation (e.g., a reading test) in which the student is provided with specific instructional materials, urged to do his best, and induced to cooperate (in the sense that unsuccessful efforts may have to be repeated); then he contrasts it with a *free-to-do*, or *on-his-own*, situation (e.g., voluntary leisure-time reading) in which the individual does whatever he wishes. Ojemann observes that those who stress stating instructional objectives have ignored this distinction between *controlled motivation* and *on-his-own* behavior. He suggests that recognizing the difference leads to awareness of the importance of including in analyses of objectives those that contribute to the student's feeling that what he is being asked to study will have personal significance or worth. Thus instead of simply stating terminal behavior in terms that reflect primarily what *you* want, Ojemann suggests that you invite students to begin a learning unit by discussing the potential significance to themselves of what they will be asked to learn. For example, in introducing a unit on specific gravity, Ojemann and Pritchett (1963) asked first-grade pupils to discuss "Why should we spend our time trying to figure out why things float?" In another situation, Finder (1965) asked pupils from an inner-city slum to discuss reasons why studying English would be worth the trouble before asking them to embark on such study.

A question often posed by students is; "What do we have to learn this stuff for, anyway?" Too often the answer of the teacher has been; "Because I'm telling you to learn it." In a sense, simply stating objectives in a specific, detailed, and explicit way reflects this answer. Ojemann suggests that a better answer is: "Okay. That's a legitimate question. Why *should* we study this? What are some ways this information might be of interest or of value to you?" Better yet, don't wait for the question to be asked. Invite students to discuss reasons for learning material before you present objectives—or, in appropriate situations, before you *write* objectives. If you provide a list of objectives after encouraging such a discussion, it would seem that students would have a different feeling about them from what is usually evoked by lists that are simply presented as something to be accomplished. In some cases, however, it may be difficult for students to anticipate some of the most important values of information. Therefore, it may be desirable for *you* to provide an explanation. Also, since it is not possible to predict how information might be used, you might explain that you are asking your students to learn certain information because experience has shown that it is *likely* to be of value. (In discussing the rationale of this book in Chapter 1, the point was made that since you have limited experience with teaching, you may not be able to recognize the value of some of the material you are being asked to learn. You were asked to accept on faith that every bit of information selected for emphasis has been chosen because it has high potential pay-off value for a teacher. In some cases, you may wish to make a similar statement.)

Listing objectives and guiding students to achieve them fit the open education themes of diagnosis, instruction, and evaluation. Allowing room for student choice, discussion, and interpretation of goals fits the themes of *provisioning,* in which children are free to move about, select, and manipulate materials and *humanness,* in which the students' own learning products are displayed and exchanged. This last point relates to Piaget's theory of development: Because the thinking of young children is different from that of adults, it may be difficult for adults to specify a series of objectives that will make sense to elementary school pupils. For example, David Elkind (1970, p. 70) points out that the original New Math program was not completely effective because it was written by adults who overlooked the differences between concrete and formal operational thought. Furthermore, the styles of conceptualization described by Kagan should be taken into account. In some cases, then, it may be preferable to state objectives in not too explicit terms to allow students to have greater choice when selecting and manipulating materials, to take advantage of student-student instruction, and to allow for variations between impulsive and reflective, analytic and thematic thinkers.

The last point in Gronlund's suggestions for stating behavioral objectives urges you to consult reference materials that help in identifying types of behavior appropriate for defining more complex objectives. Two such sources are the *conditions of learning* developed by Robert F. Gagné and the *taxonomy of educational objectives* developed by Benjamin S. Bloom and several associates.

Gagné's Conditions of Learning

Robert Gagné in *The Conditions of Learning* describes the conception of learning endorsed by most American psychologists. He notes that to understand how the newborn infant develops into an adult, consideration should be given to factors that are in large part genetically determined (growth) and those that are due primarily to environmental experiences (learning). Since many types of learning are largely dependent on events in the environment, they happen under observable conditions that can be studied scientifically. Gagné reviews the various theories of learning proposed by those who have engaged in such study and describes the prototypes which have emerged. He then observes:

> These learning prototypes all have a similar history in this respect: each of them started to be a representative of a particular variety of learning situation. Thorndike wanted to study animal association. Pavlov was studying reflexes. ...Kohler was studying the solving of problems by animals. By some peculiar semantic process, these examples became prototypes of learning, and thus were considered to represent the domain of learning as a whole, or at least in large part. Somehow, they came to be placed in opposition to each other: either all learning was insight or all learning was conditioned response. Such controversies have continued for years, and have been relatively unproductive in advancing our understanding learning as an event. (1970, p. 20)

This point of view is similar to that stressed by Dewey in the excerpts from *Experience and Education* quoted in Chapters 1 and 2 and emphasized again at the end of Chapter 5—you are more likely to profit from what has been discovered about learning if you make selected use of techniques based on different theories than to make exclusive use of just one approach. To facilitate such a procedure, Gagné describes different sets of conditions under which learning occurs. He summarizes his approach this way:

> There are as many varieties of learning as there are distinguishable conditions for learning. These varieties may be differentiated by means of descriptions of the factors that comprise the learning conditions in each case. In searching for and identifying these, one must look, first, at the capabilities internal to the learner, and second, at the stimulus situation outside the learner. Each type of learning starts from a different "point" of internal capability, and is likely also to demand a different external situation in order to take place effectively. The useful prototypes of learning are those delineated by those descriptions of learning conditions. (P. 24)

Three psychologists who have explored ways to make learning more systematic and efficient. Robert M. Gagné (upper left) is professor of educational psychology, Florida State University. He has carried out research on a variety of aspects of learning, and served as president of the American Educational Research Association in 1970.

Benjamin S. Bloom (upper right) is Charles H. Swift Distinguished Service Professor at the University of Chicago. His research and analyses of early experience, educational objectives, and mastery learning have had wide-ranging impact on psychology and education.

Robert F. Mager is research advisor on instructional systems to the American Institutes of Research and director of research, Aerospace Education Foundation. His books on how techniques of programmed instruction can be applied to learning situations have met with enthusiastic response.

This description emphasizes two components of Glaser's model of teaching: entering behavior and instructional procedures. On the basis of his analysis of the conditions of learning, Gagné proposes a hierarchy of eight progressively complex types of learning:

Signal learning. This is exemplified by the classical conditioning experiments of Pavlov, in which an involuntary reflex is activated by a selected stimulus (e.g., a dog salivates when a bell rings). Since such learning involves *involuntary* responses, it is basically different from the other seven types.

Gagné's conditions of learning

Stimulus-response learning. Notable here are Skinner's operant conditioning experiments, in which voluntary actions are shaped by reinforcement (e.g., a pigeon learns to peck a disc when progressively more precise disc-pecking movements are rewarded by presentation of food pellets).

Chaining. Individual acts previously acquired through S-R learning are combined when they occur in rapid succession, in the proper order, and lead to reinforcement (e.g., a novice driver learns to start a car by combining the skills and observations he has already acquired: checking to make sure the gearshift is in neutral, inserting the key in the ignition, turning the key, waiting to hear the motor start, releasing the key, depressing the accelerator).

Verbal association. Verbal chains are acquired through a process that includes the following elements: S-R connections already acquired in the form of words, a *coding connection* between old and new words, contiguity of each link with the following one, an indication that the new response is correct (e.g., a student of French learns that *alumette* is the word for *match* because as he learns it and as he correctly answers a question asked by the teacher he says to himself, "A *match* is used to illuminate, so the word for *match* is *alumette*").

Discrimination learning. A pupil learns to vary his responses to verbal associations as his store of them becomes more numerous and complex. The major difficulty to be overcome in this type of learning is *interference* between new and old chains (e.g., the student of French may forget previously learned verbal associations when he acquires new words. To prevent interference, he will need to thoroughly learn distinctive chains that will permit him to differentiate between words).

Concept learning. The learner responds to things or events as a class (e.g., the child learns the concept *middle* by being presented with many sets of different objects arranged in a line and by generalizing that regardless of size or shape, "middle" always refers to the one between the others).

Rule learning. The pupil learns to combine or relate chains of concepts previously acquired (e.g., a child combines the concepts *round* and *ball* when he learns that round things roll) in such a way that he is able to apply what he has learned to a wide variety of similar situations.

Problem solving   The individual learns to combine rules in a way that permits him to apply them to a wide variety of new situations (e.g., a child who understands that round things roll puts a ball in a place where it will not roll away).

Gagné argues that the more advanced kinds of learning can take place only when a person has mastered a large variety of verbal associations, which are in turn based on a great deal of stimulus-response learning. A student is more likely to grasp a concept if he is acquainted with a variety of verbal associations, more likely to understand rules if he has grasped appropriate concepts, more likely to solve problems if he has a large repertoire of rules.

Gagné's description of types of learning will be used as the organizational frame of reference for the remainder of this chapter. First, some suggestions will be offered on how you might encourage your students to master verbal associations and discriminations. Then the teaching of concepts and rules will be discussed. Finally, an analysis of techniques for teaching problem-solving, supplemented by some suggestions for encouraging creativity, will conclude the chapter.

Teaching Verbal Associations

As noted above, for students to be able to engage in more advanced kinds of learning, they must master a considerable number of verbal associations as prerequisites. Before a child can learn to read, he needs to learn the names of many things: before a high school student can perform experiments in chemistry, he needs to learn about chemical elements and terminology: before a future teacher can develop a theory of teaching, she needs to learn about the characteristics of students and the nature of learning. All the more advanced types of learning are based on the acquisition of verbal associations.

One of the clearest examples of verbal associations is *naming*. When a child attaches a sound to an object, he does so by developing an association between a stimulus and a response. Since such learning takes place through operant conditioning, it can be analyzed on the basis of the fundamental principles of this theory of learning. That is what Gagné has done in *The Conditions of Learning*, a title that reflects his major approach—the description of the conditions of operant learning for each of his eight types. In order for verbal associations (the fourth type) to be learned, the following conditions, derived from those described by Gagné, must be met:

1. Each stimulus-response connection which constitutes a part of the verbal association must have been previously learned (e.g., if a little girl is to learn to say "My doll," she must have had experience with a doll and be able to say "my" and "doll").

Learning verbal associations through chaining

2. The individual links in the chain must be presented in rapid succession and in the proper sequence (e.g., someone must give the little girl her doll and say, "My doll.").

3. The learner herself must actively make the chain of responses, because each response generates kinesthetic stimuli that become part of the next link (e.g., the little girl herself must say, "My doll.").

4. In most cases the chain must be repeated more than once in order to be learned (e.g., the little girl probably will have to hear and say "my doll" several times before she masters the phrase).

5. There must be confirmation of correct responses (e.g., when the little girl says, "My doll," someone else must smile and say, "That's right! My doll.").

6. If the learner tends to confuse one verbal association with another, selective reinforcement will be needed to clear up the confusion (e.g., if the little girl also calls her stuffed dog "my doll," it will be necessary for someone to say, "*This* is 'my doll,' *this* is 'my dog.' ").

7. If the verbal association is not used and confirmed from time to time after it has initially been learned, it may be forgotten (e.g., if the little girl fails to say "my doll" for a few days after she has first uttered this phrase, she may forget it).

All these points are based on the principles outlined in the preceding chapter in the discussion of experiments by Pavlov and Skinner. The principles include activity, repetition, reinforcement, generalization, discrimination, and extinction. In addition, Jenkins (1963) has demonstrated that the acquisition of verbal associations is greatly facilitated by *mediating links*—the *coding connections* that Gagné emphasizes as a crucial element in the learning of verbal associations.

Mediating links

You can also provide such links by arranging associations in some orderly relationship, by using verbal or visual cues, or by employing such specific aids as *mnemonic devices* (Jingles such as "*i* before *e* except after *c*").

Mnemonic devices

It has also been demonstrated (McGeoch and Irion, 1952) that extinction can be minimized if the learner is encouraged to add a new "part" or unit of learning as he rehearses previously learned parts. This kind of review is necessary because old and new associations interfere with each other, as Gagné emphasizes in his analysis of discrimination learning.

Suggestions for Teaching Verbal Associations

In the preceding chapter you were provided with some suggestions for applying operant conditioning in the classroom. The basic points emphasized were: (1) Use reinforcement. (2) When generalization occurs, use selective reinforcement to teach discrimination. (3) Organize units of study into a logical sequence. The following suggestions supplement these ideas. They are based on Gagné's conception of a hierarchy of types of learning and on the experiments described in the last two paragraphs. Now that you have been acquainted with all the prerequisite ideas organized in sequence and have been provided with some mediating links, which also illustrate progressive mastery of parts, you are ready to acquire some new ideas. But you are more likely to master the suggestions for teaching verbal associations listed below if you play an active learning role by adding applications of your own.

1. If appropriate, draw up a list of the verbal associations that your students will probably need to know in order to master a given topic.

2. Try to organize the verbal associations you have listed.

3. Use specific mediating links for verbal associations that defy organization or don't make sense.

4. Whenever possible, explain and demonstrate *why* you are asking your students to learn verbal associations.

5. Provide considerable repetition; that is, use drill, but make the drill as active, varied, and enjoyable as possible.

6. Once a bit of information has been learned, prevent extinction by combining occasional repetition with reinforcement. Have your students use the information in class discussions and tests.

1. *If appropriate, draw up a list of the verbal associations that your students will probably need to know in order to master a given topic.*

S-R psychologists emphasize the importance of specifying the desired terminal behavior as the first step in any learning situation. Gagné suggests that teachers using his hierarchy of types of learning attempt to list the specific verbal associations that students will need to master in order to learn particular concepts and rules and then assist the students to learn these verbal associations (or make sure that they already possess mastery). Although drawing up such a list may not always be possible, you are urged to spend some time analyzing the specific bits of information your students will need to know to prepare them for a given learning experience and then make an effort to teach these basic ideas before you attempt to teach more complex forms of learning.

Examples

Make a list of all the words in a primer, and make sure that first-graders are familiar with the things the words represent.

In a math class, list the symbols that will be used.

In a geography class, list the terms and place names that students will most likely need to know.

In the space below you might attempt to list the specific verbal associations you would want the students in your classes to know before you started to teach a specific topic.

_____

_____

_____

_____

In *The Conditions of Learning*, Gagné offers some examples of the learning structure of mathematics (pp. 175ff.), science (pp. 180 ff.), foreign language (pp. 190 ff.), and English (pp. 196 ff.). He lists hierarchies of things to be learned for selected topics within each of his subject areas, the hierarchies being based on his eight progressive types of learning. This is one way to map a plan for teaching a given subject. If you will be teaching one or more of the subjects outlined by Gagné, you may want to examine his examples. Even with such examples as aids, however, you may find it difficult to list verbal associations, concepts, and rules in that order because such an approach demands awareness of the *entire* structure of a given topic or subject. It may be necessary to list rules first and then work backwards. In many subjects the development of a hierarchy of things to be learned is a substantial intellectual feat.

You may find it more effective to augment Gagné's conditions with the *taxonomy of educational objectives* developed by Benjamin S. Bloom (1956) and several associates. In developing the taxonomy, Bloom collected lists of things that leading educators felt students should learn[1] and then classified the objectives into three *domains:* cognitive, affective, and psychomotor. The *cognitive* domain covers the same general types of learning as Gagné's verbal associations, concepts, rules, and problem solving. The *affective* domain relates to attitudes and values, the *psychomotor* domain to skills. (These last two major

---

[1] These lists are more detailed descriptions of the kinds of general goals (noted in Chapter 1) that Voeks describes in *On Becoming an Educated Person* (1970).

types of learning will be discussed in Chapter 8.) At this point an outline of the cognitive domain is provided (as an alternative to Gagné's hierarchy of types of learning) to serve as a framework for describing the terminal behavior you may want your students to achieve in a given topic or subject and to help you outline the verbal associations, concepts, and rules they will need to learn for each topic or subject.

If you decide to use Gagné's hierarchy or Bloom's taxonomy, in order to prevent possible frustration and the subsequent rejection of the whole idea of listing objectives, you should not expect to come up with a "perfect" list of objectives on your first try. The list of objectives for this book was derived toward the end of the development of the text, which in turn had evolved over fifteen years. For simple skills and subjects, you may find it easy to describe terminal behavior. But if your subject matter is fairly complex, it may be necessary to develop a list of goals through a lengthy process of experimentation, in which ideas emerge as you try out a variety of approaches to teaching. Only after you have gained complete familiarity with a given subject are you likely to be able to sit down and write out a reasonably coherent description of terminal behavior. Thus you may find the taxonomy described on the next few pages more meaningful *after* you have taught a year or two.

Bloom: taxonomy of educational objectives

Bloom's taxonomy is a comprehensive classification of *all* the goals he believes schools should try to achieve in their efforts to produce educated citizens. If one wanted to create a complete curriculum for the entire educational career of a student, he could use the entire taxonomy as a guide. Since you are not likely to be faced with such a master planning problem, you will probably find it more helpful to focus on those sections of the taxonomy that relate to your grade level and subject area. (When the list of objectives for this book was drawn up, only selected categories seemed appropriate. And since certain important ideas did not fit any of the sections in the published list, supplementary categories were added.)

The following outline will be most useful to you in drawing up lesson plans during your Methods course, your student teaching,* and your first years of teaching. Since it is likely to be of considerable value, you are urged to obtain the handbook containing the complete list. It is an inexpensive paperback that should be a valuable addition to your professional library. It not only presents a complete description of all the types of learning in the cognitive domain but also supplies for each type some sample test questions which might prove valuable in making up exams. The title is *Taxonomy of Educational Objectives, Handbook I; Cognitive Domain* edited by Benjamin S. Bloom.

Space is provided under each point in this abridged outline[2] for you to jot down appropriate learning experiences. If you find the taxonomy helpful, you might want to draw up your own outline, providing more room for notes.

---

[2] In this outline the headings (with the exception of "Intellectual Abilities and Skills") are the same as those in the complete taxonomy. The rest of the material is an abridgement.

Taxonomy of Educational Objectives: Cognitive Domain
Handbook I

KNOWLEDGE

Knowledge of Specifics

Knowledge of Terminology—What terms and symbols will your students need to know? (E.g., verb, noun, + −, H_2SO_4)

_____

_____

_____

_____

Knowledge of Specific Facts—What specific facts will your students need to know? (E.g., names of the states, chief exports of Brazil, the properties of H_2SO_4)

_____

_____

_____

_____

Knowledge of Ways and Means of Dealing with Specifics

Knowledge of Conventions—What sets of rules will your students need to know? (E.g., rules of etiquette, rules of punctuation)

_____

_____

_____

_____

Knowledge of Trends and Sequences—What awareness of trends and sequences will your students need to have? (E.g., nature of evolution, changes in attitudes about the role of women in American society)

_____

_____

_____

_____

Knowledge of Classifications and Categories—What classification and category schemes will your students need to know? (E.g., types of literature, types of business ownership, types of government)

_____

_____

_____

_____

Knowledge of Criteria—What sets of criteria will your students need to be able to apply? (E.g., factors to consider in judging the nutritional value of a meal)

_____

_____

_____

_____

Knowledge of Methodology—What sorts of methodology will your students need to master? (E.g., ways to solve problems in math, set up an experiment in chemistry)

_____

_____

_____

_____

Knowledge of the Universals and Abstractions in a Field
Knowledge of Principles and Generalizations—What general principles will your students need to know? (E.g., laws of heredity, laws of motion)

_____

_____

_____

Knowledge of Theories and Structure—What general theories will your students need to know? (E.g., nature of free enterprise system, theory of evolution)

_____

_____

_____

_____

INTELLECTUAL ABILITIES AND SKILLS

Comprehension

Translation—Ability to put communication into another form. What sorts of translations will your students need to perform? (E.g., state problems in own words, read a musical score, translate words and phrases from a foreign language, interpret a diagram, grasp the meaning of a political cartoon)

_____

_____

_____

_____

Interpretation—Ability to reorder ideas, comprehend interrelationships. What sorts of interpretations will your students need to be able to make? (E.g., give their own interpretation of a novel or a poem, gather data from a variety of sources and prepare an organized report)

_____

_____

_____

_____

Extrapolation—Ability to go beyond given data. What sorts of extrapolations will your students need to make? (E.g., theorize about what might happen if . . . , draw conclusions from given sets of data, predict trends)

_____

_____

_____

_____

Application—Ability to apply principles to actual situations. What sorts of applications will your students need to make? (E.g., take principles learned in math and apply them to laying out a baseball diamond, apply principles of civil liberties to current events)

_____

_____

_____

_____

_____

Analysis—Ability to distinguish and comprehend interrelationships, make critical analyses. What kinds of analyses will your students have to make? (E.g., discuss how democracy and communism differ, be able to detect logical fallacies in an argument)

_____

_____

_____

_____

Synthesis—Ability to rearrange component ideas into a new whole. What kinds of syntheses will your students need to make? (E.g., plan a program or a panel discussion, write a comprehensive term paper)

_____

_____

_____

_____

Evaluation—Ability to make judgments based on internal evidence or external criteria. What sorts of evaluations will your students need to make? (E.g., evaluate a work of art, edit a term paper, detect inconsistencies in the speech of a politician or advocate of a given position)

_____

_____

_____

_____

2. *Try to organize the verbal associations you have listed.*

Dozens of experiments in presenting short lists of words to students have been conducted (e.g., Underwood, 1964; Kimble, 1963). A typical experiment features a list of nonsense syllables (a vowel between two consonants, such as *zib*), a list of unrelated words, a list of words relating to one general topic, and a sentence. Almost invariably, the results indicate that few nonsense syllables and unrelated words are learned in a given period of time and that they are not remembered as well or as long as the related words and the sentence. These experiments emphasize why it is important to organize material and to make the most of every possible kind of mediating link. Do your best to avoid having

Classroom Questions: What Kinds?

This is the title of a book by Norris M. Sanders in which Bloom's taxonomy of educational objectives is used as the basis for structuring classroom activities. Here is an example of the use of the taxonomy in arranging a sequence of learning experiences for a social studies class:

Memory: What is meant by *gerrymandering?* (The student is asked to recall the definition given to him earlier.) . . .

Application: The mayor recently appointed a committee to study the fairness of the boundaries of the election districts in our community. Gather information about the present districts and the population in each. Determine whether the present city election districts are adequate. (The student is expected to apply principles of democracy studied in class to this new problem.)

Analysis: Analyze the reasoning in this quotation: "Human beings lack the ability to be fair when their own interests are involved. Party X controls the legislature, and now it has taken upon itself the responsibility of redrawing the boundaries of the legislative election districts. We know in advance that our party will suffer."

Synthesis: (This question must follow the preceding application question.) If current election districts in our community are inadequate, suggest how they might be redrawn.

Evaluation: Would you favor having your political party engage in gerrymandering if it had the opportunity? (1966, pp. 3–5)

Sanders notes that some students might find it difficult to get a foothold in coping with these questions and suggests a different approach for students who are not too highly motivated or creative. In this alternate technique, a list of questions is presented, and students are asked to decide which ones would be legitimate questions for collective bargaining. Some of the questions are:

How much should workers of various skills be paid?

How much vacation should workers have?

How fast should the assembly line move?

For what price should the products be offered for sale?

Who should be selected as the officers of a company?

How much should be paid to the owners of the company in dividends? (P. 132)

After studying the complete list of questions, students are presented with this synthesis problem: "What principles or standards can you devise that would help determine which of the above questions should be decided by collective bargaining?" (p. 133). This problem could be tackled on an individual basis or in group discussion.

Classroom Questions: What Kinds? contains many other examples of questions and activities for a variety of subject areas and for all grade levels. If you would like some hints on how to structure classroom experiences to develop higher level cognitive abilities, you are urged to take a look at what Sanders has to say.

students rote-memorize isolated bits of material. Whenever possible, relate new verbal associations to what is familiar, and emphasize relationships.

Stressing relationships is, of course, a major concept of field theory. Whenever you organize bits of learning, you are establishing structure, developing a pattern. However, Newman (1957) performed an experiment to demonstrate that structure may not always be desirable. He had students learn the meaning of symbols used in electrical wiring. One group was given the symbols arranged in a "logical" pattern, another group was given the symbols arranged in random order. The latter group made higher scores on a test given immediately after equal-time study sessions. It appears that for certain kinds of material, structure is not necessary, and if a teacher goes to elaborate lengths to impose structure on such material—especially structure that is beyond the comprehension of the pupils—such organization may do more harm than good. But for the most part, it is desirable for you and your students to use organizational aids as mediating links whenever possible. The taxonomy of educational objectives should assist you to provide organization and structure.

Examples

If you want students to learn the names and locations of the fifty states, organize the state names according to their position on the map rather than in alphabetical order.

To assist students to learn different chemical compounds, group those that are related. But keep in mind how generalization and discrimination function in learning. If you give too many similar terms at once, you may make things difficult rather than easy. (Further comments on this point will be made in the discussion of forgetting in the next chapter.)

In the space below note how you could organize the verbal associations you would like your students to learn for some specific topic:

_____

_____

_____

_____

_____

_____

_____

_____

_____

The Value of Advance Organizers

David P. Ausubel (1960) performed an experiment to demonstrate the value of *advance organizers* in the learning and retention of meaningful verbal material. He had college seniors spend twenty minutes studying a short passage on an unfamiliar subject. Then they were given a short, multiple-choice test to measure the degree of learning. On the basis of this test, two matched groups were formed. One group was given a short passage on quite abstract material about metals and alloys, emphasizing major similarities and differences, their respective advantages and limitations, and the reasons for making and using alloys. The control group was not given introductory material. Then both groups were asked to study a somewhat longer and detailed passage on steel. (Care was taken not to include any information *directly* related to the material on metals and alloys studied by the one group.) Three days later a multiple-choice test on the material was administered, and the group that had studied the advance information did significantly better.

Ausubel attributes the superior performance of the group that read the introductory material to the impact of *advance organizers*, which functioned as mediating links at a high level of abstraction. This permitted the students to integrate and relate the material they later studied. He suggests that teachers consider offering fairly general and abstract introductory material before presenting detailed information. Done properly, this will provide students with some structure to aid them in learning specific information. (The opening chapters of this book were written to provide you with some advance organizers.)

Advance organizers

In considering this suggestion, however, you should keep in mind Piaget's observations on intellectual development. The use of advance organizers involves comprehension at the level of formal operations (or the symbolic mode, to use Bruner's description). Ausubel used college seniors as subjects. Less mature students may be confused rather than assisted by abstract generalizations presented at the beginning of a unit. For younger students, it may be preferable to work up to bigger ideas or at least limit the use of relationships to material at a relatively low level of abstraction.

An additional point to consider has been noted by V. K. Kumar (1971), who emphasizes the desirability of taking account of student interests. (This reflects the views of Ebel and Ojemann noted with regard to using instructional objectives.) He suggests that since the instructor may not be sure the advance organizers he chooses will prove relevant to everyone, students might be invited to list what they consider are the key points in an outline of material to be covered. The instructor could then perhaps provide individualized or small-group discussion in accordance with the points selected.

---

3. *Use specific mediating links for verbal associations that defy organization or don't make sense.*

Despite all your efforts, it may not be possible (or desirable, as Newman's study indicated) to organize everything. Some things are arbitrary; for example,

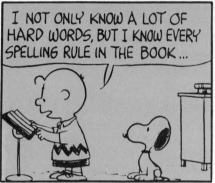

there is no logical reason why the letter *a* is shaped the way it is. In such cases you might resort to mnemonic devices. Specific mediating links assist the student to introduce at least *some* meaning into the learning of arbitrary and otherwise meaningless material.

Examples

In fourteen-hundred-ninety-two, Columbus sailed the ocean blue; *i* before *e* except after *c*; thirty days hath September . . .

If you have been taught or if you have developed on your own some mnemonic devices that have helped you master a meaningless bit of knowledge that your students will also need to know, note them in the space below:

_____

_____

_____

_____

_____

_____

4. Whenever possible, explain and demonstrate why you are asking your students to learn verbal associations.

A common complaint about education today is that it is not "relevant." Probably in some cases teachers *have* failed to consider the interests and needs of their students; hence what they are teaching is relevant only to themselves. However, in many instances students classify as irrelevant *any* material that does not have immediate practical value.

Yet in most subjects of study, students need to learn a great many verbal associations as prerequisites to understanding the concepts and principles of those subjects. If they are not assisted to persevere through the occasional drudgery of learning verbal associations, they may be unable to master not only the concepts and principles but also the exciting and rewarding bigger ideas that emerge when concepts and principles are put together. To encourage your students to reach this goal, you should do everything you can to convince them that there will likely be a delayed payoff and that valid reasons exist for committing large amounts of information to memory. And as Ojemann has suggested, you might invite students to participate in analyses of why certain information is worth learning.

You might explicitly point out that what they are now learning is preparation for later learning and explain *why* certain verbal associations and ideas need to be learned as prerequisites for mastering more comprehensive skills.

Examples

Explain to primary-grade pupils that thorough mastery of the alphabet will assist them to look up names in a telephone book, words in dictionaries, and items in encyclopedias.

In teaching sentence structure, explain why certain punctuation marks are important to know and use; e.g., explain that a capital is used at the beginning of a sentence so that the person who reads it will know that a new thought is being presented; that a period is placed at the end so that the reader will know that the thought is finished; that quotation marks are used to set off direct discourse so that the reader will know someone is talking.

In teaching mathematics, explain that the ability to supply immediately and automatically the product of 8 x 7 or any other combination of numbers facilitates computation.

If you thoroughly learned the basic principles of operant conditioning presented in Chapter 5, you are more likely to be able to understand the ideas discussed here. Also, the lists of objectives featured in this book are intended to help you not only comprehend the structure of educational psychology but also realize that learning many apparently irrelevant facts may eventually pay off.

5. *Provide considerable repetition; that is, use drill, but make the drill as active, varied, and enjoyable as possible.*

In addition to organization and mnemonic devices, you will need to use repetition in assisting your pupils to learn bits of information; this is, after all, S-R learning, which requires considerable reinforcement. But with ingenuity, you can make it fairly interesting if not actually enjoyable. A major point to keep in mind is to make learning as *active* as possible. Involve as many sense modalities as you can because active responses generate kinesthetic stimuli, which become part of the next link in the chain of verbal associations.

Examples

Have students pair off and use flash cards, or an equivalent, to drill each other.

After a new verbal association has been introduced, ask the class to supply it at frequent intervals. You might do this at the beginning and end of each period or even spring it on your pupils when you are talking to them about something else.

Use flash cards, informal team games (such as Spelling Baseball, in which you divide the class in half and throw a word to each pupil in turn), or offbeat methods of any sort. (A second-grade teacher whose pupils had been penned up in the classroom during two straight weeks of miserable weather devised a game in which she cleared the center of the room, chose three pupils, and asked them to line up against the wall. She stood at the opposite wall and dropped three cards with words written on them. The pupils sprinted across the room, picked up a card, and read the word. Then she asked each of them to make up a sentence using the word.)

Use informal, self-corrected quizzes.

In the space below you might note any additional techniques you could use to make repetition enjoyable—or at least palatable—in your classes.

Take Some Tips from Language Teaching Machines

Learning a foreign language is pretty much a matter of memorization. Twenty years ago this was done through laborious and inefficient rote memorization of essentially unrelated material. Each of the forty or fifty chapters in a text would present a list of twenty or so vocabulary words, three or four verbs, and an assortment of idioms and phrases. In many cases the phrases were not particularly related to anything and featured such improbable statements as, "The pen of my aunt is behind the big mirror on top of the old bureau in the garage." Such phrases *did* illustrate basic sentence forms, but they were difficult to work into conversation. Students were expected to learn all this material for biweekly quizzes. Class periods consisted mainly of round-robin recitation. Each member of the class would read a passage, and the teacher would correct pronunciation. Meanwhile, the rest of the class would brush up on the idioms for the quiz, doodle, or sleep. The overworked teacher would not get around to correcting the quizzes until a week after they had been written, and when they were belatedly handed back, the only feedback of interest to students was the score.

This is a classic picture of the kind of situation Skinner had in mind when he described traditional teaching as horrendously inefficient. The material was taught in a haphazard way—little or no effort was made to present a unified program of exercises; and feedback was either sparse or so delayed it did little or no good.

Today emphasis is on the conversational approach, on meaning, and on constant, immediate feedback. Instead of slaving away at silent memorization of unrelated words and phrases, the modern language student learns words and phrases that are actually used in everyday conversation. Instead of getting feedback for perhaps one-thousandth of what he says, today's student sees a word in print (in some cases he also sees a picture of what the word signifies), hears it pronounced by a native linguist, says it himself, and hears a playback of his own pronunciation. He uses his eyes, ears, and voice in learning; he makes the most of all kinds of mediating links and gets precise and immediate feedback on every word he utters. Also, the pupil systematically repeats old words as new ones are presented, putting into practice the progressive part method.

The elegant tape recorders used in language laboratories are among the most successful of all teaching machines, and they possess many of the advantages Skinner claimed for such machines: The material is presented in a logical and efficient way. Feedback is maximized. The student can proceed at his own pace and take up where he left off. The teacher can supervise an entire class at once.

Even though you are unable to use exactly the same approach as a language laboratory for monetary or other reasons, you might try to emulate language teaching machines when helping your students memorize large amounts of material. Make the memorization as natural, meaningful, and organized as possible. Encourage your students to be active as they learn—have them look at a word (*with* a picture, if the word can be illustrated), pronounce it, write it. Have students team up and give each other immediate feedback. And once a bit of material has been mastered, "program" it at frequent intervals to prevent extinction.

6. Once a bit of information has been learned, prevent extinction by combining occasional repetition with reinforcement. Have your students use the information in class discussions and tests.

For reasons already touched on, which will be discussed more completely in the section on forgetting in the next chapter, unrelated bits of information are forgotten quickly. Therefore, once such material has been mastered, it is important to repeat it and reinforce it, especially by the progressive part technique. If you are going to require your students to learn things such as the names of states and presidents, you should strengthen previously learned verbal associations by referring to them frequently and by arranging classroom situations in which your pupils will use the terms.

Examples

Make it a point to throw in review questions every now and then in class discussion and on informal exams. (For example, every week or so ask the class if they still remember when Columbus sailed, or whatever. If they don't, try another mnemonic device. You might ask members of the class to propose several possibilities.)

Keep on the alert for discussions in books, on TV, and in newspapers that tie in with the information learned. (For example, demonstrate how knowing the location of states helps clarify a newspaper account of a flood.)

In the space below you might note how you could work repetition with reinforcement into your class presentations.

_____

_____

_____

Teaching Concepts and Principles[3]

As emphasized earlier, the mastery of verbal associations is essential background for the learning of concepts and principles. However, verbal association learning is more tedious and inefficient than the higher types of learning because the formation of discrete S-R chains requires a great deal of reinforcement. Furthermore, also as noted, this kind of learning is highly vulnerable to extinction. Moreover, verbal associations—even chains of them—have limited applicability because they tend to be restricted to the physical environment. Not until the learner has mastered concepts and principles is he freed from the domination

[3] Gagné uses the term *rules* in his analysis of the conditions of learning, whereas other psychologists use *principles* to describe the same type of learning, i.e., understanding that can be applied in many situations. To emphasize this—and also because Principles is used as a heading in the lists of Key Points—this discussion features concepts and *principles*.

of physical reality; then the possibilities for further learning expand dramatically. Consequently, it is desirable for both teachers and students to concentrate on the development of concepts and principles as early and as much as possible.

Two pitfalls should be avoided, however. The first has to do with the nature of intellectual development. As Piaget and Bruner have emphasized, only the more mature children are capable of formal operations, or symbolic thinking. Gagné suggests that the reason older students are more capable of learning concepts and principles is that they have a much larger repertoire of verbal associations. The younger child is still in the process of acquiring basic ideas, and the teacher of primary grades or of introductory courses at any level should probably concentrate on helping students learn organized chains of verbal associations as opposed to emphasizing concepts and principles. It will be important for you to allow for your students' stages of intellectual development when you make plans to encourage the development of concepts.

The other pitfall is the possibility that you will push principle learning before students have mastered the basic verbal associations for a subject and that this will lead to verbal superficiality—situations in which students are able to state principles on cue but reveal by further responses that they do not really understand what they are talking about. The classic illustration of this all-too-common trap was given by William James in his *Talks to Teachers*:

> A friend of mine, visiting a school, was asked to examine a young class in geography. Glancing at the book, she said: "Suppose you should dig a hole in the ground, hundreds of feet deep, how should you find it at the bottom—warmer or colder than on top?" None of the class replying, the teacher said: "I'm sure they know, but I think you don't ask the question quite rightly. Let me try." So, taking the book, she asked: "In what condition is the interior of the globe?" and received the immediate answer from half the class at once: "The interior of the globe is in a condition of *igneous fusion*." (1958, p. 106)

If these students had been assisted in mastering concepts and principles regarding the composition of the earth, as opposed to simply memorizing meaningless phrases, they would have been able to answer the question. As Gagné puts it, "The effect of concept learning is to free the individual from control by specific stimuli" (1970, p. 182). In this case the specific stimulus was the intoning of the exact question by the teacher. Mastery of a concept is indicated by the student's ability to *generalize* beyond specific stimuli to a variety of situations—such as a question phrased in a different way. Unlike verbal associations, which are vulnerable to extinction, principles that are understood and applied are highly resistant to forgetting—in part because they are likely to be used in a variety of situations and use functions as reinforcement.

Suggestions for Teaching Concepts and Principles

Advocates of the discovery approach maintain that concepts and principles should be learned by the student himself with little direct assistance from the teacher. They argue that self-discovery leads to more meaningful and more permanent learning. However, Ausubel (1963) has demonstrated that giving the student a principle verbally is much quicker than any other teaching method and may well be as effective. The pros and cons of using the discovery approach in problem solving will be analyzed a bit later in this chapter. At this point some suggestions will be offered using the S-R approach to teach concepts and shape the development of principles. Gagné has developed an instructional sequence to guide teachers who wish to use this approach, and his sequence is the basis of the following list of suggestions. As with all types of programmed learning, first state the terminal behavior and then guide the learning so that the student achieves this behavior step by step. (For Gagné's own discussion of this sequence, see pages 195–203 of *The Conditions of Learning*.)

Teaching concepts and principles

1. *Inform students about the form of performance to be expected when learning is completed.*

Examples

Let's figure out what kinds of things roll.

Let's see if we can discover something about the composition of the earth just beneath the surface.

_____

_____

_____

_____

2. *Question students in a way that requires them to discuss the previously learned concepts that make up the principle.*

Examples

What do we mean by *round?* What are some round things in this room?

Remember when we talked about the eruption of that volcano in Hawaii?

_____

_____

_____

_____

3. *Use verbal cues to guide the students to put the principle together by linking the several concepts in the proper order.*

Examples

What do round things do if we put them down on a slanting surface?

Where did the lava come from when the volcano erupted? What temperature was the lava?

_____

_____

_____

   4. By means of questions, lead the students to provide one or more concrete applications of the principle.

Examples

If we put this basketball on the top of this slanted desk top, what will happen?

Suppose we dug a hole hundreds of feet deep on the island of Hawaii. How would we find it at the bottom—warmer or colder than on top?

_____

_____

_____

   5. If it seems desirable, use questions to encourage the students to state the principle in their own words.

At this point you are urged to select a principle you will want the students in your class to learn and then indicate in the blank space under each of the sets of examples above what you would say to the class to assist them to master the principle. If you take the time and trouble to do this, you will benefit from one of the most valuable aspects of principle learning; that is, you will learn to relate the principle to actual situations. To encourage you to do this consistently is one of the primary reasons for asking you to add applications of your own throughout this book. As you do so, you are in effect demonstrating to yourself that you understand the principle under discussion well enough to apply it; and this, in turn, means that you are more likely to remember it and use it in the future.

Teaching Problem Solving and Inquiry Methods

The final stage in Gagné's hierarchy of learning is problem solving. He places it at the end of the line because, "When problem solution is achieved, something is also learned in the sense that the individual's capability is more or less permanently changed" (1970, p. 216). In a sense all the lower states of learning are important, primarily as means to problem solving. Both S-R psychologists and field theorists agree that teachers should do everything possible to encourage students to function as independent problem solvers. They disagree, however, as to the best way to do this.

Skinner advises teachers to concentrate primarily on teaching subject matter but also condition students to pay attention, to study efficiently, and to engage in more varied behavior. If productivity and perseverance can be encouraged by systematically widening the ratios of reinforcement, programmed learning will likely foster problem solving.

Richard Crutchfield has developed some programmed techniques to try to accomplish these goals. He argues:

> It is not enough . . . that an individual merely be able to generate many new ideas; he must also have a highly aroused general set or propensity to do so, especially when confronted by cognitive tasks which require it. And he must know how best to apply his skills to the task. (1966, p. 64)

True to the associationist approach, Crutchfield maintains, "Sensitization and activation of the child's cognitive skills occur mainly through repeated experiences of their successful use by the child" (p. 64). (Note the emphasis on repetition and reinforcement.) In Crutchfield's opinion, current educational practice is seriously deficient in providing most pupils with such repeated experiences. For one thing, he points out, very few school experiences require a pupil to engage in genuine problem solving and thinking. Furthermore, many school tasks are too easy and appear meaningless; and cheap success or lack of proper reinforcement fails to shape the desired behavior. To overcome these inadequacies, Crutchfield outlines a general plan of attack that succinctly summarizes practically all aspects of teaching cognitive skills:

> Better teaching techniques for the fostering of cognitive skills must be developed. In particular, the child should be helped to identify, discriminate, and understand the nature and function of the skills involved in various kinds of cognitive tasks. He should be shown what can be done in problem solving and creative thinking through the effective use of these skills. Each child should be brought to participate actively in practicing and exploring these skills, principally through the experience of his own working through a great volume and variety of problem solving and creative thinking tasks. (Thinking should be a participant sport.) In all of this work, teaching techniques and instructional materials should be aimed toward providing immediate maximum informational feedback to the child concerning the results of his work, the effectiveness of use of his skills, the nature and sources of deficiencies in his performance. It is of paramount importance that feedback be tailored to fit the particular responses of the individual child, rather than being diffusely aimed at an entire classroom. This points to the need for development of more powerful and individualized tutor-learner feedback techniques than are now available.
>
> In curriculum materials and instructional efforts great stress should be placed on the transfer of cognitive skills. The child should be brought to understand the wide applicability of these complex skills to other subject-matter problems and to other fields. In other words, he should be deliberately taught to transfer.

The teacher must strike a balance: she must teach the skill in a sufficiently delimited manner so as to insure its being fully mastered, but she must also teach it as imbedded in a complex task, so as to insure its later transfer to similarly complex tasks where the skill is ultimately to be employed. . . .

Finally, attention must be given to the development and refinement in the child of an indispensable, overmastering cognitive skill—the skill of organizing and managing the many specific cognitive skills and resources one possesses for effectively attacking a problem. . . . This governing skill has many aspects. It involves an understanding of the nature of different types of problems and of the appropriate skills required in their solution. It involves the grasp of general strategies of problem-attack, the use of a "planning method" for breaking the problem up into manageable sequential steps. It involves a highly developed sense of timing—an inseparable attribute of almost all skills—and an ability to assemble component skills in an optimal pattern. It involves an ability to be flexible and adaptive in the use of one's often competing skills—being able to be alternatively intuitive and analytical, engaged and disengaged, serious and playful, creative and critical, seeking for complexity and striving for simplicity. And above all, it involves an understanding of how to compensate for deficiencies in certain of one's skills and how to exploit one's special talents, not only in the choice of the mode of attack on a problem, but also in the very choice of problems to work on. (Pp. 66–67)

If you decide to try to teach problem solving, you might use this description as a guide.

Crutchfield has developed some pictorial programmed materials for use in promoting problem solving skills in fifth- and sixth-grade children. He reports that the program produces "substantial increments" in performance (Olton and Crutchfield, 1969). It appears he has made good on Skinner's claim that problem solving can be taught through a program, independent of programs for teaching subject matter (see Figure 6–1, pp. 314–15).

Crutchfield: programmed approach to teaching problem solving

Field theorists share many of Crutchfield's views regarding the desirability of encouraging the development of cognitive skills. They argue, however, that the discovery approach is superior to programmed learning as a means of doing this. As they see it, a single discovery session is capable of providing the same kinds of learning produced by two or more separate programs because the pupil in a discovery session is learning subject matter while he is learning problem solving. They also object to the use of prepared programs on the grounds that such learning tends to make the student too dependent on the materials. When a student discovers things on his own, it is argued, he develops self-confidence and autonomy as a problem solver.

The field theory point of view can be traced to the educational philosophy of John Dewey. As revealed in excerpts cited in Chapters 1 and 2, he sees limitations in teacher-directed learning. He argues that true education is much more than the mere transmission of information, that education should encourage the development of the natural tendencies of the child, especially the tendency toward inquiry. He further insists that school experiences should help students

All the facts Jim and Lila have gathered about Mr. Search have given them a picture of what he is like.

5

What do you think they should do next in order to find out who Mr. Search really is?

Back home once again, Jim and Lila continue their discussion with Uncle John.

Notice that by working step by step, in an orderly way, Jim and Lila are being planful. They are using Uncle John's new guide:

Figure 6–1 Sections from a Lesson in the Productive Thinking Program

Covington, Crutchfield, Davies and Olton, Basic Lesson Five, *The Productive Thinking Program* (Charles E. Merrill Publishing Co., 1972), pp. 22–23.

learn how to inquire about things effectively instead of merely helping them to acquire information.

Dewey's ideas were interpreted and applied in unfortunate ways in the 1930s and 1940s, and he was blamed by the critics of progressive education for many of the "mistakes" of that approach to pedagogy. For example, some progressive educators oversimplified Dewey's philosophy, arguing that learning *any* factual material inevitably involves uncritical absorption of information and is therefore wrong. Even the most devoted discovery exponent of this era acknowledges that much information must be acquired before effective inquiry can take place.

A contemporary interpretation of Dewey's philosophy of education has been offered by J. Richard Suchman, who has conducted extensive experiments on *inquiry training*. Suchman points out that "learning by doing" was a gross oversimplification of what Dewey actually had in mind. Suchman suggests that a much closer approximation of Dewey's intent is summed up by the phrase "discovering by experimenting and thinking." Here is the way Suchman presents the field theory case for inquiry training:

> Concepts are ... most meaningful, are retained the longest and are most available for future thinking when the learner actively gathers and processes data from which the concepts emerge. This is true (a) because the experience of data gathering (exploration, manipulation, experimentation, etc.) is intrinsically rewarding; (b) because discovery strengthens the child's faith in the regularity of the universe, which enables him to pursue causal relationships under highly frustrating conditions; (c) because discovery builds self-confidence, which encourages the child to make creative intuitive leaps; and (d) because practice in the use of the logical inductive processes involved in discovery strengthens and extends these cognitive skills. (1961, p. 149)

Suchman suggests that in order to take advantage of these benefits of inquiry, the teacher follow certain procedures:

> The teacher can help the child by posing problems that are reasonably structured and will lead to exciting new discoveries. The teacher can also coach him in the techniques of data collection and organization that will lend power and control to his searching. (P. 150)

Suchman: discovery approach to instituting inquiry training

This description summarizes features of the discovery approach noted in Chapter 5 but places special emphasis on the techniques of inquiry. Suchman initiates such inquiry training by showing fourth- and fifth-grade children short films on such simple physics demonstrations as the following: A bimetallic knife is held over a flame, and it bends down; then it is put in water, and it strengthens out; next it is turned over and held over the flame again, and it bends up; finally it is put in water again, and it straightens out. The children are encouraged to find out "why" by asking questions that can be answered only by yes or no. Tape recordings of all sessions are made and later analyzed so that in subsequent sessions the experimenter can help the children ask more effective questions. He does this by pointing out that the most valuable questions are those that identify questions or events, that narrow the focus of inquiry, that "manipulate" the conditions of the experiment and lead to certain outcomes, that test hypotheses of cause and effect, and that check on the validity of conclusions. By the time the students in Suchman's experiments have been exposed to several films and postmortem sessions, they have become more adept at the techniques of inquiry.

Bruner uses similar methods in his discovery sessions. Some of these techniques were noted in Chapter 5, but a unit on geography will be described here to illustrate a slightly different approach to inquiry training. Bruner objects to teaching geography by having pupils memorize facts. Instead, he gives fifth-grade students blank outline maps and asks them to try to figure out where the major cities, railways, highways, etc., are located. Thus geography is presented "not as a set of knowns but as a set of unknowns" (1960a). The students are not permitted to consult books for other maps; they have to figure it out on their own by asking questions. (If you are impressed by Gagné's hierarchy of types of learning, you might feel that Bruner's approach fails to allow—in a systematic way—for the mastery of verbal associations as a prerequisite for the learning of concepts and rules.)

Bruner: discovery approach to teaching problem solving

It should be noted that not all children benefit equally from inquiry training. If Piaget's descriptions of stages of intellectual development are valid, children who have not yet reached the stage of formal operations can be expected to experience difficulty since inquiry training involves abstractions. Similarly, children who score low on intelligence tests also are likely to find it difficult to profit from inquiry training since most IQ tests measure abilities in dealing with the abstract. In addition, the different styles of conceptualization described by Kagan need to be taken into account. Children who are analytic and impulsive may find it difficult to deal with the inquiry approach. Despite these limitations, Suchman says that inquiry training should become an important part of the education of every child. Here is the way he summarizes his case:

> We do not suggest that inquiry or discovery should replace good, didactic exposition. If a child had to discover every new relationship for himself, a great deal of time and energy would be wasted. . . . But more basic than the attainment of concepts is the ability to inquire and discover these autonomously. Inquiry training is not proposed as a new way to teach science, but as a way of teaching basic cognitive skills that are just as important to the intellectual development of the child as reading and arithmetic. It belongs in the science program and in every other curriculum area that requires the performance of empirical operations, inductive and deductive reasoning, and the formulation and testing of hypotheses. (1961, p. 171)

To provide a bit of perspective, here again is Skinner's opinion on some of the limitations of trying to teach inquiry by discovery:

> The standard defense of "hard" material is that we want to teach more than subject matter. The student is to be challenged and taught to "think." The argument is sometimes little more than a rationalization for a confusing presentation. . . . In

the guise of teaching thinking we set difficult and confusing situations and claim credit for the students who deal with them successfully. (1968, p. 51)

Critics of the discovery approach have also pointed out that there is little proof it actually produces all that its advocates claim. In a review of available research on the discovery approach, M. C. Wittrock put it this way: "Many strong claims for learning by discovery are made in educational psychology. But almost none of these claims has been empirically substantiated or even clearly tested in an experiment" (1966, p. 33).

The Problem of Substantiation

To illustrate the complex and tangled nature of research on this topic, here is a description of some hypotheses about the values of the discovery approach, as well as an experiment designed to test these hypotheses.

In 1961 Bruner wrote an article entitled "The Act of Discovery." In it he argued that teaching inquiry through the discovery method benefits the learner in four ways: (1) It leads to an increase in intellectual potency. (2) It is more likely to encourage the learner to continue to discover things. (3) It provides him with some of the heuristics of discovery *as* he learns. (4) It facilitates conservation of memory because the material is organized in terms of the student's own interests and cognitive structures. (These claims are very similar to those noted by Suchman.) A few years later Bert Y. Kersh attempted to test these hypotheses by asking three groups of high school geometry students to learn two rules of addition. One group learned the rules through programmed instruction, the second group through guided discovery (tutorial instruction, which consisted of a form of Socratic questioning), and the third group by rote learning (the students simply learned the rules—no explanation of them was offered). Kersh measured the results by asking the subjects—after three days, then after two weeks, and finally after six weeks—to solve two problems, to state each rule, and to report whether or not they had made use of the rule after the formal learning period.

Surprisingly, the rote-learning group performed the best. Perhaps not so surprisingly, the guided-discovery group did better than the programmed-learning group in both the immediate and long-term tests. Kersh speculates that perhaps the superiority of the rote-learning group was due to the fact that the attempts to inject meaning into the rules for the other two groups caused an interference effect, which actually operated *against* mastery of the rules. On the basis of the results of this study (and of a related previous experiment) Kersh hypothesized:

> Learning by self-discovery is superior to learning with external direction only insofar as it increases student motivation to pursue the learning task. If sufficiently motivated, the student may then continue the learning process autonomously beyond

the formal period of learning. As a result of his added experience, the learner may then raise his level of achievement, remember what he learned longer, and transfer it more effectively. The explanation for the elusive drive generated by independent discovery is not evident, but several have been offered, including the Zeigarnik effect of superior memory for unfinished tasks and the Ovsiankina effect of resumption of incomplete tasks. It could also be explained in terms of operant conditioning; specifically, as a kind of "searching behavior" reinforced by the experimenter's comments and by the subject's own successful progress toward a solution. Whatever the explanation, the motivating power evidently does not appear in strength unless the student is required to learn almost completely without help and expends intensive effort over a period of 15 minutes or more. (1963, pp. 285–286)

Obviously, there is a lot more to problem solving than meets the eye. The results of the Kersh experiment demonstrate that many variables are involved. But how much would you generalize from this study? Did Kersh really test Bruner's hypotheses about the values of the discovery approach? Are rules of addition comparable to the kinds of activities advocated and used by Bruner and Suchman? (On the basis of a review of studies on problem solving, Carl P. Duncan [1959] concluded that teaching techniques that stress understanding appear to be no more effective than rote methods with simple tasks, but they *do* seem to be more effective with complex tasks. Are rules of addition simple or complex?) Were the Socratic tutorial sessions really comparable to the group-discovery sessions of Bruner? Was the program used with the pro-grammed-learning group well written or merely dashed off by someone who felt no enthusiasm for the project?

Before you could apply Kersh's conclusions with confidence, you would need to have all this information—and much more. The same questions pretty much apply to other experiments in this area—all of which means that, as with so many other aspects of teaching, you can't be certain which technique of encouraging transfer in problem solving is scientifically the best.

Thus close, objective scrutiny of the comparative effectiveness of programmed instruction and the discovery approach in teaching techniques of inquiry suggests, as noted earlier, that there is no trustworthy evidence that one approach is superior to the other. In *The Conditions of Learning*, Gagné argues that programmed learning leads to mastery of specific material and that this sets the stage for intuitive learning. And Crutchfield has demonstrated that cognitive skills can be taught separately through programmed instruction. While highly successful discovery sessions may produce all the by-products claimed for this method, less-than-perfect sessions may limit awareness of information (through "sharing of ignorance"), produce a hodgepodge of unrelated bits of information, lower self-confidence, and lead to a negative attitude toward learning. Taking all of this into account, it seems proper to think once again in terms of Stephens's theory of spontaneous schooling: either method may help students learn to think and solve problems provided it is used in appropriate situations by a teacher who acts with enthusiasm and confidence and makes an impact on her pupils.

Suggestions for Teaching Problem Solving

In trying to decide exactly how to make such an impact, you might consider some suggestions—derived from both S-R and field theory—as to how to teach inquiry, thinking, and problem solving. Many of the following recommendations parallel ideas presented in Chapter 5. The emphasis here, however, is on making your students specifically aware of *how* they are solving problems. According to learning theory, this should encourage them to use the techniques of inquiry in the future.

1. As a first step, teach your students the verbal associations, concepts, and principles and the necessary background information for dealing with a given area of study.
2. Encourage a classroom atmosphere conducive to free inquiry.
3. Encourage productivity of ideas—and the free expression of them before a sympathetic audience.
4. Set a good example as an intuitive thinker.
5. When appropriate, teach techniques of problem solving.
6. Keep in mind the nature of individual differences in problem solving ability.

1. *As a first step, teach your students the verbal associations, concepts, and principles and the necessary background information for dealing with a given area of study.*

In order for a student to proceed as an independent problem-solver, he needs to have mastered many verbal associations, concepts, and principles. It also seems desirable in most situations that he be in "full possession of the contributions of earlier thinkers" as Skinner suggests (1968, p. 89). And he should be thoroughly aware of general information relevant to the problem at hand. As Bruner puts it, "Intuitive thinking rests on familiarity with the domain of knowledge involved and with its structure, which makes it possible for the thinker to leap about, skipping stages and employing shortcuts" (1960b, p. 58). It also seems necessary for the pupil to have reached the formal operations stage of intellectual development, to be able to use the symbolic mode of thought. In other words, it is probably not practical to institute inquiry training much below the fifth-grade level. You might be able to teach younger pupils some of the rudiments of problem solving, but it would probably be an effort for all concerned.

Thus before embarking on a problem solving venture, your students should already have mastered the basic concepts and principles involved. If they haven't, remedy this lack; make them aware of what previous thinkers have thought (unless this would spoil discovery sessions); and make sure they are thoroughly familiar with the domain of knowledge involved. If you don't do these things, they will be likely to fail, and this will hinder rather than aid the growth of cognitive skills.

In the spaces below you might note how you could test for and provide these three basic prerequisites before organizing problem solving sessions.

What verbal associations, concepts, and principles must the students know? Have they already mastered these, or will they have to be taught?

_____

_____

_____

What and how much of the thought of previous thinkers do you want them to know?

_____

_____

_____

What background information will they need to be able to leap about intuitively?

_____

_____

_____

2. *Encourage a classroom atmosphere conducive to free inquiry.*

If you want your students to be free and intuitive, you will need to minimize restrictions and tension. If they feel too self-conscious or fear they will fail or be ridiculed, they are not likely to overcome their inhibitions and cut loose with free-swinging ideas.

3. *Encourage productivity of ideas and the free expression of them before a sympathetic audience.*

In their respective utopias, both Neill and Skinner claim an atmosphere conducive to creativity. Neill attributes the creative urge of Summerhill pupils primarily to freedom, including freedom from academic drudgery. Skinner speculates that if a Walden Two ever comes into existence, its inhabitants will be highly creative, partly because they will be free from both academic and nonacademic drudgery and also because the society will provide a constantly available, sympathetic audience. At Walden Two artists will have the opportunity to show their works to open-minded critics. Composers and dramatists will be able to have their works performed—they won't have to waste their time and energy seeking an audience to respond for the audience will always be there.

You might try to provide a limited Summerhill-Walden Two atmosphere in your classes; provide some time free from drudgery, and encourage your pupils to be productive and to express their ideas (or display their more tangible products) before a sympathetic and constructively critical audience.

4. Set a good example as an intuitive thinker.

Remember the importance of identification and imitation. As Bruner puts it:

> It seems unlikely that a student would develop or have confidence in his intuitive methods of thinking if he never saw them used effectively by his elders. The teacher who is willing to guess at answers asked by the class and then subject his guesses to critical analysis may be more apt to build these habits into his students than would a teacher who analyzes everything for the class in advance. (1960b, p. 62)

5. When appropriate, teach techniques of problem solving.

A variety of attempts have been made to analyze how the great problem solvers of history have made discoveries, with the hope that their mode of operation might be taught to others. One of the most frequently cited analyses (Wallas, 1921) describes the process of discovery as consisting of four stages:

Wallas: stages in process of discovery

Preparation—The acquisition of knowledge, the gaining of an awareness of how different ideas fit together, or the experience of being presented with a problem

Incubation—A period in which the various ideas are sorted out, sometimes in an unconscious way

Illumination—The "Aha!" experience when the solution dawns in thought

Verification—Empirical testing of the tentative solution

Perhaps *the* classic example of this process is the way Archimedes solved the problem of specific gravity. He had been asked, you may recall, to figure out if a crown was solid gold—or just gold-plated—without damaging the crown in any way. He had previously thought about the lawfulness of the universe and had a wide background of experience in many things (preparation). At first he was unable to solve the problem (incubation), but as he lowered himself into his bath one day, he suddenly grasped the solution (illumination) and ran naked down the street shouting "Eureka!" He later checked out his theory and found that it was valid (verification). Such discovery experiences are dramatic examples of insight learning.

Attempts to use these steps as a guaranteed "recipe" for discovery have not been very successful. But the following general suggestions for helping students learn some techniques of problem solving are derived from them:

a. Either present problems yourself (keeping in mind the suggestions of the various discovery advocates—Bruner, Bigge, Suchman—on exactly how to do this) or encourage your students to state problems of their own. Some teachers go a step further and require their pupils to state specific hypotheses to be tested. You might consider this approach if it seems appropriate.

b. Encourage and assist your students to find information relating to the problem. You can do this by teaching them how to use reference works, how to get the most out of the library, and the like or by using the question approach advocated by Bruner and Suchman. A limitation of using only the question approach is that students may not gain any experience with other ways of finding information. How many out-of-school problems, for example, can be solved by a question-and-answer approach?

c. Perhaps allow for an incubation period. One of the disadvantages of programmed learning, as noted earlier, is that reinforcement is usually immediate. This prevents the learner from doing some reflective thinking. The same limitation, however, *might* apply to group discovery sessions. If pupils are required to verbalize immediate solutions to a problem or ask spur-of-the-moment questions, the value of an incubation period—in which ideas are permitted to sort themselves out and jell—is eliminated. Consequently, you might experiment with a technique of presenting problems that permit pupils to do leisurely and independent ruminating before they attempt to pose an answer. It should be noted that group problem-solving sessions, in which pupils usually are frantically competing to be the first one to shout out the right answer, may destroy the relaxed atmosphere so conducive to intuitive thinking.

d. When illumination occurs, urge your students to state the solution in the form of a hypothesis if this is appropriate; in some situations the solution or observation is so obviously true it does not need to be verified.

e. Test the hypothesis or alternate hypotheses.

Encourage your students to follow the same procedure outside of class. Remember, transfer is usually not automatic, so it is wise to teach specifically for transfer. One way to encourage out-of-class transfer is to ask students to report on successful problem solving that takes place outside of school.

A different way of emphasizing many of these same techniques for developing problem solving abilities is derived from the work of Crutchfield and Suchman. Following is a list of suggestions you might want to use as a guide for shaping problem solving sessions if the list based on Wallas's four stages did not seem immediately useful.

a. Help students recognize and define problems. Assist them to perceive when a question is factual and can be solved by consulting a reference book such as an encyclopedia and when it is the type that should be dealt with by thinking about it.

b. Assist students to ask the right questions and to take a careful look at all available facts.

Habitual Set, Functional Fixedness, and Brainstorming

The incubation period in problem solving reflects the fact that the answer seldom comes immediately. One explanation for this is that previous learning may hinder rather than aid problem solving. (This is a form of negative transfer.) An example

Habitual set

is *habitual set*, the common tendency to use tried-and-true methods of solving problems or to keep on trying a relatively new solution that has worked in a recent situation. For example, Luchins (1942) had students solve some problems that involved measuring a given amount of water by using jars of different sizes. The first few problems were all solved in the same way. When slightly different problems were presented—problems that could be solved by a much simpler approach—the habitual set established by the previous experience blocked the students' perception of the easier method. (The technique of torpedoing used by Davis in his discovery method of teaching math is designed to make students aware of the impact of habitual set.) When the subjects in Luchin's study were admonished, ''Don't be blind,'' they were much more likely to look for new solutions.

A related characteristic of thinking that may interfere with problem solving is

Functional fixedness

functional fixedness, the tendency to associate certain objects only with certain familiar uses. Duncker (1945) demonstrated this mental attribute by giving subjects a problem to solve that involved using an open pair of pliers as ''legs'' for a simple flower stand. He discovered that subjects who were required to use the pliers conventionally just before being confronted with the novel-use situation were less likely to solve the problem than subjects who approached it cold.

Habitual set and functional fixedness illustrate that it is sometimes necessary to ''forget'' previous uses and solutions to things; that presenting too many aspects of a problem at one time may block rather than aid learning; and that sleeping on a problem sometimes helps. If you have ever had the experience of unsuccessfully trying to remember a name or similar bit of information, only to have it pop into your mind a little later, you may better appreciate why it makes sense to allow your students to have incubation periods when they are wrestling with problems. You may also have discovered that putting away a term paper for a few days usually helps you get a new perspective and detect flaws you were unaware of before.

In the 1950s a technique to nullify the impact of habitual set and functional fixedness was introduced. It was called *brainstorming* and consisted of having a group of people try to outdo each other in cooking up novel solutions to problems. The proponents argued that the relaxed atmosphere of such sessions would become contagious and break down inhibitions to the point where creative thinking would flourish. Initially they even argued that brainstorming would advance civilization at an accelerated pace since so many apparently ingenious ideas were concocted in such sessions. However, a careful evaluation of the ultimate value of such ideas (verification) indicated that most of them were impractical. Furthermore, a study by Taylor, Berry, and Black (1958) revealed that ideas produced by group brainstorming sessions were no better than those produced by individuals.

You might consider brainstorming sessions when they seem appropriate. Probably, a preferable basic strategy for overcoming habitual set and functional fixedness, however, would be to give students time to think about problems *independently*.

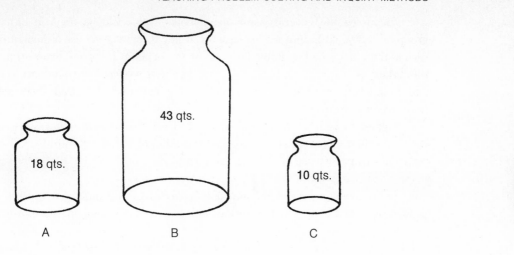

Problem 1: Given an **18** quart jar, a **43** quart jar, and a **10** quart jar; get **5** quarts.

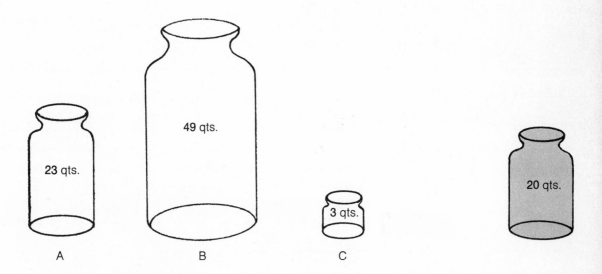

Problem 2: Given a **23** quart jar, a **49** quart jar, and a **3** quart jar; get **20** quarts.

Figure 6–2 Two Problems from Luchins' Experiment

The method used to solve the first problem may be used to solve the second one as well, but there is also a simpler solution to the second problem. If you find "habitual set" interfering with your ability to come up with the simpler solution to Problem 2, you will find the answer at the bottom of this page.

Solution to Problem 2: A-C (23−3 = 20)

Solution to Problem 1: B-A-2C (43−18−20 = 5)

c. Encourage the generation of many ideas. This could be done in either group or individual brainstorming sessions. It might include the use of heuristics such as those described by Polya. You might also explain, and even demonstrate, the nature of habitual set and functional fixedness so that your students will understand how and why mental blocks occur and recognize that there are times when a problem should be set aside for a while.

d. Suggest to your students that although a critical attitude is necessary at the verification stage, the generation of ideas should be free and intuitive. Also, point out that persistence in trying to solve problems is desirable but that stubborn persistence may block learning.

e. Try to develop persistence in problem solving by starting out with simple problems amenable to quick solution and gradually working up to thornier ones.

f. Keep in mind the value of problems that provide immediate (and individual) feedback and also the importance of making thinking a "participant sport," of teaching deliberately for transfer, and of encouraging the development of an overmastering cognitive skill.

If you can think of some specific problems to present to your classes in teaching them the techniques of problem solving, note them below:

_____

_____

_____

_____

In the space below you might take a stab at outlining a plan of attack—listing specific steps to follow—for solving the problems you noted above. You could use as a guide Wallas's four stages in the problem solving process, Polya's heuristics, or the list of points derived from the work of Crutchfield and Suchman.

_____

_____

_____

_____

A Few Qualifications

As you think about the possibility of teaching inquiry in your classes, it may be wise to keep in mind the fact that Crutchfield, Suchman, and Bruner all have worked with fourth- to sixth-grade pupils and have used mostly simple problems or demonstrations in physical science. These upper elementary-grade pupils have just achieved mastery of the symbolic mode of thought, which involves formal operations (to use the terms of Bruner *and* Piaget). Younger

Using Heuristics

The eminent mathematician Gyorgy Polya has written a book entitled *How to Solve It* (available as a paperback). Polya subtitles the book *A New Aspect of Mathematical Method* and points out that although its primary purpose is to make math more interesting, it is also designed to insure that principles learned in math courses will transfer as widely as possible. If you are going to be teaching math, you will definitely want to purchase this book. But it is valuable for all teachers who hope to make considerable use of problem solving.

The techniques discussed by Polya are sometimes called *heuristics*—strategies or devices that aid in solving problems. In many respects the heuristics described by Polya parallel the preparation-incubation-illumination-verification sequence described by Wallas. But the fact that Polya takes a slightly different tack may help you clarify your thinking about the nature of problem solving.

Here is a brief adapted outline of the basic heuristic methods described in *How to Solve It.* (For the sake of brevity, portions of the passage have been paraphrased; exact quotations are enclosed in quotation marks.)

Understanding the Problem

The first step is to "*understand* the problem. What is the unknown? What are the data? What is the condition? . . . Draw a figure. Introduce suitable notation. Separate the various parts of the condition."

Polya: suggestions for using heuristics

Devising a Plan

The second step is to "find the connection between the data and the unknown. Have you seen it before? . . . Do you know a related problem?"

Carrying Out the Plan

The third step is to "carry out the plan. Check each step. Can you see that each step is correct? Can you prove that it is correct?"

Looking Back

The final step is to "examine the solution obtained. Can you check the result? Can you check the argument? Can you derive the result differently? Can you see it at a a glance? Can you use the result, or the method, for some other problem?" (1957, pp. xvi–xvii)

An example Polya gives of how heuristics might be used to illustrate the solving of a practical problem (involving the construction of a dam, pp. 149–153) can serve as a model for structuring inquiry sessions. Suppose you structure a discussion by asking your students to analyze the economic and ecological significance of building a dam in the vicinity of the Grand Canyon. First of all, you might help students to *understand the problem* by listing *unknowns,* for example, the exact location of the dam, its shape and dimensions, the materials to be used; some of the *conditions,* for example, the need for electric power and water for irrigation, flood control, damage to fish and wild life, destruction of natural terrain; and some of the *data* needed, for example, topographic maps, geological information, figures on annual precipitation, estimates of the construction costs, projections of energy needs in that area. As the students *devise a plan,* they might be encouraged to learn about the construction and impact of other dams, and to investigate alternate sources of electric power. The actual *carrying out of the plan* would be imaginary, of course, but the importance of checking steps to *determine correctness* could be stressed as well as the point that what has been learned in attempting to solve this particular problem can be applied to other problems.

pupils may not be capable of similar types of thinking, and older students might be bored with or blasé about such demonstrations. Furthermore, simple physical science demonstrations are ideal for problem solving sessions. It seems possible that problems that are "unlawful" or that can't be answered in simple, definite terms can be frustrating to the point of producing a negative attitude toward inquiry.

You might also speculate about how much an overmastering cognitive skill really transfers. Advocates of inquiry training have tended to make lavish claims for the far-reaching value of cognitive skills, but, as noted earlier, there is little research evidence to indicate that students who have been exposed to such training actually are better able to solve problems than those who have not.

One implication of the current emphasis on inquiry training is that all people are potentially creative and should be encouraged to use this ability. Creativity will be discussed in the next section of this chapter. As an introduction to this topic, you are asked to consider these questions: If you devote too much time to teaching inquiry and cognition, will you be limiting the amount of information your students have with which to be intuitive? In other words, will it be better for you, in *your* classes, to concentrate more on information and subject matter than on how to solve problems? Or how much time should you devote to each? Those who favor inquiry training complain that the schools are producing students who know a lot but can't use what they know. But if you go too far in the opposite direction you may produce students who know all about heuristics but lack sufficient information to work with.

As you speculate about these questions, consider this observation in Gagné's *The Conditions of Learning*:

> What has learning to do with the great creative discovery? The most obvious and dependable answer is that discoveries of great social importance have been made by men with a great deal of knowledge. They are men who have acquired many kinds of hierarchies of principles. They have been deeply immersed in the principles of the discipline within which they work, and often in the principles of other disciplines also. How did they learn these principles? Just as everyone else does—by combining sets of subordinate principles; partly perhaps with the aid of verbal instruction, and partly by making the "small" discoveries that may be involved in the acquiring of the higher-order principles of any particular topic or knowledge system. (1965, p. 167)

6. *Keep in mind the nature of individual differences in problem-solving ability.*

Some people have more of a knack for being inventive than others. This may be due to a fortunate history of reinforcement, an inherited predisposition, or both. But not all students are equally effective problem-solvers. As noted earlier, there are differences among individuals in styles of conceptualization, in levels of intelligence, in levels of intellectual maturity, and in a host of unanalyzable factors (e.g., the kind of treatment the children have received from their parents), and all these contribute to differences in problem solving ability.

In using inquiry training, you might try to feature different types of problem solving for different types of thinkers. For example, Kagan (1966) has suggested that it may be necessary to teach impulsive types to be more deliberate, reflective types to be more impulsive. You might also keep in mind the likelihood that some pupils will thrive on inquiry training, others will be intimidated by it or simply not respond.

The current emphasis on inquiry training is an attempt by psychologists and educators to assist students to acquire and use general learning skills. From the theoretical point of view, much can be said for trying to teach pupils how to think and how to solve problems. From the practical point of view, this is not easy to do. But if the subject (or subjects) you will be teaching—or some aspect of it—lends itself to teaching for the transfer of cognitive skills, you are urged to make an effort to conduct inquiry-training sessions. In making this effort, you might find the following supplementary observations on creativity helpful. It has just been pointed out that even though you try to encourage all your students to become adept at problem solving, some are almost sure to be more creative than others. This pattern is found in every line of endeavor: a small number of highly productive individuals stand out. Thus an analysis of the characteristics of people who have gained eminence in a variety of fields is a logical starting point for an attempt at isolating attributes and environmental conditions conducive to creativity.

Encouraging Creativity

One of the most edifying and enjoyable accounts of the nature of creative individuals is found in *Cradles of Eminence* by Goertzel and Goertzel. This husband-and-wife team read biographies and autobiographies of 400 of the most eminent people of the twentieth century. Their book describes the generalizations that emerged as they compared notes. One of their major conclusions is, "It may be possible to be both creative and comfortable, but we suspect it is not" (1962, p. viii). They qualify this rather discouraging observation with the following conclusions:

In the childhood home of almost all those who eventually became eminent, there was an all-encompassing love of learning. "A strong drive toward intellectual or creative achievement is present in one or both parents of almost all of the 400 men and women" (p. 3). "They had driving, striving parents" (p. 9).

Many of the parents were extremely opinionated. The family attitude of neutrality and nondirective support that is championed by many contemporary psychologists was practically nonexistent.

Three out of every five of the eminent people had serious school problems. Many of them *hated* school. Only rarely were they all-around, competent, conforming students. Twenty-six were considered downright dull.

The teachers they admired the most let them go ahead at their own pace, gave them permission to work in one area of special interest, challenged them to think, and introduced them to exciting books.

Before inferences are drawn from these various findings, here are some related conclusions from a study of creativity and scientific talent done by E. Paul Torrance (1960). As a technological society, the United States is particularly interested in finding and developing future scientists, so this exhaustive survey is of considerable importance. Torrance found evidence that there is a peak of creativity at the second-grade level that tends to be squelched by demands for conformity. The curriculum, teachers, and peers all force a would-be original thinker to adjust to the norm.

Torrance also concluded that teachers are partial to the child with a high I.Q. but low in creativity. The study described the "typical" creative child in the following terms: He seems to "play around" in school; he engages in manipulative and exploratory activities; he enjoys learning (but not necessarily in school); he is intuitive and imaginative; he enjoys fantasy; he is flexible, inventive, original, perceptive, sensitive to problems, and has vital energy. In seven out of ten cases the creative student is *not* identified as intellectually gifted. The traits of "playing around," exploration, imagination, inventiveness, and energy can easily interact to produce a pest, which may account in part for the general failure to identify such children as gifted.

Suggestions for Encouraging Creativity

If the conclusions reached by the Goertzels and by Torrance are combined, it is possible to speculate on how to encourage creativity.

1. Try to emulate the family environment found in the homes of the 400 eminent individuals.

Exude a love of learning. More specifically, encourage the behavior of any pupil who shows signs of originality by recognizing and appreciating his efforts. By your own interest in everything, set an example of curiosity and inquiry.

2. Take some tips from the teachers who were admired the most by the Goertzels's 400.

As much as possible, let your pupils proceed at their own pace; permit them to immerse themselves in a specific area of interest if they become excited about it; also, introduce them to provocative books, people, things, and ideas.

3. *At the primary level especially, don't let the spark of creativity be smothered by rigid conformity to the curriculum or the standard way of doing things.*

Take a cue from the New Math; let your students figure out their own way of doing things if they prefer to.

4. *Don't require consensus on everything.*

Instead of trying to reach a compromise every time there is a difference of opinion, allow differences to flourish. Controversy can be a powerful motivating device; agreement on everything may be stultifying.

5. *Try to be open-minded about the original thinker.*

Be tolerant, if not enthusiastic, about the originality of imaginative, inventive, nonconformists even if they disrupt the blessed routine of things.

6. *Provide open-ended assignments that permit maximum opportunities for exploration, individuality, and originality.*

Developing Creative Thinking through School Experiences

Torrance is perhaps the most active worker in designing programs for encouraging creativity. The title of this supplementary note is the same as that of a concise paper he prepared for *A Source Book for Creative Thinking* edited by S. Parnes and G. Harding. (For a more complete description of Torrance's views on fostering creativity, see his *Guiding Creative Talent* [1962].) In this paper he lists twenty principles for developing creative thinking through school experiences. Some of these ideas have already been discussed in this book—in the sections on the discovery approach in earlier chapters and in this present section on teaching problem solving. In fact, a few of them have just been noted. But for emphasis and review, the complete list of twenty suggestions is given here. (For the sake of brevity, portions of the passage have been paraphrased; direct quotations are enclosed in quotation marks.)

1. "Value creative thinking." Be on the alert for new ideas, and encourage your pupils to develop all their creative talents.
2. "Make children more sensitive to environmental stimuli."
3. "Encourage manipulation of objects and ideas."
4. "Teach how to test systematically each idea." Starting as early as the third grade, show pupils how to define a problem and keep testing each idea. The heuristics described by Polya might be used as a guide.
5. "Develop tolerance of new ideas." This includes tolerance of unorthodox—and perhaps irritating—creative personalities.
6. "Beware of forcing a set pattern."
7. "Develop a creative classroom atmosphere"—a free, relaxed, unharried one.

Torrance: techniques for encouraging creativity

(*continued on p. 332*)

8. "Teach the child to value his creative thinking." Encourage students to note their ideas in concrete form whenever possible, perhaps in a special notebook set aside for that purpose.
9. "Teach skills for avoiding peer sanctions." If a highly creative pupil rubs too many classmates the wrong way, help him become more aware of the feelings of others.
10. "Give information about the creative process." You might do this by acquainting students with Wallas's four steps in problem solving and by noting some of the heuristics described by Polya.
11. "Dispel the sense of awe of masterpieces." Indicate some of the methods and difficulties experienced by famous creative people to dispel the notion that only a gifted few experience brilliant and perfect insight at the first try.
12. "Encourage and evaluate self-initiated learning." Avoid overstructuring the curriculum.
13. "Create 'thorns in the flesh.'" Ask controversial questions, and call attention to disturbing data.
14. "Create necessities for creative thinking." Confront your students with provocative problems. You might use the suggestions of Bruner and Bigge as guides.
15. "Provide for active and quiet periods." Remember the impact of habitual set and functional fixedness.
16. "Make available resources for working out ideas."
17. "Encourage the habit of working out the full implication of ideas."
18. "Develop constructive criticism"—not just criticism.
19. "Encourage the acquisition of knowledge in a variety of fields."
20. "Develop adventurous-spirited teachers." Try to put these various ideas into practice yourself. (1962, p. 45)

A program of this sort might contribute to a milieu favorable to the happy development of genius, in place of at least some of the misery which supplied the drive for most of the Goertzels's 400.

Summary

This chapter—devoted to suggestions on how you might teach different types of learning—has built upon the basic ideas presented in the preceding chapter, in which programmed learning and the discovery approach were analyzed. This accumulating sequence of ideas (the same type of sequence is found in many aspects of education) has been clarified and emphasized by Robert Gagné's description of eight progressively complex types of learning. Gagné's hierarchy serves as a frame of reference for the types of learning discussed.

One of the basic, lower-level types of learning is verbal associations; in order for a student to deal with concepts and principles with any degree of success, he must first master many facts. This task can be made easier by the way material is organized and presented and by the use of mediating links such as advance organizers. The more clearly a student grasps the structure of a given area of knowledge, the more likely he is to master higher-level concepts, which in turn leads to greater versatility in applying concepts to the solution of problems.

In assisting students to master structure, you may find it helpful to list educational objectives in a systematic fashion, perhaps in terms of Gagné's hierarchy or the taxonomy developed by Benjamin Bloom and his associates. While you can encourage problem solving by imparting to the student knowledge in the form of concepts and principles, it is also desirable to teach *techniques* of problem solving. This chapter has set forth suggestions for doing this, based on the work of Richard Crutchfield (emphasizing a programmed approach), J. Richard Suchman and Jerome Bruner (emphasizing the discovery approach), and E. Paul Torrance (emphasizing creativity).

Suggestions for Further Reading, Writing, Thinking, and Discussion

6-1 *Reading Gagné's Description of the Conditions of Learning*

Gagné's *The Conditions of Learning* (2nd ed., 1970) gives the rationale behind his classification of learning (Chapters 1, 2, and 3), explains each type of learning in detail (Chapters 4 through 8), and provides examples of how learning experiences might be guided in a systematic way by a sequence of lessons based on the classification. Gagné discusses learning hierarchies in a variety of subject areas in Chapter 9, readiness and motivation in Chapter 10, and the design of procedures of instruction in Chapter 11. If you like the idea of a carefully planned sequence of learning experiences, read one or more chapters of *The Conditions of Learning* and comment on how you might use his suggestions in your own teaching.

6-2 *Drawing up Some Guidelines for Using Instructional Objectives*

In Chapter 1, mention was made of Charles Silberman's observation that the primary cause of problems in American education is mindlessness. The development of interest in accountability also was described. If you hope to avoid a mindless approach, if you are required to demonstrate that you have brought about specific learning outcomes—or if you simply feel that it makes sense to first describe what you hope to accomplish and then take steps to do so—you will want to make use of instructional objectives. If you already have in mind a definite bit of subject matter you are sure you will present to your students, you might draw up a list of instructional objectives and work out the details of how you will determine if you have met them. If you find it difficult to look that precisely into the future, you might draw up a set of personal guidelines for preparing instructional objectives. In either case, you might consult *Preparing Instructional Objectives* (1962) or *Goal Analysis* (1972) by Robert F. Mager, *Analyzing Performance Problems* (1970) by Mager and

Peter Pipe, *Stating Behavioral Objectives for Classroom Instruction* (1970) by Norman E. Gronlund, or *Using Behavioral Objectives in the Classroom* (1972) by Daniel Tanner. (If you decide to draw up guidelines, you may wish to take into account the point made by Robert Ebel [page 287] stressing the desirability of goals that assist students to choose their own behavior and the observations of Ralph H. Ojemann emphasizing the difference between school behavior and "on-his-own" behavior [pp. 287–288].

6-3 *Examining "Taxonomy of Educational Objectives: Cognitive Domain"*

In this chapter you are provided with an abridged outline of the taxonomy developed by Benjamin Bloom and several associates in *Taxonomy of Educational Objectives: Cognitive Domain* (1956). To better understand the taxonomy and to gain insight into coordinating objectives and evaluation, examine this book. Chapter 1 describes "The Nature and Development of the Taxonomy." Chapter 2 discusses "Educational Objectives and Curriculum Development." The remainder of the book consists of definitions of the general and specific classifications followed by illustrations and exam questions. If you take a closer look at the taxonomy, record possible ways you might use it once you begin to teach.

6-4 *Looking into the Productive-Thinking Program*

Richard S. Crutchfield and his associates have developed a series of programmed picture-stories designed to "strengthen the elementary school student's ability to think." A discussion of the productive-thinking program appears in Chapter 4 ("Developing the Skills of Productive Thinking") of *Trends and Issues in Developmental Psychology* (1969) edited by Paul H. Mussen, Jonas Langer, and Martin Covington, and a curriculum library may have a complete set of the materials used in the program. The sample illustrations shown on page 314 of the text may induce you to order your own set of the lessons in the Productive Thinking Program. For information, write to Charles E. Merrill Publishing Company, 1300 Alum Creek Drive, Columbus, Ohio 43216. (A complete package of materials consists of Basic Lessons, a Teacher's Guide, a Chart of Thinking Guide, Reply Booklets, and Problem Sets workbooks.)

If you will be teaching at the upper elementary level, you will probably find the Productive Thinking Program of considerable interest. Lessons take the form of illustrated stories that a student reads and responds to. If you have the opportunity to examine these materials, describe your reactions to the program.

You might also consider using similar techniques to develop your own productive-thinking program. One possibility would be to base individual or class projects on comic books that present detective stories, perhaps even Sherlock Holmes. For insight into how a master of detective fiction provides the reader with all the clues before the detective solves the case, read an Agatha Christie mystery featuring Hercule Poirot or Miss Marple. See if you can figure out the answer before the last chapter. All the clues will be at hand. If heuristics attracts you, read and try to solve a Poirot mystery on your own. Then read another and make full use of heuristics. Poirot does, and by employing "method" and his "little grey cells" he always manages to solve a case. You might even make Agatha Christie novels the basis for a productive-thinking program at the junior and senior high school levels.

6-5 *Exploring Inquiry Training*

J. Richard Suchman has sought the same goal as Crutchfield—that is, fostering a student's ability to think or solve problems—but he favors a discovery rather than a programmed approach. To find out more about how Suchman institutes inquiry training (perhaps so that you can compare his method to that of Crutchfield) look for *The Elementary School Training Program in Scientific Inquiry* (1963) or "Inquiry Training: Building Skills for Autonomous Discovery," which appeared in Volume 7, Number 3 (1961), of the *Merrill-Palmer Quarterly*. If you read either of these, you might record your reactions and comment on how you might use techniques of inquiry training in your classes.

6-6 *Reading about Bruner's Approach to Inquiry Training*

Jerome Bruner's techniques of inquiry training are similar to, although somewhat less systematic than, Suchman's. You will find a description of how he encourages students to acquire general methods for solving problems in Chapter 3 of *Toward a Theory of Instruction* (1966). If you read this chapter, summarize your reactions to Bruner's approach and, if appropriate, tell how you might apply similar techniques in your classes.

(Note: Bruner uses exercises that are primarily mathematical. Suchman concentrates pretty much on phenomena of physical science. Crutchfield, on the other hand, features a variety of behavioral situations in his lessons. So Crutchfield's approach may be the most helpful to you in a wide range of situations.)

6-7 *Reading and Reacting to Skinner's Criticisms of the Discovery Approach to Teaching Problem Solving*

At various places in *The Technology of Teaching* (1968), B. F. Skinner criticizes the use of discovery techniques to teach inquiry or problem solving. He also offers arguments to support a programmed approach. One set of critical remarks is "Can Material Be Too Easy?" (p. 50). Skinner notes that "the teaching of truly creative behavior . . . a contradiction in terms." (p. 89). There is also a section on "Solving Problems" (p. 131), which is followed by some observations on "Productive Thinking" (p. 134), "Having Ideas" (p. 139), and "The Role of the Thinker" (p. 140). Chapter 8 is devoted to "The Creative Student." For an associationist's views on the encouragement of inquiry and creativity, read some or all of these sections and record your reactions.

6-8 *Sampling a Critical Appraisal of Learning by Discovery*

One of the main arguments for discovery learning is that it helps pupils learn to solve problems *as* they learn about other things, whereas with programmed instruction it is necessary to teach subject matter and techniques of productive thinking separately. In a 1965 conference, several outstanding psychologists made a critical appraisal of this and other claims for the discovery approach. The proceedings of the conference were reported in *Learning by Discovery* (1966) edited by Lee S. Shulman and Evan R. Keislar. The book contains articles by Bruner (Chapter VII) and Robert B. Davis (Chapter VIII) that report on favorable experiences with the discovery approach, critiques by M. C. Wittrock and Lee J. Cronbach (Chapters IV and V), and some "Psychological Insights" (Chapters X and XI), in which Robert M. Gagné analyzes the discovery approach with reference to his conditions of learning and Jerome Kagan does the same with reference to his types of thinkers. For arguments supporting and rejecting the hypothesis that by the discovery method students can learn how to solve problems *while* they are learning subject matter, read one or more chapters in *Learning by Discovery* and then record your reactions to the arguments presented on both sides.

6-9 *Finding Out More about Heuristics*

The teacher of mathematics or physical sciences is likely to find Gyorgy Polya's *How to Solve It* paperback (1954) especially interesting. The concise set of guidelines it offers might be used in encouraging students to learn to solve problems. Even if you will not be teaching math or science, you may find Polya's description of heuristics helpful and thought-provoking (and of assistance in solving Agatha Christie mysteries). If you read this book, you might note your reactions and, if possible, indicate what possibilities you see for heuristics in your classes.

6-10 *Analyzing Your Own Experiences with Habitual Set and Functional Fixedness*

The impact of factors that may interfere with students' attempts at problem solving will become clear if you analyze your own experiences with habitual set and functional fixedness. Can you remember any situations (academic or otherwise) in which use of a habitual approach to things prevented you from solving a problem? Can you remember any in which use of objects or techniques only in a "typical" way kept you from finding an easy solution? If you do not think immediately of situations like these, can you remember a time when you couldn't quite grasp a point or when a key idea eluded you at the moment you wanted it (while taking an exam, for example) only to pop into your mind later (as you were leaving a building *after* taking an exam, perhaps)? If you describe your own experiences, you might be able to assist your students to overcome similar blocks to problem solving.

6-11 *Reading about the Early Lives of Creative People*

In *Cradles of Eminence* (1962), Victor and Mildred Goertzel describe the background of four hundred eminent people who have lived in the twentieth century. Although not all of these famous individuals were creative, many of them were, and an analysis of the forces which molded their personalities sheds light on the kind of environmental experiences that seem to predispose a gifted person to develop his potential. The chapter headings summarize the main subjects discussed: Chapter 1, "Homes Which Respected Learning and Achievement"; Chapter 2, "Opinionative Parents"; Chapter 3, "Failure Prone Fathers" (half of the fathers of the four hundred were failure prone); Chapter 4, "Dominating Mothers"; Chapter 5, "Smothering Mothers" (smothering mothers produced dictators or poets—or both); Chapter 6, "Troubled Homes" (percentages from troubled homes: actors, 100 percent; authoritarian politicians, 95 percent; novelists and playwrights, 89 percent; composers and musicians, 86 percent; and military leaders, 86 percent); Chapter 9, "Early Agonies"; Chapter 10, "Dislike of School and Teachers." Some of these chapter headings may lure you to browse through *Cradles of Eminence* and relate points noted in the book to techniques for encouraging creativity in your classes.

6-12 *Examining Some of Torrance's Views on Creativity*

E. Paul Torrance has probably done more and written more about developing creativity in children than any other psychologist. For ways to stimulate your students to be as creative as possible—or at least to avoid squelching their creativity—look through one or several of Torrance's books or articles. *A Source Book for Creative Thinking* (1962) edited by S. Parnes and G. Harding contains an article by Torrance (as well as contributions by others). *Guiding Creative Talent* (1962) and *Gifted Children in the Classroom* (1965) are more extensive discussions by Torrance. If you read any of these, you might note your reactions and comment on ideas you think might be worth trying with your students.

6-13 *Examining the Views of Postman and Weingartner or George Leonard*

Leo Postman and Charles Weingartner have collaborated on two provocative books criticizing all forms of controlled education and advocating almost exclusive use of an extreme form of discovery approach. In *Teaching as a Subversive Activity* (1969), they present many of the same arguments advanced by A. S. Neill in *Summerhill* (1960) and also an extreme interpretation of the ideas first set forth by Combs and Snygg in *Individual Behavior* (1959). For a sample of the style and tone of their analysis you might read Chapter 3—"The Inquiry Method"; in it they describe the basic approach they suggest that all teachers should use and offer a set of proposals for improving education (pp. 137–140). In *The Soft Revolution*, (1971) Postman and Weingartner argue that education should be concerned not with formally presented subject matter but with relevant problems ("Schools should become institutes for social action,") [p. 28]. If this premise is accepted, they maintain it follows that students are smarter than professors, since young people are more effective in understanding and solving social ills than faculty members. For a capsule description of their philosophy read "An Open Letter" (pp. 20–37).

In *Education and Ecstasy* (1968), George Leonard makes many of the same criticisms of controlled education as Postman and Weingartner. He argues that the purpose of public education is "to prevent change" (p. 7) and that "teachers are slaves of society" (p. 8). He believes that the basic way to improve education is to increase the frequency, variety, and intensity of interaction between the learner and his environment (this is a suggestion somewhat similar to that made by Richard M. Jones in *Fantasy and Feeling in Education* (1968).) Although Leonard joins Postman and Weingartner in endorsing extreme forms of the discovery approach à la *Summerhill,* he also feels that properly used programmed techniques have their place. Unlike Postman and Weingartner who offer specific suggestions for improving education now, Leonard presents most of his proposals for reform by describing education as it might be in 2001 A.D.

All three of the books are quite thought-provoking, and if you sample sections of one of them, you might evaluate both the criticisms made as well as the proposals for improvement.

Recommended Reading in
Psychology Applied to Teaching: Selected Readings

If you would like to do further reading in books or articles mentioned in this chapter (and in the preceding "Suggestions for Further Reading, Writing, Thinking, and Discussion") without having to track down several separate volumes, you might peruse *Psychology Applied to Teaching: Selected Readings* (Boston: Houghton Mifflin, 1972). This is a collection of excerpts from books and articles from journals in psychology. The following selections provide extended commentaries on points noted in this chapter or mentioned in the "Suggestions."

Instructional Objectives: Excerpt from *Stating Behavioral Objectives for Classroom Instruction* by Norman E. Gronlund, Selection 22, p. 363. (See also Suggestion 6-2.)

Gagné's Conditions of Learning: Excerpt from *The Conditions of Learning* by Robert M. Gagné, Selection 17, p. 263. (See also Suggestion 6-1.)

Exam Questions Based on the Taxonomy of Objectives: Excerpt from *Classroom Questions: What Kinds?* by Morris M. Sanders, Selection 25, p. 389.

Encouraging Productive Thinking: "Developing the Skills of Productive Thinking" by Robert M. Olton and Richard S. Crutchfield, Selection 20, p. 313. (See also Suggestion 6-4.)

MINIMIZING FORGETTING,

MAXIMIZING TRANSFER

CHAPTER CONTENTS

EVEN IF YOU ALLOW FOR AGE-LEVEL CHARACTERISTICS AND PUT learning theory into practice in teaching verbal associations, concepts, principles, and problem-solving, you will still be faced with two problems that haunt every educator and student: *forgetting* and *transfer*.

When students are given a final examination on a subject a month or a year after they have taken the original exam, their scores drop alarmingly (R. W. Tyler, 1934). And in many subjects it is often extremely difficult to determine whether students are using what they have learned or indeed whether they have been influenced in any way by a given course. The fact is, many questions about real-life application of learning simply can't be answered scientifically. For example, some critics of professional education courses—notably the historian Arthur Bestor (1955)—have pointed out that no educator or psychologist has yet been able to prove that exposure to educational psychology leads to better teaching. This is true, but the task of controlling a sufficient number of factors to make a valid study of this question is almost impossible. Consider just one facet of the problem: How do you decide what criteria you will use to judge effective teaching?

There is the same lack of proof of transfer in all other subjects, with the possible exception of sensorimotor skills. How can you *prove* that the study of history—to turn Professor Bestor's argument back on his chosen field—has made a person better in any significant way? Those who teach the humanities speak of "transmitting disciplined thinking" and of producing "well-rounded graduates," but, as we shall see a bit later, there is no proof that they have done so. In some cases you just have to be willing to assume that a person who has done some thinking on a subject has benefited from it.

In this chapter you will be given some suggestions on how to cope with forgetting and transfer. First, causes of forgetting will be discussed, then techniques for minimizing the forgetting that is due to these causes. Next, transfer will be analyzed and ways suggested of producing maximum, permanent impact.

Forgetting

Nature and Causes

Forgetting is a problem for student and teacher alike. Right now you are bedeviled by forgetting every time you take an exam. When you begin to teach, the amount of forgetting that you encounter in your pupils may make you wonder whether teaching is worth the trouble. Unless you make a well-organized attack on forgetting, it can wipe out much that you have accomplished. In plotting preventive measures, it is important to consider *why* we forget. Here are some of the causes.

Disuse

Disuse as a cause of forgetting

The idea this word denotes is that people forget when the brain trace, which is the physical record of memory, fades away. This fading is analogous to the atrophy of a muscle that is not used. No one has yet come up with a satisfactory explanation of exactly what goes on in the brain when we learn something. There is agreement that *some* sort of change, or connection, takes place, but the exact nature of this process is yet to be pinned down. (Current research suggests that ribonucleic acid is the key.) Even so, it does seem logical to assume that a thought or idea or bit of knowledge that is used frequently becomes more strongly implanted than something that is only briefly considered, that an idea is made more permanent in individual consciousness every time it is activated.

Suppose you are able to learn the names of all the pupils in five different classes the first week of a new year. By the end of the report period, you will probably remember only the names of those pupils who ask to be called on quite often. If a student doesn't ask to be recognized until the end of the report period, you may have to mumble, "Yes?" and hope that this will sound a little bit like the actual name. Frequent repetition of names strengthens the brain trace; disuse, on the other hand, appears to cause names to fade quickly from memory.

Reorganization

Reorganization (sometimes called *distortion* or *trace transformation*) is more a description of what happens to memories than a cause of forgetting, but it merits mention. Quite frequently we don't forget things completely; a residue remains. When you are asked to supply an answer to a question about some rarely used idea, you may generalize and fill in the gaps with stray bits of related ideas you happen to remember.

Reorganization as a factor in forgetting

Reorganization is illustrated perfectly—and hilariously—in a book entitled *1066 and All That* (1931) by Walter Carruthers Sellar and Robert Julian Yeatman. This delightful little volume presents English history as a typical ex-student might recall it ten years after graduation. One example: "Joan of Ark was a French descendant of Noah, who, after hearing angel voices singing Do Re Mi, became inspired, thus unfairly defeating the English in several battles." As the authors point out in the preface, "History is not what you thought. It is what you can remember." No doubt you have had the experience of answering a test question not by writing about what the textbook author or the lecturer thought but by putting down what you could *remember*.

Repression

Some things are forgotten because they are unpleasant. This tendency to *repress*, or resist remembering, disagreeable experiences is a key concept in Freud's theory of psychoanalysis.

Repression as a cause of forgetting

Interference

In his analysis of discrimination learning, Gagné stresses the impact of interference between old and new verbal associations, a phenomenon called *retroactive inhibition.* You will tend to forget the names of former students when a new report period begins and you learn another set of names. A related factor in learning and forgetting is *proactive inhibition*, in which the old interferes with the new. You may have difficulty remembering new names because the old ones are still cluttering up your memory. Such interference is most likely to occur when similar material is involved. Remembering names is just one example. Memorizing spelling words is another; learning Spanish and French at the same time is another; studying for final exams in Psychology and Sociology at the same time is still another.

Retroactive inhibition and proactive inhibition as causes of forgetting

But even dissimilar things compete with each other since the mind can assimilate just so much at one time. As noted in the preceding chapter,

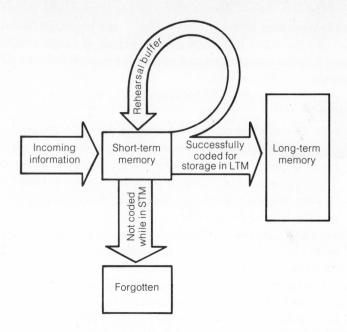

Figure 7–1 Memory Mechanisms This diagram illustrates the conception of memory that postulates *long-term storage* and *short-term storage* mechanisms. Incoming information is fed into the STM (short-term memory), and if not attended to, fades away. If, however, the information is attended to in some way (or *rehearsed*), it will be retained—at least for a short period of time. The set of memory traces maintained in STM at any one time is referred to as the *rehearsal buffer.* It is analogous to a filing cabinet with a fixed capacity—only so many bits of information can be stored, and as new items enter the rehearsal buffer, they push out old items that have not been attended to for a period of time. Information that has been rehearsed will be temporarily stored in STM. If a particular term is regarded as important, it will be *coded* and become a part of LTM (long-term memory). An individual may not be able to remember or retrieve everything stored in LTM, though, because the cues needed to identify the particular bit of information may be incomplete. This is analogous to an item that is placed in a filing cabinet under one heading, but is initially searched for under other headings. A person who examines his LTM thoroughly enough is likely to eventually retrieve the information that has been recorded.

Almost immediate loss of nonrehearsed information from STM is similar to forgetting due to *disuse.* Loss of information that was rehearsed sufficiently to remain in STM temporarily, only to be bumped out by new information, is similar to forgetting due to *interference.* Inability to retrieve information from LTM in complete or accurate form is similar to reorganized forgetting.

**The Structure of Human Memory and
Some Educational Implications**

This is the title of an article by V. K. Kumar that appeared in the December, 1971, issue of *Review of Educational Research.* Kumar provides a much more technical and exhaustive analysis of current research on memory than is presented in this chapter, but even though different terms are used, the implications are basically the same.

Those who specialize in research on memory now refer to three types of memory or storage systems (see Figure 7-1, p. 344): a sensory storage or register (SR), a short-term store (STM or STS), and a long-term store (LTM or LTS). Information is first contained in the storage register, then identified and retained in the short-term store; finally, selected information is assimilated into what is already stored in the long-term storage system. (This view parallels Piaget's theory of intellectual development in some respects.) The final phase depends to a considerable extent on what the individual *wants* to store, a point emphasized by E. Z. Rothkopf in this way; "A student has complete veto power over learning" (1970, p. 326). Among other implications noted by Kumar are these points: The short-term storage system has a limited processing capacity, which means teachers should select for learning a relatively small number of key points; students should receive ample time to learn new material through rehearsal (repetition) and be encouraged to use visual and verbal coding procedures (mnemonic devices); it is important to take into account the cognitive structure of students in assisting them to learn and remember.

Many of these points have already been noted in discussing learning; the others will be emphasized in this chapter. Thus the analysis of studies by Kumar serves to corroborate ideas that already have been developed.

---

interference is one of the major complicating factors in the learning of verbal associations.

Suggestions for Minimizing Forgetting

It is important to recognize the causes of forgetting and to try to remove them or at least minimize their influence. Here are some suggestions on how you might do so.

1. To combat disuse, use repetition, recitation, and review.
   a. Make sure your students learn things well in the first place.
   b. Make use of recitation, examples, and test questions to provide repeated exposure.
   c. Have frequent review sessions. In particular, compensate for "summer loss" and for the forgetting that occurs between the introductory and the advanced course.

346

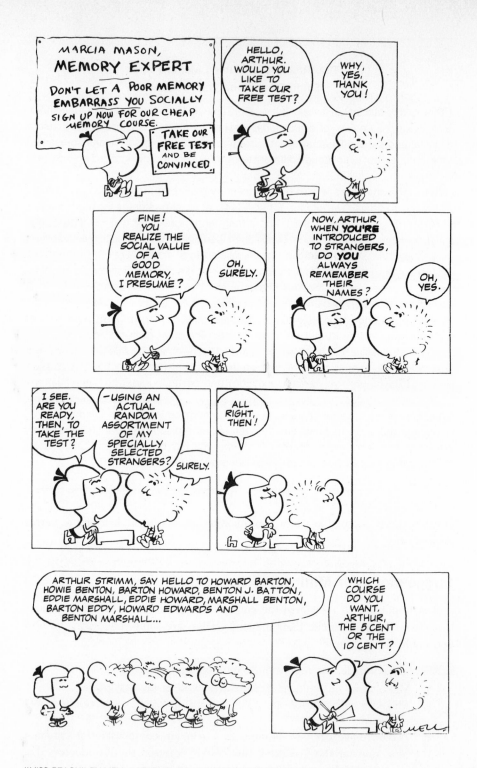

"MISS PEACH" BY MELL LAZARUS, COURTESY OF PUBLISHERS-HALL SYNDICATE

2. To prevent reorganization, or distortion, stress meaningfulness and encourage discrimination learning.
   a. Emphasize meaningfulness: deemphasize rote memorization or thoughtless repetition.
   b. If confusion becomes apparent, take up each of the conflicting ideas separately; make sure students master each one thoroughly.
3. To combat repression, make your teaching pleasant and enjoyable.
4. To minimize interference, encourage thorough learning, provide distributed study periods, alternate between intensive and relaxing activities, and make learning active.
   a. Help students really master material at the start.
   b. Use distributed study periods, especially with drill subjects.
   c. Alternate between intensive intellectual activity and relaxing pursuits.
5. Suggest to your students that they use the Survey Q3R Method of Study.

1. *To combat disuse, use repetition, recitation, review.*

   a. *Make sure your students learn things well in the first place.*

Brain traces fade more slowly if they are well established at the start. Therefore, it makes sense to encourage your students to do their original learning thoroughly. You shouldn't force students to repeat things to the point that they become bored or rebellious because this may tend to operate *against* their remembering; but you should keep them at something beyond the point of barely recalling the ideas or information.

   b. *Make use of recitation, examples, and test questions to provide repeated exposure.*

A second way to prevent disuse is to have your pupils continue to apply the idea or method learned. This is related to the points made in discussing the teaching of concepts and principles in the preceding chapter. Continue to present new ideas in as many different ways and situations as possible. One of the most direct ways to get pupils to use ideas is to give them quizzes and exams.

   c. *Have frequent review sessions. In particular, compensate for "summer loss" and for the forgetting that occurs between the introductory and the advanced course.*

Another way to prevent disuse is to incorporate frequent review sessions into your lesson plans. Be sure to do this at least before every exam, but use every opportunity to reaffirm or illustrate a previously learned point. (Many of the points noted first in Chapter 5 and amplified in Chapter 6 are being emphasized again in this chapter to take advantage of the value of repetition, reinforcement, mediating links, and the progressive part technique.)

Importance of review

If you will be teaching at the elementary level, it will be necessary to allow for the considerable amount of forgetting that takes place during the summer vacation. Studies (Bruene, 1928; Brueckner and Distad, 1923) suggest that the loss is greatest for specific skills such as spelling and multiplying fractions, rather than geography and science, and that it is more severe for incompletely mastered skills. For example, the reading skill of a first grader is more riddled by forgetting than that of a sixth grader. To offset this kind of forgetting, provide special review sessions at the beginning of the school year. In such sessions, devote most of the time to specific techniques and incompletely mastered skills.

If you will be teaching at the secondary level, it would be wise to give an informal, ungraded quiz at the beginning of every advanced course you teach. This will permit you to discover which key points the students have forgotten since they took the introductory course. If you then devote a few days to review of key ideas, with special emphasis on the forgotten points revealed by the quiz, you may be able to avoid considerable confusion and do a more efficient job of teaching.

2. To prevent reorganization, or distortion, stress meaningfulness and encourage discrimination learning.

a. Emphasize meaningfulness; deemphasize rote memorization or thoughtless repetition.

Values of emphasizing meaning and structure

To reduce confusion between similar ideas, which is the most troublesome form of reorganization, emphasize mastery of concepts and principles as much as possible. If your students really understand the idea behind something, it won't matter if they get some of the details a bit garbled. Furthermore, their use of concepts and principles may actually improve retention. R. W. Tyler (1934) found that whereas students suffered almost 80 percent memory loss for names of animal structures learned in a course in Zoology the previous year, they showed a slight *gain* in applying principles and a substantial gain—22 percent—in interpreting new experiments.

On the other hand, if students are forced to learn by rote, frequent distortions are to be expected. What's worse, the meaningless repetition may encourage the student to respond mechanically. The "igneous fusion" story is one example of this kind of rote learning. Another classic story is told of an elementary school boy who persisted in saying, "I have went." After correcting him a dozen times, his teacher finally exploded and sentenced him to write "I have gone" 100 times after school. As he reached the ninetieth repetition late that afternoon, the teacher left the room on an errand. When she returned, she discovered that the hapless pupil had finished his task and departed. On the board were 100 progressively sloppier "I have gone's," together with this note: "Dear teacher, I have wrote 'I have gone' 100 times and I have went home."

The moral of this tale is, of course, that repetition does little good unless the student is helped to *understand* his error. This story also points up the futility of requiring an excessive number of repetitions. It is usually more effective to ask an error-maker to do something the correct way a few times and *think about it* than to force him to do it 100 times, which will be so tedious and distasteful that he will almost certainly think about something else. For example, it is much better for a student who can't remember how to spell *principal* to write the word five times and make use of a mnemonic device by thinking to himself, "The principal is a pal," than to write it 100 times and think that his teacher is a louse. Furthermore, excessive repetition may actually encourage reorganization, since the repeated material may begin to look queer. (Try writing your signature twenty-five times in rapid succession and see whether you feel more—or less—sure of what you are doing.)

b. *If confusion becomes apparent, take up each of the conflicting ideas separately; make sure students master each one thoroughly.*

In his hierarchy, Gagné places discrimination learning between verbal association and concept learning to emphasize how new chains will interfere with old ones. To minimize confusion, make sure pupils learn the words in the first primers thoroughly; and if you find that your students tend to confuse the

---

A Few Things You Probably Never Knew

To illustrate the nature of reorganization, as well as the way the mind of a child works, here are a few statements originally handed in to an elementary school teacher, later published in a New York newspaper, and eventually included in an anthology by H. Allen Smith entitled *Don't Get Perconel with a Chicken*. (An earlier work of the same type was called *Write Me a Poem, Baby* [1956].)

We don't raise silk worms in the U.S. because the U.S. gets her silk from rayon. He is a much larger animal and gives more silk.
Denver is just below the O in Colorado.
An adjective is a word hanging down from a noun.
They don't raise anything in Kansas but alpaca grain and they have to irritate that to make it grow.
The Mediterranean and the Red Sea are connected by the sewage canal.
Marconi invented the Atlantic Ocean.
Abraham Lincoln was shot by Clare Boothe Luce.
When a man has more than one wife he is a pigamist.
An epidemic is a needle that puts you to sleep.
A spinster is a bachelors wife.
Chicago is nearly at the bottom of Lake Michigan.
The equator is a menagerie lion running around the earth and through Africa.
When you breathe you inspire and when you don't you expire.
A blizzard is the inside of a fowl. (1959, pp. 38–39)

These excerpts also illustrate why it is wise for a teacher to get some feedback from time to time, just to find out what pupils *really* think.

---

techniques of multiplying and dividing fractions, or adverbs and adjectives, review the conflicting ideas separately, and make sure that they understand the first one before you take up the other.

3. To combat repression, make your room and your teaching pleasant and enjoyable.

Other things being equal, pupils learn more and remember more in an agreeable atmosphere. The obvious way to avoid the negative influence of repression is to make life in your classroom as enjoyable as possible.

4. To minimize interference, encourage thorough learning, provide distrib- uted study periods, alternate between intensive and relaxing activities, and make learning active.

a. Help students really master material at the start.

Something learned well is less likely to be displaced by new material, so make sure that important ideas are learned thoroughly.

b. Provide distributed study periods, especially with drill subjects.

If you have a list of fifty spelling words to be learned, it is far better to present ten words a day during short study periods on each of several days than to give all fifty at once. This is called *distributed practice,* and the obvious reason for it is to prevent the words from interfering with one another. You are actually encouraging retroactive and proactive inhibition when you present too much material in one period. You should also use the progressive part technique to reinforce previously learned words as you present new ones.

Making use of distributed practice

In distributed practice, it is usually necessary to divide the material into small parts, which because of the *serial-position effect* (R. C. Atkinson, 1957) seems to be the best way for students to learn and retain unrelated material (e.g., spelling words). The serial-position effect is the tendency of people to learn and remember the words at the beginning and end of a long list more easily than those in the middle. When you use short lists, you in effect eliminate the hard-to-memorize middle ground.

Minimizing the serial-position effect

However, the part approach may not be the best way to assist students to learn and retain meaningful material (e.g., a role in a play). It may be preferable for the learner to concentrate on large amounts of material at once in order to make the most of overall organization and structure. Considerable research has been done on the question of the part versus the whole method, and it is difficult to pin down definite conclusions. However, the following general guidelines were offered by McGeoch and Irion after they had reviewed a large number of studies:

Relative merits of whole and part procedures

The more intelligent the subject, the more likely that the whole method will be advantageous.

The advantage of the whole method increases with practice in using it.

When practice is distributed rather than massed, the whole method becomes increasingly favorable.

Material that is meaningful and unified tends to favor the whole method.

A disadvantage of the part method is the time required to connect the separate learned parts. Methods that get around this difficulty will reduce the advantages of the whole method. (1952, pp. 501–507)

If you will be teaching a subject such as dramatics or music, which require the memorization of large amounts of material, you might want to refer to this list when the time comes to assist your students to learn a role or a composition.

c. *Alternate between intensive intellectual activity and relaxing pursuits.*

Studies of forgetting reveal that the greatest amount of interference occurs when one intellectual activity is followed by a similar intellectual activity (Gibson, 1941). The least interference comes from sleep or rest (Jenkins and Dallenbach, 1924). Thus from a theoretical point of view there are advantages in putting your students to sleep. A more practical approach is to try to schedule things so that periods of intensive intellectual activity are followed by restful or nonacademic activities.

5. *Suggest to your students that they use the Survey Q3R Method of Study.*

Francis P. Robinson (1961) has developed a method of study that takes into account research on memory. You might try it yourself and also recommend that your students practice it. The title for the technique reflects these steps:

Survey: Glance over headings in a chapter or unit of study to grasp the main points and read the final summary if there is one.

Question: Convert the first heading into a question.

Read: Read to answer the question.

Recite: Look away from the material and try to answer the question, preferably by jotting down key phrases on a piece of paper.

Repeat these steps for the other headings.

Review: After reading the entire selection, look over your notes on main points and fill in subpoints verbally or in writing. Then expose each major point and check your ability to supply the subpoints listed under it.

In addition to suggesting that your students use this technique on their own, you might adapt it for learning sessions with the entire class or small groups of students.

The Importance of Structure

Before turning away from the topic of forgetting, the importance of structure, of some sort of pattern or framework for aiding learning, will be emphasized once again. To remind you of the multiple value of structure, here is a statement from Jerome Bruner's *The Process of Education,* which amplifies the excerpt used as an advance organizer in Chapter 2:

Importance of structure

> Teaching specific topics or skills without making clear their context in the broader fundamental structure of a field of knowledge is uneconomical in several deep senses. In the first place, such teaching makes it exceedingly difficult for the student to generalize from what he has learned to what he will encounter later. In the second place, learning that has fallen short of a grasp of general principles has little reward in terms of intellectual excitement. The best way to create interest in a subject is to render it worth knowing, which means to make the knowledge gained usable in one's thinking beyond the situation in which the learning has occurred. Third, knowledge one has acquired without sufficient structure to tie it together is knowledge that is likely to be forgotten. (1960, p. 31)

In the preceding section listing suggestions for minimizing forgetting, the suggestion that you emphasize meaningfulness implied the importance of structure as a memory aid. In the next section the two other major ways in which structure helps the learner will be discussed: first, in generalizing from what has been learned to what is later encountered and, second, in generating intellectual excitement.

Transfer

Its Nature

In the discussion of forgetting, attention was focused on relatively short-term projects, for example, helping students remember material for an exam or compensating for forgetting over a summer vacation. But the true test of successful teaching is whether or not a given teacher, book, or course of study has made a more lasting impact. This long-range effect is the essence of *transfer.*

However, not all teachers have cause to be upset if pupils *do* forget factual material. If you will be teaching a subject like English literature, the main thing you may try to do is instill a love for English literature. On the other hand, if you will be teaching a subject such as typing, you will be concerned that your pupils learn and continue to use proper techniques for manipulating the machine, for using accepted forms for letters, etc. The following discussion on transfer will make more sense if you keep this distinction in mind.

To provide some historical perspective, two early theories of transfer, both now largely rejected, are discussed in the following section. The subsequent section presents the current theory that general principles, ideas, and approaches to problem solving are the types of learning most susceptible to transfer. And the final section makes some suggestions for maximizing this kind of transfer.

A Brief History of Theories of Transfer

At the end of the nineteenth century it was believed that the "mind was like a muscle," to use the most common wording. A theory called *faculty psychology* suggested that the mind was divided up into a memory faculty, a reasoning faculty, etc. Related to this was the doctrine of *formal discipline,* which held that if a student was forced to participate in rigorous mental exercise involving one of the faculties, he would strengthen and develop that faculty. The reasoning was that a boy who did fifty push-ups a day would develop formidable biceps, that a boy who memorized fifty lines of Homer would develop a formidable memory.

These theories were originated, or appropriated, by advocates of "classical" education as a defense against those who argued that there was no longer any reason for teaching Greek and Latin. When a privileged young Englishman went off to Oxford in the early 1800s, he studied Latin and Greek so that he could prepare himself for a career as a scholar or barrister or for a Byronic tour of "the glory that was Greece." Such reasons did *not* apply for a middle-class, American boy in the 1900s who planned to be, say, a shoe salesman. Therefore, the theory of formal discipline was either manufactured or appropriated to justify the continued stress on these subjects.

This defensive strategy has been used by other embattled protectors of an entrenched educational position, and it is satirized in *The Saber-Tooth Curriculum* by J. Abner Peddiwell (a pseudonym for Harold Benjamin). This delightful book describes education in Paleolithic times, when the three skills most necessary for survival were scaring saber-tooth tigers with firebrands, catching fish by hand, and clubbing woolly horses (for clothing). These three activities became the basis for the curriculum of the school. Unfortunately, however, a new ice age emerged. The saber-tooth tigers got pneumonia and died, and they were replaced by ferocious bears who weren't the least bit afraid of fire. The streams grew muddy so that fish were no longer visible to be grabbed. And the woolly horses were driven elsewhere and replaced by antelopes, which could run too fast to be killed by simple clubbing. Therefore, in time, necessity led to the development of new techniques to insure survival: Clever hunters invented a pit trap for bears and a snare for antelopes, and clever fisherman invented a net to catch the no longer visible fish.

Eventually some "radicals" suggested that since saber-tooth-tiger-scaring, fish-grabbing, and horse-clubbing were obsolete, they should be dropped from the curriculum of the school and replaced by pit-digging, net-making, and snare-setting.[1] But the wise old men who controlled the school only smiled indulgently and said:

> "Don't be foolish. . . . We don't teach fish-grabbing to grab fish; we teach it to develop a generalized agility which can never be developed by mere training (in net-making). We don't teach horse-clubbing to club horses; we teach it to develop a generalized strength in the learner which he can never get from so prosaic and specialized a thing as antelope-snare setting. We don't teach tiger-scaring to scare tigers; we teach it for the purpose of giving that noble courage . . . which can never come from so base an activity as bear-killing." [2] (1939, pp. 42–43)

In the early twentieth century the "radicals" included such men as James and Thorndike, who sought some objective evidence to test the claims of the formal-discipline advocates. James started off with a simple experiment in which he demonstrated that memorizing one batch of poems has little or no effect on the ability of a student to memorize other poems. More elaborate studies of the same type were performed by other psychologists with the same results. Thorndike (1924) applied the *coup de grâce* with an immense study comparing the school records of over thirteen thousand high school students. The comparisons were set up to determine whether the study of Latin, or of any other subject, seems to have a pervasive effect on reasoning ability. The results indicated that several subjects had more of an impact than Latin but that no subject really made much of a dent in overall performance. This mammoth undertaking received a great deal of publicity and pretty much killed off Latin and the doctrine of formal discipline.

Thorndike: no increase in intelligence from study of a subject

The impact of the Thorndike study led to an overreaction, however. Educational leaders argued that since it was apparently impossible to change a student's capacity for reasoning or memorizing by having him study the classical subjects, the curriculum should be made ultrapractical to provide specific practice for "real life" situations. An attempt was therefore made to anticipate the skills that most young American citizens would need. Unfortunately, the various subject-matter specialists found it difficult to come to an agreement, and the final curriculum often was more a result of an internal power struggle in the school district than a dispassionate appraisal of basic needs.

Limitations of "real-life" education

Even so, this new curriculum was an improvement over formal discipline, and it did much to make teaching more humane. But there were a few problems that the innovators hadn't thought of. For one thing, "real life" for most pupils was often stultifyingly dull. Fairy tales were excluded from the primers, for example, since no real girl was ever going to eat a poisoned apple and sleep

---

[1] As you can see, some people complained about lack of relevance even in Paleolithic times.
[2] And as you can see, some teachers and administrators were just as disinclined to listen to criticism and suggestions for reform.

until the kiss of true love awakened her; instead, the stories described ways to help mother in the kitchen. Math students were asked to add grocery bills instead of wasting time on geometric proofs. English students wrote letters of application instead of themes on "What Literature Means to Me." Foreign languages gave way to driver training, since about the only student who would actually use French or Spanish was the one in ten thousand who planned to live in Europe or become an interpreter.

Another problem resulted from the tremendous amount of variation among children. The curriculum planners soon discovered that it was impossible to predict what several million students were going to need in real life when they came from widely varying backgrounds and were going on to such diverse and unpredictable occupations as ditchdigging, computer operating, and astronauting. The new primers were just right only if a child had a white-collared father and an angelic mother who always smiled as she tidied up her $35,000 home. The other fifty million children didn't find this picture quite so familiar. When the "real life" approach was combined with the "whole-child" philosophy, which held that getting along with others is just as important as intellectual learning, the result was confusion and dissatisfaction with the schools on the part of many citizens and critics outside of education. (For a detailed analysis of the whole tangled debacle, consult *Let's Talk Sense about Our Schools* (1953) and *A Fourth of a Nation* (1957) both by Paul Woodring.)

Current Views of Transfer

Then the Russians launched Sputnik. Because of fear, hurt pride, and the fact that the "revolution" in education had already begun, some abrupt changes were made in educational philosophy. The blame for our inferiority in rocketry was placed on the schools, increasing the criticisms of the whole-child approach already being made. It was pointed out that real-life education seemed to be largely ineffective and that the deemphasis on academic subjects was producing something of an intellectual disaster. Added ammunition was provided by large business concerns, which reported that what personnel managers really sought were well-rounded, liberally educated humanists rather than inadequately prepared specialists in practical skills.

As a consequence of these various influences, we have returned to a certain degree of stress on theoretical subjects. Much of this shift can be attributed to a realization that since you can't possibly predict the specific skills a child will need when he gets out of school, what you should give him is first some general information so that he will know what the world is like and second some training in solving problems on his own.

The *sight*, or *whole-word* reading approach furnishes an excellent illustration of the limitations of "specialized" skills. The theorists who proposed this

Dick said, "Go, Jane.
Jump! Jump!
Jump, Jane!"

Figure 7–2 A Page from a Dick and Jane Reader

From *Fun with the Family* by Helen M. Robinson, Marion Monroe, A. Sterl Artley, et al. Copyright © 1965 by Scott, Foresman and Company. Reproduced by permission of the publisher.

technique argued that children would learn to read faster if they started out with whole words rather than letters. They thought they could anticipate all the words a child would need by listening in on nursery-school conversations and picking out the most frequently used words for inclusion in the primers. This worked pretty well as long as the child read only standard primers, but as soon as he encountered a book outside the standard series, he inevitably ran into words he had never seen before. The words might as well have been written in Greek or Chinese. He had learned to recognize words by reacting to their overall appearance, so the best he could do was try words he knew which were somewhat similar in appearance. More frequently, he just took a wild guess. And if he didn't have a parent or teacher around to tell him if his guess was correct, he was stalemated.

It took several years for the entrenched reading specialists to acknowledge these limitations of the whole-word approach and several more years for public and professional pressure to bring about a change. Most current techniques for teaching reading include the use of the alphabet or its equivalent so that a young reader can *sound out* a word he's never encountered before. Since he has heard and spoken many words, it's likely that the sound will give him a tip-off to the meaning of written form. As a result, today's reading pupil is provided with something his grandparents were given but may have been denied his parents—a general approach to reading that he can use in many situations rather than a severely limited number of specific responses (see supplementary note on the next page).

Before suggestions for maximizing transfer are offered, it may be useful to summarize the points that have been made in this chapter. First, the forgetting of specific facts is considerable, especially if they are learned mainly to pass an exam. Second, the belief that memorizing facts strengthens the mind even though the facts themselves are later forgotten is fallacious. Also because of the nature of retroactive and proactive inhibition, memorizing large doses of factual information probably weakens rather than strengthens the memory. And the idea that studying "logical" subjects, for example, Latin and Geometry, improves one's powers of reasoning is also false. On the other hand, educating students for "real life" by teaching them specialized, practical skills is unworkable mainly because it is impossible to anticipate the great variety of skills that will be required of different individuals in a rapidly changing civilization.

The best solution to this impasse seems to be to teach general principles and also approaches to problem-solving, since these two types of learning are most likely to transfer, and also to encourage the student to make individual applications as the need arises. But in order for this plan to be successful, the student must be shown that the principles are potentially useful so that when a situation arises in which they are needed, he will both remember them and recognize their applicability.

358

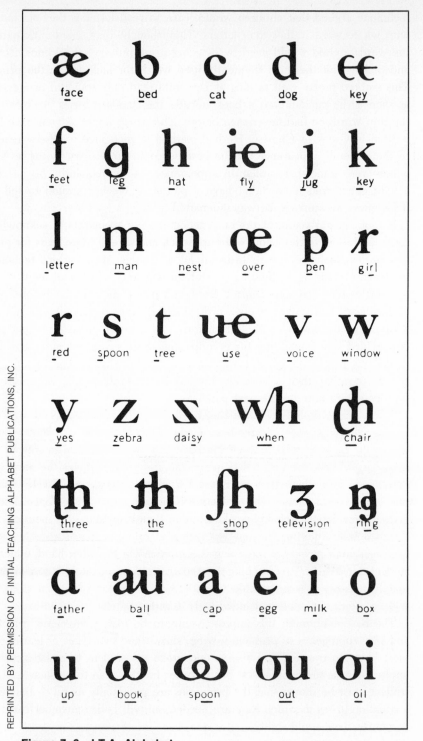

Figure 7–3 I.T.A. Alphabet

The Initial Teaching Alphabet

One ingenious approach to the teaching of reading features the use of the *Initial Teaching Alphabet*, or I.T.A. for short. This alphabet was developed by Sir James Pitman of England and consists of forty-four symbols, which are reproduced in Figure 7–3 on the facing page.

The proponents of I.T.A. point out that English is an inconsistent language. A letter can have different sounds in different words (e.g., b*one*, *one*, d*one*, g*one*). Some words are spelled the same but pronounced differently (e.g., *tear* meaning to rip, and *tear* as in crying). The long *i* sound can be spelled *aisle*, *height*, *choir*, *eye*, *pie*, *cry*, *sigh*, *buy*, *guide*, *island* (and at least twelve other ways.) The symbols used for lower-case and capital letters differ and so do those for written and printed letters. Because of these inconsistencies and the generalization they produce, learning to read through conventional methods causes confusion.

The fact that English is not a phonetic language complicates things for the beginning reader. According to Pitman, in the regular English alphabet two thousand or more visual patterns are used for the forty-four sounds of English speech. In the I.T.A. he uses just *one* pattern for each sound, which means that once the child has associated the forty-four symbols with their respective sounds, he can read any word. In addition, the child can *write* on his own at a much earlier stage. For further simplification, capital letters are omitted, and there is no difference between written and printed letters. Thus I.T.A. provides the child with a versatile, all-purpose alphabet that encourages transfer.

Suggestions for Maximizing Transfer

Here are some suggestions on how to promote the transfer of principles and the transfer of approaches to problem solving.

1. Make the situations discussed and the activities conducted in the classroom as similar as possible to those that the student encounters outside it.
2. Teach deliberately for transfer by emphasizing applications.
3. Encourage your students to apply the principles and ideas they have learned to a wide variety of situations.
4. Be alert to the possibility of negative transfer.
5. Try to "send your students away from your instruction anxious to use what they have been taught—and eager to learn more."

   1. *Make the situations discussed and the activities conducted in the classroom as similar as possible to those that the student encounters outside it.*

One of the clearest illustrations of this point is the scrimmage in athletics or the dress rehearsal in dramatics or music. An observation made by a high school principal is quoted on the next page.

I always said we were better because we spent our time playing basketball while the opponents spent their time practicing. That is, our practice periods were periods of play—just more and more basketball. There was little formal instruction, and no drill. All of the coaching was applied to actual game situations. It always showed when we played our traditional rivals—they were taught. We were so natural—and having such a good time! *They* were thinking, and it showed all over. When the pattern didn't work, someone was jerked. Our kids just did what came naturally from all those scrimmages. We got so good in basketball that the crowds finally began to drop off.

Not all coaches agree with this explanation of success, but many varsity athletes do. Some coaches become so fascinated with clever, intricate exercises and drills that they devote little practice time to actual game play. The same is often true of music teachers and occasionally of dramatics instructors. The glee club or band may spend most of their rehearsal time singing or playing exercises or concentrating on isolated sections of the pieces they are to perform. The result can be a disaster. If a band has never had a complete dress rehearsal for the big concert, never had a complete run-through, the conductor may find himself frantically singing sections of a piece when the instrumentalists get lost. This is the case with almost all skills and many academic subjects.

Providing class activities similar to those outside

If you want your pupils to apply outside of school what they have learned in school, do your best to give them "scrimmage" or dress-rehearsal experiences in class.

Examples

Throughout this book examples have been provided to indicate how principles of psychology may be applied in the classroom.

In business classes make the classroom as much like an office as possible.

In auto shop make the class as much like a garage as possible.

Use student body and class elections to teach students how to function as voting citizens.

In the space below you might note how you could feature "scrimmage" activities in your classes.

_____

_____

_____

_____

_____

2. *Teach deliberately for transfer by emphasizing applications.*

Simply to discuss general principles and to assume that your students will make applications on their own usually is not effective. In order for transfer to take place, you must teach deliberately for transfer.

Examples

In several science courses that a particular student took, considerable emphasis was placed on the scientific method. It was not until late in his college career when he encountered a first-rate teacher, however, that this student really became aware that the methods of science can be applied outside the laboratory. This exceptional teacher, instead of presenting a concept and simply hoping or assuming that his students would gain insight, continually pointed out how science can be used in everyday situations.

Twenty or thirty years ago, the subject of sex was taught by studying the birds and bees and flowers. Students were supposed to figure out on their own how this related to human beings. Because of new understanding of transfer, a more enlightened population, and the ever-increasing number of illegitimate babies born to high school girls, sex education today is more direct and specific.

In the space below you might note how you could emphasize applications in your classes.

_____

_____

_____

_____

_____

3. *Encourage and assist your students to apply the principles and ideas they have learned to a wide variety of situations.*

When you emphasize applications, point out that any given principle has almost limitless uses. If you apply a principle to only one or two situations, your students may assume that it has only limited value. Do your best to emphasize the fact that the "sky's the limit" as far as application of general ideas is concerned. (This is the same point stressed in Chapter 6 in the list of suggestions for teaching principles and in the discussion of problem solving. The point is repeated here not only to emphasize it but also to illustrate it.)

Examples

The multiple examples (in most cases more than one example is offered) and the write-in space throughout this book, together with the specific urgings to add examples of your own, have been provided to encourage you to make wide use of the various ideas discussed.

This description comes from a sixth-grade teacher:

> Lack of transfer of arithmetic processes to the solution of so-called story problems, or word problems, is notorious for bringing teachers close to tears of frustration. We forget so easily the difficulties we experienced so many years ago in the same situations.

> If one is not careful, the application of the arithmetic processes to applied problems is illustrated by two or three examples, and then the students are turned loose on problems very much like the examples. All goes well until a problem is reached which is not *exactly* like the example, and then the teachers are prone to say: "What's wrong with these children? They just don't want to think!" Our problem is that the students have not been taught to look for the similarities in apparently different problems. To try to help the students in the search for similarities in similar, but outwardly different, situations I tried the following plan:

> To an example like $3 \times 5 + 6$, I asked each child to bring in a story problem which could be solved by making the computation. The variety of problems submitted was astounding. (For example: If John, Myrtle, and Hank each see five different flying saucers, but none of them see the six hidden behind the hill, how many flying saucers are there?) These word problems were then redistributed, and the children were required to assign to each word problem the corresponding arithmetic examples. It is too early to tell just how well this is working, but I am feeling pretty optimistic about it.

Learning sets

The preceding example illustrates both the advantages and the disadvantages of teaching a general technique and encouraging a large number of similar applications. In solving many similar problems, students develop a *learning set*. This term was coined by Harry F. Harlow (1949), who did experiments with monkeys to demonstrate how they came to solve problems with almost 100 percent success after 300 trials. In effect, the monkeys were *learning to learn* as they solved the problems. However, the example described by the sixth-grade teacher indicates that in the very process of learning how to solve a particular type of problem, students tend to get into a rut, which may cause difficulty when they encounter slightly different problems. This is the same sort of contingency that Robert B. Davis (1966) tries to combat with his torpedoing technique for teaching math through a discovery approach (noted at the end of Chapter 5), and it introduces the problem of negative transfer.

4. Be alert to the possibility of negative transfer.

Negative transfer

In discussing problem solving in the preceding chapter, functional fixedness and habitual set were mentioned. And in the analysis of forgetting earlier in this chapter, retroactive and proactive inhibition were described. All these factors operate to produce *negative transfer*. Such transfer occurs when an idea that students have previously learned *impedes* the solution of the problems at hand instead of helping them to solve slightly different ones. You should be aware that such negative transfer may occur. To neutralize its impact, follow the four suggestions noted earlier in the discussion of functional fixedness and interference: (1) Emphasize that similar, though not identical approaches may be necessary. (2) Encourage students to "sleep on it" if they seem unable to free themselves from confusion during a particular session, especially during the early stages of mastery. (3) Use distributed study periods. (4) Try either torpedoing or a variation of the technique devised by the sixth-grade teacher described above under Point 3.

5. Try to "send your students away from your instruction anxious to use what they have been taught—and eager to learn more."

At the end of Chapter 1, Robert Mager observed that this should be the primary goal of a teacher. (Bruner put it differently, saying, "The first object of any act of learning . . . is that it should serve us in the future" [1960, p. 17]). Ultimately, the most important kind of transfer occurs after students have completed a grade or course, leave school, or graduate. If the experiences that took place in the classroom were properly arranged, they will be anxious to use what they have learned and, ideally, eager to learn more. Too often, though, students complete a grade or a course with the feeling that they never again want to have anything to do with the subject. In such cases, the teacher has gone to great pains to unintentionally produce negative transfer.

In *Developing Attitude Toward Learning* Mager discusses ways you might teach to produce positive rather than negative transfer. Mager is a behaviorist and a leading advocate of stating instructional objectives in specific terms. He defines "attitude" in terms of overt behavior and describes it as an objective in this way: "At the end of my influence over the student, when in the presence of the subject of _____, the percentage of approach responses made by him will be at least as great as it was when the student first arrived" (1968, p. 15). He defines an approach response as "an action that indicates a *moving toward* the subject" (p. 21). Mager gives examples of approach responses as if a private detective followed a student enrolled in a biology course and recorded all his activities. For example: "During the week, the student went to the library twelve times; spent 70 per cent of time there reading biology books . . . Tuesday evening, student attended meeting of the university biology club; broke date with favorite girl to attend" (p. 24).

Although you will be eager to increase approach responses, you also will want to reduce the likelihood of *avoidance* responses. For example: "On Tuesday, student tried to convince mathematics instructor that he should excuse him from course. [On Wednesday] failed to turn in three of four mathematics assignments on time" (p. 27). Mager observes that once avoidance responses develop, they are not likely to be reversed. Thus instruction that produces avoidance tendencies will do considerably more harm than good.

To discover the sorts of experiences that lead to approach and avoidance tendencies, Mager asked students to describe the subjects they favored the most and least and then explain why and how they got that way. Before you read the next few sentences, you are urged to jot down your own reactions to these questions in the spaces below.

Favorite subject:_____
How it got that way:_____
_____
_____
_____
_____

Least favored subject:_____
How it got that way:_____
_____
_____
_____
_____
_____

Here is the way Mager describes the results of his interviews:

> To summarize the results of the study, we can say that a favorite subject tends to get that way because the person seems to do well at it, because the subject was associated with liked or admired friends, relatives, or instructors, and because the person was relatively comfortable when in the presence of the subject or activity. A subject least favored tends to get that way because the person seems to have little or no aptitude for it, because the subject is associated with disliked individuals, and because being in the presence of the subject is often associated with unpleasant conditions. (P. 37)

On the basis of these results, Mager suggests that to increase the likelihood of approach tendencies you should do everything possible to accentuate positive conditions (e.g., provide clear instructional objectives, give students some choice in selecting what they will study, give students some control over length of study sessions, treat students as individuals) and reduce or eliminate negative ones such as pain, fear and anxiety, frustration, humiliation and embarrassment, boredom, and physical discomfort. Furthermore, you should remain aware of the importance of *modeling*; that is, behave the way you want your students to behave. (If you want your students to be enthusiastic about your subject, act that way yourself.)

In the final two chapters of *Developing Attitude Toward Learning*, Mager provides detailed instructions for *evaluating* your success in increasing approach tendencies and finding specific ways to *improve* your skill in encouraging that

Guidelines and Principles in Teaching for Transfer

In *The Transfer of Learning,* Henry C. Ellis provides a concise review and interpretation of research on transfer. He summarizes his analysis with seventeen empirical principles and five guidelines. Nine of the principles and all the guidelines are presented here to recap points noted in this chapter, as well as to review many of the ideas discussed in Chapters 5 and 6.

Empirical Principles

Over-all task similarity. Transfer of training is greatest when the training conditions are highly similar to those of the ultimate testing conditions.

Stimulus similarity. When a task requires the learner to make the same response to new but similar stimuli, positive transfer increases with increasing stimulus similarity.

Response similarity. When a task requires the learner to make a new or different response to the same stimuli, transfer tends to be negative and increases as the responses become less similar.

Learning-to-learn. Cumulative practice in learning a series of related tasks or problems leads to increased facility in learning how to learn.

Insight. Insight, defined behaviorally as the rapid solution of problems, appears to develop as a result of extensive practice in solving similar or related classes of problems.

Mediated transfer. Transfer can occur as a result of mediation due to the network of associative linkages between tasks.

Task or stimulus variety. In general, variety of tasks, or of their stimulus components, during original learning increases the amount of positive transfer obtained.

Amount of practice on the original task. The greater the amount of practice on the original task, the greater the likelihood of positive transfer; negative transfer is likely to occur following only limited practice on the original task.

Understanding and transfer. Transfer is greater if the learner understands the general rules or principles which are appropriate in solving new problems. (1965, pp. 72–74)

Guidelines for Teaching

Maximize the similarity between teaching and the ultimate testing situation.

Provide adequate experience with the original task.

Provide for a variety of examples when teaching concepts and principles.

Label or identify important features of a task.

Make sure that general principles are understood before expecting much transfer (Pp. 71–72)

type of behavior. The book is an inexpensive paperback and is highly recommended. It contains many practical suggestions you might use to increase the likelihood that your students will approach rather than avoid what you have taught them after they leave your classroom.

Summary

This chapter has acquainted you with some causes of forgetting and offered suggestions to minimize forgetting. Although you will want to help your students remember as much as possible of what they learn, you will probably be even more interested in encouraging them to apply or relate things they learn in the classroom to situations and activities outside it. Such transfer of learning is most likely to take place if you help students combine facts and concepts into principles of wide applicability and if you encourage them to develop positive attitudes toward what they have learned and to work out techniques of problem solving. In this chapter you have been provided with suggestions on how to do this—suggestions that further develop ideas analyzed in the preceding chapter, which discussed the teaching of facts, principles, and techniques of problem-solving.

Suggestions for Further Reading, Writing, Thinking, and Discussion

7-1 *Sampling Other Discussions of Forgetting and Transfer*

The analysis of forgetting and transfer presented in this chapter is brief and circumscribed. A different and perhaps more comprehensive overview of these two aspects of learning is available in other texts in educational psychology. If you would like more information, pick out two or three promising-looking recent publications at a library. You are sure to find at least a section if not a chapter devoted to forgetting and transfer. Read the appropriate sections of other texts, and outline points that impress you as informative or potentially valuable. For a concise but complete analysis of transfer, look for *The Transfer of Learning* (1965) by Henry Ellis. Excellent observations on forgetting and transfer for the elementary teacher appear in Chapters 9 and 10 of *The Learning Process and School Practice* (1970) by May V. Seagoe.

7-2 *Discovering English History as It Is Remembered*

If you will be teaching history, or have ever taken a course in the history of England, try to find a copy of *1066 and All That* (1931; paperback ed.,

1958) by Walter Carruthers Sellar and Robert Julian Yeatman. This is a description of English history as it might be recounted by a self-confident person who never learned it very well in the first place and who "reorganized" the few ideas that made an impression, filling in gaps as necessary. Chapter XLIX, for example, is devoted to "The Industrial Revelation" ("the discovery that women and children could work for 25 hours a day in factories without many of them dying or becoming excessively deformed"). In case you are unable to find this book, take a stab at writing your *own* version of a segment of history (or physics or chemistry or geography or whatever). Choose a subject you studied earlier in your academic career and compose a three- or four-page description of it. First note the few miscellaneous points you think you remember. Then let yourself go and fill in the gaps. (Write as if whatever you record will be taken as gospel by an audience of completely naive people who think you are the world's foremost authority.) After completing your account, read it and reflect on the recollection and transfer of information you once learned. If you don't remember much, does this mean you wasted your time when you studied the subject? Would you suggest dropping courses in that subject from the curriculum? If you hadn't taken that course, how would you have discovered whether it had or did not have meaning to you? Do you feel that a few miscellaneous recollections—even garbled ones—are better than no recollections at all?

7-3 *Tuning in on the Thoughts of Children*

Because they may not have matured intellectually to the point of understanding certain ideas, because ideas tend to become generalized, and because of the impact of forgetting, your students may have idiosyncratic notions about many things. You will discover this as soon as you start reading papers and exams, but meanwhile look for two assortments of gems of childish thought: *Write Me a Poem, Baby* (1956) and *Don't Get Perconel with a Chicken* (1959), both by H. Allen Smith. Art Linkletter has published similar collections of children's observations, but some of the reactions were obtained under rather contrived circumstances. Even so, you might enjoy browsing through his *Kids Sure Rite Funny* (1962) or *A Child's Garden of Misinformation* (1965). As you sample any of these books, speculate on what you could do to prevent or correct for misconceptions and garbled recollections. If some of the statements reported by Smith or Linkletter appeared on your students' exams or papers, how would you react? For example, here is a composition (reproduced in *Don't Get Perconel with a Chicken*) entitled "Adults": "Adults dont do anything. Adults just sit and talk and dont do a thing. Theres not anything duller in this world than adultry." Would you simply enjoy them or attempt to set their authors straight? How might you bring about discrimination if it is apparent that generalization has taken place? Are there any techniques for reducing children's tendency to draw false conclusions? Or is it preferable to attribute some interpretations to thought below the level of formal operations and simply let further maturation take care of things?

7-4 *Learning English with* $H°Y°M°A°N$ $K°A°P°L°A°N$

Leo Rosten is an extremely versatile man who has been a reporter, Hollywood scriptwriter, author, and editor. When he was working on his Ph.D., he taught as a "bootleg substitute for an instructor in a night school." Out of his experiences came a novel about a teacher of special classes in English for immigrants who were applying for American citizenship. The book appeared under the pseudonym Leonard Q. Ross and was called *The Education of* $H°Y°M°A°N$ $K°A°P°L°A°N$ (1937). Hyman Kaplan was the "star" pupil in the class, and the way he came to grips with English illustrates all sorts of complications resulting from generalization, reorganized forgetting, and negative transfer. (For example, Mr. Kaplan refers to a newspaper as "he" rather than "it" because it is called the "Harold Tribune.") The further adventures of Mr. Kaplan—and of his teacher, Mr. Parkhill — are chronicled in *The Return of* $H°Y°M°A°N$ $K°A°P°L°A°N$ (1959). An English teacher will find these books especially enjoyable, but Hyman Kaplan has almost universal appeal. If you read either book, comment on the techniques Mr. Parkhill used in coping with Mr. Kaplan's interpretations of English. Then describe how you might have handled things if you had been the teacher.

7-5 *Analyzing Paleolithic Education*

As a young instructor of future teachers, Harold Benjamin was struck by what he considered absurdities in American education. He found release from his frustration with the "educational establishment" by writing a satire—*The Saber-Tooth Curriculum*—under the pseudonym J. Abner Peddiwell. In a series of imaginary "lectures," a professor of education describes how education was conducted in Paleolithic times. Even though *The Saber-Tooth Curriculum* was written in 1939, many of the sacred cows ridiculed by Benjamin thirty years ago are still with us. If you enjoy satire, this book will both entertain and enlighten you. If you read *The Saber-Tooth Curriculum*, relate Benjamin's criticisms of education to current trends and practices in the schools.

7-6 *Taking a Closer Look at I.T.A.*

The English language developed with no thought to the problems of generalization or negative transfer. The unsuspecting child is forced to deal with all kinds of inconsistencies. For example, a first-grader learns how to write *I* and then discovers that it is wrong to use *I* for *eye* or *aye*. Because English is not spelled phonetically, the regular alphabet causes many problems for children learning to read. (There are twenty-two different ways the sound of *I* is spelled in different words.) Sir James Pitman's "Initial Teaching Alphabet" attempts to counteract some of the confusing elements of written English. If you will be teaching at the primary level, you might find it of interest to examine some I.T.A. materials in a curriculum library. Look through a series of books printed in I.T.A., paying attention to the way the transition is made from Pitman's special alphabet to the regular alphabet. Then note what you consider advantages of the I.T.A. as well as disadvantages. (For example, what sort of negative transfer might result from differences between the two alphabets?) If possible, interview a teacher who has used I.T.A. materials and ask for her reactions, positive and negative.

Recommended Reading in
Psychology Applied to Teaching: Selected Readings

If you would like to do further reading in books or articles mentioned in this chapter (and in the preceding "Suggestions for Further Reading, Writing, Thinking, and Discussion") without having to track down several separate volumes, you might peruse *Psychology Applied to Teaching: Selected Readings* (Boston: Houghton Mifflin, 1972). This is a collection of excerpts from books and articles from journals in psychology. The following selections provide extended commentaries on points noted in this chapter or mentioned in the "Suggestions."

The Saber-Tooth Curriculum: Excerpt from *The Saber-Tooth Curriculum* by J. Abner Peddiwell (Harold Benjamin), Selection 18, p. 290. (See also Suggestion 7-5.)

The Nature of Transfer: "Transfer and the Educational Process" by Henry C. Ellis, Selection 19, p. 299. (See also Suggestion 7-1.)

TEACHING SKILLS AND ATTITUDES

KEY POINTS

Sequences
Preconventional, conventional, and postconventional moral thinking (Kohlberg)

Classifications
Taxonomy of educational objectives, affective domain (Krathwohl, Bloom, Masia)

Studies
Edge of progressivism over traditional education (Eight-Year Study)

Concepts
Chaining
Task analysis
Beta hypothesis (Dunlap)
Learning curve, plateau

Methodology
Making a task analysis and using chaining, demonstration, and guidance to help students master skills
Taking learning curve into account to help students master skills and techniques
Noting desirable attitudes and values and providing learning experiences to lead to their development
Encouraging moral development by using procedures recommended by Kohlberg and Raths.

CHAPTER CONTENTS

IN THE DISCUSSION OF TRANSFER IN THE PRECEDING CHAPTER, SKILLS and attitudes were listed, along with general principles and techniques of problem solving, as more or less permanent forms of learning. This chapter offers suggestions for teaching these two types of learning, which constitute the remaining two domains—the psychomotor and affective—in the taxonomy of educational objectives.

Teaching Skills

In addition to verbal associations and general concepts and principles, you will probably be teaching psychomotor skills. In the primary grades, for example, you will want your pupils to learn how to print legibly. In many subjects in junior and senior high school, these skills (e.g., driving a car, operating a sewing machine, manipulating an electric typewriter, using a power saw, and swinging a golf club) may be of major if not exclusive importance. Some of the research evidence on skill learning will now be examined as a prelude to considering how to teach psychomotor abilities.

Both the armed forces and industry have been eager to make use of psychological principles to increase efficiency. Therefore, a considerable amount of research has been done on skill learning. Since this learning involves observable behavior, it is especially appropriate for behaviorists to study; many analyses of skill learning focus on S-R associations, the approach described by Robert Gagné in *The Conditions of Learning*. Gagné uses various simple skills—such as the series of acts performed in starting a car or in using a key to unlock a door—to illustrate chaining, the third form of learning in his hierarchy of types.

Conditions for Chaining

The conditions for chaining are basically the same as those for learning verbal associations, which were listed in Chapter 6:

Conditions for chaining

1. Each individual S-R connection must have been previously learned (e.g., to open a locked door, a person must be able to identify the upright position of the key, insert it into the lock, turn it, and push the door open).
2. The steps, or links, in the chain must be performed in the proper order. You could teach this either by demonstrating the proper sequence and then inviting the learner to perform or by using verbal instructions as prompts (e.g., "All right, now that you have the key in the lock, turn it, and then push the door open").
3. The individual steps must be performed in close succession to establish the chain.
4. Repetition is usually necessary if the act is to be performed easily and efficiently, since it often takes several tries to smooth out clumsy and superfluous movements.
5. The terminal step, or link, must result in success, which provides reinforcement (e.g., the door must open).
6. Once a motor skill has been learned, it can be generalized (e.g., the technique for opening one lock can be applied to opening a slightly different one). However, it may be necessary to teach the student to discriminate if there is a significant difference in the second act (e.g., opening a lock by turning the key counterclockwise).

In analyzing the ways chains of responses are learned, psychologists have speculated quite a bit about which kinds of cues are the most helpful. It would appear that *external* cues, provided through verbal instruction and demonstration, are generally better than physical manipulation of the learner, because skills must be learned through a personal process of trial and error. A clear example of this is the baby learning to walk. The toddler must learn to master his muscles and nervous system by trying to walk, making an error, trying again, reducing the error, and so on until he becomes an expert walker. The same process is necessary in learning any sensorimotor skill—the learner has to do it himself. If someone else tries to do it for him, the process may be impeded. Consequently, it seems preferable for teachers to take this into account and provide external cues but not physical guidance when assisting students to master psychomotor skills. The basic techniques for providing such cues—demonstration and verbal guidance—will now be discussed.

Suggestions for Providing Demonstrations and Guided Practice

Here are some suggestions, based on Gagné's analysis of the conditions for learning chains, on how you might put these techniques into practice in teaching skills.

1. If possible and appropriate, analyze the skill to ascertain the specific psychomotor abilities necessary to perform it, arrange these component abilities in order, and help students to master tham in this sequence.
2. Provide demonstrations and, as students practice, give verbal guidance to aid mastery of the skill.
   a. Demonstrate the entire procedure straight through, then describe the links of the chain in sequence, and finally demonstrate the skill again step by step.
   b. Allow ample time for students to practice immediately after the demonstrations. (Remember the importance of activity, repetition, and reinforcement.)
   c. As students practice, give guidance verbally or in a way that permits them to perform the skill themselves.
   d. Give guidance in a relaxed, noncritical atmosphere and in a positive form.
3. Be alert to generalization and interference.

1. *If possible and appropriate, analyze the skill to ascertain the specific psychomotor abilities necessary to perform it, arrange these component abilities in order, and help students master them in this sequence.*

When S-R theory is applied to the teaching of a skill, the first step is to analyze the terminal behavior of the skill in order to isolate the links in the chain, then to arrange the links in the proper sequence, and finally to shape the desired behavior. Military and industrial psychologists often use this technique. First, they perform a *task analysis* to isolate the components of a skill, *Task analysis*

HOW TO START A CAR

1. Take your place in the driver's seat.

2. Fasten your seat belt.

3. Lock the doors.

4. Adjust side and rear view mirrors so you have full vision out the back window and along the driver's side of the car.

5. Make sure the gear shift is in Park or Neutral.

6. Put the key in the ignition, turn it, and step on the gas pedal.

7. Put the car into gear.

8. Release the emergency brake.

**Figure 8–1
Taking Chaining into Account in Describing How to Start a Car**

next they arrange these in the most efficient order, and then they train personnel to follow the chain exactly. Although the technique works fine for disassembling a rifle or assembling a spark plug, it may not function too well with more complex tasks. If the learner is required to concentrate too much on the separate steps, this may prevent him from linking them in his own natural, fluid way.

For example, some coaches, impressed by the task analysis technique and eager to apply scientific methods to sports, will watch an expert tennis player or golfer and then describe the steps involved in serving or putting. Afterwards they assist novice athletes to follow these movements step by step. In some cases this works very well, but in others the learner gets so involved in thinking about the steps that he is distracted from developing the smooth, coordinated movement he is trying to acquire. Moreover, some learners may be forced into using a style unnatural to them. If you watch sports on TV, you are well aware how much variety there is in the way professional athletes hit a baseball or shoot a basketball. And you probably realize that professional athletes are *not* thinking, "Step one, step two, step three," as they perform.

It is told of Yogi Berra, the legendary Yankee catcher, that early in his career he encountered an efficiency-expert coach who wanted to make hitting as scientific as possible. The coach kept urging all the players to analyze what they were doing when they were at the plate. Yogi tried to follow this advice, but after striking out five straight times, he rejected the theory, saying, "How can you think and hit at the same time?" The expert performer may be handicapped if he thinks too much, but this may not be true of the novice—though even the beginner may be bothered by too much advice.

Also, some skills appear to be more teachable than others. For example, it has been hypothesized that the primary reason baseball rules were recently changed to favor the hitter more was that pitching, which is preplanned and methodical, can be taught, while hitting, which involves a spontaneous and instantaneous reaction, cannot. Many baseball men argue that hitters are born, not made. Perhaps this explains Yogi Berra's problem. The hitter doesn't have time to think; he simply reacts. As you speculate about the possibility of using a task analysis approach, you might ask yourself whether the skill is a mechanical one, which should be performed in a premeditated, unvarying way, or a spontaneous response, which must be performed more or less instinctively.

There are substantial differences of opinion about the desirability of using a programmed approach in teaching many skills. To draw your own conclusions, you might attempt a simple task analysis of a skill you will want your students to acquire, then make tentative efforts at shaping their behavior. If a step-by-step approach helps some students, continue to use it with them. But if others seem upset by analytic methods and are obviously "thinking too much," you might try a more global approach. It is possible that the analytic and global styles of conceptualization described by Kagan also apply to the learning of skills.

Skinner's programmed technique of teaching handwriting (which was described in Chapter 5) illustrates many of the advantages and disadvantages of an S-R approach to teaching skills. With this method the student is systematically helped to perform the movements necessary to write each of the letters of the alphabet. He begins by tracing the complete letter and eventually learns to perform the proper movements as the prompts (tracing models of parts of the letter) are gradually vanished, or withdrawn. When he has mastered all the letters, he puts them together into words. Thus he learns to assemble all the links in the chain through repeated activity, which gives immediate reinforcement.

However, some primary-grade teachers who watched a film on the Skinner technique speculated that the rather jerky movements many students made as they traced the letters, particularly when the tracing models consisted of only parts of the letter, might actually interfere with the acquisition of a smooth, flowing hand. No research evidence on this point is available, but it does seem that some children might respond more favorably to a global approach, which teaches them from the beginning to write each letter in one smooth motion.

Space is provided below for you to do a task analysis of a specific skill—one you would like your students to acquire—in order to determine whether an S-R approach seems feasible. (If you will be teaching a complex skill such as typing, sewing, or cooking, you will probably be given abundant information about the most efficient techniques when you take a Special Methods of Teaching course. Many complex skills have been analyzed in minute detail by teams of specialists. There are even time-and-motion studies on ways to make a sandwich and wash dishes.)

_____

_____

_____

_____

_____

_____

_____

Whether you use an analytic or global approach, the basic technique of teaching skills is to encourage the student to perform the necessary movements in sequence. In most cases you can do this by providing first a model for the learner to follow (demonstration) and second mediating links in the form of verbal instructions (guidance).

Suzuki-san Rocks the Boat

An ingenious and dedicated Japanese named Shinichi Suzuki has developed a technique for teaching children to play the violin, a technique that punctures many traditional beliefs about skill learning. Perhaps you have heard of Mr. Suzuki and have even heard some of his pupils play. Children taught by his technique learn to play the violin about as they learn to talk—by listening and imitating. He provides children with scaled-down violins and encourages them to start right out playing—by trial and error—simple tunes that they hear on records. The traditional emphasis on unending exercises is eliminated. Mr. Suzuki feels that the child is better off playing *music* since that is what he will eventually play, and he believes that this makes practice much more enjoyable.

His spectacular results raise questions about the value of the tedious exercises that some dim and distant "authority" once decreed essential for mastery. (It also raises questions about the task analysis and S-R approach, since the Suzuki technique is "natural" and global.) In the old days it was argued that because all great violinists once spent hours a day plodding through exercise books, exercises must be requisite to success. But Mr. Suzuki has produced young violinists who never slaved over drill.*

If you will be teaching any kind of skill, cognitive or psychomotor, you might ask yourself if traditional exercises and drills are necessary. For example, in teaching grammar, is a great deal of analysis (even featuring the new and elegant transformational types) really necessary? Is there any point in having children diagram sentences? Does anyone *know* that it makes a difference in their ability to speak and write? And what about calisthenics in Physical Education? As students play games, they naturally use the muscles needed to play such games, so why spend time on exercises that activate muscles used only in calisthenics? Is it possible that some exercises—both mental and physical—serve only to satisfy the teachers, who unconsciously want students to suffer as they themselves once suffered? And *as* the students suffer, isn't it possible that they are not only wasting their time but also building up a negative attitude toward a skill?

*If you would like to find out more about the Suzuki method, read "On Learning How to Play the Violin at the Age of Four Without Tears" by N. H. Pronko in the May 1969 issue of *Psychology Today*, pp. 52–66.

---

2. *Provide demonstrations, and as students practice, give verbal guidance to aid mastery of the skill.*

a. *Demonstrate the entire procedure straight through, then describe the links of the chain in sequence, and finally demonstrate the skill again step by step.*

First tell what you are going to do and then demonstrate the entire procedure, because the resulting overall impression will serve as an advance organizer.

I'M VERY PLEASED TO SEE SUCH A GOOD TURN-OUT...

WITH A LITTLE LUCK I THINK WE CAN HAVE A GOOD SEASON..

TODAY'S SPRING-TRAINING SESSION IS GOING TO BEGIN WITH A DEMONSTRATION..

LAST YEAR WE HIT INTO TOO MANY DOUBLE-PLAYS...

TWO OF OUR MEMBERS ARE GOING TO SHOW US HOW THIS CAN BE AVOIDED...

LINUS IS GOING TO BE THE SHORTSTOP AND SNOOPY IS GOING TO BE THE RUNNER GOING FROM FIRST TO SECOND WHO BREAKS UP THE DOUBLE-PLAY...

NOW, WATCH CAREFULLY.. THE PLAY BEGINS WITH LINUS FIELDING THE BALL, AND MAKING THE PLAY AT SECOND WHILE SNOOPY STREAKS TOWARD HIM..

AAUGH!!

ARE THERE ANY QUESTIONS?

If you have any doubts about your ability to perform a skill or conduct a demonstratuon, practice the night before. If you discover you can't perform the skill very well, have a student do the demonstration. A high school basketball coach once explained to his varsity team the advantages of a new way to shoot foul shots. The method sounded logical, and they were all for it until he demonstrated—and missed eight out of ten tries. The players lost confidence in him and his method. Your students won't demand that you be better than they are in all phases of the skill you teach. In many cases, however, it may be preferable to invite one of your better pupils to show a technique you can't perform particularly well yourself.

If you do perform the demonstration yourself, resist the temptation to show off. You may make your students feel too inferior to be willing to try the skill or else bore and antagonize them to the point that they will stop paying attention. For example, a wood-shop teacher in a junior high school made a practice of demonstrating the use of the various tools by starting out with an ostentatiously effortless performance of the limited skills his students would be allowed to attempt. Then as an encore he would do an advanced trick, pointing out that it was much too difficult for beginners but that he just wanted to show what *could* be done by an expert. Instead of working on their own projects, the class had to stand around and "ooh" and "ah." After a while, none of his pupils would go to him for assistance for fear they might set off another performance. (The accident rate in this shop was abnormally high.)

After you complete the initial demonstration, describe the links of the chain in the correct order (you will probably want to do a limited task analysis beforehand). Emphasize the crucial links and point out the tricky points to watch out for. It frequently helps to list such points on the board and refer to them as you demonstrate the skill again step by step. For example, in demonstrating to first-graders how to print p and q, emphasize which side of the letters the vertical line goes on. In teaching biology students how to set up a microscope, list the proper sequence of steps.

b. *Allow ample time for students to practice immediately after the demonstrations. (Remember the importance of activity, repetition, and reinforcement.)*

Allow plenty of time for everyone to have a crack at the skill immediately after it has been demonstrated. After arousing pupils' interest by showing them something new, it is illogical—and a bit unfair—to force them to divert their attention to something else. If you don't have enough equipment for all your students, it is probably better to demonstrate to only a half or a third of the class at a time. Also, in order to maximize reinforcement, it is desirable to set up practice sessions in such a way that you are free to circulate around the class and provide specific suggestions on an individual basis.

Providing guidance

In planning practice sessions, keep in mind that learning is more likely to take place if your students are active, if you permit them to perform the skill many times, and if you arrange the sessions so that they receive immediate reinforcement for every response. If most of the class has trouble with one particular phase of a skill, review this part and again demonstrate the proper way to do it. In fact, it is a good policy to give spontaneous demonstrations whenever you discover even a few individuals making the same mistake. Students are likely to pay closer attention to these popular-demand demonstrations than to the formal, and perhaps somewhat artificial, ones.

c. As students practice, give guidance verbally or in a way which permits them to perform the skill themselves.

It is tempting to give manual assistance in many skills, for example, by taking a first-grader's hand in yours and pushing it around the paper in an effort to improve his printing. As noted earlier, this kind of guidance does little good and may even cause added difficulty. The student must learn to master his own muscles and nerves. If he is a passive instrument with you at the controls, he gains nothing from the experience. When he is later required to perform the skill, his only resources will be his own brain and body. You may get a satisfying feeling that you are speeding up the learning process when you do things for a pupil, but you are actually forcing him to depend on you and cheating him of practice.

d. Give guidance in a relaxed, noncritical atmosphere and in a positive form.

Most students, especially older ones, are self-conscious about trying new psychomotor skills for fear they will make mistakes and look silly. You can minimize this feeling by encouraging a devil-may-care approach. The more relaxed a novice is, the more likely he is to give it a try. (A relaxed, unhurried atmosphere should not be reserved only for discovery sessions.)

Emphasizing the right way to perform a skill is usually the most helpful kind of guidance. But when a student has an especially stubborn problem in mastering a particular skill or one aspect of it, deliberate exaggeration of the error may be helpful. This technique, sometimes referred to as the *Beta hypothesis,* was first described by Knight Dunlap (1949). Exasperated by a quirk in his typing technique that caused him to type "hte" for "the," Dunlap deliberately banged out several dozen "hte's" and to his surprise discovered that he had purged the "hte" demon from his system. On reflection he concluded that he had previously fixated the wrong response to the point that it had become an automatic, unthinking reaction. By deliberately *thinking* about the error, he had been able to bring it under his control and relearn the right response. Subsequently, Dunlap applied the Beta hypothesis to the treatment of stuttering. Encouraging children to exaggerate their stuttering seemed to help in many cases.

Beta hypothesis

Coaches have used the Beta hypothesis to help athletes. Divers who habitually make an awkward movement are told to exaggerate the error in practice and then relearn the dive from the beginning. If you encounter a pupil who keeps doing the wrong thing and can't seem to help himself, you might have him exaggerate the error and then start all over again to learn the correct technique. In addition, if *you*, the teacher, demonstrate an error in an extreme way, especially when students first encounter the trouble spot, this will help make them aware of the tricky mistake they are making. Doing this in a good-natured way may reduce some of the tension that often accompanies awkwardness.

3. *Be alert to generalization and interference.*

Generalization and interference occur with skill learning just as they do with cognitive learning. A student may encounter difficulty learning a new skill if he generalizes by applying specialized movements previously learned in performing a related but different skill (e.g., using a baseball swing to hit a golf ball). Interference occurs when an old skill introduces an element of confusion to the performance of a new one. If you have ever had to alternate between driving a car with a stick shift and one with an automatic transmission, you have had direct experience with negative transfer in the psychomotor domain.

To correct for generalization, the best approach may be to explain to the learner that the new skill requires special movements of its own. To cope with interference, probably the best policy is to help the learner remain constantly aware that he is performing a skill in which interference is likely to occur. For example, the driver switching from one type of shift to another might repeat often to himself, "I'm driving a car with a stick shift." (When Sweden changed from left-lane to right-lane driving, an extensive, systematic campaign was conducted to inform all drivers about the nature of negative transfer and to keep them thinking, "Drive on the right.")

As you observe the attempts of your students to master a new skill, you will probably detect certain general trends in the way they progress. These trends have been studied systematically and have been plotted graphically in the form of learning curves.

Implications of the Learning Curve

When the progress of an organism in learning a skill is plotted on a graph, the most typical pattern is illustrated in Figure 8–2, p. 382. This curve is a highly oversimplified presentation of a complex process, and some psychologists argue that learning curves either represent a nonexistent phenomenon or are too unreliable to be of value. But if the concept is not taken too literally, it can be useful in pointing up some trends in skill learning (and also related trends in cognitive learning).

Think back to your own efforts at learning a foreign language or geometry, typing or tennis. You probably got off to a slow start the first week or so. Just how slow the start was depended mainly on how much previous experience

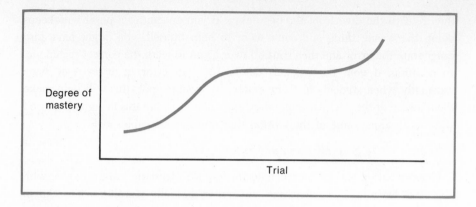

Figure 8–2   A Hypothetical Learning Curve

in related skills you brought with you. If you took French before Spanish, for example, you had a big jump on your fellow students in Spanish class. Even so, your first efforts were undoubtedly a bit clumsy. After you got the hang of it, though, you probably went through a period of rapid improvement. The first flush of success usually makes a new activity enjoyable to the beginner and motivates him to keep trying. It is likely that you eventually reached a leveling-off stage. When that happened, your continued mastery of the activity probably depended on whether it had a special appeal for you or whether you were required to go on using it. If you took Spanish or Geometry only to satisfy a college requirement, you undoubtedly forgot most of it. If you periodically used your typing skill to prepare term papers, it is likely that you maintained a fair degree of proficiency. If you enjoyed tennis so much that you played twice a week, you probably came close to achieving your potential.

Suggestions Derived from the Learning Curve for Teaching Skills

The learning curve provides some supplementary suggestions for teaching skills.

Implications of the learning curve

1. When presenting a new skill, give extra assistance and encouragement to the slow starters.
2. Make the most of initial interest and enthusiasm.
3. When a leveling off of interest or improvement occurs, either encourage continued practice to maintain the skill or help students master advanced techniques.

1. *When presenting a new skill, give extra assistance and encouragement to the slow starters.*

The initial rate of learning a skill depends on a person's readiness and innate ability. Pupils who have had considerable previous experience with an activity or have a special affinity for a skill or subject will learn much more rapidly during the first few days than those who do not. Inexperienced pupils may need special attention and encouragement the first few days. Otherwise, the way some of their classmates whizz along may destroy their self-confidence and squelch their eagerness to try.

2. *Make the most of initial interest and enthusiasm.*

As earlier noted, once students have experienced some success, they are especially susceptible to encouragement, so make the most of their excitement about improving. Eventually, though, a point at which no further improvement is discernible will be reached.

3. *When a leveling off of interest or improvement occurs, either encourage continued practice to maintain the skill or help students master advanced techniques.*

If the leveling off occurs after satisfactory performance has been attained, occasional practice is usually sufficient to enable the students to maintain the skill.

If you want your pupils to develop *maximum* proficiency, however, you will need to be alert to these *plateaus* in the learning curve—periods of no apparent improvement. They are called plateaus because this is what they resemble on a learning curve diagram—a flat surface at a higher level than the original level of learning.

Plateaus

The phenomenon first received attention in a study of how novice telegraphers learn to send and receive Morse code (Bryan and Harter, 1897). The study revealed that after a few weeks of training most of the students hit a plateau that lasted a week or two and then experienced another spurt of learning. Analysis suggested that the telegraphers had initially reacted to each letter as a separate entity and that after they had developed considerable skill in sending and receiving in this way, their improvement leveled off. Then suddenly, and more or less unconsciously, they started thinking in terms of words rather than letters. They reacted to the word *the*, for example, as one unified burst of dots and dashes instead of three discrete letters.

Perhaps the main point to remember about plateaus is that they are common. Since you will not always be able to identify them or make specific suggestions to your pupils on how to shorten or eliminate them, the best policy is probably to do what you can to encourage continued effort. Without encouragement, a student may quit just when he is on the verge of attaining genuine proficiency.

This point is related to the argument that a person must learn a great many verbal associations before he can "leap about" intuitively. If you ever took music lessons, for example, it may be that you were forced to keep practicing during a phase when you wanted to chuck the whole thing. But if you persevered, perhaps you learned to play so well that you could devote your thoughts to the subtleties of interpretation rather than to the proper placement of your fingers and arms. At that point you probably began to enjoy yourself.

Once a skill has been almost perfected, extinction is usually no longer a problem. A person rarely forgets how to swim or ride a bicycle. The most logical explanation for this is that a great many repetitions are necessary to master the skill in the first place and that the exercise of the skill even for a short time provides abundant reinforcement. For example, if you know how to type, consider the number of times you must have hit each key as you practiced. Add to this the number of times you hit each key every time you type a term paper. In view of the thousands or millions of repetitions and reinforcements involved in the mastery and use of a skill such as typing, swimming, and riding a bicycle, it is not surprising that a person who has not used such a skill for several years can quickly get back into the swing of it.

Performing highly complex psychomotor skills is extremely involved and difficult to understand. For example, although several athletes may have essentially the same level of basic proficiency, one or two will become stars, and the others will be mediocre performers. And when individual players are combined into a team, their performance is even more baffling and unpredictable. Every season teams classified as inferior by past performance and overall ability upset teams rated as outstanding. The most plausible explanation is the *attitude* of the participants.

Attitude also plays a definite and puzzling role in cognitive learning. Students who apparently have all the abilities needed to perform a given activity sometimes experience learning blocks that prevent them from successfully combining the abilities. Furthermore, the attitude of a student toward a subject or skill may be the primary determinant of how much he will remember and use. A student who has a highly efficient but rather cold teacher may master the principles of mathematics but develop such a negative attitude in the process that he will avoid the use of math in and out of school. On the other hand, a student who has a somewhat disorganized but highly enthusiastic teacher may know less at the end of the course, but he may have acquired such a positive feeling toward math that he will continue to read and learn about mathematical concepts.

Field theorists consider attitudinal reactions the most important aspects of learning. S-R theorists prefer to concentrate on observable behavior, and it is only recently (as in Mager's *Developing Attitude Toward Learning*) that they have shown interest in such hard-to-measure factors. But although attitudes are elusive and difficult to study scientifically, it is apparent that they influence the acquisition and use of both cognitive and psychomotor abilities. Consequently, it is important to examine some of the research data on attitude development and use it for speculating about the possibility of systematically encouraging desirable attitudes.

Teaching Attitudes and Values

Not many years ago, when the "whole-child" philosophy was the most popular theory of education, attitudes were considered more important than subject matter. As Burton P. Fowler, president of the Progressive Education Association, put it, "We endorse, by common consent, the obvious hypothesis that the child rather than what he studies should be the centre of all educational effort" (1930, p. 159). And perhaps you have heard the cliché, "I don't teach subject matter; I teach children." Report cards in the 1930s and 1940s frequently devoted more space to citizenship than to academic performance. It was felt that the schools should concentrate on creating "citizens for democratic living" other than mere scholars. In most (but not all) school systems this is no longer the case for a variety of reasons, some noted earlier, including the launching of Sputnik, changes in educational philosophy, and the "cult-of-efficiency" emphasis.

Critics of the whole-child approach pointed out that most teaching goals were too vague to be even recognized, let alone achieved. They also complained that the lack of priorities in the schools and the elimination of many academic subjects were producing a nation of illiterates. The titles of three books critical of progressive education reflect the nature of the indictment: *Quackery in the Public Schools* (1953) by Albert Lynd, *Educational Wastelands* (1953) by Arthur Bestor, and *The Diminished Mind* (1954) by Mortimer Smith.

The subsequent counterreaction to the whole-child approach greatly decreased the emphasis on citizenship, but most educational theorists still acknowledge that attitudes and values are an important aspect of education. Strong differences of opinion exist, however, on how the schools can encourage or teach desirable attitudes. There is also considerable controversy on how much classical academic education, as compared with progressive education, contributes to the development of personality and character.

Differences of opinion among humanists, educators, scientists, and citizens were never more evident than in the 1950s when the prevailing progressive approach to education was attacked by Lynd, Bestor, and Smith, as well as by Admiral Hyman Rickover and many others. The major argument between the two factions—the entrenched educationists and their critics—centered around the question of transfer. The educationists argued that the whole-child approach produced the most lasting kind of impact on children. They sought to equip students with general attitudes and techniques of learning. The humanists argued that liberal education and the development of the intellect were the most vital goals of learning.

The Eight-Year Study

An investigation that had served to put the progressive education theory "on the line" was carried out by a group called the Commission on the Relation of School and College. The purpose of this investigation, named the Eight-Year Study because it spanned that period of time, was described by Wilford M. Aiken in *The Story of the Eight-Year Study* in these terms:

> We are trying to develop students who regard education as an enduring quest for meanings rather than credit accumulation; who desire to investigate, to follow the leadings of a subject, to explore new fields of thought; knowing how to budget time, to read well, to use sources of knowledge effectively and who are experienced in fulfilling obligations which come with memberships in the school or college community. (1942, p. 144)

Eight-Year Study: progressivism over traditional education

In 1932 thirty secondary schools had been invited to disregard the usual curriculum and provide progressive education to the hilt for four years. They were encouraged to experiment in their teaching to try to achieve the goals just described. Over three hundred colleges agreed to take part in the venture by waiving their formal admission requirements. This was essential since few of the test schools taught traditional courses. In the experiment the collegiate careers of fifteen hundred graduates of the progressive high schools and those of matched graduates of traditional high schools were compared. Generally speaking, the experimental school graduates scored slightly but consistently better in both academic and nonacademic performance. (For details, see Aiken's book.) On the basis of these findings, the progressive educators argued that education which consists of "an enduring quest for meanings" is as good as, if not slightly better than, a traditional curriculum. However, it seems prudent to consider this observation by Lawrence Cremin in his book *The Transformation of the School*:

> The excitement of the venture seemed to infuse the work of students and teachers alike. Student yearbooks spoke with self-conscious seriousness about the aims and ends of education, while teachers reported a heightened sense of participation in educational policymaking. Old lesson plans were scrapped, and new material introduced; there were conferences galore, to plan, to execute, to appraise. In short, there was all the thrill, the vigor, and the commotion that attaches to any reform enterprise—so much so that probably *anything* attempted would have succeeded better than what had come before. (1961, pp. 254–255)

What Cremin is describing here is a massive Hawthorne effect, but it also reflects the observations of Combs and Snygg mentioned so many times in this book—that how a subject is taught may be more important than what is taught, that attitudes acquired with learning may be more important than subject matter.

The Eight-Year Study had less impact on education than you might expect. Cremin attributes this to the fact that foundation interest in the study was so great that the participating schools were flooded with money, and when the money was cut off at the end of the experiment, so were the programs. In addition, the results of the study were reported in 1942, when everyone was preoccupied with the war. But perhaps the main reason was that the study was buried by a concerted attack on the progressive movement by humanists, scientists, and lay citizens, an attack that gained momentum in the 1950s.

The clearest statement of what the critics, particularly the humanists, disliked about progressive education was presented in *The Restoration of Learning* (1955) by Arthur Bestor. Bestor not only mounted a systematic critique of progressive education but also presented an eloquent defense of classical, academic education. He argued, "The schools are the only institution which will provide intellectual training," and by the words *intellectual training* he meant "the deliberate cultivation of the ability to think." He wrote, "To transmit the power of disciplined thinking is the primary responsibility of education." The ability to think is developed best, he asserted, by training in the basic academic disciplines —history, English, science, mathematics, and foreign languages. He also expressed the traditionalists' argument that liberal education produces graduates who possess the values and attitudes that are reflected in sympathetic understanding of social problems.

If Bestor's argument is analyzed with reference to the discussion of transfer presented in the preceding chapter, it can be questioned on several counts. First of all, the evidence from the Thorndike study on formal discipline indicates that exposure to traditional academic subjects does not have an effect on reasoning ability. Then the Eight-Year study, even allowing for the Hawthorne effect, reveals that the progressive approach to education is just as capable of producing thoroughly competent college students as the traditional curriculum. In addition, Bestor implies that the "power of disciplined thinking" will be an automatic byproduct of a liberal education, yet the research reviewed by Ellis indicates that it is necessary to make a deliberate effort to teach for such transfer. Account also should be taken of Mager's observations. Too much stress on "intellectual training" may obligate instructors to make up examinations that demand large amounts of detailed information and to follow stringent grading practices. This would cause all but the top students to feel they have little aptitude for many subjects. As a result, they would be predisposed to avoid any contact with such subjects in the future, and negative transfer will have been produced. Finally, there is evidence from a study by Philip E. Jacob (1957) that college students who took many of the liberal arts courses recommended by Bestor showed no greater sympathetic understanding of social problems at the time of graduation than those who had taken few such courses.

It appears, then, that if you hope to encourage your students to develop attitudes that previously have been attributed to a liberal education, you will have to be systematic about it. On the next few pages you will be asked to consider, among other things, the personal qualities you will need to express as a teacher in order to influence the attitudes and values of your students. In the concluding pages of this chapter you will be given some suggestions on how to encourage desirable moral characteristics. As background for these discussions, some observations on the nature and origin of attitudes are in order.

Origins and Development of Attitudes and Values

The attitudes and values of a student are the product of a lifelong interaction between inherited predispositions and environmental experiences. Children seem to develop attitudes through a process of absorption: they react to things they see and hear, and they imitate their parents and peers. They are usually not aware that they are being influenced. If a child's parents over a period of years make frequent negative comments about school and teachers, it will not be easy for a teacher who must deal with large numbers of students for only a short time to change the resulting ingrained attitude of the child toward school. If a child comes from a home in which the parents never read anything—not even a newspaper—and the primary source of "culture" is a TV set tuned to crude programs, it will not be easy for a teacher of literature to convert him in five, fifty-minute periods a week. If a child watches his parents lie and cheat and flagrantly break laws as a matter of daily routine, it will not be easy for a teacher to inculcate honesty and respect for the law. Some teachers *do* succeed in accomplishing all these things, but it is certainly not easy.

The long-term, subtle development of attitudes and their consequent ingrained nature probably account for much of the rapid fading of gains made in Head Start programs, to note just one example of the inadequacy of a brief positive experience to counteract a lifetime of negative experiences. If the school cannot influence the parents to adopt some of the values it is trying to inculcate in students, little permanent change is likely to occur. (And if the school *does* succeed in changing the values of students—as in the Higher Horizons program—without influencing the values of their parents or peers, serious conflicts may develop.)

And consider the conclusions of the Jacob study. By the time a student enters college he has had eighteen years of attitude-forming experiences. Is it surprising that a college teacher who sees a student only three days a week and who may never have personal contact with him or even know his name has little impact on his way of thinking? By the time a student reaches high school, his attitudes are well on the way to being formed. His parents, siblings, and playmates as well as his overall environment have profoundly influenced the traits he inherited. In high school and college, the peer group is a powerful factor. The student may be influenced more by the behavior of his friends than by the beliefs of his parents or teachers.

Then there is the generation gap. Many high school and college students go to great lengths to demonstrate their contemptuous rejection of what they regard as the hypocritical values of the adult society.

Taking note of all this should help you develop a realistic (but not defeatist) view of your chances of exerting a permanent impact on the attitudes and values of your pupils; here are some suggestions you might use as guidelines.

Suggestions for Encouraging Desirable Habits, Attitudes, and Values

1. List the habits, attitudes, and values you wish to encourage.
2. Do your best to provide learning experiences that will lead to the development of the habits, attitudes, and values you want to foster.
3. Make use of object lessons—when illustrative incidents occur in the course of events, take advantage of them.
4. Be aware of your student's level of moral development and encourage understanding of more advanced thinking about attitudes and values by presenting "moral dilemmas" and by clarifying values.
5. Apply learning theory—associate pleasant and positive experiences with the behavior and values you want to encourage.
6. Set a good example. Keep in mind the importance of modeling, identification, and imitation.
7. Keep your personal prejudices under control.

1. *List the habits, attitudes, and values you wish to encourage.*

As with other types of learning, the logical way to start the task of encouraging desirable habits, attitudes, and values is to specify those you have in mind. Some teachers object to such an attempt as worthless, which may be the case if the list consists of glittering generalities. But if you think about it a bit, you should be able to come up with some specific values and forms of behavior you would like to foster. As noted earlier, if you hope to promote the transfer of certain habits, attitudes, and values, you should teach specifically for this.

Listing attitudes and values to be encouraged

Examples

Many elementary and some secondary report cards include citizenship categories, for example, "gets to work promptly," "respects school property," etc. If your school uses such cards, you might take this list as a guide. Not only would it serve as the basis for your value and attitude development program, it might also make it easier for you to determine grades.

In preparing to teach a subject, as you define the terminal behavior you want to help your students achieve, think in terms of the *affective* as well as the cognitive domain. (For example, in addition to teaching social science students knowledge and generalizations, you might try to inculcate an open-minded attitude toward the opinions of others; in addition to teaching business students how to type, you might encourage neatness.)

If you would like to try to develop a systematic list of affective goals, you might consult the second volume of *Taxonomy of Educational Objectives,* which presents a classification of educational objectives for the affective domain similar to the taxonomy developed for the cognitive domain in the first volume. For maximum benefit you should read the entire *Handbook II,* but a brief summary is provided here to show you what the classification of affective objectives is like. The authors—David R. Krathwohl, Benjamin S. Bloom, and Bertram B. Masia—describe an "erosion" of affective objectives in education, which they attribute to three factors: the difficulty of evaluating such outcomes, the fear that tampering with personal values is equivalent to indoctrination, and the very slow development of affective characteristics. They point to evidence that affective factors must be specifically taught and say that the assumption that values are an automatic by-product of certain kinds of cognitive behavior has not been corroborated by any kind of proof. (They refer to the Jacob study as well as to other less ambitious evaluations.) The significance of these findings for the teacher has already been noted: You will probably have to teach just as specifically for attitudes and values as you do for cognitive learning.

For further information regarding the summary of the taxonomy presented below[1] and for examples of test items you might use to evaluate each goal, see *Taxonomy of Educational Objectives, Handbook II.* Space is provided under each point for notes or comments you may care to make either now or after you have embarked on your teaching career.

Taxonomy of educational objectives: affective domain

Taxonomy of Educational Objectives: Affective Domain
Handbook II

Receiving (Attending)—"The learner [becomes] sensitized to the existence of certain phenomena and stimuli."

    Awareness—What sorts of attitudes or awarenesses do you want your students to have? (E.g., "awareness of aesthetic factors in dress, furnishings, architecture," etc.; "recognition that there may be more than one acceptable point of view" on a question)

_____

_____

_____

_____

[1] The headings in this summary are exactly the same as those in the complete taxonomy. All other exact quotations are enclosed in quotation marks.

Willingness to Receive—What sorts of *tolerances* would you like to encourage your students to develop? (E.g., "tolerance for a variety of types of music"; "listens to others with respect"; "increase in sensitivity to human need and pressing social problems")

_____

_____

_____

Controlled or Selected Attention—What sorts of attributes that untrained observers frequently ignore would you like to encourage your students to recognize? (E.g., listens for rhythm in poetry or prose read aloud, "sensitive to the importance of keeping informed on current political and social matters," looks for construction details in garments or furniture)

_____

_____

_____

Responding—The learner does something with or about the phenomena.
Acquiescence in Responding—What sorts of habits of self-discipline would you like to encourage in your students? What specific kinds of regulations do you want your students to comply with? (E.g., "completes his homework," "obeys the playground regulations," obeys rules in an industrial arts shop, "willingness to comply with health regulations")

_____

_____

_____

Willingness to Respond—What kinds of voluntary habits relative to your subject would you like your students to adopt? (E.g., voluntarily searches for information, practices rules of safety, voluntarily reads books and magazines, participates in a variety of constructive hobbies and recreational activities)

_____

_____

_____

_____

Satisfaction in Response—What kinds of habits that arouse positive feelings of satisfaction would you like your students to develop? (E.g., "finds pleasure in reading for recreation"; "listens with pleasure to good music"; "enjoyment of literature, intellectually and aesthetically, as a means of personal enrichment and social understanding")

_____

_____

_____

Valuing—The learner displays consistent behavior reflecting a general attitude.
Acceptance of a Value—What sorts of beliefs (emotional acceptance of a proposition) would you like your students to develop? (E.g., "desires to attain optimum health," "increased appetite and taste for what is good in literature")

_____

_____

_____

Preference for a Value—What kinds of values would you like your students to develop to the point of their feeling a sense of active identity with a given concept or idea? (E.g., writes letters to agencies, organizations, or newspapers in order to express opinions; "initiates group action for the improvement of health regulations")

_____

_____

_____

Commitment (Conviction)—What sorts of ideas would you like your students to entertain with considerable conviction? (E.g., "loyalty to the various groups in which one holds membership," "loyalty to the social goals of a free society . . .")

_____

_____

_____

Organization—The value system of the person is internalized.
Conceptualization of a Value—What sorts of wide-ranging conceptions would you like to try to develop in your students? (E.g., "attempts to identify characteristics of an art object which he admires," "forms judgments as to the responsibility of society for conserving human and material resources")

_____

_____

_____

Organization of a Value System—What might you do in your classes to contribute to the formation of a desirable system of values by your students? (E.g., begins to form judgments as to the major directions in which American society should move," "develops techniques for controlling aggression in culturally acceptable patterns")

Characterization by a Value or Value Complex—In effect, the attitude and value system becomes a way of life.

Generalized Set—What could you do in your classes to encourage your students to develop encompassing attributes of character? (E.g., develop a conscience, develop a consistent philosophy of life)

If the classification is not completely clear to you, it may help to note that the outline proceeds in terms of progressively inclusive behavior. At a superficial level a student may be merely aware of the existence of a given subject. But if you have sufficient impact on his thinking, your subject may literally become a way of life for him. At the intermediary levels of behavior described, your students might be influenced to varying degrees without developing a total commitment to a particular point of view.

The taxonomy may be more meaningful and useful to you if you concentrate on the first three categories. The development of advanced commitments and beliefs represented by the final categories is likely to occur long after you lose contact with your students. Even so, you may find that points toward the end of the outline will help you identify some affective goals for your classes—although you may never find out whether you have achieved any measure of success in helping students attain them.

2. *Do your best to provide learning experiences that will lead to the development of the habits and attitudes you want to foster.*

If you do come up with a list of habit and attitude goals, do some thinking specifically about how you might encourage such attitudes.

Examples

A kindergarten teacher tried to encourage perseverance by having her pupils begin the year with short-term projects and toward the end of the year undertake more ambitious tasks (e.g., each child made his own paper chains for the class Maypole).

If you want pupils to respect school property, repeatedly emphasize the importance of taking care of things.

This book, by presenting both sides of key issues and urging you to examine the "motives" and emotional involvement of the advocates of the issues, has encouraged you to be openmindedly skeptical about new developments in education.

In the space below you might note some specific techniques for encouraging the development of the habits, attitudes, and values you listed earlier. (If you decide, for example, that you would like to encourage awareness of the importance of keeping informed, *how* can you do this?)

_____

_____

_____

_____

3. *Make use of object lessons—when illustrative incidents occur in the course of events, take advantage of them.*

Encouraging desirable attitudes and values

In attempting to inculcate attitudes and values, you will find it is often more effective to use natural situations than to devise formal presentations. (This technique was suggested in Chapter 4 for helping elementary-grade pupils develop such traits as honesty and generosity.)

Examples

If a pupil damages something which belongs to someone else, point out why it is important to respect the property rights of others.

Introduce your students to books written to build desirable attitudes. There are several series of these books, some that use animal characters.

Use current events to illustrate the nature of certain kinds of behavior (e.g., discuss the causes of riots, or point out the importance of being informed about propositions on ballots).

4. *Be aware of your students' level of moral development and encourage understanding of more advanced thinking about attitudes by presenting "moral dilemmas" and by clarifying values.*

Lawrence Kohlberg (1966, 1969) has developed a theory of moral development that is a more elaborate version of Piaget's distinction between moral realism and relativism. He has devised a series of hypothetical situations describing *moral dilemmas,* for example, should a boy tell his father about a brother's misdeed? These are presented to children and their responses rated with reference to three levels of moral thinking: preconventional, conventional, and postconventional. (Each level is subdivided into two stages.) Just as *operations* are the key to Piaget's stages of intellectual development, *conventional* moral thinking is the key to Kohlberg's stages. The child at the *preconventional* level interprets moral situations in terms of physical consequences (e.g., punishment) or out of deference to power or prestige (e.g., the desire to avoid trouble). The child at the *conventional* level interprets moral situations in a conforming (conventional) way, first by wanting to please others and later by showing respect for authority and because of a desire to maintain the social order for its own sake. The adolescent at the *postconventional* level makes independent moral judgments; he recognizes that the rules of the social order are somewhat arbitrary and makes decisions in terms of general ethical principles and his own conscience. (This level is similar to Piaget's moral relativism stage.)

Kohlberg: Stages of moral thinking

These stages can be illustrated by reactions to the moral dilemma involving a boy telling his father about a brother's misdeed:

Preconventional.   "He'd better not or he'll get beat up." (Punishment)

"He should keep quiet because his brother might squeal on him." (Avoid trouble)

Conventional.   "If my father finds out later, he won't trust me." (Respect for authority)

"We should always tell the truth. Otherwise, no one can trust anyone else." (Maintain the social order)

Postconventional.   "I need to weigh what my brother did and why he did it." (Consideration of general moral principles)

"He thought he could trust me—I have to consider that." (Coming to terms with one's conscience)

Just as Piaget argues that the child advances through the stages of intellectual development in sequence, Kohlberg maintains that children must pass through lower stages of moral development in order to become capable of postconventional thinking. And just as Piaget urges the teacher to pay heed to the intellectual level of the child in planning learning experiences, Kohlberg recommends the teacher to take note of the level of moral development of their pupils in assessing their reactions to moral situations and in planning character education.

The Kohlberg stages are not clearly related to specific age levels, particularly since many individuals never progress beyond the conventional level. However, the switch from preconventional to conventional thought typically takes place around the end of the elementary grades. Consequently, elementary-grade pupils may not be capable of interpreting moral situations in terms other than punishment or avoiding trouble. (Kohlberg notes: "It does not seem wise to treat cheating as a genuine moral issue among young children" [1966, p. 26]). Furthermore, they may not be able to respond to efforts at moral education which are beyond their level of understanding.

Kohlberg suggests that teachers ask questions and listen to the explanations their students give for moral judgments to gain insight into their level of moral thought. He also suggests that moral dilemmas be presented so that students will be confronted with "a sense of uncertainty as to the right answer to the situation in question" (p. 23). Ideally, these discussions should aim at communicating ideas one level beyond that of the pupils who are participating. In addition, pupils should be encouraged to apply moral judgments to their own actions. Finally, he urges teachers to try to avoid being overly concerned about classroom rules and routines since these tend to apply only to the school environment. To encourage moral development that will permit your pupils to deal with problems unrelated to school routines, you should encourage analysis of "broader and more genuinely moral issues" (p. 26).

Encouraging moral development (Kohlberg)

To put these recommendations into practice, you might set aside certain periods for discussion and analysis of moral dilemmas. To begin, you could describe a situation from your own experience and ask students to write about what they think they would have done. These explanations could be used to assess the general level of moral thinking of the class, and further situations might be described to encourage more advanced thinking. To stimulate your students to apply moral reasoning to their own behavior, you might ask them to write about their own experiences with moral dilemmas and then have them exchange experiences and interpretations in informal small group discussions.

You could also consider the possibility of arranging for your students to actually *experience* moral dilemmas. Jane Elliott, a third-grade teacher in a small town in Iowa was so deeply affected by the assassination of Martin Luther King, Jr., she devised a technique for providing her pupils with direct experience with prejudice. Her basic technique, which is reported in the television documentary "The Eye of the Storm" and in *A Class Divided* by William Peters, could be used as a model for similar learning situations. She divided the class on the basis of eye color, and told the students that brown-eyed people are better, cleaner, more civilized, and smarter than blue-eyed people. The "superior" brown-eyed students were given extra time at recess, allowed to go to lunch first, sit in the front of the room, and were extensively praised for correct answers. The "inferior" blue-eyed students were required to use paper cups rather than the drinking fountain, were not allowed to use the equipment on the playground, and were treated as stupid when they gave wrong answers.

Just a few hours under this regime led to startling changes in the behavior of the students. Brown-eyed pupils became convinced of their superiority, to the point of mistreating blue-eyed classmates and then demanding an apology; formerly confident blue-eyed children became tense, clumsy, and unsure of themselves. The following week, the roles were reversed and the blue-eyed

Mrs. Elliott allowed the blue-eyes such special privileges as going first to lunch when she gave them the "superior" role first enjoyed by the brown-eyes, who had to wear paper collars as a sign of their "inferior" status.

Photograph by Charlotte Button for the ABC News documentary program *The Eye of the Storm.*

children were decreed superior and given all the privileges. Despite the fact that the now-inferior brown-eyed children were aware that this was just a temporary "game," they reacted intensely and seemed to become convinced that they now *were* inferior. The only difference between the two phases of the experiment was that the blue-eyed children who had experienced discrimination first were noticeably less vicious in their treatment of their "inferior" classmates. After a few days, the experiment was concluded and the pupils were asked to discuss it and write about it—which they did with great animation and also insight. The experiment was repeated the next year, with slight variations, including the use of paper collars to identify inferior pupils. Even though some of the students were aware of what had taken place the previous year, they still responded as if the changes were genuine.

You should keep in mind that some teachers who have used this technique have encountered criticism from parents, school board members, and citizens—which suggests that you secure approval from local school authorities and the parents of your pupils before such an experiment is put into practice. If you prefer not to use such a drastic technique, or if it would not be appropriate for your grade or subject area, you might devise variations of the Elliott method by asking your students to engage in less extreme forms of role playing; for example, have students play the roles of a boy who has just dented the fender of the family car and his best friend who saw him do it. Explain that the guilty driver is thinking of blaming it on a hit-and-run driver, the friend wants him to tell the truth. After the students act out how they would behave in such a situation, ask them to analyze it—preferably on a postconventional level of reasoning involving discussion of moral principles and examination of one's conscience.

A different approach to encouraging moral development has been proposed by Louis E. Raths, Merrill Harmin, and Sidney B. Simon, who in *Values and Teaching* recommend *values clarification*. They define values as personal guides that give direction to behavior and suggest that they develop through a seven part process. In order for a value to develop, they believe it must be "chosen freely from among alternatives after thoughtful consideration of the consequences of each alternative" (1966, p. 30), that it must be cherished (i.e., the person is happy with the choice) to the point of willingness to affirm the choice publicly, and that it must repeatedly "give direction to actual living" (p. 29).

Encouraging moral development (Raths)

Raths and his colleagues have developed several techniques to assist students in clarifying their values by encouraging them to go through the stages in this process. One method involves discussions that stress individual responses to situations in which there are no "right" answers. To lead students through the stages, you might ask questions such as these:

Choosing freely:
   Where do you suppose you first got that idea?
   Are you the only one in your crowd who feels this way? . . .

Choosing from alternatives:

What else did you consider before you picked this?

What's really good about this choice which makes it stand out from other possibilities? . . .

Choosing thoughtfully and reflectively:

What would be the consequences of each alternative available?

Have you thought about this very much? How did your thinking go? . . .

Prizing and cherishing:

Are you glad you feel that way?

Is it something you really prize? . . .

Affirming:

Would you tell the class the way you feel some time?

Would you be willing to sign a petition supporting that idea? . . .

Acting upon choices:

I hear what you are for; now, is there anything you can do about it?

Have you made any plans to do more than you already have done? . . .

Repeating:

Have you done anything already? Do you do this often?

Will you do it again? (Pp. 63–65)

As leads for topics for such discussions, Raths and his colleagues urge you to listen for statements made by your students that reflect *attitudes* ("I'm for . . .," "I'm against . . .," "The way I see it . . ."), *aspirations* ("Someday I'm going to . . .," "If all goes well . . ."), *purposes* ("We're thinking about . . .," "When I get this . . . I'm going to . . ."), *interests* ("My hobby is . . .," "I got this catalog on . . ."), and *activities* ("After school I usually . . .," "Last weekend we . . ."). You might structure analyses by asking students to write about and later discuss topics that reflect such observations or by presenting a provocative situation; "You are in a group of persons with whom you would like to be friends. Two members of the group begin to tease a nearby girl who has a very strange face. Others in the group join in, although a few are silent" (p. 96). Students might be asked to write what they think they would do, what other alternatives are available, what explanations for different responses might be, etc.

If you feel that you would like to arrange clarification sessions, you will find more complete information and suggestions in *Values and Teaching* or *Values Clarification: A Handbook of Practical Strategies for Teachers and Students* (1972) by Sidney B. Simon, Leland W. Howe, and Howard Kirchenbaum.

5. Apply learning theory—associate pleasant and positive experiences with the behavior and values you want to encourage.

Keep in mind that "the way subject matter is taught may be more important than what is taught." If you want your students to like your subject and learning in general, make your classroom as pleasant and enjoyable as possible, and do your best to make the subject matter interesting and stimulating.

6. Set a good example. Keep in mind the importance of modeling identification, and imitation.

In the analysis of Mager's *Developing Attitude Toward Learning* in the preceding chapter, the importance of *modeling* as a source of positive transfer was noted. The key role that imitation plays in learning has been studied and stressed by Albert Bandura (1962). In summarizing the results and implications of dozens of studies, Bandura observes, "We have found that almost any learning outcome that results from direct experience can also come about on a vicarious basis through observation of other people's behavior and its consequences for them" (1967, p. 78). The implication of this conclusion is that you should behave the way you want your students to behave. This same point was emphasized by Combs and Snygg in their observation that "how you teach may be more important than what you teach." Young pupils, especially, learn many things—particularly ways of behaving—by imitation. They identify with parents and teachers, and they do what they see admired elders do. This fact underlies one explanation offered of why girls get off to a better start in school than boys. Girls find it natural to identify with and imitate the female teachers they encounter when they enter school, and boys do not. At the secondary level, students are probably more inclined to identify with teachers than with parents, perhaps because they are in conflict with their parents and also because younger teachers are closer to them in age. This factor contributes to the fear of some parents that their adolescent offspring will be brainwashed by younger teachers. Regardless of the grade level you teach, you should keep in mind that you will serve as a model for your students.

Examples

If you want your pupils to be prompt, neat, and respectful of school property, be that way yourself.

If you want your students to be enthusiastic about literature, for instance, manifest enthusiasm yourself.

If you want your students to be tolerant of differing opinions, you yourself should be tolerant of differences of opinion expressed in class.

In the space below you might note specific forms of behavior you would like your pupils to imitate. Then try to set an example.

_____

_____

_____

_____

Using Russian Methods to Encourage Social Responsibility

In *Two Worlds of Childhood: U.S. and U.S.S.R.,* Urie Bronfenbrenner compares child rearing and educational practices in Russia and the United States. He concentrates on the process of socialization and takes as the primary criterion for judging the worth of each society "the concern of one generation for the next" (1970, p. 3). After extensive observation in Russia, Bronfenbrenner concluded that life in a Soviet family involves a considerable amount of affectionate but restrictive handling of young children and stress on obedience and discipline. Russian schools emphasize self-reliance and the development of a positive social attitude. These qualities are encouraged by group games, communal responsibilities, role playing, and systematic reports. Group competition is used to a considerable extent, and members of a group are encouraged to keep each other in line, to rate each other, and to discipline each other.

When he compared his observations of Russian children to their counterparts in America, Bronfenbrenner concluded that in terms of inculcating concern of one generation for the next, Russia was superior to the United States. The primary reason for America's poor showing is, he suggests, that children in this country are no longer brought up by their parents but by television and by their peers who are segregated by age. Lack of contact with parents and children of different ages causes social disruption that leads to lack of concern for others.

As a corrective, Bronfenbrenner suggests that we consider using some of the practices used by the Russians. He cites the work of Bandura and others in pointing up the importance of modeling as a means for encouraging desirable types of behavior. Ideally, the child should see that the model is regarded as competent and is rewarded for the competency; and the model should be someone who is considered a major source of support and control in the child's environment and also considered similar to the child himself. Several models are better than one, and the child is more likely to actually imitate if he observes that the model's behavior leads to a desirable outcome.

Bronfenbrenner recommends that teachers encourage greater concern for others by consciously setting a good example, by reinforcing children who manifest desirable behavior, and by using teams and group competition to encourage social responsibility. He observes, "Surely the most needed innovation in the American classroom is the involvement of pupils in responsible tasks on the behalf of others within the classroom, the school, the neighborhood, and the community" (p. 156). If you would like more information on how Russia encourages social responsibility and how Bronfenbrenner believes we might do the same, read at least Chapters 2 and 6 of *Two Worlds of Childhood*.

---

7. *Keep your personal prejudices under control.*

Because attitude formation is a subtle and often unconscious process, it is especially important that you do not inflict your personal biases on your pupils. A distinction should be made here between arousing enthusiasm for your subject and forcing your nonacademic opinions upon a captive audience. Do your best to avoid taking advantage of your prestige and power to entice or force students into adopting your personal opinions.

Summary

In this chapter you have been acquainted with some suggestions for teaching skills and encouraging desirable attitudes. The two basic techniques for assisting students to master skills are demonstrations first and then guided practice. As students practice, you should keep in mind the typical learning curve and the possibility that if they reach a plateau, they may need extra encouragement and instruction in advanced techniques.

Differences of opinion exist regarding the best way to teach attitudes. These differences center around the question of transfer (which was discussed in the preceding chapter) and stem partly from the conflicting beliefs of educators and humanists. Educators have argued that emphasis on the "whole child" and adoption of a progressive approach produce graduates who will eventually become well-rounded citizens. Humanists have maintained that in the process of learning "classical" subjects, the student acquires not only knowledge but also a deeper and more sympathetic appreciation of human values. Attempts to substantiate these claims have failed to provide clear-cut evidence that either approach actually produces a noticeable change in student behavior. Consequently, there is now general agreement that the teaching of attitudes and their transfer must be approached in the same way as any other type of learning—first by describing the kind of behavior desired and then by doing everything possible to encourage such behavior. The chapter concluded with some suggestions on how to do this.

Suggestions for Further Reading, Writing, Thinking, and Discussion

8-1 *Playing the Role of an Efficiency Expert*

When a teacher or psychologist performs a task analysis, he is functioning in the same way as an efficiency expert in a modern industrial concern. Time-and-motion studies are frequently carried out in industry and the military in order to find the most efficient way to do a given task and also to facilitate instruction. In certain business and military situations, in which a devotee of task analysis is in charge, virtually *everything* is done "by the numbers." To become more aware of the pros and cons of making a task analysis and chaining the steps to be followed in acquiring a skill, imagine that you are a dedicated efficiency expert. Describe how routine activities (such as getting dressed or eating breakfast) could be made as efficient as possible or how a task-analysis fanatic might set up a family schedule to increase efficiency around the house, or select some other activity of your own choosing. After you have written your satire, analyze it and note any points it illustrates about the pros and cons of performing a task analysis.

8-2 *Checking on the Possibility of Analytic and "Global" Types*

Jerome Kagan has described impulsive or reflective and analytic or thematic types of thinkers. It seems likely that there are also differences in the way individuals function physically. For example, some students respond more readily to a programmed approach to learning a skill; others prefer a discovery approach. Furthermore, certain skills ideally call for a step-by-step treatment, whereas in other types of performance individuality and freedom might be limited by a standard way of doing things. If you expect to be teaching a variety of skills, which ones might you subject to a programmed technique and which ones might be taught in a more open-ended fashion? How would you handle a "global" type of student who balked at step-by-step methods of instruction or an analytic type who seemed lost when told to "just go at it"? Would you insist that all students learn the same skill in the same way?

8-3 *Analyzing Demonstrations You Have Witnessed*

Demonstrations are a very common pedagogical device. If you would like to sort out your thoughts with regard to this form of teaching, think back to good and bad experiences you have had with teachers who used this method of instruction. Describe the best and the worst demonstrations you can remember. Then analyze why you were favorably or unfavorably impressed and try to compose a set of guidelines to follow when *you* give demonstrations.

8-4 *Analyzing Experiences with Negative Transfer*

The negative-transfer effect that a previously learned skill may have on the mastery of a new skill can be exasperating, time-consuming, and frustrating. Think back to skills you have learned and try to recollect any problems you encountered due to negative transfer. One student, for example, had learned to play the violin and then decided to take piano lessons. On his violin music, the numeral *1* appeared over the notes to be played with the first finger. On his piano music, the numeral *1* was placed over the notes to be played with the *thumb*. It was so difficult to overcome the tendency to use his forefinger in response to a *1* in the music that the student gave up piano lessons in disgust. Analyze this situation, or a similar one you experienced yourself, and describe how you might assist someone to overcome the confusion induced by negative transfer. (If you had been the teacher of the piano student, how might you have helped him use the thumb rather than the first finger?)

8-5 *Analyzing Experiences with a Plateau*

Many learning curves have plateaus. You will surely recall learning situations in which you reached a point of no apparent improvement, only to go on eventually to a higher level of performance. Describe such an experience and then indicate what a teacher might have done to help you cope with or overcome the plateau in your curve of learning.

8-6 *Designing a Curriculum to Accomplish the Goals of the Eight-Year Study*

Wilford M. Aikin described the purpose of the Eight-Year Study in these terms:

> We are trying to develop students who regard education as an enduring quest for meaning rather than credit accumulation; who desire to investigate, to follow the leadings of a subject, to explore new fields of thought; knowing how to budget time, to read well, to use sources of knowledge effectively and who are experienced in fulfilling obligations which come with memberships in the school or college community. (1942, p. 144)

In many ways those words describe what contemporary college students often feel should be the purpose of higher education. Assume you are placed in charge of developing a new college. How will you organize the curriculum, plan classes, and carry out evaluation to achieve the purpose outlined above (or a credo you yourself evolved)? After describing your "ideal college," analyze it with reference to some realities of higher education in the United States today—a high student-teacher ratio, limited funds, the "demand" for some measure of academic achievement. Could changes be effected *within* the present structure of higher education to bring it closer to your "ideal"? Or would a complete departure be necessary?

8-7 *Programming Attitudes in "Walden Two"*

One of the most striking features of B. F. Skinner's utopia described in *Walden Two* centers around the way desirable attitudes are reinforced and undesirable attitudes eliminated. The novel describes child-rearing techniques that encourage perseverance and patience and eliminate jealousy. If the possibility of shaping attitudes and values interests you, read Chapters 12, 13, and 14 of *Walden Two*. You might record your reactions, first noting whether you think the techniques would *really* work if used exactly as described in the novel, then indicating whether you think similar techniques are applicable in a typical American home or classroom.

8-8 *Using Programmed Techniques in Developing Vocational Instruction*

Programmed instruction is rather common in military and industrial situations for teaching skills of various kinds. If you will be teaching a course that involves training in specific skills, you are urged to purchase a copy of *Developing Vocational Instruction* (1967) by Robert F. Mager and Kenneth M. Beach, Jr.

The authors have had wide experience in industry, in behavioral research, and in teaching. In their words, "*Developing Vocational Instruction* is designed to aid both the skilled craftsman who is preparing instruction through which to teach his craft, and the experienced vocational or technical instructor who is interested in improving his present course or finds it necessary to prepare a new one." They also point out, however, that the book "is not specific to subject matter or vocation, and it applies to many academic as well as vocational and technical areas." If you will be teaching a craft or vocational skill or if you would like to know how to make a job description, carry out a task analysis, derive course objectives, and develop lesson plans (among other things), read *Developing Vocational Instruction* and note your reactions.

8-9 *Learning More About Teaching Skills*

For complete, technical information about skill learning you might consult *Acquisition of Skill* (1966) edited by Edward A. Bilodeau. For concise, application-oriented discussions of teaching athletic skills, see *What Research Says to the Teacher: Physical Education in the Elementary Schools* (1963) by Anna S. Espenschade, *What Research Says to the Teacher: Physical Fitness* (1963) by Paul Hunsicker, or *Teaching Physical Education* (1966) by Muska Mosston. (This last book includes a chapter on the use of discovery methods in physical education.)

Recommended Reading in *Psychology Applied to Teaching: Selected Readings*

If you would like to do further reading in books or articles mentioned in this chapter (and in the preceding "Suggestions for Further Reading, Writing, Thinking, and Discussion") without having to track down several separate volumes, you might peruse *Psychology Applied to Teaching: Selected Readings* (Boston: Houghton Mifflin, 1972). This is a collection of excerpts from books and articles from journals in psychology. The following selection provides extended commentary on points noted in this chapter and mentioned in the "Suggestions."

Programming Attitudes: Excerpt from *Walden Two* by B. F. Skinner, Selection 7, p. 73. (See also Suggestion 8-7.)

PART

MOTIVATION

MOTIVATION:

THEORY AND APPLICATIONS

Classifications
*Hierarchy of needs: physiological, safety, belongingness and love, esteem,
    self-actualization, knowing and understanding, aesthetic (Maslow)*
Deficiency needs, growth needs (Maslow)
Bad choosers, good choosers (Maslow)

Experiments
*Setting of realistic goals by successful students, unrealistic goals by students
    who have failed (Sears)*

Concepts
Nature of a choice situation (Maslow)
Level of aspiration (Hoppe)

Theories
Growth motivation (Maslow)
Competence (White)
Achievement motivation (McClelland and Atkinson)
Behaviorist-associationist interpretation of motivation

Methodology
Satisfying deficiency needs, encouraging growth choices
Encouraging the setting and maintaining of realistic levels of aspiration
Making judicious use of praise, reducing the negative impact of blame
Using objectives and Goal Cards (Programmed approach)
Inducing dissatisfaction in the life space (Discovery approach)
Using incentives
Avoiding excessive competition
Encouraging the desire to achieve

CONTENTS

SO FAR, YOU HAVE BEEN ACQUAINTED WITH THE CHARACTERISTICS of students at different age levels, with speculations about how they learn, and with suggestions on how to facilitate the learning, remembering, and transfer of facts, concepts, skills, and attitudes. But there remains the problem of why some pupils seem to have so much more desire to learn than others. And you will be concerned with how to arouse the interest of your students, particularly those who lack zest for learning. What this boils down to is *motivation*.

Interpretations of motivation reflect differences between the Lockeian and Leibnitzian points of view, which were presented in the discussion of development and learning in Chapter 5. The Lockeian view, as you will recall, stresses that a human being begins life as a *tabula rasa* (blank slate) that is subsequently "filled in" through interaction with the environment. This concept of development is currently reflected in the guided experience position and in programmed learning, whose aim is to shape the learner's behavior. Leibnitz conceived of man as purposive and self-directed, a notion now reflected in the natural view of development and in the discovery approach.

The behaviorist-associationist-environmentalist view of learning and development is based on the five presuppositions that Allport traces to the Lockeian view: that what is external and visible is of primary importance, that learning is the substitution of one effective stimulus for another or of one response for another, that what is small and molecular is of greater concern than what is large and molar, that animals and humans are basically equivalent, and that what comes earlier in development is more fundamental than what comes later. Those who endorse this position study motivation by analyzing observable behavior, attempt to trace associations built up between stimuli and responses, concentrate on specific reactions, do much of their research on animals, and emphasize the importance of early experiences.

Early behaviorist-associationist experiments in motivation involved observing the behavior of rats that had been deprived of food and noting the way reinforcement led to associations between stimuli and responses. On the basis of such experiments, a conception of motivation was proposed that stressed the importance of physiological drives and the way these serve as the basis for other motives. For example, it was suggested that a student would be motivated to learn in order to earn praise from a teacher because early in life phrases such as the "good boy" uttered by his mother as she fed him were associated with his hunger being satisfied.

Behaviorist-associationist view of motivation

In time, further experiments revealed that although this explanation might account for some aspects of motivation, it placed too much emphasis on the satisfaction of physiological drives. A number of investigators (e.g., Butler, 1953) demonstrated that young animals with all their physiological drives satisfied would engage in many types of behavior simply to satisfy their curiosity or to manipulate things. This led to recognition that not all behavior is necessarily derived from physiological drives, but the behaviorist-associationist view of motivation still places great emphasis on external behavior and on the ways in which responses are reinforced.

Skinner's experiments with rats and pigeons illustrate this view of motivation. The animal is deprived of food before it is placed in the learning situation. When it makes a move toward the desired terminal behavior, it is reinforced with a food pellet. Those who favor an operant conditioning approach follow the same general procedure in the classroom, making allowance for the obvious fact that the physiological drives of most students will be reasonably satisfied. Just as the rat is reinforced with food each time it responds in the desired way, students are reinforced for each correct answer by being given praise, prizes, candy (the human equivalent of a food pellet), or sometimes money. If a teacher experiences problems in encouraging students to learn, the behaviorist-associationist is likely to maintain that it is because conditions have been improperly arranged or because reinforcement has not been supplied in an advantageous manner.

Those who endorse Leibnitzian views, and believe that human beings are not blank slates but purposive and self-directed, are bothered by the assumption that students need to be motivated by being supplied with rewards for specific actions. Advocates of the natural view of development and the discovery approach stress that learning activity should be—and can be—its own reward. Abraham H. Maslow has developed the most systematic description of a theory of motivation based on this view. (His general view of development and behavior was outlined in Chapter 2.)

Maslow's Theory of Growth Motivation

Maslow first described sixteen propositions he felt would have to be incorporated into any sound theory of motivation. (These are discussed in Chapter 3 of *Motivation and Personality*.) Maslow eventually proposed a theory of *need gratification* (or *growth motivation*) that he felt met these propositions. He refers to need gratification as "the most important single principle underlying all development," adding that "the single, holistic principle that binds together the multiplicity of human motives is the tendency for a new and higher need to emerge as the lower need fulfills itself by being sufficiently gratified" (1968, p. 55). He elaborated on this basic principle by proposing a hierarchy of needs, starting with *physiological* needs at the bottom and working up through *safety* needs, *belongingness* and *love* needs, *esteem* needs, the need for *self-actualization*, and the desires to *know* and to *understand* and culminating in *aesthetic* needs (described in Chapter 4 of the same book).

Maslow's hierarchy of needs

In Maslow's theory of growth motivation, when a person has the lower *deficiency* (or D) needs (physiological, safety, belongingness and love, esteem) satisfied, he will feel motivated to satisfy the higher *being* (or B) needs (self-actualization, knowing and understanding, aesthetic)—not because of a deficit but because of a *desire* to gratify the higher needs. Being needs are the basis for self-actualization, and Maslow spent several years studying and describing the characteristics of consistently self-actualizing persons. (He defines self-actualization as "an episode or spurt in which the powers of the person come together in a particularly efficient and intensely enjoyable way" (1968, p. 91.) A good part of *Toward a Psychology of Being* is devoted to these descriptions, and you will probably find them of considerable interest. Maslow felt that the study of mentally healthy individuals was necessary because previous theories of motivation, particularly Freudian theory, were based on study of people who were mentally ill. Maslow felt that the primary reason human beings were not seen as capable of self-direction by early theorists who analyzed motivation was due to the type of individual studied. He argued that observation

Maslow: growth motivation

of mentally healthy individuals leads to a different conclusion than that proposed by Freud. He notes:

> Observation of children shows more and more clearly that healthy children *enjoy* growing and moving forward, gaining new skills, capacities and powers. This is in flat contradiction to that version of Freudian theory which conceives of every child as hanging on desperately to each adjustment that it achieves and to each state of rest or equilibrium. According to this theory, the reluctant and conservative child has continually to be kicked upstairs, out of its comfortable, preferred state of rest *into* a new frightening situation. (1968, pp. 23–24)

Differences Between Deficiency and Growth Needs

A key aspect of Maslow's theory is the distinction between deficiency and being (or growth) needs. These differences are described in Chapter 3 of *Toward a Psychology of Being* and can be summarized as follows:

Differences between deficiency and growth needs

1. A person acts to get *rid* of deficiency needs (e.g., hunger); he *seeks* the pleasure of growth needs.
2. Deficiency motivation leads to reduction of disagreeable tension and restoration of equilibrium; growth motives maintain a pleasurable form of tension.
3. The satisfying of deficiencies *avoids* illnesses; the satisfying of growth needs *produces* health.
4. The satisfying of deficiency needs leads to a sense of relief and satiation; the satisfying of growth needs leads to pleasure and a desire for further fulfillment.
5. Deficiency-need gratification tends to be episodic and to result in consummation (e.g., eating three meals a day); growth motivation is continuous and never-ending.
6. Deficit needs are shared by all members of the human species; growth needs are idiosyncratic because every person is different.
7. The fact that deficit needs can be satisfied only by other people leads to dependence on the environment and to a tendency to be other-directed (e.g., the person must be sensitive to the approval of others); growth needs are satisfied more autonomously and tend to make one self-directed.
8. In contrast with the growth-motivated individual, the deficit-motivated person is more dependent upon others, whom he sees primarily as need-gratifiers rather than as individuals in their own right; consequently, he is limited in interpersonal relations.
9. The deficit-motivated person tends to be self-centered; the growth-motivated person is capable of being problem-centered and of perceiving situations and people in a detached way.
10. The deficit-motivated person must depend on others for help when he encounters difficulties; the growth-motivated person is more able to help himself.

Competence, Equilibration, and Adequacy

Maslow is not the only psychologist to stress need gratification as opposed to deficit motivation. Robert W. White wrote a classic paper on motivation in which he analyzed dozens of theories and hundreds of studies to explain his dissatisfaction with the behaviorists' emphasis on drive reduction. He summarized his argument in this way:

> [This] survey indicates a certain unanimity as to the kinds of behavior that cannot be conceptualized in terms of primary drives. This behavior includes visual exploration, grasping, crawling and walking, attention and perception, language and thinking, exploring novel objects and places, manipulating the surroundings, and producing effective changes in the environment. The thesis is then proposed that all of these behaviors have a common biological significance: they all form part of the process whereby the animal or child learns to interact effectively with his environment. The word *competence* is chosen as suitable to indicate this common property. Further, it is maintained that competence cannot be fully acquired simply through behavior instigated by drives. It receives substantial contributions from activities which, though playful and exploratory in character, at the same time show direction, selectivity, and persistence in interacting with the environment. Such activities in the ultimate service of competence must therefore be conceived to be motivated in their own right. It is proposed to designate this motivation by the term effectance, and to characterize the experience produced as a *feeling of efficacy*. (1959, p. 331)

White: competence motivation

This emphasis on a drive for competence "motivated in its own right" is similar to Maslow's contention that "healthy children enjoy growing and moving forward, gaining new skills, capacities and powers."

Jean Piaget's principle of *equilibration* also stresses self-regulation. He feels that the child progressively attains a higher degree of equilibrium at each stage of development. Piaget acknowledges the same growth motivation concept proposed by Maslow when he says that the organism has "a fundamental need which is that of the organism's development" (1963, p. 170).

Arthur Combs and Donald Snygg postulate that all behavior can be attributed to one need: *adequacy*, "a great driving, striving force in each of us by which we are continually seeking to make ourselves ever more adequate with life" (1959, p. 45). This is obviously much like Maslow's need for gratification and White's concept of competence.

The last four of these points are of most direct concern to teachers. You should keep in mind that in your classroom you will be the primary source of satisfaction of the deficiency needs of your students, that they will depend on you and that they will therefore have a tendency to be self-centered.

Implications of Maslow's Theory

The implications for teaching Maslow's theory of motivation are provocative. One down-to-earth implication is that a teacher should do everything possible to see that the lower-level needs of students are satisfied so that they will be

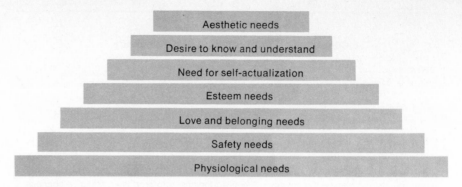

Figure 9–1 Maslow's Hierarchy of Needs

Abraham H. Maslow, ''A Theory of Human Motivation,'' *Psychological Review,* Vol. 50, 1943, pp. 370–396. Copyright 1943 by the American Psychological Association, and reproduced by permission.

more likely to function at the higher levels. Your students will be more likely to be primed to seek satisfaction of the need to understand and know in your classes if they are physically comfortable, feel safe and relaxed, have a sense of belonging, and experience self-esteem. To help you keep this in mind, Figure 9–1 presents Maslow's list of needs arranged in a literal hierarchical form.

Since the satisfying of deficit needs involves dependence on others and since teachers have the primary responsibility for what takes place in the classroom, it is worth emphasizing again that you will play an important role in the need gratification of your students. The more effective you are in assisting them to satisfy their deficit needs, the more likely they are to experience growth motivation.

Even though you do your best to satisfy the lower level needs in this hierarchy, however, it is apparent that you are not likely to be successful in establishing a situation in which all of your students will always function at the highest levels. To note just one example, a child who feels that his parents do not love him or that his peers do not accept him may not respond to your efforts to show you react favorably. And if his needs for love, belonging, and esteem are not satisfied, he is less likely to be in the mood to learn. It is only under close to ideal circumstances that the higher needs emerge. Perhaps even more important to theorizing about education, it is only when the higher needs come into play that a person is likely to choose wisely when given the opportunity.

*Bad choosers and
good choosers*

Maslow emphasizes this point by making a distinction between *bad choosers* and *good choosers.* When some people are allowed freedom to choose, they seem consistently to make wise choices; most people, however, frequently make choices which are self-destructive. Maslow explains this by describing growth as it takes place under ideal circumstances, and how it more often actually occurs. He says:

> Growth takes place when the next step forward is subjectively more delightful, more joyous, more intrinsically satisfying than the previous gratification with which we have become familiar and even bored; ... the only way we can ever know what is right for us is that it feels better than any alternative. The new experience validates *itself* rather than by any outside criterion. It is self-justifying, self-validating. ...
>
> Then arise the inevitable questions, What holds [the child] back? What prevents growth? Wherein lies the conflict: What is the alternative to growth forward? Why is it so hard and painful for some to grow forward? Here we must become more fully aware of the fixative and regressive power of ungratified deficiency needs, of the attractions of safety and security, of the functions of defense and protection against pain, fear, loss, and threat, of the need for courage in order to grow ahead.
>
> Every human being has *both* sets of forces within him. One set clings to safety and defensiveness out of fear, tending to regress backward, hanging on to the past, *afraid* to grow...., *afraid* to take chances, *afraid* to jeopardize what he already has, *afraid* of independence, freedom and separateness. The other set of forces impels him forward toward wholeness of Self and uniqueness of Self, toward full functioning of all his capacities, toward confidence in the face of the external world at the same time that he can accept his deepest, real, unconscious Self. (Pp. 45-46)

Growth, as Maslow sees it, is the result of a never-ending series of situations offering a free choice between the attractions and dangers of safety and those of growth. If a person is functioning at the level of being needs, the choice will ordinarily be a progressive one. However, Maslow adds:

> In this process, the environment (parents, therapists, teachers) is important in various ways, even though the ultimate choice must be made by the child:
>
> a. It can gratify his basic needs for safety, belongingness, love and respect, so that he can feel unthreatened, autonomous, interested and spontaneous and thus dare to choose the unknown.
>
> b. It can help by making the growth choice positively attractive and less dangerous, and by making the regressive choice less attractive and more costly. (1968, pp. 58-59)

The first point emphasizes the suggestion made earlier that you should do everything possible to gratify deficiency needs to encourage growth. The second point can be clarified by a simple diagram Maslow has devised to illustrate a choice situation (1968, p. 47):

Enhance the dangers   Enhance the attractions   *Nature of a choice situation*

Safety ←——————— < person > ——————→ Growth

Minimize the attractions   Minimize the dangers

Maslow's theory of motivation is congruent with the views of Dewey, Piaget, Combs and Snygg, Neill, and advocates of both free and open education. Because it is assumed the child will choose wisely if given the chance, the basic approach to education they endorse involves arranging attractive learning situations so that students can select the activities they feel have personal appeal or value. Instead of having the teacher supply reinforcement, the self-chosen activity of the child becomes its own reward. In order to encourage this kind of education, however, it is necessary—once again—to seek an optimum balance between freedom and control. This is the problem Dewey analyzed so searchingly in the excerpts from *Experience and Education* quoted in Chapter 2, and it is a theme that has been touched on in every chapter of this book. The open education approach has been suggested as the most promising solution, since it combines freedom with guidance. In deciding how you might seek a balance between the motivational aspects of these two factors, you will need to consider interrelationships between safety and growth.

Interrelationships Between Safety and Growth

The distinction Maslow makes between safety and growth has been analyzed in different terms by other theorists. One of the first descriptions of the push-pull nature of many decisions was provided by the German psychologist F. Hoppe (1930) who analyzed *level of aspiration*. He observed that a person tends to raise his goals after success and to lower them after failure. This process protects him from continual failure or from too easy achievement, which does not provide a feeling of accomplishment. The level of aspiration is set as a compromise between two conflicting tendencies: the desire to avoid disappointment accompanying failure, which forces aspirations down, and the desire to succeed at the highest possible level, which pushes aspirations up. However, in some cases the protective mechanism is thrown out of balance. If the person sets goals that are too high, he will inevitably fail. If he sets goals too low, he is robbed of a sense of achievement no matter what he does. The ideal situation is for a student to maintain a realistic level of aspiration.

Hoppe: level of aspiration

The impact of aspirations was demonstrated in an experiment by Pauline Sears (1940), who worked with three groups of upper elementary school subjects. A "success" group was composed of children who had had a consistent history of success in all academic subjects. A "failure" group consisted of pupils with the opposite sort of record. A "differential" group was made up of children who had had successful experiences with reading but unsuccessful experiences with arithmetic. The subjects were given a series of twenty speed tests in arithmetic and reading. After the first trial, they were asked to estimate the time it would take them to do the next section. Then half of the pupils in each group were exposed to a "success condition"—they were lavishly praised

Sears: successful students set realistic goals

for their performance after most (but not all) of the next nineteen trials. The other pupils in each group were exposed to a "failure condition"—they were criticized rather severely for poor work after most (but not all) of the next nineteen trials. After each trial, all subjects were asked to estimate their time for the next test.

Pupils who were exposed to the "failure condition" showed greater discrepancies between their estimated and their actual performance. They were also much more variable in the way they reacted—some tending to set consistently lower goals, others setting impossibly high goals for themselves. The pupils with previous histories of academic success were somewhat better able to cope with the experimental "failure condition"; their discrepancies and variability were not so extreme. The "success condition" pupils (even those with a previous history of failure), on the other hand, set realistic goals for themselves, with a tendency to put them slightly above the actual level of performance.

The Need for Achievement

J. W. Atkinson (1964) has developed a theory of motivation embodying a more comprehensive interpretation of Hoppe's level of aspiration. His theory is also derived from the conception of *achievement motivation* proposed by David McClelland (1961). McClelland believes that in the course of development, human beings acquire a *need* for achievement, and he has conducted research to demonstrate the degree to which it varies among individuals. Atkinson hypothesizes that differences in the strength of the need for achievement can be explained by postulating a contrasting need to avoid failure. Some people, he suggests, are success-oriented, others have a high degree of anxiety about failure. By experiments similar to those conducted by Sears, Atkinson (1960) showed that a success-oriented person is likely to set goals for himself of intermediate difficulty (i.e., he has a 50/50 chance of success), whereas anxiety-ridden persons set goals that are either very high or very low. (If such a person fails on the hard task, no one can blame him; and he is almost sure to succeed on an easy task.) Atkinson believes that the tendency to achieve success is influenced by the probability of success and the attractiveness of achieving it. A strong need to avoid failure is likely to be developed if a person experiences repeated failure and if he sets goals beyond what he thinks he can accomplish.

McClelland and Atkinson: achievement motivation

The similarity of this conception to Maslow's theory of motivation and to Hoppe's interpretation of level of aspiration is apparent. All three emphasize that it is necessary to take into account the fear of failure in arranging learning experiences. The same point has been stressed by John Holt in *How Children Fail* (1964) and by William Glasser in *Schools Without Failure* (1969) and *The Identity Society* (1972). Glasser argues that in order for a person to succeed at life in general, he must first experience success in one important aspect of his life. For most people, that one important part should be school. But the

traditional approach to education, which emphasizes comparative grading, allows only a minority of students to feel successful. Thus most students feel that they are failures, and their motivation to achieve in other aspects of their lives is depressed. This is the basic argument Benjamin Bloom makes in advocating learning for mastery, and it is related to Erikson's theory of development, which stresses the importance of encouraging initiative and industry (rather than doubt and guilt), and to Harry Stack Sullivan's emphasis on the importance of a positive self-concept produced by favorable reflected appraisals.

Implications of Views of Motivation

Before offering suggestions for developing classroom techniques in motivation, an analysis of the implications of the various theories that have just been outlined is offered as background.

The behaviorist-associationist view of motivation emphasizes that it is necessary for a teacher to supply reinforcement in order to guide learning. Although such an approach is appropriate and effective in some situations, if used to excess it is likely to lead to a conception of motivation that may become extrinsic, manipulative, materialistic and repressive.

When a person indulges in an activity primarily because he will earn a reward, the motivation is *extrinsic*—as contrasted with *intrinsic* motivation, in which

the person engages in an activity for its own sake. Some activities may provide their own reinforcement, but the associationist's conviction that it is a mistake to leave anything to accidental contingencies of reinforcement leads them to feel uncomfortable about such activities. Instead, they prefer conditions that are arranged to *produce* specific kinds of behavior. Since these situations are arranged rather than natural, a person may not find them self-reinforcing, and this will make it necessary for reinforcement to be supplied. In many cases, the reinforcement that is supplied is not directly related to the activity and is therefore extrinsic.

Once a teacher accepts the principle that arranged contingencies are preferable to accidental ones and decides to supply reinforcement for almost all responses, she is virtually committed to behavior manipulation. Stimulus situations must be devised and responses in a desired direction must be reinforced, which is likely to cause problems because of the necessity to supply different and more satisfying reinforcements. A student is likely to cease to respond if any particular technique is used too often (which will cause the reinforcement to lose its appeal), and when learning becomes more difficult he may demand greater rewards for greater effort. Consequently, praise may become ineffective; after the first dozen or so pieces of candy or the equivalent may seem unappetizing; the chance to indulge in a self-selected activity may not be considered worth the trouble. It seems almost inevitable that excessive use of rewards will lead to a materialistic "What will I get out of this?" attitude.

And as soon as a student realizes that he is in a situation where no one is around to supply a pay-off, he is likely to abruptly drop an activity.

When reinforcement is supplied by others, a depressive effect may occur because of factors such as those outlined by Maslow in his comparison of deficiency and growth needs. The fact that deficit needs can be satisfied only by other people leads a deficit-motivated person to be sensitive to the approval of others and dependent on them, thereby limiting his interpersonal relations and reducing his confidence in solving problems on his own. Ideally, the student should be encouraged to be autonomous, to see others as individuals in their own right (not just as suppliers of reinforcement), and to be capable of helping himself. The behaviorist-associationist view of motivation thus stresses deficit motivation and may limit growth motivation.

Some advocates of behavior modification take pains to note that the techniques they use are for early training only and that the ultimate goal is to encourage eventual self-directed behavior. However, few books or articles on behavior modification actually give instructions as to how a teacher can bring about the transition. Erikson's theory of development and Sullivan's observations on the self-concept, both of which stress the importance of having children feel confident about their ability to control their own behavior, make clear the difficulties of designing reinforcement schedules to wean a child from control.

In his theory of motivation, Maslow asks you to have trust in the human organism and to allow freedom of choice. At the same time, he urges you to remain aware of the complexity of motivation and to be aware that the good chooser is the exception rather than the rule. Neill and Holt and some other champions of free education advocate complete freedom of choice. This view, however, fails to take into account Maslow's observations that being needs likely lead to wise choices are more likely to come into play when teachers gratify the lower-level deficiency needs of their students and make growth choices attractive. The free education view also overlooks the hierarchical nature of learning described by Gagné in *The Conditions of Learning*. Problem-solving, intuitive thinking, and creativity are the most satisfying and valuable kinds of learning experiences—the kind that occur during episodes of self-actualization. But in order to become capable of such learning, a person must first master verbal associations, concepts, and principles. Few children can be expected to have the maturity and foresight to realize this and to persevere through the sometimes minimally rewarding work of mastering basic information. If given complete freedom, they may respond only to aspects of the learning environment that have immediate, superficial appeal and never come to grips with a field of study. If diverted from mastering information that has great potential value, and that might lead to genuine employment of a subject, they are seduced by the attractions of safety into making bad choices.

In light of all of this, it is apparent that once again some sort of balance between control and freedom seems desirable. In thinking about how to develop such a conception of motivation, consider the following list as goals to strive for in arranging learning. Many of them are similar to goals noted earlier.

Goals to Strive for in Arranging Motivational Experiences

1. Take into account Maslow's hierarchy of needs, particularly the distinction between deficiency and growth needs.
2. Remain aware that teachers are in a key position to gratify deficiency needs—which can be satisfied only by others.
3. Keep in mind Maslow's description of a choice situation and the desirability of enhancing the attractions of growth choices while minimizing their dangers.
4. Try to see that learning experiences encourage students to develop a realistic level of aspiration and to become success-oriented.
5. Do everything possible to minimize anxiety and failure and to maximize feelings of initiative and industry and the development of a positive self-concept.
6. Maximize intrinsic motivation, self-direction, and the enjoyment of doing something for its own sake.
7. Minimize extrinsic motivation, manipulation, and overtones of materialism.
8. Take into account the need to supply encouragement when students are engaged in mastery of background information that will have a delayed pay-off.

The following suggestions are offered as starting points for developing ways to achieve these goals.

Arousing and Sustaining Interest in Learning

1. Do everything possible to satisfy the deficiency needs—physiological, safety, belongingness, esteem.
   a. Allow for the physical condition of your pupils.
   b. Make your room physically and psychologically safe.
   c. Show your students that you take an interest in them and that they "belong" in your classroom.
   d. Arrange learning experiences so that all students can gain at least a degree of esteem.
2. Enhance the attractions and minimize the dangers of growth choices.
3. Direct learning experiences toward feelings of success in an effort to encourage a realistic level of aspiration, an orientation toward achievement, and a positive self-concept.
   a. Make use of goals and objectives that are challenging but attainable.
   b. Provide knowledge of results (by emphasizing the positive).
   c. Consider the advantages and disadvantages of symbolic or material rewards.

4. Be alert to the damaging impact of excessive competition.
   a. Encourage cooperation by making use of variations of the committee approach.
5. For students who need it, encourage the development of a desire to achieve.
6. Take advantage of natural interests, try to create new ones, and encourage learning for its own sake.
7. Provide encouragement and incentives for learning that is essential but not intrinsically appealing.

Satisfying deficiency needs

1. *Do everything possible to satisfy the deficiency needs—physiological, safety, belongingness, esteem.*

   a. *Allow for the physical condition of your pupils and the classroom.*

Examples:

Be aware that your students may occasionally be hungry or thirsty. (This sounds obvious, but it is frequently forgotten.) Permit snacks on an individual basis or have a routine—or occasional nonroutine—snack break.

Have a change of pace or a break when appropriate. With young children, make allowance for flexible nap time.

Make a habit of checking the room temperature. Ask your *class* if the room is too warm or cool.

In the space below, you might note other practices you can follow to satisfy physiological needs.

_____

_____

_____

   b. *Make your room physically and psychologically safe.*

The need for safety will likely be satisfied by the general classroom climate you establish, although physical factors of safety may be involved, particularly with young pupils. In one kindergarten, for example, several children were worried about the possibility of fire after seeing TV news coverage of a fire in the school. In most cases, however, you can best ensure safety by establishing a relaxed, secure classroom environment.

Examples:

If you see that a pupil fears something—for example, being bullied by older pupils on the playground, fire, enclosed places—explain that you will offer protection or that adequate precautionary measures have been taken, or that you will give him a nonthreatening place in the room.

Establish a classroom atmosphere in which students know what to expect and can relax about routines. Do everything you can to make your room a place that is psychologically safe, be alert to things you do that are unnecessarily threatening, and try to see things from your students' point of view in an effort to detect anxiety-producing situations.

As much as possible, establish classroom routines in which students can take the initiative, for example, don't require recitation—wait for students to volunteer; don't force students to participate in new activities—let them try when they feel ready.

A humiliating or embarrassing experience may so generalize that a student comes to hate or fear everything connected with a classroom. So go out of your way to make such a student feel comfortable and secure.

In the space below, you might note other ways to make your classroom an inviting, secure place:

_____

_____

_____

   c. *Show your students that you take an interest in them and that they "belong" in your classroom.*

Examples:

Learn and use names as fast as you can.

Follow the open school practice of keeping detailed records for individual pupils and refer to accomplishments specifically.

Whenever possible, schedule individual tutorial or interview sessions so that you can interact with all students on a one-to-one basis.

If a student is absent because of an extended illness, send a get-well card signed by the entire class.

To encourage *esprit de corps* have class planning sessions or have "sharing", that is, invite students at *all* grade levels to talk about interesting experiences or make appropriate announcements.

In the space below, you might note other ways to make students in your classroom feel they "belong."

_____

_____

_____

d. Arrange learning experiences so that all students can gain at least a degree of esteem.

Examples:

Play down comparisons, encourage self-competition.

Make use of mastery learning.

Permit students to work toward individual goals.

Give individual assistance to slow-learning students.

(Further suggestions for satisfying esteem needs will be presented with subsequent points.)

Encouraging growth choices

2. *Enhance the attractions and minimize the dangers of growth choices.*

When you first begin to teach, you might keep a copy of Maslow's diagram of a choice situation in your top desk drawer. Refer to it when the need arises and ask yourself: Am I setting things up to encourage effort or encouraging the student not to try? If you establish situations that cause pressure, tension, or anxiety, your students will choose safety and do their best to remain uninvolved. But if you minimize risks and make learning seem exciting and worthwhile, even the less secure students may feel impelled to join in.

Examples:

Don't penalize guessing on exams.

Don't impose restrictions or conditions on assignments if they will act as dampers: For example, "You must hand in all papers typed and with no erasures or strike-overs." Some students may not even start a report under such conditions.

Avoid "do-or-die" situations such as single exams or projects.

To encourage free participation, make it clear that you will not grade students on class recitation.

Point out and demonstrate the values of learning and the limitations and disadvantages ("dangers") of not learning; for example, note that knowing how to multiply and divide is necessary for personal bookkeeping and also that errors will lead to problems and perhaps the necessity to have someone else do the work for you.

In the space below, note other ways to make safety choices appear unattractive or "dangerous" and make growth choices desirable and unthreatening.

_____

_____

_____

Checking on Contact Difficulty, Conditions, and Consequences*

In Chapter 10 of *Developing Attitude Toward Learning,* Robert F. Mager provides a check list you might use in analyzing your own instruction with the aim of increasing your students' approach responses and decreasing their avoidance responses. (*Approach* and *avoidance* are the terms behaviorists use to describe what Maslow depicts in his "choice" diagram.) Mager provides lists of questions under the headings *contact difficulty, contact conditions,* and *contact consequences.* Following is an abridged version of his list:

The Instructor

Contact Difficulty. What does the instructor do that makes it easy or difficult for the students to experience the subject?

Does he speak loud enough for all to hear easily?

Does he allow or encourage questions?

Contact Conditions. What does the instructor do to make it easy or difficult to stay in contact with the subject?

Must students remain inactive for long periods of time?

Is he interested in teaching students or is he more interested in keeping order?

Does *he* behave as he wants his students to behave?

Contact Consequences. What happens to the students when they do work with, or manipulate, the target subject?

How are their questions answered? With interest? With hostility?

With insult, ridicule, or disdain? Are they ignored?

Does the instructor use subject matter as an instrument of punishment?

Instructional Materials and Devices

Contact Difficulty. Do the materials facilitate or inhibit student contact with the subject?

Do type size and style make it difficult to read the material?

(Ask a student.)

Are the materials easy to get at?

Contact Conditions. How easy or difficult is it to continue to use the materials?

Is it easy to see the place or importance of the materials, or do students consider them nuisances?

What is the reading difficulty?

Contact Consequences. What is the result of using the course materials?

Do students suffer from "relevance confusion"? Do they come away wondering why the materials were used?

Are they frustrated because they had to watch while other students performed the experiments, made the adjustments, or took the measurements?

The Physical Environment

Contact Consequences. Would the student's work *improve* as a result of *leaving* the student to experience the subject?

Does the student have adequate work space?

Does the seating arrangement facilitate distraction?

Contact Consequences. Would the student's world *improve* as a result of *leaving* the environment in which he was closeted with the subject?

Is the student anxious to get away from the environment?

Is the student relieved when he leaves the environment? Why?

*(Abridged from pages 87–91 of *Developing Attitude Toward Learning.*)

3. Direct learning experiences toward feelings of success in an effort to encourage a realistic level of aspiration, an orientation toward achievement, and a positive self-concept.

Hoppe described aspiration level and Sears illustrated its impact in her study of students who worked under success- and failure-oriented conditions. McClelland's theory of achievement motivation and Atkinson's development of it further emphasize how some people are success-oriented, others anxiety-ridden. Glasser maintains that in order for a person to succeed at life in general, he must first experience success in one important part of his life—particularly in school. Erikson stressed the importance of developing initiative and industry, Sullivan the significance of a positive self-concept. All these theorists emphasize the vital importance of feeling success. If students experience early failure in any learning experience, they will either lose interest or actively avoid further learning—which could bring more failure. Consequently, it is vital to try to arrange learning experiences so that students will experience success. In order to feel successful, it is necessary first to establish goals that are neither so low as to be unfulfilling nor so high as to be impossible and then to know that they have been achieved. Thus there is a two-step process: establishing goals and receiving knowledge of results.

Encouraging a realistic level of aspiration

a. Make use of goals and objectives that are challenging but attainable.

At the beginning of Chapter 6, instructional objectives were discussed. It was pointed out that the basic technique is derived from Skinner's rat and pigeon experiments, in which the first step is to state the desired terminal behavior. Those who favor programmed instruction advocate the use of objectives stated in behavioral terms, primarily to make instruction more efficient, but they also suggest that objectives be used to arouse, sustain, and direct student interest. When objectives are used for purposes of motivation, however, it is especially important to take into account the observations by Ebel and Ojemann and invite students to participate in the selection of goals. If you simply state objectives as what you intend to have your students learn, you are unlikely to get the reaction you would get if you assisted your students to establish their own goals—or at least to think along with you as you explain why the goals are worthwhile. This will shift the emphasis from extrinsic to intrinsic motivation.

In developing goals to serve a motivating function, you may want to use the techniques recommended by Mager and Gronlund to help shift the emphasis from teacher direction to student choice. Having a specific goal to shoot for is one of the best ways to arouse and sustain interest, and you might assist your students to state objectives in terms of a time limit, a minimum number of correct responses, the proportion of correct responses, or a sample of actions.

Examples:

"Why don't you see if you can get that report done in the next thirty minutes?"

"Here is a list of ten scientists whose work is described in the third chapter of the text. Why not try to describe a key experiment for at least seven of them by the end of the period?"

"You got six out of ten on this spelling quiz, why not try for at least eight out of ten on the retest?"

"After reading this article on the laws of motion, see if you can state them in your own words and give two everyday examples of each."

The form of these examples implies that you are inviting students to participate in the development of their own objectives. Although this is a desirable policy to follow, it may not always be possible or appropriate to stick to it. In many situations you may find it necessary to set goals yourself. In making decisions regarding presentation of goals, consider the advantages and disadvantages of programmed instruction and the discovery approach.

If you set goals by means of programmed instruction, the student may or may not be given a detailed description of the terminal behavior, but he will at least know he is working toward improving his spelling or learning about the relationships between heat and light or whatever. He will also have what amounts to a long series of specific goals in the form of frames in the program. Each time the student supplies a correct answer, he has achieved a goal of sorts, and this may motivate him to continue more than awareness of the general purpose of the program.

There are ways other than programs to apply S-R theory to encourage goal-directed behavior. The use of *Goal Cards* provides a semiprogrammed approach. A Goal Card is a detailed series of tasks to be completed by the student. It does not lead him to reach these goals as a program would; it merely enumerates things to be accomplished. Figure 9-2, p. 428, is a Goal Card used in the first grade in Winnetka, Illinois.

Programmed approach to setting goals: goal cards

As you can see, this is a highly specific list of things to be achieved. The proponents of Goal Cards (Bauernfeind, 1965) argue the following: pupils who use them are highly motivated, especially when they record their own progress; the cards facilitate communication between teachers (e.g., a substitute teacher can discover just how much a given pupil knows); "test items are practically written"; the cards are invaluable in parent-teacher conferences. Everyone knows exactly what the child knows and where he is in the curriculum. (The Science Research Associates Reading Lab has many of the same characteristics and advantages; a pupil reads a series of stories, tests himself, and records his progress.)

A program or Goal Card provides one type of incentive or purpose—a specific set of tasks to be performed. With some variations, it could be used with almost any subject matter. All you need do is draw up a list of things to be accomplished, put them in order, and encourage your students to work their way through the items.

However, if you will be teaching a subject that lacks clearly specifiable terminal behavior or if you feel uncomfortable about being that precise in shaping the

Pupil _____ Teacher _____ Year _____

Check

Can count 10 objects .... _____
Can read and write numerals up to 10 .... _____
Recognizes number groups up to 5... _____
Recognizes patterns of objects to 10.. _____
Can read and write numerals to 20 .... _____
Can count objects up to 100 .... _____
Recognizes numbers to 100 .... _____
Can read and write numerals to 50 .... _____
Recognizes addition and subtraction symbols................................ _____
*Understands meaning of the inequality signs .... _____
Can count objects:
    by 2's to 20... _____
    by 5's to 100.. _____
    by 10's to 100... _____
Recognizes geometric figures:
    triangle.. _____
    circle .... _____
    quadrilateral... _____
Recognizes coins (1¢, 5¢, 10¢, 25¢)... _____
Knows addition combinations 10 and under using objects .... _____
Knows subtraction combinations 10 and under using objects................. _____
Recognizes addition and subtraction vertically and horizontally .... _____
*Can construct simple plane figures with straightedge and compass....... _____
Shows understanding of numbers and number combinations:
  (check one)
    1. using concrete objects .... _____
    2. beginning to visualize and abstract .... _____
    3. makes automatic responses without concrete objects......... _____
*Can tell time:
    1. hour... _____
    2. half hour.. _____

*(Goals starred are not essential for all students)

_____

Comments:

Reprinted with permission of Superintendent of Schools, Winnetka, Illinois. Note: Only the first part of the Goal Card is reproduced here.

Figure 9–2   Math Goal Card

learning of your students, you might prefer a field theory approach to providing goals. Morris L. Bigge (1964), perhaps the most consistent of field theorists, suggests that the teacher select problems for discovery sessions by thinking in terms of the life space. To motivate students through application of field theory principles, Bigge maintains, the teacher should try to induce a sense of dissatisfaction in them. This will stimulate students to seek a solution in order to regain equilibrium in the life space. Since dissatisfaction will function as tension, a field of forces will be set up favoring goal-directed behavior. The types of situations Bigge proposes for structuring discovery sessions (noted in Chapter 6) illustrate this concept: switching the subject matter, introducing disturbing data, permitting students to make mistakes.

Goal Cards provide incentives which are specific and tangible, but they are open to the usual criticism of S-R theory; i.e., they tend to limit individuality, lend an assembly-line aura to learning, and restrict learning primarily to what the teacher has decided in advance should be learned. If they are used as the basis of examinations, the student may think of learning as a means to an end—getting a grade. This is an extrinsic kind of motivation, and forgetting will probably occur as soon as the exam has been written.

The discovery-method problem that arouses tension in the life space avoids these disadvantages, but the very subtlety of stimulating dissatisfaction which will lead to learning may make it difficult to arrange. Furthermore, the lack of clearly defined terminal behavior may prevent some students from achieving a sense of closure, which will either lead to continued tension in the life space or divert their attention to something else. As usual, you have to pick and choose and balance alternatives. If you are dealing with material which involves clear terminal behavior, Goal Cards might be ideal motivating forces. If you are dealing with feelings and attitudes, motivating students by inducing a sense of dissatisfaction might be more appropriate. (This discussion of goals reemphasizes points made earlier in explaining the lists of Key Points, or objectives. Key Points for each chapter are offered in order to provide a workable compromise between goals that are too specific and those that are too vague. If you respond favorably to the Key Points technique, you might provide your students with a list of such points for a chapter in a text, a unit, or a lecture.)

Regardless of the approach you take when you set goals for your students, keep in mind the importance of success as a basis for the development of a realistic level of aspiration and an orientation toward achievement. Don't set impossibly high standards, and try to avoid situations in which only a minority of students can succeed. In the traditional approach to grading, success in the form of As and Bs can be achieved by only a few students, and it is frequently necessary for them to "defeat" their classmates in order to succeed. The result is apparent: Many pupils have had all desire to learn suppressed because they realize that when only the top 30 percent get respectable grades, the 70 percent at the bottom simply can't win. If you want most of your students to have

A Different Opinion on the Value of Goals

Emphasis on goals is not appropriate for all subjects or teaching styles. Even if appropriate, goal-directed behavior may have unfortunate repercussions, as noted in Chapter 1. In *How Children Fail,* John Holt argues that too much emphasis on guided learning (such as the practice of basing test items on Goal Cards) makes students answer-centered rather than problem-centered. Schools ''are a kind of temple of worship for right answers'' (1964, p. 40). As a consequence, students become *producers* (interested only in providing answers teachers want) rather than *thinkers* (capable of coming up with their own answers). He also believes that the demand for right answers that results from goals being made too specific causes children to become obsessed by a fear of failure. If they can't achieve the goal (supply the answer), they have failed. The more specific the question, the more specific the failure when the question can't be answered. To avoid failure, students resort to all sorts of strategies to bluff their way through assignments.

Holt ignores the fact that a pupil who is working his way through a program or Goal Card is getting frequent positive reinforcement, which he might not get in a free-learning situation. Even so, it is important to keep in mind Holt's observation about answer-centered teaching. If you get too carried away with specific goals and Goal Cards and terminal behavior, you may easily create the kind of failure-dominated atmosphere he describes. Moreover, in some situations, providing a goal for a given activity would be absurd.

---

the desire to learn, it is obvious that you should set goals that they can achieve and provide extra assistance and encouragement (and not public humiliation or evidence of failure) for those less adept at achieving the standards that have been set.

Examples:

Make use of techniques of open education: Let students choose activities on their own, encourage students to learn from each other, use tests not to compare students but to diagnose weaknesses and to set the stage for remedial instruction, and provide as much individualized instruction as possible.

Use the mastery approach: State objectives, arrange learning materials to assist students to achieve them, use tests to determine if the goals have been met, provide remedial instruction for those who need it, let students take tests as many times as they need to in order to achieve the established standard of performance.

b. *Provide knowledge of results (by emphasizing the positive).*

In assisting your students to experience success as a means for establishing a realistic level of aspiration, it will be essential for them to receive detailed information about their performance. In a programmed approach, this will be supplied automatically when the student responds to a question in a program or compares his performance to criteria included in a set of instructional objectives. As noted earlier, the subtlety of the discovery approach (which stresses reducing tension in the life space) may not always provide a sense of accomplishment. In discovery sessions—and in many other classroom situations—knowledge of performance will be supplied by comments you make. If you make observations on recitation, ask questions in a discussion or on an exam, or provide comments on papers of various kinds, the kind of feedback you provide may make the difference between producing feelings of success or failure. Consequently, you should do your best to comment favorably on successful performance and avoid calling attention to failure, particularly the kind that is already apparent.

Advocates of behavior modification urge teachers to make broad use of praise as a reinforcer—to the point of suggesting that you shape your own behavior to increase your productivity as a praiser. Even if you don't use behavior modification techniques, you will almost automatically praise pupils for perceptive comments in class discussion, excellent written work, considerate behavior, etc. Richard E. Farson points out that it is important to remain aware of some "hidden" aspects of praise. He offers these hypotheses:

> Praise is not only of limited and questionable value as a motivator, but may in fact be experienced as threatening.
>
> Rather than functioning as a bridge between people, it may actually serve to establish distance between them.
>
> Instead of reassuring a person as to his worth, praise may be an unconscious means of establishing the superiority of the praiser.
>
> Praise may constrict creativity rather than free it.
>
> Rather than opening the way to further contact, praise may be a means of terminating it. (1968, p. 110)

Farson notes that research on the impact of praise does not clearly substantiate its value. Frequently, reproof is just as effective, which suggests that the safest conclusion is that *some* response motivates people better than no response at all. He goes on to comment on how defensive people are about praise. (He suggests you note how frequently people react to it by saying things like "Well, *I* like it" or "It was just luck.") He explains this as suggesting that praise is an evaluation and that any evaluation is threatening. He also notes that when a person praises us, he is sitting in judgment; if praise is accepted, it puts us under an obligation to behave accordingly. To gain insight into these aspects of praise, he suggests that you ask yourself how you feel when you receive praise, that you note what you say in response to it, that you analyze how you feel when you give praise, and that you speculate about what you are trying to accomplish with it.

In *Between Parent and Child* (1965) (and also in *Between Parent and Teen-ager,* 1969, and in *Teacher and Child,* 1971), Haim Ginnott distinguishes between desirable and undesirable praise, which emphasizes some of the same points made by Farson. Undesirable praise focuses attention on a child's character and personality—for example, "Good boy" or "I'm proud of you." Desirable praise emphasizes the child's efforts and accomplishments—for example, "That's a good point" or "You've really improved your spelling." Ginnott agrees with Farson that praise may intimidate a child if he feels obligated to live up to the evaluation. When you praise the students in your classes, you might keep in mind these observations.

Making judicious use of praise

Although you should be aware of some of the complications of praise, you should also be aware of the negative impact of blame. If you are disappointed with a class or with a particular student, or if you feel tired and frustrated because things aren't going well, you may find yourself reacting with negative comments. If this occurs, keep in mind the possible consequences. An extremely negative reaction to an error may induce panic, making it impossible for the pupil to think enough to replace the wrong response with the right one. When you praise a pupil for a correct response, realize that you are saying in effect, "That's right; do it again." When you reprimand a pupil for a wrong response, you are saying, "That's wrong; stop it." But if you fail to help the pupil find the right response or frighten him so that he is unable to think, he is forced to choose between doing nothing at all or repeating the original response.

Reducing the negative impact of blame

When a pupil is told when he does the wrong thing but not when he does something right, he never has the chance to experience success. Continual failure leads to fear and depression. It also often leads to attempts to escape. It is natural to avoid attempting something if failure is inevitable, as has been pointed out previously. Sometimes the student does this by lowering his level of aspiration. Sometimes physical escape in the form of sickness or truancy is the result. Perhaps the most dangerous kind of escape is withdrawing into the world of fantasy.

Since the student gains nothing from failure, why do so many teachers use sarcasm, ridicule, and punishment? Probably because *they* gain something from the experience; berating pupils and watching them squirm provide a sense of satisfaction and power, especially to weak and insecure people. Teachers have been known to burst into a teacher's room to brag about how they had just routed a student or class. Such demonstrations of power are tempting, and it may be well to watch yourself in your initial reactions as you assume control of a class.

c. *Consider the advantages and disadvantages of symbolic or material rewards.*

As noted in the discussion of performance contracting and behavior modification in Chapter 5, many behaviorists advocate the use of material rewards. You were asked at that point to speculate about the advantages and disadvantages of the technique. At this juncture, the question is raised again, this time with

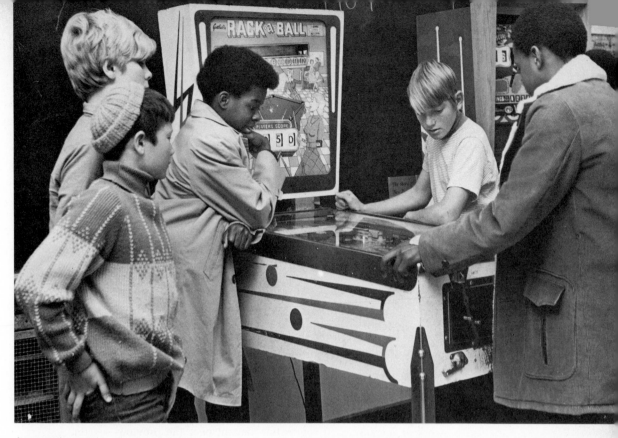

A reward room in a junior high school where tokens earned for academic achievements may be used to play pinball.

Courtesy of Dr. Joan Webster, Grand Rapids Public Schools, Director, Contract Learning Projects

reference to the behaviorist view of motivation. Those who favor behavior modification support the Lockeian view and believe that it is necessary to shape behavior by supplying reinforcement. If students do not learn, it is because they have not been presented with a properly designed sequence of stimuli or a satisfactory chain of reinforcements. This view is illustrated most clearly by techniques used by performance contractors who deal with children who have learning problems. In most cases performance contractors use tangible rewards. Dewey Lipe and Stephen N. Jung comment on this point in a review of studies involving incentives. They note: "Central to the emphasis on incentives is the belief that the newer educational programs of the past decade have not produced impressive results and have especially failed the so-called 'deprived student'" (1971, p. 249). In an effort to assist "deprived" students to succeed, behavior modifiers have used a wide variety of incentives. Lipe and Jung mention the following in their review:

Providing fruit, cookies, and sandwiches at snack time only to children who behave as they said they would.

Using the school-furnished lunch as a reinforcer along with candy, goldfish, clothes, and jewelry.

Providing candies, trinkets, toy cars, and dolls for a successful performance.

Making public records of those who perform successfully by circling numbers on cards, writing names on the blackboard, placing marbles in a holder, writing out tickets.

Using incentives Providing tokens in the form of play money, poker chips, or washers that can be traded in for candy, toys, games, or special privileges.

Allowing children to watch the first part of an interesting movie but not letting them see the last part unless they complete an assignment.

Using a timer to record the number of minutes all students in the class are engaged in study and rewarding them on the basis of the time recorded.

Turning on a light at the desk of each student who makes overt signs of studying and rewarding him according to the amount of time the light is on.

Dividing a "reinforcement" room into three areas marked off by different colors and having different games and activities in each area. To get into the most desirable area, students have to get 90 percent or better on daily classroom work or increase their scores ten percent over the previous session.

If you ever decide to use such incentives, you now have quite an assortment to choose from. Before you do, you are urged to consider the possible disadvantages of controlled education discussed earlier (particularly at the end of Chapter 5 and the beginning of this chapter).

(A variation of using incentives that fits a student-directed approach is to encourage pupils to reward themselves for goals they have selected. This will be discussed a bit later.)

4. Be alert to the damaging impact of excessive competition.

In the traditional public school that uses comparative grading practices, competition is used as a basic motivating force. The excerpts from John Gardner's *Excellence* (1961) noted in Chapter 1 emphasize the problems of balancing the values of competition (which may lead to great achievements) with their dangers (which cause failure and loss of confidence). There is no denying that competition is a fact of life in a meritocracy and that successful people often do extend themselves when they compete. But if competition becomes excessive in a school situation, students may think of learning only as a means to an end (being better than others); they may be more interested in their relative position in a class than in their actual performance. Only a few students will be able to experience success, and the tendency to make safety rather than growth choices will be increased.

A Psychoanalytic View of Learning

This is the title of an article by Michael Maccoby in which he comments on the dangers of excessive competition and the use of extrinsic motivation. He observes:

> Teaching through [competitive] games may inject rich doses of excitement and learning drive into many students who will as a result increase their test scores. But there is the danger of furthering the formation of an alienated-competitive character. Many of the children will become dependent on competition to stimulate them. Winning will become their real interest: they will prefer being first to understanding the nature of things. Because they will learn only what is necessary for success, their relatedness to knowledge will be superficial. Studies . . . indicate that game-like competition not only narrows the breadth of their learning but can increase anxiety about losing, causing for some children paralyzing conflict and learning blocks. Many of the most independent, self-activating children need to work at their own pace and are upset by extrinsic rewards and punishment. (1971, p. 32)

Maccoby suggests that attempts to speed up learning through competition and extrinsic motivation may produce graduates who possess an *alienated-competitive* attitude or the *consumer mentality*. The former entails a compulsion to win and a concomitant loss of sense of self, the latter a depression that the person tries to overcome by constantly searching for new forms of excitement and entertainment.

To encourage the development of more productive character traits, Maccoby offers four principles:

1. Schooling should provide the discipline needed for the development of the self (the ability to concentrate, to think critically, and to communicate).
2. Education should reinforce the natural development of the self (by encouraging independence, discipline, and commitment).
3. In teaching, a constant effort must be made to clarify the purpose of study and to make explicit values implicit.
4. Teaching techniques should develop the student's activeness (self-direction and purpose).

To avoid these disadvantages, encourage students to compete against themselves, try to give each pupil some experience with success by arranging situations in which all students have a fairly equal chance in a variety of activities, and make use of group competitive situations that stress fun rather than winning.

Avoiding excessive competition

Examples:

Have each pupil set his own goals, and keep a private progress chart.

Follow the open education technique of keeping a separate folder for each student rather than a grade book that indicates only relative performance.

Give recognition for such virtues as punctuality and dependability.

Give recognition for skill in arts and crafts, music, special interests, and hobbies.

Use games such as *spelling baseball*. Divide the class into two approximately equal teams. Each time a pupil spells a word correctly, award his team a base. Four bases and the team has a run. Each misspelled word is an out. No team members are eliminated, and the pressure is reduced considerably. If some unfortunate makes too many outs, you can feed him a fat pitch in the form of an easy word his next time at bat. In order to avoid overidentification in a particular team, use different players for each game. (If permanent teams are set up or if you overemphasize the competitive nature of the game by offering a prize, the technique may backfire.)

a. *Encourage competition by making use of variations of the committee approach.*

Some educational theorists suggest that since competition leads to feelings of failure for so many pupils—and friction between the competitors—it should be replaced by a cooperation that is to be encouraged through the use of committees. About fifteen years ago the committee approach and group dynamics were all the rage. The popularity of this technique was an outgrowth in part of the "cult of efficiency" in American education; the team approach was being used in industry, so business-oriented educators decided to try it in the schools. Dozens of arguments in favor of group work were propounded, among them the following: Students would learn to work with others and would thus be prepared for democratic living and future team ventures later in life. Students would gain valuable experience in discovering answers for themselves. The efforts of the group would be superior to those of any single member of the group.

In actual practice these advantages are not always realized (as you may have found through personal experience). Group members sometimes come to dislike each other intensely, especially if one person ends up doing most of the work. The things students learn are not necessarily related to the subject of study. One highly enthusiastic committee, for example, prepared a skit that featured elaborate papier-mâché masks (to identify the types of characters depicted). The group also rented a theater, baked cookies, and made coffee for the postpresentation "reception." Thus they learned all about how to make papier-mâché masks, how to reserve rooms, how to bake cookies and make coffee—but little or nothing about the topic assigned for study (age-level characteristics) because the "incidentals" occupied their study time. Other committees became adept at ordering films and securing guest speakers but failed to come to grips with the subject of study. As for the alleged superiority of group effort, the demand for consensus when a group is preparing a report often leads to lowest-common-denominator results. (Although the committee approach often leads to such situations, in many cases it is appropriate and functions successfully.)

A feature of programmed instruction is that each student works individually. The discovery approach is almost always marked by group interaction. Herbert A. Thelen has experimented and written at length about the way groups learn through the process of inquiry. Not surprisingly, Thelen is a field theorist, and he endorses many of the same ideas advocated by Bruner, Combs and Snygg, and Bigge. However, he places special emphasis on group dynamics. Here is his capsule description of the method:

> The first requirement for group investigation is a teachable group: one which can develop a sense of common cause, one whose members can stimulate each other, and one whose members are psychologically compatible and complementary. The students are assigned to a consultant (teacher) who confronts them with a stimulus situation to which they can react and discover basic conflicts among their attitudes, ideas, and modes of perception. On the basis of this information, they identify the problem to be investigated, analyze the roles required to "solve" it, train themselves to take these roles; act, report and evaluate the results. These steps are illuminated by reading, possibly by some short-range personal investigations, and by consultation with experts. The group is concerned with its own effectiveness, but its discussions of its own processes are related to the goals of the investigation. (1960, pp. 81–82)

Here are some further suggestions of Thelen for creating desirable group investigation situations: "The groups for learning should be small enough so that each individual can be heard, can have a contributing role, and can become well acquainted with the others. This suggests a maximum size of fifteen" (p. 133). The group should be "able to find common cause fairly readily" (speak the same language) but also be "able to get into temperamental conflict"; (for example, "react differently to the same reality stimulus; there should be the possibility of clashes" (p. 133).

Thelen notes the wide individual differences in the way students approach subjects, in the kinds of group situations they respond to, in the kinds and amounts of instruction they need in order to work effectively, in ideas about who should make the decisions to guide learning, in the kinds of "support and clash" that stimulate them to learn, in the amount of knowledge and experience they bring to bear in an investigation, and in a host of other factors. "Thus, we see that every group is a growing, changing organism" (p. 134).

To illustrate some of the imponderables in group work, Thelen describes two committee-approach learning situations, a unit on "How do different people live?" in the second grade and a student-produced television series on the history of a community put on by a high school class.

The second-grade children, perhaps under the influence of a Walt Disney "True Life Adventure," chose *prairie dogs* for their subject of study despite the efforts of the teacher to convert them to the Algonquin Indians (about whom she had a great deal of information from previous years). The dismay of the teacher turned to delight as the children not only came through with a smashing dramatic production about prairie dogs but also learned a great deal about how animals *and* people live. The TV series, on the other hand, turned out much the way the papier-mâché mask episode (described earlier) did. The students gained a lot of experience in taking photographs and lettering signs and solving lighting problems, but the production "incidentals" prevented them from thinking or learning about history. (This brings up an interesting question. If you endorse the Combs and Snygg argument that *how* a student feels about learning is more important than *what* he learns, what do you do when you have a bunch of committees working happily away on projects that have nothing to do with the curriculum? Is it better to have a class ecstatically laboring on incidentals or somewhat less enthusiastically engaged with genuine subject matter?)

Thelen summarizes the rationale for group investigation in these terms: "The heart of the method of group investigation is to arrange things in such a way that the students have the experience of creating a group dedicated to the furtherance of inquiry in the appropriate domain of knowledge" (p. 147). If this summary doesn't give you a clear idea of how to go about using group techniques, see Chapters 7 and 8 in his *Education and the Human Quest*.

5. For students who need it, encourage the development of a desire to achieve.

Despite your efforts to gratify deficiency needs, enhance the attractions of growth choices, arrange learning experiences to produce a realistic level of aspiration and a feeling of success, and play down the negative impact of competition, some of your students will still lack confidence about their ability to learn. In such cases you may try to assist students to acquire a general motive to achieve. McClelland (1965) has demonstrated that it is possible for groups of individuals, in intensive training sessions of one to three weeks, to be instilled with needs to achieve that will be reflected in accomplishments far beyond their previous efforts. Although McClelland's technique would be difficult to use in a school setting, some of the practices he follows might be adapted for small-group or individual sessions with students who appear to lack motivation to succeed. In McClelland's training sessions, he does everything possible to make individuals feel that they can develop a motive to achieve, to show them how the motive will be beneficial, to make acquisition of the motive appear to be an improvement in their self-image, to encourage the achievement of concrete goals, to keep records of progress, and to establish an atmosphere of warm and honest support.

David A. Kolb (1965) based an Achievement Motivation Training Program on the work of McClelland, Atkinson and others. As with McClelland's program, intensive training sessions were provided (as part of a summer school program). In the opening session, the participants (underachieving high school boys) were given information intended to make training work and were acquainted with characteristics McClelland has found typical of high achievers: personal responsibility for actions, willingness to take moderate risks, the desire for knowledge of results of actions. In subsequent sessions the boys competed in miniature racing-car contests, took various tests, and played the role of manufacturer.

In all of these activities, they were urged to analyze their reactions and to constantly think about how they could improve their need for achievement. After the training had been completed, its effectiveness was revealed by higher grades. As with McClelland's program, it would be difficult to follow the exact procedures used by Kolb in a regular school setting, but it would be possible to encourage students to emulate the qualities of high achievers by taking personal responsibility for attempting work (perhaps in the form of a contract), being willing to shoot for goals beyond those considered safe, and being eager to receive detailed knowledge of results. A. S. Alschuler (1968) used essentially this approach by organizing learning tasks as self-competitive games in which the student is responsible for setting his own goals and is graded on his own terms.

Encouraging the desire to achieve

Another technique for assisting students to become better achievers was developed by J. S. Sorensen, E. A. Schwenn, and J. Bavry (1970), who devised a checklist for self-ratings by elementary grade students regarding *prosocial behaviors* (Figure 9-3, p. 440). Students rated themselves and then participated in individual and small-group conferences with their teacher in which each category on the list was defined by recalling or identifying instances of the behavior described. Then each child was asked to select one or more types of behavior in which to improve and to check both his present rating and desired rating. At the next conference, he rated himself to determine if improvement had been achieved. The teacher supplied reinforcement in the form of praise for all improvement, kept a conference record to make note of progress and problems, and asked the pupils to describe reasons why working toward improvement would benefit them. Teacher ratings of student behavior after the program had been completed indicated that most students indeed made significant improvement in the types of behavior listed.

Sorensen, Schwenn, and Herbert J. Klausmeier (1969) used a similar approach to motivate elementary pupils to indulge in more reading. Many books were made available in the classroom, forms for reporting titles of books read were provided, and conferences with the teacher were arranged. At these conferences, teachers were urged to keep in mind these motivational procedures:

Modeling: doing such things as telling the child that he (the adult) reads frequently and likes to read; being engaged in reading when the child comes in for the conference and starting to read a book as the child leaves the conference. Modeling also includes such procedures as informing the child of the reading behavior of a possible model and indicating the value of independent reading to other persons who may serve as models for the child.

Reinforcement: smiling, nodding affirmatively, saying "good," "fine," etc., when the student shows that he has independently read a book or pages in a book. The adult also reinforces positive attitude statements about reading either made spontaneously by the child or in response to questions.

Name _____ Sex _____ Age _____ Date _____

Directions:

Put an X under column 1 if you almost always have to be told to do the job.
Put an X under column 2 if you usually have to be told to do the job.
Put an X under column 3 if you sometimes do the job yourself and sometimes have to be told to do the job.
Put an X under column 4 if you usually do the job yourself.
Put an X under column 5 if you almost always do the job yourself.

	1	2	3	4	5
1. I listen to the teacher.					
2. I begin schoolwork right away.					
3. I correct mistakes.					
4. I work until the job is finished.					
5. I work when the teacher has left the room.					
6. If I make mistakes, I still keep working.					
7. I work on learning activities in free time.					
8. I get to class on time.					
9. I do extra schoolwork.					
10. I do my share in class projects.					
11. I read during free time.					
12. I ask questions about schoolwork.					
13. I have pencil, paper, and books ready when they are needed.					
14. I move quietly to and from my classes.					
15. I listen to the ideas of others.					
16. I help my classmates.					
17. I pick up when the work is finished.					
18. I take care of my clothing, books, and other things.					
19. I take care of the school's books, desks, and other things.					
20. I follow directions					

Source Herbert J. Klausmeier, Juanita S. Sorensen, and Elizabeth Ghatala, 1971 "Individually Guided Motivation Developing Self Direction and Prosocial Behaviors." *Elementary School Journal.* 71(6). p. 344

Figure 9–3 Checklist of Prosocial Behavior

Feedback: informing the child of progress by telling him how many books or pages in a book he has completed. Feedback was also given on any improvement in word recognition or comprehension skills.

Goal-setting: helping the child select the next book of an appropriate difficulty level and length. The reading of the book or books then becomes the child's goal for the next conference. (1969, p. 351)

The reading frequency and achievement of almost all students increased as a result of this program—and even control pupils who were not included in the experiment showed improvement, indicating that the interest in reading became contagious.

If you despair over the lack of confidence, interest, or motivation of your students, you might try to encourage the development of the motive for achievement by using variations of the techniques just discussed. With modifications, they could be used with all grade levels and with all types of students.

6. *Take advantage of natural interests, try to create new ones, and encourage learning for its own sake.*

In the preceding section, techniques for aiding the development of motivation were discussed. Some advocates of free education—for example, Neill and Holt—argue that if schooling is arranged properly, such training is unnecessary; if the child follows his natural interests, he will learn all he needs to know. For reasons already discussed regarding the balance between freedom and control, this policy seems unworkable for most situations. The open education approach, which stresses freedom of choice and cooperative planning and also teacher guidance, appears to have greater promise. By this approach, the student is given considerable freedom to select activities because of their intrinsic interest. The kinds of activities selected from free-choice situations can be used as guidelines for arranging learning experiences likely to appeal to students. May V. Seagoe surveyed reports on such experiences and concluded that children's interests result from successful experience and familiarity. Among the "points of appeal that emerge from studies of specific interests," she lists the following:

(a) the opportunity for overt bodily *activity*, for manipulation, for construction, even for observing the movement of animals and vehicles of various sorts; (b) the opportunity for *investigation*, for using mental ingenuity in solving puzzles, for working problems through, for creating designs, and the like; (c) the opportunity for *adventure*, for vicarious experience in make-believe, in books, and in the mass media; (d) the opportunity for *social assimilation*, for contacts with others suitable to the maturity level of the child (ranging from parallel play to discussion and argument), for social events and working together, for human interest and humanitarianism, and for conformity and display; and (e) the opportunity for use of the new in real life, making the new continuous with past experience and projecting it in terms of future action. (1970, p. 25)

You might use these points as a basis for trying to create new interests.

Examples:

Ask your students to note their interests and hobbies on a card, then use the information to plan individual and group learning activities.

Try to make sure that initial experience with a new topic will be successful (by using the level-of-aspiration techniques noted previously).

Have students go to the board, move around and participate in class discussion—not just sit at their desks.

Use discovery-approach techniques to provide opportunities to investigate. Set up learning centers with provocative displays and materials such as these suggested by C. M. Charles:

APPRECIATION CENTER for observing paintings, poems, sculptures, arrangements, etc.

ART ACTIVITY CENTER equipped for drawing, painting, modeling, etc.

COMMUNICATIONS CENTER equipped for listening to, viewing, and dramatizing music, stories, and guided activities

DISPLAY CENTER for showing and observing collections, projects, and hobbies

GAMES CENTER where students can use instructional games, puzzles, and similar aids

LIBRARY AND READING CENTER containing both commercial and student-made reading materials

SCIENCE CENTER equipped for observation and project work

SOCIAL SCIENCE CENTER stocked with maps, charts, documents, reference books, etc., along with materials and equipment for constructing (1972, p. 105)

Permit and encourage considerable interaction between students, either in groups or in pairs.

Continually point out how new learning relates to previous learning and how it can be applied to other class situations.

In attempting to arouse new interests you might employ techniques used by advertisers and by the creators of "Sesame Street" and "The Electric Company." Use intensity, size, contrast, and movement to attract attention. Make use of color, humor, and exaggeration to introduce a topic or make a point. Use audiovisual devices of all kinds—films, tapes, charts, models, etc.

Examples:

Redecorate part of your room the night before presenting a new unit, then have the class help you finish it up.

Make full use of the audiovisual aids available from the school, district, or county.

Students working in the media center of the Matske Elementary School in Houston, Texas. The media center is located between instructional areas, so that the children have easy access to the audio-visual materials and reference works.

If you are a frustrated actor or actress, ham it up on occasion; make a dramatic production out of a demonstration.

In considering use of such techniques, it might be worth noting this criticism Michael Maccoby has leveled at "Sesame Street:"

Programs such as "Sesame Street" excite the children, but only recently has the question been asked (by the BBC) of what character traits are developed. Exciting learning through TV may further the consumer mentality in children, fostering their need for constant stimulation, for being entertained and "turned on." Other methods of learning the alphabet or numbers might take longer, but they might also emphasize *active* character traits, particularly concentration and the child's development of individual rhythms of work. We must consider the possibility that whatever the content of the programs, TV as a medium for teaching may have negative effects on character development, particularly if not combined with activating classroom discussion. (1971, p. 33)

Even if Maccoby exaggerates the possible dangers of "Sesame Street," it is worth keeping in mind that it is at times desirable to stress that some learning should be indulged in just for its own sake. The demand for "relevance" is related to this point. As defined by some people, relevance implies "immediate, practical, obvious value." True, learning experiences that fit the description are likely to have appeal, but there will be problems if you attempt to make *all* learning relevant. Jacques Barzun has commented on the complications of trying to make all learning exciting and relevant.

> "Exciting" is not . . . synonymous with "interesting," it is usually its opposite. In excitement, time goes fast and thought is blurred. In a stretch marked by interest, time goes slowly, every minute is savored and its passing regretted. No doubt interest can rise to excitement, but these very words indicate a climax that draws its power from previous calm. Composers whose pieces bang away with kettledrums and cymbals from start to finish are not exciting, but boring; those who develop an idea from quiet beginnings to the highest tension and clearest resolution produce the greatest satisfaction. Students will readily think of other parallels from life.

> So true is this that even modern, sophisticated excitement-seeking students will respond to a genuine academic use of calm, will learn the pleasures of drudgery, and enjoy the application of discipline. For discipline (which includes drudgery) does not simply prevent or restrain: it *demands;* and demand—contrary to excitement—arouses and directs action. . . . The net result of this quieter but sterner pursuit is the *possession* of knowledge and the delight of possession, which differs radically from the sense of having lived from riot to riot or gone through a ritual to "qualify."

> Nor is this all: what has been acquired with a will is always "relevant." It has become part of the structure of the mind and thus acts in every subsequent situation. . . .

> The belief that a curriculum can be devised and kept relevant to the present is an illusion: whose present, in the first place, and relevant for how long? Students differ in tastes, knowledge, and emotional orientation. What concerns (or "excites") one four-year generation will bore the next, as anyone can verify by reference to popular music. And so it is with literature, politics, and the current view of creeds and crises. (1968, pp. 38–39)

It would seem desirable on some occasions to try to inculcate a feeling that many of the most satisfying human experiences are neither wildly exciting nor highly relevant.

Examples:

Offer history not only as a means for interpreting current events but also because of the sheer interest of finding out about how earlier people lived and why certain events occurred.

Point out that many aspects of art, music, and literature are not "practical" but represent an attempt on the part of the creator to express his feelings to others. (Many of Maslow's examples of self-actualization center around artistic creation.)

A skit from "The Electric Company" teaching recognition of the "ph" consonant.

Encourage students to learn about nature simply to increase their appreciation of it.

Set an example by commenting on things that strike you as interesting, even though they are not "practical." (A very successful French teacher was so enamored of her subject that she occasionally leaned against the blackboard, giving the impression that her ecstasy was so great that she needed support—she would then gaze upward and say with great conviction and fervor, "Isn't French *interesting!*")

7. Provide encouragement and incentives for learning that is essential but not intrinsically appealing.

It is a good policy to appeal to intrinsic interests as much as possible, but there are many learning situations that have overtones of drudgery. Few students are enthusiastic about learning to spell or to multiply and divide, yet these skills are important if not essential. Because of the hierarchical nature of many learning situations—as exemplified by Gagné's conditions of learning—you may need to stimulate, persuade, inspire, and cajole students to learn some material that is essential for everyday living or subsequent learning. In such situations, you may feel it necessary to resort to progress charts, gold stars, and other

---

Push Back The Desks

This is the title of an inexpensive paperback by Albert Cullum that contains many suggestions for making required elementary school subjects exciting and appealing. Among other things, Cullum describes how to:

Arrange a *Parade of Presidents* in which each pupil selects a president of the United States and presents a "State of the Union" message to the rest of the class, each member of which takes the part of a member of Congress.

Teach geography by presenting *Adventure Hunts,* in which the pupils imagine they are detectives trying to keep on the track of a person who travels to various parts of the United States.

Have the class build a replica of *King Tut's Tomb* and then encourage students to play the role of archeologists. Instead of "digging" for mummies, however, the students use flashlights to find problems, puzzles, graphs, and other items dealing with numbers that are written on cards tacked to the inside walls of the tomb. Each problem has a number and a point score, and after a student figures out his answer, he deposits it in a box designed as a sarcophagus. After each "dig" answers are discussed, and at the end of the year, fancy certificates are presented to the archeologists who, by accumulating sufficient points, made a minimum number of successful "digs."

---

kinds of incentives. In making use of such extrinsic motivation, however, do your best to play down overtones of manipulation and materialism. This might be done by pointing out that the awards are merely a crutch or an aid and by encouraging students to remain aware of this fact. An excellent way to do this is to have them set their own incentives, or supply them in the form of objectives.

Examples:

"I know that memorizing spelling words is not the most interesting thing in the world, but it's easier for us to understand each other if we all spell the same way. Try making up a chart to help you keep improving; give yourself an apple or something else each time you hit your goal."

"If you have trouble concentrating on this chapter, write out a short answer to each of these ten questions."

"Learning the names of these trees may seem to be drudgery, but when you know them all, we will really be able to cover some fascinating topics. See if you can learn them all by Friday."

The use of key points and margin notes in this book is intended to give you some specific goals to look for as you read.

To sixth graders, hand out dittoed sheets of twenty questions based on articles in each section of a morning newspaper. Each student is provided with a copy of the paper and competes against himself to discover how many of the questions he can answer in the shortest period of time. (Typical questions: Why is the Senator from Mississippi upset? Who got the assists on Bobby Hull's record-breaking goal? What did Miss Peach say to Marcia?)

Create a *Renoir Room* (or the equivalent) in which reproductions of Renoir paintings are displayed on all the walls and the students are encouraged to find out as much as they can about the painter.

Have students read and dramatize Shakespeare and Chaucer.

Have students read the poems of Longfellow and paint murals depicting scenes from the poems.

Arrange for after-school panel discussions during which students exchange opinions and interpretations of a particular book they have read.

Many other techniques for making required elementary school subjects interesting and enjoyable are described in *Push Back the Desks.*

(Additional suggestions for arousing and sustaining interest are presented in the next chapter. These are described with reference to disadvantaged students, but they might be used with all students.)

Summary

In this chapter on motivation you have been acquainted with Abraham H. Maslow's distinction between deficit motivation and growth motivation, with his hierarchy of needs, with his characterization of development as a never-ending series of choices involving safety and growth, and with his argument that most people, because they tend to be bad rather than good choosers, need guidance.

The interrelationships between safety and growth emphasized by Maslow are also stressed in Hoppe's concept of level of aspiration and in Atkinson's theory that the need for achievement is the result of a balance between success-orientation and anxiety about failure.

The behaviorist-associationist view of motivation emphasizes that teachers should try to control and shape behavior by the way they arrange learning situations and by how and when they supply reinforcement. Although this has the advantage of making teachers aware of how their behavior influences that of their pupils, it tends to lead to motivation that is extrinsic and materialistic. Students may come to expect a reward for everything they do, and it may be difficult to design reinforcement situations and schedules that assist them to eventually become self-directed.

Maslow's theory of motivation seems more promising as a guide for teachers since he calls attention to the importance of satisfying deficiency needs and encouraging growth choices, the desirability of arranging learning situations to lead to feelings of success, and the damaging impact of excessive competition. The observations of McClelland and Atkinson provide ideas and techniques that might be used to encourage students who lack this quality to develop a general desire to achieve.

Suggestions for Further Reading, Writing, Thinking, and Discussion

9-1 *Reading Maslow's Own Account of His Theory of Need Gratification*

The second edition of Abraham H. Maslow's *Toward a Psychology of Being* (1968) is filled with so much insight into so many aspects of human behavior and adjustment that you are urged to buy a copy for repeated reference. The headings of the major sections of the book indicate the general topics discussed: Part I, "A Larger Jurisdiction for Psychology"; Part II, "Growth and Motivation"; Part III, Growth and Cognition"; Part IV, "Creativeness"; Part V, "Values"; Part VI, "Future Tasks." If you have time only to sample the book at the moment, read Chapter 1, in which Maslow describes his conception of sickness and health; Chapter 3, in which he differentiates between deficiency and growth needs; Chapter 11, in which he contrasts bad choosers and good choosers; or Chapter 14, in which he lists forty-three basic propositions of a growth and self-actualization psychology. (The propositions in Chapter 14 pretty much summarize all his observations on motivation.) Summarize the points made in any parts of Maslow's book you read, and add your own observations.

9-2 *Reading a General Analysis of Motivation*

The treatment of motivation in this chapter is limited and oversimplified. For more background, read an appropriate chapter in a general or introductory psychology text. (Almost any introductory psychology text will contain a chapter on motivation.) If you find a concise analysis of motivation, summarize it and relate it to points made in the text.

9-3 *Analyzing Your Own Motivation*

Insight into theories of motivation sometimes results from self-analysis. How energetically do you pursue different goals? Do you have a fairly consistent level of aspiration, or do you exert yourself in only a few areas of behavior? What forces drive you to try to achieve at a high level in certain activities? Can you relate your drives to psychological needs? Do you sometimes feel compelled to regain a sense of equilibrium? Do you engage in some of your activities as a means to "expression"? If those questions do not seem simple to answer, analyze your behavior at different times in terms of Maslow's hierarchy. Do you find evidence that you are more likely to want to learn or to satisfy an aesthetic desire when your lower-level needs have been taken care of? If you note exceptions, how might you explain them? (E.g., are thoughts of hunger and discomfort displaced by the sight of the love of your life?) If you gain any insight into your own motives, describe and comment on your-self-analysis.

9-4 *Analyzing the Forces That Shaped Famous People*

In speculations about what motivates people to strive and achieve, the question of determinism is of key importance. An earlier discussion offered various observations on determinism, with special reference to two explanations of what factors "produced" Shakespeare. Was he primarily the product of contingencies of reinforcement, or did he inherit some sort of "divine spark" of inspiration? Now that you have more information on motivation, choose some famous person you know something about, or would like to learn about, and analyze—as best you can—the forces that made him great. Or browse through *Cradles of Eminence* (1962) by Goertzel and Goertzel and consider the common factors they found in the backgrounds of famous people. Is there evidence to back up Freud's suggestion that in some cases extreme efforts in the arts or politics are due to sublimation of the sex drive? Or analyze the lives of the eminent people described by Goertzel and Goertzel (or any group of your own choice) with reference to Shakespeare's "theory" of motivation: "Some are born great, some achieve greatness, and some have greatness thrust upon them." You may conclude that psychologists haven't come up with any better way to summarize motivation since those words were written over 350 years ago. If any of these questions or suggestions appeal to you, record your reactions.

9-5 *Analyzing the Forces That Shaped Acquaintances*

If you find it difficult to analyze your own behavior and feel more attuned to the present than the past, you might turn your attention to the forces that influenced individuals you have known. Can you think of an acquaintance who appears to have a tremendous desire to succeed in certain areas of endeavor? . What forces in his background might have made him that way? After you record your speculations, try to relate them to one or more of the theories of motivation that have been discussed and comment on any implications that seem to emerge.

9-6 *Contrasting Bad- and Good-Choice Situations*

Maslow makes a distinction between bad and good choosers. To become more aware of what he means by this, analyze your own feelings and behavior with regard to choice situations. Maslow describes growth as a never-ending series of decisions between safety and growth and suggests that a person is more likely to make a good choice if he feels confident and self-accepting. If the person feels threatened, he may be unable to resist selecting a safe—but perhaps undesirable—form of behavior. Think back to choice situations you have faced recently. When you decided to try something and it proved to be an exhilarating experience, did you feel confident and self-accepting prior to the decision? Can you figure out what made you that way? If you procrastinated about a choice and finally took a safe way out by avoiding the situation or reacting in a manner that provided little if any satisfaction, what was it that made you feel threatened? Could you—or someone else—have reduced the threat somehow? If possible, relate your analysis to how you might function as a teacher. What could you do to establish a classroom environment where your students would feel confident and unthreatened enough to make good choices and have more frequent self-actualizing experiences?

9-7 *Analyzing Level of Aspiration*

Maslow's distinction between bad and good choosers is essentially a generalized version of Hoppe's observations on the level of aspiration. Hoppe suggested that a person's level of aspiration in a given situation is a compromise between two conflicting tendencies: (1) the desire to avoid disappointment accompanying failure, which operates to force aspirations down, and (2) the desire to succeed at the highest possible level, which pushes aspirations up. If you find it difficult to analyze a choice between safety and growth as suggested in exercise 9–6, you might attempt an analysis of your level of aspiration in one or two situations. For example, at the beginning of a course when you determined the grade level you hoped to achieve, what factors influenced your decision? If the evaluation in the course seemed to be threatening, did you set your aspirations at the C level? How did you react when you got your grade on the first exam? If you set your aspiration level low for one course and high for another, what factors influenced your decision? Record your reactions to one or more of these questions and then describe how you might assist *your* students to set high—but realistic—levels of aspiration. What could you do to help them achieve a desirable compromise between the two tendencies to avoid disappointment and to succeed at the highest possible level?

9-8   *Speculating about the Pros and Cons of a Structured Curriculum*

A. S. Neill argues that a free, self-demand approach to education is most likely to permit a child to respond favorably to learning experiences. He is against any sort of structured curriculum, particularly one in which a student is required to take certain courses or to learn material predetermined by a teacher. Robert Gagné, on the other hand, believes that students learn best when learning experiences are arranged systematically so that verbal associations serve as the basis for concepts and principles, which eventually lead to problem solving. Inevitably, this approach involves direction by a teacher who "requires" students to learn certain things in a certain way. If you are undecided about these two points of view, think about the subject or subjects you will be teaching. Could some topics be approached in a free way whereas others might need to be prearranged and presented in sequence? A different way of looking at this question would be to think about courses you have taken. Would you have preferred more freedom with some subjects, and did you wish the instructor had been better organized and done more structuring with others? Note your reactions to either of these sets of ideas, and comment on the implications.

9-9   *Analyzing the Advantages and Disadvantages of Competition*

Presently in American education there is a move to reduce competition between students. Excessive competition obviously has many disadvantages; most disturbing is the amount of threat involved, which tends to lead to safety rather than growth choices. But competition has values too, and certain dangers would follow if all competitive effort were eliminated. John Gardner, former Secretary of Health, Education and Welfare, has analyzed the problem of encouraging and maintaining constructive striving in the United States in three short books. *Excellence* (1961) stresses the importance of high standards. *Self-Renewal* (1965) examines ways individuals and societies might resist the negative impact of apathy and lowered motivation. *No Easy Victories* (1968) describes the difficulties of achieving and maintaining excellence and self-renewal. If you have the opportunity to read one of these books (all three are quite concise), you might summarize Gardner's views and state your reactions.

9-10   *Assessing Your Reactions to the Committee Approach*

You may find it helpful to assess any personal experiences you have had with the committee approach in order to decide whether, when, and how to use this technique in teaching. If you have been a member of a committee, record your reactions, perhaps by listing desirable and undesirable aspects of the experience. Then describe how you might make the most of the things you liked while eliminating or reducing the disadvantages. If you feel enthusiastic about group learning, sample Chapters 7, 8, and 9 of *Education and the Human Quest* (1960) or Chapters 1, 2, and 10 of *Classroom Grouping for Teachability* (1967), both by Herbert A. Thelen. Thelen, probably the leading exponent of the group approach, has much to offer. Summarize the points made by Thelen and add your own reactions.

9-11 *Recording Your Own Reactions to Praise and Blame*

You may be more alert to the impact of praise and blame on student behavior if you record your own reactions to these two types of teacher response. Think back to teachers you had, and to specific incidents in which you (or a classmate) were exposed to desirable kinds of praise or undesirable kinds of blame. When you were praised for doing well, what were your reactions? If you were ridiculed or humiliated or severely criticized for poor schoolwork (not for deportment), what were your reactions? Can you recall any experiences which were so distasteful you still have a negative emotional response just thinking about them? After recording your recollections, comment on the implications and perhaps draw up a list of do's and don'ts to follow when *you* become the person who dispenses praise or blame.

9-12 *Reacting to a Humorous Programmer's Views on Goals and Motivation*

Robert F. Mager is an advocate of programmed instruction. Most psychologists who are attracted by the more precise and technological aspects of teaching seem to suppress any hint of levity in their writing. Mager, however, has an irrepressible sense of humor. His two short books mix humor with common sense and practical suggestions on how to use programmed instruction in motivating students. Both books are available in paperback and would be valuable additions to any teacher's professional library. In *Preparing Instructional Objectives* (1962), Mager suggests how educational objectives can be specified in such a way that students are encouraged to demonstrate their achievement of the objectives. In *Developing Attitude Toward Learning* (1968), he offers observations on how to teach so that your pupils will have more favorable feelings about your subject after studying under your direction than before they met you. (From one point of view, this is the single most important goal a teacher should try to reach.) If you read either or both of these books, note points made by Mager that strike you as especially promising and indicate how you might use these ideas when you begin to teach.

9-13 *Obtaining More Complete Information on How to Encourage a Desire to Achieve*

If you are intrigued by the possibility of helping students acquire a need to achieve, you will want to read more complete accounts of how this has been done. David C. McClelland provides a book-length description of his theory in *The Achieving Society* (1960) and a more concise view in "Toward a Theory of Motive Acquisition," *American Psychologist,* 20 (1965): 321–333. In addition, articles by and about McClelland are featured in the January 1971 issue of *Psychology Today.*

J. W. Atkinson explains his conception of the need to achieve—as well as many other theories of motivation—in *An Introduction to Motivation* (1964). David Kolb describes how he put the McClelland-Atkinson ideals into practice in "Achievement Motivation Training for Underachieving Boys," *Journal of Personality and Social Psychology,* 2 (1965): 783–792. A description of a variety of techniques, including the use of the "Checklist for Student Self-ratings of Prosocial Behaviors" was provided in the section titled "A System of Individually Guided Motivation" (pp. 339–355) of *Learning and Human Abilities: Educational Psychology* (3rd ed., 1971) by Herbert J. Klausmeier and Richard E. Ripple. If you sample one or more of these books or articles you might draw up your own list of guidelines for helping students acquire a need to achieve.

Recommended Reading in
Psychology Applied to Teaching: Selected Readings

If you would like to do further reading in books or articles mentioned in this chapter (and in the preceding "Suggestions for Further Reading, Writing, Thinking, and Discussion") without having to track down several separate volumes, you might peruse *Psychology Applied to Teaching: Selected Readings* (Boston: Houghton Mifflin, 1972). This is a collection of excerpts from books and articles from journals in psychology. The following selections provide extended commentaries on points noted in this chapter or mentioned in the "Suggestions."

Maslow's Theory of Growth Motivation: "A Theory of Human Motivation" by Abraham H. Maslow, Selection 21, p. 338.

Using Objectives to Arouse, Sustain, and Direct Interest: Excerpt from *Stating Behavioral Objectives for Classroom Instruction* by Norman E. Gronlund, Selection 22, p. 363.

Views of Motivation: "What Does Motivation Mean to S-R Associationists and Gestalt Field Theorists?" by Morris R. Bigge, Selection 23, p. 371.

Problems Stemming from Too Much Concern about Relevance: "Students or Victims" by Jacques Barzun, Selection 4, p. 32.

Maslow's Theory of Need Gratification: Excerpt from *Toward a Psychology of Being* by Abraham H. Maslow, Selection 30, p. 452. (See also Suggestion 9-1.)

10 TEACHING THE DISADVANTAGED

KEY POINTS

Facts

Many pupils from disadvantaged backgrounds suffer from poor health and diet, live under poor conditions in shattered family situations, have a negative attitude toward school, are more attracted by practical and vocational than theoretical and academic aspects of schooling, have limited language skills and a slower rate of learning, lack school know-how, and have a poor self-concept.

Trends

Preschool compensatory education (Head Start) extended through third grade by Follow-Through programs.

Reports

Children from disadvantaged backgrounds benefit if placed in classes with students who possess greater educational strength (Coleman Report)

Concepts

Destiny control

Methodology

Programmed techniques for teaching the disadvantaged. Presentation of series of preplanned lessons with emphasis on reinforcement.

Discovery approaches to teaching the disadvantaged: Emphasis on more or less spontaneous development of lessons based on ideas contributed by students. Stress on interpersonal relationships.

Satisfying deficiency needs, encouraging growth choices.

Encouraging feelings of success and a positive self-concept.

Promoting the desire and skills to do well in school.

CONTENTS

IN THE PRECEDING CHAPTER, MASLOW'S OBSERVATIONS ON MOTIVATION were presented to serve as an organizational frame of reference for analyzing motivation and developing techniques for teaching. His hierarchy of needs emphasizes that students are not likely to be eager to learn unless their deficiency needs have been satisfied and that they are more likely to make growth choices when the opportunity to learn appears attractive and unthreatening. In the suggestions for arousing and sustaining interest based on Maslow's observations (as well as those of Hoppe, McClelland, Atkinson, Erikson, Sullivan, and Bloom), special emphasis was placed on the importance of encouraging feelings of success and avoiding a sense of failure. These observations apply to all students, but they have a special significance for disadvantaged students.

The term "disadvantaged" applies to students who are also referred to as culturally deprived, underprivileged, needy, etc. Some critics object to such labels on the grounds that they create a fatalistic image that may lead to stereotyping and a self-fulfilling prophecy reaction. These possibilities do exist, but the risks can be minimized if you remain aware of them. And there are advantages to taking into account the special learning problems of students who *are* at a disadvantage.

Inequality of Educational Opportunity

In Chapter 1, the concept of education as the "great equalizer" and the role of the school in a meritocracy were examined. The traditional public school emphasis on survival of the fittest has been accepted as fair until recently when the Coleman Report, and the follow-up analyses of it in *On Equality of Educational Opportunity* edited by Mosteller and Moynihan, presented evidence that our educational system seems to perpetuate existing differences. Students who enter school at a comparative disadvantage tend to remain at a disadvantage; those who possess characteristics that permit them to respond favorably to school experiences are rewarded by admission to institutions of higher learning, and degrees from such institutions serve as passports to affluence.

Advocates of the critical-period viewpoint believed that a disadvantaged background could be cancelled out by enriched early experience, and they were instrumental in establishing Head Start programs. Children who attended Head Start schools undoubtedly benefited in many ways, but they were still at a disadvantage when confronted with the primary-grade curriculum. As a result,

Follow-Through extension of Head Start

Follow-Through programs[1] have been established in an effort to extend through the third grade the kind of compensatory education provided by Head Start. It is too early to tell if these programs have been successful, since they were first instituted in 1968; the success of early instruction can be measured only by later school performance. Although some directors of Follow-Through programs are optimistic, many critics doubt that any school program could overcome some of the handicaps of the disadvantaged.

The primary conclusion of the Coleman Report was that social class has a greater impact on later school achievement than any other factor. Corroboration of this conclusion by others has led Jencks (1972a, 1972b) to argue that the only way to reduce inequality is to change the basic social structure of this country. If we turn to socialism, he asserts, and "eliminate" the disadvantaged by reducing disparities between the affluent and the deprived, the impact of an improved total environment will make it possible to reduce inequalities.

---

[1] Each community which qualified for Follow-Through funds was permitted to select its own director, who was responsible for setting up a pilot program in such a way that the effectiveness of his methods could be measured. The programs vary from those that are pure behavior modification to those that are discovery oriented. Several specific programs will be described later in this chapter.

An anti-busing rally in Washington, D.C.

At the moment, this does not seem to be a realistic possibility, particularly when negative reactions to busing and integration are considered.

In the Coleman Report, evidence was presented to substantiate the claim that "if a minority pupil from a home without much educational strength is put with classmates with strong educational backgrounds, his achievement is likely to increase" (1966, p. 22). This conclusion had much to do with the busing policy that has stirred such controversy. It was argued that attendance boundaries that decide which school a child will attend are determined by the surrounding neighborhood. Because of economic factors and

Coleman Report: positive impact of "educational strength"

Ability Grouping or De Facto Segregation?

Ability grouping is a device for coping with individual differences between pupils in readiness to learn and in speed of learning. Since it is difficult for a teacher to present material to pupils of all levels of ability at one time, either classes are divided into groups within a particular room or pupils are placed in "streams" or "tracks." (Reading groups in the primary grades are an example of the in-class approach; the X-Y-Z system in high school exemplifies the stream or track approach.)

Although ability grouping supposedly makes students feel less threatened, lets them learn more easily, and allows teachers to do a more effective job, there is no clear-cut evidence that children learn any better in a group approach than in nongrouped classrooms (Thelen, 1967). And the Coleman Report stressed that interest in learning was stifled in classes consisting entirely of students from disadvantaged backgrounds. Thus it is possible that an apparently ineffective technique is being used to worsen the very conditions that Coleman felt were so inimical to the education of the disadvantaged, that is, separating children with high and low "educational strengths."

In most cases, initial group placement is based on test data or limited observation. Typically, total test scores are used, yet children who earn similar overall scores vary considerably in specific abilities. Thus they may actually be more similar in some respects to children placed in other groups. What happens to a child who is misplaced in a low group in the first grade? In terms of the expectation of the teacher (consider her thoughts as she sits down with the group labeled "slow")

---

building and other restrictions, there is considerable homogeneity in income and background within a neighborhood. So children from affluent and poor neighborhoods are segregated from each other, which results in educational strengths and weaknesses also being segregated. Busing was suggested as a means for establishing a ratio of advantaged and disadvantaged students in all classrooms so that those with less strength would benefit from association with more favored peers. Upper- and middle-class parents feared that their children would be adversely affected by the presence of disadvantaged pupils. This, together with questions regarding freedom of choice (and perhaps anxiety that a larger proportion of capable individuals might make it more difficult for advantaged children to compete later in life) has led to the current restrictions on busing.

A different approach to equalizing opportunity has been attempted in Forest Hills, New York. It was reasoned that inner city children are at a special disadvantage, and so it was proposed that instead of busing children back and forth to achieve a balance, low-rent housing should be provided closer to middle-class residential areas so that the desired ratio would be achieved through neighborhood integration. Resistance has been so intense that the program has been delayed, and it does not seem likely that integrated housing is any more of a realistic solution than busing.

and the way later stages are built upon previous stages in ability grouping and especially in track and stream schools, it seems possible that the entire academic career of a child will be determined the moment he is placed in his first group. That this is not an imaginary danger is attested to by the fact that the superintendent of schools in Washington, D. C., was forced to resign because he insisted on a track plan, and parents of pupils placed in the slow groups successfully argued in the courts that their children were caught in a trap.

Advocates of grouping maintain that a child can switch tracks if it becomes apparent that he has been misplaced. However, in their study on the impact of expectation Rosenthal and Jacobson found that teachers seemed to resent pupils who didn't behave "as advertised" and that this tended to limit reevaluation. Whatever the reasons, teachers in track schools rarely recommend shifts. And one study (Daniels, 1961) noted that teachers overestimated by 400 percent the amount of shifting that actually did occur.

If you find yourself teaching in a school that requires you to use ability grouping, do everything possible to make the most of techniques that permit you to work with pupils at the same general level, but at the same time do your best to resist or overcome the disadvantages just noted. One solution would be to use an open education approach, and stress individual learning. Group instruction could be provided for students having similar difficulties with specific aspects of the curriculum. This would let you concentrate on learning problems, not on children who are labelled as slow, average, or fast.

Taking all of this into account, the current state of affairs regarding education of the disadvantaged might be summed up this way: It appears that preschool compensatory programs such as Head Start have not been completely successful; Follow-Through programs are likely to help, but the "hidden curriculum" of the middle-class home will probably continue to provide children from such homes with a learning advantage; attempts to make all classrooms or all homes middle-class so that the hidden curriculum will affect all children do not seem very realistic at this point.

Some educators, such as George Dennison and Jonathan Kozol, argue that the only solution is to set up small, neighborhood *minischools* in the belief that it is impossible to bring about improvement within the present structure of the public schools. As pointed out earlier, even though this plan may have great merit, it does not seem a workable alternative for more than a small fraction of disadvantaged students. It is an incontrovertible fact that most children, particularly lower class children, will continue to attend public schools. Apparently, then, the most promising course of action would be an all-out effort by all public school teachers to do everything they can to follow a *value-added* approach to education—that is, as much as possible provide instruction according to the needs of different pupils so that almost all will achieve at respectable levels. This book as a whole offers ideas on how you might do this, but the remainder of this chapter is devoted to specific suggestions for teaching the disadvantaged.

As background for these suggestions, a description of factors typical of disadvantaged pupils will be summarized, followed by an overview of programs and techniques designed to improve the education of such students.

Factors Typical of the Disadvantaged

In *The Culturally Deprived Child*, Frank Riessman provides a detailed description of factors typical of disadvantaged children. The following list, although supplemented by observations of others, is based primarily on his analysis:

Lack of an educational tradition in the home

Negative attitude toward school   Anti-intellectualism and discontent with schools

Antagonism toward school and teachers

Vocational orientation   Vocational rather than academic orientation

Poor health and diet   Poor health, inadequate diet, frequent moves, noisy and crowded homes

Shattered family life   Shattered family life, many fatherless homes

Limited language skills   Limited language and reading skills

Insufficient school know-how   Insufficient school know-how, for example, how to listen and respond in class, how to prepare for and take tests

Preference for practical   Interest in the practical as opposed to the abstract

Preference for physical rather than verbal learning

Slower rate of learning   Slower rate of learning

Inadequate motivation to achieve remote goals (pessimistic about chance for a college education, anxiety about being out of place in college)

Poor self-concept   Poor estimate of self, lack of confidence in school, fear of failure

Victimization by overt discrimination in the form of older school buildings, larger classes, poorer teachers, higher teacher turnover, tests

Negative influences in the forms of subtle and often unintentional discrimination, for example, patronizing or condescending attitude on the part of teachers, lower expectations, and the impact of the self-fulfilling prophecy

Recognizing these factors, a considerable number of programs for educating the disadvantaged have been developed. Becoming aware of techniques used

by specialists in compensatory education, should assist you to select and develop methods of your own. In keeping with a major theme of this book, these programs will be analyzed by contrasting programmed with discovery approaches.

Programmed Techniques for the Disadvantaged

Sullivan's Approach to Programmed Reading

Although programmed reading was not developed specifically for use with the disadvantaged, it has proved especially successful with such students. One of the earliest and most comprehensive programmed reading systems was developed by M. W. Sullivan and several associates. The degree to which this technique has been preplanned is indicated by the fact that *The Teacher's Guide for the Prereader* is 64 pages long, whereas the guide for the first series (which covers only part of the entire program) is 451 pages long. The reason for the size of these guides is that instructions for every step of the program are provided in detail. (Figure 10-1, p. 462, lists the instructions the teacher is to follow in presenting the first page of the Prereader; Figure 10-2, p. 463, is a page from the Prereader on which students are to print the appropriate words.)

462

Teacher's Key	Student Response
Look at the page on the right. (Hold your book up and point to it.)	
On the page you see some lines like this. (Draw eight horizontal lines on the board.) On the left side of the top line you see a letter. (Draw a letter *a* at the left of the top line on the board.)	
Who can tell me the name of this letter?	*a*
You all remember how to make the letter *a*. First I draw a circle, like this. (Draw a circle on the board to the right of the letter *a*.)	
Now *you* draw a circle in your book to the right of the letter *a*. Make the circle just touch the line, the way I did.	(Students draw circle.)
After I've made the circle, I draw a straight line down the side of the circle like this. (Finish the letter *a* on the board.)	
Now you finish the letter *a* in your book by drawing the straight line.	(Students draw straight line.)
Now I'm going to make another letter *a*. First I draw the circle. (Draw it to the right of the second *a*.) Then I draw the line. (Draw it.)	
In your book, write the letter *a* just like this one. (Point to the *a* that you just made.)	(Students write *a*.)
Now I want you to go ahead and fill up all the lines on the page with letter *a*'s. I'll come by and help you while you work.	(Students fill page with *a*'s.)
(Check each student's work, making sure that he draws first the circle and then the line, that he writes his letters on the horizontal lines, etc.)	
Now I want you to turn to the next page of your book like this. (Demonstrate by turning the page.)	

Reprinted from Teacher's Guide to *The Prereader* by Cynthia D. Buchanan © 1968 Sullivan Associates with permission of McGraw-Hill, Inc.

Figure 10-1 Instructions for Presenting First Page of Prereader in Sullivan Program

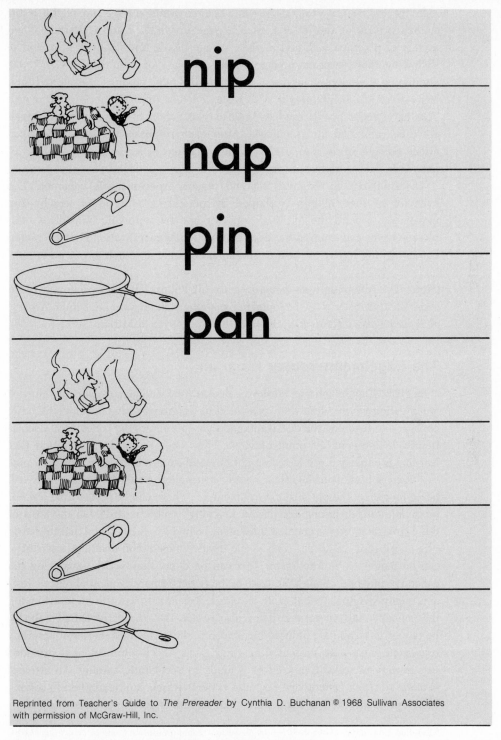

nip

nap

pin

pan

Figure 10–2   Page from Prereader in Sullivan Program

In the Sullivan approach, the student first prints a page full of the letter *a*, then a page of the letter *i*, then a page in which *a* and *i* alternate, then a page of *n*'s, then *a*, *i*, and *n*, then a page of *p*'s, and finally *i*, *n*, *a*, and *p*. Following that he prints a page of *an*'s, a page of *in*'s, then *in*'s and *an*'s alternating. Eventually, he prints *pan* and *pin* under pictures of each and then is given a series of pictures next to which he is to print the appropriate word. This basic technique is used to build a vocabulary of several words, which are then combined into sentences. After each response, the student is given either corroboration and praise by the teacher or immediate feedback by uncovering the correct answer.

The similarity to Skinner's rat and pigeon experiments is apparent: The behavior of the children is shaped by presenting a series of step-by-step movements toward the terminal behavior and by supplying immediate reinforcement for each step in the desired direction. Generalization is counteracted by contrasting letters and words similar in appearance (such as *pin* and *pan*).

(Note: The following four techniques are all Follow-Through programs. More complete descriptions can be found in *Experiments in Primary Education: Aspects of Project Follow-Through* by Eleanor E. Maccoby and Miriam Zellner.)

The Engelmann-Becker Program

Siegfried Engelmann and Wesley C. Becker (two leading advocates of behavior modification whose ideas were presented in Chapter 5) have developed a basic approach to teaching the disadvantaged that epitomizes the behaviorist-associationist-environmentalist point of view. They operate on the assumption that learning is entirely a product of environmental experiences. As Engelmann puts it: "Even if he is working alone, with no 'teacher' present, [the pupil] is still being taught by the physical environment. . . . There can be no learning (except in trivial, autistic instances) without teaching" (1968, p. 461). On the basis of this assumption, they argue that intelligent behavior is learned and that therefore "less intelligent" children—such as the disadvantaged (and mentally retarded)— can be taught to be intelligent. This can be done, they say, by analyzing the concepts and operations that lead to high performance on intelligence tests and then providing students with programmed units to assist them in achieving the concepts and operations. They also reason that the disadvantaged should be taught in systematic fashion the academic skills they lack. Series of carefully organized lessons are presented at a fast pace, and reinforcement is provided in a variety of ways. Every effort is made to accelerate learning. An attempt is made to teach generalized response systems which can be applied to solving future problems, and to shape traits like attentiveness and perseverance.[2]

Programmed approaches to teaching the disadvantaged

[2] Detailed information about the Engelmann-Becker technique can be found in *Preventing Failure in the Elementary Grades* (1969) by Engelmann, *Distar Instructional System* (1969) by Engelmann et al., and *Teaching: A Course in Applied Psychology* (1971) by Becker, Engelmann, and Thomas.

The Behavior Analysis Program

Donald Bushell, Jr., has developed a programmed approach that uses systematic reinforcement in the form of recess, snacks, art, and stories to teach study skills (e.g., learning when to talk and when to be silent, staying with assigned tasks) as well as subject matter. The teacher and also mothers, who act as assistants, are seen as behavior modifiers.

The Instructional Gains Program

Lassar Gotkin uses various learning games in a programmed approach. One of these, *Matrix Games*, consists of cards with a dozen or so pictures of children engaging in various activities. A child is given one of the cards and directed by the teacher or by a fellow student to "put a red circle around the boy drinking milk," or the teacher might cover up one of the squares and ask the pupils to figure out what the "secret" picture is. The games are designed to provide a sequence of learning experiences that proceed in such small steps that almost every response will be correct. Learning is active, can be carried out by assistants or the children themselves, and feedback is immediate and almost always positive. In stressing the values of games that children can handle themselves, Gotkin makes this observation: "If there's anything about ghetto life, it's that the kids have been underlings. Their parents have been underlings, and then the kids have been underlings. I'm interested in Child Power—that the kid should be learning to manage himself" (1970, p. 56).

The Primary Education Project

Lauren Resnick has developed a technique patterned after the model of teaching proposed by Robert Glaser, that is a variation of Individually Prescribed Instruction (described in Chapter 6). Skills needed by disadvantaged students were first analyzed, and then a series of learning units was prepared. The entering behavior of each pupil is determined by tests, then each starts at the appropriate point and works his way through the series. Three classes of skills are emphasized: orienting and attending, perceptual-motor, and conceptual-linguistic. As much as possible, the students learn by interacting with the materials and each other. The teacher supplies reinforcement such as praise, gold stars, or tokens and gives assistance where necessary.

Steven Daniels's Gerbils, Goldfish and Games Approach

In *How 2 Gerbils 20 Goldfish 200 Games 2,000 Books and I Taught Them How to Read* (hereafter referred to simply as *How 2 Gerbils . . .*), Steven Daniels describes an approach that combines aspects of behavior modification with discovery techniques. He feels that it is important for the teacher of students from slum areas to function as a leader, and in the opening pages of his book he describes what happened when he failed to do this in the first year he taught. He then describes specific techniques for establishing control (e.g., state rules and enforce them) but notes that "keeping classroom order is primarily the product of a significant and engaging curriculum" (1971, p. 33). This is true because, "When you got nothin', you got nothin' to lose." So the solution is to give students something to lose—an engaging curriculum. To develop and maintain such an atmosphere, Daniels has devised a variety of techniques, some paralleling those advocated by behavior modifiers (but based more on a philosophy of self-selection than complete external control) and some similar to open education methods. (Daniels is an ideal model if you aspire to becoming a "romantic Machiavelli".)

As reinforcement, he pays children ten cents for erasing the board (so they can earn lunch money), provides three *Games Certificates* each year that can be used to substitute free activity for reading on days when no one feels like reading, he makes use of Grandma's Rule by using preferred activities as incentives for completing less preferred ones, he posts a Reading Progress board on which students can chart their progress, and he has developed a series of books arranged in order of difficulty. (All of these techniques, it should be noted once again, emphasize a good deal of freedom in self-direction on the part of the students. They are not controlled by the instructor as much as in techniques previously described.)

Daniels uses discovery techniques by surrounding students with books and games and providing for considerable choice (to the point of establishing a Do-Nothing Corner), using role playing and psychodrama, exposing students to problem solving situations (such as giving them bus tokens, then dropping them off at various points in the city and giving a prize to the student who gets to City Hall first), and having *Games Day* every Friday.

Daniels's book is crammed with practical advice and ingenious ideas for educating the disadvantaged (or any type of student, for that matter), and you are urged to put this at the top of your list of books to buy for your professional library.

Discovery Approaches for the Disadvantaged

Although widespread interest in developing techniques to provide better education for disadvantaged children is a recent development, some methods for teaching such children were put into practice many years ago. Two educators who anticipated the current interest in teaching children from deprived environments by using what today are called discovery techniques were Maria Montessori and Sylvia Ashton-Warner.

Maria Montessori   Maria Montessori was born in the Italian village of Chiaravalle. After showing great promise early in life, she gained admission to the University of Rome and eventually earned the first medical degree ever given to a woman in Italy. She was influenced by the theories and educational methods for training retarded children developed by the French physicians Edouard Seguin and Jean Marc Itard and founded a school for retarded children in which she put their ideas into practice. Her experiences in teaching the retarded led to an appointment as a lecturer in pedagogy at the University of Rome, which in turn led to the request that she establish a nursery school for tenement children. The Casa dei Bambini, as the school was called, attracted worldwide attention, and Montessori schools were established in many countries between 1910 and 1920. As trends in education changed, the Montessori approach seemed less appropriate, and interest in the method waned. The Montessori movement in Italy was halted when the Fascists closed her schools. She moved to Barcelona and worked there until the Spanish Civil War forced her to move to the Netherlands. She was again forced to move at the outbreak of World War II and spent the war years in India. After the war, she returned to the Netherlands, where she lived and taught until her death in 1952.

The Montessori Method

Within the last few years, Montessori schools have become popular again after a fifty-year period of relative obscurity. In many cases, such schools enroll children from affluent homes, perhaps because it has become voguish to do so. The use of Montessori methods with the overadvantaged children is something of a paradox since the original techniques were developed for use with the underadvantaged. This came about as a result of Montessori's training and early interests. She began her career as a medical doctor and spent her earliest professional years working with mentally retarded children and in public health. She became involved in education when she was asked by the director-general of the Roman Association for Good Building to create a nursery school that was to be part of a model tenement project. Because of her training, early interests, and the nature of the school she was asked to develop, she stressed cleanliness, order and housekeeping skills as well as reading, writing, and arithmetic. The techniques Montessori developed to encourage such learning anticipated many aspects of both the discovery approach and programmed learning.

In terms of basic assumptions, Montessori advocated the views of Leibnitz rather than Locke. She noted, "*Environment* is undoubtedly a *secondary* factor in the phenomena of life; it can modify in that it can help or hinder, but it can never *create*" (1912, p. 105, italics in original). She referred to prizes and punishments as "the instrument of slavery for the spirit" (p. 21) and recalled that "all human victories, all human progress, stand upon the inner force" (p. 24). In contrast to Engelmann, who maintains that "there can be no learning (except in trivial, autistic instances) without teaching," Montessori observed that "a man is not what he is because of the teachers he has had, but because of what he has done" (p. 172).

Although Montessori advocated the Leibnitzian view, she also urged teachers to observe and experiment, noting that "the more fully the teacher is acquainted with the methods of experimental psychology, the better will she understand how to give the lesson" (p. 107). Montessori combined these two ideas by suggesting that teachers observe the natural, spontaneous behavior of children and then arrange learning experiences to encourage its development. She recommended that lessons be brief, simple, and objective (carried out with objects, and independent of teacher control) and that they not be arranged "to make the child feel that he has made a mistake" (p. 109).

A Montessori classroom, showing some of the Montessori apparatus and children using (left) the knobless cylinders (muscular coordination) and (right) the number cards.

COURTESY OF THE AMERICAN MONTESSORI SOCIETY

CHARLES HARBUTT/MAGNUM PHOTOS, INC.

The techniques and apparatus Montessori developed reflect a combination of what today are discussed in terms of discovery and programmed methods. She stressed activity and self-direction but at the same time provided children with "programmed" materials—for example, form boards arranged in sequence and designed to provide immediate feedback. She used what today are called activity centers, but she also urged the teacher to use repetition in daily associations between stimuli and responses. ("The lessons in nomenclature must consist simply in provoking the association of the name with the object" [p. 225].) She also stressed that the teacher should determine if what today is called terminal behavior had been achieved. ("The teacher must always test whether or not her lesson has attained the end she had in view" [p. 225].) She encouraged children to interact and to teach and learn from each other but also presented lessons to build a hierarchical series of skills in much the same manner Gagné recommends today. For example, in teaching reading and writing she first encouraged practice in handling a pencil, then presented the alphabet in the form of large letters cut out of sandpaper (to permit the child to use several senses at once), then had the child select the letter, trace it and draw it, and finally had the children combine letters into words. (In the Montessori system, the child writes before he reads. Unfortunately, the fact that English orthography is nonphonetic—i.e., a sound cannot be determined simply by the combination of letters used to write it—makes her approach difficult to use, unless, perhaps, the ITA alphabet is used.) Numerals were also presented in sandpaper form, and addition, subtraction, multiplication, and division were taught with blocks and rods.

Obviously Montessori was a brilliant innovator. Some of her techniques were based on assumptions that are not appropriate to the American disadvantaged child in the 1970s, but if you will be teaching younger children, you are urged to read at least one book by or about Montessori. (Suggestions will be offered at the end of the chapter.)

Sylvia Ashton-Warner's Organic Approach

In 1958, Sylvia Ashton-Warner published her novel *Spinster*, in which she described techniques for teaching disadvantaged Maori children in New Zealand. In *Teacher* (1963) she gives a detailed explanation of her approach, the heart of which is *organic reading*, a pedagogical method that epitomizes the Leibnitzian viewpoint just as the Sullivan approach epitomizes the Lockian position. (As you read this description of Ashton-Warner's approach, you are urged to compare it with Sullivan's programmed technique.)

The meaning of *organic* in Ashton-Warner's approach is summed up in these statements; "First words must have intense meaning for a child. They must be part of his being" (1963, p. 33). When five-year-old Maori children first came into her room, Ashton-Warner invited them to come up to her, one by one, and ask her to print a word on a large card. (The child's name was also printed on the corner of the card.) The child said the word after it had been printed, took it to a mat (serving as a desk), and traced it. After each child had been given a word, all the cards were collected and put in a box. The next day the cards were dumped on the floor, and the children took out their words, after which they chose a partner and exchanged vocabulary. As this was being done, the children came up individually to ask for another word. From time to time, the children were asked to read their cards. If they were unable to read any particular word, the card was destroyed. When a *Key Vocabulary* of thirty words for each child had been accumulated, the children were encouraged to write their own key words and, after being provided with additional general vocabulary, to write sentences. During these writing periods, which were limited to twelve children at a time, Ashton-Warner circulated around the group and gave individual assistance. Each day, new words were printed on the board so that all could see them. When a sufficient vocabulary had been acquired, each child wrote a story, which he then read to and exchanged with other children. Thus the children created their own texts. In addition to reading and writing, the children also were free to select from many activities and took frequent field trips that were used as the bases for stories, singing, and dancing.

Discovery approach: development of ideas expressed by students

The First Street School of George Dennison

In *The Lives of Children,* George Dennison describes the short, turbulent history of the First Street School. Dennison explains how he was influenced by Tolstoy, Dewey, Neill, Ashton-Warner, and others in developing the principle that education is a preparation not for later life but for "the present lives of children" (1969, p. 9). To put his philosophy into practice, he created a minischool consisting of twenty-three students and varying numbers of teachers who lived in the neighborhood. Because of the nature and size of this school and because Dennison was unable to sustain it for more than two years, it does not serve as a model for direct imitation in a public school. However, in Chapter 12 of his book, Dennison offers suggestions for those who see merit in the approach, and the Appendix consists of comments on teaching techniques by other educators who endorse the First Street philosophy.

Jonathan Kozol's Free School Approach

In *Death at an Early Age,* (1967) Jonathan Kozol exposed the deplorable conditions of life in a Boston ghetto school. In *Free Schools* (1972) he describes the kind of school he has created as an alternative. To understand his approach, it is important to take into account the anguish, rage, and frustration of his first experience with teaching. Although Kozol would like to endorse the free philosophy as advocated by Neill and Dennison, he is obviously imbued with a mission—to help black children work their way out of the ghetto. To do that, he argues, they must be equipped with certain skills (such as reading), and taught how to survive and beat the system. (As Kozol uses the word, "free" refers more to freedom from the stultifying impact of public education than it does to a self-directed approach.) He does everything possible to encourage self-direction but recognizes that formal instruction is necessary if students are to learn the skills they will need. He provides this description of what he considers an ideal free school:

> There is, within the school, a lot of emphasis on what the old-time teachers used to call "the basic skills." There is also a visible presence of high energy and fun, pupil irreverence and adult unprotectedness, . . . a warm, reassuring and disarming atmosphere of trust and intimacy and good comradeship between children and adults, a sense of trust that builds at all times on the recognition of the difficult conditions that surround their school and of the dangers which exist for each and every one of them on the outside.

Discovery approach: stress on interpersonal relationships

> There is also something in this school which is too rare in many of the Free Schools that I know: a real sense of stability and of sustained commitment in regard both to the present lives and to the future aspirations of the children in the school. . . . [The teachers] are not afraid to give their kids direct instructions, straightforward criticism or precise and sometimes bitter admonitions. They like *Summerhill* but they do not think it is the only good book ever written. (1972, pp. 74–75)

Herbert Kohl's "Spontaneous Interest" Approach

Herbert Kohl describes his experiences of teaching in a sixth-grade class in a Harlem elementary school in *36 Children* (1967), and in *The Open Classroom* (1969) he offers some general suggestions derived from these experiences (and later ones). The Kohl approach is not so much a systematic program of instruction as a general philosophy of taking advantage of spontaneous interests, although a few features (e.g., activity centers) of the British open education technique are recommended. You are urged to read *36 Children* to discover how he converted spontaneous class comments into units on myths, themes on "My Block," autobiographies, fables, an alphabet book, and a class newspaper. His basic approach is summarized in this excerpt from *The Open Classroom*:

> I considered my role in [the] class was to bring in things to share with the students and to be available to help them. I brought books and articles and poems to class, and left them there. Sometimes we talked about them though often we didn't. However, my bringing what I cared about to the class made it easier for them to bring things that were important to them.
> One has to be patient with freedom and have as rich an environment as possible available for students so there will be things they can choose to do. One cannot

ask pupils to be free or make choices in a vacuum. There is no limit to what can be brought to class to enrich the environment. A partial list would include:

—second-hand books

—old magazines

—scraps of wood, metal, and cloth discarded by factories

—old billboard posters

—parts of broken machines—cars, TV's, radios, toasters, etc.

—tape recorders and tape

—old toys

—old clothes to be used to create a classroom costume closet

—a sewing machine and needles and thread

—discarded advertising materials such as signs, posters, booklets, sales tags, handbills

—comfortable old furniture or rugs

—light fixtures, flashlights, wire, bulbs, batteries

—typewriters

—posters and buttons of all sorts (1969, pp. 99–100).

The "Open Education" Approach of Hilda Taba and Deborah Elkins

Kohl titles one of his books *The Open Classroom,* but his basic technique of teaching is much closer to what is referred to in this book as *free* education than to what is called *open* education. Techniques for teaching the disadvantaged that exemplify open education have been developed and practiced by Hilda Taba and Deborah Elkins, who explain their approach in *Teaching Strategies for the Culturally Disadvantaged* (1966). The original description of their work appeared in 1950, thus anticipating the open education movement of today, but their methods are essentially the same as those now being developed in Britain and North Dakota.

The basic guidelines for instructional strategies recommended by Taba and Elkins include continual diagnosis to discover gaps in knowledge and areas in need of attention and the simultaneous pursuit of objectives in these areas: knowledge, thinking, attitudes, and skills; providing for heterogeneity; pacing learning by providing "bite-size" chunks arranged in hierarchical fashion; structuring learning to allow for tangibility, concreteness, and overt activity; extensive use of dramatization, playmaking, and role-playing; and providing experiences in observing and interviewing.

Sylvia Ashton-Warner

Jonathan Kozol

George Dennison

KARL BISSINGER

James Herndon

Herbert Kohl

Stephen Daniels

The implementation of these guidelines can be illustrated by a unit on "Human Hands." The unit was introduced at a concrete level by asking students to trace their hands and using the tracings as a basis for discussing the beauty and similarity of hands and then as a stimulus for writing on "Important Things My Hands Can Do." The descriptions provided were then analyzed and tallied on the board under different categories to encourage awareness of concepts. The final list of categories was reproduced and added to the written theme as the beginning of an individual notebook for each pupil. Then the teacher read a story, and students were asked to discuss how hands were used by the characters; afterward, the original categories were revised and expanded. For homework, the students were asked to observe an adult for thirty minutes and write down everything the person did with his hands. These reports were discussed, tallied, categorized and added to the notebooks, following which each student summed up his general observations on hands in a short paragraph that was later reproduced in a booklet and distributed to the members of the class. Next, Help Wanted ads in newspapers were analyzed to illustrate how hands are used in many different occupations, magazines were distributed and students asked to cut out pictures of hands, and newspaper articles on hands were collected. All of these were used in group discussion and as the basis for written exercises to be added to the notebooks.

Additional themes using the same general techniques were "Walls in Our Life" and "Aspirations." The purpose of the latter topic was to build understanding of goals and encourage the development of realistic aspirations, and it featured interviews with parents and other adults, the dramatization of original plays, and role-playing (some students acted as employers, others as job aspirants).

As this brief description indicates, Taba and Elkins recommend teaching techniques that illustrate many of the themes of open education described by Walberg and Thomas: manipulation, movement, considerable discussion, instructional materials written by students, continual diagnosis, individual notebooks. *Teaching Strategies for the Culturally Disadvantaged* offers detailed suggestions for setting up and carrying out social studies units for secondary school students, although the basic methods described could be adapted for use at almost any grade level or subject. It is one of the most practical how-to-do-it books on open education *and* the education of the disadvantaged, and it is highly recommended.

James Herndon's Experiments with Creative Arts and Other Things

In *The Way It Spozed to Be* (1968), James Herndon describes his initial experiences in grappling with life in a public junior high school; in *How to Survive in Your Native Land* (1971) he describes later experiments with "survival" in American education. During his first year as a teacher, Herndon struggled to find ways to arouse interest in the standard curriculum by using student-led groups, tape recorders, games like Scrabble, trips to the library, a Friday "film orgy" (complete with candy), and play reading. At the conclusion of *The Way It Spozed to Be,* he expresses the fatalistic view that what he did probably made no difference and that there was little hope for change. However, he decided to give teaching another try, and in *How to Survive in Your Native Land* he describes how he (and his colleagues) induced his students to invent their own language, drop notes in bottles off the Golden Gate bridge, pretend to be Peace Corps workers, invent an island, and engage in a variety of other learning experiences. Eventually, he found a school where he was allowed to unveil *Creative Arts*—a two-hour block of time during which students voluntarily (with parental permission) participated in a no-assignment, no-grade curriculum. When they weren't making abundant use of their *Permanent Hall Passes,* students in C. A. built monster kites, drew elaborate mural maps, and wrote, produced, directed and starred in a scintillating film epic, *The Return of the Hawk.*

Despite the apparent success of many of his ideas in regular and C. A. classes, Herndon expresses doubts about the value of any kind of schooling. He also speculates that C. A. and other forms of free education work only because they are better than the regular curriculum. He suggests that the burden is shifted from teacher to kids and that teachers may set up such classes in the hope that their students will show them how to teach. Perhaps Herndon is so hard on himself because he began his career with high hopes and did not fully realize the magnitude of the job he was tackling. If Coleman and Jencks are correct—and there is considerable evidence that they are—the primary reason that educating the disadvantaged rarely works to perfection is because of the crushing impact of the entire environment in which students exist. As some observers have pointed out, the schools are attempting too much. Herbert Kohl, in expressing his disappointment about the lack of permanent change in his students, notes "One year is not enough." Herndon seems to have been bothered by the same feeling. But it is apparent from reading his books that he did have a substantial positive impact on his pupils, and it seems certain that all of them learned more than they would have if left to their own devices. Herndon feels uncomfortable about using many of the ingenious teaching techniques he developed because at heart he is a believer in freedom. But it would appear that when he did exert leadership, his students learned more than he might like to admit. The problem of reconciling freedom and control that Kozol analyzes so openly in *Free Schools* seems to surface only occasionally in Herndon's books. Herndon's struggle to reconcile freedom and control is illustrated by the following excerpt from *The Way It Spozed to Be,* which summarizes much of his philosophy of education. He is commenting on the kind of advice (other than such down-to-earth suggestions as where to get films, how to make up easily corrected tests, etc.) given to new teachers by older colleagues.

This advice was a conglomeration of dodges, tricks, gimmicks to get the kids to do what they were spozed to do, that is, whatever the teacher had in mind for them to do. It really involved a kind of gerrymandering of the group—promises, favors, warnings, threats, letting you pass out or not pass out paper, sit in a certain place or not, A's, plusses, stars, and also various methods for getting the class working before they knew it. The purpose of all these methods was to get and keep an aspect of order, which was reasonable enough, I suppose. But the purpose of this order was supposed to be so that "learning could take place." So everyone said—not wanting to be guilty of the authoritarian predilection for order for its own sake—while at the same time admitting that most of the kids weren't learning anything this way. Everyone agreed that our students were on the average a couple of years below grade level, everyone agreed that was because they were "deprived" kids, but no one agreed that simply because nothing was going on the way they were doing it, they ought to try something else.

It's not my purpose or even desire to criticize these teachers—they were as good or better than most and they had a difficult job—but frankly I could never come to terms with their attitude. They knew a certain way, or ways, to teach. They knew how to get control of the class and, that established, some ways to present the material they thought important. The control didn't work consistently because the kids were not easily threatened, having little to lose. Promises were fairly successful at the beginning of the year, but their power steadily declined as the kids saw through them or were disillusioned about their value. The material which was so important, which had to be "covered," was supposed to lead toward understanding, broader knowledge, scientific method, good citizenship or, more specifically, toward better writing, speech, figuring, grammar, geography, whatever it was. But actually what was happening was that they were presenting the students, every day, with something for them either to do or not-do, while keeping them through order from any other alternative. If a kid couldn't or wouldn't do his assignment, he had only the choice of not-doing it, of doing nothing. Almost every teacher admitted that this last was the choice of half the class on any given day.

The kids who chose to do the assignment seemed rarely to benefit from it; even if they did the speller conscientiously, their written work remained badly spelled. The A's promised as a prize for hard work didn't materialize. The result was that these teachers faced, every year, the certain knowledge that the first day of school was the best they could hope for, since the progress and morale of the class could only be downhill. The only question left was whether or not they could hold out. (1968, pp. 76–78)

If Herndon has expressed feelings you have also wrestled with, you are urged to consider the open education approach as a means for a teacher to provide guidance and direction and at the same time avoid a "do or not do" situation.

(Note: The following four techniques are all Follow-Through programs. More detailed descriptions can be found in *Experiments in Primary Education* by Maccoby and Zellner.)

The Education Development Center Approach

David Armington uses the British open school approach as a model for a program that stresses having a variety of activities, a flexible time schedule, pupil interaction, and considerable self-management.

The Bank Street Program

Elizabeth Gilkeson and Herbert Zimiles use an approach that reflects the themes of open education described by Wahlberg and Thomas. Students are free to choose activities, the teacher analyzes the learning of each pupil and provides individualized instruction. Considerable emphasis is placed on language development and on relating classroom experiences to nonschool situations.

The Cognitively Oriented Approach

David Weikart uses the theories of Piaget as a basis for a program in which the child moves from the simple to the complex and from the concrete to the abstract. Pupils first use their own bodies to experience concepts and then move to verbal and finally conceptual levels. The following is an example of how this is done.

> At first, our children play boat by having a real, life-sized boat to get into. Later, they can play with a toy-sized boat, but one that looks like a real boat—isn't too much stylized. Later they can use an ash tray as though it were a boat. We put each child into this sequence, and try to start with toys at the right level of abstraction for the child. We find it very hard to get the teachers to use the motoric level. (1970, p. 37)

The Tucson Early Education Model

Marie Hughes and Ronald Henderson have developed a program to assist Mexican-American children to overcome English deficiencies, gain experience in manipulating objects, and develop a sense of the sequence of events. Stories told by the children are recorded and class experiences described in illustrated books (a technique similar to that used by Ashton-Warner). Following is a description of the Tucson reading program:

> When we are trying to teach reading, we try to make it functional; it must be related to experiences the child and his friends have had, it must be useful to the child to be able to read the labels so he can tell what is available where—so he can get the things he wants. We make a lot of use of the primer typewriter to label everything, and then use the labels in referring to materials, places, etc. The better teachers can use this environment easily. Our assumption is that the

children are less motivated if you use a more formal program to unlock the recurring environment. (1970, p. 40)

In addition, efforts are made to inculcate positive attitudes toward school, to build the ability to persist, and the expectation of success.

Summary of Points Covered

At this point, a summary of what has been covered so far is offered to serve as background for the teaching suggestions that follow.

There is considerable evidence that the traditional approach to education in America perpetuates inequality of opportunity more than it functions as an "equalizer." The "hidden curriculum" of the upper- and middle-class home, where children spend much more time than they do in school, has a greater impact than classroom experience. Attempts to compensate for this by providing Head Start and Follow-Through experiences do not seem to be sufficient. Busing, low-rent housing in middle-class neighborhoods, and other socialistic programs are meeting with considerable resistance. Thus it appears that the best solution available is for all teachers to make a concerted effort to use a value-added form of education. To put such a program into practice, students who need more assistance to achieve instructional objectives should be provided with extra attention and instruction. In establishing guidelines for doing this, the characteristics of the disadvantaged should be taken into account along with programs developed by those who have specialized in the education of underprivileged pupils.

The list of suggestions for arousing and sustaining interest in learning in the preceding chapter applies to all students, but the same outline is now offered as a framework for noting additional techniques that apply more specifically to the disadvantaged. Many of these are derived from the programs just described.

Suggestions For Teaching the Disadvantaged

1. Do everything possible to satisfy the deficiency needs—physiological, safety, belongingness, esteem.
   a. Allow for the physical condition of your pupils.
   b. Make your room physically and psychologically safe.
   c. Show your students that you take an interest in them and that they "belong" in your classroom.
   d. Arrange learning experiences so that all students can gain at least a degree of esteem.
2. Strive to enhance the attractions and minimize the dangers of growth choices.
3. Direct learning experiences toward feelings of success in an effort to encourage a realistic level of aspiration, an orientation toward achievement, and a positive self-concept.

4. Be alert to the damaging impact of excessive competition.

5. For students who need it, encourage the development of a desire to achieve.

6. Take advantage of natural interests and try to create new ones, and encourage learning for its own sake.

7. Provide encouragement and incentives for learning that is essential but not intrinsically appealing.

1. *Do everything possible to satisfy the deficiency needs—physiological, safety, belongingness, esteem.*

Satisfying deficiency needs

    a. *Allow for the physical condition of your pupils.*

Many children from disadvantaged homes are in poor health, have an inadequate diet, and must cope with noisy and crowded living conditions. As a result, it may be necessary to pay special attention to their physical condition.

Examples:

Check whether your students have had breakfast. If many have not, inquire about the availability of breakfast programs provided by college or other groups, see if the school cafeteria might provide breakfast as well as lunch, or supply some fruit and cereals on your own.

Follow Daniels's technique of paying children for chores such as erasing the board, either in lunch money or in apples, cookies, and the like.

Stress the importance of a good diet.

When students seem sleepy, provide frequent breaks and rest periods.

Make maximum use of a school nurse to diagnose and treat health problems and to emphasize the importance of cleanliness and a good diet.

If you can think of other ways you might compensate for unsatisfied physiological needs of disadvantaged pupils, note them below.

_____

_____

_____

    b. *Make your room physically and psychologically safe.*

Many disadvantaged children live in environments in which physical safety cannot be taken for granted. (In *How 2 Gerbils. . .* , Daniels describes the jungle atmosphere that may be created by neighborhood gangs.) Consequently, you have an opportunity to make your room seem a haven. Herndon observes:

> I often wondered how they got along outside my classroom. In the world of and around [the school], most of the kids were scared—scared of failure, scared of being black, scared of their new shoes, scared of tearing their clothes,

Varying Views on the Education of the Disadvantaged

One of the first books on the disadvantaged was *The Culturally Deprived Child* by Frank Riessman. It concisely describes the problems involved in educating the disadvantaged and offers specific suggestions to teachers. However, many of Riessman's conclusions and proposals were by necessity personal interpretations, hypotheses, and extrapolations derived from his own experience. Patrick Groff (1964) took seventy-eight statements from Riessman's book and asked about three hundred teachers of the culturally deprived to indicate how much they agreed or disagreed with them. Many of the "endorsed" statements have been used in explaining the characteristics of the disadvantaged and the implications for teaching presented in this chapter. However, the following few supplementary points of agreement and disagreement have not yet been mentioned. The teachers *agreed* with Riessman on the following statements:

Natural leaders in the class should be sought out and won over.

Strong demands and firm, unyielding rules are needed from a definite and authoritative teacher who sets up a highly structured classroom with strict routine and order.

Flexible, nongraded classes should be used.

The teachers *disagreed* with Riessman on these points. Thus a substantial number of experienced teachers in effect endorsed an opposite interpretation.

The disadvantaged child lacks a sense of competition in school.

The system of personal marks should be replaced by group competition.

The disadvantaged child best likes the three R's and least likes social studies, literature, and the arts.

The disadvantaged child sees little value in books and discussions.

The disadvantaged child does not like to work in short spurts with frequent breaks.

Segregating the disadvantaged by ability or achievement should not be undertaken.

The teacher should expect initial hostility and nonacceptance from the disadvantaged.

The best teacher of the disadvantaged is one who identifies with the underdog.

The white teacher should not treat Negro children with informality. They see this as disrespect.

The teacher cannot take a gentle approach with the disadvantaged child.

Teachers should use suggestions and demonstrations of their superior physical strength.

If you read Riessman's book, it would be wise to read Groff's article as well. It appears in the October 1964 issue of *Exceptional Children.*

scared of not knowing how to do right, scared of not getting a pencil or a piece of three-hole lined paper upon which they would be too scared to write anything much if they got it. Perhaps the students of 7B fell back, outside the classroom, as individuals, into this scariness and became apathetic or violent or ugly, or called each other watermelonhead. I really don't know. It seemed as if in the classroom they had found something reasonable to respond to, as often an individual kid will find in school some promise which is kept, something sensible or even beautiful, something not available in their homes or families or in their blocks, and so come to live really only at school, even sometimes to love it and find in it the same joy and despair as any lover. (1968, pp. 33–34)

Examples:

Establish routines and firm control, but do it in a positive way so that less secure students realize you will protect them from possible physical harm and so all pupils will feel that your room is a place where they can feel unthreatened.

Be consistent, honest, warm, firm, and fair.

    c. *Show your students that you take an interest in them and that they "belong" in your classroom.*

Examples:

Go out of your way to know students on an individual basis.

Encouraging a positive self-concept

Consider using Daniels's technique of sending birthday and Christmas cards.

Because many disadvantaged students come from minority groups, another aspect of "belonging" may be of concern to you. Within recent years, interest in developing pride in the heritage of one's own ethnic group has increased. You might attempt to encourage such feelings in an effort to satisfy the need to belong.

Examples:

Place pictures of successful members of different minority groups on bulletin boards, encourage students to read and write biographies of them and to discuss their work.

Invite such individuals to talk to your class.

Search for books and materials that emphasize the positive achievements of minority group members, for example, the *Negro Heritage Library.*

Refer to the booklist in Chapter 11 of Daniels's *How 2 Gerbils. . .* for titles in which either black or Puerto Rican characters play significant roles. Or consult the appendix of *A Handbook for Teaching in the Ghetto School* by Sidney Trubowitz for a bibliography of books "which portray Negro characters, reveal the cultural heritage of the Negro, or tell of lives of Negroes who have made significant contributions to the total American culture" (1968, p. 147).

Because there are so many fatherless homes, invite retired men of different ethnic backgrounds to visit your class and describe the kinds of jobs they held.

If they seem to establish rapport with your students, consider asking them to assist you in small-group or individual instruction.

The Special Problems of Spanish-Speaking Disadvantaged Students

Although many black children use variations of English that do not completely jibe with the English used by authors of texts and by teachers, they still have general familiarity with standard English. This is not always the case with Puerto Rican and Mexican-American children. In many school districts, rules prohibit the use of any language other than English on the grounds that the best way to encourage its mastery is to *force* both pupils and teachers to use it. (This is the reason Governor Ronald Reagan of California gave when he vetoed a bill that would have provided funds for bilingual education.) What these rules and the policy of "forced" English fail to take into account has been described by Philip D. Ortego in this way:

> When Chicano children are punished for breaking "no-Spanish" rules, they are being reprimanded for the crime of speaking the only language they know. They are being pressed into thinking of their language as "wrong" and "inferior," and the more this continues the more they become hostile, resentful, and alienated from society, from their families, and even from themselves. Thus, the Spanish-speaking child who encounters stern and imposing prohibitions against using his language not only is traumatized by a conflict he does not readily understand but is forced into a position of repudiating his cultural identity or else of perishing within the educational process. (1971, p. 64)

In recognition of such factors, the Bilingual Education Act of 1968 was passed. (A few states, e.g., Massachusetts, also have passed laws providing extra funds for bilingual education.) It provides for programs that present the initial instruction of Spanish-speaking children in that language and also the gradual introduction of English so that the child will be truly bilingual. (As some advocates of the program point out, the result is the same as programs to encourage English-speaking children to learn a foreign language in the elementary school.) Although the intentions of the act are praiseworthy, implementation has been slow because of the lack of qualified teachers and inadequate funds and materials.

If you have Spanish-speaking children in your classes, you might seek information and assistance from Spanish departments in colleges or universities and from chapters of MECHA (*Movimiento Estudiantil Chicano de Azatlan*), the national Chicano student organization. Or, obtain one of these publications: *A Forgotten American: A Resource Unit for Teachers on the Mexican American* (1969) by Luis F. Hernandez, *Montezuma's Children* (1971) by Philip D. Ortego, *Mexican American Education: A Selected Bibliography* (with ERIC Abstracts), ERIC/CRESS Supplement No. 2 (available from Superintendent of Documents, U.S. Government Printing Office, Washington, D.C., 20402; Stock Number 1780-1063, price $2.50).

Encourage the development of "black is beautiful" feelings (or the equivalent).

Consider developing a limited program similar to one used in the Multi-Culture Institute of San Francisco. Encourage pupils from various ethnic and religious backgrounds to get together at designated periods and prepare presentations for the rest of the class illustrating and explaining the art, music, beliefs, and ceremonies of their particular group. On special holidays, have the entire class participate in the celebration, including the preparation and enjoyment of appropriate foods.

If you can think of other ways to convert feelings of rejection because of a minority group background to feelings of belonging, note them in the space below.

_____

_____

_____

_____

_____

_____

d. *Arrange learning experiences so that all students can gain at least a degree of esteem.*

Many disadvantaged children, particularly those from minority groups, have a poor estimate of themselves as a result of many factors including living conditions, actual experiences with discrimination, stereotyped conceptions created by films and television (consider the image of the American Indian presented in most westerns), and observation of the difficulty their parents experience in improving their lot. This point was emphasized in the Coleman Report as *destiny control*, which refers to an individual's feeling that he can shape his own future. The report considered it "to have a stronger relationship to achievement than . . . all other 'school' factors together" (1966, p. 23). All these factors highlight the degree to which efforts should be made to assist disadvantaged students to satisfy their esteem needs. This might be accomplished in part by techniques just described in discussing belonging, but the most promising approach is to do everything possible to assist students to feel that they can be successful, to encourage self-control, and to provide background in skills that will pave the way for success in higher education. (W. Arthur Lewis (1969) points out that although blacks make up 11 percent of the population, they have 2 percent of the jobs at the top, 4 percent of the jobs in the middle, and from 16 to 40 percent of the jobs near and at the bottom. He maintains that since blacks will always be a minority, they should strive

Destiny control

Encouraging feelings of success

THE EMPEROR OF ICE CREAM

By Barbara

Once upon a time there was an emperor, and he said, "The only emperor is the emperor of ice cream." Everyone knew that wasn't true, but they were Afraid to say anything. One day a man came up to him and said, "I'm the emperor of ice cream." When the emperor heard this he said: "I am the emperor of ice cream." They started to Argue. There was a great war. The two emperors fought Fiercly. THEE Emperor of ice cream won. The emperor smiled and said, "The only emperor is the emperor of ice cream

to become successful in a predominantly white world and that the only way to do so is by gaining traditional (white) higher education and by learning to interact with whites.)

Examples:

Use the Montessori approach as a model. Try to set up learning situations that are brief, simple, carried out with objects, independent of teacher control, and so arranged that the child is not made to feel he has made mistakes.

Use materials such as the *Matrix Games* developed by Gotkin to encourage "Child Power," whereby students manage their own learning and get away from the feeling they are underlings.

Be especially wary of degrading criticisms. At the same time, avoid hypocritical praise.

Constantly remind yourself of Ginott's distinction between desirable and undesirable praise: praise the act, not the child.

Make use of student-created materials: books, plays, newspapers, stories, decorations. Follow the Taba and Elkins procedure of "publishing" student work in the form of a class "text."

Follow the advice of Daniels: "The best method I've found for creating self-esteem is to let my students, to the fullest possible degree, run the class. Aside from the fact that they will teach and lead one another better than I can, they feel trusted, important, and worthy of respect" (1971, p. 91).

This list of techniques brings up a question about the use of behavior modification with the disadvantaged. Some teachers have felt that it is important to provide a steady diet of reinforcement in the form of praise or tangible rewards and in this way attempt to build the confidence and self-esteem of their students. The assumption is that the environment must be controlled by others which leads to the question of if and how outer control can then be transferred to inner control. When classroom activities are almost all planned and prepared and controlled by the teacher, students may well get the feeling that they are not trusted or worthy of respect. On the other hand, if the teacher goes too far in the direction of freedom, the students may be overwhelmed by the magnitude of the task of educating themselves. A workable compromise seems to be to follow the open education approach: provide direction but still allow individual choice and at the same time encourage students to develop some of their own materials and to learn from each other.

A page from a book written and illustrated by students of Herbert Kohl.

The Higher Horizons Program

In 1956 a program was instituted in a New York junior high school with the following purpose: ''to identify, stimulate and guide into college channels able students from low socioeconomic homes.''* The project was given the title ''Higher Horizons,'' and it has received a good deal of publicity because the aims were fulfilled in dramatic fashion: Thirty-nine percent more students eventually were graduated from high school compared with pre-Higher Horizons years; three and a half times more students went to college than previously. Although these results are impressive, Higher Horizons has been criticized. It has been pointed out that the expanded budget, the lower pupil-teacher and pupil-counselor loads, and the zeal of those involved to ''prove'' they could do it made the program somewhat unrealistic as a model for all school districts.

Whatever the validity of such criticisms (which may explain why similar programs have not become a fixture in more school systems), the techniques used can be of value to any teacher in a secondary school in which there are disadvantaged students. If your school district lacks an organized program, you may be able to develop a miniature, private version of Higher Horizons. Here are some of the techniques used in New York:

To identify those with potential and to ascertain strengths and weaknesses, a variety of test instruments were used.

Pictures of Negro and Puerto Rican doctors, physicists, and journalists were displayed in the classroom to instill motivation and develop the self-image of the students.

Special remedial reading classes of five and six pupils each were organized. *All* teachers, regardless of what subjects they taught, devoted the first ten minutes of each class to drills in reading.

---

2. *Enhance the attractions and minimize the dangers of growth choices.*

Many disadvantaged children see learning as threatening or not worth the effort, and they conceive of not attempting to learn as safe. As Daniels puts it, "When you got nothin', you got nothin' to lose." And Herndon has pointed out that many disadvantaged students may choose to engage in horseplay or defiance because it is considered preferable to appear bad than stupid. He also describes some elaborate and ingenious techniques his pupils devised to make it appear that they knew more than they actually did. Maslow's diagram of growth choice thus takes on special significance when dealing with the disadvantaged, so do everything possible to make growth (in the form of learning) attractive and unthreatening.

Encouraging growth choices

Examples:

Don't require students to perform in front of their peers unless they choose to do so.

Book fairs and circulating libraries of paperbacks were started. Students who read a certain number of books were given recognition (e.g., badges that said "Readers Are Leaders").

An intensive counseling service was established to provide guidance concerning career and college possibilities.

A cultural program was initiated. Groups of students were taken to movies and concerts—after having been prepared for the experience by discussing what to look or listen for, what it would be like, etc.

Classrooms were opened after school hours to provide a quiet place to study. Counselors made arrangements with parents in crowded apartments to turn television sets off between certain hours so students could complete their homework. (The counselors also persuaded younger brothers and sisters not to pester scholars at work.)

Parents were involved in school programs through meetings, home visits, and letters. Workshops were organized to give parents the opportunity to discuss career possibilities for their children.

Obviously many of these techniques are beyond the resources of an individual teacher, but they do suggest the direction you might take if you would like to attempt to develop some type of Higher Horizons project of your own.

° Reports on the Higher Horizons project appeared in *Strengthening Democracy*, Vol. 9, No. 4, March–April, 1957, and Vol. 12, No. 4, May, 1960, published by the Board of Education of the City of New York.

Provide positive feedback in private and personal ways.

Follow Daniels's lead and make learning so lively and interesting that students will find safety (not joining in) unattractive.

If you can think of other ways to make growth choices seem especially attractive to disadvantaged students, note them in the space below:

---

3. *Direct learning experiences toward feelings of success in an effort to encourage a realistic level of aspiration, an orientation toward achievement, and a positive self-concept.*

For reasons discussed in commenting on satisfying esteem needs, unless the disadvantaged pupil is given assistance, he is quite likely to be predisposed more toward failure than success. This is likely to be true even for kindergarten children because of the early environment in the slum home. Robert D. Hess and Virginia Shipman (1965) observed mother-child interaction in disadvantaged homes and found, typically, that the mothers were inattentive and unresponsive to the child, used impoverished language, tended to lack self-confidence and destiny control, were disorganized in the way the home was run, and functioned as much at the preoperational level as their offspring. It is this sort of background that leads to the restricted range of experience and limited language and reading skills of the disadvantaged. Head Start and other preschool experience might partially overcome the impact of such a milieu, and many preschool programs provide parent education and involvement; but even with such assistance, the disadvantaged child may not possess the necessary background for success in school and lack confidence in his ability to learn. When all children in a class come from the same kind of deprived background and share the same feelings of pessimism, a form of reciprocal fatalism may develop. (This is the reaction Coleman hoped could be counteracted by busing.) Consequently, it is essential to set up learning experiences so that disadvantaged students will gain the knowledge and skills they lack and experience success, because this will encourage the development of a realistic level of aspiration, which in turn will pave the way for subsequent fruitful learning and feelings of success.

Because programmed instruction provides a step-by-step learning procedure and reinforcement for every response, it has proved especially successful with disadvantaged students. Even some of the most devoted advocates of a free approach have admitted this. Here is an observation made by Wilbur Rippy (who taught at a New York City version of Summerhill) which appears in the appendix of Dennison's *The Lives of Children*:

> In a society that makes such a big deal out of learning, and out of, say, learning to read in the first few grades, a child will be made to feel like a dummy unless he complies. The freedom of choice—which ideally would protect his own needs—becomes illusory because he is swayed by pressures that are almost ubiquitous. The school must give him every conceivable support in this; and I would favor teaching methods which increase the child's own effectiveness and independence as fast as possible. In the teaching of reading, the best method is one that aids the child in "breaking the code." The method should be clear, decisive, and quick. The child's increase in competence will bring pleasure. . . .
>
> For the above reasons, I've used the Sullivan Programmed Reader, the Merril Series, and the Stern materials. The Sullivan Programmed Reader is quite a shock to an adult who is concerned with good literature, whatever that is. Yet it quickly teaches the child to read. Too, it relieves him of gratuitous adult aid and of much well-meant but superfluous (and often confusing) adult attention. I've found that children who have started with the programmed material have quickly branched out to other reading. They also become more able to "do their own thing," for they gain the skills quickly and then are able to write their own stories, cartoons, and books without relying all the time on adults.

Some kids dislike the Programmed readers, or might start on them and soon tire. In such cases, I've made other material available—the Merril, or Stern material. The teacher's manual recommends using the Programmed reader day after day, as an unbroken series, but this is unwise and I have never done it. Some teachers feel that programmed materials will create a programmed child, but I have never seen any evidence of this. The Programmed reader seems more likely to rescue the child from the diffuse and ineffective teaching so often seen in schools.

I am still surprised that I can recommend these materials. You know my interest in literature, but perhaps you don't know that for many years I supported and taught an individualized reading program somewhat akin to Sylvia Ashton-Warner's. In using the programmed materials I was forced to the conclusion that the child was soon liberated from his dependency, and was able to communicate the images, ideas, and feelings which lie at the heart of the "basic skills." (1969, pp. 297–298)

You might use these observations as a starting point for drawing your own conclusions about achieving a balance between programmed and discovery approaches to teaching the disadvantaged. In addition, consider using these techniques for assisting students to experience feelings of success, develop a realistic level of aspiration, and an orientation toward achievement.

Examples:

Use Daniels's *Reading for Pleasure* technique. Obtain (even if you have to buy them yourself) hundreds of books; spread them around the room, invite students to pick out a book, read it to themselves or friends, and post titles read on a Reading Progress Board. Or use Daniels's list of books graded in terms of difficulty to provide a more open version of the SRA (Science Research Associates) Reading Lab. (For instructions on how to set up such a program, together with a list of the books arranged by levels, see pp. 135–150 of *How 2 Gerbils . . .*)

Encouraging feelings of success

When students are self-conscious or have doubts about their ability to do something well, put everyone under a handicap; Herndon had his students paint left-handed and with huge brushes when they expressed fears that their efforts at art would look inept.

Use the open education approach of having students set individual goals in consultation with you and use techniques (noted in the preceding chapter) under the following headings:

Make use of goals and objectives that are challenging but attainable.

Provide knowledge of results by emphasizing the positive.

Use the Taba and Elkins unit on "Aspirations" as a model for assisting students to understand such concepts as why people strive for goals and also to learn what sorts of jobs are available and what is involved in getting a job.

If you can think of other ways to make disadvantaged students feel successful in school work and develop a realistic level of aspiration, note them in the space below:

_____

_____

_____

4. *Be alert to the damaging impact of excessive competition.*

Most people enjoy competition only when they have a reasonable chance to come out on top. When a disadvantaged child is forced to compete in academic work against those who come from richer backgrounds, he has little chance to win. It is especially important, then, to hold down competition between students from varying backgrounds. When students are grouped either unintentionally or as a consequence of school boundary lines, and all have approximately the same background, the use of games and light-hearted competition might help to arouse interest. But in other situations, it is probably wise to avoid competition as much as possible.

Examples:

Both Herndon and Daniels made extensive use of games in their classrooms. Herndon used Scrabble and Spin-the-Pointer (described on page 131 of *The Way It Spozed to Be*), and Daniels set aside every Friday as Games Day and also had three special Games Days during the year. In order of preference, the ten best classroom games for these days were:

1. Checkers
2. Playing cards
3. Monopoly
4. The Game of Life
5. The Newlywed Game
6. Go to the Head of the Class
7. Ker-Plunk
8. Tip-it
9. Jigsaw puzzles
10. Spill and Spell

Daniels also describes these competitive techniques:

The Reading Progress Board was one of the external motivational devices that I used to encourage the children's reading. One wall of the room was covered with dark Portuguese cork. Each student had his name affixed along the bottom, with a colored map-flag pinned over it. As his group finished a book and passed the test, his flag advanced two of the twelve total spaces on the board. If he reached the top by the end of the school year, he was appropriately rewarded—a giant Sugar Daddy candy sucker.

Another incentive that was very effective was the "Group of the Week." The best group each week (a subjective decision, as are most decisions) had its picture taken in full color. The photograph was posted on the wall, and each child got a Hershey bar. A well-read classroom marches on its stomach! (1971, pp. 60–61)

5. *For students who need it, encourage the development of a desire to achieve.*

Most disadvantaged students are likely to need such encouragement. Consider some of the characteristics listed at the beginning of this chapter: lack of an educational tradition in the home, anti-intellectualism and discontent with schools, antagonism toward schools and teachers, vocational rather than academic orientation, inadequate motivation to achieve remote educational goals.

The middle-class child, typically, comes from a home in which doing well in school is stressed in a variety of ways, and he enters school eager to learn. This eagerness may be snuffed out in part, but the ultimate goal of attending college is almost a certainty and serves as a long-term motivator. The slum child typically enters school with negative or at least neutral feelings about learning and with little hope that he will ever attend college. Therefore, he is not likely to see much reason to strive for high grades. Consequently, it may be necessary to attempt to encourage the development of a desire to achieve in almost all disadvantaged pupils. Techniques described in the preceding chapter can be used for this purpose, but additional attention might be paid to providing school know-how and sophistication and in making learning seem worthwhile.

Examples:

Use the achievement training techniques developed by Kolb (based on the work of McClelland and Atkinson): encourage students to emulate high achievers by taking responsibility for attempting work, being willing to shoot for high goals, and being eager to receive detailed knowledge of results.

Promoting the desire and skills to learn

Stress the importance of doing well on exams, give practice in taking exams, supply hints on how to allow for different types of questions, for example, if there is no penalty for guessing, answer all the questions.

Use the Checklist for Student Self-Ratings of Prosocial Behaviors (Fig. 9-3, p. 440) to assist students to improve their study skills.

Emphasize that learning *does* pay off. Invite former students who have gone on to college and secured good jobs to speak to the class and emphasize the importance of doing well in school.

Exude confidence in the ability of your students to learn, and guard against low expectations and the impact of the self-fulfilling prophecy.

The Philadelphia Motivation Program

In *Got No Time to Fool Around*, Rebecca Segal describes the *Motivation Program* of the Philadelphia public schools, which is similar in many respects to New York's Higher Horizons program. The credo of the program is described this way: "The "M" program is composed of four fundamental parts of a coherent program designed to enrich, broaden, and motivate . . . selected students. These are curricular enrichment, parent and community involvement, cultural enrichment, and tutoring" (1972, p. 47).

The program is put into effect by selecting students who impress teachers as showing promise but who lack motivation and identifying them as "M" students. They participate in an induction ceremony and receive pins that identify them as participants. Teachers—and special counselors in the "Motivation Office"—do everything possible to build up the self-concept of "M" students, arrange for tutorial assistance, organize field trips to colleges, provide tickets for plays and concerts, and give assistance for gaining admission to college and winning scholarships.

In order to stay in the program, the students must take extra classes in English and Math, earn at least a "B" average, and do outside reading. In addition, parents are urged to attend group discussions on ways to help their children do well in school. To demonstrate the values of making an effort to do well in school, the achievements of "M" graduates are reported, and students who are accepted at college and those who receive scholarships are given special recognition.

Like New York's Higher Horizons, features of the Philadelphia program require school-wide cooperation, but any teacher can put into practice what is considered to be a key to its success—taking a personal interest in students.

If you can think of other ways to encourage the development of a desire to achieve, including ideas derived from the techniques mentioned in the preceding chapter, note them in the space below.

---

6. *Take advantage of natural interests, try to create new ones, and encourage learning for its own sake.*

Until recently, a major problem of educating disadvantaged pupils was that almost all school materials were developed to appeal to the interests of a hypothetical middle-class child. Fortunately, more attention is now paid to developing instructional materials that are relevant to the experiences of the disadvantaged. ("Sesame Street" is an excellent example of this.) However, some

The Parkway Program in Philadelphia, a high school started in 1969, has no school building and no grades, but instead uses the resources of the urban community. Students and teachers, who must volunteer for the program, devise their own curriculum. Here, a Parkway student gives a chemistry demonstration to elementary school children.

of the characteristics of disadvantaged learners need to be taken into account in providing experiences that will be compatible with their "natural" tendencies toward learning. These factors include limited language skills, interest in the practical as opposed to the abstract, and preference for physical rather than verbal learning. To allow for these tendencies, emphasize language and physical experience, try to base abstractions on concrete experience, and take advantage of experiences that students bring up themselves.

Examples:

Use variations of the Ashton-Warner technique by using words and ideas requested by your students as the basis for lessons, the development of student-created materials, and student interaction.

Use the Kohl approach of building units on comments made in class.

Follow the Taba and Elkins procedure of starting off a unit with a concrete, physical activity; have students trace their hands.

Make reading functional, as described by Ronald Henderson of the Tucson program.

Get into the habit of verbalizing extensively and try to get your students to respond.

Use psychodrama. Have students act out situations. (For a description of this technique, see page 75 of *How 2 Gerbils . . .*)

Use role-playing. For example, instead of having students read about the Constitutional Convention, have them act it out.

Use the classroom courtroom described on page 142 of *Up the Down Staircase* as a guide for setting up similar activities.

Use the Weikart technique (based on Piaget's theory) of having younger students learn the concept of boat by first getting into a full-sized boat (or facsimile), then into a stylized boat, and eventually thinking of objects like ashtrays as boats.

In language class, have students write autobiographies or themes on "My Block" and the like.

In math class, hand out mail order catalogs, give each of the students a hypothetical sum of money, and have them fill out an order including shipping and sales tax charges.

Teach problem-solving by using Daniels's technique of giving students bus tokens, dropping them off at various points around town, and giving a prize to the one who gets to City Hall first.

Be prepared for more than the usual amount of "What do we have to learn this stuff for, anyway?" and try to make "impractical" subjects such as literature appealing by encouraging students to write and illustrate their own books and experience the values of such activities directly.

If you can think of other ways to take into account the practical, physical, concrete orientation of disadvantaged students, note them in the space below.

_____

_____

_____

_____

7. Provide encouragement and incentives for learning that is essential but not intrinsically appealing.

Under ideal circumstances, it makes sense to try to build learning experiences to assist students to eventually reach the kinds of goals described by Voeks. As pointed out at the end of the preceding chapter, in order to achieve many of these goals, it is usually necessary to take into account the hierarchical nature of learning as exemplified by Gagné's conditions of learning and to provide a foundation in the form of mastery of verbal associations, concepts, and principles. Because such basic learning has a delayed payoff and is not always intrinsically appealing, you are urged to provide encouragement and incentives to give your students a boost. Implicit in this suggestion is the assumption that a carefully arranged curriculum can be devised to assist students to become well-educated persons and that it is important to be conscientious about providing necessary background information. When dealing with the disadvantaged (and, often, the advantaged), concern about arranging instruction in a hierarchical form may develop into a compulsion to "cover" subject matter. Some teachers become so obsessed with the idea that students must pass tests on certain material that is considered basic or vital, they fail to recognize that such learning may be pointless at best and destructive at worst. It may be destructive because not enough allowance can be made for students who have not mastered the most basic material, and the further they go in school, the further behind they get. As a result, rigidly adhering to an ideal curriculum dooms a large proportion of the class to confrontation with material they cannot understand, which in turn produces failure. James Herndon describes this situation in typically incisive fashion.

> Whatever class, age group, grade, section it is, in a public school, the subject matter is carefully arranged so that some of the kids will already know it before they get there. Then, for a little while in the primary grades, the school will try to teach those who didn't know it already. But it doesn't really work. It doesn't work because the winners keep intruding, raising their hands in advance of the question, or because while the teacher works with the losers on what the winners already know the winners are free to read or draw or talk to one another and therefore learn other stuff and when the loser gets into the second grade, having learned what the school demanded that he knew before he entered the first grade, the second grade will have assessed what the winners know and the losers don't and produce that as the subject matter for the year. Later on, of course, the school will refuse to teach the losers at all. *In all public schools in the United States* the percentage of kids who cannot really read the social studies textbook or the science textbook or the directions in the New Math book or the explanations in the transformational grammar book is extraordinarily high. Half the kids. The school tells everyone that reading is the key to success in school, and no doubt it is, a certain kind of reading anyway. Does the school then spend time and effort teaching those kids who can't read the texts how to read the texts? . . . Well of

course the school says it ain't got money for all them remedial reading teachers, otherwise it would love to teach everyone to read. But it does have money enough for a million social studies teachers to teach Egypt to groups of kids, a small percentage of whom already know everything about it, a larger percentage of whom know enough to copy the encyclopedia, the text, or other kids' homework, and another large percentage of whom can't do anything but sit there, get in trouble, provide jobs for counselors and disciplinary vice-principals and consultants and psychologists (all of whom get paid to deal with problems the school causes every day) and become an unending supply of failure for the school. (1971, pp. 94–96)

Herndon and Daniels and other teachers of the disadvantaged have correctly analyzed this situation, hence they concentrate on teaching reading. Kozol goes a step further. He argues that for the disadvantaged, being a "well educated person" means being able to "wage guerilla warfare with credentials" (1972, p. 38). He agrees with Lewis in stressing that the best thing the schools can do for slum children is to equip them with skills to compete in a middle-class white world. If this argument is endorsed, the kind of learning most essential to disadvantaged students would seem to be that which would equip them to get satisfactory grades, pass tests, and meet requirements. Although it will obviously be necessary to master some subject matter in order to do this, the fundamental skills center around reading, study habits, and test-taking skills—plus a feeling of self-confidence and the conviction that it is possible to achieve.

The Coleman Report and subsequent studies indicate that current educational programs for the disadvantaged are insufficient to overcome the impact of the hidden curriculum of the environment. In theory, changing the environment is the most logical way to solve this problem. Considering current attitudes toward socialism, busing, and integration, this solution does not appear to be realistic. Consequently, the only hope is to try to provide disadvantaged children with the kind of education most likely to increase their chances of helping themselves.

The kind of learning that is essential for the disadvantaged, therefore, is quite different from that for the student who has benefited from an enriched environment. It is unlikely that any kind of public school education will ever bring about complete equality of educational opportunity, but if you concentrate on assisting the disadvantaged to develop skills that will help them beat the educational system, they will at least have a better chance than if they were left to struggle by themselves.

Summary

In this chapter you have been acquainted with observations on the nature and extent of inequality of opportunity in American education, the characteristics of the disadvantaged, descriptions of programmed and discovery approaches to teaching the disadvantaged, and suggestions for teaching the disadvantaged.

Suggestions for Further Reading, Writing, Thinking, and Discussion

10-1 *Sampling Sections of the Riot Commission Report*

The *Report of the National Advisory Commission on Civil Disorders* exhaustively analyzes the causes of ferment in American society. It is organized around three questions: What happened? Why did it happen? What can be done? As a future teacher, you will probably find many sections of the Riot Commission Report interesting. Since the complete document is over seven hundred pages long, you may wish to read only sections of it. In that case, look at Chapter 8, "Conditions of Life in the Racial Ghetto," or the section on education in Chapter 17, "Recommendations for National Action." If you read either of these sections, or others of your own choice, summarize the points made and add comments of your own.

10-2 *Analyzing Interpretations of "Equality of Educational Opportunity"*

The Riot Commission Report presents a general analysis of the education of the disadvantaged. A more specific evaluation of problems of inequalities in education is offered in *Equality of Educational Opportunity* (the Coleman Report). The report itself is extremely detailed and lengthy, but you will find a brief analysis of Coleman's major conclusions, together with a review of criticisms made by others, in an article by Christopher Jencks, "A Reappraisal of the Most Controversial Educational Document of Our Time," which appeared in the *New York Times Magazine* of August 10, 1969, or in an article by Catherine Caldwell titled "Social Science as Ammunition," which appeared in the September 1970 issue of *Psychology Today*. More comprehensive analyses are to be found in *On Equality of Educational Opportunity* (1972), edited by Frederick Mosteller and Daniel P. Moynihan, which consists of fourteen articles by psychologists, sociologists, and statisticians. In addition, Christopher Jencks offers a book-length interpretation of the Coleman Report—plus research of his own—in *Inequality: A Reassessment of the Effect of Family and Schooling in America* (1972). If you read any of these analyses of the nature and impact of inequality in American education, summarize the main points and note your own reactions. (You might also be on the alert for critiques and analyses of the Jencks book. It seems likely to arouse considerable controversy.) The significance and ramifications of busing are discussed in *Busing: A Moral Issue* (1972) by Howard Ozmon and Sam Craver.

10-3 *Sorting Out Your Thoughts on Ability Grouping*

The Coleman Report suggested that placing disadvantaged children in the same class might produce a form of reciprocal fatalism. At present there is considerable controversy over desegregation in American schools. Attempts to integrate students of disadvantaged backgrounds into middle-class schools are often blocked or sidestepped in one way or another. Some educators argue that it is desirable to group students on the basis of ability. Advocates of this position might not be upset by segregation because such a policy leads to a form of ability grouping. Other educators, impressed by the Coleman Report, feel that any educational arrangement that separates students from rich and poor environments is undesirable since it perpetuates the tendency for the fortunate child to be given extra opportunities and for the unfortunate child to remain at a disadvantage. Those who favor ability grouping point out that merely placing a disadvantaged child in a room with middle-class pupils is not always beneficial; the student from a poor environment may be intimidated or humiliated by the ease and speed of learning demonstrated by his luckier classmates.

How the educational handicaps of the disadvantaged can be overcome is perhaps the most important problem of contemporary American education. Examine the issues and try to come up with your own solution. Perhaps you could describe an overall policy you would recommend and then list some specific interim measures to be used until a general solution is found.

10-4 *Recording Your Reactions to Integrated Education*

Attempts to "integrate" higher education are being made on many college campuses. Programs and scholarships provide minority-group students with increased opportunities to get a college education since a college degree is recognized as being almost a necessity for many types of jobs. When these programs were in the planning stage, it was hoped that interaction between students from different backgrounds would lead to the lowering of barriers between ethnic groups. This hope has seldom been realized because the members of some minority groups have tended to keep to themselves. In the very process of seeking identity, they have caused a polarizing rather than an integrative reaction. If you have had any personal experience with such a situation, record your reactions. Can you think of any techniques or approaches which might permit minority group students to maintain a sense of identity but also become "integrated" at the same time? In the absence of some form of interaction, how will minority groups ever become participating members of society at large? What are the advantages and disadvantages of reducing distinctions between different groups of Americans? If you have not been directly involved with this situation, but find the question interesting, you might read "The Road to the Top Is Through Higher Education—Not Black Studies" by Arthur Lewis, in the May 11, 1969, issue of the *New York Times Magazine*. Summarize the points made by Lewis and note your reactions.

10-5 *Reading a Personal Account of Life in Ghetto Schools*

The formal reports noted in exercises 10-1 and 10-2 cover the educational problems of disadvantaged children in a comprehensive way. Within the last few years, several accounts of the experiences of individual teachers in ghetto schools have been published. Edward R. Braithwaite described what it was like to teach in a London slum in *To Sir, with Love* (1959). Bel Kaufman's *Up the Down Staircase* (1964), a fictional narration of life in a New York City high school, is probably the most widely read exposition of life in a big-city school. At about the time *Up the Down Staircase* was establishing itself on the best-seller lists, three young men were either starting or finishing descriptions of their experiences in ghetto schools. Jonathan Kozol accepted a position as a substitute teacher in a Boston elementary school. He held the position for about six months before he was dismissed, at which time he expanded the notes he had taken into *Death at an Early Age* (1967). Herbert Kohl told what it was like to be a teacher in a Harlem sixth grade in *36 Children* (1967), and James Herndon commented on academic life in an Oakland junior high school in *The Way It Spozed to Be* (1968) and described further experiences with teaching in a different junior high in *How to Survive in Your Native Land* (1971). At the same time Herndon was finishing his second book, Stephen Daniels described his experiences in a Philadelphia junior high school in *How 2 Gerbils, 20 Goldfish, 200 Games, 2,000 Books and I Taught Them How to Read* (1971), and Pat Conroy gave an account of what it was like to teach in a two-room school house on Yamacraw Island off the coast of South Carolina in *The Water Is Wide* (1972). Any of these books will give you awareness of what it is like to teach disadvantaged students. If you read one of these accounts—or another you discover on your own—comment on points which impress you the most.

10-6 *Reading Accounts of Teaching the Disadvantaged to Pick up Teaching Techniques*

The books noted in the preceding exercise might be read not only for a general impression of what it is like to teach the disadvantaged but also to gain ideas for teaching techniques. If you want to read them for this purpose, you might browse until you find a section describing teaching techniques, or sample sections beginning at the pages indicated in the following books:

To Sir with Love, pp. 65, 85, 98.

Up the Down Staircase, pp. 63, 114, 129, 139, 142, 191, 199.

36 Children, pp. 27, 34, 44, 61, 64, 114, 129, 137, 176.

The Way It Spozed to Be, pp. 130, 139, 144.

How to Survive in Your Native Land, pp. 24, 44, 145, 155.

How 2 Gerbils, etc., pp. 39, 48, 57, 66, 71, 73, 91, 94, 98, 112, 124, 132, 150.

10-7 *Examining Descriptions of Approaches to Teaching the Disadvantaged*

In addition to reading the personal accounts noted in the preceding exercise, you might examine books devoted to descriptions of teaching techniques or books of readings made up of collections of articles on various aspects of the education of the disadvantaged. Five books of the first type are: *The Culturally Deprived Child* (1962) by Frank Riessman, *Teaching Strategies for the Culturally Disadvantaged* (1966) by Hilda Taba and Deborah Elkins, *The Disadvantaged: Challenge to Education* (1968) by Mario D. Fantini and Gerald Weinstein, *A Handbook for Teaching in the Ghetto School* (1968) by Sidney Trubowitz, and *Experiments in Primary Education: Aspects of Project Follow-Through* (1970) by Eleanor E. Maccoby and Miriam Zellner. Among the more carefully edited books of readings are *The Disadvantaged Learner* (1966) edited by Staten W. Webster, *Education of the Disadvantaged* (1967) edited by A. Harry Passow, Miriam Goldberg, and Abraham J. Tannenbaum, and *Reaching the Disadvantaged Learner* (1970) edited by A. Harry Passow.

10-7 *Speculating about the Impact of "Skillful" Child Rearing*

As reports of the "fade" reaction of Head Start programs have accumulated, some theorists have concluded that the failure of preschool experiences to have a permanent impact is due to too little, too late. It has been suggested that an intensive program of stimulation should start in infancy. Another proposal is that the child-rearing practices of different mothers should be observed, the performance of their children should be noted, and the techniques used by mothers who "produced" bright children should then be practiced by *all* mothers. Advocates of this approach predict that it will, in effect, lead to the development of uniformly bright children. Record your reactions. Do you favor the idea? Do you think it will work? Do you see any possible dangers or disadvantages? If you should read an analysis of the child-rearing techniques used by the parents of some highly successful person, would you feel confident about using the same techniques with your children? (If you would like to read a complete account of techniques being advocated, look for *Experience and Environment: Major Influences on the Development of the Young Child* (1973) by Burton L. White and Jean Carew Watts.)

10-8 *Learning About Child Rearing in a Kibbutz*

Many disadvantaged children come from shattered family situations where either or both parents may be frequently or permanently absent. At one time, child psychologists felt that consistent care from a particular caretaker was essential for normal development, but reports of the success of communal child-rearing practices in Israel have led to a revision of this hypothesis. In an Israeli kibbutz, children are reared in a communal atmosphere and respond favorably. In *The Children of the Dream* (1969) Bruno Bettelheim, an eminent psychiatrist, describes life in a kibbutz and suggests—among other things—that this approach to child rearing would be highly beneficial to disadvantaged children from broken homes. Other descriptions of kibbutz life are provided by Melford E. Spiro in *Kibbutz: Venture in Utopia* (1963) and *Children of the Kibbutz* (1965). If you would like to learn more about communal child rearing, particularly as a means for reducing the impact of family disintegration on disadvantaged children, you might read one of these books and note your reactions.

10-9 *Reading About Migrant Children, Poverty, and Desegregation as Described by Robert Coles*

Robert Coles, a psychiatrist, was strongly influenced by Erik H. Erikson. He has spent ten years studying the forces that shape the lives of children, particularly those of migrant workers in the rural South. He offers his interpretations in a trilogy—*Children of Crisis: A Study of Courage and Fear* (1967), *Children of Crisis: Migrants, Mountaineers, and Sharecroppers* (1972), and *Children of Crisis: The South Goes North* (1972)—and also in *Still Hungry in America* (1969) and *Uprooted Children: The Early Life of Migrant Farm Workers* (1970). He analyzes the impact of desegregation in *The Desegregation of Southern Schools: A Psychiatric Study* (1963). Coles also offers his observations on socially handicapped children in *Dead End School* (1968) and on children of the middle class in *The Middle American: Proud and Uncertain* (1971), written in collaboration with Jon Erikson.

10-10 *Reading about Minority Group Life in America*

Listed below are books you might read to become acquainted with perceptions of those who have experienced minority group existence in America. If you read one of these books you might note points you feel are of significance to teachers.

Blacks: *Black Boy* (1945) by A. Richard Wright, *Invisible Man* (1947) by Ralph Ellison, *Notes of a Native Son* (1953) by James Baldwin, *Manchild in the Promised Land* (1965) by Claude Brown, *Soul on Ice* (1968) by Eldridge Cleaver, *Black Rage* (1968) by William Grier and Price Cobbs, *Black Self-Concept* (1972) by James A. Banks and Jean D. Grambs, *Black Psychology* (1972) edited by Reginald Jones.

American Indians: *Custer Died for Your Sins* (1969) by Vine Deloria, Jr., *Bury My Heart at Wounded Knee: An Indian History of the American West* (1971) by Dee Brown.

Mexican-Americans: *Chicano* (1970) by Richard Vasquez, *Barrio Boy* (1971) by Ernesto Galarza, *Chicanos: Our Background and Our Pride* (1972) by Nephtali DeLeen, *I Am Joaquin* (1973) by Rodolfo Gonzalez.

Puerto Ricans: *Growing Up Puerto Rican* (1972) by Paulette Cooper.

10-11 *Becoming Acquainted with the Montessori Method*

If you would like to learn more about the Montessori Method, you have a wide choice of books to examine. Montessori's own descriptions of her approach can be found in *The Montessori Method* (1912, paperback edition 1964), *Dr. Montessori's Own Handbook* (1914, paperback edition 1965), and *Spontaneous Activity in Education* (1917, paperback edition 1965). If you read any of these books, you may find that you are intrigued as much by the style of writing as by the descriptions of how Montessori developed her approach to preschool education. For descriptions by others, with suggestions for adapting the original techniques for use in contemporary America, consult *The Montessori Revolution* (1962, paperback edition 1966) by E. M. Standing, *Learning How to Learn: An American Approach to Montessori* (1962) by Nancy M. Rambusch, and *Montessori: A Modern Approach* (1972) by Paula Lillard. If you sample any of these descriptions of the Montessori Method, you might note techniques that strike you as worth trying in your own classroom.

PART

5

EVALUATION

11 EVALUATING CLASSROOM LEARNING

KEY POINTS

Trends
Comparative grading develops as result of competition in a meritocracy, concern about selection through "grading on the curve"
Tradition of comparative grading being questioned as disadvantages are recognized

Classifications
Taxonomy of educational objectives

Criteria
Test evaluation criteria: standard situation, permanent record of behavior, and comparison with standard answers

Experiments
Cheating by almost all children when stakes sufficiently high (Hartshorne and May)

Concepts
Competitive system leads to opportunities for gifted, causes problems for less able (Gardner)
Need to deal with individual differences wisely and humanely (Gardner)
Halo effect, cognitive dissonance, projection, unconscious likes and dislikes
Importance of an adequate sample

Methodology
Writing and scoring classroom exams
Making out report cards
Drawing and interpreting frequency distributions
Computing and interpreting mean and median
Using a mastery learning approach

CHAPTER CONTENTS

THE PRECEDING TWO CHAPTERS STRESSED THAT FOR STUDENTS TO BE eager to learn, their needs for safety, belonging, and esteem should be satisfied, and they should be encouraged to make growth choices rather than safety choices. In many respects, the single most effective approach in attempting to achieve these purposes is to try to arrange instruction so that almost all students will experience some degree of success. The sense of success contributes to the development of a realistic level of aspiration, encourages the emergence of a need for achievement, and sets the stage for achievement later in life. Any approach to grading that causes many students to feel they have failed appears illogical and destructive when it is analyzed in reference to these points.

In most schools in America, students are graded by being compared to each other, a system that can cause many students to feel unsuccessful. As background for devising ways to improve the system of educational evaluation, the sources of the tradition of comparative grading should be considered.

Origins of Comparative Grading

Most early societies were based on the principle of hereditary privilege. Education was provided only for children from families of wealth and power since it was assumed that the children of working class parents needed only enough training to permit them to engage in the same menial activities as their parents. As meritocratic societies came into being, compulsory education laws were passed to insure that all children would be exposed to the potential benefits of schooling. It was assumed that this would give all children, regardless of background, the chance to earn a place in the world through their own efforts. However, in order to provide all with an opportunity to succeed, open competition seemed essential. This led to the development of the traditional public school, in which a survival-of-the-fittest policy prevails. In order to find out who the most deserving students were, it seemed essential to compare them, and so the A-to-F grading scale came into being. The basically competitive nature of America also played a part in the evolution of competitive grading. Business enterprises competed for the most capable individuals, and so pressures developed for the schools to train and identify the most promising scientists, technologists, industrialists, and businessmen. This led to a form of education that concentrated on selecting the most likely candidates and giving them the best schooling. For many years this seemed an ideal system; only recently was it recognized that disadvantages and inequities existed in a meritocratic approach.

Competition as source of comparative grading

A child who does well when he first begins school will qualify for classes and programs in junior and senior high that will gain him admission to a reputable college or university, which in turn will make him attractive to business corporations or open the doors to graduae school. An advanced degree from a prestige university then becomes a passport to jobs with high influence and remuneration. This makes a great deal of sense when considered from the point of view of the gifted students, or professors in prestigious universities, or personnel directors of large corporations but not from the viewpoint of the huge number of losers who are victimized by the system.

Testing in an elementary school (top), high school students taking an exam that will help determine their eligibility for college (middle), and adults taking a civil service exam (bottom).

Some theorists argue that a meritocracy can be sustained only by a stringent process of selection. In *The Rise of the Meritocracy*, the English sociologist Michael Young observes: "Educators realized full well [that] clever children had to be caught young if they were to achieve, as adults, the highest standards of which they were capable,[1] and with the growth in complexity of science and technology, only the highest standards were high enough. Scientists, whose best work is often done before they are 30, need from the earliest possible years to get an intensive education" (1959, p. 43).

In addition to emphasizing the need for early identification of the gifted, Young points out that when hereditary privilege was the basis for societies, the less competent aristocrat might graciously recognize the fact that he was often served by his betters (in the series of novels of P. G. Wodehouse, Bertie Wooster and all his aristocratic friends openly acknowledge the superiority of his valet, Jeeves); and the individual born into a working class family could always rationalize his lack of achievement by saying he never had a chance. But in a meritocracy, the successful man may become unsympathetic and elitist because he feels he is successful entirely as a result of his own achievements, and the unsuccessful man may have to admit to himself that he has been given the chance—and has failed. For reasons noted in discussing the Coleman Report, and in related studies, it is apparent that neither of these conclusions may be valid in many situations, even though the individuals involved may think so. The twentieth-century son of well-to-do, ambitious parents who attends superior public schools in an affluent neighborhood and qualifies for admission to an Ivy League college may have just as great an advantage over a slum child who attends a ghetto school as that which the son of an eighteenth-century duke had over the offspring of one of his scullery maids.

Can We Be Equal and Excellent Too?

John Gardner has pointed out other difficulties of a meritocratic approach in *Excellence*, subtitled *Can We Be Equal and Excellent Too?* He notes that societies of hereditary privilege were doomed by the industrial revolution, which made it essential that "the individual be free to bargain (and be bargained for) in the open market on the basis of his capacity to perform, without regard to other criteria of status" (1961, p. 4). He then notes:

> But release from hereditary stratification brought problems as well as opportunities for the individual. Sometimes it gave him only the freedom to be crushed by the new forces of industrial society. And while it offered him freedom to achieve, it placed a new burden of responsibility and pressure on him. Among the consequences were not only exhilaration but anxiety, not only self-discovery but fear....

[1] For a fascinating fictional account of what might happen if a clever child were "caught young" and assisted to achieve, read *The Child Buyer* by John Hersey.

In a society of hereditary privilege, an individual of humble position might not have been wholly happy with his lot, but he had never had reason to look forward to any other fate. Never having had prospects of betterment, he could hardly be disillusioned. He entertained no hopes, but neither was he nagged by ambition. When the new democracies removed the ceiling on expectations, nothing could have been more satisfying for those with the energy, ability and emotional balance to meet the challenge. But to the individual lacking in these qualities, the new system was fraught with danger. Lack of ability, lack of energy or lack of aggressiveness led to frustration and failure. Obsessive ambition led to emotional breakdown. Unrealistic ambitions led to bitter defeats.

Competitive system leads to dangers as well as opportunities

No system which issues an open invitation to every youngster to "shoot high" can avoid facing the fact that room at the top is limited. (1961, pp. 18–20)

Gardner observes, "The sorting out of individuals according to ability is very nearly the most delicate and difficult process our society has to face" (p. 71). Since it is so delicate and difficult, there is a temptation to overreact to the painfulness of the sorting-out process. This may lead to a different kind of problem. Gardner comments:

At times our desire to protect young people from invidious comparisons has produced serious confusion in educational objectives and a dangerous erosion of standards. Such consequences, whether rare or frequent, are a legitimate cause for concern. Because of the leveling influences which are inevitable in popular government, a democracy must, more than any other form of society, maintain what Ralph Barton Perry has called "an express insistence upon quality and distinction." When it does not do so, the consequences are all too familiar: the deterioration of standards, the debasement of taste, shoddy education, vulgar art, cheap politics and the tyranny of the lowest common denominator. (P. 73)

And he adds:

The traditional democratic invitation to each individual to achieve the best that is in him requires that we provide each youngster with the particular kind of education which will benefit *him*. That is the only sense in which equality of opportunity can mean anything. The good society is not one that ignores individual differences but one that deals with them wisely and humanely. (P. 75)

Need to deal with individual differences wisely and humanely

Gardner then suggests that the best way to achieve this goal is to "cultivate diversity in our higher educational system" (p. 83). But in addition to diversity, he argues that we should stress excellence in all kinds of learning, not just in ultraacademic programs:

We must never make the insolent and degrading assumption that young people unfitted for the most demanding fields of intellectual endeavor are incapable of rigorous attention to *some sort of standards*. It is an appalling error to assume—as some of our institutions seem to have assumed—that young men and women incapable of the highest standards of intellectual excellence are incapable of any standards whatsoever, and can properly be subjected to shoddy, slovenly and trashy educational fare. . . .

... We must learn to honor excellence (indeed to *demand* it) in every socially accepted human activity, however humble the activity, and to scorn shoddiness, however exalted the activity. (Pp. 85–86)

To achieve these goals, Gardner argues we must find ways to solve this problem:

How can we provide opportunities and rewards for individuals of every degree of ability so that individuals at every level will realize their full potentialities, perform at their best and harbor no resentment toward any other level? (P. 115)

Some of the ingredients of a solution proposed by Gardner are avoiding labels, providing multiple and repeated opportunities for students to learn, providing different kinds of instruction for students who differ in ability, and stressing a pluralistic approach to values and a philosophy of individual fulfillment. Open education, a value-added view of instruction, and learning for mastery are techniques that have been developed to put into effect the solution proposed by Gardner, but the tradition of comparative grading is so strongly entrenched that there is still resistance to these techniques.

The meritocratic nature of American society has had much to do with comparative grading, but there are other contributing causes that have resulted from trends in education and psychology.

The Impact of the Normal Curve and of Carnegie Units

Impact of "grading on the curve"

At the beginning of this century, precise measurement of large numbers of people together with the development of statistical procedures led to recognition of the normal (bell-shaped) curve. This created the assumption that not only physical characteristics but also intelligence and achievement were distributed "normally," so teachers were required or urged to evaluate students by grading "on the curve." This policy was also instituted because of concern about academic standards and the limited number of openings in colleges and universities. Before community colleges became prevalent, only a small proportion of high school graduates could be accepted by institutions of higher learning. It was assumed that only gentleman scholars or those in need of preprofessional education would go to college. Consequently, most high schools were required to rank their graduates in terms of grade-point averages to facilitate the process of selection. Furthermore, *Carnegie units*, which indicated the number of courses in a high school curriculum that colleges thought were the best preparation for liberal or professional education, became the justification for subjects taught at lower levels of schooling. Starting in kindergarten, school systems would not only begin to sort students, they would also arrange the curriculum primarily to prepare students for college—even though only the favored minority would ever seek admission. (Carnegie units still dominate the high school curriculum, despite the fact that the nature of higher education now includes much more than liberal and preprofessional education.) Although there are now almost enough colleges of all types to accommodate most high school graduates, the existence of a prestige hierarchy perpetuates emphasis on ranking the students.

Perhaps the most damaging aspect of a highly competitive grading approach is the impact it has on the self-concept of students and the expectations of teachers. When students first compete for grades, those who rank low when they are initially tested in the primary grades begin their school careers with a sense of failure that leads to feelings of inadequacy and perhaps rejection. Those in the top third of the class may develop a sense of initiative and industry, a positive self-concept, and have their need for esteem satisfied; but the lower two-thirds are likely to experience guilt and inferiority, react to low grades as negative appraisals, and gain no satisfaction of their needs for belonging and esteem. Furthermore, after an initial evaluation, the first-grade teacher—despite herself—is likely to be a victim of high or low expectations, which will be perpetuated when subsequent teachers test children to determine their relative position or examine previous report cards and test scores. Even if the teacher conscientiously avoids looking at previous reports, the experience of the students is likely to have made them function as good or poor learners. Thus the self-fulfilling prophecy mechanism will take effect. The same set of reactions will continue throughout a student's career.

Disadvantages of comparative grading

Even a student who has earned a grade-point average that places him in the top third of his class may have his confidence and eagerness to learn squelched if he ranks in the bottom third on the first exam in any course. If the final grade is based on only two or three exams, the usual (and understandable) reaction is to give up on the course and study just to get by. Or if considerable pressure exists to get high grades because of admission or job requirements, the student may feel driven to try to steal exam papers, use crib sheets, or buy a professionally written term paper.

Gradual awareness of these and other factors has led more and more people to question comparative grading practices. In place of highly competitive education, many schools are turning to individualized instruction (as in the open education approach), a value-added conception of education, and learning for mastery. Rather than presenting a standard curriculum in a standard way and dividing students into categories in terms of how well they respond to it, there is a trend toward finding ways to assist almost all students to meet a respectable level of achievement. Ignoring, humiliating, or punishing less successful students is giving way to an increasing awareness that they should be provided with extra assistance so that they can experience feelings of success and develop confidence in their ability to learn. It should be stressed, however, that this approach to evaluation does not eliminate tests and grades. Doing away with all kinds of evaluation has been suggested by many students and by some educators, but it does not seem appropriate for open education, value-added, or mastery approaches. To explain this conclusion, some of the problems that would ensue if tests and grades were eliminated will now be noted, and an analysis of the advantages and disadvantages of grading practices will be offered.

As undergraduates have been given more control over the way colleges and universities function, they have tended to make revision of the traditional grading system the top-priority item. In some colleges students have persuaded faculty to grade all courses pass-fail. Other colleges have eliminated the F grade, and the student in danger of failing is given the option of withdrawing from the course without penalty. Still other colleges have adopted the European technique—having comprehensive exams at the end of the senior year as opposed to end-of-semester exams for each course. But even at colleges that retain end-of-course evaluations, many students are eager to replace written examinations with informal "global" reactions. Or they argue that they would prefer a personal evaluation to a test score or a letter grade. Letters of recommendation or the professor's general reactions to a series of comprehensive papers are proposed as alternatives to the grade point average.

These innovations highlight some of the disagreeable and resented aspects of traditional tests and grades. Because they are less threatening, they have considerable appeal. However, these less rigorous forms of evaluation contain hidden disadvantages. If you are considering using some of these methods in your own classes, you may find the following analysis of formal evaluation procedures especially interesting (and perhaps provocative).

Even though you favor a free approach to evaluation, such a technique may not work below the college level. The major reason is that you probably will be dealing with groups of largely unselected students. It is possible to use a pass-fail or letter-of-recommendation approach in a small college with low teacher-pupil ratios, low class-loads and students who are carefully chosen from the top 10 or 15 percent of all high school graduates. (It is possible, but for reasons to be examined later, it may not be desirable.) It is next to impossible to do so at the below-college level, where the typical teacher-pupil ratio is high, teachers have heavy class-loads and the aim is to provide education for all students, not just for those who are most successful in academic subjects.

To illustrate some of the hidden problems involved, assume that you have strong negative feelings about formal exams and grades. You oppose them so much, in fact, that you plan to base grades on your own personal impressions of students. If you decide to be intuitive, you will be especially vulnerable to certain psychological mechanisms that come into play whenever human beings react to each other. Here is a summary of some of these mechanisms.

Mechanisms That Interfere with Objectivity

If you use only your personal impressions to determine whether a student gets an A or an F, the only way to find out what your pupils are thinking is to listen to their comments in class discussion or note how they react to your questions. How many pupils out of a class of thirty are going to be able to recite frequently? And if you ask questions, how will you pick out the pupil to give an answer? Suppose you do it by calling on students in alphabetical order.

The first pupil on your roll sheet gets the first question, and it's an easy one. What's more, it's early in the day, and you are in a good mood. Everyone can answer it, but you don't know this as you make a mental note that the top-of-the-alphabet student responded correctly. By the time you get to the last student on the list, you are tired and irritable and ask an extremely difficult question. He can't answer it. No one else in the class can either, but you aren't aware of this.

Or suppose the luckless tail-ender gives a whole series of brilliant answers during the first part of the grade period, but the day before grades are due he says something utterly stupid. All those favorable impressions might be wiped out by one unfortunate blooper that sticks in your mind.

Or suppose a particular pupil says something stupid the first day, which reminds you that one of the less charitable teachers in your school once labeled this individual the dumbest student she had encountered in twenty years. Your first impression is likely to be, "This one really *is* a lunkhead." No matter what that pupil says during the rest of the year, you may think of him as a lunkhead and interpret his remarks accordingly.

Another student, on the other hand, makes a good first impression. Everything she says seems to be a pearl of wisdom because she is attractive, neat, friendly, polite, and attentive, because her father is a surgeon, and because she just won an essay contest.

Compare this pupil to the son of the policeman who just gave you a ticket for going forty-five in a twenty-five-mile zone. And suppose the same boy is given to nose-picking, a habit you have always found obnoxious, and looks alarmingly like a rough kid who gave you a bloody nose when you were in the third grade.

These are just a few of the factors that will influence your judgments. Do you think you could still be fair in evaluating the students? Some teachers insist that they *can* allow for all such factors. Many of these influences are so subtle, however, that a person is not aware of them. You can't allow for something you are unconscious of.

Here is a description of specific mechanisms affecting the perceptions of different individuals when they react to each other.

The Halo Effect

There is a tendency for prior information, or one impression or characteristic, to influence all other impressions. In the examples just given, a positive halo was induced by a student's appearance and background, which perhaps was

516

associated with stereotypes. A negative halo was attached to a student because of a remark made by another teacher, his resemblance to a childhood nemesis, and a disagreeable habit.

Cognitive Dissonance

Cognitive dissonance

We like to think that our attitudes and beliefs form a consistent, logical pattern. If we are exposed to evidence that might lead to incongruities or inconsistencies in our perceptions, we make an effort to reduce this "dissonance," either by perceiving selectively or by supplying an explanation. Once a halo has been established, there will be a tendency to pick out things that fit under it and ignore those that don't. If one of your favorites says something dumb, you either forget it or excuse it. If a student you have come to think of as dull says something brilliant, you attribute it to luck or to help from someone else.

Projection

Projection

One is prone to interpret the behavior of others in terms of his own personality—to "project" his thoughts and feelings upon others. If a certain pupil strikes you as "my kind of kid," projection will aid him. On the other hand, if you associate the policeman's son with the traffic ticket, you may see him as an incorrigible cheater. Not wishing to acknowledge a weakness of your own character, you project it to a scapegoat. Projection may seem a bit mysterious, but in essence it is summed up by the familiar statement: "It takes one to know one." Most of us have a hard time knowing ourselves, but if we find that we are very much concerned about a certain trait in others, this may well be an unrecognized trait in our own personality.

Unconscious Likes and Dislikes

The "mysterious" quality of projection is related to a final point. One of Freud's major contributions to psychology was his revelation of the importance of the unconscious. As Freud pointed out, only a small fraction of our memories and experiences are within the scope of consciousness—that is, capable of being thought of at will. Many more of our experiences are in the realm of the unconscious; they persist as memories and may influence our behavior, but they cannot be examined or understood because we are not aware of them.

Unconscious likes and dislikes

All of us have certain likes and dislikes in regard to physical and personality traits. Some of these we think we understand: "I don't like kids with red hair and freckles because the bully who used to beat me up every other day when I was in the third grade had red hair and freckles." But many other preferences or aversions are based on memories we are not aware of. It is therefore impossible for anyone to be completely fair or unprejudiced in reacting to others. You may be able to handle *some* of your conscious prejudices, but the far more numerous unconscious influences are beyond your control.

No matter how hard you try to maintain objectivity, your reactions to your pupils will be swayed by the halo effect, cognitive dissonance, and projection. One reason psychologists urge using controlled techniques of evaluation is that they minimize the impact of these unsystematic influences. To illustrate, consider the following characteristics of formal tests.

Characteristics of Tests

Standard Situation

On most tests all students are required to answer the same questions. This eliminates the situation described earlier in which one student, through the luck of the draw, gets an easy question and a less fortunate student gets a difficult one.

Characteristics of tests that might be used as test evaluation criteria

Permanent Record of Behavior

Written exams mean answers recorded in permanent form. If you rely on intuitive reactions to class recitation, then projection, the halo effect, and cognitive dissonance can run wild. The earlier example of a pupil who says something stupid late in the report period that wipes out previous good impressions illustrates only one possible error. All impressions based on casual observation and recorded only in memory are susceptible to selective perception. Remember that memory is being exposed to the influence of the unconscious. Having a permanent answer to scrutinize doesn't guarantee avoidance of the influence of the psychological mechanisms just discussed, but it does let you go back over your evaluation several times if necessary in an effort to eliminate the influence of transitory moods and feelings. You can't do that with a recollection that was distorted and limited by the subjective factors to begin with and is vulnerable to further distortion by subsequent events.

Fixed Set of Criteria

When you ask all pupils to react to the same questions and you have their answers in permanent form, you can compare each answer to a fixed criterion. The test-maker prepares a key of the correct answers, which indicates how many points each part of an answer is worth. Then he compares each test to the key. If he takes care not to look at the name on the first page of the test, the influence of such factors as name, facial features, habits, and other prejudicial conditions or situations is eliminated. There are still potential contaminating factors—handwriting, grammar, sentence structure, etc.—but if

Do Some Reflecting on Teachers, Tests, and Subjectivity

To clarify your understanding of these points, reminisce a little. Do you recall incidents involving you or some of your friends in which the "subjectivity" of the teacher showed? How did it feel when you were on the receiving end of such discriminatory tactics?

As you think back over your years in school, which types of tests did you consider most fair? Which types struck you as most unfair? Did the fair tests possess the three qualities just described? If not, why *did* you feel favorably disposed toward them?

the grader makes an effort to remain aware of such factors, their influence can often be reduced to such an extent that they have no significant impact on the final score.

The purpose of this survey has been to convince you that formal testing procedures can yield fairer and more accurate evaluations than unsystematic observations. With this background, consider the following advantages of formal evaluation procedures. (They are related to topics discussed in the preceding six chapters.)

Potential Advantages of Formal Evaluation Procedures

1. Evaluation provides feedback, which often functions as reinforcement, which in turn is an essential part of learning. (Noted in discussion of learning in Chapter 5.)
2. Tests help guarantee that a student will master basic facts and skills en route to mastery of concepts and general abilities. (Noted in discussion of the teaching of facts, concepts, and skills in Chapter 6.)
3. In studying for exams, students usually learn material with reasonable thoroughness, which helps assure that material will be remembered. Furthermore, distortions and faulty generalizations may be cleared up by the wrong answers being corrected. (Noted in discussion of forgetting in Chapter 7.)
4. Exams require students to try out their ideas under rigorous circumstances that limit "fudging." In the absence of such control, many students might never really test their ideas (or their abilities) in a literal sense. (Noted in discussion of problem solving in Chapter 8.)
5. Tests may be the only way to get many pupils to learn many important things. Test scores function as specific goals. Most students need incentives

even to approach their full potential. Sometimes a student studying for an exam discovers a new interest. (Noted in discussion of goals in Chapter 9.)

6. Specific feedback may permit a student to compete against himself. (Noted in discussion of competition in Chapter 9.)

7. Under proper circumstances, performance on tests may provide a detailed analysis of the strengths and weaknesses of pupils. This information can be used in a variety of ways by teachers, counselors, and students themselves. (Noted in discussion of level of aspiration in Chapter 9 and in the discussion of teaching disadvantaged students in Chapter 10.) Evaluation also assists a teacher to improve her own performance. In the absence of feedback, it is practically impossible for a teacher to make systematic efforts to change things for the better, whereas the very process of writing and reading exams aids the organization and presentation of subject matter.

For these advantages of tests to work out in practice, evaluation must be carried out under the best possible conditions. The rest of this chapter discusses techniques you might use to create favorable circumstances.

Reconsider for a moment the *Taxonomy of Educational Objectives: Cognitive Domain*, first noted in the discussion of the teaching of facts and concepts in Chapter 6. The six major classes in the taxonomy are:

Knowledge—Can students recall information?
Comprehension—Can students explain ideas?
Application—Can students use ideas?
Analysis—Do students see relationships?
Synthesis—Can students combine ideas?
Evaluation—Can students make judgements?

These categories reflect evaluations of one kind or another, although the last class is most directly concerned with them. This is not surprising since the psychologists who developed the taxonomy were members of a committee of college and university examiners interested in improving assessment procedures. The evaluation emphasis of the authors is revealed by an important feature of the book—illustrative test items at the end of each section of the taxonomy (another argument in favor of your buying the book).

In Chapter 6 you were invited to use the taxonomy as a basis for developing specific goals for your classes. At this juncture you are asked to make it a basis for determining whether or not your goals have been reached. In considering these two ideas—goals and evidence that goals have been reached—you will find it instructive to again compare S-R associationism and cognitive-field theory. The S-R theorist, who favors programmed learning, starts out by describing the terminal behavior he wants to produce. He writes his program to lead the student to this very specific goal (e.g., knowing how to spell *manufacture*, understanding how a flashlight works). All is simple and straightforward. Things are not nearly so precise for the advocate of the discovery approach. The goals

Taxonomy of educational objectives as a basis for evaluation

of discovery units are often difficult to pin down (e.g., understanding man). Since the goals are vague in many cases, it may be next to impossible to determine whether or not they have been achieved.

If you have favored the discovery approach over programmed learning up to this point, take a moment to analyze the values of more structured learning experiences in relation to the potential advantages of evaluation listed above. Generally speaking, a programmed approach is more likely to make the most of those advantages than a less structured learning situation. Feedback is much more frequent and systematic in a programmed approach; the mastery of a sequence of steps leading to specified terminal behavior is almost guaranteed; the use of a large number of questions provides a continuous series of goals; and the very explicitness of the technique permits a systematic analysis of strengths and weaknesses. Unless discovery sessions are consistently successful, students may feel that they are not getting anywhere and therefore fail to experience reinforcement; the disorganized nature of many discovery sessions may actually work against the mastery of ideas in a logical and efficient sequence; the atmosphere may become so relaxed that few students will exert themselves; and since the desired learning often centers around elusive feelings and attitudes, it may be impossible to analyze strengths and weaknesses.

Disadvantages of Formal Evaluation Procedures

Although the potential advantages and the characteristics of tests just discussed should be kept in mind, so should the disadvantages of evaluation. If you share the views of many student critics of education, the whole business of evaluation is what bothers you most about schooling. Critics of evaluation procedures frequently stress the four points listed below:

1. Too much emphasis on grades limits creativity and individuality of expression. Consequently, grades may discourage rather than encourage learning that is personally relevant to the student.
2. Grades put too much pressure on the student. Learning should be an enjoyable experience; it is too often tension-filled and disagreeable. Students should not be forced to compete with each other to earn high grades.
3. Information learned for a test is only a means to an arbitrary end—a grade. Much of what has been learned will be forgotten as soon as the grade is achieved.
4. Teachers are too authoritative. Students are forced to spit back exactly what the book or professor says. This is not only degrading, it entails punishment if a student doesn't learn what he has been told to learn.

Theme: On Returning to School After Summer Vacation.

No one can deny the joys of a Summer vacation with its days of warmth and freedom.

It must be admitted, however, that the true joy lies in returning to our halls of learning.

Is not life itself a learning process? Do we not mature according to our learning? Do not each of us desire that he

YES, MA'AM? OH... WHY, THANK YOU..I'M GLAD YOU LIKED IT..

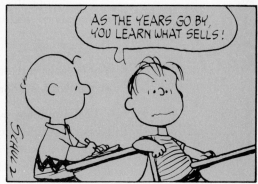

AS THE YEARS GO BY, YOU LEARN WHAT SELLS!

Goals to Strive For in Improving Evaluation

Upon examining the problems of eliminating grades entirely, the mechanisms that interfere with objectivity, the characteristics of tests, the potential advantages of formal evaluation procedures, and the disadvantages of evaluation, the following goals to strive for in improving evaluation emerge:

Do everything possible to arrange evaluation experiences so that they lead to feelings of success.

Minimize public comparisons and competition among students.

Be aware that learning ability is not the same in all pupils, but use this knowledge as the basis for a value-added approach to education; that is, give extra assistance to those who need it.

Do everything possible to make evaluations fair and objective—guard against the halo effect, cognitive dissonance, projection, and the impact of unconscious likes and dislikes.

Make the most of the characteristics of tests; provide a standard situation, obtain records of performance in permanent form, compare student performance to a fixed set of criteria.

Try to use tests so that they emphasize reinforcement of correct responses and not punish wrong responses.

Arrange evaluation so that it identifies omissions and weaknesses that need to be corrected before the student moves on to more advanced material.

Try to use evaluation as a motivating device by encouraging students to set and achieve respectable (and realistic) goals.

Stress the importance of establishing and meeting standards. As much as possible, use tests to promote self-competition and improvement.

Set up exams so that they provide feedback for you to use in improving instruction.

When appropriate, state specific instructional objectives, determine if they have been reached, and take steps to supply remedial instruction.

Do everything possible to reduce pressure and tension.

Try to make tests functional in the sense that students recognize or are made aware that the information requested is being learned for good reasons.

Before offering suggestions based on these goals, it should be noted that you probably will be required to assign grades, regardless of your personal feelings about them or the type of school in which you teach. Even if you secure a position in a free school, you may find that you will be asked to evaluate your pupils; if you teach in a public school, it is almost a certainty. In the elementary grades, you may be allowed to use designations such as "satisfactory" or "needs improvement," but at the secondary level, you are almost sure to have to assign grades on a scale from A to F. Grading appears to be an unavoidable feature of higher education in a meritocracy. Undergraduate and graduate degrees are necessary for many preferred jobs, and the number of applicants is usually greater than the available openings. Even if this is not the case, graduate education requires so much personal interaction between students and teachers, and therefore such an investment in time and money, most universities feel compelled to admit only graduate students who have demonstrated that they have the ability and perseverance to engage in sustained and high level learning. Consequently, some sort of evidence of previous success in schooling is essential in making judgments about the potential of candidates. Some experimental colleges that began by using general descriptions of performance and samples of work in lieu of grades have now switched to letter grades simply because their graduates had difficulty gaining admission to graduate school.

Although admission to colleges and graduate schools is a primary reason you are likely to be asked to assign grades, parents also exert pressure on schools to evaluate students. Naturally enough, parents want to know how their children are doing in school. Some of their reasons may be unfortunate (e.g., a desire to exert pressure for harder work if a son or daughter is not earning a high enough grade-point average, or to qualify for the college the parents have selected); but the fact remains, parent interest in grades is so high, many schools that have experimented with more global and personal evaluations have been forced to switch back to letter grades. Current interest in accountability probably has increased this tendency—grades not only provide information about students but also about the teacher. If you assign blanket B's, you may be accused of trying to cover up your inadequacies as a teacher.

In light of all this, as you speculate about how to improve evaluation, it would be prudent to assume that you will be required to evaluate your students in terms of some sort of scale, usually one that reflects three to five levels of performance.

Suggestions for Improving Testing

The suggestions on the following pages are intended to help you to control the influence of the mechanisms that lead to subjectivity, to take advantage of the favorable characteristics of tests, and to develop goals to strive for in improving evaluation.

1. As early as possible in a report period, decide when and how often to give tests.

   Writing and scoring classroom exams

   a. Consider distributing a course outline on the first day of class. (Remember the value of goals.)

    b. Announce tests and other assignments well in advance. Give a detailed description of what will be covered, how it will be evaluated, and how much it will count toward a final grade.

    c. Be considerate in scheduling.

2. Prepare a content outline of the materials to be covered on each exam, and take care to test on each part. (Doing this will enable you to get a good sample.)

    a. Take into account the kinds of terminal behavior you hope to achieve.

    b. Select the type or types of questions most likely to measure the desired terminal behavior accurately and efficiently.

3. Make up the questions aiming for clarity, objectivity, and ease of grading.

    a. Be certain the instructions and questions are clearly understood. (Doing this will help provide a standard situation.)

    b. Do your best to write questions that reduce subjectivity to a minimum and are relatively easy to score.

4. Make up and use a detailed key.

    a. Evaluate each answer by comparing it to the key.

    b. Be willing and able to defend the evaluations you make.

5. When grading is completed, if possible analyze each question in an effort to improve future exams.

    1. *As early as possible in a report period, decide when and how often to give tests.*

        a. *Consider distributing a course outline the first day of class. (Remember the value of goals.)*

    The response from your students will be more positive if, on the first day of class, you take the trouble to describe the organization of a given unit or course and provide information on all tests and assignments. (The reasons for doing this were discussed in the analysis of goals in Chapter 9.) Students will feel more comfortable if they have such an outline and will be more motivated to get to work. In addition, *you* will benefit from having a clear idea of what you hope to accomplish. You not only will be better organized but perhaps also will avoid the agony and inefficiency of making up exams on the spur of the moment.

        b. *Announce tests and other assignments well in advance. Give a detailed description of what will be covered, how it will be evaluated, and how much it will count toward a final grade.*

    If the test is to be used as a learning device as well as a means of evaluation, provide specific goals. If you are coy or absentminded, you may discourage careful study. Consider these two announcements and imagine how you might react to each: "We'll have an exam in a week or so; it, uh, will cover, uh, everything we've discussed so far" versus "We'll have an exam next Wednesday; it will be on the material covered in class starting with the topic of _____, and on pages 216 through 275. There will be five short-answer, essay questions and a fifteen-item matching question on that mimeographed outline I handed out." Which set of goals would look more attainable to you? Which would be more likely to motivate you to actually prepare for the exam? And suppose the first teacher then gave you a fifty-item true-false test on a twenty-five page section of the text (out of 400 covered so far), whereas the second gave you exactly the kind of test he said he would. How would you feel about each class the next time an exam was scheduled? What would be your attitude toward doing a conscientious job of studying?

For the most part, it seems preferable to announce tests well in advance. Pop quizzes tend to increase anxiety and tension and to force students to cram on isolated sections of a book on a day-by-day and catch-as-catch-can basis. Simple homework assignments or the equivalent will encourage more careful and consistent study than pop quizzes. When tests are announced, it is comforting to a student to know exactly what material he will be held responsible for, what kinds of questions will be asked, and how much a given test or assignment will count toward the final grade.

If you assign term papers or the equivalent, list your criteria for grading the papers (e.g., how much emphasis will be placed on style, spelling and punctuation, research, individuality of expression). In lab courses most students prefer a list of experiments or projects and some description of how they will be evaluated (e.g., ten experiments in chemistry, fifteen drawings in drafting, five paintings in art, judged according to posted criteria).

c. *Be considerate in scheduling.*

You may reduce antagonism toward tests if you are thoughtful about scheduling them—or about scheduling deadlines for other assignments. For one thing, it is a bit unfair to have exams on Monday. A student ought to be able to enjoy the weekend without having the threat of an exam to nag him. Another unreasonable tactic is to set the deadline for a term paper or project the day after a vacation.[2] It's human nature to put off some things until the last minute, and the guilt and uneasiness aroused by procrastination can spoil an entire holiday. In the upper grades you might also consider such occasions as a big game, a dance, or elections. And, if possible, allow students to choose between two or three dates you have selected for exams or deadlines so the majority can pick a day when they will not be loaded down with other assignments.

---

[2] In end-of-course evaluations at the college level, a significant number of students have reported that they appreciate prevacation deadlines—even though they may at first be irritated at the thought of getting to work early in a quarter or semester.

2. Prepare a content outline of the material to be covered on each exam and take care to test on each part. (Doing this will enable you to get a good sample.)

a. *Take into account the kinds of terminal behavior you hope to achieve.*

If you have drawn up lesson plans or otherwise described the terminal behavior you are aiming for, you already have such an outline. If you have not done this by the time the first test is due, it is almost essential to make amends at that point. The more precisely and completely goals are described at the beginning of a unit, the easier and more efficient evaluation (and teaching) will be. Using a clear outline will help assure an adequate sample of the most significant kinds of behavior.

When the time comes to assess the abilities of your pupils, it will be impossible to observe and evaluate all relevant behavior. You can't listen to more than a few pages of reading by each first-grader or ask history students to discuss on an exam more than a few pages of the hundred or so assigned. Because of the limitations imposed by large numbers of students and small amounts of time, your evaluation will have to be based on a *sample* of behavior—a three- or four-minute reading performance, questions covering perhaps one-tenth of the material assigned for an exam. It is therefore important to obtain a representative, accurate sample.

Importance of an adequate sample

Examples:

At the elementary level, perhaps the report card (if your school uses a detailed list of skills and abilities) can serve as the basis for determining what you will evaluate.

If a test is on material presented in class, outline what you have covered, and make up questions from each section.

If the test is on text material, ask questions from every part of the assigned reading, including at least one question from every major section of the book.

b. *Select the type or types of questions most likely to measure the desired terminal behavior accurately and efficiently.*

The cognitive and affective taxonomies of educational objectives will help you decide what kinds of questions to use. For example, mastery of knowledge can be measured most efficiently by objective tests. Application of skills and ideas can be measured best by performance tests. Objectives centering around analysis, synthesis, or evaluation are appropriate topics for essay exams. If you are systematic about listing goals, with or without use of the taxonomies, you will probably discover that no single kind of question is appropriate for all types of learning. This is often an advantage, since it provides a wider base for evaluation and is likely to reduce feelings of pressure somewhat.

Examples

On many elementary school report cards a pupil is not given an overall mark in reading but is graded on oral reading, reading speed, comprehension, etc.

In English, the grade might be based both on ability to write themes and on understanding of grammar and punctuation as measured by a formal test.

In a physical education class you might grade on knowledge of the rules of the game as well as performance.

In a biology class, a pupil might be graded on his ability to handle a microscope or do a dissection as well as on his knowledge of the text.

When the time comes to decide what kinds of questions to use and how many of each type, you may be tempted to settle for those that are easiest to write or that you personally preferred as a student. A better procedure is to look over the following points contrasting essay and objective tests. Most test items are variations of these two basic types of questions, and the listing below indicates the advantages and disadvantages of each type. The seven points are from *Essentials of Educational Measurement* by Robert L. Ebel. (For more detailed information you are urged to read the book, which is an exceptionally clear analysis of evaluation.) Note that Ebel seems to be writing here primarily about the comprehensive essay exam.

An essay test question requires the student to plan his own answer and to express it in his own words. An objective test item requires him to choose among several designated alternatives (1972, p. 123)

An essay test consists of relatively few, more general questions which call for rather extended answers. An objective test ordinarily consists of many rather specific questions requiring only brief answers. (P. 126)

Students spend most of their time in thinking and writing when taking an essay test. They spend most of their time reading and thinking when taking an objective test. (P. 130)

An essay examination is relatively easy to prepare but relatively tedious and difficult to score accurately. A good objective examination is relatively tedious and difficult to prepare but relatively easy to score accurately. (P. 131)

An essay examination affords much freedom for the student to express his individuality in the answer he gives, and much freedom for the scorer to be guided by his individual preferences in scoring the answer. An objective examination affords much freedom for the test constructor to express his knowledge and values but gives the student only the freedom to show, by the proportion of correct answers he gives, how much or how little he knows or can do. (P. 131)

An essay test permits, and occasionally encourages, bluffing. An objective test permits, and occasionally encourages, guessing. (P. 136)

The distribution of numerical scores obtained from an essay test can be controlled to a considerable degree by the grader; that from an objective test is determined almost entirely by the test. (P. 137)

If the term *essay exam* is expanded to include short-answer essay as well as comprehensive essay, the following seven points of comparison might be added to those noted by Ebel[3]:

1. In scoring an essay exam, the teacher gains insight into how and why a student gave a wrong answer. This provides specific and valuable information that can be used in a variety of ways. Scoring an objective test usually indicates only that a student selected a wrong answer; it does not reveal the line of thought that led to its choice (though a separate analysis may be made later).

2. An essay test is likely to be analyzed in some detail, particularly since it is rather easy to go over the test with the entire class in a short period of time. On a multiple-choice test, frequently only the score is reported to students because reviewing all the questions in class or individually would be prohibitively time-consuming. To do the job properly, you would need to explain—for each question—why the right alternative was correct and why the three or four wrong alternatives were incorrect.

3. The secretarial aspects of preparing essay tests are fairly undemanding, especially if the questions can be written on the board. The secretarial task of preparing objective tests, particularly multiple-choice tests, is often burdensome. If no secretarial help is available, it may take hours to type up stencils and run off, collate, and number the exams (numbering is necessary to check for missing copies).

4. Essay questions are usually easy to remember. This fact increases the possibility that students in one class will pass on the entire contents of a test to students in other classes. Consequently, it may be unfair to use exactly the same assortment of essay questions more than once, a circumstance that limits the chance of improving a test for future use and also makes comparisons between classes less precise. Objective (especially multiple-choice) questions are harder to memorize and pass on to other students, so an objective test can be used, improved, and used again, and the same test can be given to more than one class.

5. The teacher who uses essay tests spends the bulk of her exam time reading student answers. This is an undeniably tedious job but does provide insight into faulty generalizations, misinterpretations, and omissions that can lead to better instruction and student performance. The teacher who uses objective tests spends the bulk of her exam time writing questions—and perhaps doing secretarial chores. With multiple-choice tests the greatest amount of time is devoted to devising *wrong* answers. This activity is not likely to help instruction, although it may improve testing.

---

[3] Many of these points are derived from observations made by Banesh Hoffmann in *The Tyranny of Testing*, a searching analysis of the possible dangers of too much concern for "objectivity" in evaluation.

6. Since an essay exam is open to a certain amount of adjustment in the way answers are scored, the result may be higher student morale; but it should be recognized that reevaluations are highly vulnerable to the halo effect, cognitive dissonance, and projection—even though the teacher does her best to control for them. Answers to objective questions are usually nonnegotiable. This inflexibility may cause a certain amount of resentment, but it does eliminate subjectivity.

7. On essay tests it is possible to give a student credit for a "lukewarm" answer. Such adaptability tends to reduce anxiety and pressure and also permits the grader to give partial credit for reasoning. On objective tests some right answers may be chosen for completely illogical reasons, some wrong answers for logical, defensible, and ingenious reasons. These responses may occur with only a few questions, and the errors may not alter the total score significantly, but awareness of this aspect of objective testing will bother some students to the point of bitterness, especially if they are not given an opportunity to explain their answers.

(A technique for permitting students to explain why they selected certain answers will be noted later.)

A type of test question that compromises between multiple choice and essay is the short-answer item. It can be especially effective in assisting you to achieve many of the goals noted earlier. You provide students with a standard situation, obtain answers in permanent form, and can make up a detailed key to use in evaluating answers, but you also permit a degree of freedom for individual interpretation. In addition, short-answer questions require students to recall information and express it in their own words, which is a more demanding and realistic form of behavior than choosing among alternatives provided by someone else. Furthermore, you will get insight into the thinking that led to misinterpretations and will thus have information you can use to provide specific remedial instruction. This information will not only help the student, it will also help you improve your teaching and your testing.

Writing good test questions is a fine art, and you are likely to find that your first efforts will cause considerable confusion. Even veterans of twenty or thirty years of test-writing still find it difficult to anticipate aspects of a question that will be vague or misleading. Consequently, you will want to make it a habit to evaluate your tests. Many test specialists believe that the best way to do this is to select items that discriminate most effectively between high and low scores. Although the process of selecting items that discriminate and rejecting those that do not makes sense if the aim is to highlight differences in the test-taking abilities of students, it has limitations when it is examined from a pedagogical point of view—or from an operant conditioning position. The aim of a teacher should be to assist as many students as possible to learn as much as possible. In this sense, exams function not only as evaluation devices but also as programs. And programs should be written to maximize the proportion of correct answers. If there are too few questions that most students (particularly the less able ones) can answer, the students most in need of encouragement are reinforced the least. When exams are thought of as programs, items (frames) that assist almost all students to realize they understand the point should be retained, not eliminated.

In analyzing the effectiveness of the questions you write, you might use *clarity* as the primary criterion. If a question makes it possible for students to explain to you (and to themselves) that they understand an objective, retain it. If it causes confusion, either reject it or examine the errors and misinterpretations and rewrite it. This is not intended as a suggestion that you make questions artificially easy, just that you do everything possible to make them clear.

3. *Make up the questions, aiming for clarity, objectivity, and ease of grading.*

   a. *Be certain the instructions and questions are clearly understood. (Doing this will help provide a standard situation.)*

The first of the test characteristics mentioned previously was that all students are in the same (standard) situation. With essay tests this is the case only if all pupils interpret the questions in essentially the same way. To help guarantee such response, try to refine out all traces of ambiguity when you make up questions.

At first, in constructing tests you may tend to make questions rather vague, rationalizing that the brighter students will know what you want and that interpreting the question properly is a measure of their ability. This is not necessarily a valid argument. Some students may misinterpret a question and write an excellent "wrong" answer. Then you face a dilemma: Should you give credit for such an answer or give a zero because what you expected was not forthcoming? After a certain amount of pondering, punctuated by loud squeals of protest from outraged victims, you may become convinced that you are responsible for helping every student understand exactly what is called for. Otherwise the test becomes a guessing game. It reveals how shrewd a pupil is at figuring out what is wanted, not always how much he really knows about the subject matter. To avoid this pitfall, try to be complete and specific in writing questions. Even when you have done your best and congratulate yourself that you have removed every trace of ambiguity, probably some pupils *still* won't get what you are driving at. Therefore, you are urged to clarify exam questions at any time—even after the exam has started.

Some teachers categorically refuse to answer questions about a test that is in progress. There are arguments in favor of this policy if multiple-choice tests are being used, although even then many students appreciate occasional clarification. But with essay tests such a policy may reduce the likelihood of a standard situation and also increase tension. To ease things, urge students to come up and ask for clarification during the test, or circulate so that they can ask questions.

Skinner's Observations on Testing

In *The Technology of Teaching*, Skinner makes several criticisms of current testing procedures. For one thing, he says, when a pupil studies for a test, he does so primarily to avoid *not* knowing—he reads as a form of avoidance. Further, "Almost all educational measurement emphasizes accuracy" (1968, p. 176). But, says Skinner, "The most easily measured products of education are not necessarily the most valuable," and he goes on, "Very often the responses which are most readily accepted as signs of knowledge are precisely those which are least likely to form part of a successful repertoire" (p. 245). For example, a chemistry student may be asked to reproduce the periodic table on a test. This is simple to test and simple to evaluate, but how much does it indicate about the student's ability as a chemist? "A test score gives us little assurance that the student will make use of what he knows" (p. 246).

Skinner is especially critical of multiple-choice questions. He points out that they not only put a premium on accuracy but provide prompts in an undesirable way. Multiple-choice tests confront the student with complete answers. Thus they do not show whether the behavior involved in selecting an answer is strong enough to take place without prompts. If it is not strong enough, it will appear only when elicited by an appropriate question. Yet, "Answers to questions are a relatively rare form of behavior" (p. 245).

Although Skinner does not make the following point in a specific way, it is derived from his observations: Although multiple-choice tests are popular because they are easy to score, they confront the student with three or four times as many wrong answers as right answers; typically, he gets no feedback on specific questions (unless the instructor goes over every question in class or in private conferences, which is the exception rather than the rule). It might be argued, then, that the act of selecting an answer is perhaps the only reinforcement the student receives. If he chooses a wrong answer, he is reinforced for a wrong answer—especially if he thinks to himself as he blackens the appropriate column, "Ha! I *know* I got that one right."

You might even suggest that they write out a paragraph or two to show you the line of thought so that you can tell them whether they are on the right track.

It is sometimes argued that spelling out exactly what is wanted tips off the less perspicacious students and reduces the accuracy of the test. But how important is this point? The answer is the important thing, and it is almost invariably a more accurate reflection of the student's knowledge than his interpretation of the question. Furthermore, the student who is a bit tense during an exam tends to act like a drowning man grasping at a straw—if there is a familiar word or phrase in a question, he reacts to a minor point and madly starts writing an answer without reading the rest of the instructions. By going out of your way to clarify questions, you minimize indiscriminate responses. Such reactions indicate nervousness rather than ignorance, and you will come closer to finding out what the student knows if you prevent it.

b. *Do your best to write questions that reduce subjectivity to a minimum and are relatively easy to score.*

Multiple-choice and other questions have a clear advantage over essay exams in objectivity and ease of scoring. But even essay exams can be made objective and relatively easy to score by use of a detailed key—also by concealing the name on the paper as you are reading it.

4. *Make up and use a detailed key.*

One of the most valuable aspects of a test is that it permits comparison of the permanently recorded answers of all pupils according to a fixed set of criteria. Use of a complete key can do more to reduce subjective influences than anything else. Such a key can save you time and trouble, not only in grading papers but also in defending your evaluation of questions.

You will often detect misleading words or statements in a question when working out *your* answer to it. What's more, you may be able to clarify what you want and provide a standard format at the same time by the way you arrange a question on the page. Suppose you want students to consider the point under present discussion. If you simply say, "Discuss the importance of using a key," each pupil may take a slightly different approach in what he writes. You will have to read each answer very carefully and credit points as each major idea is discussed. This will take a great deal of time. In effect, it will be necessary to analyze the organization of the answer in order to grade the content. But if you ask first of all for a discussion of the use of a certain point as it relates to the general characteristics of tests, leave a blank space for the answer (indicating it will be worth five points, say), and do the same for the other subpoints, the standard organization and format will make grading quicker.

a. *Evaluate each answer by comparing it to the key.*

This suggestion points up the desirability of devising questions and arranging a format in such a way that grading will be easy. Whenever possible, indicate the exact number of points you have awarded to each answer. The more precise your designations, the more satisfied your students are likely to be and the more complete your knowledge of results.

b. *Be willing and able to defend the evaluations you make.*

You will probably get few complaints if you have a detailed key and explain to the class how each answer was graded when exams are returned. To a direct challenge about a specific answer to an essay question, your defense might be to show the complainer an answer that received full credit and invite him to compare it with his own. If he responds, "I *still* don't see why I didn't get full credit," about all you can say is, "Well, I didn't think you did a complete or clear job in your answer. Take a look at this answer and see if you think yours is as good." You will probably get a reluctant acceptance of the decision, but even if you don't, the attempt may reduce the likelihood of a permanent grudge leading perhaps to poor work the rest of the report period or year.

A major disadvantage of multiple-choice tests is that they provide so little detailed knowledge of results. And precise, specific knowledge of results is extremely important to efficient learning. It is next to impossible to go over a multiple-choice test in class; at least one student will have picked out each of the wrong alternatives and will want to explain why—while the other members of the class doze, or fume as they wait to give *their* explanations, or make out a list of right answers to pass on to someone in the other section. Going over a fifty-item test may take hours. It may even take hours with just one student, particularly if he is a divergent thinker or argumentative.

A partial solution to this problem is to let each student pick out three to five questions that he thought were graded wrong and explain to you in a five-minute individual conference why he selected his answer. (A variation is to allow students to explain on the test itself why they picked certain answers.) If his reasoning seems valid, you might give whole or partial credit for the answer. This policy may reduce the resentment and pressure that students associate with multiple-choice tests and also give you the chance to receive feedback. Such knowledge of results can help you improve not only your test questions but also your teaching and the learning efficiency of your students.

5. When grading is completed, if possible analyze each question in an effort to improve future exams.

Not only do properly graded exams provide students with valuable knowledge of results, they can also give you valuable insight into your skill as a test-maker (and teacher). A basic criterion for judging a test is to check on whether it actually measures what it is intended to measure. To obtain such information, conduct a postmortem after each test. Even as you are grading essay exams, you will usually recognize that some questions are vague and misleading and perhaps think of ways to improve them. It is prudent to record these ideas on your key as you grade papers so that they will be available when you need them later. More information will come from students who register complaints—if you permit them to complain.

With multiple-choice and other objective tests, you are not likely to become aware of which questions are effective and which can be improved unless you carry out a systematic item analysis. Many test specialists do this by grouping students in the top and bottom 27 percent of the class and comparing the way they answered each question. (For details on why you choose 27 percent and how to go about the analysis, see exercise 11-11 at the end of the chapter.) Such an analysis will disclose the difficulty of each item and show which questions discriminated best between good and poor students. The obvious drawback to this procedure is the amount of time it takes.

Should You Ever Change a Grade?

Some teachers categorically refuse to change a grade once a paper has been evaluated and returned. It is argued that the teacher will be exposed to too much pressure if he agrees to listen to complaints and that the "operators" will talk their way into a higher score through persistence or cajolery while the shy, silent types take their lumps. All this is true, and you can save yourself a lot of trouble if you issue an "all decisions are final" ultimatum, but there *are* counterarguments.

For one thing, you will almost always have to read papers rapidly. It is possible to skip a key word or phrase in an essay exam or term paper and give an unfairly low score. In addition, you may be tired and irritable toward the end of a grading session and unconsciously toughen your standards. Or, if you grade papers in several separate sessions, you may not maintain a consistent mood or interpretation of the key. Then there is the factor of relativity—any paper you grade after an exceptionally good (or bad) paper may suffer (or benefit) by comparison.

For all these reasons, consider the use of limited gripe sessions after handing back papers. If you feel a student has a legitimate complaint, you might change the score. If you feel he is a borderline case who is *only* trying to talk his way from a C+ to a B—, you might stay firm. One technique for dealing with an aggressive complainer is to say that you will look over his paper that evening and report back if the score is changed. This eases the pressure you may experience if the student is peering over your shoulder and pushing you hard. If you permit a student to "interpret" what he "really meant," you will be giving him an unfair advantage. To be consistent, you would have to invite all other students to interpret their answers as well—which would be impossible in most cases, unless you permit a five-minute conference for everyone who wants it.

One final point has to do with the defense of different kinds of grades. If you favor the open-ended approach to teaching, perhaps you intend to use a single, comprehensive term paper as the basis for the final grade in a course. Suppose you give a student a B on such a paper, and it turns out that if he had received an A, he might have been admitted to his first-choice college. He asks you to look over the paper again. You do this very carefully but become even more convinced that it's a B. You can't pin down all your reasons but have a general, intuitive feeling that it is definitely not in a class with the papers to which you assigned A's. Consider the way he will feel (and how you will feel) when you try to explain this to him. Then imagine how both of you would feel if you had used quizzes, exams, and several short papers and were able to point to a set of ten numerical scores in your gradebook. If it were possible to show him that his total was thirty points below that of the student who got the lowest A, do you think he would feel less resentful about his grade than he would under the single-paper circumstances?

Some testing specialists have suggested that a less onerous way to get the same information is to hand back exams and have students indicate by a show of hands whether they got each question right or wrong. Although this does save the teacher a lot of work, it is potentially embarrassing to students and also maximizes the likelihood that the answers to all of the questions will circulate through the school.

An alternative is the complaint-conference approach noted earlier. If students are permitted to discuss three to five questions with you, you will find out a good deal about specific test items and how they may be improved. You will also learn which ones discriminate between good and poor students. In addition, you will gain insight into *why* students selected wrong answers, which will assist you to do a better job of teaching. The straight item-analysis approach does not provide the latter information. In order to use either test-analysis technique, however, you will need to go over the right answers. While this is most desirable pedagogically, it may be unfortunate from a testing point of view since students in other classes may get tips on the test, which will tend to reduce its validity. About the only solution is to build up a file of questions and use a slightly different assortment each year.

In evaluating your tests, you must be cognizant of their general level of difficulty. Analyze them to be sure they are not unreasonably difficult. Keep in mind points made in previous chapters in regard to providing goals, the disadvantages of intense competition, the fact that success is necessary for the development of realistic goals, and the fact that being flunked is often interpreted as punishment. Making one or two test questions "challenging" is one thing. Going all out to flunk as many students as possible is another. You may discover that you have overestimated the ability of your pupils when you first make up exams, particularly at the high school level. (You may assume that the pupils have as much specialized knowledge of a subject as you have.)

To decide whether your exams are on an appropriate level of difficulty, check for consistency. If some students do an excellent job but most do a poor job, low scores may be due to lack of study. If *all* pupils get low scores, it is probably the teacher who is at fault—because of ineffective presentation, questions that are too hard, overly rigorous scoring, or a combination of these factors. Perhaps the worst consequence of unrealistically difficult exams is that they encourage cheating. Several articles recently published report that the high school student of this era does not feel guilty about cheating. According to some interviewers, cheating is accepted as a matter of course because "everybody does it." It is depressing to think the situation is as black as this, but cheating on exams does exist. The every-man-for-himself philosophy of American life has been blamed, but probably more fault lies with the emphasis on grades as the basis for entrance to college. Experimental studies of honesty (Hartshorne and May, 1928) reveal that almost anyone will cheat if the pressure is extreme enough. Some people will cheat most of the time and a few will hardly ever, but practically everyone has a "breaking point." It seems sensible, therefore, to

Hartshorne and May: cheating due to pressure

do everything possible to make exams just and reasonable. If you go out of your way to confound the test-takers or if you resort to trickery, you are literally inviting pupils to fight back by cheating.

Few students are so callous that they can ignore feelings of guilt, even if they regard the use of crib sheets or the equivalent as somewhat justified. The probable consequence will be an intensification of negative attitudes toward you and your subject, which will block present and future learning. The best way to avoid this is to be fair and objective about tests and grades. More specifically, give your students questions that will keep them busy. Trying to pick up stray bits of information from a neighbor's paper or from a crib sheet is a time-consuming business. Ask questions that require everyone to write for the entire period.

One more point about cheating: An effective teacher does the best he can to put temptation behind the pupil. Perhaps you can remember teachers who seemed almost to *encourage* cheating. A more constructive policy is to make a quiet "announcement" if you think you detect skulduggery: "A couple of people seem to be curious about papers other than their own. Let's have independent effort." This warns the backslider, but in such a way that the situation can usually be handled with a minimum of ill feeling.

Report Cards

Because American schools must deal with millions of pupils, almost inevitably you will be asked to fill out report cards. They may possess more disadvantages than advantages, but they appear to be unavoidable. This section offers suggestions on how to assign final grades fairly and expeditiously.

The task of making out report cards is subject to a number of restrictions. Perhaps the major one is that in most cases you must distill all your reactions to a student into a single letter-grade, which places him in one of three or five gross categories. The most agonizing decision a teacher is forced to make is the placing of that thin, somewhat arbitrary line between two letter-grade levels. You may make a gesture toward a finer distinction by recording A— or B+ in your grade book, but the fact remains: The official grade is registered as either an A or a B. About the only way you can assuage your guilt and frustration over the luckless wretch who falls just *below* the line is to consider that half a dozen other teachers are also reacting to him. (This is the case at the secondary level. In the lower grades you may be the sole evaluator.)

Report cards come in a baffling range of sizes, shapes, types, and even colors. They vary from a semiannual letter to the parents to a four-page inventory covering every conceivable academic and nonacademic pursuit. However, most of them fall into a similar pattern.

Report cards for the elementary level usually have two major sections: one for academic achievement and the other for "social growth," "attitudes," or "citizenship." (During recent years there has been a sharp diminution in the amount of space devoted to the latter type of behavior. This reflects disenchantment with "life-adjustment" education.) The teacher is ordinarily required to grade each pupil on his ability in reading, arithmetic, language, spelling, handwriting, social studies, health or science, music, art, and physical education. Often subcategories are found under reading, writing, and arithmetic. For example, you may have to rate a pupil on his ability in oral reading, reading comprehension, and library participation. In most cases grading is on the five-step A to F scale. At the primary level and occasionally in upper elementary classes, a three-step system is used: "above average," "satisfactory," "needs improvement." Many elementary school cards also distinguish between actual achievement and estimates of ability, effort, or aptitude. These categories and other subheadings such as "social growth," "attitudes," and "citizenship" are usually labeled either "satisfactory" or "unsatisfactory."

In secondary school the great majority of report cards are austere affairs which call for a stark A, B, C, D, or F for each subject. Sometimes a catchall "citizenship" column is added; almost invariably it is reserved for negative reactions—either a check mark or a U for unsatisfactory.

Suggestions for Making Out Report Cards

There are bound to be report cards that vary from the "typical" ones just described. Even so, the common elements they are all likely to share justify offering the following suggestions:

1. Before classes begin, examine a copy of the card used in your school, and make sure you are aware of the local ground rules for grading. *Making out report cards*
2. Pick out the important and reportable areas.
3. Test and observe specifically for the gradable skills.
4. Whenever possible, compute subtotals "as you go."
5. If you must grade "citizenship," take special care to guard against the halo effect, cognitive dissonance, and projection.
6. Do your best to make separate and independent evaluations of achievement and "citizenship."

   1. Before classes begin, examine a copy of the card used in your school, and make sure you are aware of local ground rules for grading.

Some decisions regarding grades must be made on a school- or district-wide basis. In order to provide a degree of consistency so that all teachers of a given class or subject apply roughly similar standards, guidelines regarding grades and distribution are sometimes necessary—especially in schools that use grouping systems such as the ungraded primary or the X-Y-Z system. Consequently, it is important to be clearly aware of local ground rules before you begin to develop lesson plans or to plot tests and assignments.

Report Card

"He is highly creative. His art work often takes interesting and unexpected turns."

"He is straightforward, honest and has a well-developed sense of fair play."

"Billy has good habits of personal hygiene and takes pride in his appearance."

"He seems to understand that Little Clocks run down and is very good about rest time."

2. *Pick out the important and reportable areas.*

As you study the card, select the most important *and* gradable categories, and decide how to work within the local regulations. The more elaborate cards at the primary and elementary levels have thirty or forty categories to be evaluated several times a year. It is impossible to make systematic observations of more than a few skills and abilities, so if you are confronted with an extremely detailed card, you may be forced to pick out those skills you and other teachers

---

Some Observations on Parent-Teacher Conferences

Teachers at the elementary level usually must report student progress in whole or in part through parent conferences. In some schools this means "interpreting" a standard report card to the parents and in others, simply giving an oral analysis of strengths and weaknesses. Parents often dislike the latter kind of report unless the teacher shows them something specific to back up her remarks. One parent, for example, said that she and her husband got the same answer to all their queries about their son's progress: "He's doing just fine." He was doing "fine" even in reading, although he was two grade levels below the level he should have been. The parents suspected that the teacher didn't *know* their son's status.

If your school features parent conferences, keep in mind that unless you have kept systematic records of student performance, your only recourse will be to keep smiling (and perspiring) and repeating, "He's doing just fine." Picture an interview with aggressive parents who have ambitions for their son far exceeding your estimate of his abilities. Whether an actual report card is used or not, life will be much simpler if you can support your judgments with evidence. Such evidence will also permit you to do a better job of teaching.

---

and consultants consider most important. The primary teacher is most likely to face this problem. As the children progress through school, the report cards gradually approach that ultimate, one-letter judgement.

3. *Test and observe specifically for the gradable skills.*

This suggestion is intended for the primary teacher because of the complexity of the report cards. If each pupil must be judged on such specific qualities as oral reading, reading comprehension, and library participation, making out thirty report cards can be onerous. Preparing for this chore ahead of time simplifies it. For example, every day you might have an oral reading period during which five or ten pupils read. If each pupil reads five times during a report period and you grade his performance on a ten-point scale, the points can be totaled and a distribution prepared before the deadline. A simple glance at your distribution then permits you to assign grades quickly and easily. Without such a system, you may find yourself at 2:00 A.M. the morning grades are due desperately dredging your memory for recollections of how well each pupil can read. Resorting to this haphazard alternative brings into play the halo effect, cognitive dissonance, projection, and the influence of the unconscious.

4. *Whenever possible, compute subtotals "as you go."*

If you plan ahead and space tests and exercises over the grading period, you can also get a jump on the usual last-minute rush of calculating and assigning grades. (In the example noted above, each pupil's set of five scores might have been totaled after he had completed his fifth oral reading.) This means determining just a few sets of totals each day for several days as opposed to undergoing a hectic all-night session. In the upper levels, you might sum up the points for homework, papers, quizzes, and exams a few weeks before the final. Marking finals is almost always a pressure-filled task, and if on top of that you must add up five or ten numbers for each of thirty to five-times-thirty pupils, you may be reduced to a state of exhaustion coupled with panic. It's much easier to add just one number to the subtotal and proceed from there to final distribution and grades. This policy will put you in a position also to provide the pupils with their relative positions going into the final exam. As a teacher you may have some misgivings about the desirability of doing this, but since most students clamor for such a semifinal report you may feel obligated to supply it.

5. If you must grade "citizenship," take special care to guard against the halo effect, cognitive dissonance, and projection.

Given the choice, you may prefer to avoid grading pupils on their "citizenship." How to define it is the first problem. Even with a workable definition, the difficulties involved in observing for it with accuracy are so great that you would have little time left for teaching or evaluating scholastic performance. When you are forced to evaluate such factors as "shows self-control" or "considers the rights of others," consider the *anecdotal report* as a device for making your reactions more systematic and less subjective. The anecdotal report takes several forms, but a common technique is to take a pad of paper or an inexpensive notebook and put the name of each pupil at the top of a page. Five minutes or so at the end of each day is all that is necessary to conduct a postmortem of the day's events. This could become almost automatic. Try to remember and record things that turned out well and things that didn't, and in the latter case analyze what went wrong so that you can prevent a similar disaster in the future. As you recollect what happened, make an effort to recall specific incidents involving individual pupils.

For example, two boys got in a fight as they were lining up for recess; a not-so-bright pupil gave an outrageously wrong answer that provoked gales of derisive laughter from the class; class elections were held. As you note each event on your page for the appropriate pupil, you are making a record that may later prove valuable. If a particularly belligerent boy has a fight a day, you have evidence to back up a "needs improvement" grade under the "shows self-control'" column. If you become aware later in the year that the maladroit boy who made the dumb remark seems to have changed from an extrovert to an introvert, the reminder of his embarrassing experience could be the tipoff that this was the original cause of the shift in his behavior; building up his confidence by feeding him easy questions you know he can answer may counteract the low esteem of his classmates. Or the simple notation that a certain girl was elected class secretary for October could come in handy during a parent conference or in a conversation at Back-to-School Night or a P.T.A. meeting.

This sort of record is most appropriate for the elementary teacher, but it can also be of use to a secondary teacher. Such notes can help correct for inaccuracies resulting from distortions of memory. On the other hand, you have to guard against the influence of cognitive dissonance. The more you describe a certain kind of behavior in your notes about a pupil, the more likely you are to look for—and find—more incidents of the same kind and to ignore evidence that is dissonant. The antidote to this trap is to be aware of it and make an effort to be open-minded in noting similar behavior in other pupils.

6. *Do your best to make separate and independent evaluations of achievement and "citizenship."*

With a report card that has separate sections for scholarship and "citizenship," keep these two factors separate in your mind and in your grade book. If you are asked to distill your judgement into only one letter-grade, it will be even harder to be fair.

Perhaps as a student you considered one of your teachers hypocritical and deceitful. A common form of "deceit" is to grade a pupil below his actual achievement and explain, if challenged, that he showed "lack of effort," or "a poor attitude," or "unsatisfactory recitation." Such statements may be nothing more than thinly disguised excuses for venting personal animosities. The teacher is thinking, "I don't like you and this is my way of getting back at you." In many cases the reason the teacher doesn't like the pupil is that the pupil has made it abundantly clear that he doesn't think much of the teacher. For a teacher to exact revenge in the form of a deliberately lowered final grade is indefensible. But it's oh-so-tempting, and you may have to take particular care to avoid falling into the trap. The best safeguard is to draw the lines on your final grade distributions *before* you know which name is attached to which tally and then stick to your decision. (If the tallies are so close you have to compare papers, then make a determined effort to firmly control your emotions.)

Mention of drawing lines on final distributions introduces the problem of processing sets of scores to convert them into grades. If you are forced to deal with large numbers of students, it may be essential to use statistical techniques for clarifying relationships and making evaluations. Being pressed for time, you may have to restrict yourself to simple techniques involving the drawing of a frequency distribution and the calculation of a measure of central tendency.

Converting Scores into Grades

There are several ways to depict a distribution of scores, but the most workable is to take a sheet of lined paper and list the scores consecutively from the lowest to the highest. Then place a tally for each pupil beside the appropriate score. If you are reasonably careful to put the tallies about the same distance from the margin, you will end up with a plain indication of how the scores

Drawing a frequency distribution

are distributed. Just looking at the distribution will provide a good deal of information, but your interpretation of the relative values of the scores will be clarified if you calculate a measure of central tendency—either the *mean* or the *median*.

The Mean

Computing the mean

The mean is the arithmetical average compiled by adding up all the test scores and dividing by the number of pupils. If you have thirty to five-times-thirty listed and an exam with quite a few points, you are in for a sizable amount of calculating. It's difficult to do a sum like that in your head, and there may not be a calculating machine at hand. To simplify the job, use a frequency distribution as illustrated in Table 11-1, which depicts a hypothetical distribution of scores on a short test.

Table 11–1   Calculating the Mean from a Frequency Distribution

Score X	Tally	Frequency f	Product of score and frequency fX
47	/	1	47
46	/ /	2	92
45	/	1	45
44			
43	/	1	43
42	/	1	42
41	/ /	2	82
40	/	1	40
39	/ /	2	78
38	/	1	38
37	/ /	2	74
36	/ /	2	72
35	/ / / /	4	140
34	/ / /	3	102
33	/ /	2	66
32	/ /	2	64
31			
30	/	1	30
29	/	1	29
28	/	1	28
27	/	1	27
26			
25	/	1	25
24	/	1	24

N = 33   Sum total of scores $\Sigma fX = 1188$

$$\text{Mean (M)} = \frac{\text{Sum total of scores } (\Sigma fX)}{\text{Number of scores (N)}}$$

$$\text{Mean (M)} = \frac{1188}{33}$$

$$\text{Mean (M)} = 36$$

In using a frequency distribution, you will have a smaller list of numbers to deal with, which will make the task of addition less demanding. To make the job even simpler, it is possible to group scores by three- to five-point intervals; that is, tally all scores between 45 and 49 in one group. Although this variation makes it easier to add up totals and is often used with large distributions, it is not very appropriate for classroom use. Most of the time you will be interested in ascertaining the differences among pupils, and any scheme that tends to group them together will lead you away from the final information you desire. But there is no need to be concerned too much about calculating the mean, for the median, or middle score, tells you much the same thing and can be arrived at simply by counting until you reach the middle tally on a distribution.

The Median

To find the median of the distribution depicted in Table 11-1, take the number of scores (33), add 1, and divide by 2. (The reason you add 1 is to find the pivotal score.) The middle score of this distribution is the seventeenth from either the top or the bottom. If you count the tallies from either end, you will hit the score of 35.

Computing the median

With an odd number of scores, as on the distribution in Table 11-1, you will always land on the same score when you count from top or bottom. With an even number of scores, you will end up halfway between two tallies, which may be opposite different scores, for adding 1 to an even number of scores and dividing by 2 will always yield a 0.5 value. A simple way to allow for this is to circle both tallies that straddle the actual median. (To illustrate, add one more tally to the distribution in Table 11-1 opposite the 44 and then calculate the median. You should arrive at a median of 35.5.) The median is not only simpler to calculate than the mean but also less likely to be influenced by extreme scores, and for practical purposes it is a perfectly adequate measure of central tendency.

What you eventually do with your distribution of scores and your measure of central tendency after you calculate it depends on several factors. If you favor the goals for improving evaluation noted earlier, you will want to avoid—as much as possible—using a distribution that exaggerates differences between pupils. In many cases, you will be unable to completely avoid comparisons. In a large school in which several teachers handle multiple sections of a course, a degree of standardization between teacher and classes is often considered necessary. The same applies to X-Y-Z classes or the equivalent. For the assignment of final grades to be reasonably fair, final distributions will probably have to be interpreted according to school or department guidelines.

If you *are* required to make comparisons, however, you are urged to do everything you can to avoid a situation in which only a fixed minority of students can earn high grades. Some students are bound to do better than others, and it is fair and proper that superior performance be acknowledged. But if this is done in such a way that a substantial number of other students are made to feel inadequate and incapable of learning, it is a destructive policy. It makes more sense to encourage all students to strive for a superior level of performance by announcing that there is room at the top for everyone who can prove his ability. This means that as much as possible, you should concentrate on grading according to levels of performance rather than relative standing. The learning for mastery technique permits you to do this, and the chapter will conclude with a detailed description of this approach. Before turning to mastery learning, however, some observations on the GPA are offered to indicate why *some* means of assigning grades is likely to be essential.

Observations on the GPA

The thought of assigning grades may arouse negative feelings if you share the dislike of many of your fellow students for grade-point averages. The GPA is often seen by the same students as the embodiment of all that is evil about evaluation. Confronted with arguments that *some* kind of evaluation is necessary to establish and maintain standards, to screen candidates for graduate school, teaching, and the other professions, and to provide feedback for various reasons, only the most extreme critics still maintain that the abolishment of grades is possible. The thoughtful acknowledge that evaluation in some form is essential and offer alternatives to the use of the GPA as the primary criterion for assessing performance. The commonest recommendations are:

1. Pass-fail in all courses
2. Comprehensive examinations of one kind or another, for example, matriculation exams at the end of the senior year, exams before entrance to graduate school, tests administered by industrial concerns to screen job applicants
3. Letters of recommendation
4. Copies of term papers and the like.

You are invited to analyze these suggestions with reference to the discussion of evaluation presented in this chapter.

The appeal of pass-fail rests on the fact that it reduces pressure and is therefore thought more likely to encourage study because the student wants to learn, not just get a good mark. (When this point is made, it is often phrased as if learning for personal value and learning to get a grade are mutually exclusive. The implication is that you can do one or the other but not both. In thinking this over, you will probably realize that no such distinction really exists.) However, in actual practice, pass-fail tends to *decrease* the effort expended because of the lowest-common-denominator effect. As John Gardner has pointed out, the best way to motivate people to make the most of their abilities is to establish and enforce standards. The standard in pass-fail systems gravitates toward the level of those who just pass. In rare institutions with very select students, this level may be respectable; in most schools and colleges, it is mediocre.

Another disadvantage of the pass-fail system is unreliability (inconsistency). Peters and Van Voorhis (1940) have pointed out that whenever only a few categories are used (such as the two in a pass-fail system), the results are less consistent. The likelihood that a given teacher will come up with a different grade on a second evaluation of borderline students, or that different teachers will assign different grades, increases as the numbers of categories decreases.

Comprehensive exams have appeal because a student who has never experienced them is prone to think he would prefer a single major ordeal to repeated minor ones. Yet the pressure on students faced with climactic exams (as in Europe and Japan) is so great that many of them are driven to neurosis or suicide. This is not to say that the grading system in the United States never leads to such tragic reactions, but for the most part a series of circumscribed evaluations is easier to take than a few do-or-die, comprehensive blockbusters. If you will think about the problems of getting a fair and adequate sample by means of two- or three-day exams that attempt to measure *all* that has been learned in four years, as well as the problems involved in evaluating such exams, you may gain a new appreciation for biweekly quizzes.

Taking into account the halo effect, cognitive dissonance, projection, and unconscious likes and dislikes (and the vague and innocuous reports written by teachers in big universities who have limited contact with the large numbers of students), would you really prefer to take your chances with letters of recommendation? Suppose the most influential person who is asked to write about you gives the impression that he took an immediate dislike to you the first time you met and that things have been getting worse rather than better?

In view of the unreliability of global judgements, would you want a group of unknown evaluators to assess your term papers? How would such judges rank large numbers of applicants in order of merit? Where could competent judges who would have sufficient time to read quantities of papers be found? How could anyone be sure that the papers submitted by fellow students who were also seeking acceptance were actually written by them?

If you will apply the criteria for good measuring devices described in this chapter to these alternatives to the GPA, you may come to realize that grades and report cards have the major advantage that they can be made fair and valuable in a variety of ways. If your GPA is used to determine whether you possess certain minimum qualifications for teaching, for example, you are being assessed on the basis of the reactions of up to forty different teachers who have observed your performance for a period of months and evaluated you more or less systematically. The result is likely to be a more valid and reliable sample of your academic behavior than any of the alternatives just noted. However, the GPA might indeed be made more flexible: Students might take some courses pass-fail—or mastery-nonmastery. Since the learning for mastery approach shows considerable promise as a technique for minimizing many of the disadvantages of grades, it will now be discussed in detail.

Learning for Mastery

An approach to evaluation that will permit you to assign grades in terms of the traditional A-to-F pattern but still meet the goals for evaluation described earlier is the technique of learning for mastery. As with many "new" educational developments, the general idea of mastery learning was introduced and experimented with years ago. In the 1920s, Carleton Washburne (1922) devised the *Winnetka Plan*, and Henry C. Morrison (1926) developed a similar scheme at the University of Chicago Laboratory School. Both defined mastery in terms of objectives, provided students with well-organized learning units, used tests to determine if students had achieved the objectives at the completion of a unit, and provided remedial instruction for students who needed it. Although the technique was popular in the 1930s, it was largely forgotten in the '40s and '50s, probably because attacks on the "softness" of the schools and the drive to surpass Russian achievements in space put emphasis on identifying and selecting the most promising students. Then in the 1960s, critics began to describe some of the unfortunate by-products of highly competitive education, and at the same time, programmed techniques—particularly those stressing instructional objectives and units of study—were being perfected. Thus the stage was set for the reemergence of the concept of learning for mastery.

John B. Carroll (1963), in his "Model of School Learning," proposes that the focus of instruction should be the *time* required for different students to learn a given amount of material. He suggests that the degree of learning is a function of the *time allowed, perseverance, aptitude, quality of instruction,* and *ability to understand instruction.* This model puts emphasis on a value-added conception of teaching: Teachers should allow more time and provide more and better instruction for students who learn less easily and rapidly than their peers.

Benjamin Bloom used the Carroll model as the basis for mastery learning. The traditional approach, he argues, promotes the concept that if a normal distribution of students (with respect to aptitude for a subject) is exposed to a standard curriculum, achievement will be normally distributed following instruction. This approach, Bloom maintains, fosters the expectation on the part of both teachers and students that only a third of all students will adequately learn what is being taught, which leads to a disastrous self-fulfilling prophecy.

This set of expectations, which fixes the academic goals of teachers and students, is the most wasteful and destructive aspect of the present educational system. It reduces the aspirations of both teachers and students; it reduces motivation for learning in students; and it systematically destroys the ego and self-concept of a sizable group of students who are legally required to attend school for 10 to 12 years under conditions which are frustrating and humiliating year after year. (1968, p. 1)

Here is the alternative Bloom suggests:

Most students (perhaps over 90 percent) can master what we have to teach them, and it is the task of instruction to find the means which will enable our students to master the subject under consideration. Our basic task is to determine what we mean by mastery of the subject and to search for the methods and materials which will enable the largest proportion of our students to attain such mastery. (P. 1)

(The latter statement reflects Bruner's opinion that we should "begin with the hypothesis that any subject can be taught effectively in some intellectually honest form to any child at any stage of development," as well as Skinner's view that most students should be able to complete a properly written program.)

Although Bloom's approach is basically similar to the technique used in the 1920s by Washburne and Morrison, the widespread and effective use of mastery learning did not occur until the formulation of desirable ways to devise instructional objectives (such as the books by Mager and Gronlund), sophisticated descriptions of the hierarchical nature of learning (such as Bloom's taxonomy of educational objectives and Gagné's conditions of learning), and complete instructional systems (such as Glaser's Individually Prescribed Instruction or Atkinson's Computer Assisted Instruction). Another factor that has contributed to the improvement of mastery learning is the distinction between *formative* and *summative* evaluation first pointed out by Michael Scriven (1967). In most cases, evaluation is used to indicate a level of performance at the conclusion of a unit of instruction; that is, it sums up how much learning has taken place. Scriven suggests that more attention should be paid to evaluation that forms part of the teaching-learning process and provides continuous feedback to improve learning and instruction. Tests would thus be used to "form" learning in that they would help to diagnose weaknesses and make remedial instruction easier.

Ingredients for A Successful Mastery Approach

Carroll observes that "teaching ought to be a simple matter if it is viewed as a process concerned with the management of learning" (1971, p. 29) and suggests that the function of the teacher is to follow this procedure:

Specify what is to be learned.

Motivate pupils to learn it.

Provide instructional materials [to foster learning].

[Present] materials at a rate appropriate for different pupils.

Monitor students' progress.

Diagnose difficulties and provide remediation.

Give praise and encouragement for good performance.

Give review and practice.

Maintain a high rate of learning over a period of time. (Pp. 29–30)

The open education approach—as described by Walberg and Thomas—makes use of many of these procedures. Although the teacher allows for considerable student initiative rather than specifying what is to be learned, open education makes allowance for different rates, stresses diagnosis of learning difficulties, provides remedial instruction, supplies recognition for good performance, makes allowance for review and practice, and encourages a high rate of learning over a period of time. If you will be teaching at the elementary level, in particular, you may wish to follow procedures of open education. However, you may wish also to experiment with the sequence exactly as outlined by Carroll. The following suggestions, which can be adapted for use at any grade level and in any subject area, are based on Carroll's outline.

Suggestions for a Mastery Learning Approach

Using a mastery learning approach

1. Go through a unit of study, a chapter of a text, or an outline of a lecture and pick out what you consider to be the most important points—that is, those you wish to stress because they are most likely to have later value or are basic to later learning.
2. List these points in the form of a goal card, instructional objectives (as described by Mager or Gronlund), or key points or the equivalent. If possible, arrange the objectives in some sort of organized framework, perhaps with reference to the taxonomy of educational objectives or Gagné's conditions of learning.
3. Distribute a list of the objectives at the beginning of a unit, and tell your students that they should concentrate on learning them and that they will be tested on them.
4. Consider the possibility of making up some sort of "study guide" in which you provide specific questions relating to the objectives and a format for students to organize their notes.
5. Make up exam questions on the objectives (based on the study guide questions, if you provide them).
6. Arrange these questions into at least two (preferably three) alternate exams for each unit of study.

7. Make up tentative criteria for grade levels for each exam and for the entire unit or report period, for example: A—not more than one question missed on any exam, B—not more than two questions missed on any exam, C—not more than four questions missed on any exam.

8. Test students either when they come to you and indicate they are ready or when you feel there has been ample opportunity for all students to have learned the material. Announce all exam dates in advance, remind students that the questions will be based only on the objectives you have noted, indicate the criteria for different grade levels, and emphasize that any student who fails to meet a desired criterion on his first try will be given a chance to take an alternate form of the exam.

9. Grade and return the exams as promptly as possible, go over questions briefly in class (particularly those that more than a few students had difficulty with), and offer to go over exams on an individual basis. Make allowance for individual interpretations, and give credit for answers you judge to be logical and plausible, even though they differ from the answer you expected.

10. Schedule make-up exam times, and make yourself available for consultation and tutoring the day before. (At the same time that make-up exams are given, you can give the original exam to students who were absent.)

11. If a student improves his score on the second exam but still falls below the desired criterion, consider a "safety valve" option; that is, invite him to provide you with a filled-in study guide (or the equivalent) at the time he takes an exam a second time or give an open-book exam on objectives that were missed to see if he can explain them in other than written examination terms. If you feel the student does this satisfactorily, give credit for one extra answer on the second exam.

12. To supplement exams, assign book reports, oral reports, papers, or some other kind of individual work that will provide maximum opportunity for student choice. Establish and explain the criteria you will use to evaluate these, but stress that you want to encourage maximum freedom of choice and expression. (Some students will thrive on free choice, but others are likely to feel threatened by open-ended assignments. To allow for such differences, provide specific directions for those who need them, general hints or a simple request that "original" projects be cleared in advance for the more independent thinkers.) Grade all reports "pass" or "do over" and supply constructive criticisms on those you consider unsatisfactory. Announce that all "do over" papers can be reworked and resubmitted within a certain period of time. Have these reports count toward the final grade, for example, three reports for an A, two for a B, one for a C. (The student should also pass each exam at the designated level.)

This basic technique will permit you to meet the goals listed earlier, to work within a traditional A-to-F framework but in such a way that you increase the proportion of students who do superior work without lowering standards.

It also permits you to make the most of the procedures suggested by Carroll.

The advantages and also some further explanations of the steps in the suggested procedure will now be discussed.

The Values of Stating Objectives

Teachers who do not make use of objectives, typically, make up exams by haphazardly scanning a text or other form of instructional material for information that seems appropriate for exam purposes. Exams are usually written under pressure, so it often turns out that the material selected is whatever happens to fit into question format most easily. Unfortunately, such information is rarely of primary importance (names, dates, and statistics are examples of information that is easy to work into questions). However, because students read primarily to prepare for exams, they will feel obliged to concentrate on such information when they study. Skinner emphasizes this point when he observes, "What is taught often tends to be simply what can be measured by tests and examinations" (1968, p. 235), and he adds, "A predilection for scorable right answers distorts our definition of knowledge" (p. 245). If you have ever studied for an exam by deliberately seeking sections of the text you thought the instructor might use in test questions, you know what Skinner means.

In light of research on remembering and transfer, such an approach to testing appears irrational. A traditional test is something of a guessing game. If a student is simply told that he will be tested on a hundred pages of text, for example, he may devote much of his study time to trying to anticipate what will be asked and the rest of the time memorizing to the point of being barely able to recall the information until the test is written. If he has been diligent, shrewd, and lucky, the student will be able to answer most of the questions on the exam. If he has not fathomed the mind of his instructor, he will be unable to answer many questions even though he has studied hard, and he is likely to leave the examination room brooding about all the "junk" he learned that turned out to be valueless. (When passing tests is the primary goal in the class, any information that cannot be used in answering questions is likely to be considered worthless.) The student is also likely to make a resolution not to "waste" so much time studying for the next exam.

Because of factors such as these, the traditional approach to grading favors forgetting and works against remembering because it increases the likelihood of interference and reorganization, because no attempt to seek structure or interrelationships is made, and because preparing for and taking tests is likely to be seen as a disagreeable experience that the student will tend to repress. To avoid this kind of situation, you are urged to pick out objectives before you organize a unit and make up exams, choose only information you feel

is likely to have high pay-off value, stress the relationships between points you select, and do everything possible to assist and persuade your students to thoroughly learn a relatively small number of objectives. You are also urged to give them the opportunity to make up for a bad start by trying a second time. This approach is much more likely to lead to genuine understanding and to encourage transfer than the one-shot technique that is so common in American classrooms.

Perhaps you are wondering at this point if telling students what to study in advance will limit their reading of the material. This reflects a concern about "covering" a course that was noted in the preceding chapter with reference to some of Herndon's observations. Many instructors, particularly those who favor a Lockeian view (either by design or because of their approach to teaching) believe that all learning must be shaped entirely by the instructor. If a particular topic is not discussed in a lecture or covered by an exam question, it is assumed that it will not be learned. You probably know from your own experience that some courses set up to provide encyclopedic coverage of a subject are more likely to lead to superficial learning, concern only about giving the teacher exactly what he wants, and a desire to sell the text the day after the final.

National Assessment

If you are convinced of the values of objectives, you have several sources to turn to as guides for selecting and describing them: the books by Mager and Gronlund, Bloom's taxonomy, Gagné's conditions of learning. Still another source is reports from *National Assessment of Educational Progress.* Ralph W. Tyler was most responsible for the development of this program. He explained the need for national assessment this way:

> Because education has become the servant of all our purposes, its effectiveness is of general public concern. The educational tasks now faced require many more resources than have thus far been available, and they must be wisely used to produce maximum results. To make these decisions, dependable information about the progress of education is essential; otherwise we scatter our efforts too widely and fail to achieve our goals. Yet we do not now have the necessary comprehensive and dependable data. . . . This situation will be corrected only by a careful, consistent effort to obtain valid data to provide sound evidence about the progress of American education. (Tyler, 1966, p. 2)

To obtain such data, the National Assessment program was instituted in 1964. First, a comprehensive list of educational objectives was drawn up by committees of scholars, public school personnel, and lay citizens. Then questions were written by teams of specialists to determine how well these objectives were being achieved. Next these questions were formed into tests in ten subject areas: citizenship, science, writing, music, mathematics, literature, social studies, reading, art, and career and occupational development. A sample group was selected consisting of 25,000 nine-year-olds, 28,000 thirteen-year-olds, 28,000 seventeen-year-olds, and 9,000 young adults between the ages of 26 and 35. The tests have been administered to these groups according to a cycle, with two subject areas being covered each year. The results are reported in terms of geographic region, size of community, type of community, sex, color, and socioeducational background. (No data on specific students, school districts, cities, or states is provided.) The information gives data on general trends (e.g., big cities and small towns are low in science and writing) and specific questions (e.g., only 29 percent of the seventeen-year-olds tested knew that in human females, the egg is released an average of fourteen days after menstruation begins).

The purpose of the reports is to alert teachers to general areas and specific bits of information that may need special attention if a systematic effort to improve instruction is to be made. You can obtain information about National Assessment, including a list of all reports and bulletins, by writing to National Assessment of Educational Progress, 1860 Lincoln Street, Suite 300, Denver, Colorado 80203.

Figure 11–1   Page from the *National Assessment of Educational Progress*

National Assessment of Educational Progress, April, 1973 (''Recognizing Literary Works and Characters,'' 1970–71 Assessment)

Exercise R308

Ages 13, 17, Adult
Objective IA

Many people or animals that we read about in books become so well-known that we can name them just from a picture. Above is a picture of a man who appears in a story.

What is the name of the <u>man</u> in the picture?

Write your answer on the line provided.

<u>*Sherlock Holmes*</u>

	Age 13	Age 17	Adult
Acceptable responses	57.2%	78.5%	75.6%
Unacceptable responses	7.2	4.7	3.2
I don't know.	34.8	15.7	19.9
No response	.8	1.1	1.4

When you provide a list of objectives for a text, you are saying to the student (either directly or indirectly): "These are the points I think are important, and I am asking you to learn them because they are most likely to equip you with ideas you will be able to use later. The other information in the book is for you to interpret and use in your own way." If you are successful in using objectives in your teaching, your students are likely to react to this approach by scanning the text as they prepare for your exams. In the process, they may well discover sections that they will read on their own or that they will later examine more completely when they are under less academic pressure. Even if it doesn't always work out this way, they probably will have a more useful repertoire of thoroughly learned and organized ideas than if they were required to attempt to cover everything.

The Values of a Study Guide

If you have time to devise some sort of study guide, you will not only assist your students to master the objectives but also open up possibilities for alternatives to final exams. Such a guide might consist simply of a page of specific questions with blank spaces under each. Or it could take the form of a program or of a few general questions. Regardless of its form, the existence of a guide provides students with suggestions and incentives for study. It also means you can use safety-valve options with formal exams or replace formal exams with take-home or open book exercises or with oral interviews. You might handle these yourself, or you can have students test each other by following the procedure suggested by Keller (see pp. 260–261). A variation of the Keller approach has been developed by Gerald Dykstra (described in Carroll, 1970, p. 37). He has created a technique in which primary grade pupils not only are asked to pass a test on a unit themselves but also to teach it to another pupil before going on to the next unit. Flash cards are used for the testing. (This technique could be used with students at all grade levels, and completion or short-answer tests might be used instead of flash cards.)

The choice regarding open- or closed-book exams will depend on grade level and subject area, as well as your feelings about exam pressure. When you provide students with lists of objectives in advance and announce that they will have more than one opportunity to take an exam and that you will do everything possible to assist them to improve their performance, you remove some of the most anxiety-producing aspects of testing, particularly since you substantially reduce competition between students. Even so, some students will still feel pressure; many will complain about being required to memorize material, arguing that if they need to know something they can look it up. In making a decision about open or closed book exams, take into account that memorization will lead to overlearning and that thoroughly learned material is more likely to transfer. In many situations, we have to act on the spur of the moment or be prepared to see new relationships, so it is not always possible to look things up. In addition, it is necessary to become *equipped* to look things up by learning information well enough in the first place to know that it exists and where it is available. Finally, remember that *preparation* precedes *inspiration* in the process of discovery and that a person can "leap about intuitively" (as Bruner puts it) only after he has mastered the structure of a field of knowledge.

If you do decide on closed-book exams, you might point out to students who complain of test anxiety that the best solution is to be thoroughly prepared. Since students will know in advance what will be stressed, all that is needed for a relaxing test experience is thorough knowledge. Answering questions with skill and confidence can lead to feelings of self-esteem, satisfaction, and even enjoyment; but some students have never felt this way because they have been convinced that they could never do well or have always attempted to get by with the least amount of effort. The mastery approach makes it possible to change these attitudes. (It should also be noted that some students panic just as much over an open-book exam or an interview as they do over a traditional closed-book exam.)

Various Uses of Formative and Summative Evaluation

Scriven and Bloom suggest that formative tests be nongraded and used to prepare students for summative evaluation at the completion of a unit. Although this may be the best policy for some types of material, you may wish to follow the suggestions outlined here and have a series of short exams that function as both formative and summative tests. If a final summative exam is used as the basis for the final grade, students may feel considerably more pressured than if they are asked to take a series of exams. Scriven and Bloom recommend that units be arranged in hierarchical fashion. If you do this, nongraded exams that determine a student's readiness to go on to the next unit are appropriate. But if you develop units that are not based on a hierarchical structure, which you may discover will be the rule more than the exception, you may find that basing the final grade on a series of tests will be the best plan.

Should you decide to follow this procedure, consult Figure 11-2, page 558 for a suggested format for your grade book. If the grade book you are provided does not lend itself to such a recording technique, you might purchase a columnar pad designed for accountants. Using a series of exams and the grade format suggested will let you provide immediate feedback regarding progress, make-up exams, need for remedial work, and overall performance. It eliminates having to compare students and the need to laboriously total up scores and make frequency distributions before assigning final grades.

558

Figure 11-2 Suggested Format for Recording Progress in a Mastery Learning Approach

Name of Student	1st Exam Number Wrong		2nd Exam Number Wrong		3rd Exam Number Wrong		1st Paper or Project	2nd Paper or Project	Final Grade
	1st Try Form	2nd Try Form	1st Try Form	2nd Try Form	1st Try Form	2nd Try Form			

NOTES: Indicate *Form* of exam to make sure student is given a different set of questions if retested. Indicate absence by *a*. Mark papers or projects P (Pass) or R (Redo). If a Redo paper is resubmitted and evaluated as a Pass, cross out R and place a P next to it.

Determining Criteria for Different Letter Grades

One of the most crucial decisions in a mastery approach centers around the criteria you establish for different grade levels. If you hope to defend the grades you give to parents, fellow teachers, and administrators, you should do everything possible to make sure that an A in your class is equivalent to that given by colleagues. This is especially important because James H. Block (1971) has reported that the proportion of A grades in mastery classes is typically higher than in traditional classes. This is not because of low standards, but because more students are motivated to do A and B work. Therefore, you should be prepared to defend your grades by retaining copies of exams and the keys used to evaluate them and by explaining the criteria you developed for different grade levels.

In establishing criteria, refer to the discussion on instructional objectives in Chapter 6, particularly the observations of Mager (p. 285) and Gronlund (p. 286). You might set up standards for an exam in terms of the percentage of correct answers, a minimum number of correct answers, the number of correct answers provided within a given time limit, or a sample of applications. An approach that has worked well in practice is to make up 10-question exams, grade each answer plus or minus, and use these standards: zero or one wrong—A, two wrong—B, three or four wrong—C, more than four wrong—D or F. Plus or minus grading has definite advantages. It not only provides a definite number of correct and incorrect answers but also simplifies and speeds up grading. If you make up exams with an equivalent number of questions but evaluate each on a 5-point scale, you will be forced to read each answer with great care and then make a studied judgment of its relative value. If you use a plus-minus

---

Dealing with Resistance to Mastery Learning

If you can prove that students who earn high grades in your class deserve such grades, you are not likely to encounter a great deal of resistance to mastery learning. Some parents of students who have always earned A's may complain, some administrators may worry about "erosion of standards," and teachers who use comparative approaches may snipe at you because your students are more enthusiastic about you as a teacher, but positive reactions will probably more than offset such criticisms. If you encounter massive resistance, however, you might attempt to educate the critics by asking them to observe your students in action, examine your tests, and read some of the books on mastery learning noted at the end of this chapter. If resistance is so extreme that you are forbidden to use the mastery approach—or if you are not impressed by the mastery approach—you may wish to consult the books on traditional evaluation approaches noted at the end of the chapter.

---

approach, you simplify both the judging and the totaling of the final score. In many cases, you will find that the answer is obviously right or wrong and that you can evaluate it in a matter of seconds. For answers that are marginal, you can read more carefully, and if you eventually do mark them minus, you can be comforted by the fact that the student will have another chance. And it is obviously much simpler to simply count the number of wrong answers than it is to add up ten scores ranging in value from 1 to 5. With practice, you may find grading exams so quick that you will be able to provide feedback the next day.

Providing Remedial Instruction

For students who do not meet the criterion on a first try at any exam, remedial instruction might be provided by the following techniques noted by Bloom and James H. Block (1971): small-group study sessions in which two or three students who experience difficulty get together and go over their errors and help each other find and correct for omissions; individual tutoring; suggestions that the student reread the material; provision of alternate learning materials (in the fashion of a branching program), in the form of workbooks, programmed units, audio-visual materials, or academic games and puzzles; and reteaching.

The way you schedule make-up exams will depend on how you provide remedial instruction. In the Keller approach, students are allowed a retest as soon as they feel they are ready. You might use this technique if you can set aside a particular part of the school day for the purpose. You may find it simpler, however, to set aside specific preannounced times when retests (and also make-up tests for absentees) can be taken. Students who have already met the criterion for that exam can, for example, work on supplementary reports (if you decide to require them) or read for pleasure. Experience has shown that students will procrastinate if given too much freedom to select retest dates. To help them make the most of what they remember from a first try at preparing for an exam and also from remedial study and instruction, you are urged to schedule retest dates no later than two weeks after a first exam. If you use the technique of having a series of short tests serve both formative and summative functions, you will not need to give a comprehensive final exam. Consequently, you can schedule the last make-up exam in place of the final. When your students realize that those who meet the criterion for each test will not have to take an exam during the final exam period, they will have a potent incentive for doing well the first time.

If you do use a series of tests, you are urged to have students meet a criterion for each test rather than averaging their scores. The reason for this is that students who do well on the first exam may taper off toward the end of a report period and go to elaborate lengths to estimate the least amount of effort required to end up with a high final grade. To maintain high output and also to guarantee that a student who did poorly on a particular set of objectives will make a second effort to improve his performance, it seems preferable to establish the requirement of meeting the criterion on each test.

Providing Encouragment, Support, and Safety-Valve Options

If you decide to use a mastery approach and provide remedial instruction and retests, you are almost certain to discover that some students still will not meet the criterion for an A or a B on individual tests. In many cases, this will be because they have not studied diligently enough. If you teach in the upper grades (in particular) and expose students to mastery learning for the first time, some who have been identified as C or D students from the first grade on will probably have developed a habit of not studying very hard. They are likely to have figured out that there is little point in exerting themselves if they get only a second-rate reward for their efforts. It may take considerable encouragement on your part to assist such students to overcome the habits of a school lifetime and strive to do their best. In other cases, test anxiety may be the cause of poor performance. In such cases, you might go out of your way to make students feel relaxed. One technique is to invite anyone who isn't sure he is on the right track to come up during exams and ask you for an indication of "warm" or "cold" for any particular answers. If an answer isn't what you are looking for, supply a subtle hint. In still other cases, poor performance may be due to a deficiency in the intellectual skills and aptitudes involving memory and interpretation of test questions. For such students, you might use the technique suggested earlier: Tell them to do an especially conscientious job of writing out study notes and to bring these with them and hand them in along with the exam when they take the retest. If a student still fails to meet the criterion, look over his notes; if they reflect careful and diligent study, give credit for one more question. (Experience has shown that it may be necessary in a few cases to make sure a student is handing in his own notes. A simple way to check on this is to compare the handwriting on the exam and on the notes.)

Does a Mastery Approach Lower the Value of High Grades?

At this point the question may come to mind: Does a student who takes an exam a second time and still fails to meet the criterion deserve yet another opportunity to earn an A or B by completing additional work (such as doing an especially conscientious job of filling in his study guide)? Does this debase the grade or render it "meaningless"? In analyzing these questions, consider traditional grading practices, which stress the sorting-out function. In many courses, tests and grades are designed specifically to distinguish between high-scoring and low-scoring students. (This is especially true when item-analyses are carried out for the purpose of selecting questions that discriminate between high and low scorers.) A student who earns a high grade in a traditional course, however, may do so primarily because he possesses a particular set of characteristics and abilities that come into play only in the contrived and artificial test situation. Those who do not possess these traits find it difficult if not impossible to meet standards for an A or B, and unless they are given encouragement and assistance in improving (which is the exception rather than the rule), may become convinced that they cannot learn. It seems much more sensible to do everything possible to encourage all students to do superior work by searching for ways to assist those with weaknesses to compensate for their deficiencies.

If it seems illogical to go to what may seem elaborate lengths to assist a student to earn an A in a mastery scheme by providing an option that does not stress memorization or test-taking skills, consider the logic of a relative standing policy, which makes it necessary for a teacher to sort into four or five gross categories students distributed over a range of total scores. Typically, the difference between the lowest A and the highest B (for example) will be a few points out of several hundred. If a student is very close to a higher grade, why not extend him an invitation to improve instead of "punishing" him for not answering quite enough questions correctly?

One of the most destructive, illogical, and inconsistent aspects of the traditional grading approach is that it tends to make an instructor feel guilty if too many of his students earn A's. This is likely to be interpreted as a desecration of academic standards, and instructors who have a reputation for assigning only a tiny proportion of A's may be thought of as the "best" teachers in a school. If the overall amount of learning that takes place in the classes of such instructors is taken into account, they probably deserve the opposite reputation for reasons outlined by Mager in *Developing Attitude Toward Learning*. One of the most positive contributions of mastery learning may be that it will encourage you to make extraordinary efforts to assist all of your students to do A work—which is, after all, what you should try to do. Furthermore, you may find that your students will develop a class esprit de corps. Instead of creating a dog-eat-dog atmosphere in which students study by themselves, keep their notes secret, and pray that classmates will do poorly (to hold the average down), they are likely to be eager to study with each other, willing to share insights and perhaps to go out of their way to help less gifted classmates meet the criterion for an A or a B.

Being Realistic About Mastery Learning

Although this discussion of mastery learning has been intended to make you enthusiastic about the approach, you should be aware that it is not a panacea. For one thing, some students will disappoint if not infuriate you by the lengths they will go to in trying to beat the system—even after you have done everything in your power to make the system fair, just, and sensible.

Under a mastery approach, you are most likely to be able to improve the learning, attitudes, and self-concept of the typical C student. Those who have previously felt incapable of competing for high grades will usually give it a try under a mastery scheme, and many who try are likely to put out more effort, learn more, and earn higher grades than they ever have under comparative educational practices. Students who find it difficult to learn, however, may feel even more inadequate under a mastery approach than a traditional approach for reasons noted by Young and Gardner. When every opportunity to learn is provided, and the slow student is still unable to respond and do as well as his classmates, he must face the fact that he can no longer blame the system.

Mastery learning reduces competition and comparisons, but it does not eliminate them. Students who learn easily will meet the criterion for an A with little effort; they are likely to go through the required sequence so rapidly that they have considerable time for independent study. Those who learn slowly will engage in a constant battle to keep up with the required work. Herndon described the inevitable result: Because the "winners" learn faster and can engage in more self-selected study, they will probably get farther and farther ahead of the "losers." Despite suggestions that prestige colleges ought to practice open admissions, it is most unlikely that they will do so. Furthermore, the number of jobs at the top of a scale based on interest, pay, and influence will always be limited. A mastery approach cannot by itself alter the fact that students who learn easily and rapidly are still likely to be rewarded by admission to the best colleges and to get the best jobs. Even so, you may discover that a mastery approach is well worth the extra time, effort, and trouble it requires. It is likely that a greater proportion of your students will learn more, enjoy school more, develop better attitudes toward learning, and feel more confident and proud of themselves than they would under comparative grading techniques. Just don't expect miracles, and be prepared for the fact that some of your students—no matter how hard they try or how much assistance you give them—will still be unable to do as well as most of their classmates in the time available. This may be due to handicaps caused by a disadvantaged environment, to negative attitudes engendered by previous schooling, to the fact that you will be unable—by yourself—to satisfactorily satisfy their deficiency needs, or to genetic factors. All of these causes, but most particularly the last one, lead to speculations about the extent to which learning is dependent on intelligence, a topic that will be covered in the next chapter.

Summary

The competitive nature of a meritocratic society and the interests of colleges, universities, and business corporations in the selection process has brought about a tradition of comparative grading in this country. It is only recently that educators have become aware that this grading policy creates a situation in which teachers are led to expect that only a minority of students can learn and in which most students are made to feel unsuccessful and to lose interest in learning.

Even though many students and teachers advocate eliminating grades, it is not likely that this will be possible because of pressure from parents and the need for some measure of student progress. Since teachers are required to make evaluations, it is important to attempt to minimize the impact of mechanisms that interfere with objectivity—by making use of tests and by taking into account the advantages and disadvantages of tests and grades.

An approach to evaluation that seems to maximize advantages and minimize disadvantages is learning for mastery. In this approach, instructional objectives are noted, students are assisted to master them, tests are used to determine if mastery has been achieved, remedial instruction is provided, and a second opportunity to demonstrate mastery is provided.

Although mastery learning is likely to encourage students to learn more than they would under comparative grading, it is important to take pains to establish procedures that will guarantee that students meet respectable standards.

Suggestions for Further Reading, Writing, Thinking, and Discussion

11-1 *Examining Your Own Dissatisfactions with Tests and Grades*

This chapter includes comments on student criticisms of tests and grades. If you have strong negative feelings about these matters too, draw up your own list of complaints, then analyze it to see whether the disagreeable aspects could be minimized or eliminated. As you describe your plan for reform, however, keep in mind conditions under which you are almost sure to have to work. For example, most teachers in American public schools are required to assign grades on an A to F scale (or the equivalent); the GPA of a student may determine his eligibility for college or for a job; parents will be just as interested in grades as their children (if not more interested). These points are mentioned so that you will think about ways to improve evaluation *within* the present structure of the public education system rather than proposing sweeping changes that would have little or no chance of being adopted in the schools.

11-2 *Reacting to Arguments in Favor of Tests and Grades*

A number of arguments in *favor* of tests and grades are noted in this chapter. Since you will soon be dispensing rather than receiving grades, try to be open-minded about these points. Does John Gardner's suggestion that grades motivate students to work up to high standards seem valid? According to Gardner, the schools are the primary agency for doing the preliminary sorting out of able and less able individuals in our society—in which performance is a major determinant of status. Do you feel that the schools should undertake this sorting?

If you would prefer an approach to education in which comparisons between students were minimized, what alternative methods of selecting capable individuals can you propose? If the GPA in high school is not used in determining who will be admitted to college, how *should* the places in different kinds of colleges be filled? Does competition for grades assist students to make the most of their abilities? By establishing and maintaining high standards, does a teacher help students set respectable levels of performance and gain experience that will permit rigorous self-analysis? Although you may feel bitter about grades, perhaps you should at least entertain the possibility that evaluation has some desirable aspects that ought to be retained even as we seek improvements in the overall system of evaluation. If this basic question interests you, record your thoughts on the subject in writing.

11-3 *Speculating about Cheating*

Whether or not you approve, the fact remains that the schools *do* perform the preliminary sorting out of able and less able individuals. You may question the kind of ability that current school practices "reward," but the GPA (or equivalent) is unlikely to diminish in importance within the next few years. Because considerable pressure to get high grades is exerted on students in American schools, a significant number of pupils feels driven to cheat. Analyze your own experiences and feelings regarding cheating as a first step to speculating about how pressure for grades could be reduced in your classes. Knowing that you will almost surely be required to assign grades—probably with reference to some sort of distribution—what might you do to lessen your students' tendency to cheat? (As you record your thoughts, concentrate on specific techniques that might be applied within the present system.)

11-4 *Analyzing Your Own Experiences with Subjectivity*

To gain greater insight into the impact of mechanisms that interfere with objectivity, examine your own experiences with reference to the concepts noted in the text. Have you ever realized at a later time that your initial feelings about a certain individual were dominated by one good or bad characteristic that caused a halo effect? Did you ever find it difficult to believe an action or a report that was contrary to what you expected of an acquaintance? Could your irritation at a habit in someone else perhaps be due to your dislike of acknowledging that you have the same habit yourself? Have you ever reacted very favorably or unfavorably to an individual you met for the first time without understanding exactly why? Record one or more incidents of the type just described, and draw implications from them as you approach the point of interacting with large numbers of students.

11-5 *Analyzing Tests with Reference to the Criteria Noted in the Text*

You might be able to increase the likelihood that your first exams will bring about a favorable reaction in your students if you take the time to analyze exams *you* have especially liked and disliked. Write a description of the one you liked best and least. Then refer to the characteristics of tests noted in this chapter. Did you favor a test that involved a permanent record of behavior you and the teacher could reexamine as often as desired? Were your answers evaluated according to a reasonable, clear set of scoring standards? If the test you liked best did not have these characteristics, what *were* the qualities that made you respond favorably? If the test you disliked had some of these characteristics but still seemed unsatisfactory, why were you bothered? Record your reactions and, if possible, come up with a set of do's and don'ts to follow in making up exams.

11-6   *Comparing Your Reactions to Objective and Essay Tests*

This chapter includes a comparison between objective tests and essay exams. If you will be teaching at the secondary level, it might be of interest to carry out a similar analysis of your own. For example, you might compare observations made by Banesh Hoffmann in his book *The Tyranny of Testing* (1962) with those offered by Henry Chauncey and John E. Dobbin in *Testing: Its Place in Education Today* (1963). Hoffmann is a distinguished mathematician who felt that psychologists and educators were too involved in testing to recognize certain weaknesses and inconsistencies of objective tests. Chauncey is president of Educational Testing Service and Dobbin an influential member of the same company (the leading publisher of standardized tests). In Chapter 3 of *The Tyranny of Testing*, Hoffmann describes some problems of grading essay exams. In Chapter 4 he discusses "Objectivity and Ambiguity." Among other things, he points out that *objective* is a misnomer, since the term refers only to the process of grading. The person who decides which multiple-choice answer is correct is making just as subjective a judgment as the person evaluating an essay answer. In Chapter 5 he criticizes the emphasis on the "best" answer and suggests that the person taking the test is required to attempt to fathom how the mind of the test-writer functions. In Chapter 6 he argues that multiple-choice tests discriminate against the brightest, most creative students. Chauncey and Dobbin present counterarguments in a section beginning on page 77 of *Testing: Its Place in Education Today* and in the Appendix, "Multiple-Choice Questions: A Close Look." If you are undecided about the relative merits, strengths, and weaknesses of multiple-choice and essay tests, compare the views of Hoffmann with those of Chauncey and Dobbin, or make an analysis of your own. At the conclusion of your analysis, you might list some general guidelines to follow when you write exam questions.

11-7   *Making up Sample Test Items*

A good way to become aware of the difficulties and complexities of evaluation (as well as to understand different types of tests) is to devise some test questions. Take a chapter or two from this text and compose several kinds of questions—say, three to five multiple-choice, three to five completion, five true-false, a matching question (if the material seems appropriate), three short essay, and one or two long essay questions. Be sure to make up your key as you write the questions. Then ask one or two classmates to take your test. Request that they not only record their answers but also add any critical remarks about the strengths and weaknesses of specific items. Summarize the answers and criticisms and draw up a list of guidelines to follow when you construct classroom examinations.

11-8 *Analyzing the Systematic Asking of Questions to Help Students Use Ideas*

In *Classroom Questions: What Kinds?* (1966) Norris M. Sanders describes how to write and pose questions which require students to *use* ideas rather than simply remember them. Sanders bases his approach on the taxonomy of educational objectives. The hierarchical nature of learning stressed in the taxonomy is too often ignored, he feels, when questions are asked. Teachers are partial to memory-level questions, and thus restrict students to the bottom of the hierarchy of learning. The memorization of facts should not be an end in itself, but a means to permit the student to interpret ideas, make applications, analyze, and synthesize. Proper use of questions helps the student perform these higher-level operations *as* he answers. In *Classroom Questions: What Kinds?* Sanders devotes a chapter to questions which might be used in testing each of the categories in the taxonomy: memory, translation, interpretation, application, analysis, synthesis, and evaluation. Many examples are offered, and each chapter concludes with questions designed to test the reader's understanding of the discussion. For more on the possibility of using the taxonomy of educational objectives not only to plan lessons but also to make up questions, secure a copy of *Classroom Questions: What Kinds?* (it is an inexpensive paperback). Outline the ideas you regard as most valuable, perhaps in the form of a personal "handbook" on how to make systematic use of classroom questions.

11-9 *Speculating about the Possibility of Schools without Failure*

William Glasser, a psychiatrist, has analyzed traditional approaches to education and concludes that American schools cause too many students to fail. How we might reverse this trend is the subject of *Schools Without Failure* (1969). Glasser feels that the first years in school are of crucial importance and that overemphasis on memorization and grades leads numerous children to be labeled or to think of themselves as failures early in their academic careers. His prescription for reform advises "involvement, relevance and thinking." He recommends group discussion as the basic pedagogical method, argues for greater emphasis on having students relate what they learn in school to their lives outside it, and suggests that a grading system in which a student gets either a Pass or a Superior (but never an F) be substituted for the usual system. Perhaps because of his medical background, Glasser proposes a simple, definite diagnosis and prescribes simple, definite treatment. For an overview of *one* way schools might attempt to minimize failure, you might read *Schools Without Failure.* Chapter 1 is devoted to a general analysis of the problem, Chapter 6 is a critique of tests and grades, and Chapter 10 consists of Glasser's description of how teachers should use group discussion as *the* main approach to teaching. [Glasser gives other suggestions in his more recent book, *The Identity Society* (1972).] If you would prefer different analyses of some of the same points Glasser covers, you might read John Holt's observations on failure (*How Children Fail,* 1964), Banesh Hoffman's critique of grades (*The Tyranny of Testing,* 1962), the discussions of the discovery approach provided by Jerome Bruner (*Toward a Theory of Instruction,* 1966), Morris L. Bigge (*Learning Theories for Teachers,* 1964), or Herbert A. Thelen (*Education and the Human Quest,* 1960). If you read Glasser's book or one of the others, summarize the arguments presented and add your own reactions.

11-10   *Drawing up a List of Guidelines for Learning for Mastery*

If you are impressed by the arguments of Glasser and Holt regarding the negative impact of failure, you may wish to use an alternative to traditional comparative grading. Holt advocates an "intellectual smorgasbord" with emphasis on free choice and self-direction; Glasser recommends group discussion. Both believe that grades should be eliminated. Such methods are appropriate and effective in certain situations, and you may wish to use them from time to time. It is not likely that you will be able to rely on either technique exclusively, however, because of the organization and administration of public schools in this country. You may find that learning for mastery is a more satisfactory way to reduce the impact of failure while still working within a system of letter grades. If you would like to learn more about this technique for the purpose of drawing up a detailed set of guidelines, consult *Mastery Learning: Theory and Practice* (1971) edited by James H. Block (a concise paperback), or *A Handbook of Formative and Summative Evaluation of Student Learning* (1971) edited by Benjamin S. Bloom, Thomas Hastings, and George F. Madaus (a volume that provides encyclopedic coverage).

11-11   *Examining More Comprehensive Analyses of Traditional Evaluation*

If you are not convinced that mastery learning will work to your advantage, or if you find yourself in a situation where you will be required to use comparative grading, you may wish to do further reading on traditional approaches to evaluation. (You may also discover—regardless of the approach to evaluation you take—that you would like more detailed suggestions on test construction than those provided in this chapter.) An excellent collection of somewhat technical discussions on ways to improve evaluation is *The Evaluation of Instruction* (1970) edited by M. C. Wittrock and David E. Wiley. For general discussions of testing consult *Evaluating Pupil Growth: Principles of Tests and Measurements* (4th ed., 1971) by J. Stanley Ahman and Marvin D. Glock, *Test Construction: A Programmed Guide* (1970) by Lowell A. Schoer, *Measurement and Evaluation in Psychology and Education* (3rd ed., 1969) by Robert L. Thorndike and Elizabeth Hagen, or *Constructing Achievement Tests* (1968) by Norman E. Gronlund. Especially recommended is *Essentials of Educational Measurement* (1972) by Robert L. Ebel. In Chapter 5 Ebel describes "How to Plan a Classroom Test." In Chapters 6, 7, and 8 he gives specific suggestions for writing essay, true-false, and multiple-choice items. Ebel also comments on how to judge the quality of the exams you write (Chapter 13) and tells how to analyze marks and marking systems (Chapter 12). If you read sections of Ebel's book, or sample sections of other books on testing, you might summarize points you think will be most valuable when you begin to measure educational achievement.

Recommended Reading in
Psychology Applied to Teaching: Selected Readings

If you would like to do further reading in books or articles mentioned in this chapter (and in the preceding "Suggestions for Further Reading, Writing, Thinking, and Discussion") without having to track down several separate volumes, you might peruse *Psychology Applied to Teaching: Selected Readings* (Boston: Houghton Mifflin, 1972). This is a collection of excerpts from books and articles from journals in psychology. The following selections provide extended commentaries on points noted in this chapter or mentioned in the "Suggestions."

Suggestions for Writing Classroom Exams: "The Need for Better Classroom Tests" by Robert L. Ebel, Selection 24, p. 378. (See also Suggestion 11–11.)

Writing Specific Types of Test Questions: Excerpt from *Classroom Questions: What Kinds?* by Norris M. Sanders, Selection 25, p. 389. (See also Suggestion 11–8.)

Possible Weaknesses of Multiple Choice Exams: Excerpt from *The Tyranny of Testing* by Banesh Hoffmann, Selection 27, p. 412. (See also Suggestion 11–6.)

Possible Strengths of Multiple Choice Exams: "Selecting Appropriate Tests" by Henry Chauncey and John E. Dobbin, Selection 26, p. 398. (See also Suggestion 11–6.)

Mastery Learning: Excerpt from *Mastery Learning: Theory and Practice,* by James H. Block, Selection 28, p. 420. (See also Suggestion 11–10.)

12 EVALUATING ACHIEVEMENT AND LEARNING ABILITY

KEY POINTS

Terminology
Standardized test
Age-level scale, IQ (Stanford-Binet)
Verbal Scale score, Performance Scale score (WISC, WAIS)
Individual test, group test

Criteria
Allowance for measurement errors in interpretation of group test scores

Concepts
Normal probability curve
Standard deviation; z scores, T scores
Stanines
Intellectual operations (Guilford)

Methodology
Administering standardized achievement tests
Interpreting scores: grade-equivalent, percentile rank, standard

CHAPTER CONTENTS

AT THE CONCLUSION OF THE PRECEDING CHAPTER YOU WERE cautioned not to expect any approach to teaching—including learning for mastery—to create a situation in which *all* pupils learn at a superior level. Even under the best of circumstances, some will learn with comparative ease, some will experience difficulties no matter how hard they try. Recognition of this has led to considerable discussion about the causes of such differences and what, if anything, might be done to increase the proportion of individuals who learn easily. There is substantial evidence and general agreement that learning ability is dependent to a considerable degree on general intelligence. Thus speculations about the causes of and solutions to differences in learning rates should take into account the nature of intelligence.

In almost every chapter of this book, differences of opinion have been noted regarding the degree to which environmental experiences shape behavior. Up to this point, these differences have centered around how much choice the individual has (or should have) in determining his own behavior. The behaviorist-associationist-environmentalist position stresses that in development, learning, and motivation, the experiences a person has—in terms of sequence and reinforcement—are the primary determinants of behavior. The natural view of development, open education and discovery learning, and theories of growth motivation stress that the individual exerts considerable control over his own destiny. Implicit in this view is the conviction that allowance should be made for inherited tendencies and predispositions.

B. F. Skinner expresses the environmentalist position in the following observations on heredity as a cause of behavior:

> The doctrine of "being born that way" has little to do with demonstrated facts. It is usually an appeal to ignorance. "Heredity," as the layman uses the term, is a fictional explanation of the behavior attributed to it.
>
> Even when it can be shown that some aspect of behavior is due to . . . genetic constitution, the fact is of limited use. It may help us in predicting behavior, but it is of little value in experimental analysis or in practice control because such a condition cannot be manipulated after the individual has been conceived. (1953, p. 6)

Aldous Huxley expressed the opposite point of view in this way:

> In the course of evolution nature has gone to endless trouble to see that every individual is unlike every other individual. We reproduce our kind by bringing the father's genes into contact with the mother's. These hereditary factors may be combined in an almost infinite number of ways. Physically and mentally, each one of us is unique. Any culture which, in the interests of efficiency or in the name of some political or religious dogma, seeks to standardize the human individual, commits an outrage against man's biological nature. (1958, p. 26)

Far from agreeing with Skinner that environment is responsible for the larger part of behavior, Huxley states, "All the available evidence points to the conclusion that in the life of individuals and societies heredity is no less significant than culture" (p. 120).

He goes on to reply to Skinner's assertion that attention should be focused on conditions that can be manipulated. After pointing out that biological variability is greater in man than in lower species of animals, Huxley adds:

> The Will to Order, the desire to impose a comprehensible uniformity upon the bewildering manifoldness of things and events, has led many people to ignore this fact. They have minimized biological uniqueness and have concentrated all their attention upon the simpler and, in the present state of knowledge, more understandable environmental factors involved in human behavior. (P. 125)

Lacking the ability to impose genetic uniformity upon embryos, the rulers of tomorrow's over-populated and over-organized world will try to impose social and cultural uniformity upon adults and their children. To achieve this end, they will (unless prevented) make use of all the mind-manipulating techniques at their disposal. (P. 128)

Thus Huxley warns us against the conditions that he described in his novel *Brave New World* (1932).

Although differences of opinion such as those reflected by the statements of Skinner and Huxley are found in almost all aspects of education, views on the relative influence of heredity and environment are expressed with special concern—and sometimes vehemence—when the causes of intelligence are analyzed. People probably began to argue about the degree to which individuals are born smart or stupid at the time language developed. But current discussions on the nature-nurture question might be traced to a book published by the brilliant English scientist Sir Francis Galton in 1869. Interest in the theory of evolution proposed by his cousin, Charles Darwin, led Galton to investigate the intelligence of eminent men of his day. His general conclusion is reflected by the title of his book: *Hereditary Genius*. Galton based his conclusion on the fact that eminent men tend to run in families. He did not at first recognize that the England of his day was a society based on hereditary privilege and that the presence of many intelligent people in the same families could be explained just as logically by arguing that they came from a superior environment. However, he was interested in gathering information about intelligence in order to make a more systematic study of the question and was largely responsible for establishing the mental test movement.

The advent of the industrial revolution and the rise of the meritocracy brought people greater freedom to make the most of their intelligence, regardless of their background. At the same time, techniques for measuring intelligence were developed, and the debate about the causes of intelligence that continues to this day began in earnest. When a society is organized so that people are given considerable freedom to achieve success through their own efforts, those with the most intelligence and ability move to the top. Under such circumstances, children of eminent men and women tend to do well, but many individuals who come from humble beginnings also achieve eminence. The success of the son of a Nobel Prize winner might be attributed either to inheritance or environment, but suppose his father was himself the son of a common laborer? Since the environment (at least within the family) was inferior, a logical explanation would be that he was born with an exceptional brain. On the other hand, perhaps the experiences he had in school accounted for his success; so if it were possible to discover the nature and sequence of these experiences, other children might be exposed to them and perhaps acquire the same characteristics.

Within the last few years support for this latter view has gained momentum in the United States, and enthusiasm for environmental determinism might be said to have reached its peak when the Head Start programs were instituted. The popularity of the environmentalist view in contemporary America might be traced to the traditional American belief that "all men are created equal" and that any man who works hard enough can succeed, to the endorsement of the Lockeian view by American psychologists, and to research on critical periods suggesting that since early deprivation may lead to a permanent handicap, early training may lead to permanent improvements. Many behavioral and social scientists believe that we should be able to systematically create what previously has occurred by accident, and in the 1960s they succeeded in persuading the government to finance Head Start. As noted in Chapter 3, it was argued that exposing disadvantaged children to enriched early experience would substantially improve intelligence and the ability to learn. You will recall that J. McV. Hunt, the theorist who probably had more to do with the development of Head Start than any other individual, argued that "with a sound scientific educational psychology of early experience, it might become possible to raise the level of intelligence as now measured . . . by thirty points of IQ" (1961, p. 267).

When Head Start graduates entered elementary school, they were observed with special interest. The results of objective analyses of their success in school came as a blow to environmentalists: when evaluated at the end of first grade, children who had been exposed to Head Start programs did no better than children from similar backgrounds who did not attend. The report of the U. S. Commission on Civil Rights offered this conclusion: "None of the compensatory education programs appear to have raised significantly the achievement of participating pupils, as a group, within the period evaluated by the Commission" (1967, p. 138). It was then argued that the lack of success might have been because there was too little training or that what little there was came too late. To correct for the first weakness, Follow-Through programs (described in Chapter 10) were instituted. To correct for the second weakness, research was undertaken to try to discover the kinds of early experiences that successful students are exposed to. If these experiences could be isolated, mothers of underachieving children could then be provided instruction in exposing their children to effective early education curricula in their homes. The most comprehensive program of this type is the Harvard Preschool Project (White and Watts, 1973). The way mothers treat their children in home situations has been analyzed, and the children have been divided into A (able) and C (poorer than average) types. The procedure is to ascertain what the mothers of the A children do, then teach other mothers to do the same. It is hoped that the outcome will be improved development.

In a related set of studies Jerome Kagan has analyzed the differences between middle- and lower-class mothers. Middle-class mothers are more inclined to entertain their children and to interact with them in ways that contain an element of surprise. They are also more likely to help a child in distress. Thus the middle-class child gains an awareness that he has an effect on the world.

A Harvard Preschool Project field worker observing the behavior of a child under natural circumstances.

TED POLUMBAUM

A child who is not attended to may learn helplessness and impotence, which may be the beginning of a sense of fatalism about destiny control. Kagan says that "we should think of changing the behavior of mothers of poor children during the first two years of the child's life"; he feels that this goal is important enough to merit a "major national commitment" (Pines, 1969, p. 16).

Although it seems to make sense to try to discover what the mothers of high-achieving children do and then persuade all other mothers to do the same, a number of difficulties may be anticipated. First, why do mothers who seem to have a natural tendency to do all the "right" things produce some children who are high achievers and others who are low achievers? Since children from the same family background vary so much, there must be more to superficial techniques than meets the eye; evidently no single set of prescriptions will work for all children. In some cases the "ideal" environment might do more harm than good.

The fact that children who are exposed to the same general set of child-rearing practices turn out differently can be explained in a number of ways. Some of the explanations highlight further difficulties in trying to discover *the* optimum approach. The possibility of genetic differences is always present. Perhaps some of the A children described by White are high achievers mainly because they inherited favorable traits. The chief cause of a child's superiority may be his own characteristics rather than the way his mother handles him. If a child with less than average genetic potential is exposed to child-rearing that is appropriate only for especially bright children, he may become frustrated or develop an unrealistic level of aspiration.

A related point has to do with Maslow's observations about children's tendency to select what is right for them when they are free to choose. There is the danger that exposing all children to a particular set of child-rearing practices will prevent this freedom of choice and lead to problems both in personality development and in motivation. In a sense, the guided-experience advocates are suggesting that they know what is best for all children. Maslow feels that only the child can know what is best for his own needs and that he should have as much freedom of choice as possible.

The Jensen Controversy

It is still too early to tell if Follow-Through or the Harvard Preschool Project will succeed in increasing the learning ability of disadvantaged children. Although the existence of these programs indicates that the environmentalist view is still strongly endorsed, the lack of success of Head Start has created doubts about this position, doubts that have been intensified in the minds of many by the publication of articles presenting evidence in favor of the genetic view of intelligence. Such articles have appeared regularly over the past fifty years, but a recent report that attracted international attention was "How Much Can

We Boost IQ and Scholastic Achievement?" by Arthur R. Jensen, which appeared in the Winter 1969 issue of the *Harvard Educational Review*. Jensen argued that attempts at compensatory education (such as Head Start) failed because they were based on the belief that intelligence is almost exclusively the result of environmental experiences. He presented considerable evidence to substantiate the view that heredity plays a much greater role in determining intelligence, and he suggested that it would be more fruitful to take into account genetic differences in planning educational programs—as opposed to attempting to "create" intelligence. The most controversial part of the Jensen article was his claim that there are clear-cut differences between the average IQ's of different ethnic groups and that certain groups—blacks, for example—might benefit more from instruction that stressed associative learning more than conceptual learning.

The Jensen article aroused a storm of protest, and he was subjected to considerable harassment and even threats of bodily harm. The critiques that quickly appeared included complaints about his interpretation of statistics and his basic premises and also statements that he was a racist and white supremacist. (If you would like to read the original Jensen article plus commentaries by seven critics, see *Environment, Heredity, and Intelligence* (1970), Reprint Series No. 2, of the *Harvard Educational Review*.)

Fuel was added to the fire when William Shockley, a Nobel Prize winner and professor of engineering science at Stanford University, argued that, within certain limits, "an increase of one percent in Caucasian ancestry raises Negro IQ an average of one point for low IQ populations" (1971, p. 244). In the September 1971 issue of *The Atlantic*, Richard Herrnstein of Harvard analyzed the history of intelligence testing and reviewed research on the relative influence of heredity and environment on intelligence and concluded that 80 to 85 percent of the variability in IQ is due to genetic factors. Then H. J. Eysenck, an eminent English psychologist, published *The IQ Argument* (1971) in which he carried out much the same sort of analysis as Herrnstein and came to essentially the same conclusions.

Environmentalists have responded to these arguments by referring to evidence indicating that minority-group children are victims of deprived early environments (Hunt, 1961; Deutsch, 1964), claiming that there is an "IQ conspiracy" because most intelligence tests have been designed to favor middle-class whites and discriminate against lower-class minority group children (Garcia, 1972). They argue that minority-group children do poorly on IQ tests because they have not been equipped with skills to pass tests (Mercer, 1972) and suggest that minority-group children respond negatively to white testers and that they are not confident about taking tests or motivated to do well because they are influenced by a negative self-fulfilling prophecy (Watson, 1972). However, it is possible to cite evidence (e.g., Shuey, 1966; Jensen, 1969; Eysenck, 1971) to refute all these hypotheses.

To make it possible for you to gain some perspective for evaluating these arguments, the nature and measurement of intelligence will now be analyzed.

A Plea for Openness in Discussing
the Nature-Nurture Question

Some critics of Jensen, Shockley, and Herrnstein have argued that they should be prevented from presenting their views and that their work should not be discussed. This led a group of fifty eminent scientists to sign the following document (which was published in the July 1972 issue of *American Psychologist,* p. 660) and submit it to the American Psychological Association:

> Background: The history of civilization shows many periods when scientific research or teaching was censured, punished, or suppressed for nonscientific reasons, usually for seeming to contradict some religious or political belief. Well-known scientist victims include: Galileo, in orthodox Italy; Darwin, in Victorian England; Einstein, in Hitler's Germany; and Mendelian biologists, in Stalin's Russia.
>
> Today, a similar suppression, censure, punishment, and defamation are being applied against scientists who emphasize the role of heredity in human behavior. Published positions are often misquoted and misrepresented; emotional appeals replace scientific reasoning; arguments are directed against the man rather than against the evidence (e.g., a scientist is called "fascist," and his arguments are ignored).
>
> A large number of attacks come from nonscientists, or even antiscientists, among the political militants on campus. Other attackers include academics committed to environmentalism in their explanation of almost all human differences. And a large number of scientists, who have studied the evidence and are persuaded of the great role played by heredity in human behavior, are silent, neither expressing their beliefs clearly in public, nor rallying strongly to the defense of their more outspoken colleagues.
>
> The results are seen in the present academy: it is virtually heresy to express a hereditarian view, or to recommend further study of the biological bases of behavior. A kind of orthodox

The Nature and Measurement of Intelligence

One of the difficulties in drawing conclusions about research on intelligence is that there is no universally agreed-upon definition of intelligence. As a result, different people mean different things when they talk about this quality. It is especially important to keep this in mind when discussing comparative scores, since much may depend on the test used to determine the scores. The conception of intelligence that a test author has in mind when he starts to work determines the kinds of questions he writes, which in turn determines the final score. Consequently, it is important to take into account how writers of intelligence tests define the quality they seek to measure.

Definitions of Intelligence

There is general agreement that the most widely used and *respected* tests of intelligence are the Stanford-Binet and the Wechsler tests. Lewis Terman, the driving force behind the development of the Stanford-Binet tests, designed

environmentalism dominates the liberal academy, and strongly inhibits teachers, researchers, and scholars from turning to biological explanations or efforts.

Resolution: Now, therefore, we the undersigned scientists from a variety of fields, declare the following beliefs and principles:

1. We have investigated much evidence concerning the possible role of inheritance in human abilities and behaviors, and **we believe such hereditary influences are very strong.**
2. We wish strongly to encourage research into the biological hereditary bases of behavior, as a major complement to the environmental efforts at explanation.
3. We strongly defend the right, and emphasize the scholarly duty, of the teacher to discuss hereditary influences on behavior, in appropriate settings and with responsible scholarship.
4. We deplore the evasion of hereditary reasoning in current textbooks, and the failure to give responsible weight to heredity in disciplines such as sociology, social psychology, social anthropology, educational psychology, psychological measurement, and many others.
5. We call upon liberal academics—upon faculty senates, upon professional and learned societies, upon the American Association of University Professors, upon the American Civil Liberties Union, upon the University Centers for Rational Alternatives, upon presidents and boards of trustees, upon departments of science, and upon the editors of scholarly journals—to insist upon the openness of social science to the well-grounded claims of biobehavioral reasoning, and to protect vigilantly any qualified faculty members who responsibly, teach, research, or publish concerning such reasoning.
We so urge because as scientists we believe that human problems may best be remedied by increased human knowledge, and that such increases in knowledge lead much more probably to the enhancement of human happiness than to the opposite.

---

them to measure a general factor (McNemar, 1942), which might be described as the ability to deal with abstractions. David Wechsler, the chief originator of the Wechsler Intelligence Scale for Children (WISC) and the Wechsler Adult Intelligence Scale (WAIS), has defined intelligence as "the aggregate or global capacity of the individual to act purposefully, to think rationally and to deal effectively with his environment" (1944, p. 3). There are ten subtests on the WISC and WAIS, each specifically intended to measure one aspect of the aggregate of abilities described by Wechsler.

The distinction between general and specific abilities is perhaps the major point of difference in definitions of intelligence. Charles Spearman (1927), one of the earliest authorities on intelligence, spoke of a "g" (for "general") factor, plus several "s" (for "specific") factors. L. L. and Thelma G. Thurstone (1941), specialists in the statistical technique of factor analysis, isolated several specific factors, referred to them as primary mental abilities and developed a test to measure six of them. The test did not prove very successful, perhaps because later factor analyses (Anastasi, 1968) revealed that despite the Thurstones' efforts to the contrary, it still seemed to be measuring a general factor. More recently,

J. P. Guilford (1959) has proposed a multifactor theory that suggests that intelligence can be divided into 120 components. All of this indicates that there are many ways of looking at intelligence and that the way you define it will determine how you try to measure it.

The appraisal of intelligence is further complicated by the fact that it cannot be measured directly. If scientists ever find the organic basis of intelligence, it may then be possible to measure general learning ability through the use of an X-ray or an EEG or some future electronic device or chemical analysis.[1] Until that time, however, our efforts must be confined to measuring the overt manifestations of the functioning of the brain. And that is why intelligence is so elusive. It all depends on what manifestations you choose to observe. Some theorists define intelligence as what is measured by an intelligence test. This may sound like double-talk, but the intent is not to dodge the issue; it is to emphasize that any estimate of intelligence depends first and foremost on the questions asked in the effort to measure it.

Nature of Intelligence Tests

An intelligence test consists of questions that the test-maker believes will yield an adequate sample of the subject's ability to deal with the types of problems the test-maker considers indicative of intelligence (as he defines it). This is the crucial point in appreciating the values and limitations of intelligence tests.

Sir Francis Galton, who was instrumental in initiating the mental test movement, emphasized that a test consists of the *sinking of shafts at critical points* (1890, p. 373). When you set out to measure intelligence, the crux of the matter is: What are "critical points"? You have to try to select sample bits of behavior that you hope will be "critical" or indicative of a general ability, yet make your questions fair to all.

The major confounding factor is differences in educational opportunity. Remember, you hope to get an estimate of general learning ability. This means taking into account that some children benefit from an especially rich home and school environment. Obviously, the capacity of a child to learn is a function of both his inherited potential and his experiences. But since the test-maker is interested in a general capacity, he wants to avoid, as much as possible, measuring abilities that are largely the result of a particular set of home or school experiences. If he asks questions too directly related to a specific kind

---

[1] John Ertl, director of the University of Ottawa's Center for Cybernetic Studies, has developed an electronic device called the *neural efficiency analyzer*, which he claims measures the brain's physical ability to learn. The time it takes for flashes of light to register as changes in a subject's brain wave patterns gives an index of speed of information transmission, which, according to Ertl, serves as a bias-free index of intelligence. The predictive value of neural efficiency scores has yet to be established, but you may encounter reports on studies now underway. For details of the present state of knowledge about Ertl's device, examine the front-page article in the *APA Monitor* for March 1973.

of home or curriculum, he will be measuring only how well a child has responded to those experiences. What about the child who has *not* been exposed to that set of home or curriculum experiences? You can't really say he's dumb, because you haven't given him the chance to demonstrate that he's bright. To avoid this sort of handicap, the test questions should be based on situations common to practically all children. Whether they have learned from the exposure is what you hope to discover, but you must try to make sure they have had the opportunity to learn in the first place.

One more point regarding intelligence tests has to do with the score. No intelligence test score is an "absolute" measure. This is a fact many people—parents especially—fail to grasp. A common misconception about the IQ is that it is a once-for-all judgment of how bright a person is. In fact, the score on an intelligence test is merely a qualified guess about how successful a child is—as compared to other children—in handling certain kinds of problems at a particular time. If a child is retested, even with the same questions, he is quite likely to get a different score. If the second test consists of entirely different questions, he is almost certain to get a different score.

Individual Intelligence Tests

To elucidate the series of points that have just been made, a description of the Stanford-Binet, the WISC, and the WAIS, including a brief account of their origin, will now be presented.

The Stanford-Binet

The successful testing of intelligence began with a brilliant Frenchman named Alfred Binet. In the late 1890s the school authorities of Paris asked Binet if he could develop some sort of device to differentiate between pupils who were capable of doing regular schoolwork and those who were mentally retarded. Until that time, attempts at measuring intelligence had centered around compiling a composite score of physical attributes and reactions. For example, a final score might be derived from height, weight, size of head, visual acuity, and reaction time. When such scores were compared with teacher estimates of ability and success in school, little relationship was found.

Binet decided that an entirely different approach was called for. He reasoned that the basis for intelligent behavior was more likely to be discovered through an examination of the "higher thought processes": reasoning, the capacity to grasp concepts, and the ability to deal with the abstract. (Terman based his definition of intelligence on that of Binet.) Accordingly, Binet began to write test questions that he hoped would measure these qualities. But immediately he found himself faced with a vexing problem: How could he get some

Sir Francis Galton (1822–1911)   Alfred Binet (1857–1911)

uncomplicated and easy-to-obtain evidence on whether his questions did indeed measure intelligence? His solution was brilliant and simple. Binet decided to operate on the assumption that the average older child is more intelligent than the average younger child. He tried out his questions on children of different ages, and if older children were able to answer them more consistently than younger ones, he assumed the questions were measures of intelligence. Binet found that the age at which certain questions were more readily grasped than at younger age levels also provided a convenient basis for organizing the test

Age-level scale   items; he therefore grouped his questions by age levels. If a particular question was not answered by more than a few four-, five-, or six-year-olds but was comprehended by a noticeably larger proportion of seven-year-olds, he placed it at the seven-year level.

That Binet had reasoned logically was proved by the fact that his age-level scale was the first intelligence test really to work; it succeeded to a considerable degree in differentiating between bright and dull pupils. Unfortunately, Binet died at the prime of his life, before he could perfect his brainchild. For a number of years other test-makers contented themselves with little more than slight revisions or translations of the original Binet. A literal English translation of the test, by the way, proved essentially invalid—it did not differentiate very clearly between the bright and the dull. If you will think back to the point about a test's being a fair and an adequate sample, you will find the major explanation for this result. Binet's questions were within the realm of experience of a child growing up in Paris but were foreign (both figuratively and literally) to the experience of a child growing up in New York City or River City, Iowa.

Not until a man who matched Binet in imagination, creativity, and drive appeared on the scene were American teachers able to benefit from the

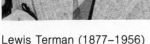

Lewis Terman (1877–1956)   David Wechsler (1896–   )

Frenchman's innovation. The man was Lewis Terman of Stanford University. Building on Binet's ideas, Terman came up with the first really successful intelligence test for use with American children. He modestly called the test the Stanford-Binet, honoring the university that sponsored the research instead of claiming the credit he deserved. The first test was published in 1916. A few years later Terman and his associates started work on an improved revision of this original test, and after ten years of effort the 1937 Revisions of the Stanford-Binet Scales, Forms L & M, were published (Terman and Merrill, 1937). In 1960 a third revision of the Stanford-Binet appeared (Terman and Merrill, 1960).

The Stanford-Binet is an individual test, given by one examiner to one subject *Individual test* at a time. Since most of the responses are recorded by the tester, the person taking the test answers most questions verbally—not by writing or marking his own responses. Thus it is essential that the person who administers the test be well trained and experienced. This is not a test a teacher can take out of a storeroom and administer after a five-minute inspection of the manual because, as the preceding chapter emphasized several times, a standard situation is required if a test is to be valid. In order to ask questions and present items on the Stanford-Binet in the standard way decreed by Terman and his associates, a considerable amount of memorizing and practicing is necessary.

When an experienced tester gets ready to give a Stanford-Binet, he first ascertains if the child to be tested is regarded as markedly below average in intelligence. The reason for this is that the first questions should be within the capability of the child. Starting slightly below the rough estimate of a child's ability makes it possible to establish a *basal age*—a level at which a subject handles all items successfully. Once the basal age is set, testing continues until

A. M. LOVE, JR.

Figure 12–1 Items from the Stanford-Binet Intelligence Scale. Materials used to test the intelligence of young children. Verbal materials are also used but mainly with older children and adults.

the child fails all tests at some age level. This is called the *ceiling age.* By that time the tester usually has covered several age levels and asked a good many questions, which will insure a fairly complete sample. It remains to score the answers according to the detailed instructions in the test manual and compute the IQ. This is done by dividing the mental age by the chronological age and multiplying by 100.

IQ:MA divided by CA multiplied by 100

Assume that a six-year-old first grader is being considered for acceleration (skipping) to the third grade. Before a final decision is made, the teacher, principal, and parents would like an estimate of his IQ. The tester can be pretty sure that such a child is able to handle questions at the five-year level with ease, so he starts there. Here is an abbreviated description of the testing for the first two age levels. (For typical materials used, see Figure 12-1.)

Five-year Level

First test Completing a simplified, stylized drawing of a man. The scoring is based not on artistic ability but on completeness, that is, on how many details (legs, arms, hands, mouth, eyes, nose, etc.) have been added.

Second test: Folding a 6- by 6-inch square of paper into a double triangle after watching a demonstration.

Third test: Defining *ball, hat* and *stove.* Must get two definitions out of three.

Fourth test: Copying a square printed on the record blank. Must perform one out of three trials satisfactorily.

Fifth test: Identifying similarities and differences in pairs of pictures. Must get nine out of twelve correct.

Sixth test: Arranging two triangular pieces of cardboard to form a rectangle. Must make correct arrangement two out of three times.

Six-year Level

First test: Defining at least six out of a list of forty-five vocabulary words. (These are arranged in order of difficulty. Testing stops after six consecutive failures.)

Second test: Explaining the differences between two objects, such as *wood* and *glass.* Must get two out of three.

Third test: Telling which feature is missing in a series of "mutilated pictures." Must get four out of five.

Fourth test: Picking out three, ten, six, nine, and then seven cubes from a pile of twelve, to demonstrate the ability to count. Must count at least four of the five trials correctly.

Fifth test: Completing analogies such as "A bird flies, a fish . . . ." Must get three out of four.

Sixth test: Solving two out of three simple pencil mazes by tracing the proper pathway.

At the higher levels the child will be asked to tell what is foolish or absurd about short statements, indicate how objects are the same or different, comprehend and apply analogies, and solve a variety of mathematical and other kinds of problems—to mention just a few of the many recurring types of questions.

The WISC and WAIS

Although the Stanford-Binet is preferred by many testers, two individual tests developed by David Wechsler and the Psychological Corporation are also widely used. You are likely to see the letters WISC and WAIS occasionally on cumulative folders. As noted earlier, these tests are based on a different concept of intelligence from Binet's and Terman's, and may be more appropriate in some situations, particularly when information is desired about nonverbal intelligence.

David Wechsler was a psychologist at Bellevue Hospital in New York City when he felt impelled to do something about the lack of an effective intelligence test for adults. (The 1937 Stanford-Binet was not very useful beyond the age of fifteen.) Wechsler felt that intelligence was an aggregate of abilities, not a single general ability. Accordingly, he developed a test (which he called the Wechsler-Bellevue) to measure several specific mental abilities (Wechsler, 1944).

The original Wechsler test filled a definite need and was widely used. However, it was described by one authority in testing (Anastasi, 1958) as a "crude though promising instrument." Because the criticism was deserved, the Psychological Corporation, an independent testing concern, collaborated with Wechsler on a revision of the Wechsler-Bellevue designed especially for children. The WISC was published in 1949. A few years later a revised Wechsler-Bellevue for adults came out, the WAIS. These two revisions are very similar to the original Wechsler-Bellevue—to the point of retaining some of the exact questions—but as test instruments they merit much more respect and confidence.

To give you a clearer idea of the nature of the Wechsler tests, here is a description of the subtests on the WISC:

Verbal Scale

First test: General Information. Questions that measure knowledge of such matters as distances between cities, names of explorers, etc.

Second test: General Comprehension. Questions intended to measure practical judgement and common sense; for example, "What is the thing to do when you cut your finger?"

Third test: Arithmetic. Arithmetic problems of the type found in most elementary school textbooks.

Fourth test: Similarities. Items that require the subject to tell how two things are alike, for example, a peach and a plum.

Fifth test: Vocabulary. Words the subject is asked to tell the meaning of.

A supplementary or alternate test is sometimes used that requires the child to repeat a series of spoken numbers.

Performance Scale

First test: Picture Completion. A series of incomplete pictures intended to discover whether the subject can describe what is missing.

Second test: Picture Arrangement. A series of comic-strip type cards that must be arranged in the proper order so that they tell a story.

Third test: Object Assembly. Scrambled pieces to be formed into pictures, for example, a horse.

Fourth test: Block Design. Printed pictures of mosaic designs to be reproduced by arranging colored blocks.

Fifth test: Coding. A key consisting of symbols paired with nine digits and a test blank with a long list of scrambled digits. The subject is asked to write as many of the symbols in the corresponding blank spaces as he can. (The child below the age of eight is asked to work with a simpler code.)

A supplementary or alternate test to Coding is Mazes. The subject must work his way out of pencil mazes by starting in the center and progressing to the edge without entering blind alleys.

With the exception of the Picture Completion test, all scores in the performance tests are based on time and accuracy. This means a premium is put on speed.

In scoring a subject's responses to the various subtests, the tester first converts the raw scores to standard scores. From the total of the standard scores three deviation IQ's are computed: one for the Verbal part, one for the Performance part, and a Full Scale quotient based on all the tests. (Since the WISC and WAIS are not age-level scores, the IQ's are calculated with reference to tables of norms, not by dividing mental age by chronological age.)

WISC and WAIS: verbal and performance scores

The Stanford-Binet and the Wechsler tests are individual tests that must be administered by a trained examiner. It takes at least an hour and frequently two hours to give one of these tests and another thirty minutes or more to score it. Consequently, they are usually restricted to a very small number of cases, for example, students being considered for special classes for the mentally retarded. For most pupils, group tests are often the only measures that are economically feasible for assessing intelligence.

Group Tests of Mental Ability

Group tests of intelligence are often called tests of mental ability or scholastic aptitude, but they attempt to measure the same general ability (or abilities) as individual tests of intelligence. Widely used group tests include the Lorge-Thorndike Intelligence Tests, the Kuhlmann-Anderson tests, the Otis Quick-Scoring Mental Ability Tests, the Henmon-Nelson Tests of Mental Ability, and the California Test of Mental Maturity. Note the plural form in most of these titles. The measures consist of from four to twelve separate scales, reflecting a multifactor conception of intelligence.

Although group tests are considerably less expensive than individual tests, they are usually not as reliable or valid. Because of the nature of individual differences, it is impossible to anticipate all the ways various students will respond to instructions or specific questions on a test. An examiner who gives a Stanford-Binet or a WISC can do a great deal to clear up misunderstandings and to probe for more complete answers as he asks the questions (without destroying the standard situation). A teacher proctoring a room of thirty students working on a group test is unable to make such adjustments. Consequently, errors of measurement multiply when group tests are used. The score may be distorted by misunderstanding of the instructions, misuse of the answer sheet, a panic reaction to the teacher's use of a stopwatch, anxiety induced by the awareness that a classmate has already finished, and the like. In addition, group tests often put a premium on reading speed, and this one factor may influence many scores disproportionately.

Allowance for measurement errors in judging group test scores

For all these reasons, group test scores should be interpreted even more cautiously than individual IQ scores—and regarded as tentative estimates, not absolute scores. Whenever possible, it is desirable to get more than one test score of mental ability before making decisions or even inferences about student potential.

Using Test Scores to Individualize Teaching

Now that you have some familiarity with tests of intelligence and mental maturity, you are equipped to make some inferences about the claims of environmentalists that such tests are middle-class oriented, that they discriminate against lower-class minority-group children, that the attitude of the tester (or the nature of the test-taking situation) might lead to lower scores for such children. All of these arguments have some validity: the items on the Stanford-Binet and Wechsler are much more familiar to middle-class than lower-class children, the standardization groups did not include a representative sample of minority-group children, the great majority of individuals who give tests of intelligence are middle-class whites, middle-class children are likely to be more test-wise. Even so, Shuey, Jensen, and Eysenck present evidence that account has been taken of these factors in many studies, yet there are still differences in IQ among different groups.

Thus there are no simple, unequivocal interpretations regarding the distribution of intelligence. And because of the complexity of measuring IQ and the difficulties of taking into account all variables, it is also impossible to come up with any definitive statement about the relative influence of heredity and environment. Authorities may cite the same studies and come up with diametrically opposed conclusions. If you would like to make up your own mind on the question, you are urged to read comprehensive analyses by defenders of each position. For this purpose, you might examine these books: *Intelligence and Experience* (1961) by J. McV. Hunt, *Environment, Heredity, and Intelligence*, Reprint Series No. 2, Harvard Educational Review (1970), which includes the Jensen article and several critiques, and *Intelligence: Genetic and Environmental Influences* (1971) edited by Robert Cancro (an exceptionally good collection of articles by seventeen contributors—including Jensen and Hunt—who have specialized in the study of intelligence)

Before you engage in such study, however, you might ask yourself if there is any point in trying to come to a definite conclusion on the questions of group differences and the exact proportion of intelligence attributed to heredity and environment. Even if group differences do exist, will it make any difference in your classroom? Because of the nature of actuarial prediction and overlap, you could not be sure that a particular member of a minority group identified as high or low in intelligence actually is high or low until you give him a chance to prove it—which is the best policy anyway. And even if only 20 percent of the variability of intelligence is due to environmental factors (as many hereditarians claim), that would still be enough to make you want to provide the best possible learning environment for each pupil. If these propositions sound logical, you may wonder why there is so much concern about intelligence tests. The reason is that test scores may exert a profound influence on the educational career—and the entire life—of a child.

Individual and group intelligence tests were developed primarily to make *predictions* about relative ability. They were devised at a time when it was believed that the primary function of public education ought to be the selection of the most promising candidates for college admission. Considerable stress was placed on grouping and on determining if students seemed to have the potential to cope with advanced learning. Most tests were standardized to produce a normal distribution of scores, since this approach emphasized differences and facilitated selection procedures.

This conception of education is being questioned. There is now more emphasis on a value-added view and on criterion-referenced rather than normative grading. Instead of using tests to accentuate differences between pupils, they are frequently being used to try to find ways to assist all pupils to learn at a high level. If this point of view is endorsed, there is no point in speculating about group differences and the precise degree to which intelligence is determined by nature or nurture. It is more important to use tests to diagnose strengths and weaknesses of individual pupils in order to establish the most effective learning environment.

Because many critics have concentrated only on certain aspects of Jensen's observations on intelligence, particularly those that have been sensationalized

Arthur Jensen

Richard J. Herrnstein

J. McV. Hunt

by the press, they have overlooked the fact that this is precisely the procedure he recommends. The final paragraph in his article in the *Harvard Educational Review* sums up his major recommendation:

> If diversity of mental abilities, as of most other human characteristics, is a basic fact of nature, as the evidence indicates, and if the ideal of universal education is to be successfully pursued, it seems a reasonable conclusion that schools and society must provide a range and diversity of educational methods, programs, and goals, and of occupational opportunities, just as wide as the range of human abilities. Accordingly, the ideal of equality of educational opportunity should not be interpreted as uniformity of facilities, instructional techniques, and educational aims for all children. Diversity rather than uniformity of approaches and aims would seem to be the key in making education rewarding for children of different patterns of ability. The reality of individual differences need not mean educational rewards for some children and frustration and defeat for others. (1969, p. 117)

This is the same basic point made by many educators who have been praised for their sympathetic understanding of minority groups. When Jensen suggested that Negroes may learn better through associative rather than conceptual methods, he was attacked as a racist and white supremacist. Yet there is virtual unanimity of opinion among those who have written books and articles on the education of the disadvantaged (noted in Chapter 10) that they have a vocational rather than an academic orientation, have limited language and reading skills, have greater interest in the practical than the abstract, and prefer physical to verbal learning. Most programs for teaching the disadvantaged, including Head Start and Project Follow-Through, have operated on these assumptions. Yet it would seem that the basic assumption of these programs is that minority-group children learn better through concrete, associative learning. Jensen is not suggesting that test scores be used to make decisions about the superiority or inferiority of different groups, he is suggesting that they be used to improve learning by identifying the learning aptitudes and styles of different individuals to set the stage for planning instruction.

This trend toward identifying aptitudes and styles has been developing for a number of years. It is based on the conception of intelligence proposed by J. P. Guilford, on identification of several types of cognitive styles, and on what is referred to as *aptitude-treatment-interaction.*

Guilford's Conception of Intelligence

Guilford's view of intelligence is a more systematic and complete elaboration of the "s" factors hypothesized by Spearman and the primary mental abilities described by the Thurstones. He hypothesizes five intellectual *operations,* four *contents,* and six *products.* The five operations, which are listed below, are especially important for speculating about ways to improve instruction.

1. *Cognition.* "Immediate discovery, awareness, rediscovery, or recognition of information in various forms; comprehension. . . ."
2. *Memory.* "Retention or storage, with some degree of availability, of information in the same form in which it was committed to storage."
3. *Convergent Production.* Using information in a way that "leads to one right answer or to a recognized best or conventional answer."
4. *Divergent Production.* Productive thinking "in different directions, sometimes searching, sometimes seeking variety."
5. *Evaluation.* Ways in which we "reach decisions as to the goodness, correctness, suitability or adequacy of what we know, . . . remember, and . . . produce in productive thinking." (1959, pp. 470–475)

A few implications of Guilford's description of different operations indicate the significance of his theory: A student low in memory will need a different kind of instruction from one low in cognition, any approach to teaching that stresses a single route to a learning goal (such as a linear program) is not likely to appeal to or be understood by all students, and divergent thinkers might be at a disadvantage on tests perfected through item-analysis techniques.

Cognitive Styles

In Chapter 5, Kagan's description of impulsive-reflective and analytic-thematic styles of thinking were noted. Samuel Messick has described several other cognitive styles that "represent a person's typical modes of perceiving, remembering, thinking, and problem solving" (1970, p. 188). He summarizes them in this way:

> *Field independence versus field dependence*—"an analytical, in contrast to a global, way of perceiving [that] entails a tendency to experience items as discrete from their backgrounds and reflects ability to overcome the influence of an embedding context" (Witkin and others, 1962).
>
> *Scanning*—a dimension of individual differences in the extensiveness and intensity of attention deployment, leading to individual variations in vividness of experience and the span of awareness (Holzman, 1966; Schlesinger, 1954; Gardner and Long, 1962).
>
> *Breadth of categorizing*—consistent performances for broad inclusiveness, as opposed to narrow exclusiveness, in establishing the acceptable range for specified categories (Pettigrew, 1958; Bruner and Tajfel, 1961; Kogan and Wallach, 1964).
>
> *Conceptualizing styles*—individual differences in the tendency to categorize perceived similarities and differences among stimuli in terms of many differentiated concepts, which is a dimension called *conceptual differentiation* (Gardner and Schoen, 1962; Messick and Kogan, 1963), as well as consistencies in the utilization of particular conceptualizing approaches as bases for forming concepts—such as the routine use in concept formation of thematic or functional relations among stimuli as opposed to the analysis of descriptive attributes or the inference of class membership (Kagan, Moss, and Sigel, 1960; Kagan and others, 1963).

Cognitive complexity versus simplicity—individual differences in the tendency to construe the world, and particularly the world of social behavior, in a multidimensional and discriminating way (Kelley, 1955; Bieri, 1961; Bieri and others, 1966; Scott, 1963; Harvey, Hunt, and Schroder, 1961).

Leveling versus sharpening—reliable individual variations in assimilation in memory. Subjects at the leveling extreme tend to blur similar memories and to merge perceived objects or events with similar but not identical events recalled from previous experience. Sharpeners, at the other extreme, are less prone to confuse similar objects and, by contrast, may even judge the present to be less similar to the past than is actually the case (Holzman, 1954; Holzman and Klein, 1954; Gardner and others, 1959).

Constricted versus flexible control—individual differences in susceptibility to distraction and cognitive interference (Klein, 1954; Gardner and others, 1959).

Tolerance for incongruous or unrealistic experiences—a dimension of differential willingness to accept perceptions at variance with conventional experience (Klein and others, 1962). (Messick, 1970, pp. 188–189)

At the present time, we do not have tests that will permit you to determine with any degree of confidence which of Guilford's types of intelligence or which of these cognitive styles an individual pupil may possess. Efforts to do so are being made, but in a review of such attempts to take account of aptitude-treatment-interaction, Lee J. Cronbach and R. E. Snow (1969) concluded that at this stage, attempts to match learning strategies to types of learning ability have not yet succeeded.

Even if clear guidelines are not yet available, however, you might still remain aware of the existence of types of intelligence and cognitive styles, and then try to adjust learning situations to fit the individual child. Perhaps the best single technique to use is to provide a variety of approaches to instruction and permit each pupil to choose the one he prefers. This is what the open education approach attempts to do. You might also make tentative use of scores on tests your students have already taken or will take as a part of a school test program. Even though you may not wish to use tests to make individual comparisons, it is almost certain that you will be provided with test scores indicating differences among your students. Tests are a part of American life, as you can no doubt attest from personal experience.

If you attended kindergarten, you may have taken one or more readiness tests to determine your preparedness for first grade. In the primary and elementary grades you probably took achievement or mental maturity tests as often as every year to determine your progress and perhaps for grouping purposes. Testing probably tapered off a bit in junior and senior high school, but you undoubtedly took at least one standardized test before you were accepted for admission to college. If you applied for a scholarship, you may also have taken the National Merit Award Exams or the equivalent. If you decide to go on to graduate school, you are likely to be asked to take the Graduate Record Exam before you will be considered for admission. Once you leave

Competency, Accountability, and Testing

Two trends in American education that indicate the extent to which you may be personally involved with tests are *competency-based teacher certification* and *accountability*.

A committee appointed by the U.S. Office of Education has published a report titled "The Power of Competency-Based Teacher Education," in which it is suggested that the current teacher certification procedure—which emphasizes college course work, references, and interviews—be supplemented or replaced by assessment of teacher knowledge, demonstrations of teacher competence under actual classroom situations, and measurement of pupil achievement under brief or long periods of instruction. Thus you may be asked to take tests to prove your knowledge of subject matter and of principles of teaching, and your pupils may be given tests to measure your productivity as an instructor. The committee recommended that pupil performance *not* be stressed too heavily, because of technical problems and the complexities of measurement. Some states, however, already have established guidelines for using pupil performance as a primary determinant of teacher competence. In 1972, for example, the California legislature voted to put accountability into effect. The exact implementation of the policies established will be up to local school districts, but the general guidelines stipulate that the learning potential of students for different subjects is to be estimated at the beginning of each school year and that teachers will be held accountable for bringing students up to the designated performance levels. School districts are thus faced with the task of measuring before and after

college and apply for a job, you may be asked to take some sort of exam, particularly if there is a large number of applicants. If you decide to try the Peace Corps for two years before starting your teaching career, you will be asked to take the Peace Corps Entrance Test. And even after you secure a teaching position you may be required—for reasons of accountability—to take exams at frequent intervals to prove your competence. In all of these tests, your score is reported in such a way that you are compared to others. The same is likely to be true for your students. Even though you do your best as a teacher to operate on the assumption that all of your pupils will be capable of doing superior work, you are likely to be asked to administer tests that will yield scores emphasizing relative standing.

If you are impressed by the value-added conception of education, you might attempt to use these tests not to sort students into levels of ability but to plan instructional programs for individual pupils. Scores on tests of mental ability might be used to help identify students who are likely to experience difficulty with standard instructional materials. Scores on achievement tests might be

performance, and teachers will have to arrange instruction to produce proof that their students have learned.

From the point of view of legislators and taxpayers who want proof of teacher efficiency and productivity, these regulations are seen as a step in the right direction. From the point of view of educators (and the U.S. Office of Education committee), the problems of implementation seem enormous. How will estimates of potential be made? If tests are used, who will devise or select them? How will estimates of potential be made to ensure that teachers are not asked to do the impossible? Will teachers be forced to "teach to the test" in order to survive? If the chief concern of teachers and pupils is high test scores, what impact will this have on classroom atmosphere, particularly at the end of the year? Will it be possible to use an open education approach in such a situation? Can tests be devised—particularly for subjects that do not stress acquisition of knowledge—that will accurately reveal the amount of learning that has taken place? Will learning be even more equated with the ability to answer test questions than it is now?

These are just a few of the questions that will have to be answered before the California version of accountability can be assessed. The fact that accountability has been made into law in some states is an indication of a trend you will need to consider. One obvious point is that you will need to become aware of the nature and significance of testing and also know how to interpret test scores. Another is that comparative grading may work against a teacher expected to bring individual pupils up to specified levels of performance. Only students who earn high grades are likely to be motivated to do their best. Therefore, in order to encourage almost all students to learn close to capacity, mastery learning may be essential.

---

used to identify areas and skills in need of improvements. In making inferences, however, you should remain aware of the limitations and potential dangers of using test scores too literally. For these reasons, it will be desirable for you to learn about the nature, administration, and interpretation of standardized tests.

It is likely that your students will have taken (or will take) tests of mental ability, achievement, and perhaps aptitude. As already noted, tests of *mental ability* are designed to measure intellectual potential—abilities, such as reasoning or verbal facility, that are the product of inherited tendencies and *general* home and school experiences. *Achievement* tests are intended to measure the amount of understanding of specific subject matter—how much learning the student has achieved in various subject areas as a result of studying those subjects. Tests of special *aptitudes* are used to make predictions about how well an individual will handle different kinds of tasks or jobs and are most commonly used in vocational guidance. Typical aptitudes measured by such tests include clerical skills, motor coordination, form perception, and finger dexterity.

Standardized Achievement Tests

An achievement test published by one of the concerns that specialize in such measuring instruments is devised in essentially the same way as a classroom test—up to a point. First, the terminal behavior is specified (usually on the basis of a survey of courses and curricula relating to the subject or subjects). Then the types of questions most likely to measure the various aspects of the terminal behavior are chosen. Next the questions are written. Most classroom tests are given to students at this point and then scored, but the achievement test is subjected to several more operations before it is put into use. The nature of these procedures is indicated by the term *standardized*.

Standardized tests

After the questions for an achievement test are written, they are arranged into a trial form and presented to a representative sample of students. The answers given by these students are then subjected to the item-analysis technique described in the preceding chapter. Items that appear to be most valid in terms of how well they discriminate between high- and low-scoring students are put into the final test. This test is then given under carefully controlled conditions to a representative assortment of thousands of students to obtain comparative samples of performance. The results are published as norms, which permit a teacher to compare a particular pupil or group of pupils to students from all over the country.

Use of standardized achievement tests imposes two tasks on the classroom teacher: administration and interpretation of scores.

Administering the Tests

Administering standardized tests

The most important point to keep in mind about administering achievement tests is the need for a standard procedure. What this boils down to is the necessity for following to the letter the instructions for giving a test. Otherwise the scores of some pupils may be distorted by factors that were not present when the test was standardized—and so may reduce the value of the normative data. To illustrate, the experience of two teachers in a small school district will be described.

One teacher taught in a school with an easygoing, pleasantly addlepated principal, the other under a very efficient, well-organized principal. A notice was sent to each school announcing that achievement tests were to be administered on a given day. The relaxed principal took a quick glance at the memo, put it on top of the pile on his desk, and forgot about it. The other principal obtained copies of the test booklet and called a special teachers' meeting devoted to familiarizing everyone with the nature of the test and its administration.

When the tests were delivered to the schools on the specified day, the casual principal took them around to his teachers, said, "You're supposed to give these today," and wandered off. The efficient principal had the booklets distributed to the classrooms, where both the students and the teachers were poised and prepared. It happened that this particular test featured a rather unorthodox answer sheet. All the teachers who were forced to give the test on the spur of the moment did not catch this, and even those who did discover it were unable to alert their pupils to it very effectively. The teachers in the other school had warned the students ahead of time and quickly demonstrated the way to record answers before the students got to work. Needless to say, the scores earned by students in the two schools varied considerably.

This may be an extreme, atypical example, but it does emphasize the need for insuring that your students have the opportunity to respond to achievement tests in the standard manner prescribed by the test publisher. You should read the Teacher's Manual that accompanies every reputable achievement test and follow the instructions faithfully. Usually included is information on preparing pupils, advance seating arrangements, pencils and scratch paper, distributing and collecting the test booklets and answer sheets, enforcing time schedules, and answering questions. Since achievement test scores may play a significant role in the academic careers of your pupils, it is important to maximize the validity and reliability of these tests by providing the standard testing situation.

Interpreting the Scores

When you use your own exams and are dealing with groups of thirty students, you may be able to analyze scores without the aid of too many statistical procedures. When you utilize tests developed by independent testing concerns for nationwide use, it is impossible to interpret scores without the assistance of norms reported in the form of some sort of statistical concept. Consequently, information usually is provided to make it possible to interpret a given student's raw score by norms for a class, school, district, or state, or for the entire nation.

Interpreting scores of standardized tests

One of the biggest problems confronting the developer of a standardized test is how to make allowance for the unique characteristics of the various school systems. For example, if a given topic or technique is taught a year earlier in one district than it is in another, it is desirable to take this into account in interpreting the results within a given district. Generally speaking, the most useful comparisons are those made at the local level, since most students in a particular district have been exposed to a reasonably uniform curriculum. If normative data are not available at the local level, you will need to be especially careful in making inferences about the significance of a score.

No matter what sorts of norms are available, however, you will need to know how to interpret different types of scores. Most achievement test scores are reported on profiles developed by the test publisher in terms of some or all of the following: grade-equivalents, percentile ranks, standard scores, or stanines. At one time or another you are likely to encounter each of these.

Grade-Equivalent Scores

Grade-equivalent scores

The grade-equivalent score is established by interpreting raw scores in terms of grade levels. A student who made a grade-equivalent score of 4.7 performed at the level the average fourth-grader in the standardization group achieved by the seventh month of the school year. The grade-equivalent is used most often at the elementary level, but because it may lead to misinterpretations, it is not as popular as it once was. One problem with grade-equivalent scores is the tendency to interpret a score that is above a student's actual grade level as an indication that he is capable of consistently working at that level, which might lead parents to agitate for an accelerated promotion. Such a score shows that the student did somewhat better on the test than the average student a grade or two above him, but it does not take into account the possibility that he lacks knowledge of certain skills covered in the grade he would skip if demands for acceleration were granted.

Percentile Ranks

Percentile ranks

The most widely used score for achievement tests is the *percentile rank*. This score indicates the percentage of students who are at or below the score of a given student. It provides specific information about relative position. A student earning a percentile rank of 87 did better than 87 percent of the students in the particular normative group being used. He did not get 87 percent of the questions right—unless by coincidence—and this is the point parents are most likely to miss. They may have been brought up on the percentages grading system—with 90 and above an A, 80 to 90 a B, and so on down the line. If you report that a son or daughter has a percentile rank of 50, some parents are horror-struck or outraged, not understanding that the child is average, not a failure. In such cases the best approach is probably to emphasize that the percentile rank tells the percentage of cases below the child's score. You might also talk in terms of a hypothetical group of 100; for example, a child with a percentile rank of 78 did better than 78 out of every 100 students who took the test, and 22 out of 100 did better than he did. (For diplomatic reasons it might be better to skip the number who did better than a child who scored below the fiftieth percentile.)

Although the percentile rank gives simple and direct information on relative position, it has a major disadvantage: The difference in achievement between students clustered around the middle of the distribution is often considerably less than the difference between those at the extremes. The reason is that most scores *are* clustered around the middle of most distributions of large groups of students. The difference in raw score between students at percentile ranks 50 and 51 may be one point. But the difference between the student with a percentile rank of 98 and the one ranked 97 may be ten or fifteen points of raw score because the best (and worst) students scatter toward the extremes. This quality of percentile ranks means that ranks on different tests cannot be averaged. To get around the difficulty, standard scores are often used. Standard scores are expressed in terms of a common unit—the standard deviation—that will now be described.

The Standard Deviation

This statistic indicates the student's degree of deviation from the mean. It is most valuable when it can be related to the normal probability curve. Figure 12-2 shows a normal probability curve indicating the proportion of cases to be found within three standard deviations[2] above and below the mean.

Standard deviation

The normal curve is a mathematical concept that depicts a hypothetical distribution of scores. Such a perfectly symmetrical distribution rarely if ever occurs in the real world. However, since many distributions of human characteristics or kinds of performance do resemble the normal distribution, it is often assumed that such distributions are "normal" enough to be so treated. Thus information derived by mathematicians for the hypothetical normal distribution can be applied to the approximately normal distributions that are found in actuality. (An important thing to remember: When this assumption is made in regard to learning ability, it may lead to the expectation that only a few students are capable of superior work.)

Normal probability curve

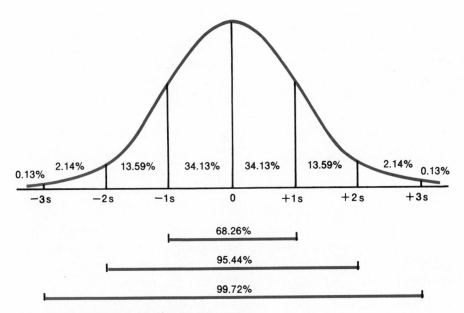

Figure 12-2   The Normal Probability Curve

[2] Several abbreviations of standard deviation are regularly used, including SD, σ, or s. Because SD seems most directly related to the actual term, it is used in the discussion in this text as well as in Table 12-1. However, to acquaint you with the symbol s also, s is used in Figures 12-2 and 12-3, although some statisticians might prefer σ because a theoretical distribution is depicted.

Table 12-1 Calculating the Standard Deviation (Using the Frequency Distribution from Table 11-1)

Score X	Frequency f	Deviation (X-M) d	Deviation squared (X-M) d²	Product of frequency and deviation squared fd²
47	1	11	121	121
46	2	10	100	200
45	1	9	81	81
44				
43	1	7	49	49
42	1	6	36	36
41	2	5	25	50
40	1	4	16	16
39	2	3	9	18
38	1	2	4	4
37	2	1	1	2
36	2	0	0	0
35	4	−1	1	4
34	3	−2	4	12
33	2	−3	9	18
32	2	−4	16	32
31				
30	1	−6	36	36
29	1	−7	49	49
28	1	−8	64	64
27	1	−9	81	81
26				
25	1	−11	121	121
24	1	−12	144	144
N = 33			Sum total of fd² (Σfd²)	= 1138

$$\text{Standard deviation (SD)} = \sqrt{\frac{\text{Sum total of fd}^2 \quad (\Sigma \text{fd}^2)}{\text{Number of scores} \quad (N)}}$$

$$\text{Standard deviation (SD)} = \sqrt{\frac{1138}{33}}$$

$$\text{Standard deviation (SD)} = \sqrt{34.4848}$$

$$\text{Standard deviation (SD)} = 5.87$$

The derivation of the normal probability curve is quite technical. The computation of a standard deviation for a group of test scores is relatively simple. To illustrate, Table 12-1 and the list below offer an example and a description of the computation of standard deviation for the data recorded in Table 11-1.

1. Compute the mean (i.e., add up all scores and then divide by the number of scores). Symbolically: $\frac{\Sigma X}{N}$, where Σ = sum total, X = score, and N = number of scores.

2. Find the difference between each score and the mean. Symbolically: d = X − M, where d = difference, X = score, and M = mean.

3. Square all the differences and add them. Symbolically: Σd^2, where Σ = sum total and d^2 = differences squared.

4. Divide the sum of the squared differences by the number of scores. Symbolically: $\dfrac{\Sigma d^2}{N}$, where Σd^2 = sum of differences squared and N = number of scores.

5. Compute the positive square root of this figure. That square root is your standard deviation. If you measure off three standard deviations above the mean and three below the mean, you should include practically all scores in your distribution if you have a close to normal distribution.

Keep in mind that without a more or less normal distribution of scores, it is unwise to make inferences about relative position in terms of the normal probability curve. Only when large numbers of unselected students are tested do distributions of scores tend to take on the characteristic bell shape. Test publishers establish norms with large, representative student populations, so scores based on the normal curve can be used in interpreting results of standardized tests. Standard scores have been developed for this purpose.

Standard Scores

The first step in deriving standard scores is to calculate a standard deviation, as illustrated in Table 12-1. The next step is to determine the position of a given score within the distribution. The standard score provides this information; it tells how far a raw score lies from the mean of a distribution in terms of the standard deviation of the distribution. One type of standard score—the z score—is based on a mean of 0 and an SD of 1. The sign of the z score (+ or −) indicates whether the score is above or below the mean. Suppose you have a distribution of scores that yields a mean of 40 and a standard deviation of 5. For a raw score of 45, the z score is computed thus:

z scores

$$z = \frac{X - M}{SD}, \qquad z = \frac{45 - 40}{5} = \frac{5}{5} = +1.$$

This z score tells you that the pupil who got a raw score of 45 is one standard deviation above the mean.

In order to avoid negative z scores (which are found for all raw scores below the mean) and decimals (which are found for scores not falling exactly at standard deviation division points), T scores have been devised. T scores use some arbitrary number as the mean. With many T scores, 50 is the number chosen, although 100 is used with some intelligence tests and 500 is used on the Graduate Record Exam. To get a T score, simply multiply the z score by 10 (to get rid of the decimal) and add the product to 50. For a negative z score (which you would get if the raw score was below the mean), you *subtract* the product (10z) from 50. In the example of a raw score of 45, which had a z-score equivalent of +1, you get a T score of 60, as follows:

T scores

$$T = 50 + 10z,$$
$$T = 50 + (10)(1) = 50 + 10,$$
$$T = 60.$$

If you want T scores but not z scores, you can proceed directly to the calculation of T scores from raw test scores by using the following formula:

$$T = 50 + \frac{10(X - M)}{SD}.$$

For the example of a raw score of 45, a mean of 40, and a standard deviation of 5, you would get a T score of 60, as follows:

$$T = 50 + \frac{10(X - M)}{SD},$$
$$T = 50 + \frac{10(45 - 40)}{5} = 50 + 10 = 60.$$

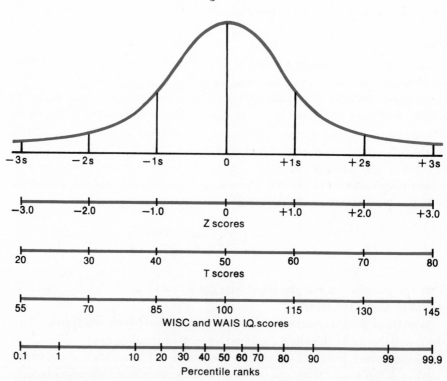

Figure 12–3   Relationship between T scores, z scores, WISC and WAIS Scores,* and Percentile Ranks

*Both the WISC and the WAIS have a mean of 100 and a standard deviation of 15. The 1960 revision of the Stanford-Binet uses standard scores, which have a mean of 100 and a standard deviation of 16. For all practical purposes this one-point difference is of no significance; hence you can interpret Stanford-Binet IQ's by referring to the WISC and WAIS scale on the diagram.

To grasp the relationship between percentiles, z scores, and T scores, examine Figure 12–3. This diagram shows each type of scale marked off below a normal curve. It supplies information about the interrelationships of these various scores, *provided* the distribution you are working with is essentially normal. In a normal distribution, for example, a z score of +1 is the same as a T score of 60 or a percentile rank of 84; a z score of −2 is the same as a T score of 30 or a percentile rank of about 2. (In addition, note that the distance between the percentiles that are clustered around the middle is only a small fraction of the distance between the percentile ranks that are found at the ends of the distribution.)

Stanines

During World War II, Air Force psychologists developed a new statistic that is now being used by many publishers of standardized tests. It is called the *stanine* (an abbreviation of "standard nine-point scale"), reflecting the fact that it is a type of standard score and that it divides a population into nine groups. With the exception of stanine 1 (the lowest) and stanine 9 (the highest), these groups are spaced in units of half a standard deviation, as indicated in Figure 12–4.

Stanines

If you are mathematically inclined and fond of symmetry, you can immediately sense why test publishers use stanines. When teachers or administrators divide classes, they usually find that having three groups is the most workable arrangement. First-grade teachers have the "Robins," "Bluebirds," and "Sparrows"; high school principals make up X, Y, and Z classes. So all you have to do when you subdivide is put pupils who are in stanines 1, 2, and 3 in the slow group, those in stanines 7, 8, and 9 in the fast group, and those in stanines 4, 5, and 6 (the majority) in the average group. It looks and sounds very neat, but unfortunately it's not that simple.

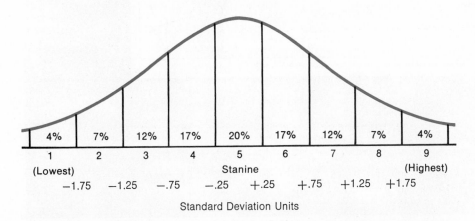

Figure 12–4   Percentage of Cases in Each Stanine (with Standard Deviation Units Indicated)

FORM **W**

Stanford Achievement Test

PRIMARY II BATTERY

TRUMAN L. KELLEY • RICHARD MADDEN • ERIC F. GARDNER • HERBERT C. RUDMAN

NAME Harris (*last*) James (*first*) J. (*initial*)

BOY ☑ GIRL ☐ GRADE 2 TEACHER Mrs. Anderson

SCHOOL George Washington DATE OF TESTING 68 (*year*) 6 (*month*) 9 (*day*)

CITY OR TOWN Gridley DATE OF BIRTH 60 (*year*) 1 (*month*) 7 (*day*)

STATE Kansas AGE 8 (*years*) 5 (*months*)

	GRADE SCORE	PERCENTILE RANK*	STANINE* (1 2 3 4 5 6 7 8 9)
Word Meaning	3.1	60	6
Paragraph Meaning	3.1	60	6
Science & Social Studies Concepts	4.6	89	8
Spelling	2.6	40	5
Word Study Skills	1.8	12	3
Language	2.5	28	4
Arithmetic Computation	4.2	98	9
Arithmetic Concepts	4.7	94	8

*Percentile Ranks and Stanines based on tables for Beginning ☐ Middle ☐ End ☑ of grade (check one)

HARCOURT, BRACE & WORLD, INC. NEW YORK

Figure 12–5 Stanford Achievement Test-Profile

Reproduced from Stanford Achievement Test, copyright © 1964–1966 by Harcourt Brace Jovanovich, Inc. Reproduced by special permission of the publisher.

Some test publishers cite the success of the Air Force pilot selection program as evidence that the stanine scale can effectively classify people. However, they fail to point out that the Air Force used a *battery* of about twenty tests. Many of these measured such sensorimotor factors as coordination and reaction time. Most school achievement tests are susceptible to many more errors of measurement than the Air Force battery; thus any attempt to split a small group into nine subsections, or even three subsections, should be made cautiously. Grouping based on stanine scores (or any scores) should be tentative.

Figure 12–5 is a profile used in reporting scores on the Stanford Achievement Test. Obviously, you will need to understand percentile ranks, standard scores, and stanines in order to interpret it. Most reputable test publishers provide detailed guides to help you interpret and make the most of student profiles. But it is usually assumed that you have some familiarity with the general considerations and specific statistics just described.

For reasons noted earlier, you are urged to use information on test profiles to assist individual pupils to learn more effectively, not to make comparisons among pupils. As a matter of fact, you may be forbidden by law to administer tests for purposes of making comparisons. In some states, it has been successfully argued that most standardized achievement and mental ability tests favor white middle-class students and discriminate against all others. Since the tests have been used to group students, it is argued that they perpetuate inequalities because students with the most educational strength are separated from those with the least. Even if you begin your teaching career in a state that does not impose any restrictions on use of tests for grouping, you may wish to act (as much as possible) as if this were the case. Even if you do this, however, you should not lose sight of the fact that there *are* differences in intelligence and learning ability and that these will have a substantial impact on the success of individual pupils not only in school but also later in life. Furthermore, if you decline to use the results of tests or tell your students they are unimportant, you may only postpone the inevitable. Most colleges are likely to continue to use tests, and so are business corporations and governmental agencies. Consequently, this chapter ends on the same note as the preceding one on classroom evaluation: Don't expect all of your students to perform at the same level.

Is It Possible to "Equalize" Intelligence?

As Bloom has pointed out, there are disadvantages in assuming that learning ability is distributed normally—teachers may be led to expect that only a few students can learn at a respectable level. Although the reasons for making a literal interpretation of a normal distribution of learning ability have been discussed at length in this book, is has also been stressed that it is wise to keep in mind that people do differ in their ability to learn, that there are a limited number of openings at the top of the job hierarchy, and that the most capable people are likely to get such jobs. Some behavioral and social scientists believe that if we succeed in equalizing environmental opportunities, all people will become equal in ability. Other theorists (e.g., Herrnstein and Eysenck) have argued that if this occurs, the heritability of intelligence and other traits will be just as great if not greater because they will be attributable solely to heredity. Those who specialize in the study of environmental conditions are reluctant to accept the possibility of inherited differences. For example, in testimony before the Senate Committee on Education, Jensen reported that the Newsletter of the American Anthropological Association urged its members to burn all copies of the *Harvard Educational Review* that contained his article. But inherited differences do occur, and there is no logical reason to assume that the brain is less affected by genetic factors than height or any other physical characteristic. Robert Cancro has observed, "The only way we can deny a significant genetic contribution to intelligence is by denying the very existence of the trait itself" (1971, p. 59).

Inherited differences in intellectual capacity may not be distributed according to a perfectly normal curve, but there are undeniable variations among individuals. Up to this point, attempts to reduce these differences have not been notably successful, and past experience suggests that current claims that ways have been found to increase intelligence should be accepted only tentatively until further investigation and attempts to replicate are made. For example, thirty years ago Bernardine G. Schmidt (1946) claimed that she had discovered an educational technique that was capable of raising the IQ's of students identified as mentally retarded. Samuel A. Kirk (1948) made a thorough investigation of her claims and found numerous methodological and statistical errors. Furthermore, Schmidt declined to explain her methods, which made it impossible for others to attempt to replicate her efforts. Kirk (1958) later made a carefully controlled attempt to improve the intelligence of mentally retarded children using a variety of methods and intensive individualized instruction. He concluded that it was not possible to do much to improve the IQ's of children whose retardation was due to organic causes (e.g., brain injury) but that considerable improvement was shown by children whose retardation was due to cultural factors. This was especially true of children who came from institutions—their control group counterparts who remained in the institution and received no preschool education showed no improvement and also dropped on follow-up tests. (These findings are consistent with other studies of children—and animals—reared in deprived environments.) Control-group children from normal home situations lagged behind their counterparts who had received preschool education before they entered school, but they achieved almost identical IQ's by the end of first grade. S. L. Guskin and H. H. Spicker (1965) found the same tendency for control-group children to catch up with experimental-group children who had been exposed to preschool training. (These results might be interpreted in a number of ways: as evidence against the critical period concept, as an indication that testing young mentally retarded children yields unreliable scores, as an indication that the original diagnosis of mental retardation was erroneous, that any kind of positive school experience will assist children to increase their intelligence, that the slower maturation rate of mentally retarded children means that they benefit more from later schooling than they do from preschool training.)

Ten years ago, Carl Delacato (1959, 1963, 1966) and Glenn Doman claimed to have discovered a technique for "recirculating brain patterns" so that retarded children would become average or above average in intelligence. Melvyn P. Robbins (1960) used their methods under carefully controlled conditions (and made allowance for such factors as the Hawthorne effect and the experimenter

---

Causes of Mental Retardation

As you speculate about the significance of experiments in raising intelligence, it may be of assistance to consider causes of mental retardation. There is considerable agreement about these causes:

Biochemical disorders, for example, phenylketonuria (PKU) and galactosemia

Chromosomal abnormalities, for example, an extra chromosome leading to Mongolism (Down's Syndrome)

Infectious diseases contracted by the mother during the first months of pregnancy, for example, rubella (German measles) and hepatitis

Drugs taken by the mother during pregnancy (and perhaps before pregnancy)

Poor maternal diet before and during pregnancy

Brain injury due to anoxia (lack of oxygen) or birth complications

Infectious diseases contracted by the child after birth, for example, encephalitis and meningitis

Ingestion of drugs and poisons after birth

Deprivation or mistreatment during early life, particularly during the first four years

Existence in a deprived, sterile, or nonstimulating environment during the entire period of development

There is considerable *disagreement* about the following factor as a cause of mental retardation: inheritance of a particular type of brain. Some analyses of the causes of mental retardation do not even mention this possibility, whereas others emphasize that it is the most important single explanation for differences in intelligence. The evidence relating to this question is voluminous, complex, and open to varying interpretations. But you might ask yourself how you feel about this question: Do you believe that some people are *born* with a better brain than others?

bias effect) and found no differences between experimental and control groups. In addition, Doman and Delacato withdrew from a government-sponsored study of their methods and declined to answer questions put to them by ten professional and voluntary organizations concerned with handicapped children. (This is reported in the August 1968 issue, Vol. 17, No. 4, of *Children Limited*, the Newsletter of the National Association for Retarded Children.) At the present time, the work of Rick Heber (1970) at the "Milwaukee Project" is attracting considerable attention. Press reports claim that he has succeeded in raising the IQ's of disadvantaged preschool children by thirty points. Ellis B. Page (1972) has pointed out, however, not only that such claims are unwarranted but also that methodological weaknesses of Heber's approach tend to invalidate any results of the project.

Some Final Speculations on Intelligence

In view of the claims and counterclaims about the possibility of raising the IQ, it may be instructive to keep in mind the distinction between intelligence and a score on an intelligence test. In much of the research cited in support of the raise-the-IQ claims, a higher score on a test is taken as evidence that overall intellectual ability has been correspondingly increased. This assumption is open to question. Consider, for example, some experiments regarding the impact of nursery school experience on IQ. Heber (1968) reviewed the results of twenty-nine intensive, preschool programs for disadvantaged children and found that although five- to ten-point gains were common (measured at the time the child left the preschool), gains of more than ten points were rare. In addition, a fade reaction has been reported in most long-term studies of Head Start training (Jensen, 1969). This evidence, it might be argued, suggests that special nursery school experience helps children answer questions on intelligence tests with slightly more success but that the advantage disappears when different questions are asked. Or, to put it another way, no permanent impact is made on their general intellectual ability.

Early in this chapter, intelligence was defined as that which is measured by an intelligence test. Temporary increases in IQ score can be explained in part by referring to this definition. If a child attends a nursery school, the attitudes and skills he develops will make him a more sophisticated test-taker. First, he will build confidence in reacting to adults other than his parents. This will give him a better chance to respond favorably to the tester when a follow-up examination is administered. Second, he will play with many of the materials that are used in tests, for example, form boards, blocks, beads, pictures. In a sense he will get practice in handling intelligence test items. These two factors in themselves might conceivably produce IQ gains of five to ten points. Does a higher score due essentially to the fact that a child feels *en rapport* with a tester who administers a follow-up exam mean he is more intelligent? Does a higher score earned by a child who has been "practicing" the items on the test mean that his overall intellectual capacity has increased correspondingly? Suppose an enterprising businessman announces plans to manufacture exact duplicates of the test items on the Stanford-Binet and the WISC, to be sold under the trade name "Make-a-Genius Playthings." For orders over $50, a copy of the verbal items in these tests will be included as a bonus. Will such playthings increase a child's overall intellectual ability, or will they merely equip him to take intelligence tests?

Observations on intelligence made earlier in this chapter also noted that intelligence cannot be measured directly, that the indirect measurement of intelligence is based on evaluating the reactions of an individual to a series of standard situations (questions), and that the goal of the test is to obtain a numerical score that indicates how well the individual's ability to deal with the test questions (whatever that ability may be) will be used in dealing with similar questions. Moreover, in order for this goal to be achieved the test must consist of a fair and adequate sample of questions. If a child is given special training in answering test questions, does his performance reflect a "fair" sample? Or is it a loaded and artificial sample indicating that he will perform equally well *only* when placed in similarly loaded and artificial situations?

Two University of Chicago professors who felt that the Stanford-Binet is too middle-class oriented and that it discriminates against lower-class children, devised what they hoped would be a "culture-free" test—the Davis-Eells Games. Arguing that inappropriate questions were the primary reason disadvantaged children scored lower on the Stanford-Binet, they deliberately set out to try to make their test fair to lower-class children. It turned out to be a wasted effort because middle-class children got higher scores on the test and also because the scores had little predictive value. What Davis and Eells tried to do, in a sense, was to create the appearance that the disadvantaged are as good at taking tests as are middle-class children. But a test score is not the same thing as intelligence, and educational programs explicitly or inadvertently designed to increase a test score do not necessarily have an impact on the other-than-test behavior of the child.[3]

To further clarify these points, an analogy is offered. Assume that eyesight is roughly comparable to the kind of intellectual capacity a child possesses

---

[3] In an article on recent Head Start programs, Pines (1969) reported that J. McV. Hunt has arranged for mothers of disadvantaged children to watch the administration of intelligence tests. The mothers are then encouraged to coach their children on the test items. Coached children attain an average IQ of 110 compared to an IQ of 80 for uncoached children. Thus Hunt has succeeded in bringing about the 30-point IQ increases he predicted. However, only the later school performance of these children will show whether the gain reflects an increase in general intelligence or merely a higher test score.

(in the sense that the visual acuity of the child is determined, within limits, by inheritance). Assume, now, that a particular child has extremely poor vision. If you helped the child memorize the materials used in testing his vision, would you be improving his sight? With training, he could pass the test with a perfect score, but would he see any better? What might happen if on the basis of the test the child was placed in a situation in which he had to have perfect vision? Would he be able to perform satisfactorily? Or would it make more sense to get an *accurate* estimate of his sight and assist him to make the most of the actual vision he possessed?

This is not a perfect analogy, for intelligence has less specific physical limits than vision. It is generally assumed that most people use only a fraction of their potential brain power. Thus regardless of the physical limitations of the brain, functioning intelligence might be increased by application of a "sound scientific educational psychology of early experience"—or programmed problem-solving sessions, or inquiry training, or whatever. Even taking this into account, the danger remains: If a child is given what amounts to training in taking tests, he may be prevented from learning in a more natural and perhaps permanent way, and he may be placed in educational situations beyond his true capacity.

This point can be illustrated by an analysis of the theories and techniques of Siegfried Engelmann, perhaps the most outspoken advocate of the view that intelligence can be taught. (Engelmann was mentioned previously in connection with behavior modification techniques [Chapter 5], and a Follow-Through project based on behavior modification principles [Chapter 10]). Engelmann's philosophy of teaching for intelligence can be summed up by this statement:

> If intelligent behavior is learned just like any other behavior, then teaching is highly relevant to the development of intelligent people. There are two approaches to demonstrating that intelligent behavior is learned: one is to present evidence of the effects of teaching on IQ scores; the other is to present a logical analysis of the issue. [In Engelmann (1971)], evidence is given that during two years of direct instruction based on Engelmann's approaches to teaching, disadvantaged four- and five-year-olds gained an average of 24 IQ points on the Stanford-Binet Intelligence Test. A wide variety of studies could be cited to show that when children are taught more intensively and effectively, they do better on intelligence tests. A second approach to the demonstration is through a logical analysis of the behavior defined as intelligent. It is that approach that is taken in this [book].
>
> The major thrust of the argument to be presented is that what is measured on intelligence tests involves various combinations of operations under the control of concepts. Therefore, if the teacher knows how to teach concepts and operations, she knows how to make people "intelligent." This is not to say that some people are not more readily taught than others, or that genetics makes no difference. The point to be made is that intelligent behavior does not come with the baby;

it is learned. Intelligent behavior is the product of learning interactions with an environment. If teachers know how to induce behavior that is considered intelligent, they know how to make people smarter. (Becker, Engelmann, and Thomas, 1971, p. 389)

In *Give Your Child a Superior Mind,* Engelmann tells parents how he thinks they can make their children smarter. The dust-jacket notes indicate that if at age five a child who has been taught according to the methods described is not able to read 150 words a minute, add columns of figures, tell time, subtract, multiply, divide, solve algebra equations, and score high on the first IQ test, the price of the book will be refunded. This book and similar descriptions by Engelmann (Chapters 27 and 30 of *Teaching: A Course in Applied Psychology* by Becker, Engelmann, and Thomas) indicate that "teaching concepts and operations" could also be described as teaching how to give correct answers on the Stanford-Binet. It might also be noted that although he indicates that he *could* cite a wide variety of evidence to show that children can be taught to do better on intelligence tests, he does not do so. Furthermore, his study is too recent to tell if the increase in IQ he claims he has produced will be permanent. (The claim of 24 points is misleading and exaggerated, since a control group that was not given any instruction gained an average of 5 points, making an average gain of 19 points. You should also be aware that the experimental group consisted of only twelve children.) In order to determine that Engelmann has increased intelligence rather than merely raised test scores, the subjects of his study should be tested at intervals after the training has been discontinued.

Engelmann not only recommends teaching the types of items that appear on the Stanford-Binet, he also advocates accelerating the rate of learning:

> . . . Children can be made more intelligent than they were when they came to the teacher if she teaches them concepts and operations *at a faster than "normal" rate.* How far she can go will be a function of her skill in motivating the children, holding their attention, and presenting good routines for teaching concepts and operations. (Becker, Engelmann, and Thomas, 1971, p. 440)

In advocating this policy, Engelmann argues that Piaget's suggestion to teachers that they allow children to learn at their own pace is poor advice. To prove his point, he set out to teach six-year-old children the concept of specific gravity, then invited Constance Kamii, an advocate of the Piaget view, to test the children to determine whether or not they had gained genuine understanding. Kamii (1972) concluded that the children had gained only partial understanding of the concept, that they still functioned at the preoperational level, and that they applied the rule they had learned in rote fashion. Engelmann argued that this seemed to be the case only because the children lacked information that would have been necessary for them to use the rule with understanding. He claimed that they could be taught this information and then would be able to apply the concept. Kamii evaluated this argument and

A ACHIEVE

READ MOTHER THE ALPHABET.

B BEND

I'M NOT GOING TO LET YOU PLAY WITH YOUR EDUCATIONAL TOYS UNTIL YOU READ MOTHER THE ALPHABET.

C CAREER

IF YOU DON'T GET STARTED NOW YOU'LL BE BEHIND ALL YOUR LIFE. READ MOTHER THE ALPHABET.

D DIRECTION

THE LITTLE GIRL DOWN THE HALL IS A YEAR YOUNGER THAN YOU ARE AND SHE READS THE ALPHABET.

E EDUCATE

ABCDEFGHI JKLMNOP QRSTU- VWXYZ!

ALL YOU HAVE TO DO IS EXPLAIN TO HIM.

F FIFTY

HE'S REALLY VERY OLD FOR HIS AGE.

discovered that the children had to be told what information they would need. (They were not able to ask for it on their own.) To Engelmann, this difficulty presents no problem, since "there can be no learning (except in trivial, autistic instances) without teaching" (1968, p. 461). But not endorsing this view does present difficulties. If you attempt to teach intelligence by anticipating all of the concepts and information a child will need and then shaping his behavior so that he learns it, what will happen when he encounters situations you have not anticipated? Advocates of open education approaches argue that the time Engelmann spends in training children should be devoted to open-ended learning experiences, in which children are free to learn at their own pace and in their own way. It is argued that this will lead to more permanent learning, and since the child will gain experience with solving problems as he learns, he will be equipped to handle new situations when he encounters them.

Environmentalists believe that it should be possible to increase intelligence. Thus far, they have not offered conclusive proof that anything other than a temporary increment in test scores can be produced by special training. With greater knowledge and improved techniques, however, programs such as Follow-Through may succeed in assisting children from disadvantaged backgrounds

---

Consciousness III or a Meritocracy?

In *The Greening of America*, Charles Reich predicted that the spread of what he called Consciousness III would lead to a society in which no one would judge anyone else and "the whole concept of excellence and comparative merit" (1970, p. 243) would be rejected.

At the conclusion of his article in *The Atlantic,* Richard Herrnstein summarizes his conclusions in the following form:

1. If differences in mental abilities are inherited, and
2. If success requires those abilities, and
3. If earnings and prestige depend on success,
4. Then social standing (which reflects earnings and prestige) will be based to some extent on inherited differences among people. (1971, p. 58)

Those who favor the Reich view argue that the "revolution" he predicts cannot be resisted and that of their own accord, Americans will reduce elitism in our society; that is, they will do everything possible to arrange conditions to move away from the assumption that some people have more ability than others. Herrnstein suggests that society is actually moving in the opposite direction.

Which view do you think is the most realistic appraisal, and what are the implications regarding assumptions about intelligence, learning ability, and the things that should take place in the schools?

---

to make better use of their potential and to improve their general learning ability. The assumption that intelligence is distributed normally has likely helped bring about the pessimistic belief that only a minority of children have high capability and that many children with considerable potential have not been assisted to do as well as they might. You are urged to operate on the assumption that all children can learn at a respectable level. At the same time, you are urged to take into account that no matter what you do, you will not succeed in making all children equal in either subject matter mastery or learning ability. If you strive to create the impression that this is so, you may misdirect your efforts. It would seem more prudent to concentrate on providing students who lack test-taking skills with instruction on how to take tests rather than by attempting to equip them with answers to tests you know they will be given, since they will eventually have to take tests (and deal with test-like situations) without your assistance. You should do everything you can to assist them to develop study skills and perseverance, since they will need to learn on their own. You should strive to encourage them to develop a need for achievement, a positive self-concept, and confidence in their abilities. But you should also try to arrange instruction so that they develop a realistic level of aspiration.

We do not presently know how to equalize ability. Many people doubt that we ever will, but even the most ardent environmentalist admits that some people are, at present, more capable than others. And by and large, the most capable people are likely to win the most desirable jobs. A person should be encouraged to strive for the highest possible goals, but if he competes for a place beyond his abilities, he is doomed to failure. It is a mistake to underestimate what an individual might be able to do, but it may be just as much of a mistake to do the opposite.

Summary

In this chapter, the background and current state of the nature-nurture controversy have been analyzed. In the 1950s and 1960s, the environmental view of intelligence was widely endorsed, and it was hypothesized that a proper arrangement of learning experiences would make it possible to substantially increase intelligence. The failure of Head Start and recent interpretations of the degree to which genetic factors limit and influence intelligence by Jensen and others have led to questions about the extent to which IQ's can be altered.

In order to evaluate the nature-nurture question it is necessary to bear in mind how intelligence is defined and measured. But instead of attempting to arrive at a definite decision regarding the nature and extent of differences in IQ, it would seem more constructive to use intelligence test scores to individualize instruction by taking into account types of intellectual operations and cognitive styles. In addition, data available on profiles that summarize the results of the standardized achievement tests almost all American students take at frequent intervals can be used to diagnose strengths and weaknesses and plan instruction.

In making efforts to use test scores to improve instruction, there may be advantages in assuming that until ways are found to equalize intellectual ability, there always will be differences in intelligence, and that some students therefore will learn more easily than others. Teachers should approach instruction with the expectation that all pupils can learn, but they should also remain aware that some students are certain to be more teachable than others. Failure to acknowledge this may lead to unrealistic levels of aspiration and inevitable failure by less able students.

Suggestions for Further Reading, Writing, Thinking, and Discussion

12-1 *Analyzing Your Experiences with Standardized Tests*

Do you recall taking a standardized test that seemed exceptionally well or badly administered? (For example, did you ever have a teacher who seemed confused about how to proceed or who made a great show of using a stopwatch or the like?) Do you recall any situation in which the scores you received on a standardized test had undesirable repercussions? (For example, did you ever have a teacher who seemed to evaluate you more in terms of your test profile than on the basis of what you considered your actual performance? Did you find your previously high self-confidence shaken by a low test score and come to doubt your ability to do good work?) After describing any negative or positive experiences you have had with standardized tests, draw a "moral" for each experience.

12-2 *Taking an Individual Test of Intelligence*

If you wonder what it is like to take an individual test of intelligence, you might check on the possibility that a teacher of a course in individual testing needs subjects for practice purposes. (In most courses of this type, each student is required to give several tests under practice conditions.) Look in a class schedule for a course in psychology or education designated Individual Testing, Practicum in Testing, or something similar. Contact the instructor and ask him whether he wants subjects. If you do find yourself acting as guinea pig, jot down your reactions to the test immediately after you take it. Would you feel comfortable about having the score used to determine whether you would be admitted to some program or would qualify for a promotion? Did the test seem to provide an adequate sample of your intelligence? Were the kinds of questions appropriate for *your* conception of intelligence? Record your reactions and comments on the implications.

12-3 *Evaluating a Standardized Test*

In most school systems the selection and use of standardized tests is supervised by a specialist in testing. It is possible, however, that you will have to make your own evaluation of a test or several alternate tests. To find out the kinds of information available for evaluating standardized tests, examine the seventh *Mental Measurements Yearbook* (1972) edited by O. K. Buros, or look for a recent copy of the *Review of Educational Research*, published by the American Educational Research Association. Issues of this journal entitled "Psychological Tests and Their Uses," "Educational Tests and Their Uses," and "Methods of Research and Appraisal in Education" contain references to new tests and to research findings with old tests. Select two or more tests designed for the same general purpose (by examining the catalogs of test publishers or obtaining sample copies from a test library), and compare them on the basis of the following factors:

Title

Year of publication

Purpose as described by test publisher

Group to which applicable

Cost of test booklets

Cost of answer sheets

Time required

Types of scores

Evidence of validity: size and nature of standardization group, evidence regarding relationship of scores on given test to scores on other tests, etc.

Evidence of reliability: method of estimating consistency of scores, size and nature of sample

Estimate of ease of administration, clarity of instructions, etc.

Kinds of scores and how reported

Comments of reviewers in *Mental Measurements Yearbook* and/or *Review of Educational Research*

After making your comparison, indicate which test you prefer and explain your reasons why.

12-4 *Evaluating the Significance of Guilford's Five Mental Operations*

To gain greater insight into J. P. Guilford's factors of intelligence, you might speculate about the significance of his five mental operations—cognition, memory, convergent production, divergent production, and evaluation. Guilford suggests that most forms of evaluation place too much emphasis on only one or two of these operations. As you consider making up tests of your own, give some thought to this point. Were many of the tests you have taken as a student designed to tap only one or two of the operations described by Guilford? Did this have a detrimental effect—and if so, how did it influence you in an undesirable way? How might you avoid or minimize the harmful effects of tests that measure only a limited type of intellectual ability?

12-5 *Examining the Pros and Cons of Assessing Creative Potential*

A number of tests to measure creative potential have been devised, primarily because some studies (e.g., Getzels and Jackson, 1962), indicate that measures of intelligence do not necessarily reflect mental operations associated with creativity. Taking into account different types of intelligence is to be desired as a means for broadening the assessment of abilities, but it is possible that a creativity score *causes* just as many problems as it eliminates. Suppose, for example, that the students in your classes were given a test of creativity and the scores were reported to you. What would you do with them? Would you place children with high scores in special groups or give them special opportunities to demonstrate their ability? Would you evaluate assignments with reference to the scores—i.e., look more carefully for signs of creativity in the work of those who earned high scores? Would you distrust your own judgment that the work of a pupil was highly creative if you knew he had a low score on the test? Or would you be better off simply encouraging *all* pupils to be as creative as possible and not be concerned about an estimate of creative potential, on the assumption that creativity flourishes when there are abundant opportunities for each person to express himself in his own way? If you are intrigued by the question of the use or abuse of measures of creativity, record your observations and perhaps list some guidelines for encouraging free expression that you might apply in your classes.

12-6 *Learning More About Technical Aspects of Testing*

If you would like more complete information and group tests of intelligence and achievement, see *Essentials of Psychological Testing* (3rd ed., 1970) by Lee J. Cronbach or *Psychological Testing* (3rd ed., 1968) by Anne Anastasi.

For more complete information on statistics, you might look up one of the following books (simpler books are noted first, more comprehensive texts last): *A Primer of Statistics for Non-Statisticians* (1958) by A. N. Frantzblau, *A*

Simplified Guide to Statistics for Psychology and Education (1962) by G. M. Smith, *Statistics for the Teacher* (1963) by D. M. McIntosh, *Elementary Statistical Methods in Psychology and Education* (1960) by Blommers and Lindquist, *Statistics for the Classroom Teacher, a Self-Teaching Unit* (1963) by Townsend and Burke, *Statistics in Psychology and Education* (5th ed., 1951) by H. E. Garrett, and *Psychological Statistics* (3rd ed., 1962) by Quinn McNemar.

PART

6

INDIVIDUAL DIFFERENCES

AND ADJUSTMENT

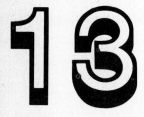

TEACHING

EXCEPTIONAL STUDENTS

KEY POINTS

Classifications
Custodial, trainable, and educable levels of mental retardation

Criteria
Mental retardation: subaverage general intellectual functioning associated with impaired adaptive behavior (A.A.M.D. definition)
Characteristics of the trainable and the educable mentally retarded
Detecting visual handicaps
Detecting hearing handicaps

Studies
Self-sufficiency of graduates of classes for the educable retarded in later life (Charles)
Superior behavior and adjustment of students early identified as intellectually gifted (Terman and Oden)

Concepts
Low convulsive threshold as explanation of epilepsy

Methodology
Teaching slow learners
Teaching rapid learners
Teaching the visually handicapped
Teaching pupils with impaired speech
Teaching the hard of hearing
Teaching and dealing with epileptics

CHAPTER CONTENTS

IN THE PRECEDING TWO CHAPTERS, IT WAS EMPHASIZED THAT YOU should do your best to assist all of your pupils to learn at a respectable level but that you should be aware that they will differ in ability. Even though distributions of intelligence and learning ability may not be perfectly symmetrical, there will always be some students who possess relatively more—or less—of these capacities. This chapter is concerned with such students and also with those who are exceptional in other ways. Although the primary focus will be on the extremes, the same general considerations apply to students who vary from the average to a lesser extent, which includes almost all pupils. Consequently, the teaching techniques to be described apply to all classes. If you keep this in mind, you can learn something about special classes for exceptional students and pick up teaching techniques for your own use as well.

✓ *Teaching the Slow Learner*

In an effort to communicate with each other more effectively, people attach labels to things. Scientists are especially prone to do so and have developed a nomenclature for a great variety of qualities and conditions, including levels of intelligence. The scientist is usually more systematic than the layman in making classifications but even he can't escape all semantic pitfalls. When a scientist uses words to denote elusive qualities (such as intelligence), his hearers tend to lose sight of the fact that the verbal symbol is just an abstract representation of what is referred to, not the thing itself. This tendency has unfortunate results when an IQ score is considered to be the same as intelligence (a point that was analyzed in the preceding chapter). It also leads to confusion when certain labels are used for different levels of intelligence.

Not many years ago, children of the lowest intelligence were called feeble-minded. Semanticists perform a valuable service when they point out the negative impact of such words. *Feebleminded* has overtones of fatalism, and eventually the term *mentally retarded* took its place. For some people, even that is too negative, and they use *intellectual inadequacy* instead. This discussion is intended not to ridicule the evolution of a euphemism but rather to emphasize that although *feebleminded, mentally retarded,* and *intellectually inadequate* refer to exactly the same group of children, you may *think* of them as denoting different groups. Different images are evoked because of the varying ideas, experiences, and individuals you associate with each of these words. And because the images evoked by words vary from one individual to another, people's reactions to the same words vary too. The purpose of this slight digression is to help you avoid being trapped by the confounding snares of semantics when children who are deficient in intelligence are discussed. Any classification is made up of labels for the general characteristics of certain types of children. The label does not *endow* the child with a certain fixed set of characteristics; it is simply a descriptive verbal symbol that facilitates communication.

✓ Classifications of the Mentally Retarded

In recent years there has been a trend toward classifying people at the lower levels of intelligence into two categories: the *mentally defective,* that is, individuals whose mental impairment is due to brain injury, disease, or accident; and the *mentally retarded,* that is, individuals who have no identifiable organic cause for their inability to learn. This classification is favored by the National Association for Retarded Children, and it was introduced to minimize the semantic complications just discussed. The N.A.R.C. feels that the traditional classification of *idiot, imbecile,* and *moron* is undesirable because the terms are too frequently misused in everyday speech—usually in a derogatory way. Although the reasoning behind the defective-retarded classification is sound, its emphasis on causes makes it less appropriate for teachers than a more recent

The A.A.M.D. Definition of Mental Retardation

The American Association on Mental Deficiency's statement on mental retardation has been widely hailed as the best definition to date. Here is an abridged version:

know this

A.A.M.D. definition of mental retardation

> Mental retardation refers to subaverage general intellectual function which originates during the developmental period and is associated with impairment in adaptive behavior. . . . *Subaverage* refers to performance which is greater than one Standard Deviation below the population mean of the age group involved on measures of general intellectual functioning. Level of *general intellectual functioning* may be assessed by performance on one or more of the various objective tests which have been developed for that purpose. . . .
>
> The definition specifies that the subaverage intellectual functioning must be reflected by *impairment in adaptive behavior*. Adaptive behavior refers primarily to the effectiveness of the individual in adapting to the natural and social demands of his environment. Impaired adaptive behavior may be reflected in: (1) maturation, (2) learning and/or (3) social adjustment. These three aspects of adaptation are of different importance as qualifying conditions of mental retardation for different age groups.
>
> Rate of *maturation* refers to the rate of sequential development of self-help skills in infancy and early childhood. . . . *Learning* ability refers to the facility with which knowledge is acquired as a function of experience . . . [and] is particularly important as a qualifying condition of mental retardation during the school years.
>
> *Social adjustment* is particularly important as a qualifying condition of mental retardation at the adult level where it is assessed in terms of the degree to which the individual is able to maintain himself independently in the community and in gainful employment as well as by his ability to meet and conform to other personal and social responsibilities and standards set by the community. . . .
>
> Within the framework of the present definition mental retardation is a term *descriptive* of the *current* status of the individual with respect to intellectual functioning and adaptive behavior. Consequently, an individual may meet the criteria of mental retardation at one time and not at another. A person may change status as a result of changes in social standards or conditions or as a result of changes in efficiency of intellectual functioning, with level of efficiency always being determined in relation to the behavioral standards and norms for the individual's chronological age group. (Heber, 1961, pp. 3–4)

Much of the discussion in this section will make more sense if you refer to this definition from time to time. Your attention is directed especially to the last paragraph about *current* status and the changes that may occur from time to time.

three-level approach, which is now widely used in place of the idiot-imbecile-moron designations. Its labels, *custodial, trainable, educable,* reflect the sort of educational arrangements provided. Table 13-1 presents the IQ range and frequency of individuals classified as custodial, trainable, and educable.

Custodial-trainable-educable classifications of mentally retarded

Table 13-1 IQ Range and Frequency of Types of Mental Retardation

Classification	IQ	Approximate Frequency
Custodial	0-24	1 in 500
Trainable	25-49	1 in 100
Educable	50-75	2 or 3 in 100

Table 13-2   MA Ranges for the Three Levels of Mental Retardation

Classification	Approximate MA range
Custodial	0-3
Trainable	4-7
Educable	8-12

Unless you have had considerable experience interpreting IQ's, these numbers will not mean very much to you. A more easily grasped way to describe the three levels is in terms of mental age, or MA. The ranges for these levels are indicated in Table 13-2.

The highest figure in each category represents the peak intellectual level likely to be attained at *maturity*. This means that a person accurately classified as a custodial type will never exceed the intelligence of a normal three-year-old child. You should keep in mind that there is much variation among individuals lumped under each heading and that these items are arbitrary divisions made for what sometimes amounts to administrative convenience. In planning educational programs for thousands of children, it is essential to be able to refer to a child with an IQ of 51 as *educable* and one with an IQ of 49 as *trainable*. Different educational provisions may be established for them by law. In terms of their general behavior, however, they may often be indistinguishable. The children are essentially the same; the label is different.

Custodial Mentally Retarded

As just noted, individuals classified as the custodial mentally retarded rarely develop beyond the intellectual level of three-year-olds. This does not mean that they develop normally until they are two or three and then suddenly stop. A child at the custodial level may continue to mature intellectually for several years, but from the very beginning the rate of development is slower. As a result, children who are this severely retarded are usually identified within the first years of life. A pediatrician may note the retardation during a physical examination, or the parents may come to realize that the child is markedly slower in walking and talking than other children of the same age.

Quite often the tip-off that the child is retarded takes the form of physical anomalies of one kind or another. Defects of intelligence are, unfortunately, frequently coupled with physical defects, even though one does not directly cause the other. Mongoloids are a case in point.[1] Individuals classified as mongoloids have somewhat oriental-looking eyes, a small skull, a round flat face, abnormalities of both hands and feet, and poor teeth. Their intellectual capacity is usually in the upper custodial or the low trainable range.

To picture the kind of limits imposed by an IQ of less than 25, consider the repertoire of behavior of a two-year-old. Then imagine this behavior as

[1] The technical term for mongolism is *Down's Syndrome*.

The A.A.M.D. Classification of Mental Retardation

While the custodial-trainable-educable classification is regarded as most appropriate for teacher use, you should be aware of another popular classification scheme. The American Association on Mental Deficiency feels that standard deviation units are especially useful for classifying the mentally retarded. Since it is possible that you will later encounter the A.A.M.D. classification, the table below is provided for your future reference.

Word description of retardation	Level of deviation in measured intelligence	range in SD value	Corresponding range in IQ scores for tests with SD	
			15 (WISC)	16 (Stanford-Binet)
Borderline	−1	−1.01 to −2.00	70–84	68–83
Mild	−2	−2.01 to −3.00	55–69	52–67
Moderate	−3	−3.01 to −4.00	40–54	36–51
Severe	−4	−4.01 to −5.00	25–39	20–35
Profound	−5	Below 5.00	Under 25	Under 20

Source: Halbert B. and Nancy M. Robinson, *The Mentally Retarded Child,* Copyright © 1965. Reprinted with the permission of McGraw-Hill Book Company, Inc. Data adapted from Heber, 1961.

the ultimate performance of a mature adult. You will realize that custodial mentally retarded of high level may learn to say a few words and understand a few more but are capable of no more than rudimentary communication. They can walk, although clumsily, but their all-round coordination is usually so poor that they cannot handle small objects with any dexterity. They may be able to learn to take care of themselves in a minimal way but will probably always require assistance for such things as washing and dressing. In most cases custodial types have to be cared for all their lives, frequently in institutions which are set up to maintain twenty-four-hour custodial care; hence the term *custodial*. It is not very likely that you will encounter children at this level in the public schools. Their retardation is so extreme that they are usually identified by the time they would ordinarily be eligible for kindergarten or first grade.

Trainable Mentally Retarded

To obtain a rough estimate of the capabilities of a mature individual at the trainable level of retardation, think of a first grade child. (Children at the lower end of this range will resemble the custodial type.) A first grader can speak intelligibly, though his vocabulary is small. He can read and write in a rudimentary way; he can be trusted to take care of himself quite well and can be expected to perform simple household tasks or run errands. The individual

Characteristics of trainable mentally retarded

A Downs Syndrome boy names tools in a prevocational shop class. Later, the instructor helps place the boys in jobs.

like a 1st grader with

with an IQ of 25 to 49 has this same repertoire of skills but is more likely to have physical abnormalities, to be in poor health, and to speak poorly.

Although individuals at the trainable level are capable of independent, responsible action for short periods of time, they need close supervision all their lives. In school they are almost sure to be placed in special classes. The word *trainable* is used in referring to these classes, because it is widely agreed that the children cannot be educated in the usual sense of the word. When they reach maturity, graduates of trainable classes should ideally have part-time employment at a Sheltered Workshop or similar subsidized business operation; they are incapable of competing for jobs on the open labor market. In a Sheltered Workshop or Work Training Center for the Handicapped, the trainable level person may be gainfully employed and kept busy. Since round the clock supervision will be necessary anyway, it is eminently sensible to permit the person to be productive—rather than constantly worrying about what may happen when an individual with the body of an adult and the mind of a child is faced with the problem of occupying himself. It makes sense from an economic standpoint as well. If a graduate of a trainable class is employed, even part time, he is helping to support himself instead of existing as a dependent.

The children at Central Cooperative School (Webster Parish, La.) for the trainable mentally retarded learn to handle themselves competently in the cafeteria, choosing their food, carrying their own trays, and eating properly.

Educable Mentally Retarded

Children who score in the IQ range of 50 to 75 vary considerably more than those on the two lower levels just discussed. Because IQ divisions are arbitrary, the child with an IQ in the 50s will behave very much like the trainable mentally retarded just described. As the IQ approaches 75, the kind of behavior expected of an average upper-elementary-grade child is likely to be found. A fifth- or sixth-grader is capable of a good deal of independent action; and, as we shall see, many graduates of classes for the educable retarded can lead normal lives to the degree that they can earn salaries sufficient for them to marry, raise families, and buy homes. As for learning, however, many school systems acknowledge that such children are incapable of responding to the standard curriculum. Consequently, in numerous schools students with IQs below 75 are placed in special classes.

Characteristics of educable mentally retarded

Children at this level are usually normal in physical appearance. They may have a decent vocabulary as far as *verbal* communication is concerned, and at the younger ages their social maturity may be close to par. But when they are asked to deal with the abstract—in learning to read or to comprehend mathematics—their retardation becomes apparent. Most children who eventually are placed in educable classes enter school and attend regular classes for part, if not all, of their schooling. Thus it may be up to you (as the person in the best position to assess academic ability) to initiate procedures that can eventually lead to the placement of a child in a special class. You should therefore have some familiarity with procedures for identifying the mentally retarded, the nature of special classes, what they aim to accomplish, and how well they succeed.

Identifying Students for Placement in Classes for the Mentally Retarded

The recommendation for placement in a class for trainable or educable retarded is rarely, if ever, based solely on an IQ test. The decision is usually made after the consideration of several kinds of evidence. In most cases this will include the judgment of a number of teachers, which means that the child is given years of opportunity to show that he is capable of responding to the standard curriculum. If the results of personal observation and testing by one or more teachers suggest mental retardation, an examination of group test scores is in order. If those scores corroborate the initial diagnosis, an individual test is given, and if that is indecisive, frequently another individual test. Quite often a thorough physical examination is requested.

This process results in the best possible estimate anyone can come up with regarding the intellectual level of the child. Evaluation is not restricted to a forty-minute sample of test behavior but is based on systematic and unsystematic observation by a variety of people over an extended period of time. If all the evidence points to intelligence below that needed for coping with the regular curriculum, the child may be recommended for a special class.

Goals of Classes for the Educable Mentally Retarded

Listing the goals of special education for the mentally retarded is perhaps the most concise way to describe such classes. Samuel A. Kirk and O. Johnson list these purposes of a program for the educable mentally retarded:

1. They should be educated to get along with their fellow men; i.e., they should develop social competence through numerous social experiences.
2. They should learn to participate in work for the purpose of earning their own living; i.e., they should develop occupational competence through efficient vocational guidance and training as a part of their school experience.
3. They should develop emotional security and independence in the school and in the home through a good mental hygiene program.
4. They should develop habits of health and sanitation through a good program of health education.
5. They should learn the minimum essentials of the tool subjects, even though their academic limits are third to fifth grade.

6. They should learn to occupy themselves in wholesome leisure time activities through an educational program that teaches them to enjoy recreational and leisure time activities.

7. They should learn to become adequate members of a family and a home through an educational program that emphasizes home membership as a function of the curriculum.

8. They should learn to become adequate members of a community through a school program that emphasizes community participation. (1951, p. 118)

Learning Characteristics of the Educable Mentally Retarded

In helping the mentally retarded pupil achieve these goals, the teacher needs to take into account learning characteristics of such students. The pupil who is below average in intelligence typically experiences difficulty in dealing with abstractions and in making generalizations. Because he functions at a mental-age level that seldom exceeds that of the average, upper-elementary grade pupil, he is not likely to be capable of formal operational thought. His thinking will be preoperational (he is likely to classify things by a single feature and not be concerned about inconsistencies) or in terms of concrete operations (he may be able to master some aspects of reversibility but unable to develop or test hypotheses). The inability to generalize means that it is necessary to try to anticipate situations he is likely to encounter and then give specific instruction on how he might cope with them.

Another way to emphasize this point is to note that the mentally retarded student is not able to benefit from nonspecific instruction or incidental learning. A child of average or above-average intelligence is able to accommodate and assimilate ideas on his own. This is one of the basic assumptions on which open education is based—that the student is capable of selecting his own learning experiences and integrating them into his own conception of the world. Because the mentally retarded pupils are not able to do this, the assumptions of guided learning and the techniques of programmed instruction are particularly appropriate for educating them.

Suggestions for Teaching Pupils with Below-Average Intelligence

If both the educational goals of the mentally retarded and the characteristics just described are borne in mind, suggestions for teaching students who are below average in intelligence can be noted. The following teaching recommendations developed by Kirk reflect the degree to which assumptions of guided learning, principles of operant conditioning, and techniques of programmed instruction are considered ideal for educating the mentally retarded.

1. *Never let the child fail.* Organize materials and use methods which lead the child to the right answer. Provide clues where necessary. Narrow the choices he has in responding. Lead him to the right answer by rewording the question or simplifying the problem. Never leave him in a failure, but carry him along until he finds success.

2. *Provide feedback so that he knows when he has responded correctly.* Learning is facilitated when the child has knowledge of whether his response is correct or not. If his response is incorrect, let him know it, but let it be only a way station in finding the correct response. Lessons should be so arranged that the child obtains an immediate feedback on the correctness of his answer. This is one of the principles used in any good programmed learning procedure. If a child is learning to write the word *dog*, for example, he covers the model, writes the word, then compares his response with the model, thus getting feedback on his effort.

3. *Reinforce correct responses.* Reinforcement should be immediate and clear. It can be either tangible, as in providing tokens, candy, etc., or it can be in the form of social approval and the satisfaction of winning a game.

4. *Find the optimum level at which the child should work.* If the material is too easy, the child is not challenged to apply his best efforts; if too difficult, he faces failure and frustration.

5. *Proceed in a systematic, step-by-step fashion* so that the more basic necessary knowledge and habits precede more difficult material.

6. *Use minimal change* from one step to the next to facilitate learning.

7. *Provide for positive transfer of knowledge from one situation to another.* This is facilitated by helping the child generalize from one situation to another. By presenting the same concept in various settings and in various relationships, the child can transfer the common elements in each. Itard, for example, when training the Wild Boy of Aveyron, noted that the boy learned to select a particular knife from a group of objects in response to the written word *knife*, but that when a knife of a different shape was substituted he could not respond. The child had not generalized the concept of *knife*; he had failed to transfer the understanding of the label to knives in general.

8. *Provide sufficient repetition of experiences to develop overlearning.* Many teachers have said, "Johnny learns a word one day but forgets it the next day." In such cases, Johnny probably had not had enough repetition of the word in varying situations to insure over-learning, that is, learning to the point where he will not forget it readily. Mentally retarded children seem to require more repetitions of an experience or an association in order to retain it.

9. *Space the repetitions of material over time* rather than massing the experiences in a short duration. When a new concept is presented, come back to it again and again, often in new settings, not as drill but as transfer to a new situation.

10. *Consistently associate a given stimulus or cue with one and only one response in the early stages of learning.* Do not tell the child, "This letter sometimes says a and sometimes says ah." Teach him one sound at a time until it is overlearned and then teach the other sound as a different configuration in a new setting. If the child has to vacillate between two responses he will become confused.

11. *Motivate the child toward greater effort by:* (a) reinforcement and the satisfaction of succeeding, (b) variation in the presentation of material, (c) enthusiasm on the part of the teacher, and (d) optimal length of sessions.

12. *Limit the number of concepts presented in any one period.* Do not confuse the child by trying to have him learn too many things at one time. Introduce new material only after older material has become familiar.

13. *Arrange materials with proper cues for attention.* Arrange materials in such a way to direct the pupil's attention so that he will learn to attend to cues in the situation that will facilitate his learning, and to learn to disregard those factors in the learning situation that are irrelevant.

14. *Provide success experiences.* Educable mentally retarded children who have failed in the regular grades and then been placed in a special class may have developed low frustration tolerance, negative attitudes toward school work, and possibly some compensatory behavior problems which make them socially unpopular. The best way to cope with these problems is to organize a day-to-day program presenting the child with short-range as well as long-range tasks in which he succeeds. The self-concept and the self-evaluation of the child are dependent upon how well he succeeds in the assignments given to him. Thus a special class teacher must be very careful to see not only that the child does not fail but also that he experiences positive success and knows that he has succeeded. Although this principle is applicable to all children it is particularly necessary with children who are retarded. They face enough failures in school and in life without having to repeat them over and over again in a classroom situation. (1972, pp. 214–216)

The following are O. P. Kolstoe's suggestions for teaching specific tasks:

1. The tasks should be uncomplicated. The new tasks should contain the fewest possible elements, and most of the elements should be familiar, so he has very few unknowns to learn.

2. The tasks should be brief. This assures that he will attend to the most important aspects of the tasks and not get lost in a sequence of interrelated events.

3. The tasks should be sequentially presented so the learner proceeds in a sequence of small steps, each one built upon previously learned tasks.

4. Each learning task should be the kind in which success is possible. One of the major problems to be overcome is that of failure proneness. This major deterrent to learning can be effectively reduced through success experiences.

5. Overlearning must be built into the lessons. Drills in game form seem to lessen the disinterest inherent in unimaginative drill.

6. Learning tasks should be applied to objects, problems, and situations in the learner's life environment. Unless the tasks are relevant, the learner has great difficulty in seeing their possible importance. (1970, pp. 22–23)

Graduates of EMR Classes Twenty Years Later

Now that you have been acquainted with the nature of special classes for the mentally retarded, it will be instructive to take a look at what happens to the graduates of these classes. A number of follow-up studies have been

What Kinds of Jobs Do The Mentally Retarded Hold?

According to the United States Department of Labor, two million mentally retarded persons are working in private industry. A million more of America's six million retarded could be employed, it is estimated, if they were properly trained. What kinds of jobs can they be trained for? Here is a brief list: They can be butchers, salesclerks, messengers, mechanics, waitresses, maids, stockboys, painters, carpenters, upholsterers, manicurists, mail-sorters, elevator operators, welders, and weavers.

Businessmen who hire graduates of classes for the mentally retarded point out some reasons why they prefer such workers: If they don't understand something, they will admit it; brighter persons might try to bluff. They are less likely to daydream (and throw a monkey wrench in the machinery) when assigned tedious, repetitive jobs. They are more punctual, steady, loyal, dependable, and eager to please than "average" workers.

If a child is diagnosed early in life as mentally retarded and given the opportunity to attend special classes, upon graduation he will probably receive employment assistance—proper training and contacts with placement agencies. You might keep this in mind if you must help decide special-class placement.

Charles study: self-sufficiency of EMR graduates in later life

conducted, one of the most comprehensive by W. A. Charles (1953), who obtained information from 151 persons formerly enrolled in special classes for the educable retarded. Only those with an IQ below 70 had been eligible for the classes. At the time of Charles's study, these individuals had an average age of forty-two, which meant they had spent more than twenty years providing for themselves in an unsheltered world. On the whole, they coped surprisingly well. The most telling statistic to back up this assertion is that over 80 percent were self-supporting. What's more, most of them were leading normal lives, in the sense that they were married, raising families, and living in their own homes. (It is of interest to note that the IQ range of their offspring was 50 to 138, with a mean of 95.)

Statistics compiled for the retarded group and for the average American citizen showed two main distinctions. First, the death rate was about twice as high for the low-IQ men. It was explained that this was due to the kind of common-labor job, often dangerous, that many of the special-class graduates held. Lack of sufficient intellectual alertness to recognize potentially hazardous situations caused several violent deaths. Also, there was a greater tendency for the special-class graduates to commit minor law infractions. This might be attributed to lack of ability to comprehend subtleties of legal regulations and to poor judgement. The general conclusion remains favorable, though. One cautionary note is that the mentally retarded do less well during periods of economic depression.

Are Special Classes Beneficial or Harmful?

Although the results of Charles's follow-up study could be interpreted as favorable to special-class instruction, over the last few years considerable criticism has been expressed regarding the placement of children in special classes. Analyses of the students who are assigned to such classes reveal they contain a disproportionate number of disadvantaged minority group children, particularly those from bilingual homes. For reasons noted in the preceding chapter, it is argued that the tests used to identify these children are biased and unfair. And once a child is placed in a class for the mentally retarded, it is argued, he is treated as if he *were* mentally retarded and therefore prevented from making the most of his potential. But even in cases in which the identification procedures have been considered fair and complete, some educators question the policy of placing children of below-average intelligence in special classes.

Research on the relative benefits and harm of special class placement has provided conflicting results. G. O. Johnson (1950) found that mentally retarded children tended to be isolated or rejected by their classmates when they attended regular classes. Elizabeth A. Welch (1967) discovered that mentally retarded elementary schoolchildren who spent half the school day in special classes and half in regular classes earned higher achievement scores and decreased in self-derogation compared to students who spent all of their time in special classes. S. L. Guskin and H. H. Spicker (1968) reviewed available research and concluded that children in special classes are better adjusted and have a better self-concept than those who remain in regular classes. H. Goldstein, J. Moss, and Laura J. Jordan (1965) discovered that lower-level educable retarded make better educational progress in special classes, whereas those at the upper levels (75 to 85 IQ) tend to do better in regular classes. Lloyd M. Dunn (1968), a leading specialist in the education of the mentally retarded, has observed that placing students in special classes often occurs for reasons of expediency or because regular-class teachers are not willing to take the trouble to work with slow learners. He recommends that special-class placement be resorted to only after account has been taken of sociocultural deprivation.

Kirk, whose suggestions for teaching slow learners were quoted earlier, makes these recommendations:

1. Children should be assigned to special classes for the mentally retarded only after a differential psychoeducational assessment indicates that the child shows a general mental retardation requiring a special program geared to his abilities. These classes should be comprised of children who, on the whole, have lower IQ's than children now so assigned.
2. Children with learning disabilities and children from minority ethnic groups whose background of experiences places them at a disadvantage in relation to the general population should remain in the regular grades but be helped by itinerant and resource teachers to adapt to the regular grades and establish adequate learning habits.

3. Regular elementary education, through more individualized instruction and teachers better informed on learning characteristics of educationally retarded children, should adapt to a large proportion of children they are currently referring for special education. (1972, p. 202)

The development of open education techniques and criterion-referenced grading accords with Kirk's recommendations. It would seem that many of the problems facing students who are below average in intelligence have stemmed from an inflexible curriculum and comparative grading practices. If each student is assisted in setting individual goals, allowed to engage in learning designed to meet his own style and abilities, and evaluated with reference to standards of performance, many of the slow learner's problems are likely to be reduced or eliminated. However, below a certain point, this may not be the case, as suggested by the conclusions of Goldstein, Moss, and Jordan. It appears that students whose IQs are in the 75 to 85 range (when these scores have not been distorted by biased tests) may be negatively influenced by the lowest-common-denominator effect of special-class instruction. If they attend regular classes, they may be "pulled up" by their more gifted classmates. But below the 75 IQ level, the student may be better off in a special class. If you are ever asked to participate in a decision regarding special-class placement, you are asked to consider these points; also take into account that most special classes are limited to 15 students or less, which means more individual attention.

Teaching the Rapid Learner

Regardless of how well we succeed in helping children make the most of their intelligence, there will always be a fortunate minority who function at an especially effective level. This section examines the nature and education of rapid learners.

Characteristics of Rapid Learners

For information on what the intellectually gifted are like, there is one source in a class by itself, the five-volume *Genetic Studies of Genius* by Terman and Oden, both of Stanford University. These volumes consist of a succession of reports on the characteristics of fifteen hundred of one year's crop of the brightest children in California from the time they were in elementary school to midlife. Since these reports are available in most college libraries, only a few selected results and conclusions will be noted here.

The overall impression one receives from the volumes is that individuals of superior intelligence are generally superior in other respects as well. On the average they are taller, healthier, better coordinated, and better adjusted than others. They do exceptionally well in school. After graduation they hold

Terman and Oden study: superior behavior and adjustment of gifted

important positions in the professions and in management and earn salaries considerably above the average. Marital happiness is rated as significantly greater than the norm, and the divorce rate is lower.

Gifted individuals beget children who are still in the superior category (average IQ, 133) but not as high as their parents (IQ, over 140). This is referred to as *regression toward the mean.* Although some high-IQ parents produce children even more intelligent than themselves, the tendency is for very bright parents to have children with IQs somewhat below their own; the measured intelligence of the children moves back (or regresses) toward the average. (The same is true at the opposite end of the distribution. Low-IQ parents tend to produce children more intelligent than themselves, but still below average.)

For details about any of these statements regarding gifted individuals, see *Genetic Studies of Genius: The Gifted Group at Mid-Life* (Terman and Oden, 1959).

Educational Programs

The identification of gifted pupils is almost invariably based on an individual intelligence test, although teacher judgment and group test scores also play a part.[2] Once the rapid learner has been identified, he may be placed in one or more of the following programs.

Enrichment

This is the most common administrative arrangement. The basic idea is to have the child remain in the regular class and avoid possible negative effects of separating him from his average classmates. This caution is praiseworthy, but enrichment sometimes turns out to be nothing but an empty phrase. If the regular teacher is told to provide the enrichment and still teach thirty-five others, she will find it difficult to do much of anything. Preferable techniques are having the enrichment activities provided by an outside teacher or releasing the regular-class teacher to individually instruct the gifted. During the first few years you teach, you will probably be responsible for some form of enrichment, and do-it-yourself techniques will be discussed after other educational programs for the gifted are mentioned.

Acceleration or Skipping a Grade

You are no doubt familiar with this procedure; perhaps you experienced it. Opinions differ as to whether acceleration is a good idea. One argument against it is that it damages the social adjustment of the child. Presumably, if he is skipped, his small size will make him stand out, and he will be unable to

---

[2] For an excellent list identifying characteristics of the gifted, see *Identifying Children with Special Needs* by Kough and DeHaan (1955).

participate in the social give-and-take of the classroom. This sounds plausible, and undoubtedly it occurs in a few cases, but substantial evidence contradicts both parts of the supposition. Terman, among others, found that accelerated pupils were rated as better adjusted—socially and academically—than their fellow geniuses who remained with their age-mates. He went so far as to recommend that almost any child with an IQ over 140 should be skipped at least one grade. If this seems hard to accept, consider two things: (1) the likelihood that the accelerated child will *not* be a physical misfit because of the range of maturity to be found at any particular grade level and (2) the fact that social behavior and interests are more a function of mental age than chronological age.

It is doubtful that you will ever be asked to take the sole responsibility for deciding whether a child should be skipped a grade. But if you are teaching at the primary level, you may well initiate consideration of such a move. When a certain pupil learns everything in a small fraction of the time his classmates require and you simply don't have time to give him the individualized instruction he needs, keep an open mind about acceleration.

Perhaps the biggest drawback to skipping a grade is that the teacher who inherits the accelerant may have to scramble to fill in the work missed. Many school districts meet the problem by providing either individualized or group instruction for a month or so in the summer. If such a program exists in your area, there should be little reason to hesitate to recommend a pupil for skipping.

Finally, it should be mentioned that not all pupils who are accelerated look upon their new status as an unmixed blessing. Some children are better off unaccelerated. A child who seems perfectly happy with his age-mates and is somewhat immature in non-intellectual characteristics might be better off where he is even if his IQ merits acceleration. In this case your judgment and that of the principal, the psychologist who gives the individual test, and the parents are usually considered—along with the feelings of the child.

Advanced Standing

Acceleration is usually confined to the elementary grades, but an administrative arrangement for permitting skipping at the secondary level is to have the brightest pupils go through junior high in two years with a summer session sandwiched in between. The curriculum is set up so that the rapid learner can be just that. Another procedure allows high school seniors to take college-level courses for credit. Sometimes a pupil—if he is permitted to take enough units—can enter college as a sophomore.

Correspondence Courses and Tutoring

In small school districts one or two brilliant children are occasionally found several dozen IQ points higher than the other above-average pupils. One way to provide for them is tutorial instruction. In some cases this is given by a principal or teacher with released time. Because of the expense, the solution is more likely to be a correspondence course. Combining these two techniques has met with a good deal of success. Called the Sponsor-Correspondent Plan, its purpose is to establish a liaison between the brilliant pupil and someone with training and experience in the area of the pupil's greatest interest. Often the person who serves as a sponsor is a retired expert in the field.

Suppose a brilliant pupil in a small high school is fascinated by inorganic chemistry. Because of his intellect and his single-minded drive, he learns more about the subject than his teacher—who also teaches three other subjects—knows. The teacher asks a nearby college or professional organization if it knows of a retired inorganic chemist who might enjoy assisting a young enthusiast. If such a person is found, the sponsor and the pupil correspond with each other and, as often as circumstances permit, have personal conferences. Highly successful experiences with this technique have been reported, and if you find yourself teaching in a small school and bedeviled by an embryonic Einstein, it could be your salvation.

Special Classes

The remaining programs for gifted pupils consist of special class groupings of selected individuals. Sometimes, all the brightest pupils from a number of elementary schools are segregated early in the grades and placed in an accelerated curriculum. In large cities, often an entire school is made up of such classes. But even more frequently the brightest pupils attend special classes in selected subjects for part of each day. They remain in the regular class most of the day and progress through the curriculum at the standard rate.

The main disadvantage of the full-time, segregated-class technique is that the initial choosing of pupils is crucial and virtually final. After a year or so it may be too late to introduce late bloomers or misjudged rejects into the class. The part-time, special-class plan permits much greater flexibility. One of its big advantages is that continued attendance in the supplementary special classes is usually contingent upon consistent above-average work in the regular class. This tends to motivate the majority of the bright pupils to keep doing their best. It also permits any child who has the brainpower and motivation to earn a place in the special class.

Since most special-class programs are schoolwide, you probably will not have to take any individual initiative in preparing for them. At this point, more detailed consideration will be given to the administrative arrangement for gifted pupils that does demand individual teacher initiative—enrichment. (If you use any sort of individualized approach [e.g., open education, mastery learning] in your classes, you will be faced with the problem of providing study suggestions for students who finish assigned work faster than others. The following suggestions apply to all such students, not just those who have exceptional ability.)

Enrichment Techniques

Horizontal and Vertical Enrichment

Most discussions of enrichment techniques distinguish between *horizontal* and *vertical* enrichment. Horizontal enrichment consists in giving a rapid learner who has finished an assignment ahead of everyone else more material at the same general level of difficulty. The vertical approach involves giving him more advanced work of the same general type. Take a math period as an example. Assume that you have started the class on a workbook assignment in math. About the time you get your pencil sharpened and turn around to start giving individual help, you bump into your 146-IQ student, who has come up to announce that he has finished and ask what you would like him to do next. One reaction is to say, "Go back to your seat and do the next five pages of problems." If these problems are at the same level of difficulty, that's horizontal enrichment. If the forest of waving hands signaling the need for special help induces panic, a vertical enrichment assignment may be forthcoming: "Why don't you read the next chapter and see how well you can handle those problems we are going to take up next month."

These examples emphasize the pitfalls of literal horizontal or vertical enrichment. If you assign the fast workers more of the same, it won't take them long to figure out that there is little point in making much of an effort. This can ruin motivation, destroy the ability to concentrate, and squelch interest. Terman found that one of the things his geniuses disliked the most about school was tedious, repetitious drill. On the other hand, if you urge the rapid learner to take off on his own, what will happen when you reach next month's problems? The more often you resort to vertical enrichment assignments that simply anticipate what is to come, the bigger the problem becomes. Before long you are rummaging around the storeroom for next year's text. And that can *really* lead to a mess when the clear, innocent voice pipes up to announce to the teacher of the next higher grade that he's already finished the standard text. Mrs. So-and-so gave it to him.

To avoid such unpleasantness, use some discretion in applying horizontal and vertical enrichment. Don't let an assignment of more of the same seem like punishment. If the skill in question is not likely to be improved substantially by more repetition (e.g., problems in addition), find some related exercises of equivalent difficulty (e.g., a book of math "puzzlers"). In reading classes, permit the child to read several other books at the same level of difficulty instead of stultifying him with an additional dose of primer material. In high school classes, have optional extra assignments for the fast workers.

If you choose to give an assignment at a more advanced level, take care not to anticipate what is to be covered in ensuing semesters and years. Try to obtain curriculum materials that will supplement, not duplicate, the standard curriculum. A series of books from a different publisher is the most logical

Techniques for teaching rapid learners

source of such materials, and most school districts have consultants who can help you obtain what you need. In any event, it pays to do some planning. Trying to take care of enrichment problems by tossing spur-of-the-moment instructions over your shoulder as you dash off to provide remedial help for the slow learners is ineffective at best and potentially disastrous.

Individual Study Projects

One of the most effective ways to provide enrichment when straight horizontal or vertical techniques fail to fill the gap is through the assignment of individual study projects. These assignments should probably be related to some part of the curriculum. If you are studying Mexico, for example, the rapid learner could be permitted to devote free time to a special report on some aspect of Mexican life that intrigues him. On the other hand, if the gifted child has a hobby—say, writing short stories or poems—it might be preferable to let him turn to this pursuit in his free time, even though it is tangential.

To provide another variation of the individual study project, you could ask the rapid learner to act as a research specialist and report on questions that puzzle the class. An incident in a third-grade classroom illustrates this technique. A child asked about sponges and triggered a whole series of related questions that the teacher couldn't answer. There happened to be a boy with an IQ of 150 in this class, and he was asked to spend his reading period with the encyclopedia and give a report on sponges the next day.

Still another individual study project is the creation of an open-ended, personal yearbook. Any time a child finishes the assigned work, he might be allowed to write stories or do drawings for such a journal. When possible, though, unobtrusive projects are preferable. Perhaps you can recall a teacher who rewarded the fast workers by letting them work on a mural (or the equivalent) covering the side board. If you were an average student, you can probably testify that the sight of the class "brains" having the time of their lives splashing paint around the wall was not conducive to diligent effort on the part of the have-nots sweating away at their workbooks. Reward assignments should probably be restricted to individual work on unostentatious projects.

The individual study project is essentially the same thing as *independent study*—one of the most popular educational innovations of the moment. Those who favor independent study point out that the traditional school has been too rigid about the way the curriculum is presented. They question the idea that every subject should be taught to equal numbers of pupils for equal periods of time every day. They also feel that too much teacher direction may be undesirable. These critics of traditional schooling believe that team teaching and flexible scheduling are to be preferred, particularly in conjunction with independent study. (Not *all* independent study is done as a part of team teaching or flexible scheduling, but in most cases it seems to be a "package deal.")

How Should You Handle an Obnoxious "Genius?"

Imagine that you are teaching in a third grade. It is the end of the first month of school. A new boy is assigned to your room. During his first week in class he manages to antagonize just about everyone. He gets perfect scores on all his work and makes sure the entire school is well aware of this. He shouts out answers to questions when you call on other children. (He gives the impression that he can't help doing this—he is just bursting with information.) He makes remarks about the stupidity of children who can't answer as rapidly or as accurately as he does. When he recites, he somehow works in all kinds of slightly relevant information he has memorized. He even corrects you on particular points (you spoke of "crocodiles" when you should have said "alligators"), and upon looking the matter up, you discover that he is right. How could you encourage him to be humbler without squelching his undeniable gifts?

Independent study, they say, allows for infinite variety; it allows for individual differences better than any other method of pedagogy and provides greater satisfaction and depth of learning; and it encourages self-regulation and self-responsibility in learning. Furthermore, this approach presumably fits well with what is known about transfer, since the skills used in independent study in school are essentially the same as those likely to be used in later out-of-school study. Finally, it is argued that independent study is excellent preparation for college.

Various types of independent study can be engaged in—ranging from homework assignments to teacher-directed individual study to a completely independent "thesis." In some cases the contract approach is used, and the student agrees to prepare a paper on a topic he submits to the teacher. In other cases a student meets with a teacher in individual tutorial sessions and writes a series of short papers on topics that emerge from discussion. In still other instances a student works on a programmed unit.

This brings up one of the most controversial points about independent study. Some enthusiasts (e.g., Trump, 1959) argue that it is appropriate for *all* children, regardless of age and intelligence. Others point out that it does not work very well with certain students and that the prediction of which ones will take to the method is difficult. Willard J. Congreve, principal of the University of Chicago Laboratory School, has had a good deal of experience with independent study. When it was first introduced in his school, he notes, "It became apparent that some students just could not bring themselves to use the option days in a manner conducive to learning" (1965, p. 32). When students were given the opportunity to comment freely on the program, their responses "ranged along the entire continuum from total support of the program to complete rejection" (p. 33). Some felt the program was too restrictive; others thought it far too permissive.

Some resented any teacher interference; others desired more structure and guidance. Generally speaking, students with high IQ scores, high grade-point averages, and high scores on college aptitude tests chose the most independent projects; those with low scores and grades chose more "dependent" projects. (The University of Chicago Laboratory School has an atypically above-average school population.) Sixty percent of the students responded favorably to independent study; from their point of view the major advantage of the program was that it "provided them with an opportunity to learn more about themselves and how they studied" (p. 37). Congreve summarizes his general conclusions:

> In spite of the long-held notion about teen-agers desiring freedom to work out their own destinies, when given the opportunity to plan their programs, to select modes of study and to take the consequences for these selections, only about half of the freshman students in a high ability student population really are comfortable with such a situation and wish to have it continue. A sizable percentage of them (about fifteen percent) are so uncomfortable with this situation that they react almost violently against the idea of having been subjected to it. On the other hand, a similar percentage (again about fifteen percent) are tremendously enthusiastic about the program and feel cheated when such opportunities are terminated. (P. 39)

If your school has an independent study program, you undoubtedly will be given specific instructions on how it should be structured. But for your own edification, you might read *Independent Study* (1965) edited by David W. Beggs III and Edward G. Buffie. Keep in mind, too, that not all students respond favorably to the plan. Consequently, if all pupils are forced to try independent study, individual differences may be squelched just as much as they are in a lecture course given for fifty minutes five days every week.

Supplementary Reading and Writing

A common complaint about modern American education is that pupils don't do enough reading and writing. At any grade level an excellent enrichment goal is to try to remedy relative illiteracy. Encourage the capable students who have time on their hands to spend it reading and writing. A logical method of combining both skills is the preparation of book reports. It is perhaps less threatening to call them book *reviews* and emphasize that you are interested in personal reaction, not in a précis or abstract. Some specialists in the education of the gifted have suggested that such students be urged to read biographies and autobiographies. The line of reasoning is that potential leaders might be inspired to emulate the exploits of a famous person. Even if such inspiration does not result, you could recommend life stories simply because they are usually interesting.

Development of Creative Hobbies

At the elementary level, a rapid learner might devote spare class time to a hobby—providing it is appropriate. If the pupil has an interest in poetry or rocks or butterflies, encouragement from you may lead to future specialization.

At the secondary level, pupils who are gifted in your particular subject might be urged to spend class time on a paper for an essay contest, or a Science Fair project, or a dress or desk to be entered in the county fair. A related point is that you should help high school seniors who are talented in your field to apply for scholarships. Some schools, and teachers, place winners each year, basically because they take the trouble to assist logical candidates.

Identifying and Teaching Handicapped Students

Although exceptionality in intelligence and general learning ability is found in almost any class—even homogeneously grouped classes have relatively slow and relatively fast students—you may encounter other kinds of exceptionality from time to time. In the event you take the lead in identifying a child who is handicapped in some way, you may find that you are expected to make special educational provisions for the student. The remainder of this chapter focuses on the identification of certain types of exceptionality and provides a brief list of suggestions for teaching the blind and partially sighted, the deaf and hard of hearing, students with impaired speech, and those with some form of epilepsy.

✓ The Blind and Partially Sighted

Identifying children who need special education because of visual handicaps may very well be instituted by a teacher. Although the handicap of a blind child is usually apparent to almost everyone, a less severe but still damaging visual handicap is often not recognized until an eye specialist conducts a thorough examination. Perhaps the logical person to recommend such an examination is the teacher. You will be in a position to observe the child in situations that demand normal vision. Here are some symptoms of visual problems (derived from a discussion in Dunn, 1963, pages 421-422) that you will be likely to notice:

Identifying students with visual handicaps

Holding a book abnormally near or far from the eyes.

Walking overcautiously; faltering, stumbling, or running into objects not directly in the line of vision.

Rubbing the eyes frequently. (Some children look as if they are attempting to "brush away" the blur.)

Frowning and distorting the face when using the eyes; tilting the head at odd angles when looking at objects.

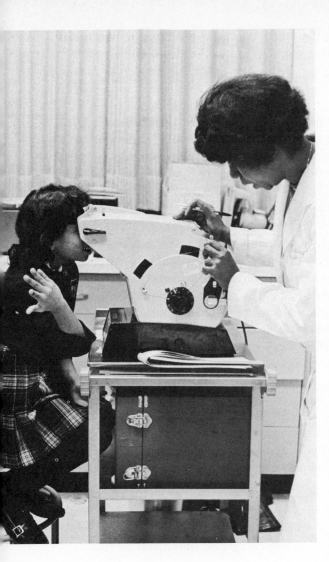

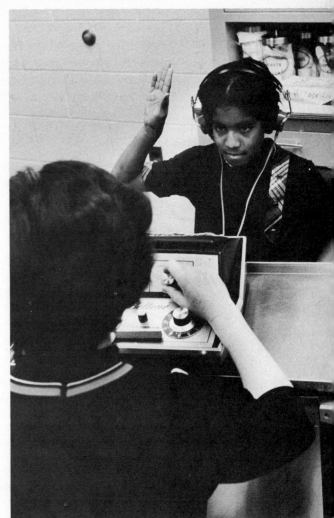

Child taking a vision test.

MARION BERNSTEIN

Child taking an audiometer (hearing) test.

DE WYS, INC.

Indicating undue sensitivity to normal light levels by squinting or other facial signs of irritation.

Performing inconsistently when reading print at different distances, for example, on the board and in a book.

Any suspicion that a child has a visual problem for the above or related reasons should prompt you to alert the school nurse or the parents or both. The child with a severe problem will be eligible for special schools or classes. If the problem is less incapacitating, you will want to consider special teaching techniques in your classroom.

Most states have special schools for blind children, not to mention such nationally famous institutions as the Perkins School in Watertown, Massachusetts. Many workers with the blind favor educating blind children in the specialized environment of a school created expressly for that purpose. In some cases, however, particularly at the secondary level, the parents or local school authorities prefer to have the child remain in a regular classroom. The numerous organizations that offer aid to the blind usually acquaint blind children and their parents with the resources available. For your own information, and in case you encounter a family that is unaware of these resources, here is an abbreviated list.

The Seeing Eye Dog Guide program, Morristown, New Jersey.

The Library of Congress Division for the Blind provides free reading materials in the form of braille, talking books, and tape recordings. (They even pay the postage.) These materials are distributed through thirty regional libraries. Look for the address of the one in your area, or contact the American Foundation for the Blind)

The American Foundation for the Blind at 15 West 16th Street, New York, provides consultative services and scholarship funds and publishes *The Braille and Talking Book Review* as well as monographs on educational techniques.

The American Printing House, a private Kentucky corporation located at 1839 Frankfort Avenue, Louisville, publishes catalogs of braille and talking books, tape recordings, etc.

The Hadley Correspondence School of Winnetka, Illinois, provides a wide range of home correspondence courses.

The Perkins School in Watertown, Massachusetts, sells braille typewriters and a stylus and slate for "handwriting."

A local chapter of Lions International, the Variety Club, or the Delta Gamma Foundation will sometimes supply funds for the purchase of a small portable tape recorder and other materials and devices.

If you are wondering what it is like to teach a blind pupil in a regular class, here is a description of a blind college student. He came to class with a tape recorder. He recorded the lecture and class discussion and, back in the dorm after class, transcribed the recording on his braille typewriter. Before the semester started, the text had been recorded for him on tape by an inmate at a state penitentiary. He took exams by typing out his essay answers on a conventional typewriter and by having a reader record answers to multiple-choice questions.

Many cities and counties provide special classes for the partially sighted, but if you are asked to teach such a child in the regular class, materials are likely to be available from the Special Education section of your school district. If materials are not readily available or if you must take the initiative for planning an educational program on your own, here is a list of sources to contact:

The American Foundation for the Blind, 15 West 16th Street, New York. It provides a variety of literature about the education of the partially sighted.

The National Society for the Prevention of Blindness, 79 Madison Ave., New York. This organization supplies information about the prevention of blindness. (It no longer offers other types of information on blindness.)

Stanwix Publishing House, 3020 Chartiers Avenue, Pittsburgh, Pennsylvania. It publishes many materials in large type.

In addition, several publishers print large-type versions of standard texts and workbooks, and the American Optical Company sells a Projection Magnifier that optically enlarges the print of texts that have standard type size.

For complete information and suggestions regarding teaching techniques for the partially sighted, you are urged to take advantage of the resources listed above. One general rule of thumb should be mentioned in closing this section on children with visual handicaps: Be alert to the aggravating effect of glare. Materials with large-sized print alleviate this problem. Many children with poor vision are rendered even less capable of seeing when they are forced to look at glaring surfaces. Permit them to experiment until they find a location in the room that is free of reflected light. Do not use dead white or coated paper if you can avoid it. Encourage the partially sighted child to tilt the top of his desk or use a lapboard so that light does not reflect directly back into his eyes.

Techniques for teaching students with visual handicaps

The Deaf and Hard of Hearing

In many states school children have to take a hearing test every two or three years. Such tests are set up so that the preliminary screening is done in groups. Occasionally a child at the borderline slips by because of the difficulties of testing large numbers of children. Or a hard-of-hearing child transfers into the school district just after the test date. Or a hearing problem begins to develop shortly after a test. (Medical authorities have expressed concern about the literally deafening impact of much popular music. Teen-agers who listen to rock music may suffer a noticeable hearing loss.) For these and similar reasons keep in mind the following *symptoms of poor hearing*, which could tip you off that an audiometer test is called for:

Identifying students with hearing handicaps

Peculiar listening posture; habitual turning of the head to position one ear toward the speaker.

Inattention and slow response; lack of interest in general conversation.

Mistakes in carrying out instructions or frequent requests to have instructions repeated.

Irrelevant answers.

Spotty educational record with poor work in subjects that require hearing the spoken voice. Work depending on written directions may be done well.

Voice peculiarities—monotone, high pitch, too soft or too loud.

Faulty enunciation and mispronunciation of words.

Repeated colds, earaches; ear discharge

Tendency to look at another person's lips, rather than his eyes, in face-to-face situations.

If you find it hard to understand the behavior of a student, consider the possibility of a hearing problem. It is most important to detect a hearing loss as early as possible. For one thing, most hearing difficulties detected before the age of eight can be counteracted. For another, a major educational handicap may result if a child with limited hearing manages to conceal his disability—or remains unaware of it. In fact, the hearing difficulty may prevent him from grasping the rudiments of basic skills. A bright child sometimes compensates for defective hearing by resorting to brilliant improvisations to adjust to his condition. In the process he may exhaust himself mentally and physically and miss out on the fundamental skills that his less capable but normal-hearing classmates are grasping with ease.

Like blindness, total deafness is likely to be detected early in life. A deaf adult who has received special education may be able to react so skillfully to a world built around sound that he is indistinguishable from his more fortunate fellow citizens. The deaf *child* simply cannot develop the necessary skills by himself. The main reason is that he will not be able to learn how to talk unless he is given a highly specialized kind of schooling.

If you ever turn off the sound on your TV set to obtain blessed relief from a commercial, you get a rough idea of what the deaf child is up against. *You* know, of course, the gist of what the huckster is saying, and you have had years of experience in listening to words. Chances are, you have also had a nauseating overexposure to the words of the commercial—which is why you turned off the sound. Contrast your inability to react to the picture of what is being said with the predicament of a child who has *never* heard any word.

Even when they do learn to talk, children who are deaf from birth never learn to pronounce words faultlessly because of lack of feedback, and in some cases incorrect pronunciation may be the only indication you will receive that the person you are conversing with is deaf. Because of the problems of teaching a deaf child, special schools are found in most states. It is next to impossible for a regular classroom teacher with thirty other pupils even to begin to teach a deaf child. Individual attention and much special training are required, and progress is facilitated by elaborate and expensive equipment.

The hard-of-hearing child may be eligible for a special class if one is available. But you are likely to have some hard-of-hearing pupils in your own classes, either because they are not eligible for a special class or because such classes do not exist in the local school system or the school district. In such cases you might consider two remedial measures. First, you could inquire about the possibility of receiving specialized assistance from the school speech therapist, a speech clinic attached to a college, or a summer school or camp sponsored by the Crippled Children's Society (or the equivalent). The child with a hearing loss needs the help of specialists to determine whether a hearing aid is advisable and to learn speech (or lip) reading. Usually speech training is desirable to enable him to increase the vocabulary of words he can pronounce properly. Second, there are certain things you can do on your own:

1. *Use preferential seating.*

> *Techniques for teaching students with hearing handicaps*

By trial and error, find the spot in the room where the child can hear best. This is likely to be in the front of the room, but because of peculiar acoustics in different settings, it may be elsewhere. Ideally, the child should sit where he can hear you as well as his classmates. If he has better hearing in one ear, a seat placed at an angle in the appropriate front corner of the room might make it simpler for him to tune in on most of what you say as well as recitation by classmates.

2. *Take special care to speak clearly.*

This seems almost too obvious to mention, but unless you are a speech major or minor, attention has probably never been called to your elocution. A deliberate effort to improve the clarity of your speech will benefit the hard-of-hearing child—and everyone else.

3. *Try to remember to face the class whenever you speak.*

This may also seem obvious, but many teachers address half of their remarks to the blackboard. Guard against this as much as you can. Face the class not only to gain maximum effectiveness from voice projection but also to permit the hard-of-hearing child to benefit from watching your lips. In regard to this last point, make an effort to recognize and to check any nervous habits that might obscure your lips, like scratching your nose or pushing back your glasses.

4. If the hard-of-hearing child does not understand something, rephrase it instead of repeating it verbatim.

The specialist who offered this suggestion gave two reasons for it. First, repeating the same phrase tends to focus attention on the child's handicap and is likely to make him self-conscious. But, in addition, probably some of the sounds you used were especially difficult for the child to hear. A different set of sounds gives him another assortment to choose from, so to speak, and at the same time provides additional clues for him in figuring out what you are saying.

These suggestions should help you cope with many hearing problems. However, if it is solely up to you to take the initiative in planning for the education of a deaf or hard-of-hearing child, the following sources of information will be helpful:

The National Association of Hearing and Speech Agencies, 919 18th Street NW, Washington, D.C., publishes a variety of pamphlets and acts as a clearinghouse on problems of the hard of hearing and the speech impaired.

Deafness Speech and Hearing Publications, Inc., publishes abstracts of articles on deafness and speech. Editorial offices are located at Gallaudet College. You may obtain information about publications on deafness and speech impairment by writing the Office of Public Information, Gallaudet College, Kendall Green, Washington, D.C.

Local chapters of the Crippled Children's Society, often in conjunction with the Shriners, offer financial aid for physical examinations and the purchase of hearing aids, as well as for treatment in clinics and attendance at camps.

Students with Impaired Speech

A handicap that is often related to poor hearing is impaired speech. A nonhandicapped person learns how to talk properly by receiving feedback in the form of his own voice. Since the deaf person cannot hear the sounds he is making, other kinds of feedback are substituted. Sometimes, for example, the child is asked to feel his throat. Sometimes he speaks into a microphone, and the sound waves are converted into visual images on a screen resembling a TV tube. The child with a hearing loss almost invariably has a speech problem, but because he does not hear how strange his voice sounds to others, he may not be bothered about this as much as the speech-impaired child who *does* get feedback. Supplementary measurements or the opinion of a specialist may be necessary to detect certain sight or hearing handicaps. But the child with a speech problem proclaims it to the world every time he opens his mouth. Only when we stop to consider how much we depend on oral communication do we begin to comprehend why the entire life of a speech-impaired child seems to revolve around his voice.

A child who is ashamed to speak is not only prevented from participating in academic activities but also cut off from others socially. Although teen-age lovers might be satisfied to spend an hour together without talking, almost every other social situation is predicated on the verbal interchange of ideas and reactions. The child who is unwilling to talk is isolated. As a dedicated member of a speech and drama department frequently puts it, "Speech is the star performer in the drama of interpersonal relationships." Less obvious but perhaps more important is the key role language plays in maintaining mental health. When we use words to express our feelings, we release tension and often gain some understanding of ourselves.

The relationship between speech and mental health is circular. Good speech can contribute to good adjustment; poor speech frequently contributes to poor adjustment. At the same time, poor adjustment quite often causes poor speech. Some speech therapists maintain that *every* speech problem is a manifestation of psychological conflict. Even if this is not always the case, a very common consequence of impaired speech is the development of problems of adjustment.

As soon as you become aware of a speech defect in a child, arrange for assistance from the speech therapist on the staff of the city or county school district. You may not be able to treat the problem yourself, but you *are* in a position to ease the reactions of the child and his classmates to the condition, particularly in the case of stuttering. This particular impairment is especially likely to cause tension not only in the child but in the rest of the class as well. Here are some suggestions for coping with stuttering. (Many of them were supplied by a young man who had struggled with stuttering for twenty-two years. Thanks to some teachers who put these ideas into practice, he overcame his handicap, became a teacher himself, and is now a superintendent of schools.)

1. Try not to show you are upset.

Suggestions for coping with stuttering

The pupils in the room will take a cue from you. If you seem repulsed or bothered when a child starts to stutter, the class will probably react in the same way. Even if you *are* upset, do your best to conceal it.

2. Go out of your way to show the child you accept him as he is.

Most children who stutter have been subjected to numerous experiences of rejection—by parents, peers, and teachers. They need positive reinforcement to compensate for this backlog of negative reactions.

3. *Don't force the child to recite; encourage him to volunteer.*

If you follow a policy of compulsory recitation, you might make an exception for the pupil who stutters. Inform him privately that he is invited to speak up when he wants to but that you will never call on him. (You will probably get a more relaxed response from the entire class if you apply this rule to *all* pupils.)

4. *If the child asks to recite and then starts to stutter, control the temptation to "say it for him."*

The child knows what he wants to say all too well. Finishing a word or sentence for him does not assist him in any way. In effect, you are calling attention to his inability to speak normally. A child often stutters mainly because his parents have expressed concern about his nonfluency. What such a child desperately needs is someone who *doesn't* get upset when he begins to stutter.

5. *Don't praise a child when he says something in a relatively fluent manner.*

This is a natural impulse, but it is a rather backhanded compliment. You may be relieved and pleased that he has spoken so well, but praising him tends to make what is a normal performance seem abnormal. Instead of being complimentary, your remark may become unintentionally sarcastic.

6. *Try to build up confidence through nonverbal activities.*

Many stutterers lack self-confidence. Anything you can do to demonstrate to the child and his peers that he is capable in matters other than speech will help him develop sufficient poise to minimize the effects of the stuttering. You might point out accomplishments in subtle ways and perhaps arrange situations so that the child is sure to do well.

If these suggestions are not sufficient to help you handle pupils with speech problems, the best agency to get in touch with is the National Association of Hearing and Speech Agencies, 919 18th Street NW., Washington, D.C.

Students with Epilepsy

The final type of exceptionality to be discussed is the least understood. Epilepsy is more common than cerebral palsy, polio, multiple sclerosis, and tuberculosis *combined*, but much ignorance and misunderstanding are associated with it, sometimes with tragic consequences. Parents may become terrified; the child may be filled with anxiety because the threat of a seizure is ever present; in too many instances the epileptic is driven to suicide.

Some parents have such an irrational dread of the word *epilepsy* that they "shop around" medical centers until they find a doctor who diagnoses the ailment as something else. This is not intended as a slur on the medical profession.

Certain types of epilepsy are difficult to identify, except by a neurologist, and the general practitioner can do only his best. But the extent to which parents will shy away from a thorough neurological examination is both pathetic and alarming. Ignorance about epilepsy is so widespread that until 1965 our national immigration laws prohibited epileptics from becoming citizens. In several states it is illegal for epileptics to marry. In a few states epileptics can be sterilized against their will. In some school districts epileptics are prevented from attending regular classes. For every business concern that will hire a known epileptic, there are possibly a dozen that will not. To illustrate how archaic such laws and practices are, here are some facts about epilepsy.

Epilepsy is a neurological disorder characterized by seizures. There are two main forms: *grand mal* and *petit mal* (French for "big sickness" and "small sickness"). A person who has grand mal seizures loses consciousness and falls down. For a few minutes the body twitches convulsively, and the person is likely to salivate, giving the appearance of foaming at the mouth. These violent tremors are followed by a coma lasting anywhere from a few seconds to several hours. Petit mal epilepsy is much less severe. In its mildest form it may consist simply of a blank stare for a second or so. In other cases the person loses motor control for a few seconds. He may drop things or stand motionless unaware of what is going on around him, but he does not fall. A teacher may think such a pupil is daydreaming.

Epilepsy is *not* contagious. It is caused by damage to the brain and nervous system as a result of birth injuries, accidents, tumors, infectious diseases, and other bodily disorders. The question of whether epilepsy is inherited is a thorny one. Some of the literature distributed by epilepsy organizations states categorically that it is *not*. The motives of those who make this assertion are praiseworthy, since they are attempting to remove the stigma attached to the term, but in the strict sense they have overstated their case.

Many medical specialists are of the opinion that a person may inherit a *low convulsive threshold*. To explain what is meant by that phrase, the analogy most commonly presented in books and articles will be offered. The causes of epilepsy are represented as the water in a reservoir. They are held in check by a dam (the convulsive threshold). Under normal conditions the dam is high enough to hold back the causes. But if injury, disease, emotional involvement, or some combination of them increases the volume of the reservoir, it may overflow. The overflow takes the form of the seizure. In some instances the causes are so extreme that no threshold can hold them in check. In others, the person may inherit a low threshold. An individual with a low threshold may develop epilepsy from causes that would ordinarily be held in check. This is why it may be more accurate to modify the statement that epilepsy is not inherited to read, "A person may inherit a *predisposition* toward epilepsy in the form of a low convulsive threshold."

Low convulsive threshold

But what if a person does inherit such a predisposition—is he doomed to a life of misery and helplessness? He shouldn't be. Even if he has a low convulsive threshold, the "dam" can usually be built up artificially through the use of seizure-preventing drugs. At the present time, medical reports reveal that four out of five epileptics respond to medication. In half of all cases, seizures can be brought under complete control. There is no reason for epileptics not to marry, and unless both sides of the family tree show a consistent history of epilepsy, there should be little hesitation about having children. An increasing number of enlightened employers are hiring epileptics and if they have consistent control of their seizures, epileptics should be able to drive cars.

By far the biggest handicap in the life of an epileptic is the ignorance of his fellow citizens. We tend to fear what we don't understand, and the common reaction of a group of people witnessing a grand mal seizure is fear coupled with revulsion and sometimes panic. If you have an epileptic in your class, you have the opportunity to perform a much-needed job of educating his classmates on the nature of this disease and thereby lessening their fear.

It would be desirable if parents informed school authorities about the presence of epilepsy. But because of the stigma attached to the word, you will not be likely to find a note in a cumulative folder warning you that a child is subject to seizures. If you *do* find such a note, probably the best policy is to anticipate the possibility of a seizure. You might give a brief talk on epilepsy (a concise, inexpensive book will be recommended at the end of this section), obtain one or more films (from the sources to be listed), or have a nurse or doctor present a simple lecture. A seizure is frequently explained by likening it to "an electrical storm in the brain." You could ask the child to explain to the class how he feels during the seizure and to say whether he experiences an "aura," or warning, that he is about to have an attack. (With an extremely shy or self-conscious child, it is probably better not to ask him to talk about his attacks.)

If and when a grand mal seizure does take place, either in a known epileptic or in a case that takes you completely by surprise, here is a suggested list of things to do and *not* do:

Suggestions for dealing with epileptic seizures

✓1. Try to maintain your composure.

Be calm and matter of fact in reacting to the seizure. If you show you are afraid or confused, the class will take the cue and behave accordingly.

✓ 2. If you are in a position to do so, break the fall of the person.

Once he is on the floor, do not try to restrain him in any way, but *do* move any furniture or other objects away from him.

✓ 3. Do not try to put something between the person's teeth.

Experience has shown that this is likely to do more harm to the epileptic or the would-be assistant than the contingency it is supposed to prevent, that is, the tongue being bitten. Even if the tongue *is* bitten, it will heal quickly.

4. *Once the person regains consciousness, help him to a quiet place.*

Preferably, take him out of the room or at least out of sight of his classmates to a place where he can rest.

5. *Discuss the seizure with the class.*

Explain what caused it, and pass on the suggestions just noted for dealing with future seizures. If a child has frequent seizures, you might assign one or two close friends to act as assistants.

For more complete information, and films and pamphlets, contact:

The National Epilepsy League, 222 North Michigan Avenue, Chicago, Illinois.

The National Easter Seal Society for Crippled Children and Adults, 2023 West Ogden Avenue, Chicago, Illinois.

Also check with the local Public Health Department to determine whether there is a local or state society.

An excellent, inexpensive book on epilepsy is *Epilepsy, What It Is, What to Do About It* (1958) by Tracy J. Putnam.

The importance of an enlightened approach to understanding children with epilepsy cannot be overemphasized. There is a very direct relationship between the frequency and severity of attacks and the psychological state of the individual. A common trigger of seizures is emotional tension and stress. A person with a predisposition toward epilepsy who is filled with anxiety about his condition and the reactions it provokes in others finds himself in a vicious circle. The more nervous he becomes, the greater the likelihood of a seizure; the more frequent the seizures, the greater the degree of nervousness.

A child with epilepsy whose parents live in terror of his seizures is caught in a trap. If his teachers and classmates react the same way, the trap becomes inescapable. If you can prove to the epileptic pupil that you accept and understand him, your confidence may be contagious enough to influence the other pupils in the class and the epileptic himself. The epileptic's behavior may be dominated by his condition only a few seconds a month; the behavior of others may dominate his entire life. The seizures he experiences are simply a natural way his nervous system gains release from excessive pressure. As a teacher, you are in an excellent position to reduce such pressure by an attitude of confidence and acceptance and by recognizing occasional seizures for what they are—perfectly natural forms of behavior.

Summary

In this chapter you have been provided with information regarding the characteristics and identification of slow learners, rapid learners, and handicapped students and with suggestions on how to arrange learning experiences for each of these types of exceptional pupils.

Suggestions for Further Reading, Writing, Thinking, and Discussion

13-1 *Observing in a Special Class*

In case you have ever considered becoming a teacher of a special class, you might ask your instructor to help make arrangements to visit such a classroom. Most large school districts have classes for trainable and educable mentally retarded students, as well as separate classes for the blind and partially sighted, for the deaf and hard-of-hearing, and for children with cerebral palsy and related conditions. Following your observation, describe the characteristics of the pupils that seemed most noticeable or record your general reactions.

13-2 *Reading a More Detailed Account of Mental Retardation*

If you are interested in mental retardation, you might wish to do some further reading to supplement the brief analysis in the text. You will find a concise discussion of mental retardation with emphasis on teaching in *The Mentally Retarded Child in the Classroom* (1965) by Marion J. Erickson. For a comprehensive account of the causes of mental retardation and a penetrating analysis of ramifications of retardation, look for *The Mentally Retarded Child* (1965) by Halbert B. Robinson and Nancy M. Robertson. A briefer account, emphasizing educational planning and techniques, is *Mental Retardation: An Educational Viewpoint* (1972) by Oliver P. Kolstoe. Samuel A. Kirk provides considerable information in concise form in Chapters 4, 5, and 6 of his *Educating Exceptional Children* (2nd ed., 1972).

13-3 *Sampling Suggestions for Teaching Rapid Learners*

Since it is widely believed that American schools do not pay sufficient attention to exceptionally bright students, perhaps you will want more information on teaching the gifted. *Gifted Children in the Classroom* (1965) by E. Paul Torrance, *Teaching the Gifted Child* (1964) by James J. Gallagher, and *Curriculum Planning for the Gifted* (1961) edited by Louis A. Fliegler are especially recommended, although you will probably find several other books on the subject in any college library. If you do further reading about teaching rapid learners, summarize points you think might serve as guidelines when you begin to teach.

13-4 *Reading More Detailed Accounts of Handicapped Children*

If you are interested in teaching children with specific types of handicaps, you might wish to do further reading. For a brief account of visual, hearing, speech, and other problems, look up a text on the exceptional child. *Educating Exceptional Children* (2nd ed., 1972) by Samuel A. Kirk is particularly recommended, but you will probably find several similar books in a college library. For more detail on a specific handicap, consult a teacher of a special class or look in a library card catalog. A concise, inexpensive source of ideas for teaching all types of exceptional children is *Helping Children with Special Needs* (1956) by Robert F. DeHaan and Jack Kough. You might select points from your reading that impress you as important and summarize the information for future reference.

13-5   *Speculating about Life in a Meritocracy*

Numerous arguments have been presented in favor of merit pay or merit advancement, each individual's career depending on objective assessment of his abilities, with the most capable people in positions of influence, and the less capable in jobs appropriate to their lower level of functioning. In many respects, our society is already moving in this direction; it is very common for organizations to use tests to decide among candidates for a given job. The English sociologist Michael Young has written a fascinating interpretation of what might happen if a society became a pure meritocracy. He emphasizes the difficulties that may arise if concern with measurement of abilities gets out of hand. You are urged to read *The Rise of the Meritocracy* (1959). Do you think events would occur in the manner postulated by Young? If not, note your own speculations. You might also attempt to relate the observations of Young to special education. Do some points in *The Rise of the Meritocracy* highlight the possible dangers of too much identification, segregation, and education of above- or below-average individuals?

13-6   *Reacting to a Fictional Account of the "Manipulation" of a Genius*

John Hersey was disturbed by the extreme reaction of some Americans to the launching of Sputnik. In many areas an all-out campaign was initiated to identify brilliant children and then offer them a speeded-up curriculum in an effort to produce "instant scientists." In his novel *The Child Buyer* (1960), Hersey describes what might have occurred if this tendency had gone too far. While Hersey's account is exaggerated, it does emphasize certain dangers involved in any attempt to *force* growth. If you have ever wondered about the possible disadvantages of attempting to "push" a child prodigy in a desired direction, you will enjoy reading this novel. Record your reactions.

14 TEACHING TO ENCOURAGE NEED GRATIFICATION

CHAPTER CONTENTS

THE PRECEDING CHAPTER OFFERED SUGGESTIONS ON HOW TO ADJUST teaching for students who differ substantially from most of their classmates. Although some variations in student behavior may be due to the kinds of exceptionality just described, most can be traced to personality traits. All children are exceptional in terms of personality since everyone is unique. This chapter will deal with the question of how you might attempt to understand and allow for the diversity and individuality of behavior.

First of all, some factors that determine personality will be discussed. Further observations on Abraham Maslow's theory of motivation will then be offered as a basis for some suggestions on how to teach to maximize need gratification and aid adjustment. Because need gratification is so hard to achieve, however, many of your students will inevitably have difficulty adjusting. To help you understand and perhaps ameliorate adjustment problems, an analysis will be made of types of frustrations, some common reactions to these, and the kinds of reactions that often indicate extreme problems. Then some proposals will be made on what you might do to help. The chapter will conclude with a discussion of techniques you might use to aid students with learning blocks.

Determinants of Personality

Determinants of personality

There are many ways of describing personality and dozens of theories of personality, but this analysis will be restricted to an examination of the determinants of personality developed by Henry A. Murray and Clyde Kluckhohn (1948). Murray and Kluckhohn describe four types of personality determinants: constitutional, group membership, role, and situational. *Constitutional* determinants are inherited characteristics and predispositions (sex, height, facial features, body chemistry, etc.). *Group membership* determinants include the general culture (e.g., American, French, Japanese) in which a child is reared and all the cultural subgroups that influence personality development (such as class, family, peer group, friends). *Role* determinants include not only the general, more or less permanent self-concept of a person but also the specific and variable roles he assumes in different situations (reflected, for instance, in the behavior of a boy who feels self-conscious about writing a poem in English class as contrasted with his behavior as captain of the football team). *Situational* determinants are all the experiences of the individual that contribute to the development of his personality—not only those that have a cumulative impact because they are repeated over and over but also traumatic or especially significant, single experiences that alter the entire course of his life.

If you take into account the fact that any student's personality is the product of a tremendous number of such determinants, interacting in complicated ways, you will not be surprised that it is often hard to understand behavior. (For in-depth study of how the determinants of personality interact, you are urged to read a text or take a course in either developmental psychology or the psychology of personality.) The difficulty of understanding personality development is compounded by theorists' lack of agreement about the relative significance of the determinants. Differences of opinion—among hereditarians and environmentalists, among critical-period advocates and believers in "natural" development, among associationists and field theorists—are especially complex in regard to personality. However, an approach that provides a reasonably firm basis for speculating about behavior is based on the concept of need gratification.

Maslow's Theory of Need Gratification

In Chapter 2, Maslow's theory of motivation was used to sum up the basic assumptions of the natural development and open education points of view. In Chapter 9, his hierarchy of needs and diagram of a choice situation served as background for discussing ways to arouse and sustain interest in learning. Here, Maslow's theory, hierarchy, and growth-choice diagram serve as a framework for discussing ways of setting the stage for need gratification.

A brief review of the aspects of Maslow's theory that have previously been noted will structure the discussion that follows. Maslow maintains that each individual has an essential inner nature that is shaped by environmental experiences. The impact of experience is determined by how the individual reacts to situations involving a choice between safety and growth. If the individual makes growth choices, he will achieve need gratification. If he makes unwise safety choices, his inner nature will be frustrated or denied and sickness will result. An individual is more likely to make growth choices if the deficit needs (physiological, safety, love and belonging, esteem) have been satisfied. Since these needs can be satisfied only by others, the way the child is reacted to by parents and teachers is of great significance. Even though the ultimate choice between safety and growth in any situation must be made by the child, parents and teachers can supply support and assistance by gratifying deficit needs and by making growth choices attractive and unthreatening.

Behavior as continual series of choices between safety and growth

This summary emphasizes that the most promising techniques you might use to encourage your students to experience need gratification have already been discussed—in the chapters on learning, motivation, and evaluation. If you can make your students feel safe and accepted in your room and assist them to learn, they are likely to experience feelings of belonging and esteem and be encouraged to make growth choices that can lead to self-actualization. If you avoid or minimize situations in which students feel threatened, rejected, or inferior, they are more likely to make growth choices.

The Dynamics of Adjustment

To gain additional insight into how to make positive alternatives attractive, examine Figure 14-1 below, a diagram of a choice situation derived mainly from the work of Kurt Lewin. Representing the basic dynamics of adjustment, it shows one of the simplest and clearest ways deficit needs determine behavior.

Lewinian diagram of process of adjustment

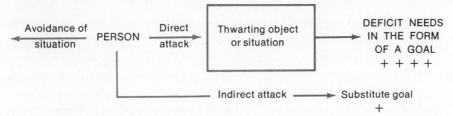

Figure 14–1   An Adjustment Diagram

Derived from the work of Kurt Lewin and from a conception suggested by Dashiell (1949), which was further developed by Shaffer and Shoben (1956).

The adjustment process is instigated by a deficit need, which produces disagreeable tension. To reduce the tension, the person must react in some way, and his action usually is an attempt to overcome a thwarting object or circumstance. If a person is hungry, for example, he needs to either prepare or obtain food. If a child feels left out, he needs to gain the feeling he belongs by experiencing acceptance by parents, teachers, or peers. After various exploratory attempts to reduce the tension, sooner or later the person is driven to make a choice. In an ideal situation the chosen reaction satisfies the need. In a less than ideal situation, the chosen reaction is inadequate and the sense of relief is incomplete. The degree of satisfaction gained depends on whether the person achieves his original goal, accepts a less satisfying but reasonably adequate substitute goal, or fails to reach any goal at all.

Since individuals can meet most deficit needs only by overcoming a frustrating circumstance, awareness of common reactions to frustration may bring better understanding of the behavior of your pupils and also provide leads on how you might be able to make desirable choices attractive.

Types of Reactions to Frustration

A very common reaction to frustration is aggression. Most of the time when we are thwarted, we get mad, but the anger can be expressed in positive, neutral, or negative ways. Occasionally, the aggression provoked by frustrating circumstances is channeled into creative effort. Certain truly sublime artistic works were inspired, in a sense, by anger. It is reported that Richard Wagner was stimulated to compose his magnificent *Die Meistersinger* because he was stung by a critic's accusation that he was incapable of writing counterpoint—among other things. Wagner's reaction was to compose an opera that permitted him to defend his musical style and at the same time "lecture" hidebound reactionaries who were behind the times. He presented his arguments in the form of some of the most brilliant contrapuntal passages ever composed. And for good measure, Wagner made the clown-villain of *Die Meistersinger* a very thinly disguised caricature of the unfortunate offending critic.

In many cases the natural impulse when frustrated is to fight back at the thwarting object or person. This sort of behavior is very apparent in young children. If you try to restrain a child who is engaged in a tug-of-war over a tricycle, you may receive a kick or a punch. Most adults learn enough self-control to suppress such direct attacks, but they resort to insidious indirect forms of aggression as substitutes. The switching of aggressive feelings from the original source to some other person or object is called *displacement*. The directing of the displaced anger at a particular person or group of persons is called *scapegoating*, a widely prevalent source of prejudice.

Sources of Creativity Other Than Anger

Although creative works are sometimes motivated primarily by aggression, a deficit-motivation theorist would be likely to attribute creative activities to secondary drives derived from biological needs. Thus he might trace a great novel or painting or symphony to an acquired drive originally associated with the satisfaction of a physiological need. Whiting and Child (1953), for example, have proposed a theory of behavior systems to explain how this could occur. They suggest that in the process of satisfying the hunger drive, children learn that they are dependent on others and that later in life some persons strive to demonstrate their *resistance* to overdependence on others and as a consequence manifest creativity.

A Freudian, however, might attribute a great novel to the fact that the writer practiced celibacy and maintain that his creative efforts were due to sublimation of the sexual drive.

A growth-motivation theorist, on the other hand, would stress exploratory and manipulatory tendencies. Maslow, for instance, emphasizes self-actualization and argues that an individual has within him a powerful *desire* to develop his potential to the fullest extent. Once the lower-level motives on Maslow's hierarchy are satisfied, the person may be motivated to express himself just for the sake of self-actualization.

Defense mechanisms

A person confronted with a blocked-goal situation may weigh the various alternatives—including those involving aggression—and then decide to choose a somewhat less appealing substitute goal that appears easier to achieve. However, because the substitute goal is not as satisfying as the original choice, he may need to resort to a *defense mechanism* to soothe his ego. Realizing that he has compromised himself, he must defend his pride. Perhaps the commonest type of defense mechanism is *rationalization,* whereby we give socially acceptable "reasons" for our behavior. Other frequently used defenses include *identification* with those who are successful in reaching the original type of goal and *compensation*—overachievement in a substitute form of endeavor to offset lack of achievement in a more desired area.

Another natural reaction to a frustrating situation is to simply "leave the field," to use a term of Lewin's. The poor student who plays hooky, the shy child who goes off by himself, the hippie who drops out—all react by withdrawing from the scene. The unfortunate aspect of such reactions is that they are not really solutions, so the person rarely experiences satisfaction. The tension remains and may build up and lead to undesirable behavior.

Even if the individual does not withdraw physically, he may escape through fantasy. An occasional daydream can serve as a safety valve or make a grim situation bearable. It can also pave the way for success. But too much dreaming may render the personal world of fantasy so satisfying that one is unwilling or unable to relinquish it in favor of reality, and mental illness follows.

There is often no clear-cut point at which a psychologist can say that reasonable adjustment ends and mental illness begins. However, in some cases a frustrated pupil may develop a pattern of overt defiance and disruption. Such behavior may be unacceptable to others and lead to restrictions, punishment, or treatment, but the obstreperous student has chosen a reaction to frustration that has merit from a mental health point of view. He gains release for his pent-up emotion, even though he does it in a destructive way. For this reason the pupil who is a behavior problem may be less likely to develop serious forms of mental illness. Yet because his behavior is upsetting to others, he attracts more attention than a pupil on the verge of a neurosis or psychosis.

*Wickman study:
behavior problems rated
very serious by teachers*

This paradoxical situation was first brought to notice when Wickman (1928) asked teachers and psychotherapists to note the kinds of behavior they regarded as most "serious." The teachers rated such overt acts as stealing, cheating, and disobedience most damaging. The psychotherapists, on the other hand, considered sensitiveness, unsocialness, suspiciousness, and fearfulness more serious than behavior problems. This difference of opinion was thought to stem from teachers' concern over behavior that threatened them or disrupted the class. The psychotherapists, taking into account that aggressive actions release tension, focused on those forms of behavior that were likely to escape notice but predisposed the pupil to serious maladjustment later in life. Alexander Tolor, William L. Scarpetti, and Paul A. Lane (1967) repeated the Wickman study and found that experienced teachers of their era were more aware of the potential dangers of withdrawal; inexperienced teachers tended to regard aggressive and regressive behavior as abnormal, whereas psychotherapists perceived them to be normal. Recognition of these various reactions to frustration should guide your endeavors to help students make wise choices in how to react. Keep in mind that the goals set by the student are often the key. A student with an impossible goal is virtually doomed to choose one of the less satisfying reactions. Consequently, one way to encourage good choices is to encourage goals that you are reasonably sure students can achieve. But also try to steer your students toward seeking direct rather than indirect forms of satisfaction so that they will not be forced to make extensive use of defense mechanisms. Finally, you should do everything possible to divert students from reactions of withdrawal; these are the least satisfying choices and often lead to serious adjustment problems.

Dealing with Adjustment Problems

Although a teacher can do quite a bit to help a pupil satisfy his needs, it is inevitable that at least a few students in your classes will exhibit symptoms of poor adjustment. Sometimes basic needs are frustrated by parents. Sometimes, predisposing factors in the personality of the child prevent adequate adjustment.

Keep in mind that not even the best teacher in the world is able, alone, to rehabilitate some children who are caught in the trap of poor adjustment.

When a person gets started in the wrong direction in satisfying his needs, it is of utmost importance to detect this as early as possible. The longer he resorts to a certain defense mechanism or neurotic reaction, the more rigid he becomes and the more he resists making a change. One of the biggest difficulties a psychotherapist faces is convincing a neurotic client to let go of the behavior pattern that is dominating his life. (This problem is depicted very clearly by Maslow's diagram of the choice situation.)

The neurotic has found something to cling to, and even though it is not completely successful, it does provide a modicum of security. Before he can free himself to embark on a more gratifying course, he has to build up enough confidence to abandon his own solution. In a sense the aim of the psychotherapist is to persuade and assist the person who has selected an unsatisfactory and unacceptable reaction to frustration to replace it with a more satisfying and constructive form of behavior. The earlier the attempt is made, the easier it is. As an observer with no direct personal or emotional ties to your pupils, you are in an ideal position to detect signs of poor adjustment. If you report them to the proper authorities, psychotherapy can be undertaken before a neurosis or psychosis develops.

Estimates of Pupil Adjustment

Many estimates have been made of the proportion of well-adjusted and poorly adjusted pupils in a typical class or school. The estimates vary depending on the standards established and the types of evaluation used, but two sets of figures are offered to give you some indication of what to expect in the classrooms.

Ivan N. Mensh and co-workers (1959) based the following estimate on ratings of over eight hundred third-grade children:

Well-adjusted: 20 percent

No Significant Problems: 52 percent

Subclinically Disturbed: 20 percent

Disturbed: 8 percent

C. E. Ullman (1952) found that when teachers and psychotherapists made independent judgments, they were in substantial agreement that 8 percent of the pupils in public school classrooms were maladjusted. The ratio of boys to girls was 4 to 1.

R. G. Stennett (1966) estimated that 22 percent of the pupils in the elementary grades of a school district were moderately or severely "emotionally handicapped."

MARION BERNSTEIN

Symptoms of Adjustment Problems

To give you something specific to look for, a list of symptoms indicative of difficulties in adjustment is offered at this juncture. You should, however, guard against the temptation to use it as the basis for "analyzing" all your pupils, your friends, or even yourself. It is important to remain aware of symptoms of poor adjustment, but overdiagnosis should be scrupulously avoided.

Symptoms of adjustment difficulties

1. *Depression, unsocialness, fearfulness, and suspiciousness.* These are the first four symptoms noted by psychotherapists and, ranked in order of seriousness, in a repeat of the Wickman study done by C. E. Thompson (1940). As you can see, they are not likely to be obvious and are most frequently found in the pupil who withdraws—literally and figuratively. Perhaps the only additional comment necessary is that "unsocialness" should not be equated with "individuality." The key to the difference is the attitude of the "loner." If the pupil who remains aloof seems satisfied with his lot and does not exhibit the other symptoms, you should probably honor his decision to avoid the crowd. If, on the other hand, the isolate seems depressed and furtive, he may be revealing that he is experiencing little need gratification.

2. *Persistent patterns of undesirable behavior.*   One hallmark of neurosis is persistent behavior. If a particular pupil reacts to almost all frustrations with the same type of defensive behavior, this may be a tip-off that adjustment problems exist. The mentally healthy person is confident and flexible. The mentally ill person is insecure and afraid to experiment. A pupil who suffers from chronic fatigue, seems "nervous" about everything, and worries excessively about insignificant problems may be caught in a neurotic pattern of rigidity.

3. *Extreme, inappropriate reactions.*   Even a well-adjusted person may get angry if pushed far enough or attempt to withdraw temporarily if embarrassed. But when a person explodes over a minor irritation or dissolves into tears at a mild rebuff, he may be signaling that the immediate experience was only the last straw. The *real* reason for the inappropriately extreme reaction is probably the existence of more complicated and permanent difficulties.

4. *Lack of Contact with reality.*   One thing that sets the psychotic apart from the normal is lack of contact with the real world. If a pupil thinks in terms

of impossible goals for himself or seems hard to reach or daydreams excessively, he may be indicating that the real world is too much for him to handle and that he is trying to create a private world of his own.

5. *Compulsive behavior giving the appearance that the person can't help himself.* Sometimes a pupil may give the impression that he is *compelled* to behave as he does. The troublemaker may seem bewildered by his actions; the fearful pupil may appear to be perplexed or even dazed by his response. In a sense such pupils *are* driven by forces beyond their control. When this point is reached, it is time for professional assistance.

Difficulties of Providing Psychotherapy

The reasons for seeking professional assistance become apparent when account is taken of the nature and difficulties of providing psychotherapy.

1. *Need for specialized knowledge and training.* The person who is properly authorized to perform psychotherapy is the trained professional. In many states psychologists must pass professional qualification examinations similar to those required for medical doctors. A clinical psychologist is expected to earn a Ph.D. degree and to have undergone an intensive internship. An individual on the counseling staff of a school district is usually required to have an M.A. plus some internship experience. Understanding what lies behind the behavior of any individual requires a kind of training and experience that a regular classroom teacher is virtually prevented from obtaining. A person is no more equipped to perform psychotherapy after taking a psychology course or two than he would be to perform surgery after a semester of biology.

Difficulties of providing psychotherapy

2. *Conflicting roles of a teacher-therapist.* A psychotherapist endeavors to establish a climate of permissiveness. He tries to convince the client that "anything goes" as far as he is concerned. This sort of atmosphere is necessary so that the person will be willing to express thoughts and feelings that society might find unacceptable or shocking. A high school girl, for example, who hates her mother probably has many adjustment problems at home and at school as a result of this conflict. If she admitted her feeling to others, their responses might arouse negative reactions in her that could lead to a sense of guilt and even worse forms of behavior. A psychotherapist tries to establish a relationship in which there are few rules or limits. A teacher, on the other hand, seeks a relationship with a class in which rules and limits *are* recognized. If a teacher tries to be both an authority figure and a psychotherapist, the two roles will conflict. The almost inevitable result will be feelings of confusion and distrust, which will probably not be restricted to the teacher and a particular pupil but may envelop the entire class.

"MISS PEACH" BY MEL LAZARUS. COURTESY OF PUBLISHERS-HALL SYNDICATE.

3. *Emotional involvement.*   Several sections of this book have urged objective, unemotional evaluation of pupil performance. The pervasive influence of subjectivity has been discussed at length. If you tried to act as a part-time "psychotherapist" with a certain pupil, it would be virtually impossible to remain objective in reacting to the schoolwork of that pupil. This is not to say that you should avoid empathizing with any of your pupils. It is simply to suggest that any relationship that puts you in the role of "psychotherapist" will lead to conflicts. You should take an interest in your students so that you can offer a certain amount of individualized instruction; thus the interest should be that between teacher and pupil, not that between therapist and client.

4. *Discontinued support.*   As a rule, psychotherapy is a long-drawn-out process. Adjustment problems are almost always the result of years of causal experiences, and improvement is usually not possible through short, simple treatment. In effect, the psychotherapist must attempt to rebuild a personality. Ideally, he will meet with his clients several hours a week for a year and often for several years. In the early stages of treatment he must be available to provide support at frequent intervals. As the treatment progresses, the patient becomes more independent and the visits are gradually reduced. Few teachers are in a position to meet these demands. If you are chosen to act as a psychotherapist by a pupil or if you offer to serve in this capacity, you may find that you have little free time.

In the early phases of a therapeutic relationship the patient often has an insatiable appetite for talking to his confidant. There are various explanations for this attachment, but the important point is that the patient *demands* attention. A specialist in the counseling office is given time to supply it; a teacher is not. If you are conscientious in your role as a therapist, you may find yourself under considerable pressure to get your schoolwork done. In self-defense, perhaps you will be forced to refuse to see the pupil or to invent committee meetings or other appointments. If the pupil has come to depend on your sympathy, such evasive behavior can lead to increased difficulty. To avoid this contingency, many schools appoint a counselor to progress through the grades with a certain group of pupils, thus guaranteeing continuity of treatment. The counselor can provide this, but the teacher can't, and that is why the wise teacher arranges for a pupil who seeks frequent counsel to meet with a trained professional.

Suggestions for Acting as a Sympathetic Listener

For the reasons just discussed, it is not prudent for a teacher to attempt to act as a psychotherapist, but there are times when a teacher is the person best qualified to serve as a sympathetic listener. Some pupils confide in a teacher

they respect and like but in no one else. Many students, especially at the high school level, have a negative attitude toward the counseling office. In one survey (Arnold, 1965) high school teachers estimated that their students would be twice as inclined to seek help from a teacher as from the counselor. They felt that a student with adjustment problems is more likely to turn to someone he is familiar with and that many counselors seemed to be so busy with testing and scheduling that they had little time for therapy.

A voluntary trip to see a counselor, moreover, is a bald admission that a problem is too big to be handled alone. Being able to acknowledge that outside assistance is needed is often the biggest and most important step in the process of psychotherapy. When a pupil seeks you out as the first stage in admitting the existence of trouble, you should be sympathetic enough to let him talk about it. If you interrupt with, "I'm sorry, but you'd better go see someone in the counseling office," your crude rejection may prevent the very behavior you intended to encourage.

The arguments of the preceding section were aimed at discouraging you from setting yourself up as a psychotherapist; they were not intended to recommend *complete* aloofness. By exercising care and ingenuity, you ought to be able to act as a sympathetic listener without running too much risk of encountering the problems just noted. If it becomes apparent that a pupil is becoming too dependent on you, you might subtly arrange for someone in the counseling office to take over. Meanwhile, take a cue from the methods the counselor is likely to employ.

Techniques of Nondirective Therapy

The kind of treatment many counselors are likely to use is known as *nondirective* therapy. It is also sometimes referred to as *client-centered* therapy. The terms are intended to convey some basic premises—that the person himself has the ability to solve his own problems, that he should direct his own rehabilitation, and that he (not the therapist) should be the center of the therapeutic interview. This technique was developed by Carl Rogers (1951), who insisted that earlier forms of psychotherapy, such as psychoanalysis, were dominated by the clinician and made the client too dependent on the therapist. Under nondirective therapy the client is given subtle assistance by the clinician, but he solves his own problems. It is argued that this experience better prepares him to solve future problems independently, whereas the client who has undergone psychoanalysis or the equivalent may feel that he has to return to the analyst whenever new difficulties crop up.

Rogers: non-directive, or client-centered, therapy

Following is a brief outline of the basic techniques of nondirective therapy:

The therapist develops rapport.

The therapist establishes a warm, friendly relationship so the pupil will feel he can confide in him.

The therapist accepts the feelings expressed.

The therapist does not make value judgments. Even if the actions or thoughts of the pupil are unacceptable by society's standards, they are acknowledged as "natural" forms of behavior.

A feeling of permissiveness is established.

As a result of the first two techniques, the pupil should begin to feel that almost "anything goes" in the therapeutic situation. He is encouraged to say exactly what he thinks. The only limitation on his behavior is that he be anchored to the world of reality. It is necessary to set *some* boundaries to therapeutic discussions in order to accomplish this. There are limiting factors in nearly everything we do, and it is important to keep in mind that if a person is to adjust to society, he must live within such limits.

The therapist accepts, reflects, and clarifies the feelings expressed so that the pupil gains insight into his behavior.

This is the deceptively simple part of nondirective therapy. An uninformed person given the opportunity to observe a clinical interview might conclude

PHOTO BY LILO

Carl R. Rogers   Rogers was born in Oak Park, Illinois, in 1902 into a prosperous family of a strictly religious, hard-working, and affectionate businessman who later turned to scientific farming. After earning his B.A. degree at the University of Wisconsin, where he was elected to Phi Beta Kappa and Phi Kappa Phi, Rogers entered Union Theological Seminary to prepare for the ministry. His study there, however, led to a deep interest in psychology, which he pursued at Columbia University, earning an M.A. and Ph.D. Rogers organized and headed for twelve years the Counseling Center at the University of Chicago, practicing and further developing his technique of client-centered counseling and therapy; he also counseled and taught at the University of Wisconsin. The author of several books, this noted psychologist-psychotherapist is at present Resident Fellow at the Center for Studies of the Person in La Jolla, California. In 1946 Rogers served as President of the American Psychological Association and in 1956 headed the American Academy of Psychotherapists.

that the therapist was being paid for simply sitting around and nodding sympathetically. There is a great deal more to it than that. The therapist does nod sympathetically, but he also "reflects" the feelings expressed so that they become clarified. An expert nondirective therapist is so adroit that the client feels that whatever insight he has gained is entirely the result of his own efforts.

The therapist does not attempt to direct in any way, nor does he hurry the client.

At no time does the therapist try to short-cut the procedure by explaining or prescribing. Even when he understands the problem early in the therapy, he permits the client to set the pace and to work out the solution on his own. This takes patience—and time. (If you would like to read a detailed case history featuring nondirective therapy, look for *Dibs: In Search of Self* (1964) by Virginia Axline.)

If a troubled pupil screws up his courage, contrives to find you alone, and blurts out a confession that he has a problem, you are urged to act as a sympathetic sounding board. In doing so, try to remain aware of the techniques just described. The very act of expressing troublesome feelings will release tension. Often, merely talking about a problem is all a person needs. With a problem of greater magnitude, however, the relief may be only temporary. In that case someone in a position to do a great deal of listening over a long period of time is called for. But a troubled pupil will hardly feel inclined to confer with someone in the counseling office if his initial request for assistance is snubbed.

Acting as a sympathetic listener

One final note on psychotherapy. The comment that a psychotherapist is a highly trained specialist may have given the impression that referring a student with a problem to a counseling office will take care of everything. Unfortunately, it's not quite so simple. A pupil who has problems severe enough to merit the attention of a psychotherapist has probably been building up to such a dénouement for years. The most sensitive and effective therapist in the world would not be able to bring about a simple, immediate cure—even if he had time to see the pupil every day. Most public school counselors must operate under tight restrictions. They usually serve hundreds of pupils and are lucky if they can see a pupil for an hour each week. These scattered sessions must sometimes be devoted to helping the pupil release tension rather than to planning and carrying out a program of rehabilitation.

Furthermore, any program of remediation is likely to involve teachers. It is often difficult or impossible to work with the parents, who may be at the root of the trouble; they may resent unsolicited advice on rearing their child and refuse all invitations to consult with school authorities. As the teacher, you will not be bound to the pupil by emotional ties, and you will be readily available to the counselor. But more than availability is involved. You will be in the best possible position to help a poorly adjusted pupil since you have some control over his behavior during the most significant hours of his day. You are also in a better position than the therapist to do something about satisfying his basic needs.

In school districts in which case loads are extremely heavy, a counselor never sees the pupil whose behavior is considered unacceptable or undesirable. Instead, the counselor spends his time with the teacher or teachers. This strategy acknowledges that the counselor can't hope to accomplish anything in a thirty-minute, biweekly interview and that he is better off assisting the person who has daily contact with the pupil and can arrange for satisfaction of basic needs. You should not assume that sending the name of a pupil to the counseling office will produce a miraculous change in behavior. If any miracle is to occur, you will likely be asked to play a part in bringing it about. Consequently, it is important to recognize that the best way you can encourage need gratification in your pupils is to help every one of them learn as much as he can. If you succeed in doing that, the odds favoring adjustment will be much improved.

Learner-Centered Teaching and Sensitivity Training

Learner-centered teaching (sensitivity training)

In a recent book Carl Rogers (1969) has proposed extending his psychotherapy techniques to teaching. Both teachers and students, he suggests, should gain greater understanding of themselves through intensive group experiences. He describes this approach as *learner-centered teaching*, which emphasizes its similarity to client-centered therapy. (Learner-centered teaching is essentially an "ultimate" version of the discovery approach.) Variations of the Rogers technique have been developed by others and are referred to as *sensitivity training* or by a variety of other labels including T-groups, basic encounter groups, intensive workshops, transactional analysis, and human relations training.

As conceived by Rogers, learner-centered teaching assists the participants to "share in the exploration of their interpersonal attitudes and relationships" (1964, p. 15). Whereas the first learner-centered groups consisted primarily of teachers and administrators, Rogers now advocates teaching courses in high school and college with similar methods.

Several variations of sensitivity training go a step or several steps beyond the techniques developed by Rogers; many of them incorporate an emphasis on physical sensation to supplement the verbal interaction of Rogers-style groups. The Esalen Institute of Big Sur, California, is the primary force behind this extension. Esalen has received a great deal of publicity; you may have read about the techniques it employs to stimulate participants to greater awareness of themselves and others through physical manipulation and interaction. The method has been dubbed "feel and tell" because participants are encouraged (or required) to drop their inhibitions, tell just how and what they think, and physically feel each other.

Although the popularity of sensitivity training seems to be declining, it is still used in some college and high school classes. Some participants report that the experience has been immeasurably rewarding. Others complain that they have been pushed to the brink of insanity. This brings up a crucial point about extreme forms of sensitivity training: They are in effect forms of psychotherapy and should be conducted only by those who have had extensive training in clinical psychology. If you are intrigued by what you read and hear about various kinds of sensitivity training, keep in mind the psychotherapeutic overtones involved before you volunteer to participate in such a group or initiate an experimental session or course with your pupils. And if you decide to try the less extreme forms, ask yourself whether "personal development" is being pursued at the cost of mastery of subject matter—mastery that may lead more directly to need gratification than expressions of feelings.

In sorting out your thoughts on learner-centered teaching, you might find some suggestions by Rogers helpful. The following description summarizes his views. Rogers speaks of *experiential learning* and suggests that three elements appear essential to a climate in which this kind of learning can take place:

1. The individual must be "in contact with, be faced by, a real problem" to which he desires to find a solution (1967, p. 58).
2. Once clear awareness of the problem is established, certain attitudes must be established: *realness* or *genuineness*—the teacher must be a "real person" in his relationships with his students and "meet them on a person-to-person basis"; *acceptance*—"a prizing of the student, a prizing of his feelings and his opinions"; and *empathic understanding*—"the ability to understand the student's reactions from the inside" (pp. 59-60).
3. There must be resources—material, written and personal—to facilitate learning.

The similarity of these techniques to both nondirective therapy and the discovery approach is apparent. Most of the ideas emphasized by Rogers have been advocated by Bruner, Combs and Snygg, Bigge, and Thelen. Perhaps the most important difference between Rogers's approach and an ordinary discovery session is the focus on personal interaction between teacher and students. Since experiential learning does resemble the discovery approach so closely, all the advantages and disadvantages that accrue to the latter apply to sensitivity training as well.

And since Rogers's approach to learning is so directly related to client-centered therapy, it seems reasonable to expect that experiential learning will share many of the advantages and disadvantages of this method of treatment as well. Successful experiential-learning sessions will probably lead to greater self-awareness, just as successful therapy sessions do. However, the dangers and limitations of therapy also apply, particularly to more extreme forms of sensitivity training. There are both risks and rewards in the development of deep, interpersonal relationships between teacher and student. Before you consider experimenting with experiential learning, reread the section in this chapter on difficulties in providing psychotherapy (pp. 669–671).

Early in this chapter Maslow's description of the differences between deficit motivation and growth motivation was presented. In a way, sensitivity training can be regarded as an attempt to bring about growth motivation, which seems a very sensible thing to try to do in view of the obvious desirability of this type of motivation. The more students are able to free themselves from mere satisfaction of deficit needs and to function as self-actualizing individuals, the better. The freedom, acceptance, and emphasis on individuality that are hallmarks of experiential learning would appear likely to encourage self-actualization. But it may be helpful to keep in mind Maslow's distinction between bad choosers and good choosers.

Probably not all students are able to respond equally well to experiential learning. Maslow, Rogers, and Moustakas all stress the desirability of permitting students as much free choice as possible. They also point out that the teacher's role is to make growth choices attractive and to provide resources of various kinds. Thus even in sensitivity training, the teacher should supply direction and guidance, and some students will need more guidance than others. As pointed out earlier, self-actualization tends to take place only after the lower, deficit

---

Functioning as an Authentic Teacher

If the brief description of Rogers's approach to education is not sufficiently clear, you will find *The Authentic Teacher* by Clark Moustakas a valuable source of information on a sensitivity-training approach to teaching. The subtitle of this book, "Sensitivity and Awareness in the Classroom," reflects Moustakas's contention that there are three ways the teacher contributes to the healthy development of the self:

> First, through confirming the child as a being of non-comparable and non-measurable worth, in his individual ways and as a whole person; second, by being authentically present and open to honest encounters with children and by being a resource for learning and enrichment; and third, by making other resources available . . . based on the child's own interests, wishes, directions and patterns of expression, enabling the actualization of unique potentials and the expansion of reality by furthering interest, meaning and relatedness. (1966, pp. v-vi)

Moustakas emphasizes the desirability of encouraging students to express their feelings and the need for the teacher to become an effective listener by trying to see the child as he sees himself.

needs have been satisfied. If too much time is devoted to somewhat contrived attempts to *force* the satisfaction of growth needs, deficit needs may go unmet—leaving the student further behind than if the teacher had concentrated on satisfying those needs that can be met only through the intervention of others. (One of the distinguishing features of growth needs, you will remember, is that they are autonomous and self-directed.)

Advocates of sensitivity training argue that most people use only a fraction of their potential and that the disinhibiting effects of encounter-group experiences permit much fuller use of basic capacities. This may be the case, but there is often the implicit assumption in this argument that once a person has overcome his inhibitions, he will automatically be more creative. Not taken into account is that in order to be creative, a person must first master many facts, concepts, and skills; he must also exercise considerable self-discipline. If too much time is spent encouraging freedom and not enough time is devoted to mastery of information and skills, the result may be individuals who have the proper *attitude* for creativity but lack the essentials for functioning in a genuinely creative manner. A "free" person who is ignorant and clumsy perhaps uses even less of his potential than a well-informed, highly skilled individual who is somewhat inhibited. All of which might mean that the emphasis in most school situations should be on subject matter and skills and that sensitivity training to encourage free expression should be conducted on a voluntary basis outside the classroom.

Teaching Students with Learning Blocks

In your efforts to help every pupil learn as much as he can, you will encounter some students who have learning blocks of one sort or another. The difficulty may occur only with a particular subject (e.g., reading) and may be due to physiological factors (e.g., lack of dominance). However, many learning blocks have emotional bases, and sometimes a pupil is so emotionally disturbed he is incapable of learning anything at all in a regular classroom. Quite frequently a pupil with such a pervasive problem disrupts the rest of the class. Consequently, there is increasing awareness of the need for special classes for emotionally handicapped or disturbed children. If you have a pupil who appears to be totally involved in trying to maintain even a modicum of adjustment or one who can't seem to respond to a particular subject, it would be wise to inquire about a special class. If the behavior of the pupil is disruptive enough to upset the functioning of the class, you will almost be forced to seek outside assistance.

Some pupils have learning blocks but are not so disturbed that they qualify for a special class. In this final section you will be acquainted with some techniques for working with such emotionally disturbed learners. As in the case of exceptional students (discussed in the preceding chapter), methods developed for use with extreme learning-block cases may be adapted for the regular classroom. Although the procedures to be described have been evolved in special clinical settings, they provide valuable suggestions you could incorporate into your own teaching practice.

Once again a contrast between associationism and field theory will serve as an organizational frame of reference. It so happens that among the current approaches to working with emotionally disturbed children, one method almost literally applies the principles of operant conditioning to the problem; an opposite method was devised by Jerome Bruner, whose technique reflects the discovery approach. Here is a brief description of these two procedures, together with some suggestions for applying them in the classroom.

Educational Engineering with Emotionally Disturbed Children

Frank M. Hewett has developed some techniques for dealing with emotionally handicapped children that use principles of behavior modification to produce *educational engineering.* First he postulates a hierarchy of educational tasks (Figure 14-2) based on the developmental theories of Freud and Havighurst and on Skinner's notion of acquired or secondary reinforcement. Each of the seven levels is considered in terms of "three essential ingredients in all learning situations—a suitable educational task, provision for meaningful learner reward, and maintenance of a degree of teacher structure and control" (1968, p. 43). The tasks begin as simple contact between teacher and pupil, then progress to tasks emphasizing routine and order, and then graduate to the ultimate level—self-directed achievement. At first tangible rewards are provided in the form of check marks and candy. Later the reward is gradually transformed into task accomplishment (finishing an assignment), then social reinforcement (words of praise from the teacher), and finally intrinsic, end-in-itself behavior.

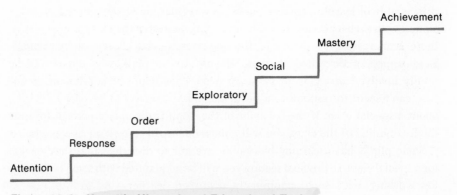

Figure 14–2   Hewett's Hierarchy of Educational Tasks

Adapted from *The Emotionally Disturbed Child in the Classroom* by Frank M. Hewett. Copyright 1968 by Allyn and Bacon, Inc. Reproduced by permission of the publisher.

Hewett leads his pupils through this hierarchy by making use of *Work Record Cards* (Figure 14-3). At the start of each day, a student in a special class is given one of these cards, which contain many squares. He keeps the card with him all day and receives a check mark for everything he accomplishes—for example, two checks for starting an assignment (attention level on the hierarchy of tasks), three for following through (response level), up to five for various qualities demonstrated in a given performance (order, exploratory, social, or mastery level.) The check marks are awarded on a fixed-interval schedule, that is, every fifteen minutes, not only to provide a steady stream of reinforcement but also to standardize the number of marks given and to reduce competitiveness. At the end of the week (or at shorter intervals) the student exchanges his completed cards for candy or a toy. (As noted, eventually these extrinsic rewards are eventually replaced by intrinsic ones.)

If a child seems unable to respond to a given assignment, he is transferred to another task, allowed to choose another task, or placed in a one-to-one tutoring situation, or he is put in isolation for a certain number of minutes, which prevents him from accumulating check marks. The technique chosen depends on the child and the situation.

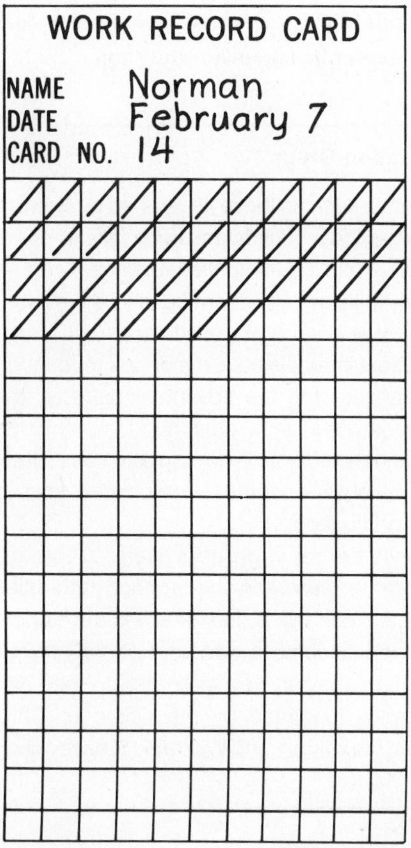

Hewett: using work record cards with the emotionally disturbed

Figure 14–3 Work Record Card Developed by Hewett In special classes for the emotionally disturbed, pupils are led through Hewett's hierarchy of educational tasks (see Figure 14–2) by means of the Work Record Card shown at right. A child is given a card a day, and for each task he accomplishes he receives one or more check marks. At the week's end he trades his completed cards for candy or toys.

Adapted from *The Emotionally Disturbed Child in the Classroom* by Frank M. Hewett. Copyright 1968 by Allyn and Bacon, Inc. Reproduced by permission of the publisher.

In commenting on the regular-class applicability of these methods, Hewett notes:

> It is not *what* you give the child in exchange for his check marks, *how much* you give him, or its *monetary value* that is the crucial determiner of its real worth. These considerations constitute the "small idea" inherent in the check-mark system. The "big idea" is that the child's accomplishments are being acknowledged in a systematic fashion and that he comes to recognize that his behavior controls certain consequences. Despite the author's plea for such placement of "big" and "little" ideas in perspective, some teachers upon reading this text will undoubtedly rush out, buy a large stock of candy, begin to pass it out rather haphazardly in the classroom, and then wait for a teaching miracle to occur. Such an approach may produce results initially, but it can be predicted with some certainty that its effectiveness will diminish fairly quickly. There is no magic in giving tangible rewards, including gold stars which have been used in education for years. It is the system with which such rewards are associated that will guarantee their success. Knowledge of the relationship of rewards to learning is ancient, but their systematic usage to help foster more adaptive behavior in the classroom is new and relatively unexplored in special education. (1968, p. 254)

If you have a pupil who finds it hard to concentrate or one who has had so little reinforcement that his incentive to learn is low, you might institute the Work Record Card system. In a sense this approach is simply an elaboration of the Goal Card technique described in Chapter 9. The major difference centers

---

"Behavior Modification Drugs"

In addition to behavior modification techniques such as those developed by Hewett, drugs that are frequently referred to as "behavior modification drugs" have come into use during the last few years. The label has been applied because certain types of medication modify the behavior of children with learning disabilities that are due to hyperactivity and distractability. It has been discovered that some drugs (e.g., amphetamine) that have a stimulating effect in adults have the opposite reaction on children. (When the body chemistry changes with the advent of puberty, the effects of the drug also change.) Such drugs have been prescribed for children who manifest hyperkinetic behavior disturbance problems, and in many cases they reduce the symptoms to the point that a previously uncontrollable child is able to respond to instruction in a normal classroom situation.

The use of drugs to treat hyperkinetic children has aroused a storm of protest in some areas, with complaints ranging from the assertion that school authorities are actively encouraging dope addiction to suspicion that a conspiracy is developing to drug children into docile conformity. If you become aware that some of your pupils are taking drugs to control hyperkinetic behavior, you may wish to take into account some observations made by a panel appointed by the Office of Child Development of the U.S. Department of Health, Education, and Welfare. (A description

---

around the policy of providing a check mark every few minutes rather than at the completion of an assignment. For children who have difficulty persevering until they finish a task, you might try fixed-interval reinforcement.

If you have time to work with students with learning disabilities on an individual basis and favor programmed learning, you might look into a system developed by Robert E. Valett. He has developed techniques for diagnosing and correcting for weaknesses in fifty-three basic learning abilities. You can find complete information about his methods in *The Remediation of Learning Disabilities* (1967), *The Psychoeducational Inventory of Basic Learning Abilities* (1968), and *Programming Learning Disabilities* (1969).

Bruner on Coping and Defending

In his discovery sessions with elementary-grade pupils, Bruner found himself intrigued by the question: "How do organisms benefit from past experience so that future experience can be handled with minimum pain and effort?" (1966, p. 130). He felt that he might gain some insight into this question by working with children with learning blocks.

In tutorial sessions with such children he found it useful to distinguish between *coping* and *defending*. In Chapter 7 of *Toward a Theory of Instruction*, he notes that *coping* "respects the requirements of problems we encounter while

---

of the report appears on page 6 of the *APA Monitor* for April 1971 (Vol. 2, No. 4.) It was reported that minimal brain dysfunction and hyperkinesis are to be found in approximately 3 percent of all school age children, that "stimulant medications are beneficial in only about one-half to one-third of cases in which trials of the drug are warranted," that when successful, the drugs improve the child's "attention, learning and social abilities," and that "there is no evidence to show that the proper use of amphetamines in treating (children) leads to subsequent addiction in later life."

The panel made the following recommendations for the proper use of drugs for hyperkinetic behavior: diagnosis by a doctor (with account taken of the child's environment and family relationships as well as physical and psychological factors), close supervision of treatment, and parental understanding and cooperation. It was stressed that "While it is entirely proper for school personnel to draw parents' attention to an individual child's behavior problems in school, teachers and school administrators should scrupulously avoid any attempt to force parents to accept any particular treatment. With parental permission, they should collaborate with the physician in the total program for the child." A final point was that a child should not be given sole responsibility for taking his own medication.

---

still respecting our integrity" (1966, p. 129). *Defending*, on the other hand, "is a strategy whose objective is avoiding or escaping from problems for which we believe there is no solution that does not violate our integrity of functioning" (p. 129). A child who defends (rather than copes) devotes most of his energies to trying to avoid problems which threaten him.

Bruner suggests that defending is the result of three characteristics of early learning: the importance of action, the fact that ideas are not isolated from their motivational or emotional context, and the inability of a young child to delay gratification once he has completed a task. Thus "early, more turbulent forms of learning are extrinsically motivated—being controlled and shaped by gratifications outside of learning itself" (p. 133). Because early learning is derived from action and is so dependent on extrinsic factors, subject matter is too likely to become intertwined with emotion. To overcome emotional involvement, a "denaturing process" may be required, and Bruner suggests that cognitive learning is the ideal framework for this process. First, it assists the child to "develop a system of cognitive organization that detaches concepts from the modes of action that they evoke" (p. 134). (This takes place when a child progresses through the enactive, iconic, and symbolic stages of intellectual development.) Second, "It requires the development of a capacity to detach concepts from their affective contexts" (p. 134). (This occurs when the child learns something for the sake of learning, not to please someone else.) Finally, "It demands a capacity to delay gratification so that outcomes of acts can be treated as information rather than simply punishing or rewarding" (p. 134).

Bruner's description of the conditions that may lead to learning blocks reflects his interest in cognitive development and his preference for the discovery approach in learning. Whereas Hewett uses principles of programmed learning and carefully designed schedules of reinforcement to overcome learning blocks, Bruner suggests that four conditions be arranged or encouraged in therapeutic discovery sessions: stimulation, play, identification, and freedom from drive and anxiety. Bruner comments on their importance:

Bruner: using the discovery approach with learning blocks

> With respect to stimulation, what is crucial is that the child have an opportunity to grow beyond enactive representation with its action-bound immediacy and beyond iconic representation with its strong susceptibility to affective link-age.... Varied stimulation with relative freedom from stress is about the only way we know of promoting such growth.
>
> With respect to play and playfulness, it is first of all an attitude in which the child learns that the outcomes of various activities are not as extreme as he either hoped or feared—it involves learning to place limits on the anticipated consequences of activity....
>
> As for identification, recall that willingness to learn, particularly in middle-class families, and particularly among boys, is a prime way of expressing identification with family ideals. One way in which learning becomes highly charged with conflict is through conflict with a family competence model who stands for, and gives rewards for, learning. There are many ways in which identification conflicts arise, but the consequence of most of them is that the child ends up with a rejected

competence ideal and no adequate pattern to guide his growth. Whether, in the case of a boy, he is the victim of a father who systematically and sarcastically attacks his son's efforts at mastery, or of one who, as a staff therapist put it, "tip-toes his way through life," the result is that the child fails to develop the sense that he can prevail by his own efforts.

Finally, the matter of freedom from excessive drive. There is good evidence that too strong an incentive for learning narrows the learning and renders it less generic, in the sense of its being less transferable. Where learning is dominated by strong extrinsic rewards and punishments, it becomes specific to the requirements of the particular learning task. (1966, pp. 134-136)

Thus Bruner suggests that a child with a learning block might overcome his handicap by receiving varied stimulation free from stress in a situation that permits him to identify clearly and positively with a competence model. This amounts to having a tutor provide a therapeutic kind of support that eventually leads to intrinsic learning. In this way the child is assisted to switch from defending to coping. Here is how Bruner summarizes his observations on helping children with learning blocks:

What seems to be required for a proper growth of respect for the requirements of problem solving is a "defusing" of intellectual activity from the demands of immediate action, effect, and drive. We have suggested that such a defusing depends upon a child's having the conditions necessary for playfulness to develop, upon his having an adequate competence model available, and upon the experience of intrinsic reward for increased competence that can start a career of "learning for its own sake." These produce coping. (P. 147)

Actually, Hewett and Bruner share many ideas regarding learning blocks. But Hewett applies the techniques of operant conditioning in a thoroughly systematic way, whereas Bruner uses a variation of the discovery approach that also includes many aspects of nondirective therapy. Hewett carefully shapes behavior and then vanishes prompts to lead up to intrinsic learning; Bruner's is a more intuitive, "personal" approach to the same goal. If you ever find yourself trying to assist a child with a learning block, consider both sets of ideas. Hewett's hierarchy of educational tasks and Work Record Card technique featuring systematic reinforcement might be feasible. Or you could ask a teacher aide to provide tutorial sessions using Bruner's suggestions. Or you might try a combination of the two. As in devising teaching techniques for many other aspects of learning, it is possible to combine features of associationism and field theory. Because the student with a learning block may desperately need tangible evidence of success, however, an initial learning situation that provides regular and direct reinforcement does seem preferable to one in which improvement occurs slowly and subtly. For this reason the use of a Work Record Card may be a better means of initiating remedial measures than a nondirective, discovery approach. Once the pupil begins to respond and starts to work his way up Hewett's hierarchy or to progress toward some of the goals noted by Bruner, a field theory approach may be more appropriate.

Troubleshooting Learning Blocks

If some of your pupils appear stymied by some or most of the curriculum, the cause of the block may or may not be emotional. The trend in American education is for a school, district, or state to select one particular approach to teaching a given subject. Because of the nature of individual differences—and the types of factors discussed in the analysis of limitations of age-level characteristics in Chapter 3—probably no single method will be appropriate for all pupils. Some will have difficulty in school simply because they do not conform to the hypothetical "typical" child the theorists had in mind when they planned the curriculum. In attempting to analyze learning blocks, consider the possibility that a pupil is atypical in terms of the following qualities (all of which have been discussed in earlier chapters of this book):

Readiness and Level of Maturation. Is the pupil an atypically slow or fast maturer? Is he so far ahead of his classmates that he is bored? Is he a slow maturer? Does he appear as ready to learn as the others? If not, what might be done to adjust the curriculum to the appropriate level of maturation? (Your answer to that last question will depend on your position in regard to "natural" versus guided-experience development.)

Stage of Intellectual Development. Does the curriculum take into account Piaget's stages of intellectual development? (To refresh your memory, refer to the discussion in Chapters 3 and 4.) Are you asking a pupil at the preoperational level to do work that requires concrete operations? Are you asking pupils to function at the level

Summary

In this chapter you have been asked to speculate about personality and adjustment. Each of your pupils will be a unique individual continuously reacting to situations in terms of inherited predispositions and ever-accumulating and ever-changing environmental experiences. As described by Maslow, much behavior is due primarily to deficit motivation, which is a necessary basis for growth motivation, which in turn sets the stage for self-actualization.

Since deficit needs can be satisfied only through interaction with others and since teachers are often among the most important people in the lives of students, you will be in a position to help your students achieve growth motivation. You might attempt to do this by arranging learning situations so that they gratify the basic needs for safety, belongingness, and esteem and also by making growth choices attractive in situations in which a student must choose between safety and growth.

You will need to take into account the way a student responds to frustration of his needs and encourage constructive reactions. Despite your efforts, some students will probably fail to achieve satisfaction of their needs and will be

of formal operations before they have reached that stage? If a child does appear to be at a lower level, should you try to speed up his development or give him assignments appropriate to his level?

Intelligence. May the learning difficulties be due to an abnormally low or high general intelligence? What scores does the pupil have on tests of mental maturity? Are they consistent? Should you request that an individual test be given? If intelligence does seem the primary factor, what can you do about it? (For some suggestions on teaching both slow and fast learners, see Chapter 13.)

Type of Intellectual Operation. Does the pupil seem to be a convergent or a divergent thinker (as described by Guilford)? Are you asking a convergent thinker to be divergent most of the time (or vice versa)? Can you present assignments that will permit each type of thinker to function satisfactorily or that will help one type to function as effectively as the other?

Cognitive Style. Is the pupil analytic or thematic, reflective or impulsive (as described by Kagan)? Does he exhibit a cognitive style similar to one of those described by Messick (pp. 592–593)? Can you present assignments that will permit each type to have some opportunities appropriate to his natural style? How can you help a pupil with one style learn to function in terms of the other style?

If you find yourself baffled by the inability of a pupil to learn some things, take note of these factors before you consider the possibility that the block is due to emotional problems. It may simply be a case of your not recognizing the nature and extent of individual differences.

---

more or less forced into responding in unfortunate ways. In such cases it is important to recognize indications of unsatisfactory adjustment as early as possible and to recommend professional counseling.

Some students will encounter frustrations because of specific learning blocks. The chapter concluded with some suggestions for handling such problems by means of techniques based on principles of programmed learning and the discovery approach.

Suggestions for Further Reading, Writing, Thinking, and Discussion

14-1 *Speculating about the Complexity of Personality*

You may gain fuller appreciation of the complexity of personality if you speculate about factors that influence behavior. The first part of *Personality in Nature, Society and Culture* (1948) by Murray and Kluckhohn has a complete description of the various determinants of personality development. You might take this section—or the suggestions offered in Chapter 3 of *Lives in Progress* (1966) by Robert W. White, which includes information on methods and also notes some precautions—and "analyze" either yourself or a close acquaintance. Do your best to list all the factors that led to the development of personality, then comment on your reactions to this attempt to gain awareness of the depth and complexity of individuality.

14-2 *Sampling Some of Maslow's Views on Adjustment*

If you did not do additional reading about Maslow's theory of need gratification earlier (in connection with motivation), you may wish to sample *Toward a Psychology of Being* (2nd ed., 1968) after thinking about the dynamics of adjustment. In Part I of this book Maslow describes the basic rationale of his theory. In Part II he explains the differences between deficiency motivation and growth motivation. Part VI is devoted to "Some Basic Propositions of a Growth and Self-Actualization Psychology." For a fairly definite set of guidelines for helping your students become self-actualizers, read at least these parts of Maslow's book and perhaps note your reactions for future reference.

14-3 *Drawing a Diagram of Your Own Behavior*

You will gain greater understanding of the diagram of adjustment in this chapter if you try a pictorial representation of some of your own behavior. First, draw a diagram of a choice situation you have encountered recently. Analyze your feelings about the situation and classify your final choice as one of safety or growth. Then ask yourself whether you made your decision because of the balance between dangers and attractions as depicted in the diagram on page 659. Next, speculate about situations centered around a specific goal (e.g., earning an "A" in some course, making the varsity in a certain sport, attracting the attention of a member of the opposite sex, being elected to an office). Did you sometimes achieve the exact goal you sought? What were your feelings when this occurred? Did you sometimes find it necessary to divert your attention to a substitute goal? How did you feel about that? Finally, can you recall being so completely thwarted by your inability to achieve the goal that you avoided the situation completely? What was your inner response on that occasion? Could someone else (e.g., a teacher) have helped you deal with the frustrating situations? Note your reactions to the situations described and comment on the implications of your reactions.

14-4 *Describing Your Defense Mechanisms*

Maslow estimates that only one out of a hundred people is a self-actualizer. Since consistent satisfaction of needs is so rare, almost everyone resorts to defense mechanisms from time to time. (Even the best self-actualizer probably rationalizes a bit now and then.) You may become more alert to the nature and impact of defense mechanisms by analyzing your own use of them. Think about your recent behavior and pick out at least one instance of rationalizing, of gaining satisfaction by identifying with others, or of engaging in one activity as compensation for lack of achievement in another activity. Perhaps this will increase your sympathy for and understanding of these forms of behavior in your students.

14-5 *Sampling "Lives in Progress"*

In *Lives in Progress* (1966), Robert W. White describes the various factors that influence personality by means of three detailed case histories. His analysis of the forces that determine personality uses a different frame of reference from Murray's and Kluckhohn's. White shares many of Maslow's views, notably the convictions that a person "is himself a center of energy and an active agent in changing his material and human surroundings" (page iv), that it is important to stress natural growth and constructive activity, and that much can be gained by studying *normal* people. The three case histories—of a physician and scientist, a businessman, and a housewife and social worker—illustrate this last point. The descriptions provide a good deal of insight into personality and behavior. If you think you would enjoy a comprehensive analysis of a life in progress, read at least one of the case histories in White's book and sample his general analysis of factors that influence personality. Chapter 4 is devoted to social forces. Chapter 6 to biological roots, and Chapter 8 to the psychodynamics of development. The final chapter, "Natural Growth During Young Adulthood," contains observations you might find helpful in your own continuous personal growth and constructive activity. A way to do this would be to outline the points made by White and add your own reactions.

14-6 *Sampling Rogers's Views on Behavior, Therapy, and Education*

Carl Rogers developed the technique of client-centered therapy twenty years ago and has since applied the same basic idea of growth of the self to other aspects of living, including education. For a concise description of Rogers's philosophy, look for "Learning to Be Free," an essay in *Conflict and Creativity* (1963) edited by Farber and Wilson and also in *Person to Person: The Problem of Being Human* (1967) by Rogers and Stevens. The latter volume includes three more essays by Rogers, as well as related discussions by others who share his philosophy. In *Freedom to Learn* (1969) Rogers comments on varied aspects of his view of education and presents descriptions of actual classroom applications in the elementary grades and at the college level. If you read one or more sections in any of these books, you might summarize the points made, and add your own reactions.

14-7 *Participating in or Finding Out About Encounter Groups*

If you are curious about sensitivity training, you might interview someone who has participated in an encounter group or join one yourself. (Campus bulletin boards often have notices announcing encounter groups of one kind or another.) Before you actually participate in an encounter group, however, you might find it helpful to read some recent analyses of their weaknesses and strengths. Rogers gives his views in *Carl Rogers on Encounter Groups* (1972). Kurt W. Back comments on his experiences in *Beyond Words: The Story of Sensitivity Training and the Encounter Movement* (1972), an excerpt of which appears in the December 1972 issue of *Psychology Today* under the title "The Group Can Comfort But It Can't Cure" (pp. 28–35). William R. Coulson gives an account of his experiences and views in *Groups, Gimmicks, and Instant Gurus: An Examination of Encounter Groups and Their Distortions* (1972). Morton A. Lieberman, Irvin D. Yalom, and Matthew B. Miles carried out a controlled experiment on encounter groups and present their conclusions in *Encounter Groups: First Facts* (1973), an excerpt of which appears as "Encounter: The Leader Makes the Difference" in the March 1973 issue of *Psychology Today* (pp. 69–76). The last paragraph of this article offers these observations:

> Encounter groups present a clear and evident danger if they are used for radical surgery to produce a new man. The danger is even greater when the leader and the participant share this misperception. If we no longer expect groups to produce magical, lasting change and if we stop seeing them as panaceas, we can regard them as useful, socially sanctioned opportunities for human beings to explore and to express themselves. Then we can begin to work on ways to improve them so that they may make a meaningful contribution toward solving human problems.

14-8 *Reading about Sensitivity and Awareness in the Classroom*

Clark Moustakas has written a book on teaching that combines many of Rogers's ideas with Maslow's. Some specific suggestions for using sensitivity-training techniques in the classroom appear in *The Authentic Teacher* (1966). In this book Moustakas makes general observations on his philosophy of teaching and suggests how this philosophy might be put into practice in the kindergarten (Chapter 4), at the early elementary-grade level (Chapter 5), in the later elementary grades (Chapter 6), and in high school (Chapter 7). If you think you would like to consider some variation of the sensitivity-training approach in your classes, sample the ideas of Moustakas and note those which strike you as most promising. (Another book you might consult is *Human Teaching for Human Learning: An Introduction to Confluent Education*, 1971, by George Isaac Brown.)

14-9 *Reading a More Complete Discussion of Adjustment*

The brief treatment of adjustment presented in Chapter 14 may entice you to browse through *Mental Hygiene in Teaching* (2nd ed., 1959) by Fritz Redl and William W. Wattenberg. This exceptionally good book covers almost every aspect of adjustment likely to be of concern to teachers. (There are extended sections on classroom applications and special problems as well as general background information.) For a more comprehensive and theoretical discussion of this aspect of psychology, *The Psychology of Adjustment* (1956) by Lawrence Shaffer and Edward Shoben is recommended. If you read sections of either of these books, you might state the points that strike you as being of potential value to the new teacher.

14-10 *Tutoring a Student with a Learning Problem*

Many campuses now have educational programs providing tutors for pupils with learning problems. (CAVE—Community Action Volunteers for Education—is an example.) If such a program exists at your college, you might volunteer to serve as a tutor. Depending on the nature of the learning problem, the age of the pupil, and the subject matter—not to mention your own philosophy of education—you will perhaps use some of the techniques developed by Hewett in his educational engineering approach or those suggested by Bruner. If you try either programmed techniques or a discovery approach (or use both methods), describe your experiences and summarize your reactions for future reference. (If you would like more complete information, examine *Educating the Emotionally Disturbed: A Book of Readings*, 1969, edited by Hardwick W. Harshman.)

14-11 *Speculating about Differences Between Teaching and Therapy*

Fantasy and Feeling in Education (1968) by Richard M. Jones was called to your attention earlier in connection with Bruner's suggestions for teaching social studies. Jones's major point is that Bruner emphasizes the cognitive side of learning at the expense of imagination and emotion. Jones describes techniques teachers might use in introducing more fantasy and feeling into learning. At first glance, this would seem to be essentially the position of those who advocate sensitivity training. However, in urging teachers to place greater stress on the affective side of learning, Jones discusses some basic differences between teaching and therapy. He argues that students go to school to be taught—not treated—and adds, "If the confrontation of emotions in classrooms is not made in the primary interests of achieving instructional objectives, both the means and ends may suffer" (p. 161). If you are interested in attempting any sort of sensitivity-training approach to teaching, consider carefully Jones's comments about the differences between therapy and teaching. For example, you might evaluate Rogers's suggestions for an educational approach derived from nondirective therapy with reference to Jones's ideas. Or simply note your reactions to Jones's points. Does he convince you that imagination and emotion should be stressed more in learning, but that it is unwise for a teacher to use a primarily therapeutic approach in attempting to do this?

14-12 *Reading a Case History Which Illustrates the Process of Adjustment and the Techniques of Therapy*

A great deal of insight into the dynamics of adjustment and the nature of psychotherapy can be gained by reading a detailed case history. Two highly regarded studies are *One Little Boy* (1952) by Dorothy W. Baruch and *Dibs: In Search of Self* (1964) by Virginia Axline. These books will acquaint you with the factors that caused a child to develop serious adjustment problems and reveal how a psychotherapist helped him overcome these problems. If you read either, try to analyze the causes of adjustment problems with reference to Maslow's hierarchy of needs (that is, in what way were the needs of safety, love and belongingness, and esteem frustrated?), and to relate the techniques of therapy to Rogers's principles of nondirective therapy. (Another book which provides insight into the nature of psychotherapy is *The Child's Discovery of Himself* (1966) edited by Moustakas, in which ten therapists describe—in more concise fashion than Baruch and Axline—how children with emotional problems succeeded in overcoming their difficulties.)

14-13 *Reading a Fictional Account of Mental Illness*

Mental illness has been discussed in textbooks, portrayed in films and on television, and explored in novels. A highly regarded fictional treatment of the subject is *I Never Promised You a Rose Garden* (1964) by Hannah Green (a pseudonym used by Joanne Greenberg), the story of the experiences and treatment of a sixteen-year-old girl who retreats from reality into an imaginary kingdom. If you would like to gain insight into the nature of psychosis and its treatment, you might read this novel.

Recommended Reading in *Psychology Applied to Teaching: Selected Readings*

If you would like to do further reading in books or articles mentioned in this chapter (and in the preceding "Suggestions for Further Reading, Writing, Thinking, and Discussion") without having to track down several separate volumes, you might peruse *Psychology Applied to Teaching: Selected Readings* (Boston: Houghton Mifflin, 1972). This is a collection of excerpts from books and articles from journals in psychology. The following selections provide extended commentaries on points noted in this chapter or mentioned in the "Suggestions."

Maslow's Theory of Need Gratification: Excerpt from *Toward a Psychology of Being* by Abraham H. Maslow, Selection 30, p. 452. (See also Suggestion 14-2.)

The Impact of School Experiences on Pupil Adjustment: "Mental Hygiene and School Learning" by Fritz Redl and William W. Wattenberg, Selection 31, p. 467. (See also Suggestion 14–9.)

Learner-Centered Teaching: "Learning to be Free" by Carl R. Rogers, Selection 29, p. 432. (See also Suggestion 14–6.)

Educational Engineering with Emotionally Disturbed Children: "A Classroom Design for Emotionally Disturbed Children" by Frank M. Hewett, Selection 32, p. 491.

Using Discovery Methods to Overcome Learning Blocks: "On Coping and Defending" by Jerome S. Bruner, Selection 33, p. 504.

15 CREATING A FAVORABLE

CLASSROOM ENVIRONMENT

also read + know 607
Causes of Mental Retardation

KEY POINTS

Classifications
Influence techniques: supporting self-control, giving situational assistance, fostering reality and value appraisal (Redl and Wattenberg)

Experiments and Studies
Positive effect of democratic leadership on boys, negative effect of autocratic leadership (Lippitt and White)
High self-esteem in children whose parents set definite limits (Coopersmith)

Concepts
Causes of misbehavior: boredom; release of tension; desire for attention, recognition, and status
Self-discipline (Neill)

Methodology
Taking into account common causes of misbehavior in establishing a constructive classroom atmosphere
Using varied influence techniques to maintain constructive classroom control
Using behavior modification

CHAPTER CONTENTS

CHAPTER 14 PRESENTED SOME OBSERVATIONS ON NEED GRATIFICATION and the nature of adjustment. A feature of need gratification that complicates every individual's pursuit of self-actualization is that, as Maslow puts it, "the [person] needs not only gratification; he needs also to learn the limitations that the physical world puts upon his gratifications, and he has to learn that other human beings seek for gratification, too" (1968, pp. 163-164).

Although it seems desirable to allow each student as much freedom of choice as possible (providing he is a good chooser), certain natural tendencies must be controlled. Primary-grade children, for example, are normally inclined to be active. Yet they must learn to control their activity—at least to some extent—in the classroom. Older students may have no intrinsic interest in some subjects. Yet because learning is hierarchical, they may be required to study some things they would ignore if left to their own inclinations. Since deficit needs can be satisfied only by others, students compete with one another for gratification provided by teachers.

Thus your pupils will have to acquire some self-control, they may have to be induced to learn things they would prefer not to learn, and they will surely have to adapt to the fact that their classmates are seeking gratification, too. Even the best teacher in the world, then, is likely to have at least some trouble keeping a class under sufficient restraint so that learning can take place. This chapter aims at preparing you to establish a favorable classroom environment. Research on the impact of different kinds of class atmosphere will be noted and followed by a discussion of specific techniques for influencing and regulating behavior. The chapter concludes with some observations on the development of self-control.

Impact of Class Atmosphere

In a classic study in psychology Kurt Lewin and two associates (R. Lippitt and R. K. White) studied the impact of different kinds of leadership on group behavior. Lewin, you will remember, was a field theorist. (He was also a German Jew who was driven out of his native land by the Nazis. It is important to consider the Zeitgeist effect a democratic society would have upon the victim of a vicious autocracy.)

Lewin and his associates asked eleven-year-old boys to participate in some after-school clubs. The groups were exposed to different kinds of leadership: authoritarian, democratic, and laissez-faire. Here are the instructions that were given to the leaders as reported in an article written by Lippitt and White:

√ *Authoritarian.* Practically all policies as regards club activities and procedures should be determined by the leader. The techniques and activity steps should be communicated by the authority, one unit at a time, so that future steps are in the dark to a large degree. The adult should take considerable responsibility for assigning the activity tasks and companions of each group member. The dominator should keep his standards of praise and criticism to himself in evaluating individual and group activities. He should also remain fairly aloof from active group participation except in demonstrating.

√ *Democratic.* Wherever possible, policies should be a matter of group decision and discussion with active encouragement and assistance by the adult leader. The leader should attempt to see that activity perspective emerges during the discussion period with the general steps to the group goal becoming clarified. Wherever technical advice is needed, the leader should try to suggest two or more alternative procedures from which choice can be made by the group members. Everyone should be free to work with whomever he chooses, and the divisions of responsibility should be left up to the group. The leader should attempt to communicate in an objective, fact-minded way the bases for his praise and criticism of individual and group activities. He should try to be a regular group member in spirit, but not do much of the work (so that comparisons of group productivity can be made between the groups).

✓ *Laissez-faire.* In this situation, the adult should play a rather passive role in social participation and leave complete freedom for group or individual decisions in relation to activity and group procedure. The leader should make clear the various materials which are available and be sure it is understood that he will supply information and help when asked. He should do a minimum of taking the initiative in making suggestions. He should make no attempt to evaluate negatively or positively the behavior or productions of the individuals or the group as a group, although he should be friendly rather than "stand-offish" at all times. (1958, p. 498)

Each group of boys was exposed to all three types of leadership but in different sequences. Trained observers recorded everything that was said and done during the group meetings. They noted that the leaders carried out their instructions with considerable fidelity but concentrated on observing the behavior of the boys. Under the authoritarian leader two types of reactions occurred. Some groups responded in a submissive and apathetic way; others responded aggressively. All groups worked actively while the authoritarian leader was present, but the rate of work dropped off sharply when he left the room. All were very dependent on him and demanded much of his attention.

Under democratic leaders the boys did not produce quite as much as they did in authoritarian-led groups, but since they continued to work after the leader left the room, they produced more in the long run. They were also more friendly toward one another and, as might be expected, more group-minded. Under the laissez-faire regime the boys were unproductive in the presence of the leader. While he was in the room, they spent most of the time asking him for information rather than doing any actual work. But the teacher-*absent* activity was highest for the laissez-faire group (perhaps because their need for stimulation and activity had been frustrated).

Lippitt and White study: positive effect of democratic leadership ✓

Lippitt and White suggest that the different groups responded to the authoritarian leader in such different ways because of previous group history. Here is the way they put it:

It was clear that previous group history (i.e., preceding social climates) had an important effect in determining the social perception of leader behavior and reaction to it by club members. A club which had passively accepted an authoritarian leader in the beginning of its club history, for example, was much more frustrated and restive to a second authoritarian leader after it had experienced a democratic leader than a club without such a history. There seem to be some suggestive implications here for educational practice. (P. 511)

Two implications are, first, that you might take into account the kind of teacher (or teachers) your students had before they entered your class and, second, that you are likely to experience difficulties if you start out with a laissez-faire or democratic approach and then attempt to move toward authoritarianism.

As you read the instructions to the three types of leaders in the Lippitt and White study, you may have found yourself thinking that the authoritarian atmosphere was similar to a structured (e.g., programmed) approach, that the democratic atmosphere is essentially that of open education, and that the laissez-faire atmosphere is basically the same as Summerhill and similar schools. Within limits, these similarities may be said to exist, and some of the boys' reactions might be expected to occur in classroom situations that resemble the club atmosphere. For example, if a teacher controls virtually all aspects of the learning situation and shapes behavior by dispensing rewards, students will likely be productive when she is present but stop work as soon as her influence is withdrawn. In addition, advocates of open education admit that learning is not completely efficient in such an approach, but they maintain that there is a high level of activity regardless of what the teacher does or where she is and that group-mindedness and student interaction are high. Finally, descriptions of Summerhill indicate that students were eager to secure attention from Neill and that their overall productivity is low.

But it seems unwise to generalize too directly from this study. Because of Lewin's background, he was eager to prove that democracy was incontestably better than autocracy, and the authoritarian leaders seem to have understood this. In their relationships with the boys, they tended to be cold and domineering. A *benevolent* authoritarian leader might have encouraged the boys to be highly productive and at the same time succeeded in establishing high morale and a wholesome group spirit.

Richard C. Anderson (1959) reviewed a large number of studies on the impact of classroom atmosphere and came to this conclusion:

> The evidence available fails to demonstrate that either authoritarian or demo-cratic leadership is consistently associated with higher productivity. In most situations, however, democratic leadership is associated with higher morale. But even this conclusion must be regarded cautiously, because the authoritarian leader has been unreasonably harsh and austere in a number of investigations reporting superior morale in democratic groups. In the educational setting, morale appears to be higher under learner-centered conditions, at least when anxiety over grades is reduced. (1959, p. 213)

This summary supports the open education approach, in which the teacher supplies guidance but encourages democratic participation on the part of students; it also supports the learning for mastery approach, in which anxiety over grades is reduced.

Classroom Control

The evidence favoring learner-centered conditions and democratic leadership may make you wonder about the extent to which you should encourage self-government. Some educators advocate almost completely student-deter-mined discipline in the schools. They argue that students should have experience in determining their own behavior. This is a desirable goal but it overlooks the fact that few rules and laws in society are developed through *direct* democratic discussion by all citizens and that students should therefore learn to live with restrictions imposed by others. As Paul Woodring puts it:

> If by discipline we mean letting the child learn that there are certain restrictions and controls which society places upon the individual and that children are not exempt from these controls, there seems to be no sound psychological reason for avoiding discipline. Indeed, such discipline would seem to be an essential part of education. (1953, p. 137)

Here is Woodring's description of the *kind* of discipline that is essential to education:

> A properly disciplined classroom is one in which the rules are reasonable and in which they are so well accepted by the children that violations are comparatively rare. It is not one in which violations frequently occur and are severely punished. . . .
>
> The rules appropriate to a classroom are the rules of normal civilized behavior of individuals in a social setting. They involve courtesy and a consideration for others. (P. 136)

Advocates of the permissive approach to teaching sometimes appear to have built a straw man labeled *discipline*, which embodies all the brutal attributes of every sadistic pedagogue who ever lived. They almost suggest that you must choose between being a helpful, friendly guide or a vicious, inhuman autocrat. Although you may sympathize with their desire to eliminate unnecessarily harsh discipline in the classroom, it is a mistake to ignore the possibility that a teacher can be both firm *and* friendly.

The most effective ways to establish a favorable classroom environment are to earn the respect, if not the admiration, of your pupils and to make what you are teaching so interesting they won't even think about causing trouble. If students like you, they will want to please you, which means they will want to avoid displeasing you by causing trouble. If they are kept interested in subject matter, they won't have much inclination to think about anything else. This is a tall order, and few teachers are good enough to fill it. Until you become such an artist at teaching, here are some suggestions for creating a "properly disciplined classroom . . . in which the rules are reasonable and in which they are so well accepted by the children that violations are comparatively rare."

Causes of Misbehavior

One way to come to grips with classroom control is to think in terms of determinism. The scientist searches for causes, and it is logical to apply this approach to misbehavior. What are the *reasons* students misbehave? In many cases the reasons are unique, personal, complex, and perhaps beyond your comprehension and control. But there are some common, general causes of misbehavior that can be anticipated—and there are some techniques you can use to reduce behavior due to these causes.

Analyzing and dealing with causes of misbehavior

Boredom ✓

Many students get into mischief simply because they are bored with classwork and can't think of anything else to do. Obvious solutions: Keep them busy. Make sure they know what they are supposed to be doing (remember the importance of providing goals). Make classwork meaningful and interesting. Take readiness into account. Be certain they all have something to do at the appropriate level of difficulty and try to have several activities to choose from.

✓ Release of Frustration and Tension

For the following reasons—and many more—students must put up with considerable frustration: A teacher requires them to behave in a manner that is "unnatural." Intellectual endeavor requires mental discipline. Practically all pupils resist learning to some degree because it is effortful, and the natural inclination is to avoid work. Added resistance comes from the imposition of a course of study by outside authority. Resentment of this increases with age and is so strong in high school that almost any secondary teacher of a required course has a built-in source of difficulty. Finally, group activity compels each individual to make concessions and compromises in adapting his personal desires to the common will of the group.

When students are frustrated, tension builds up until they are forced to react. You can't prevent this, but there are constructive ways for students to release tension under your control.

Provide frequent breaks and changes of pace. Be on the alert for the point of diminishing returns. Alternate intensive, laborious activities with relaxing ones. If the class is on edge because of the weather, an impending vacation, a game, or whatever, have more breaks and allow more activity and discussion.

✓ Desire for Attention, Recognition, Status

Some students misbehave because they want attention, and negative attention is better than none at all. A pupil who is unsuccessful in schoolwork, a poor athlete, and unpersonable may seek recognition and status by being the class pest.

You can minimize this sort of behavior by offering "legal" opportunities for gaining attention and satisfaction. Have the child compete against himself. Try to "dignify" all achievements by stressing improvement. Give positive attention in the form of favorable comments and encouragement. Give recognition for many different kinds of ability.

Even if you do everything possible to prevent the development of problems by taking into account these causes, there will still be incidents of misbehavior. The following pages suggest ways to deal with them.

''Give positive attention in the form of favorable comments and encouragement. Give recognition for many different kinds of ability.''

''Provide frequent breaks and changes of pace. . . . Alternate intensive, laborious activities with relaxing ones.''

Open Education Does Not Eliminate
the Need for Control

Some people argue that teachers must resort to techniques of classroom control because they are forcing students to engage in unnatural behavior. It is hypothesized that in a completely open atmosphere, in which children are free to engage only in self-selected activities, all "discipline" problems will disappear. Although there is undoubtedly some truth to the charge that asking students to engage in contrived learning is likely to make close supervision necessary, it is not true that all need for control disappears in a free school. (Read *Summerhill* if you find this hard to believe.) Free education does not automatically lead to satisfaction of the deficiency needs of love, belonging, and esteem; and the possibility of friction between students increases as a consequence of greater opportunities for interaction with peers. The same holds true for open schools.

Some children may engage in disruptive behavior regardless of the degree of freedom they are allowed because they come from homes where they feel unloved or inadequate. Others may cause difficulties simply to attract attention. And if two belligerent boys happen to want to use the same book or material in an activity center of an open classroom at the same time, an uproar may ensue that could touch off a mild riot.

There is no denying that unnecessarily strict teachers make trouble for themselves. But it does not follow that complete "freedom" will eliminate trouble. The intent of this chapter is to acquaint you with techniques you might use to establish and maintain a classroom environment in which students have the opportunity to learn without being unduly disturbed by others and without being intimidated or coerced by the teacher. It is not intended to convince you that the only possible course of action is to make a full-time effort to trick, bribe, or threaten students into docile obedience. A reasonably controlled environment is more constructive than anarchy.

Suggestions for Maintaining Classroom Control

1. Consider establishing some class rules.
2. Be friendly but firm. Act confident, especially the first day.
3. Have a variety of influence techniques planned in advance.
4. Whenever you have to deal harshly with a student, make an effort to reestablish rapport.
5. Try to avoid threats.
6. Be prompt, consistent, reasonable.
7. Consider using behavior modification techniques.
8. When you have control, ease up—some.

1. *Consider establishing some class rules.*

As a neophyte teacher you will have a lot on your mind. During the first few weeks you may think that teaching is just one long series of crises. The more of these you can anticipate and prepare for, the less harried and desperate you will be. Anything you can do to avoid coping with problems, especially disciplinary problems, in a completely extemporaneous manner will make life easier. You can prevent a good deal of trouble by explaining the first day that certain ground rules will apply in your room. Some teachers list these rules in a prominent position on a bulletin board. Others simply state them informally in the first class. Either technique saves time and trouble later because all you have to do is refer to the rule when a transgression occurs. The alternative is to interrupt the lesson and disturb the whole class while you make a hurried, unplanned effort to deal with a surprise attack. Unless you are experienced and skilled, your improvised technique will probably be clumsy and ineffective.

If you introduce rules the first day, it is important to take a positive, nonthreatening approach. If you spit rules out as if they were a series of ultimatums, the students may feel you have a chip on your shoulder, which the unwritten code of the classroom obligates them to try to knock off. An excellent way to demonstrate your good faith is to invite the class to suggest necessary regulations and why they should be established. (Some teachers use this technique effectively; others think it's a waste of time.) Whatever your approach, encourage understanding of the *reasons* for the rules. You can make restrictions meaningful if you discuss why they are needed. Reasonable rules are much more likely to be remembered and honored than pronouncements that seem to be the whims of a tyrant.

Examples

"During class discussion, please don't speak out unless you raise your hand and are recognized. I want to be able to hear what each person has to say, and I won't be able to do that if more than one person is talking."

"During work periods, I don't mind if you talk to your neighbors. But if you do it too much and disturb others, I'll have to ask you to stop."

"I don't mind if you chew gum—provided you don't get too juicy or noisy. If it disrupts the class, I'll have to ask you to stop."

In the space below note other rules you might want to establish in your classes.

_____

_____

_____

_____

_____

_____

✓ *2. Be friendly but firm. Act confident, especially the first day.*

The first few minutes with any class are often the most crucial of all as far as discipline is concerned. Your pupils are sizing you up, especially if they know you are a new teacher. If you act scared and unsure of yourself, you will probably be in for trouble. In self-defense, you might use this scheme to turn the tables until you have a bit more confidence: Ask the students to fill out cards about themselves at the beginning of the first day of class. This will give you a chance to make a leisurely scrutiny of them as individuals. If you start lecturing right from the sound of the bell, you will be much too busy to do this, and you may misinterpret essentially innocuous reactions as threats. If you follow the card writing by having each student introduce himself, the fact that these are ordinary human beings becomes even more apparent. What is being discussed here is a form of stage fright. Perhaps you have read about singers who pick out a single, sympathetic member of the audience and sing directly to him or her. The sea of faces as a whole is frightening. The face of the individual is not. Even if you don't need to use the cards as a crutch for your confidence, introductions have other values, such as helping you learn names and making you aware of your students as individuals.

Whatever you do the first few minutes, it is important to give the impression that you know exactly what you are doing. The best way to pull this off is to be *thoroughly* prepared.

✓ *3. Have a variety of influence techniques planned in advance.*

You may save yourself a great deal of trouble, embarrassment, and strain if you plan ahead. When first-year teachers are asked to note which aspects of teaching bother them the most, classroom control is almost invariably near the top of the list. Perhaps a major reason is that problems of control frequently erupt unexpectedly, and they often demand equally sudden solutions. If you lack experience in dealing with such problems, your shoot-from-the-hip reactions may be ineffective. Initial attempts at control that *are* ineffective tend to reinforce misbehavior, and you will find yourself trapped in a vicious circle. This sort of trap can be avoided if specific techniques are devised ahead of time. Having in mind several methods of dealing with trouble will prepare you for the inevitable difficulties that arise.

However, if you find yourself being forced to use prepared techniques too often, some self-analysis is called for. How can you prevent so many problems from developing? Frequent trouble is an indication that you need to work harder at motivating your class. You might refer to the list of causes of misbehavior in the preceding section for some specific troubleshooting suggestions. Also, check on your feelings when you mete out punishment. Teachers who really like students and want them to learn consider control techniques a necessary evil and use them only when they will provide a better atmosphere for learning.

If you find yourself looking for trouble or perhaps deliberately luring pupils into misbehaving, or if you discover yourself gloating privately or publicly about an act of punishment, stop and think about it. Are you perverting your power to build up your ego or give vent to sadistic impulses?

In *Mental Hygiene in Teaching* (1959), Fritz Redl and William W. Wattenberg present a list of *influence techniques,* which has been adopted as an organizational frame of reference for the following discussion. The first three of the four sections given below are based directly on the list. All the headings (both those in capital letters and those in boldface type) are exactly as set forth on pages 348-363 of *Mental Hygiene in Teaching.*

Under each section specific examples are offered. Some are based on ideas noted by Redl and Wattenberg; some are the results of reports by students and teachers; some are based on personal experience. After each list of examples, space is provided so that you may add techniques of your own.

| Influence Techniques | *know some of the types*

SUPPORTING SELF-CONTROL

Students should be encouraged to develop self-control. This first group of suggestions is designed to foster it.

Using influence techniques to maintain classroom control

Signals. In some cases a subtle signal can put an end to budding misbehavior. The signal, if successful, will stimulate the student to control himself. (This technique should not be used too often, and it is effective only in the early stages of misbehavior.)

Examples

Clear your throat.

Stare at the culprit.

Stop what you are saying in mid-sentence and stare.

Shake your head (to indicate "No").

Say, "Someone is making it hard for the rest of us to concentrate." (Or the equivalent)

_____

_____

_____

Proximity control. Place yourself close to the troublemaker. This makes a signal a bit more apparent.

Examples

Walk over and stand near the student.

With an elementary-grade pupil, it sometimes helps if you place a gentle hand on his shoulder.

_____

_____

_____

"Stare at the culprit."

Interest boosting. Convey interest in the incipient misbehaver. This relates the signal to schoolwork.

Examples

Ask the student a question, preferably related to what is being discussed. (Questions such as "Herman, are you paying attention?" or "Don't you agree, Herman?" invite wisecracks. *Genuine* questions are to be preferred.)

Go over and examine some work the student is doing. It often helps if you point out something good about it and urge continued effort.

Humor. Humor is an excellent, all-around influence technique, especially in tense situations. However, remember that it should be *good*-humored humor—gentle and benign rather than incisive. Irony and sarcasm should be avoided.

Example

"Herman, for goodness' sake, let that poor pencil sharpener alone—I heard it groan when you used it just now."

(Perhaps you have heard someone say, "We're not laughing *at* you; we're laughing *with* you." Before you try this one on one of your pupils, you might take note that one second-grader who was treated to that comment unhinged the teacher by replying matter-of-factly, "I'm not laughing.")

SITUATIONAL ASSISTANCE

Helping over hurdles. Some misbehavior undoubtedly occurs because students do not understand what they are to do or lack the ability to carry out an assignment. Techniques for minimizing problems due to this cause were discussed in the section on causes of misbehavior under the subheading "Boredom." They are noted again here.

Examples

Try to make sure your students know what they are supposed to do and are capable of doing it.

Take readiness into account; see to it that they have something to do at appropriate levels of difficulty.

Have a variety of activities available.

Support from routines. Trouble sometimes develops simply because students do not know what is expected of them. To avoid this in-limbo situation, it helps to establish a certain amount of routine, perhaps as part of the class rules (if you resort to such rules).

Examples

Establish a set pattern for getting started at the beginning of the day or period.

Make a specific routine out of lining up for recess, lunch, etc.

At the beginning of gym classes (or the equivalent), where wild horseplay is at a maximum, establish fixed procedure for taking roll (perhaps by having students stand on numbers painted on the floor), for determining activities to be participated in, etc.

Nonpunitive exile. In some cases pupils get carried away by anger, frustration, or uncontrollable giggling. If you feel that this is nonmalicious behavior and that the student is simply not able to control himself, ask him to leave the room.

Examples

"Herman, maybe you'd better go out and get a drink of water or do push-ups in the hall or something. We'll see you back here in five minutes."

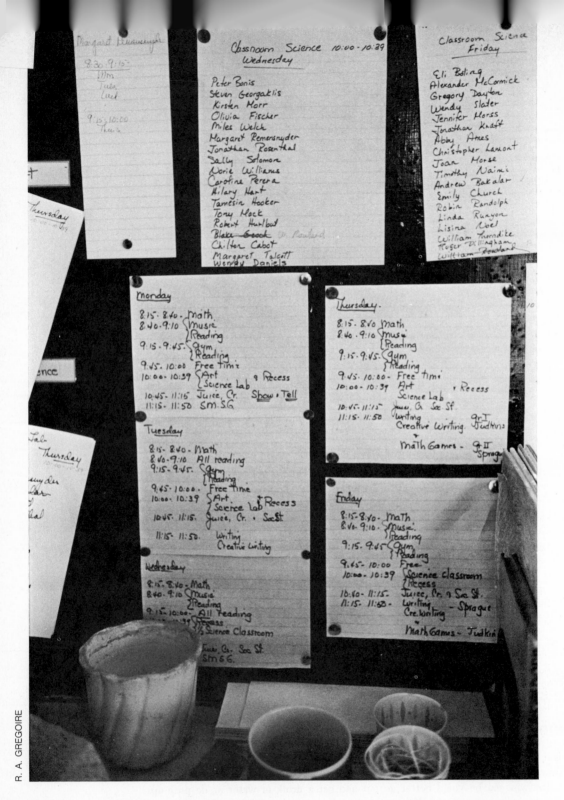

"Make sure they know what they are supposed to be doing . . . and try to have a variety of activities to choose from."

Some high schools have "quiet rooms"—supervised study halls that take extra students any time during a period, no questions asked.

Use of restraint. A student who loses control of himself to the point of endangering other members of the class may have to be physically restrained. However, such restraint should be protective, not punitive; that is, don't shake or hit. This technique is most effective with younger children; if the pupils are bigger or stronger than the teacher, it may be imprudent. (Even if the high school teacher *is* bigger, such control is usually not appropriate at the secondary level.)

Example

If a boy completely loses his temper and starts to hit another child, lead him gently but firmly away from the other pupils, or sit him in a chair and keep a restraining hand on his shoulder.

MARION BERNSTEIN

"A student who loses control of himself . . . may have to be physically restrained . . . such restraint should be protective, not punitive . . ."

✓ **Removing seductive objects.** If certain objects or fellow students are too tempting for pupils, the wise thing to do is put temptation behind them.

    Examples

        If an elementary-grade pupil gets carried away using a projector or stapler or paper cutter or whatever, put it away for a while.

        If several high school boys find themselves infatuated by a shapely, tight-sweatered, miniskirted coed, have her sit in the back of the room—behind some of the larger, dumpier girls in the class.

✓ **Anticipatory planning.** Some classroom situations are particularly conducive to misbehavior. If a certain activity seems loaded with opportunities for mischief, try to prepare the class ahead of time and emphasize the need for control.

    Example

        When an elementary school class is going to visit the local newspaper plant or the equivalent, stress the importance of not touching anything, keeping away from the machines, paying strict attention to the guide, etc.

    Most of these techniques fall under the category of prevention. The following techniques involve prevention but also function to encourage more constructive behavior.

REALITY AND VALUE APPRAISAL

As Redl and Wattenberg put it, "One of the goals of education is to enable people to increase the areas in which they can be guided by intelligence and conscience rather than by blind impulse, fear or prejudice" (1959, p. 358). The approaches to be presented now "appeal to children's sense of fairness and strengthen their ability to see the consequence of their actions" (p. 358).

✓ **Direct Appeals.** When appropriate, point out the connection between conduct and its consequences. This is most effective if it is done concisely and if the technique is not used too often.

    Examples

        "We have a rule that there is to be no running in the halls. Herman forgot the rule, and now he's down in the nurse's office having his bloody nose taken care of. It's too bad Mr. Harris opened his door just as Herman went by. If Herman had been walking, he would have been able to stop in time."

        "If everyone would stop shouting, we'd be able to get this finished and get out to recess."

✓ **Criticism and encouragement.** Sometimes it is necessary to criticize a particular student. It is preferable to do so in private, but often public criticism is the only possibility. (And it has the advantage of setting an example for other pupils.) In such cases you should do your best to avoid ridiculing or humiliating the student. Public humiliation may make a child hate you and school, arouse a counterattack, or cause withdrawal. One way to minimize the negative aftereffects of criticism is to tack on some encouragement in the form of a hint as to how the backsliding can be replaced by more positive behavior.

Examples

If a student doesn't take subtle hints (such as stares), you might say, "*Herman*, you're disturbing the class (or whatever). We all need to concentrate on this." It sometimes adds punch if you make this remark when your back is turned while you are writing on the board or helping some other student.

Act completely flabbergasted, as though the misbehavior seems so inappropriate you can't comprehend it. A kindergarten teacher used this technique to perfection. She would say, "Herman! Is that *you*?" (Herman has been belting Lucy with a shovel.) "I can't believe my eyes. I can't *imagine* you doing such a thing." And you never saw more repentant, eager-to-please students. Obviously, this gambit can't be used too often, and the language and degree of exaggeration have to be altered a bit for older pupils. But indicating that you *expect* good behavior and providing an immediate opportunity for the backslider to substitute good deeds for bad ones can be very effective—provided your pupils like and respect you enough to want to please you.

✓ **Defining limits.** In learning about rules and regulations children go through a process of testing the limits. Two-year-olds particularly, when they have learned how to walk and talk and manipulate things, feel the urge to assert their independence. In addition, they need to find out exactly what the house rules are. (Does Mommy *really* mean it when she says, "Don't take the pots out of the cupboard"? Does Daddy *really* mean it when he says, "Don't play with that hammer"?) Older children do the same thing, especially with new teachers and in new situations. The technique of defining limits includes not only establishing rules (as noted earlier) but also enforcing them.

Examples

Either establish general class rules or develop specific ones as the occasion demands. (Suggestions on how to do this were given earlier.)

When someone tests the rules, show that they are genuine and that there *are* limits.

✓ **Postsituational follow-up.** Classroom discipline occasionally has to be applied in a tense, emotion-packed atmosphere. When this happens, it often helps to have a postmortem discussion—in private, if an individual is involved, with the whole class if it was a group-wide situation.

Examples

In a private conference: "Herman, I'm sorry I had to ask you to leave the room, but you were getting kind of carried away."

"Well, everybody, things got a bit wild during those group-work sessions. I want you to enjoy yourselves, but we practically had a riot going, didn't we? And that's why I had to yell a bit. Let's try to hold it down to a dull roar tomorrow."

Marginal use of interpretation. Analysis of behavior can sometimes be made while it is occurring, rather than afterward. The purpose here is to help students become aware of potential trouble and make efforts to control it.

Example

To a restless and cranky prelunch class you might say, "I know you're getting hungry and that you're restless and tired, but let's give it all we've got for ten minutes more. I'll give you the last five minutes for some free visiting time."

The value of these techniques is that they appeal to self-control and imply trust and confidence on the part of the teacher. However, they may become ineffective if used too often, and that is why so many different techniques have been noted. The larger your repertoire, the less frequently you will have to repeat your various gambits and ploys. If the influence techniques just noted don't produce results or if they are just not appropriate, it may be necessary to resort to some form of retribution.

RETRIBUTION

When efforts at prevention and subtle control fail, you may occasionally have to resort to forms of retribution. If the misbehavior is a *fait accompli*, you have no choice but to require the guilty party to pay his debt to society. This is a part of education, too. In one sense retribution is desirable in that it presumably teaches students that they cannot break rules of conduct with impunity. But there are many negative aspects to any form of punishment. The learning-theory concept of generalization focuses attention on the major disadvantage: A punished child may come to associate hate and fear with all aspects of school and education. This suggests that you should make retribution as gentle as possible while still demonstrating to the misbehaver that he should not make the same mistake again. Here are some techniques to consider when you have no choice but retribution:

Try to "make the punishment fit the crime." This is one of the most commonly noted rules of retribution, but it is often difficult to put into practice. If you can think of compensating behavior that is directly related to the transgression, all the better.

Examples

If a student has been playing around during class, it is appropriate to have him stay in during recess and do the work that had been assigned. (If he tells you smugly that by state law he has to have recess, just tell him he has already *had* his recess.)

If a student knocks over a vase of flowers during some horseplay, have him clean it up.

_____

_____

_____

✓**Withhold a privilege.** This is related to the point just mentioned.

Example

If repeated requests to hold down the chatter go unheeded, enforce silence for a day or two. Emphasize that the privilege will be reinstated when everyone has demonstrated control.

_____

_____

_____

✓**Use detention.** This time-honored technique is not easy to apply in a day of individualized scheduling but may be effective. It is usually unwise to require work on school subjects while the culprit is putting in his time, however. A student forced to do math or reading in a situation loaded with guilt, anger, and unpleasantness may come to associate these feelings with academic matters.

Examples

If the second row from the window is fooling around instead of getting ready for recess, detain them three minutes after the rest of the class goes howling out the door.

An incorrigible talker might be asked to write a theme on "Why Talking in the Class Disturbs Others." (Perhaps he really hadn't *thought* about it.) Having students write out sentences such as "I shall not talk in class" is ineffective in most cases. The writing is often carried out automatically, and while the writer is mechanically inscribing a whole row of *I*'s, he may be thinking of what a louse you are instead of the significance of the statement. For younger children, this can be a form of torture, especially if an unrealistic number of repetitions is required. One mother, for example, stayed up until midnight giving moral support to her second grader as he laboriously wrote out *five hundred* "I will not talk in class" statements. The poor child had bleary eyes and writer's cramp and was in a state of nervous exhaustion by the time he finished. (The mother felt she had to go through with it once the task had been imposed by the teacher lest the boy decide that his parents would intercede on his behalf whenever he got in trouble. At the end of the year she did tell the teacher what she thought of her.)

_____

_____

_____

In dealing with disruptive behavior, consider "punitive" exile. One of the techniques noted by Redl and Wattenberg was "nonpunitive exile." It may also be necessary to use what amounts to *punitive* exile. A pupil who deliberately misbehaves and continues to disrupt the class—despite your efforts to get him under control—may have to be exiled in retribution. The recalcitrant pupil may be sent to a "quiet room" or to the principal's office or to any appropriate "solitary confinement" area. As with nonpunitive exile, it is usually desirable to set a time limit so the student is invited to return once he has paid his debt to classroom society.

If you routinely send misbehavers out in the hall or to a "quiet room" and require them to stay there until the end of the period, you may actually encourage mischief. Any time a pupil is bored and wants a change of scenery, he causes enough trouble to merit banishment—or escape. In other words, exile only works as retribution when what you are doing in class is reasonably interesting. (You may be able to minimize the use of exile by putting into practice the suggestions for preventing mischief due to boredom that were noted a few pages back.)

Make an appointment for a private conference. If none of the milder techniques are effective or if milder techniques are tried and only arouse more hostility, it may be well to schedule a private conference. This is preferable to a confrontation before the entire class—not only for the sake of the pupil but also for your own protection. When you find yourself face to face with the misbehaver, it is probably a good policy to let him have his say. Perhaps he just lost control, regrets his action, and wants to make amends. For your part, you might simply explain why you had to ask him to stop. It is helpful to finish such interviews on as positive a note as possible. Try to get across the point that you intend to let bygones be bygones and that you confidently expect better behavior in the future. (Some of the techniques noted under "Situational Assistance" apply here as well.)

If openly defied, appeal to an outside authority. When defiance is open and the behavior is not cut short by the suggestion of a personal conference, it's probably time to obtain an arbiter in the form of the principal or vice-principal. For example, you ask a student to go to a "quiet room" and he refuses. He either implies or directly says, "I won't go, and what are you going to do about it?" If you are a petite female lacking a black belt in judo, you won't have much of a problem deciding what to do. On the other hand, if you are a former middle linebacker and eager to show the boys in the class that you are still in shape, you might be tempted to do something dramatic. The wise course of action—regardless of your sex, size, and wrestling ability—is calmly to ask some member of the class to get the principal (or other authority designated for disciplinary control). Then go back to the lesson.

Try to avoid appealing to an outside authority unless all other measures have failed; in a sense, it is an admission that you can't handle the problem yourself. Yet you should face the fact that sometimes you will encounter such cases. There may be an impossible-to-avoid personality clash, or a pupil may be the victim of such disturbing experiences that he can't help himself, or circumstances may simply conspire to get him out on a limb. It is then far better to get the troublemaker out of the room. A running battle kept up all period or all day makes everyone suffer and severely curtails learning. It is a good idea to find out who the responsible authority is as soon as you report for your first job; you will be more than a bit embarrassed if you send a pugnacious pupil to the principal only to have him sent back two minutes later.

"... schedule a private conference ..."

How Do You Feel about Corporal Punishment or Shame and Ridicule?

From time to time an incident is reported in the newspapers that calls attention to corporal punishment. Usually, parents are suing the school system because their son (less frequently, their daughter) was paddled. The complaint centers around what this has done to the psychological well-being of the victim. In rare cases it also involves his physical well-being. What do you think of corporal punishment? What are its advantages and disadvantages? Do you approve of it or disapprove? If you approve, then how, when, to whom, and by whom should it be administered?

A related question centers around the use of shame and ridicule. Some teachers' disciplinary techniques are designed to embarrass the child in front of his peers. Perhaps you once had a teacher who resorted to placing a big piece of adhesive tape over the mouth of a talker, or drawing a small circle toward the bottom of the board and forcing the pupil to bend over and touch his nose to it, or requiring a gum-chewer to stick the wad on his nose and stand in front of the class, or the like. Certain teachers defend these methods as necessary. However, in view of the many less embarrassing techniques previously noted, this does not seem a valid argument. Do teachers who deliberately embarrass pupils do so only to teach them a lesson, or is there a sadistic element involved?

If you think of any appropriate forms of retribution used on you or your classmates that don't fit under any of the categories discussed, note them in the space below.

_____

_____

_____

✓ *4. Whenever you have to deal harshly with a student, make an effort to reestablish rapport.*

If you find yourself forced to use one of the more drastic forms of retribution just described, make a point of having a private "peace conference" with your antagonist as soon as possible. Otherwise, he is likely to remain just that—an antagonist—for the rest of the year. It's too much to expect the student to come to you of his own volition and apologize. *You* should institute the peace conference, then explain that the punishment has cleared the air as far as you are concerned and that he will start with a clean slate. But you shouldn't be surprised if a recalcitrant pupil doesn't respond overtly with signs or words of gratitude. Perhaps some of the causes of his misbehavior lie outside of school, and something you did or said may have been merely the last straw. But even if you get a sullen reaction, it is desirable at least to indicate your willingness to meet him more than halfway.

At the elementary level you can frequently make amends simply by giving the child some privilege, for example, passing out paper or being ball monitor at recess. One excellent teacher made it a point to praise a child for some positive action shortly after a severe reprimand.

✓ *5. Try to avoid threats.*

If at all possible, avoid a showdown in front of the class. In a confrontation before the whole group you are likely to get desperate. You may start out with a "Yes, you will"—"No, I won't" sort of duel and end up making a threat on the spur of the moment. Frequently, it will be impossible to make good on the threat, and you will lose face. It's far safer and better for everyone to settle extreme differences in private. When two people are upset and angry with each other, they inevitably appear silly at best and completely ridiculous at worst. You lose a great deal more than a student does by having this performance take place in front of the class. In fact, a student may actually gain prestige by provoking you successfully.

Perhaps the worst temptation of all is to try to get back at the entire class by making a blanket threat of a loss of privilege or detention. It hardly ever works and tends to lead to a united counterattack by the class. One elementary school teacher had the reputation of telling her class at least once a year that they would not be allowed to participate in the Spring Play-Day if they didn't

". . . avoid a showdown in front of the class . . ."

behave. By the time pupils reached this grade, they had been tipped off by previous students that she always made the threat but never carried it out. They behaved accordingly. And suppose, in a fit of pique, you tell your class that they must "all stay in forty-five minutes after school." What will you do when they start chattering in a chorus about bus schedules, car pools, music lessons, dentist appointments, paper routes, etc.? You can usually avoid such nightmares by putting a stop to the problem before it begins to snowball.

6. *Be prompt, consistent, reasonable.*

No attempt to control behavior will be effective if it is remote from the act that provokes it. For a troublemaker to comprehend the relationship between his behavior and the counterreaction, one must quickly follow the other. Don't postpone dealing with the pupil or make vague threats to be put into effect sometime in the future (such as taking away the privilege of participating in Play-Day). By the time the act of retribution comes due, the pupil has forgotten what he did wrong. He then feels resentful and persecuted and has the idea that you are acting out of sheer malice. A frequent reaction is more misbehavior in an urge to "get even." (He doesn't remember that *you* are the one doing the evening up.) On the other hand, retribution that is *too* immediate, that is, applied when a student is still extremely upset, may also be ineffective. At such times, it is often better to wait a bit before requiring restitution.

Being consistent about classroom control can save a lot of time, energy, and misery. Strictness one day and leniency the next, or roughness on one pupil and gentleness with another, invites all students to test you every day—just to see whether this is one of your good days or one of your bad ones or whether they can get away with something more frequently than others do. Having a set of rules is an excellent way to encourage yourself to be consistent.

Harshness in meting out retribution encourages rather than discourages more extreme forms of misbehavior. If a pupil is going to get into a lot of trouble for even a minor offense, he will probably figure he should get his money's worth. In the early days of Merrie England all offenses—from picking pockets to murder—were punishable by death. The petty thief quickly became a murderer; it was a lot easier (and less risky) to pick the pocket of a dead man and, since the punishment was the same, eminently more sensible. The laws were eventually changed to make punishment appropriate to the degree of the offense. Keep this in mind when you dispense justice.

7. *Consider using behavior modification techniques.*

Many of the techniques that have been noted—particularly stating rules, using techniques planned in advance, and being prompt and consistent—are used in a highly systematic fashion in the behavior modification approach to classroom control. In Chapters 5 and 9 you were acquainted with the techniques of behavior modification, including systematic use of praise and Premack's principle (Grandma's rule). Principles of operant conditioning are also applied in maintaining class control. Wesley C. Becker, Siegfried Engelmann, and Don R. Thomas suggest these strategies for classroom management:

Using behavior modification

1. Specify in a positive way the rules that are the basis for your reinforcement. Emphasize the behavior you desire by praising children who are following the rules. Rules are made important by providing reinforcement for following them. Rules may be different for different kinds of work, study, or play periods. Limit the rules to five or less.
   As the children learn to follow the rules, repeat them less frequently, but continue to praise good classroom behavior.

2. Relate the children's performance to the rules. Praise behavior, not the child. Be specific about behavior that exemplifies paying attention or working hard: "That's *right*, you're a hard worker." "You watched the board all the time I was presenting the example. That's paying attention." "That's a good answer. You listened very closely to my question." "Jimmy is really working hard. He'll get the answer. You'll see."
   Relax the rules between work periods. Do not be afraid to have fun with your children when the work period is over.

3. Catch the children being good. Reinforce behavior incompatible with that which you wish to eliminate. Reinforce behavior that will be most beneficial to the child's development. In the process of eliminating disruptive behavior, focus on reinforcing tasks important for social and cognitive skills.
4. Ignore disruptive behavior unless someone is getting hurt. Focus your attention on the children who are working well in order to prompt the correct behavior from the children who are misbehaving.
5. When you see a persistent problem behavior, look for the reinforcer. It may be your own behavior. (1971, p. 171)

Your reactions to these strategies, as to previously discussed applications of operant conditioning, will depend on your feelings about guided experience as opposed to free education and also your general conception of the causes of behavior (whether they are due entirely to experience or are the result of a degree of inner choice).

The behavior modification approach calls attention to the ways your students will respond to your behavior, to the need for consistency, and to possible ways you might inadvertently reinforce the very behavior you would like to prevent. However, the same possible weaknesses noted in evaluating applications of principles of operant conditioning to learning and motivation also apply to classroom control: Techniques described by Becker, Engelmann, and Thomas may be effective only with young children, your role in the class may be that of manipulator and dispenser of rewards, extensive use of reinforcement may lead to satiation, control will be extrinsic. In addition, some of the disadvantages of autocratic and dominative classroom atmospheres may result if you are too concerned about shaping behavior.

To make the most of the advantages of behavior modification while minimizing the disadvantages, you might follow the procedure recommended in discussing motivation and urge students to shape their own behavior. You might do this by asking them to help you establish rules when rules seem necessary and to control their own behavior, perhaps by using a checklist such as that devised by Sorensen, Schwenn, and Bavry (Figure 9-3, p. 440).

A question that comes to mind most directly in regard to behavior modification techniques, but also applies to this entire discussion of classroom control, is: How much control is really necessary? For example, if you insist that your students line up with precision to go out to recess, are you doing so to avoid a jam at the door, or are you perhaps enjoying the power of knowing that you can get pupils to obey your commands? If you shape conscientious work at desks by praising only students who do their work quietly and with apparent industry, are you doing so to instill desirable study habits or perhaps to make classroom life easier for you?

If you find that you are devoting considerable time to shaping classroom behavior, you might analyze your motives: Is the behavior you are trying to produce really necessary and beneficial, or are you controlling for the sake of control? Children should learn to control their impulses and to respect the rights of others, but they should also learn to be self-sufficient and to be capable of making independent decisions. If students are conditioned (and that is exactly what occurs in behavior modification) to respond without thinking when a person in authority gives a command, their capability for independent thought and action may be diminished. In *Brave New World* (1932), Aldous Huxley described a society in which techniques of classical conditioning were used to make citizens easier to control. The application of principles of operant conditioning is not as extreme, and the consequences are more susceptible to analysis by those who are manipulated, but the end result of using too much behavior modification could lead to the sort of behavior that Huxley described in his novel.

8. When you have control, ease up—some.

It is extremely difficult, if not impossible, to establish a controlled atmosphere after allowing anarchy. Don't make the mistake of thinking you will be able to start out without any control and suddenly take charge. It may work, but in most cases you will have an armed truce or a cold war on your hands. It is far better to start out on the strict side, and then ease up a bit after you have established control. (Remember the results of the Lippitt and White study: Groups that started out under democracy resented authority.) Being strict doesn't mean being unpleasant or dictatorial; it simply means that everyone in the room is aware that they are expected to respect the rights of others.

Establishing Self-control

In sorting out your thoughts in regard to general classroom control and specific influence techniques, you might consider the question of *self*-control. The human infant starts life completely dependent on his parents for survival. As he matures, he is encouraged and assisted to develop increasingly greater independence. Perhaps the most important single goal of development is for the child eventually to become an autonomous individual. A qualification to this independence is that he should be able to make constructive compromises with the restrictions imposed by society. These include group codes that are necessary to permit people to get along with one another and laws and regulations that are established and enforced by those in authority. The problem is: How do you encourage a child to become self-controlled and independent, yet able to accept the essential limitations imposed by others without either losing his individuality or becoming so upset by not being wholly free that he is unable to function constructively? A related problem centering around self-control is: What is the best way to encourage children to become self-reliant and persevering?

Some theorists maintain that the development of self-control is the concern of the parents and that the schools have no business interfering in such matters. Another point of view is that since school is the primary if not the only experience with group living most young people have, it is impossible for teachers to avoid the issue of training for group living. Furthermore, school is the primary "occupation" of children, so pupils will inevitably be concerned with developing work skills and attitudes. The question therefore is not "Should teachers be concerned about such things?" but "How can teachers go about encouraging desirable traits?" With these points as a frame of reference, consider a few different opinions on the nature of self-control.

Neill on Self-discipline

At Summerhill, A. S. Neill strives to establish self-regulation of behavior. He emphasizes, however, that this does not mean a child is allowed to do whatever he pleases. There is a distinction between freedom and license. As Neill puts it, "In the disciplined home, the children have *no* rights. In the spoiled home, they have *all* the rights. The proper home is one in which children and adults have *equal* rights. And the same applies to school" (1960, p. 107).

Neill's analysis of self-discipline ✓

In evaluating these statements, you should keep in mind that Summerhill is a miniature world of fifty citizens. All decisions are made at meetings that every member of the school attends, and each individual is allowed to vote. If one pupil complains that another is doing something that disturbs him (for example, practicing his electric guitar at 3:00 A.M.), all members of the school decide if this is an infringement of individual rights. If they agree that it is, a rule is established to control the behavior. If the rule is violated, a fine is assessed or some privilege is withdrawn. Graduates of Summerhill report that this policy assists them to gain direct experience in respecting the rights of others and in understanding the need for rules and regulations. If you decide to use some modification of the Summerhill technique in establishing rules in your classroom, however, you should keep in mind that making *all* decisions by participatory democracy can be an extremely frustrating, time-consuming process. It may also be unwise to use this approach with younger pupils because they will not be capable of moral relativism, and the number of rules they suggest and the penalties they assess may become excessive. Furthermore, as a teacher you will not have the freedom to practice complete equality, since it will be your responsibility to protect school property. Neill explains the "freedom-not-license" idea in this way:

It must be emphasized again and again that freedom does not involve spoiling the child. If a baby of three wants to walk over the dining table, you simply tell him he must not. He must obey, that's true. But on the other hand, you must obey him when necessary. I get out of small children's rooms if they tell me to get out. (P. 107)

In a school situation, such a policy would be impossible to follow, since the equipment and furnishings do not belong to individual pupils as is true of the contents of a child's room at Summerhill. (Suppose a student is abusing a $300 microscope in a science activity center of an open classroom and he tells you to go away when you come over to tell him to stop. Would you do so?) Neill recognizes this problem and observes: "In actual practice, there is, of course, authority. Such authority might be called protection, care, adult responsibility. Such authority sometimes demands obedience, but at other times gives obedience" (p. 156).

In a public school classroom, the most practical way to put this philosophy into practice might be to allow students considerable freedom of choice, but within limits you establish—after you have explained or asked them to discuss *why* rules are necessary to protect the rights of others and to insure that books and equipment will not be abused so that all may be able to use them. The value of such a policy is suggested by the results of a study on self-esteem.

Values of Adult Control

In *The Antecedents of Self-esteem*, Stanley Coopersmith reports on an extensive investigation of self-esteem in elementary school pupils. Fifth-grade teachers were asked to rate their pupils on an inventory that reflected self-confidence, level of aspiration, and related factors. Several other measures were taken, and students who rated highest on self-esteem were studied intensively. The kinds of child-rearing practices used by their parents were also investigated. Here is a brief summary of some of the conclusions:

Coopersmith study: value of setting limits in encouraging self-esteem

> Parents of children with high self-esteem are concerned and attentive toward their children; . . . they structure the worlds of their children along lines they believe to be proper and appropriate and . . . they permit relatively great freedom within the structures they have established. . . .
>
> Definite and forced limits are associated with high rather than low self-esteem . . . families which establish and maintain clearly defined limits permit *greater* rather than less deviation from conventional behavior, and freer individual expression. . . .
>
> Other things being equal, limits and rules are likely to have enhancing and facilitating effects. . . . Parents who have definite values, who have a clear idea of what they regard as appropriate behavior, and who are able and willing to present and enforce their beliefs are more likely to rear children who value themselves highly. (1967, pp. 236–237)

Coopersmith offers this explanation for the results of his study:

> Well-defined limits provide the child with a basis for evaluating his present performance as well as facilitating comparisons with prior behavior and attitudes. . . . The child learns that there is indeed a social reality that makes demands, provides rewards, and punishes violations. . . . This leads to differentiation between self and environment and increases self-definition. (P. 238)

As you sort out your thoughts about the kind of leader you plan to be, you are urged to consider these conclusions. If you establish well-defined limits and allow freedom within these limits, you may help your students understand that there is a social reality that makes demands and thereby encourage self-definition and eventually self-control.

Summary

This chapter has provided a variety of suggestions for establishing and maintaining classroom control. In creating a favorable classroom climate, you should take into account the impact of the general style of leadership you use. Ordinarily, an approach that emphasizes firmness but in which the leader has regard for student opinions is to be preferred to rigid, arbitrary authoritarianism.

Another way to establish control is to analyze common causes of misbehavior and take steps to anticipate and perhaps eliminate actions stemming from them. Despite your efforts at prevention, however, incidents of misbehavior will be almost inevitable. Handling them will be facilitated if you plan specific techniques ahead of time. To this end, you have been offered a number of influence techniques and urged to add others of your own. In conclusion, you were asked to speculate about using limits to help students develop self-control.

Suggestions for Further Reading, Writing, Thinking, and Discussion

15-1 *Analyzing Class Atmospheres You Have Experienced*

The Lippitt and White study and the observations of Anderson will seem more significant if you think about the different class atmospheres you have experienced. Look again at the descriptions of democratic, autocratic, and laissez-faire leaders (pages 696–697) and recall a teacher who most closely exemplified each type. Then record your recollection of how you and your classmates reacted to the classroom atmosphere. Or compare the class atmosphere you found most agreeable as a student with the one you found most disagreeable. Regardless of your approach, try to highlight the characteristics of the desirable and undesirable class "climates" and record the implications.

15-2 *Sampling Friedenberg's Views on "Colonial Treatment" of Adolescents*

In *Coming of Age in America* (1965) Edgar Z. Friedenberg argues that American "adolescents are among the last social groups in the world to be given the full nineteenth-century colonial treatment" (p. 4). Comparing youth workers to missionaries, he suggests that even in the better high schools of America teachers and administrators are primarily concerned with "control, distrust and punishment" (p. 36). He raises a basic question in the book: What does it cost in individual freedom and dignity to provide justice and equality in a mass society? If you are concerned about excessive control of young people, Friedenberg's analysis will interest you. Chapter 1 describes the general theme of the book. Chapter 2 gives his observations on what a typical American high school is like. (Compare your recollections of life in high school with the picture offered by Friedenberg.) Chapter 3 describes his research. Chapter 4 includes a critique of teachers ("every high school student can be virtually certain that he will experience successive defeat at the hands of teachers with minds of really crushing banality" p. 181), and the final chapter concludes with prescriptions for reform (widespread use of programmed instruction and much more stringent selection of teachers). You might read some sections of *Coming of Age in America,* summarize the arguments, and note your own reactions.

15-3 *Developing a Personal List of Dos and Don'ts for Classroom Control*

The influence techniques described in this chapter may be more meaningful if you analyze your own experiences with classroom control. Think back to techniques you felt were excessively harsh or cruel. Were there incidents in which a teacher embarrassed or humiliated a child or caused considerable mental anguish? If so, describe the situation and then use it as a basis for drawing up a list of techniques to be avoided at all costs. You might also develop a set of procedures you definitely want to try.

15-4 *Sampling Neill's Views on Discipline*

In *Summerhill* (1960), A. S. Neill comments on the advantages of self-discipline. The sequence of topics in this book is a bit disorganized, but if you read "Self-Government" (page 45), "The Unfree Child" (page 95), "The Free Child" (page 104), "Obedience and Discipline" (page 155), and "Rewards and Punishments" (page 162), you will have a fairly complete picture of Neill's views on how children should learn self-control. Whether you read any of the sections noted above or a different account of Neill's views on discipline, note the points that impress you the most and add your own reactions.

15-5 *Reacting to Ginott's Suggestions on Discipline*

Haim Ginott has written two best sellers on the subject of communication between parents and their offspring. *Between Parent and Child* (1965) will be of interest to you if you will be teaching at the elementary level. *Between Parent and Teenager* (1969) is more appropriate if you will be teaching at the secondary level. The basic ideas stressed in these books are applied more directly to education in *Teacher and Child* (1971). All three books describe how parents and teachers can make use of techniques similar to those of Rogers's nondirective therapy. There is considerable emphasis on assisting the child to understand his own feelings. Suggestions are offered on how to praise and criticize, and how to achieve a balance between permissiveness and limits to help children develop responsibility, self-control, and independence. Not all of the methods described in these books can be used by teachers at all levels, and you may disagree with some of Ginott's recommendations, but as a general guide for establishing and maintaining classroom control his ideas can be quite helpful. If you read any of these books list the points you think might be useful later.

15-6 *Reading a More Complete Account of Classroom Control*

For a more comprehensive analysis of common causes of behavior problems and suggestions on how to handle them, *Mental Hygiene in Teaching* (2nd ed.,

1959) by Redl and Wattenberg is especially recommended. Chapter 10 is devoted to "Group Life in the Classroom," Chapter 11 to "The Psychological Roles of Teachers"; Chapter 13 presents a list of "Influence Techniques," and Chapter 14 notes "Some Common Dilemmas Teachers Face." Another excellent book on this subject (available as a paperback) is *Psychology in the Classroom* (2nd ed., 1968) by Rudolf Dreikurs. Part I deals with "Basic Principles," Part II with "Practical Applications." If you will be teaching at the secondary level and you want a down-to-earth list of dos and don'ts, you might browse through *The Teacher's Survival Guide* (1967) by Jenny Gray, subtitled "How to Teach Teen-agers and Live to Tell About It!" Blunt and breezy in style, the book is both entertaining and informative. If you sample one of these books, or a similar volume, note ideas that strike you as potentially valuable.

15-7 *Reading About Special Schools for "Incorrigibles"*

Two special New York City schools are described in *The Angel Inside Went Sour* (1971) by Esther Rothman and *Nine Rotten Lousy Kids* (1972) by Herbert Grossman. Rothman describes her experiences as principal of a school for girls considered impossible to handle in regular classrooms. For information about teaching such students, you might sample Chapter 5, "Requiem for a Curriculum," Chapter 6, "The Myth of Discipline," and Chapter 10, "Developing Self-Esteem: A Therapeutic Approach." *Nine Rotten Lousy Kids* is a day-by-day log kept by the teachers in a school for teen-age boys who were to be sent to residential treatment centers, state training schools, or mental hospitals. To sample this book, read one or two sections about incidents that occurred and how they were handled. If you read parts of either of these books, you might note techniques you could use with difficult-to-handle students in your classes.

Recommended Reading in *Psychology Applied to Teaching: Selected Readings*

If you would like to do further reading in books or articles mentioned in this chapter (and in the preceding "Suggestions for Further Reading, Writing, Thinking, and Discussion") without having to track down several separate volumes, you might peruse *Psychology Applied to Teaching: Selected Readings* (Boston: Houghton Mifflin, 1972). This is a collection of excerpts from books and articles from journals in psychology. The following selection provides extended commentary on points noted in this chapter and mentioned in the "Suggestions."

Factors Which Contribute to the Nature of the Classroom Environment: "Mental Hygiene and School Learning" by Fritz Redl and William W. Wattenberg, Selection 31, p. 467. (See also Suggestion 15–6.)

16 TEACHING FOR YOUR OWN SELF-ACTUALIZATION

KEY POINTS

FACTS
Teacher dissatisfactions: large classes, too much nonacademic supervision, busywork, low salaries

Studies
Problems of teachers: self-doubt, anxiety, sense of insecurity (Jersild)

Principles
Dependence of self-actualization on prior meeting of deficit needs (Maslow)
Two conflicting forces continually exerted on individual: one toward growth and health, another toward sickness and weakness (Maslow)
Self-knowledge as main road to self-improvement (Maslow)

Methodology
Dealing constructively with frustrations

CHAPTER CONTENTS

IN THE PRECEDING TWO CHAPTERS YOU WERE ASKED TO CONSIDER HOW you might teach so as to establish an atmosphere conducive to the need gratification of your students. In this chapter you are asked to consider your own self-actualization.

Self-actualization is obviously an important issue for personal reasons, but it is important for other reasons as well. As a teacher, you will be involved in relationships with students who have little or no choice in the matter. If you are frustrated by conditions in your personal or professional life, you will not only suffer the consequences yourself but also inflict them on your students. If you are angry about something, you may take it out on your pupils or infuse them with your hostility. If you are almost totally dissatisfied with teaching, you will communicate this feeling to your pupils in an unmistakable way. This short chapter is offered, then, for your students' benefit as well as yours.

Many of the ideas on adjustment discussed in Chapter 14 can be applied to your own behavior, but this chapter presents some points relating specifically to teaching and to teachers. They are organized in a pattern similar to that followed in Chapter 14. First, the adjustment sequence of a teacher is analyzed in terms of goals and frustrations, then the various reactions to frustration are noted, and the final pages offer a number of techniques for dealing with frustrations.

Goals of Teachers

Why have you chosen a career in teaching? What made you decide to prepare for a credential? What are the goals you hope to achieve, the satisfactions you hope to gain? If you are interested in self-analysis, note these in as specific a form as possible in the space below.

_____

_____

_____

_____

_____

_____

_____

_____

_____

_____

You might compare your list with the following assortment of goals and satisfactions reported by veteran teachers: enjoyment of children or young adults, pleasure in watching students learn under one's direction, desire to tell others about a particular field of study, enjoyment in associating with young people who are exploring new ideas, desire to maintain a family tradition in teaching, eagerness to do something specific about negative conditions and behavior by influencing young people in a positive way, identification with an admired former teacher, opportunity to be one's own boss (within limits) and to develop one's own ideas and theories, job security, having summers free (for travel, study, or working at a different kind of job), mastery of a skill and earning of a credential that will permit employment now and at a later time (after raising a family), desire to do something important.

As you get closer to the point of actually stepping in front of a class of your own, you are probably wondering whether you can achieve these goals and whether teaching is going to be genuinely satisfying. The only way to find out is to give it a try. Until that time, you might speculate about how well teaching permits satisfaction of the deficiency needs as described by Maslow.

Satisfying Teachers' Needs

For a teacher, safety is pretty much equated with security. In the economic sense, teaching provides considerable security—assuming that you have few and simple pleasures. With tenure, steady employment is assured. But in terms of emotional security, the teacher is not guaranteed equivalent satisfaction. In *When Teachers Face Themselves* (1955), Arthur Jersild notes that many teachers are anxious and lonely. Jersild emphasizes "search for self," his basic thesis being that a person must understand himself before he can understand others. In his book he discusses the theoretical implications of what teachers report when they are asked to try to understand themselves.

Jersild study: self-doubt and anxiety experienced by many teachers

In addition to the personal, search-for-self aspect, Jersild's book reveals that many teachers feel insecure about their jobs. Although the causes are not examined, certain factors stand out. When some students fail to learn, a sensitive teacher can't help wondering, "Is it *my* fault?" Encountering a particularly apathetic group of pupils may cause you to brood about whether there *is* any reason for studying your pet subject. Fortunately, there are usually enough signs of flickering interest to sustain you, but you may have days when you wonder whether you belong in a classroom or in business with your brother-in-law.

The needs for love and belongingness are met very directly in the lower grades. Primary-grade students often give overt indications that they like their teacher. Undisguised looks of adoration, Valentine's Day cards, presents at the end of the year—these are unmistakable signs to the primary-grade teacher that she is liked. At the secondary level, affection is not so obvious. Because of the adolescent revolt, the teacher-authority figure may be disliked. Even pupils who do admire a teacher may take pains to conceal it. If you think you have a strong need for evidences of affection, before you make a final decision about the grade level you prefer, consider the possibility that a secondary teacher may serve as a target for teen-age hostility. It should be noted, however, that many high school teachers earn respect and subtle signs of high regard from their pupils.

While teaching is a secure occupation, which helps satisfy the need for safety, it is also low-paying, which may complicate satisfying the need for esteem. Few tangible marks of "prestige" are within the means of the person who must exist solely on a teacher's salary. In our status-oriented society, this can cause a teacher to feel unsuccessful, at least in terms of material possessions. For the most part teachers earn *in*tangible, though often much more meaningful, rewards than people do in other lines of endeavor. Awareness of doing something important and assisting young people to learn and develop their potentialities may be the major source of self-satisfaction and self-esteem for a teacher, as compared with a showplace residence in an exclusive suburb, a Cadillac, and a 75-horsepower speedboat.

Common Frustrations of Teachers

In weighing the possibility of satisfying needs through teaching, it is well to be aware of some of the "realities," frustrations, and disappointments encountered in public school education. The opening chapters of this book suggested that it might be unwise to develop too complete a theory of teaching before you discover the conditions under which you will have to operate. It was noted that you will need to balance theories proposed by educators, scientists, and humanists; that your personal inclinations toward a given style of teaching may be thwarted by the preferences of your superiors; that you must allow for the influence of school boards, administrators, and parents; that you may have to abide by curriculum decisions made by state and local committees that have not asked for your opinions; that you will have to live with some frustrating conditions imposed by lack of funds, poor buildings, and the like.

Specific frustrations teachers encounter are revealed in a survey conducted by the California Senate, which will be summarized at this point. (The complete report was published by the Senate in 1965 under the title *Let Us Teach*.) A random sample of fifteen thousand California classroom teachers filled out a lengthy questionnaire regarding their reactions to teaching conditions. The final question was: "Is there any specific thing which you think calls for state action to help teachers do a better job of teaching?" The teachers' answers, in effect, represent the types of frustrations you may realistically expect to meet. (Although the survey was restricted to teachers in California, many of the same conditions are probably found in every state of the Union.) Listed below are the answers that were supplied most often by the teachers:

Teacher dissatisfactions

1. *Smaller classes.* The commonest response to the question was: Reduce the class load. In the opinion of one teacher, "More teachers leave the teaching profession for this one reason than any other—even skinflint salaries."

2. *Less pupil supervision.* Many teachers complained that the demands of supervising pupils during so-called "free" or "preparation" periods or at lunchtime prevented them from ever having a relaxing moment to themselves during the school day or even from getting off their feet for ten minutes.

3. *More clerical help.* The amount of paper work and busywork teachers are forced to do is another big reason given for leaving the field—or at least thinking about leaving it. Much of this work is regarded as unrelated to the actual process of education, and most teachers feel that it could be done by clerks.

4. *Higher salaries.* Perhaps the most significant thing about this point is that it was mentioned less often than the first three. The low pay of teachers

is a national scandal, and although things are gradually getting better, many male teachers find it necessary to engage in moonlighting. One high school teacher reported that of the seventy male teachers in his school, only two did not moonlight. Most of them reported, however, that they were willing to take on a second job in order to remain in teaching.

5. *More supplies, equipment, and textbooks.* This pretty much boils down to need for more money to finance education.

6. *Better education colleges and courses.* The main plea here was for more emphasis on practical applications and less on theory.

7. *More preparation time.* Quite a few teachers reported that they had no free time at all during the school day to devote to class preparation.

8. *More special classes and vocational schools.* The teachers felt that more classes should be established for the mentally retarded, for the disadvantaged, for the emotionally handicapped, and for students who plan to enter business or the trades instead of going to college.

Additional reasons teachers become disenchanted to the point of resigning include lack of response from students, lack of a discernible impact on pupils, and problems in controlling the class—particularly in schools that have "traditions" of unruliness.

A Different Analysis of Common Dissatisfactions with Teaching

In one survey of specific teacher dissatisfactions (McLaughlin and Shea, 1960) the following complaints were noted, in the order indicated:

Elementary Teachers
1. Excessive clerical work
2. Cafeteria supervision
3. Too many after-school meetings
4. Inadequate physical equipment
5. Low salary

Secondary Teachers
1. Low salary
2. Indifference of students to learning
3. Too many after-school meetings
4. Heavy teaching load
5. Discipline

Many of these points parallel those mentioned in the California Senate report, partly, perhaps, because the McLaughlin and Shea survey was also conducted in California. You will note that there are some differences, however, between the two reports. And there are also marked differences between the two grade levels in this second report. If you are undecided about which level you hope to teach, the list above may help you make up your mind. It is interesting to speculate why some dissatisfactions are ranked differently by the two groups. Why, do you suppose, did secondary teachers rate salary at the top of the list and elementary teachers put it fifth?

From this brief review of goals and frustrations, it is apparent that given the proper teacher qualities and school conditions, teaching can permit a person to achieve satisfaction of the psychological needs. However, it is equally apparent that many barriers prevent the easy or direct reaching of these goals. You will not know whether the satisfactions outweigh the frustrations until you have taught at least a year or two. But it will help to think ahead to how you can make your reactions constructive ones when the inevitable frustrations occur. You will remember from the discussion of reactions to frustration in Chapter 14 that a person can make a direct attack and strive to overcome a frustrating situation; he can compromise—accepting a lesser goal and resorting to a defense mechanism to ease things; or he can withdraw from the situation, either physically or psychologically.

In many situations the most constructive thing to do is to try to overcome the frustrations. But not all frustrations *can* be overcome. Suppose, for example, the school board or a state curriculum committee or a local superintendent insists that you teach (or not teach) something in a certain way. To attack the injunction directly would be pointless since you would have no chance to succeed and would probably suffer considerable mental and professional anguish in making the attempt. (And your involvement might hinder rather than aid your students.) The more sensible thing to do would be to find legal ways to teach within the limits established but in such a fashion that you would still be able to assert your individuality.

It also makes sense to try to bring about change by making suggestions through established channels. These channels are becoming more open every year, especially with the increasing acceptance of collective bargaining as a legitimate way for teachers to express themselves. Nevertheless, even if you are successful in some of your onslaughts on the barriers—and do bring about certain improvements and do find legal ways to get around restrictions—you will still encounter frustrating conditions that are not amenable to much change. This is a fact of life all teachers (and most other people) must simply face. Then you just do what you can and make the best of it. But in making the best of it, you will be more able to maintain a satisfactory personal adjustment if you keep in mind some of the better ways of handling frustrations.

Suggestions for Dealing with Frustrations

Here is a list of suggestions on how to cope with frustrations. With the exception of points 10, 11, and 13, the statements in italics are exact quotations from *Mental Hygiene in Teaching* by Redl and Wattenberg, pages 494-497.

1. *Develop self-awareness.*

Suggestions for dealing constructively with frustrations

This is Arthur Jersild's general theme in *When Teachers Face Themselves* (1955) and *In Search of Self* (1952). The basic idea is that the better a person understands himself, the less likely he is to be overwhelmed by events he cannot control. Furthermore, a person who understands and accepts himself is better able to accept and understand others. As aids in developing self-awareness, you might read either of the books by Jersild, *On Becoming a Person* (1961) by Carl Rogers, or *Toward a Psychology of Being* (2nd ed., 1968) by Abraham Maslow.

2. *Recognize new possibilities in teaching.*

This is related to the earlier suggestion that you try to "disarm" the educational enterprise. If a "standard" technique for dealing with a problem is blocked by a directive or set of conditions, find a new and different way to do it.

3. *Evaluate dissatisfactions.*

If you find yourself dissatisfied with certain aspects of teaching, try to select those portions of the problem that *can* be dealt with and become a relaxed

fatalist about the rest. (Confucius put it in the form of the familiar prayer: Give me the strength to change what can be changed, the courage to accept what cannot be changed, and the wisdom to tell one from the other.)

4. Reevaluate total load.

If you are inundated by work and pressure mounts, it will be helpful to try to eliminate or reduce certain tensions. For example, when you are driven to the brink by having to grade term papers for five classes of thirty-five pupils, don't assign term papers unless your teaching load is adjusted.

5. Look for help on specific questions.

If you are hung up on a particular frustration, ask for ideas from your principal or an older teacher or a consultant. In some cases, all it takes is a little more experience or a different perspective to reveal a simple solution. Remember the impact of functional fixedness.

6. Deliberately expose yourself to new experiences.

Anyone who is conscientious about teaching needs periods of rest and relaxation. Functioning as an inspirational pedagogue takes a lot out of a person. For this reason it may be wise to cultivate a noneducational hobby, take a nonteaching summer job, or make the most of that three-month vacation.

7. Seek satisfactions elsewhere.

If conditions in school block the achievement of psychological needs, make a deliberate effort to find satisfaction outside the classroom. For example, a high school teacher who felt unhappy about the lack of overt acceptance and admiration of his students (not because he was a poor teacher but because high school students often make it a point not to show admiration openly) became the scoutmaster of a Boy Scout troop. Another way to satisfy partly frustrated needs is to develop a creative hobby.

8. Talk it over with friends.

One purpose of psychotherapy is to provide catharsis—the release of tension. You can get much the same result by talking over your problems with others. There is obviously a limit to how much you can impose on any one person, but an occasional legitimate gripe will rarely strain relationships with a spouse, friend, or colleague, especially if you spread the gripes around and act as a reciprocal "therapist." If you are upset about something (the furnace at home went on the blink at 3:00 A.M.), talk about it and warn the class that they had better look out for you that day.

9. Stimulate group discussion.

A variation of the preceding point is "group therapy" sessions. Gripe sessions in a cafeteria or teachers' room are often an effective way to keep body and soul together, especially if there is an element of humor in them. (Looking for the humorous side of things is a fine, all-purpose method of dealing with frustrations in or outside the classroom.)

10. *Get physical release of tension.*

When frustrations build up, you might indulge in recreational activities or in physical work to gain release. Raking leaves or mowing the lawn not only helps provide catharsis but may also provide an additional reward—the satisfaction of completing a job that has to be done. (One teacher who was known for his patience and sympathy in dealing with students was a viciously competitive tennis player on the local courts. Another even-tempered pedagogue would garden whenever she felt the need to unwind. Her back yard looked like a horticultural exhibit.)

11. *Avoid taking out your frustrations on the class.*

A primary reason for seeking release of tension through gripes or creative hobbies or physical activities is to avoid punishing your students. When you find yourself frustrated—and angry as a result—it is natural to want to take it out on those thirty-five scapegoats trapped in your room, especially if they have done more than their share in contributing to your frustration. In a sense, your students are so many sitting ducks. The temptation to shoot them down is sometimes well-nigh irresistible. A certain amount of righteous indignation is probably a good thing for genuinely guilty pupils to be exposed to at the proper time, but too often an angry teacher is more at fault than the alleged provokers. If you are upset because of your own weaknesses or inabilities and compensate by bawling out the class or giving a spot quiz, the students will realize it. A frequent consequence is that they will retaliate, and then you really *will* have some frustrations to cope with.

12. *Get professional help.*

In some cases, personal problems are of such a nature and intensity that they are beyond the help that friends can give or are too extensive to be solved by any of the suggestions noted here. If you feel that you have reached this point, the sensible thing to do is seek professional assistance. Since some frustrations may drive an individual to neurosis or psychosis, you should not regard the need for such help as an admission that you are a total failure. A person who recognizes his need for help is often in better mental health than one who refuses to acknowledge the possibility.

13. *In extreme cases, execute a strategic withdrawal.*

It sometimes happens that a teacher is caught in a bind. If you find yourself teaching in a school where you seem to be penned up in a life space consisting of nothing but negative factors, it may be best to leave the field of forces.

Chains of unfortunate circumstances or personality conflicts may lead to an intolerable situation, in which case moving to a different school or a different district may be the sensible rather than the cowardly thing to do.[1] If you discover, however, that your dissatisfactions are not with local conditions or people but that you simply do not enjoy teaching and that none of the preceding suggestions help very much, it would be logical to look for a different kind of job. At stake is not only your own personal adjustment but also the well-being of your students.

Doing Something Specific and Direct about Frustrations

Most of the suggestions just offered represent compromise or withdrawal reactions. However, there is an increasing tendency for teachers to make a "direct attack on the barrier." Until recently the teacher was expected to take just about anything without complaint. Entering the profession involved a sort of voluntary commitment to martyrdom. Typical arguments were: "If you can't stand the conditions of teaching, then you don't deserve to be a teacher" or "You have to be willing to make sacrifices if you want to teach." Now more and more teachers have decided to be less passive and fatalistic. They are determined to do something about the deplorable conditions in public education and about their own destinies. The primary weapon for bringing about change is the time-honored technique of collective bargaining.

For years teachers avoided the use of this technique for fear of jeopardizing their role as "professionals." The first breakthrough came when some teachers formed local units of the American Federation of Teachers (or United Federation of Teachers) and unabashedly called such organizations labor unions. Teachers who had previously joined the "traditional" professional organization, the National Education Association, either switched to the A.F.T. or agitated for collective bargaining within the older, well-established group. The issue was clouded and sidetracked for some time because the N.E.A. includes both administrators and teachers, which some people say is akin to having labor and management in the same organization. (For an interesting account of this arrangement, together with some thought-provoking ideas on the whole issue of "teaching power," read *The Future of Public Education*, 1960, by Myron Lieberman.) In any event, the success of several A.F.T. (or U.F.T., in New York City) strikes more or less forced the N.E.A. to resort finally to "sanctions" in their efforts to initiate change. (The officials of N.E.A. were unable to bring themselves to call a strike a strike, even though a sanction amounts to practically

---

[1] If you find that your dissatisfaction with teaching is caused primarily by the structure and bureaucracy of traditional education, you might contact the Teacher Drop-out Center, Box 521, Amherst, Mass. 01002. It has been established to assist teachers to find positions in innovative, free, and open schools.

The Values of Psychotherapy

In all his books Arthur Jersild has emphasized the importance of knowledge and acceptance of self. In attempting to gain self-knowledge and self-acceptance, some teachers have undergone psychotherapy. When Jersild (1963) interviewed over one hundred teachers who had taken this course of action, most of them reported they found the decision to undergo therapy quite a struggle. The final determination to go ahead was due to intense personal problems or to a desire to live more zestfully. Many said that they were helped in their decision by support from friends and relatives. Among the benefits attributed by these teachers to therapy were the following:

Deeper insight into the nature of anxiety (90 percent)
Less disturbance over the problem of handling anxiety (90 percent)
Ability to engage in competition with better grace (many of the group)
Less need of approval or adulation from others (many of the group)

Less distress when confronted with personal problems of students (90 percent)

Considerable change in women's attitude toward their femininity (There was less change in men's attitude toward their masculinity.)

In another study by Jersild (1962), 90 percent of a different group of teachers who were asked for their opinions about psychotherapy said they believed that unconscious factors play a big part in life. About 45 percent thought it would be a good idea if many teachers were psychoanalyzed, and over two-thirds indicated that they themselves would be willing to undergo psychoanalysis if they had the time and money.

---

the same thing.) At the present time, both the A.F.T. (or U.F.T.) and the N.E.A. are becoming more and more active in agitating for change. The number of strikes, or sanctions, increases each year, primarily because so many of them lead to improvements.

When you take your first teaching job, you may well have an opportunity to choose between joining the A.F.T., the U.F.T., and the NEA. Even if you don't have that particular choice, you may have to decide whether to vote for or against a strike, or sanction. If the demands of the organization seem reasonable and you believe they will increase your effectiveness as a teacher, you might classify your behavior as a direct attack on the barrier of frustrations. In this new era the teacher is not forced to resort only to mechanisms of compromise and withdrawal, and the consequence may be not only better conditions in the schools but also better mental health for both teachers and pupils. All of this assumes that a strike is called for positive reasons and is motivated by a desire to improve conditions in the schools and hence provide better education. Some strikes or demonstrations, however, appear to stem more

from a desire to gain release of tension or to cause trouble for those in authority than from positive feelings. Such strikes often do more harm than good.

Confronted with a decision to strike or not to strike, think back to Piaget's distinction between moral realism and moral relativism. The immature person tends to interpret things literally; thus some people who argue that *any* kind of strike or demonstration is justifiable may be functioning at an immature level. The more mature person takes into account all the circumstances. In talking about academic freedom, the more mature teacher gives careful thought to the factor of academic responsibility and tries hard to use the new teacher power only when it is needed to make things better for the students who come to school to be educated.

Increasing the Possibility of Self-actualization

The preceding discussion on satisfying the needs of safety, belongingness, and esteem—and on ways of dealing with the frustration of these needs—has emphasized deficit motivation. In terms of Maslow's hierarchy, satisfying the deficit needs sets the stage for growth motivation, satisfaction of the "being" needs, and self-actualization. Many psychologists believe that in order for children to develop more of their potential (and function in a self-actualizing way), they should have contact with adults who are functioning as especially healthy and productive individuals. Since teachers have considerable influence over students, it is only natural to speculate on how you can become a self-actualizing individual—for your students' benefit as well as your own.

The first step toward self-actualization has already been discussed: Do everything possible to satisfy the deficit needs of safety, belongingness, and esteem. Once these are taken care of, the possibility of self-actualization is enhanced. Maslow has described what self-actualizing people are like (see pp. 74–96, 103–114, and 157 of *Toward a Psychology of Being*), but he says, "We know they are that way, but not how they get that way" (1968, p. 163). He suggests that in time we may be able to trace the life histories of those who consistently function as self-actualizers and use them as models for assisting others to achieve growth motivation. Unfortunately, this has not yet been done, but Maslow's observations may help you achieve a greater degree of self-actualization on your own. They will also enable you to understand why self-actualization is such an elusive experience and why you may find yourself dominated by deficit motivation. Maslow emphasizes need gratification and awareness of regressive forces and provides some general suggestions on how to encourage growth motivation:

Stage set for self-actualization by satisfying deficit needs

> The main prerequisite to healthy growth is gratification of the basic needs. (Neurosis is very often a deficiency disease, like avitaminosis.) But we have also learned that unbridled indulgence and gratification has its own dangerous conse-quences. . . . Only to the self-disciplined and responsible person can we say, "Do as you will and it will probably be all right."
>
> We must also face squarely the problem of what stands in the way of growth, that is to say, the problems of cessation of growth and evasion of growth, of fixation, regression, and defensiveness, in a word the attractiveness of psychopathology, or as other people would prefer to say, the problem of evil.
>
> Why do so many people have no real identity, so little power to make their own decisions and choices?
>
> 1. These impulses and directional tendencies toward self-fulfillment, though instinctive, are very weak, so that, in contrast with all other animals who have strong instincts, these impulses are very easily drowned out by habit, by wrong cultural attitudes toward them, by traumatic episodes, by erroneous education. Therefore, the problem of choice and of responsibility is far, far more acute in humans than in any other species.
> 2. There has been a special tendency in Western culture, historically determined, to assume that these instinctoid needs of the human being, his so-called animal nature, are bad or evil. As a consequence, many cultural institutions are set up for the express purpose of controlling, inhibiting, suppressing and repressing this original nature of man.

*Pull of positive and
negative forces*

3. There are two sets of forces pulling at the individual, not just one. In addition to the pressures toward health, there are also fearful-regressive pressures backward, toward sickness and weakness. (Pp. 163–164)

Maslow then notes that until recently these trends have tended to make people think that "man could be saved only by extra-human forces" (p. 165). The knowledge of psychopathology and psychotherapy has reached the point where we now know "that human evil is largely (although not altogether) human weakness or ignorance, forgivable, understandable and also curable" (p. 165). He then comments on the implications of the awareness that self-knowledge and self-acceptance lead to self-actualization:

*Self-knowledge as path
of self-improvement*

1. Self-knowledge seems to be the major path of self-improvement, though not the only one.
2. Self-knowledge and self-improvement are very difficult for most people. They usually need great courage and long struggle.
3. Though the help of a skilled professional therapist makes this process much easier, it is by no means the only way. Much that has been learned from therapy can be applied to education, to family life, and to the guidance of one's own life.
4. Only by such study of psychopathology and therapy can one learn a proper respect for and appreciation of the forces of fear, of regression, of defense, of safety. Respecting and understanding these forces makes it much more possible to help oneself and others to grow toward health. False optimism sooner or later means disillusionment, anger and hopelessness.
5. To sum up, we can never really understand human weakness without also understanding its healthy trends. Otherwise we make the mistake of pathologizing everything. But also we can never fully understand or help human strength without also understanding its weaknesses. Otherwise we fall into the errors of overoptimistic reliance on rationality alone.

If we wish to help humans to become more fully human, we must realize not only that they try to realize themselves but that they are also reluctant or afraid or unable to do so. Only by fully appreciating this dialectic between sickness and health can we help to tip the balance in favor of health. (Pp. 165–166)

For a more complete discussion of these ideas, you are referred to *Toward a Psychology of Being*; the final chapter consists of forty-three basic propositions summarizing all aspects of Maslow's observations on human behavior. If you would like to expand your knowledge of yourself as a step toward self-actualization, you are urged to read and ponder those points.

Summary

In this chapter you have been asked to think about the goals you hope to achieve in teaching and to speculate on the likelihood of satisfying the need

for safety, belongingness, and esteem as you teach and work toward these goals. You have been urged to take into account that satisfaction of many of your needs will depend on the reactions of your students and that the bureaucratic nature of public education in the United States is bound to cause you numerous frustrations. You have been given suggestions for dealing with these frustrations. The chapter concluded with a résumé of some of Maslow's observations on the importance of self-knowledge and self-acceptance as a basic step toward self-actualization.

Suggestions for Further Reading, Writing, Thinking, and Discussion

16-1 *Analyzing the Goals You Hope to Achieve Through Teaching*

Since you are considering devoting your professional life to teaching, you may wish to conduct a personal analysis of the goals you hope to achieve. First list the factors that led you to work toward a credential. What experiences predisposed you to choose teaching as a profession? What goals have you in mind? Then analyze these factors with respect to the needs for safety, belongingness, and esteem. From what you know about life in the schools, do you believe you will be able to satisfy your deficiency needs as a teacher? If you have wavered between teaching and a different kind of job, which alternative seems more likely to satisfy your needs for safety, belongingness, and esteem? If you have doubts about your feelings on teaching, self-analysis may help you resolve conflicts and uncertainties.

16-2 *Estimating Your Abilities to Cope with the Frustrations of Teaching*

A survey reported in this chapter lists common dissatisfactions of teachers. Frustrations arise from large classes, too much nonacademic supervision, excessive clerical busywork, and low salaries. If you are wondering how committed you are to teaching, try estimating how much these frustrations will irritate you. If you have seriously considered another sort of job as an alternative to teaching, you might ask one or two people in that line of endeavor what their major satisfactions and dissatisfactions are. Then compare their responses to those of teachers you know or to the lists of advantages and disadvantages of teaching noted in this chapter.

16-3 *Trying to Gain Greater Understanding of Behavior,* *Including Your Own*

Presently, there is considerable interest in assisting individuals to understand their own behavior better. Humanistic psychology, the discovery approach, the perceptual view of behavior, nondirective therapy, and sensitivity training—not to mention the desire of college students for personally relevant education—are all manifestations of this trend. Basic to the concern for self-knowledge is the belief that only when a person understands his own behavior can he understand the behavior of others. If you have a general interest in self-understanding or feel that you may be better able to comprehend your students' behavior by becoming more aware of your own, explore the dynamics of adjustment. Courses on this subject are offered in the psychology departments of many colleges. Encounter groups conducted by reputable and experienced leaders provide another semiformal framework for developing self-understanding. In the absence of structured situations, or if you prefer to think things through on your own, read one or more books intended to foster understanding of behavior. You might choose from the following: *In Search of Self* (1952) by Arthur Jersild, *The Art of Growing* (1962) by Robert E. Nixon, *The Transparent Self* (1964) by Sidney M. Jourard, *Lives in Progress* (2nd ed., 1966) by Robert W. White, *Toward a Psychology of Being* (2nd ed., 1968) by Abraham H. Maslow, or *Man's Search for Himself* (1950) and *Love and Will* (1969) by Rollo May.

16-4 *Finding Out More about Transactional Analysis*

One of the best selling books of 1972 was *I'm OK—You're OK* (1967) by Thomas A. Harris. An earlier best-seller on the same general theme was *Games People Play* (1964) by Eric Berne. Both books describe *transactional analysis* (T.A.). As their popularity attests, many people have found T.A. helpful in understanding human relationships.

In *Games People Play*, Berne suggests that human relationships can be understood by taking into account the interactions of the three ego states—Parent, Adult, and Child—found in all individuals. If two people interact in such a way that both function as Adults (for example, engaging in rational interchange of ideas), or if they both realize that they are in a Parent-Child relationship (for example, one person acting as a more knowledgeable and responsible guide), things will go smoothly. If, however, one person perceives a situation as an Adult-Adult relationship (for example, a teacher saying matter-of-factly to a student, "Did you finish that assignment you said you were going to do?") while the other perceives it as a Parent-Child relationship (for example, the student thinking or saying, "You're always nagging me, just like my mother"), then the crossed transaction will lead to difficulties. The bulk of Berne's book is devoted to descriptions of *games*, which are defined as "an ongoing series of complementary ulterior transactions progressing to a well-defined predictable outcome" (p. 48), that illustrate the nature and significance of transactions.

In *I'm OK—You're OK*, Harris uses a variation of Berne's Parent-Adult-Child ego states to illuminate transactions. He suggests that there are four possible interactions between people: I'm Not OK—You're OK (for example, a child disappointing his parents), I'm Not OK—You're Not OK (for example, a disturbed child perceiving himself and others negatively or with suspicion), I'm OK—You're Not OK (for example, a psychiatrist treating a patient), I'm OK—You're OK (for example, both participants functioning in a positive way and understanding each other). The purpose of T.A. as practiced by Harris is to assist people to feel that they—*and* people they interact with—are OK most of the time.

If you would like more information about T.A., read either of these books, perhaps noting insights that strike you as illuminating.

16-5 *Investigating the Rights of Teachers*

As preparation for deciding on joining a teachers' organization or union—or simply for your own information—you might want to find out more about the constitutional rights of teachers. The American Civil Liberties Union has published an inexpensive handbook by David Rubin titled *The Rights of Teachers* (1972) that gives complete coverage of this topic.

17 EPILOGUE

The intent of this book has been to help you use your own originality in applying to your teaching what is known about the principles of psychology (or, to be more precise, what one person considers the principles of psychology that are relevant to teaching). It has been argued that you are more likely to succeed in doing this if you can grasp the larger structure of psychology as a first step.

Chapters 1 and 2 noted some of the complications that will confront you as you attempt to evolve a theory of teaching. The reconciliation (and synthesis) of ideas about teaching is complicated by the fact that general trends are derived from a tremendous number of circumscribed studies and observations in education and psychology. As a result, there are many ways these bits of information can be interpreted and combined. One consequence is that there are strong differences of opinion—as you are now well aware—regarding the proper way to teach. A related consequence is that many interpretations fit selected evidence equally well. Adding to the confusion is the impact of subtle personality factors—the interest and enthusiasm and style of the teacher. It has been noted that the general impact of a teacher frequently overrides the specific techniques used. J. M. Stephens's theory of spontaneous schooling emphasizes this point: Teachers can use almost diametrically opposed techniques and yet encourage the same amount of learning. So you should feel free—if not obligated—to develop your own personal style and theory of teaching. This book has attempted to acquaint you with some of the research evidence (and some of the conflicting interpretations of this evidence) so that you can start evolving your own theory—always taking into account the restrictions imposed by the conditions and trends in public education, which are not related to purely philosophical or psychological variables.

At the present time, traditional methods of teaching are under fire. Perhaps you have actively tried to bring about change; perhaps you have restricted yourself to thinking about how you can improve things when you become a teacher. Right now you can see things from the student point of view. In a year or two you will be on the other side of the desk. For that reason you are urged to jot down at the end of the following list, which summarizes common complaints about education, your own major gripes about the kind of teaching you have experienced.

Common Complaints about American Education

1. The impersonal nature of it all, the restricted opportunities for teachers and pupils to interact in a personal way.
2. The mass-production, assembly-line, compartmentalized character of much teaching and learning.
3. The lack of "relevance" of what is taught; meaningless memorization.
4. Extrinsic motivation; overemphasis on tests and grades.
5. Authoritarian teachers who don't allow for response or individuality.

Now look at that list and think about what you might do to minimize or eliminate these "weaknesses." Many of the most vociferously raised objections to education center around the degree of mind control that is involved and the assembly-line quality of learning, which reduces personal interaction between teacher and pupil. The overt-deterministic (man is not free) S-R point of view, the guided-experience philosophy, the programmed, departmentalized, assembly-line curriculum—all these seem, at first glance, to be extensions of what is most detested about contemporary education. Conversely, cognitive-field theory (which emphasizes individuality), the "natural" view of development, classroom practices permitting much teacher-pupil interaction over a protracted period of time—all these seem to be ideal prescriptions for reform. It appears that Bruner, Snygg and Combs, Neill, and Holt are on the right track and that Skinner and the majority of American psychologists (who are S-R oriented) and educational administrators (who reflect the "cult of efficiency" approach to education) are bent on making matters worse. A closer look reveals that things are not that simple.

Many critics of education (perhaps including yourself) are agitating for a kind of education that allows greater student initiative and power in determining the curriculum, minimization if not out-and-out abolition of tests and grades, development of seminar classes in which students and teachers will be equals as they discuss "relevant" topics, and elimination of the memorization of facts. It is argued that this kind of education will produce lifelong scholars who will be intrinsically motivated to continue to learn after they leave college, human beings of integrity and individuality rather than robots ground out by the academic assembly line. If you are in sympathy with some or all of these points, consider some questions.

Does it make sense for students to determine the curriculum in all subjects? If you have devoted several years to the study of a given subject (perhaps a technical one) and set out to teach this subject to immature pupils, aren't you in a better position to decide what should be covered and in what sequence? Presumably, your students will know little or nothing about the subject, which is why they are in the class in the first place. How can they decide what should be studied if they know nothing about the topic? Presumably you will be an authority on your subject (or subjects), so it seems only logical for you to act as an authority in the way you conduct the class. If you are merely the equal of your students, you have little reason to call yourself a teacher. You are reminded of Skinner's observations that the discovery method sometimes appears to exist only to absolve the teacher of a sense of failure and that in problem solving situations the teacher may take credit for what the student masters on his own.

Those who favor a free approach to education argue that the child will learn what he needs to know when he feels the urge to do so and that he will remember what he learns because his motives for learning will be intrinsic. However, the follow-up of the Summerhill graduates emphasized a fallacy in this line of reasoning that is related to the point just made: Is it sensible to expect an immature child to know what he needs to know or might benefit from knowing? Most graduates of Summerhill reported wishing that they had had better academic training and better teaching, implying a wish that they had been given more direction by someone older and wiser than they. Implicit in direction is organization. As noted in the discussion of learning and forgetting, structure is of considerable importance. Yet self-demand education tends to be somewhat chaotic compared with the kind of learning that takes place in a well-organized curriculum. A basic question is: Is it possible to provide guidance and organization without making students feel they are being manipulated? In your own thinking about how you propose to teach, you might make this the focus of attention instead of pondering too much about whether you should provide any direction at all.

At this period in your career, you may favor eliminating memorization, all forms of extrinsic motivation, and all tests and grades. It sounds like an idyllic academic existence—teachers and pupils just sitting around animatedly discussing the things that are *really* important. If you find yourself excited about such an approach to teaching, give it a try if you can. Perhaps you will have the rare ability it takes to function as this sort of teacher. But don't be surprised if the results aren't a conspicuous or consistent success. Most students seem to need fairly tangible incentives and signs that they have accomplished something. That is why you may come to appreciate the significance of a point made in Chapter 11: An exam may be the only way to encourage pupils to learn. A year or two from now, when you observe a "surefire" discovery topic collapse with a soft thud because no one in the class bothered to do the assigned reading in the book you permitted them to choose on their own, you may become aware of some positive attributes of tests. As for memorizing facts, in time you will probably realize that in many subjects there is no substitute for some memorization and that unless your pupils are aware of the basic ideas in a field, they will be unable to engage in discussions about it.

At the present time, techniques are being perfected that hold promise for bringing about substantial improvements in education. The two basic innovations discussed in this book—open education and mastery learning—attempt to provide freedom within a framework of guidance and to use evaluation as a means to encourage almost all students to meet high standards. You are urged to give these methods a try, since they combine desirable aspects of both structured and free education.

The intent of this brief summary is to encourage you to follow John Dewey's advice and remain open-minded about all kinds of teaching, even the "traditional" approaches. If you tend to lean toward one side at the moment, don't thrust the arguments of the opposition out of your mind just yet. Chances are, you will want and need to select ideas from every source you can find when you embark on your career as a teacher.

In Chapters 1 and 2 it was stated that the primary purpose of this book is to serve as a *framework* for your theorizing about teaching, to help you *structure* your theorizing. In order for you to become a practitioner of the art of teaching capable of applying your own originality to what scientists have learned about educational psychology, you will need to remain faithful to your own individuality but at the same time be willing to learn from every possible source. (You will also have to work *within* the present organizational setup of the schools.) If you *are* faithful to your own personality, you are almost sure to be consistent. And if you are willing to learn from scientists of every breed, from other teachers, your students, and your own experiences, you may be able to make a unique contribution to the improvement of American education.

BIBLIOGRAPHY

Adams, James F., (ed.), 1973. *Understanding Adolescence*, 2nd ed. Boston: Allyn and Bacon.

Ahman, J. Stanley, and Marvin D. Glock, 1971. *Evaluating Pupil Growth: Principles of Measurement* (4th ed.). Boston: Allyn and Bacon.

Aikin, Wilford M., 1942. *The Story of the Eight-Year Study*. New York: Harper & Brothers.

Allen, Dwight W., and Eli Seifman, (eds.), 1971. *The Teacher's Handbook*. Glenview, Ill.: Scott, Foresman.

Allport, Gordon W., 1955. *Becoming*. New Haven, Conn.: Yale University Press.

Almy, Millie C., E. Chittenden, and P. Miller, 1966. *Young Children's Thinking*. New York: Teachers College, Columbia University.

Alschuler, A. S., 1968. "How to Increase Motivation Through Climate and Structure." Achievement Motivation Development Project Working Paper No. 8, Harvard University Graduate School of Education.

Amidon, E., and N. Flanders, 1963. *The Role of the Teacher in the Classroom*. Minneapolis: Paul S. Amidon & Assoc.

Amidon, E., and E. Hunter, 1967. "Verbal Interaction in the Classroom: The Verbal Interaction Category System." In E. J. Amidon and J. B. Hough (eds.), *Interaction Analysis: Theory, Research, and Application*. Reading, Mass.: Addison-Wesley.

Anastasi, Anne, 1958. *Psychological Testing*, 2nd ed. New York: Macmillan.

Anastasi, Anne, 1968. *Psychological Testing*, 3rd ed. New York: Macmillan.

Anderson, John E., 1948. "Personality Organization in Children," *American Psychologist*, 3:409–416.

Anderson, Richard C., 1959. "Learning in Discussions: A Résumé of the Authoritarian-Democratic Studies," *Harvard Educational Review*, 29:201–215.

Arnold, Stanley (ed.), 1965. *Let Us Teach*. Report published by the Senate of the State of California.

Ashton-Warner, Sylvia, 1958. *Spinster*. New York: Bantam Books.

Ashton-Warner, Sylvia, 1963. *Teacher*. New York: Simon and Schuster.

Atkinson, J. W., 1964. *An Introduction to Motivation*. Princeton, N. J.: Van Nostrand.

Atkinson, J. W., and G. H. Litwin, 1960. "Achievement Motive and Test Anxiety Conceived as Motive to Approach Success and Motive to Avoid Failure," *Journal of Abnormal and Social Psychology*, 60:52–63.

Atkinson, Richard C., 1957. "A Stochastic Model for Rote Learning," *Psychometrika*, 22:87–94.

Atkinson, R. C., and H. A. Wilson (eds.), 1969. *Computer Assisted Instruction: A Book of Readings*. New York: Academic Press.

Ausubel, David P., 1960. "Use of Advance Organizers in the Learning and Retention of Meaningful Material," *Journal of Educational Psychology*, 51:267–272.

Ausubel, David P., 1963. *The Psychology of Meaningful Verbal Learning*. New York: Grune & Stratton.

Ausubel, David P., 1968. *Educational Psychology: A Cognitive View*. New York: Holt, Rinehart and Winston.

Axline, Virginia M., 1964. *Dibs: In Search of Self*. New York: Ballantine Books.

Ayollon, T., and N. H. Azrin, 1965. "The Measurement and Reinforcement of Adaptive Behavior of Psychotics," *Journal of Experimental Analysis of Behavior*, 8:357–383.

Back, Kurt W., 1972. *Beyond Words: The Story of Sensitivity Training and the Encounter Movement*. New York: Russell Sage Foundation.

Baer, C. J., 1958. "The School Progress of Underage and Overage Students,"

Journal of Educational Psychology, 49:17–19.

Baker, H. V., 1942. *Children's Contributions in Elementary School General Discussion.* Child Development Monographs, No. 29. New York: Teachers College, Columbia University.

Baker, J. Philip, and Janet L. Crist, 1971. "Teacher Expectancies: A Review of the Literature," in Janet D. Elashoff and Richard E. Snow (eds.), *Pygmalion Reconsidered,* pp. 48–64. Worthington, Ohio: Charles A. Jones.

Baker, Robert L., and Richard E. Schutz (eds.), 1971. *Instructional Product Development.* New York: Van Nostrand Reinhold.

Baldwin, James, 1955. *Notes of a Native Son.* New York: Dial.

Bandura, Albert, 1962. "Social Learning Through Imitation." In M. R. Jones (ed.), *Nebraska Symposium on Motivation: 1962,* pp. 211–269. Lincoln, Nebr.: University of Nebraska Press.

Bandura, Albert, 1967. "Behavioral Psychotherapy," *Scientific American,* 216(3):78–86.

Bandura, Albert, and R. Walters, 1963. *Social Learning and Personality Development.* New York: Holt, Rinehart and Winston.

Banks, James A., and Jean D. Grambs, 1972. *Black Self-Concept.* New York: McGraw-Hill.

Barber, Theodore X., and M. J. Silver, 1968. "Fact, Fiction, and the Experimenter Bias Effect," *Psychological Bulletin,* 70:1–29.

Barber, Theodore X., and others, 1969. "Five Attempts to Replicate the Experimenter Bias Effect," *Journal of Consulting and Clinical Psychology,* 33(1):1–14.

Bardwick, Judith M., 1971. *Psychology of Women: A Study of Bio-Cultural Conflicts.* New York: Harper & Row.

Bardwick, Judith M. (ed.), 1972. *Readings on the Psychology of Women.* New York: Harper & Row.

Barth, Roland S., 1972. *Open Education and the American School.* New York: Agathon.

Baruch, Dorothy W., 1952. *One Little Boy.* New York: Dell.

Barzun, Jacques, 1968. *The American University: How It Runs, Where It Is Going.* New York: Harper & Row.

Bauernfeind, Robert H., 1965. "'Goal Cards' and Future Developments in Achievement Testing," *Proceedings of the 1965 Invitational Conferences on Testing Problems.* University of Illinois.

Becker, Wesley C. (ed.), 1971. *An Empirical Basis for Change in Education.* Chicago: Science Research Associates.

Becker, Wesley C., Siegfried Engelmann, and Don R. Thomas, 1971. *Teaching: A Course in Applied Psychology.* Chicago: Science Research Associates.

Beggs, David W., III, and Edward G. Buffie (eds.), 1965. *Independent Study.* Bloomington: University of Indiana Press.

Bereiter, C., and S. Engelmann, 1966. *Teaching Disadvantaged Children in the Preschool.* Englewood Cliffs, N. J.: Prentice-Hall.

Berne, Eric, 1964. *Games People Play.* New York: Grove Press.

Bernstein, Emmanuel, 1968. "What Does a Summerhill Old School Tie Look Like?" *Psychology Today,* 2(5):37–70.

Bestor, Arthur, 1953. *Educational Wastelands.* Urbana: University of Illinois Press.

Bestor, Arthur, 1955. *The Restoration of Learning.* New York: Knopf.

Bettelheim, Bruno, 1969. *The Children of the Dream.* New York: Macmillan.

Bieri, J., 1961. "Complexity-Simplicity as a Personality Variable and Preferential Behavior." In D. W. Fiske and S. R. Maddi (eds.), *Functions of Varied Experience.* Homewood, Ill.: Dorsey Press.

Bigge, Morris L., 1971. *Learning Theories for Teachers,* 2nd ed. New York: Harper & Row.

Bigge, Morris L., and Maurice P. Hunt, 1968. *Psychological Foundations of Education,* 2nd ed. New York: Harper & Row.

Bilodeau, Edward A. (ed.), 1966. *Acquisition of Skill*. New York: Academic Press.

Blackie, John, 1971. *Inside the Primary School* (American ed.). New York: Schocken Books.

Block, James B. (ed.), 1971. *Mastery Learning: Theory and Practice*. New York: Holt, Rinehart, & Winston.

Blommers, P., and E. F. Lindquist, 1960. *Elementary Statistical Methods in Psychology and Education*. Boston: Houghton Mifflin.

Bloom, Benjamin S., 1964. *Stability and Change in Human Characteristics*. New York: Wiley.

Bloom, Benjamin S., 1968. "Learning for Mastery," *Evaluation Comment*, 1(2). Los Angeles: Center for the Study of Evaluation of Instructional Programs, University of California.

Bloom, Benjamin S. and others (eds.), 1956. *Taxonomy of Educational Objectives. Handbook I: Cognitive Domain*. New York: McKay.

Bloom, Benjamin S., J. Thomas Hastings, and George F. Madaus (eds.), 1971. *Handbook on Formative and Summative Evaluation of Student Learning*. New York: McGraw-Hill.

Blos, P., 1962. *On Adolescence*. New York: Free Press.

Boring, Edwin G., 1950. *A History of Experimental Psychology*, 2nd ed. New York: Appleton-Century-Crofts.

Boring, Edwin G., and Gardner Lindzey (eds.), 1967. *A History of Psychology in Autobiography*, Vol. IV. New York: Appleton-Century-Crofts.

Bradbury, Ray, 1967. *Fahrenheit 451*. New York: Simon & Schuster.

Braithwaite, Edward R., 1959. *To Sir with Love*. Englewood Cliffs, N. J.: Prentice-Hall.

Brecher, Edward M., and the editors of Consumer Reports, 1973. *Licit and Illicit Drugs*. Boston: Little, Brown.

Bremer, John, and Anne Bremer, 1972. *Open Education: A Beginning*. New York: Holt, Rinehart, & Winston.

Bremer, John, and Michael von Moschzisker, 1971. *The School Without Walls*. New York: Holt, Rinehart, & Winston.

Britton, Edward, and J. Merritt Winans, 1958. *Growing from Infancy to Adulthood*. New York: Appleton-Century-Crofts.

Bronfenbrenner, Urie, 1970. *Two Worlds of Childhood*. New York: Russell Sage Foundation.

Brown, Claude, 1965. *Manchild in the Promised Land*. New York: Macmillan.

Brown, Dee, 1971. *Bury My Heart at Wounded Knee: An Indian History of the American West*. New York: Holt, Rinehart, & Winston.

Brown, George Isaac, 1971. *Human Teaching for Human Learning: An Introduction to Confluent Education*. New York: Viking.

Brueckner, L. J., and H. W. Distad, 1923. "The Effect of the Summer Vacation on the Reading Ability of First-Grade Children," *Elementary School Journal*, 24:698–707.

Bruene, E., 1928. "Effect of the Summer Vacation on the Achievement of Pupils in the Fourth, Fifth, and Sixth Grades," *Journal of Educational Research*, 18:309–314.

Bruner, Jerome S., 1960a. "The Functions of Teaching," *Rhode Island College Journal*, 1:35–42.

Bruner, Jerome S., 1960b. *The Process of Education*. New York: Vintage Books.

Bruner, Jerome S., 1961. "The Act of Discovery," *Harvard Educational Review*, 31:21–32.

Bruner, Jerome S., 1966. *Toward a Theory of Instruction*. Cambridge, Mass.: Belknap Press of Harvard University Press.

Bruner, Jerome S., 1971. *The Relevance of Education*. New York: Norton.

Bruner, Jerome S., and H. Tajfel, 1961. "Cognitive Risk and Environmental Change." *Journal of Abnormal Psychology*, 62:231–241.

Bruner, Jerome S., Rose R. Olver, and Patricia Greenfield, 1966. *Studies in Cognitive Growth*. New York: Wiley.

Bryan, William L., and Noble Harter,

1897. "Studies in the Physiology and Psychology of the Telegraphic Language," *Psychological Review,* 4:27–53.

Buchanan, Cynthia D., 1968. *Teacher's Guide to the Prereader.* New York: McGraw-Hill.

Bugelski, B. R., 1971. *The Psychology of Learning Applied to Teaching,* 2nd ed. Indianapolis: Bobbs-Merrill.

Buros, O. K., (ed.), 1972. *Seventh Mental Measurements Yearbook.* Highland Park, N. J.: Gryphon Press.

Bushell, Donald G., Jr., 1972. *Classroom Behavior: A Little Book for Teachers.* Englewood Cliffs, N. J.: Prentice-Hall.

Butler, R. A., 1953. "Discrimination Learning by Rhesus Monkeys to Visual-Exploration Motivation," *Journal of Comparative and Physiological Psychology,* 46:95–98.

Caldwell, Catherine, 1970. "Social Science as Ammunition," *Psychology Today,* 4(4):38–74.

Callahan, Raymond E., 1962. *Education and the Cult of Efficiency.* Chicago: University of Chicago Press.

Cancro, Robert, 1971. "Genetic Contributions to Individual Differences in Intelligence: An Introduction." In Robert Cancro (ed.), *Intelligence: Genetic and Environmental Influences,* pp. 59–64. New York: Grune & Stratton.

Cancro, Robert (ed.), 1971. *Intelligence: Genetic and Environmental Influences.* New York: Grune & Stratton.

Capa, Cornell, and Maya Pines, 1955. *Retarded Children Can Be Helped.* New York: Channel Press.

Carroll, John A., 1963. "A Model of School Learning," *Teachers College Record,* 64:723–733.

Carroll, John B., 1971. "Problems of Measurement Related to the Concept of Learning for Mastery." In James H. Block (ed.), *Mastery Learning: Theory and Practice,* pp. 24–46. New York: Holt, Rinehart, & Winston.

Channon, Gloria, 1971. *Homework: Required Reading for Teachers and Parents.* New York: Outerbridge and Dienstfrey.

Charles, C. M., 1972. *Educational Psychology: The Instructional Endeavor.* Saint Louis: Mosby.

Charles, W. A., 1953. "Ability and Accomplishments of Persons Earlier Judged Mentally Deficient," *Genetic Psychology Monographs,* 47:3–71.

Chauncey, Henry, and John E. Dobbin, 1963. *Testing: Its Place in Education Today.* New York: Harper & Row.

Chomsky, Noam, 1968. *Language and Mind.* New York: Harcourt Brace Jovanovich.

Claiborn, William L., 1969. "Expectancy Effects in the Classroom: A Failure to Replicate," *Journal of Educational Psychology,* 60(5):377–383.

Clarizio, Harvey F., 1971. *Toward Positive Classroom Discipline.* New York: Wiley.

Cleaver, Eldridge, 1968. *Soul on Ice.* New York: McGraw-Hill.

Cofer, Charles N., and Mortimer H. Appley, 1964. *Motivation: Theory and Research.* New York: Wiley.

Cohen, Harold L., and James Filipczak, 1971. *A New Learning Environment.* New York: Jossey-Bass.

Coladarci, Arthur P., 1956. "The Relevancy of Educational Psychology," *Educational Leadership,* 13(8):489–492.

Coleman, James S., 1966. *Equality of Educational Opportunity.* Washington: U. S. Department of Health, Education, and Welfare, Office of Education.

Coles, Robert, 1963. *The Desegregation of Southern Schools: A Psychiatric Study.* New York: Anti-Defamation League of B'nai B'rith.

Coles, Robert, 1967. *Children of Crisis: A Study of Courage and Fear.* Boston: Little, Brown.

Coles, Robert, 1968. *Dead End School.* Boston: Little, Brown.

Coles, Robert, 1969. *Still Hungry in America.* New York: World.

Coles, Robert, 1970. *Erik H. Erikson: The Growth of His Work.* Boston: Little, Brown.

Coles, Robert, 1970. *Uprooted Children: The Early Life of Migrant Farm Workers.* Pittsburgh: University of Pittsburgh Press.

Coles, Robert, 1972. *Children of Crisis: Migrants, Mountaineers, and Sharecroppers.* Boston: Little, Brown.

Coles, Robert, 1972. *Children of Crisis: The South Goes North.* Boston: Little, Brown.

Coles, Robert, 1972. *Farewell to the South.* Boston: Little, Brown.

Coles, Robert, and Jon Erikson, 1971. *The Middle American: Proud and Uncertain.* Boston: Little, Brown.

Colman, John E., 1967. *The Master Teachers and the Art of Teaching.* New York: Pitman.

Combs, Arthur W., 1965. *The Professional Education of Teachers.* Boston: Allyn & Bacon.

Combs, Arthur W., and Donald Snygg, 1959. *Individual Behavior,* rev. ed. New York: Harper.

Congreve, Willard J., 1965. "The University of Chicago Project," in David W. Beggs, III, and Edward G. Buffie (eds.), *Independent Study.* Bloomington: University of Indiana Press.

Conroy, Pat, 1972. *The Water is Wide.* Boston: Houghton Mifflin.

Cooley, W. W., and R. Glaser, 1969. "The Computer and Individualized Instruction," *Science,* 166:574–582.

Cooper, Paulette, 1972. *Growing up Puerto Rican.* New York: Arbor House.

Coopersmith, Stanley, 1967. *The Antecedents of Self-esteem.* San Francisco: Freeman.

Corsini, R. J., and D. D. Howard, 1964. *Critical Incidents in Teaching.* Englewood Cliffs, N.J.: Prentice-Hall.

Coser, Rose Laub, (ed.), 1969. *Life Cycle and Achievement in America.* New York: Harper & Row.

Coulson, William R., 1972. *Groups, Gimmicks and Instant Gurus: An Examination of Encounter Groups and Their Distortions.* New York: Harper & Row.

Cremin, Lawrence A., 1961. *The Transformation of the School.* New York: Knopf.

CRM Books, 1971. *Developmental Psychology Today.* Del Mar, Cal.: Communication, Research, Machines, Inc.

Cronbach, Lee J., 1970. *Essentials of Psychological Testing,* 3rd ed. New York: Harper & Row.

Cronbach, Lee J., and Patrick Suppes, (eds.), 1969. *Research for Tomorrow's Schools: Disciplined Inquiry for Education.* New York: Macmillan.

Crowder, Norman A., 1963. "On the Differences between Linear and Intrinsic Programming," *Phi Delta Kappan,* 44:250–254.

Crutchfield, Richard, 1966. "Sensitization and Activation of Cognitive Skills," in Jerome S. Bruner (ed.), *Learning about Learning.* Washington: U. S. Department of Health, Education, and Welfare, Office of Education.

Cullum, Albert, 1967. *Push Back the Desks.* New York: Citation Press.

Daniels, J. C., 1961. "The Effects of Streaming in the Primary School. Part I, What Teachers Believe," *British Journal of Educational Psychology,* 31:69–78.

Daniels, Steven, 1971. *How 2 Gerbils, 20 Goldfish, 200 Games, 2,000 Books, and I Taught Them How to Read.* Philadelphia: Westminster Press.

Dashiel, J. F., 1949. *Fundamentals of General Psychology,* 3rd ed. Boston: Houghton Mifflin.

Davidson, Sara, 1972. "Cousteau Searches for His Whale," *New York Times Magazine,* September 10, 1972, pp. 33–91.

Davis, Robert B., 1966. "Discovery in the Teaching of Mathematics," in Lee S. Shulman and Evan R. Keislar (eds.), *Learning by Discovery.* Chicago: Rand McNally.

DeCecco, John P., 1968. *The Psychology of Learning and Instruction.* Englewood Cliffs, N.J.: Prentice-Hall.

DeHaan, Robert F., and Jack Kough, 1956. *Helping Children with Special Needs.* Chicago: Science Research Associates.

Deighton, Lee C., (ed.), 1971. *The Encyclopedia of Education.* New York: Macmillan.

Delacato, Carl, 1959. *The Treatment and Prevention of Reading Problems.* Springfield, Ill.: Charles C Thomas.

Delacato, Carl, 1963. *The Diagnosis of Speech and Reading Problems.* Springfield, Ill.: Charles C Thomas.

Delacato, Carl, 1966. *Neurological Organization and Reading.* Springfield, Ill.: Charles C. Thomas.

DeLeon, Nephtali, 1972. *Chicanos: Our Background and Our Pride.* Lubbock, Texas: Trucha Publications.

Deloria, Vine, Jr., 1969. *Custer Died for Your Sins.* New York: Macmillan.

Dennis, Wayne, 1960. "Causes of Retardation among Institutional Children: Iran," *Journal of Genetic Psychology,* 96:47–59.

Dennis, Wayne, and Marsena G. Dennis, 1940. "The Effect of Cradling Practices upon the Onset of Walking in Hopi Children," *Journal of Genetic Psychology,* 56:77–86.

Dennis, Wayne, and Marsena G. Dennis, 1941. "Infant Development under Conditions of Restricted Practice and Minimum Social Stimulation," *Genetic Psychology Monographs,* 23:149–155.

Dennis, Wayne, and P. Najarian, 1957. "Infant Development under Environmental Handicap," *Psychological Monographs,* 71(7). Washington: American Psychological Association.

Dennison, George, 1969. *The Lives of Children.* New York: Vintage.

Deutsch, Martin, 1964. "Facilitating Development in the Pre-School Child: Social and Psychological Perspectives," *Merrill-Palmer Quarterly of Behavior and Development,* 10(3).

Deutsch, Martin, Arthur R. Jensen, and Irwin Katz, 1968. *Social Class, Race, and Psychological Development.* New York: Holt, Rinehart and Winston.

Dewey, John, 1916. *Democracy and Education.* New York: Macmillan.

Dewey, John, 1938. *Experience and Education.* New York: Macmillan.

Douvan, E., and J. Adelson, 1966. *The Adolescent Experience.* New York: Wiley.

Dow, Peter B., 1971. "Man: A Course of Study in Retrospect: A Primer for Curriculum in the '70's," *Theory Into Practice,* 10(3):168–177.

Dreikurs, Rudolf, 1968. *Psychology in the Classroom,* 2nd ed. New York: Harper & Row.

Dreikurs, Rudolph, Bernice Bronia Grunwald, and Floy C. Pepper, 1971. *Maintaining Sanity in the Classroom: Illustrated Teaching Techniques.* New York: Harper & Row.

Duchastel, Phillipe C., and Paul F. Merrill, 1973. "The Effects of Behavioral Objectives on Learning: A Review of Empirical Studies." *Review of Educational Research,* 43(1):53–69.

Duncan, Carl P., 1959. "Recent Research on Human Problem Solving," *Psychological Bulletin,* 56:397–429.

Duncker, K., 1945. "On Problem Solving," *Psychological Monographs,* 58(270).

Dunlap, Knight, 1949. *Habits: Their Making and Unmaking.* New York: Liveright.

Dunn, Lloyd M., 1968. "Special Education for the Mentally Retarded: Is Much of it Justified?" *Journal of Exceptional Children,* 35:5–24.

Dunn, Lloyd M. (ed.), 1963. *Exceptional Children in the Schools.* New York: Holt, Rinehart and Winston.

Durost, Walter N., and George A. Prescott, 1962. *Essentials of Measurement for Teachers.* New York: Harcourt, Brace and World.

Ebel, Robert L., 1972. *Essentials of Educational Measurement.* Englewood Cliffs, N. J.: Prentice-Hall.

Ebel, Robert L. (ed.), 1969. *Encyclopedia of Educational Research* (4th ed.). New York: Macmillan.

Eells, K., A. Davis, R. J. Havighurst, V. E. Herrick, and R. W. Tyler, 1951. *Intelligence and Cultural Differences.* Chicago: University of Chicago Press.

Elashoff, Janet D., and R. E. Snow, 1970. "A Case Study in Statistical Inference: Reconsideration of the Rosenthal-Jacobson Data on Teacher Expectancy." Technical Report No. 15, Stanford Center for Research and Development in Teaching.

Elashoff, Janet D., and Richard E. Snow, 1971. *Pygmalion Reconsidered.* Worthington, Ohio: Charles A. Jones.

Elkind, David, 1968. "Giant in the Nursery—Jean Piaget," *New York Times Magazine,* May 26, pp. 25–80.

Elkind, David, 1970. *Children and Adolescence: Interpretive Essays on Jean Piaget.* New York: Oxford University Press.

Ellis, Henry, 1965. *The Transfer of Learning.* New York: Macmillan.

Ellison, Ralph, 1947. *Invisible Man.* New York: Random House.

Engelmann, Siegfried, 1969. *Preventing Failure in the Elementary Grades.* Chicago: Science Research Associates.

Engelmann, Siegfried, 1969. "Conceptual Learning." In K. E. Beery and B. D. Bateman (eds.), *Dimensions in Early Learning Series.* San Rafael, Cal.: Dimensions Publishing Company.

Engelmann, Siegfried, 1971. "The Effectiveness of Direct Instruction on IQ Performance and Achievement in Reading and Arithmetic." In J. Hellmuth (ed.), *Disadvantaged Child,* Vol. 3. New York: Brunner/Mazel.

Engelmann, Siegfried, and Theresa Engelmann, 1968. *Give Your Child a Superior Mind.* New York: Simon and Schuster.

Engelmann, Siegfried, and others, 1969. *Distar Instructional System.* Chicago: Science Research Associates.

Environment, Heredity, and Intelligence, 1970. Reprint Series No. 2. Cambridge, Mass.: *Harvard Educational Review.*

Epstein, Cynthia Fuchs, 1970. Woman's Place. Berkeley: University of California Press.

Erickson, Marion, 1965. *The Mentally Retarded Child in the Classroom.* New York: Macmillan.

Erikson, Erik H., 1950. *Childhood and Society.* New York: Norton.

Erikson, Erik H., 1958. *Young Man Luther.* New York: Norton.

Erikson, Erik H., 1968. *Identity: Youth and Crisis.* New York: Norton.

Erikson, Erik H., 1969. *Gandhi's Truth.* New York: Norton.

Espenschade, Anna S., 1963. *What Research Says to the Teacher: Physical Education in the Elementary Schools.* Washington: National Education Association.

Evans, Gary W., and Gaylon L. Oswalt, 1967. "Acceleration of Academic Progress Through the Manipulation of Peer Influence," *Working Paper* No. 155. Kansas City: Bureau of Child Research Laboratory, University of Kansas Medical Center.

Evans, Richard I., 1968. *B. F. Skinner: The Man and His Ideas.* New York: Dutton.

Eysenck, H. J., 1971. *The IQ Argument.* New York: The Library Press.

Fantini, Mario D., and Gerald Weinstein, 1968. *The Disadvantaged: Challenge to Education.* New York: Harper & Row.

Farson, Richard E., 1968. "Praise Reappraised." In Don E. Hamachek (ed.), *Human Dynamics in Psychology and Education,* pp. 109–118. Boston: Allyn and Bacon.

Featherstone, Joseph, 1971. *Schools Where Children Learn.* New York: Liveright.

Ferster, C. B., and M. C. Perrott, 1968. *Behavior Principles.* New York: Appleton-Century-Crofts.

Festinger, Leon, 1957. *A Theory of Cognitive Dissonance.* Evanston, Ill.: Row, Peterson.

Finder, Morris, 1965. "Teaching English to Slum-dwelling Pupils." In Dwight L. Burton and John S. Simmons (eds.), *Teaching English in Today's Schools: Selected Readings,* pp. 472–481. New York: Holt, Rinehart & Winston.

Flanagan, J. C., 1968. "Program for Learning in Accordance with Need." Paper presented to the American Educational Research Association, Chicago. Palo Alto, Cal.: American Institute for Research.

Flanders, Ned A., 1951. "Personal-Social Anxiety as a Factor in Experimental Learning Situations," *Journal of Educational Research,* 45:100–110.

Flanders, Ned A., 1970. *Analyzing Teacher Behavior*. Reading, Mass.: Addison-Wesley.

Flavell, J. H., 1963. *The Developmental Psychology of Jean Piaget*. Princeton, N. J.: Van Nostrand.

Fleming, Elyse S., and Ralph G. Anttonen, 1971. "Teacher Expectancy or My Fair Lady," *American Educational Research Journal*, 8(2):241–252.

Fliegler, Louis A. (ed.), 1961. *Curriculum Planning for the Gifted*. Englewood Cliffs, N. J.: Prentice-Hall.

Fowler, Burton P., 1930. "President's Message," *Progressive Education*, 7:159.

Fox, Allan M., and Richard E. Horman, 1970. "Drug Education Activities: An Innovation," in Richard E. Horman and Allan M. Fox (eds.), *Drug Awareness*, pp. 430–441. New York: Avon.

Frantzblau, A. N., 1958. *A Primer of Statistics for Non-statisticians*. New York: Harcourt, Brace and World.

Freire, Paolo, 1970. *Pedagogy of the Oppressed*. New York: Herder and Herder.

Friedan, Betty, 1963. *The Feminine Mystique*. New York: Norton.

Friedenberg, Edgar Z., 1959. *The Vanishing Adolescent*. New York: Dell.

Friedenberg, Edgar Z., 1965. *Coming of Age in America*. New York: Random House.

Froebel, Friedrich, 1887. *The Education of Man* (W. N. Hailmann, tr.). New York: Appleton-Century-Crofts.

Furth, Hans, 1970. *Piaget for Teachers*. Englewood Cliffs, N. J.: Prentice-Hall.

Gage, N. L. (ed.), 1963. *Handbook of Research on Teaching*. Chicago: Rand McNally.

Gagné, Robert M., 1970. *The Conditions of Learning* (2nd ed.). New York: Holt, Rinehart, & Winston.

Galarza, Ernesto, 1971. *Barrio Boy*. Notre Dame, Ind.: University of Notre Dame Press.

Gallagher, James J., 1964. *Teaching the Gifted Child*. Boston: Allyn & Bacon.

Galton, Francis, 1869. *Hereditary Genius*. London: Macmillan & Co.

Galton, Francis, 1890. Statement made in footnote to an article by James McKeen Cattell, "Mental Tests and Measurement," *Mind*, 15:373.

Garcia, John, 1972. "IQ: The Conspiracy." *Psychology Today*, 6(4):40–94.

Gardner, John W., 1961. *Excellence*. New York: Harper & Row.

Gardner, John W., 1965. *Self-Renewal*. New York: Harper & Row.

Gardner, R. W., and R. I. Long, 1962. "Control, Defense and Centration Effect: A Study of Scanning Behavior," *British Journal of Psychology*, 53:129–140.

Gardner, R. W., and R. A. Schoen, 1962. "Differentiation and Abstraction in Concept Formation," *Psychological Monographs*, 76, No. 41.

Gardner, R. W., and others, 1959. "Cognitive Control: A Study of Individual Consistencies in Cognitive Behavior," *Psychological Issues*, 1, No. 4.

Garrett, H. E., 1951. *Statistics in Psychology and Education*, 5th ed. New York: McKay.

Getzels, Jacob W., and Philip W. Jackson, 1962. *Creativity and Intelligence*. New York: Wiley.

Gibson, E. J., 1941. "Retroactive Inhibition as a Function of Degree of Generalization between Tasks," *Journal of Experimental Psychology*, 28:93–115.

Ginott, Haim, 1965. *Between Parent and Child*. New York: Avon Books.

Ginott, Haim, 1969. *Between Parent and Teen-ager*. New York: Macmillan.

Ginott, Haim, 1971. *Teacher and Child*. New York: Macmillan.

Ginsburg, Herbert, and Sylvia Opper, 1969. *Piaget's Theory of Intellectual Development: An Introduction*. Englewood Cliffs, N.J.: Prentice-Hall.

Glaser, Robert, 1962. "Psychology and Instructional Technology." In R. Glaser (ed.), *Training Research and Education*, pp. 1–30. Pittsburgh: University of Pittsburgh Press.

Glaser, Robert, 1963. "Instructional Technology and the Measurement of Learning Outcomes: Some Questions," *American Psychologist*, 18: 519–521.

Glasser, William, 1969. *Schools Without Failure.* New York: Harper & Row.

Glasser, William, 1972. *The Identity Society.* New York: Harper & Row.

Goble, Frank, 1970. *Third Force: The Psychology of Abraham Maslow.* New York: Grossman.

Goertzel, Victor, and Mildred Goertzel, 1962. *Cradles of Eminence.* Boston: Little, Brown.

Goldstein, H., J. Moss, and Laura J. Jordan, 1965. *The Efficacy of Special Class Training on the Development of Mentally Retarded Children.* Cooperative Research Project No. 619. Washington, D. C.: U. S. Office of Education.

Gonzales, Rodolfo, 1973. *I Am Joaquin.* New York: Bantam.

Goodenough, Florence, 1931. *Anger in Young Children.* Institute of Child Welfare Monograph Series, No. 9. Minneapolis: University of Minnesota Press.

Goodman, Paul, 1956. *Growing Up Absurd.* New York: Vintage Books.

Goodman, Paul, 1964. *Compulsory Miseducation.* New York: Horizon Press.

Goodman, Paul, 1966. *Compulsory Miseducation and the Community of Scholars.* New York: Vintage.

Goodman, Paul, 1967. *Like a Conquered Province.* New York: Random House.

Goodman, Paul, 1969. *New Reformation: Notes of a Neolithic Conservative.* New York: Random House.

Gorer, Geoffrey, 1948. *The American People.* New York: Norton.

Gorow, Frank F., 1966. *Better Classroom Testing.* San Francisco: Chandler.

Gotkin, Lassor, 1967. *Matrix Games.* New York: New Century.

Graubard, Allen, 1972. *Free the Children.* New York: Pantheon.

Gray, Jenny, 1967. *The Teacher's Survival Guide.* Palo Alto, Calif.: Fearon.

Greco, P., 1959. "L'Apprentissage dans une Situation à Structure Opératoire Concrète: Les Inversions Successives de l'Ordre Linéaire Paré des Rotations de 180°." In J. Piaget (ed.), *Etudes d'Epistémologie Génétique,* Vol. 8, pp. 68–152. Paris: Presses Universitaire de France.

Green, Hannah [Joanne Greenberg], 1964. *I Never Promised You a Rose Garden.* New York: Holt, Rinehart, & Winston.

Grier, William, and Price Cobbs, 1968. *Black Rage.* New York: Basic Books.

Griffin, J. D. M., and others, 1940. *Mental Hygiene.* New York: American Book.

Groff, Patrick J., 1964. "Culturally Deprived Children: Opinions of Teachers and Views of Riessman," *Exceptional Children,* 31(2):61–65.

Gronlund, Norman E., 1959. *Sociometry in the Classroom.* New York: Harper.

Gronlund, Norman E., 1968. *Constructing Achievement Tests.* Englewood Cliffs, N. J.: Prentice-Hall.

Gronlund, Norman E., 1972. *Stating Behavioral Objectives for Classroom Instruction.* New York: Macmillan.

Gronlund, Norman E., 1973. *Preparing Criterion-Referenced Tests for Classroom Instruction.* New York: Macmillan.

Grossman, Herbert, 1972. *Nine Rotten Lousy Kids.* New York: Holt, Rinehart, and Winston.

Guilford, J. P., 1959. "Three Faces of Intellect," *American Psychologist,* 14:469–479.

Guskin, S. L., and H. H. Spicker, 1968. "Educational Research in Mental Retardation," in N. R. Ellis (ed.), *International Review of Research in Mental Retardation,* Vol. 3, pp. 217–278. New York: Academic Press.

Hall, C. V., 1963. "Does Entrance Age Affect Achievement?" *Elementary School Journal,* 63:391–396.

Haring, Norris G., and E. Larkin Phillips, 1972. *Analysis and Modification of Classroom Behavior.* Englewood Cliffs, N. J.: Prentice-Hall.

Harlow, Harry F., 1949. "The Formation of Learning Sets," *Psychological Review,* 56:51–65.

Harlow, Harry F., 1953. "Mice, Monkeys, Men, and Motives," *Psychological Review,* 60:23–32.

Harris, Mary B. (ed.), 1972. *Classroom Uses of Behavior Modification.* Columbus, Ohio: Merrill.

Harris, Thomas A., 1967. *I'm OK—You're OK.* New York: Harper & Row.

Harshman, Hardwick W., ed., 1969. *Educating the Emotionally Disturbed: A Book of Readings.* New York: Crowell.

Hartshorne, H., and M. A. May, 1928. *Studies in the Nature of Character.* Vol. I, *Studies in Deceit.* New York: Macmillan.

Harvey, O. J., D. E. Hunt, and H. M. Schroder, 1961. *Conceptual Systems and Personality Organization.* New York: Wiley.

Havighurst, Robert, 1952. *Developmental Tasks and Education.* New York: Longmans, Green.

Hebb, D. O., 1947. "The Effects of Early Experience on Problem-solving at Maturity," *American Psychologist,* 2:306–307.

Hebb, D. O., 1949. *The Organization of Behavior.* New York: Wiley.

Hebb, D. O., 1966. *A Textbook in Psychology.* Philadelphia: Saunders.

Heber, R. F., 1961. "A Manual on Terminology and Classification in Mental Retardation," *American Journal of Mental Deficiency,* 64, Monograph Supplement.

Heber, R. F., 1968. "Research in Education and Habilitation of the Mentally Retarded." Paper read at Conference on Sociocultural Aspects of Mental Retardation, Peabody College, Nashville, Tenn., June, 1968.

Heber, Rick, and Howard Garber, 1970. "An Experiment in the Prevention of Cultural Familial Retardation." Proceedings of the Second Congress of the International Association for the Scientific Study on Mental Deficiency. Warsaw, Poland.

Hechinger, Fred M. (ed.), 1966. *Preschool Education Today.* Garden City, N. Y.: Doubleday.

Hernandez, Luis F., 1969. *A Forgotten American: A Resource Unit for Teachers on the Mexican American.* New York: Anti-Defamation League of B'nai B'rith.

Herndon, James, 1968. *The Way It Spozed to Be.* New York: Simon and Schuster.

Herndon, James, 1971. *How to Survive in Your Native Land.* New York: Simon & Schuster.

Herrnstein, Richard, 1971. "I.Q.," *The Atlantic,* 228(3):43–64.

Herrnstein, Richard, 1973. *IQ in a Meritocracy.* Boston: Atlantic-Little-Brown.

Hersey, John, 1960. *The Child Buyer.* New York: Knopf.

Hertzberg, Alvin, and Edward Stone, 1971. *Schools are for Children: An American Approach to the Open Classroom.* New York: Schocken Books.

Hess, Robert D., and Dorene J. Croft, 1972. *Teachers of Young Children.* Boston: Houghton Mifflin.

Hess, Robert D., and Virginia Shipman, 1965. "Early Experience and the Socialization of Cognitive Modes in Children," *Child Development,* 36:869–886.

Hewett, Frank M., 1968. *The Emotionally Disturbed Child in the Classroom.* Boston: Allyn & Bacon.

Highet, Gilbert, 1957. *The Art of Teaching.* New York: Vintage Books.

Hilgard, Ernest, 1962. *Introduction to Psychology,* 3rd ed. New York: Harcourt, Brace and World.

Hilgard, Ernest R., 1963. "Motivation in Learning Theory," in S. Koch (ed.), *Psychology: A Study of a Science,* Vol. V, pp. 253–283. New York: McGraw-Hill.

Hilgard, Ernest R., and Richard C. Atkinson, 1967. *Introduction to Psychology,* 4th ed. New York: Harcourt, Brace and World.

Hilgard, Josephine R., 1932. "Learning and Maturation in Preschool Children," *Journal of Genetic Psychology,* 41:40–53.

Hill, Jae H., Robert M. Liebert, and Richard Adelson, 1968. "Vicarious Extinction of Avoidance Behavior Through Films: An Initial Test," *Psychological Reports,* 22(1):192.

Hill, Winfred F., 1971. *Learning: A Survey of Psychological Interpretations* (rev. ed.). New York: Intext.

Hoffmann, Banesh, 1962. *The Tyranny of Testing.* New York: Crowell-Collier.

Holmes, F. B., 1935. *Children's Fears.* Child Development Monographs, No. 20. New York: Teachers College, Columbia University.

Holt, John, 1964. *How Children Fail.* New York: Pitman.

Holt, John, 1967. *How Children Learn.* New York: Pitman.

Holt, John, 1969. *The Underachieving School.* New York: Pitman.

Holt, John, 1970. *What Do I Do Monday?* New York: Dutton.

Holt, John, 1972. *Freedom and Beyond.* New York: Dutton.

Holzman, P. S., 1954. "The Relation of Assimilation Tendencies in Visual, Auditory, and Kinesthetic Time-Error to Cognitive Attitudes of Leveling and Sharpening," *Journal of Personality,* 22:375–394.

Holzman, P. S., 1966. "Scanning: A Principle of Reality Contact," *Perceptual and Motor Skills,* 23:835–844.

Holzman, P. S., and G. S. Klein, 1954. "Cognitive System Principles of Leveling and Sharpening: Individual Differences in Assimilation Effects in Visual Time-Error," *Journal of Psychology,* 37:105–122.

Homme, Lloyd, 1966. "Contiguity Theory and Contingency Management," *Psychological Record,* 16:223–241.

Homme, Lloyd, and Donald Tosti, 1971. *Behavior Technology: Motivation and Contingency Management.* San Rafael, Cal.: Individual Learning Systems.

Hoppe, F., 1930. "Erfolg und Misserfolg," *Psychologische Forschung,* 14:1–62.

Horman, Richard E., and Allan M. Fox, (eds.), 1970. *Drug Awareness.* New York: Avon.

Hostrop, R. W., J. A. Mecklenburger, and J. A. Wilson, 1973. *Accountability for Educational Results.* Hamden, Conn.: Shoestring Press.

Hough, J. B., 1967. "An Observational System for the Analysis of Classroom Instruction." In E. J. Amidon and J. B. Hough (eds.), *Interaction Analysis: Theory, Research, and Application.* Reading, Mass.: Addison-Wesley.

Howe, Florence, 1971. "Sexual Stereotypes Start Early," *Saturday Review,* October 16, 1971, pp. 76–94.

Howson, Geoffrey, (ed.), 1969. *Primary Education in Britain Today.* New York: Teachers College Press.

Hunsicker, Paul, 1963. *What Research Says to the Teacher: Physical Fitness.* Washington: National Education Association.

Hunt, J. McV., 1961. *Intelligence and Experience.* New York: Ronald Press.

Hunt, J. McV., and Girvin E. Kirk, 1971. "Social Aspects of Intelligence: Evidence and Issues." In Robert Cancro (ed.), *Intelligence: Genetic and Environmental Influences.* New York: Grune and Stratton, pp. 262–306.

Hurlock, Elizabeth, 1925. "An Evaluation of Incentives Used in School Work," *Journal of Educational Psychology,* 16:145–159.

Huxley, Aldous, 1932. *Brave New World.* New York: Harper.

Huxley, Aldous, 1958. *Brave New World Revisited.* New York: Harper.

Huxley, Aldous, 1962. *Island.* New York: Harper & Row.

Ilg, Frances, and Louise Bates Ames, 1955. *The Gesell Institute's Child Behavior.* New York: Dell.

Illich, Ivan, 1971. *Deschooling Society.* New York: Harper & Row.

Informal Schools in Britain Today, 1971 and 1972. New York: Citation Press.

Inhelder, Barbel, 1953. "Criteria of the Stages of Mental Development," in J. M. Tanner and Barbel Inhelder (eds.), *Discussions on Child Development.* New York: International Universities Press.

Itard, Jean Marc, 1962. *The Wild Boy of Aveyron.* New York: Appleton-Century-Crofts.

Jacob, Philip E., 1957. *Changing Values in College.* New York: Harper.

Jacobs, Paul, Milton Maier, and Laurence Stolurow, 1966. *A Guide to Evaluating Self-Instructional Programs.* New York: Holt, Rinehart and Winston.

James, William, 1958. *Talks to Teachers.* New York: Norton.

Jencks, Christopher, 1969. "A Reappraisal of the Most Controversial Educational Document of Our time," *New York Times Magazine,* August 10, pp. 12–44.

Jencks, Christopher S., 1972a. *Inequality: A Reassessment of the Effect of Family and Schooling in America.* New York: Basic Books.

Jencks, Christopher S., 1972b. "The Coleman Report and the Conventional Wisdom." In Frederick Mosteller and Daniel P. Moynihan (eds.), *On Equality of Educational Opportunity,* pp. 69–115. New York: Vintage.

Jenkins, Gladys Gardner, Helen S. Schacter, and William W. Bauer, 1966. *These Are Your Children* (3rd ed.). Chicago: Scott-Foresman.

Jenkins, J. G., and Karl M. Dallenbach, 1924. "Oblivescence during Sleep and Waking," *American Journal of Psychology,* 35:605–612.

Jenkins, J. J., 1963. "Mediated Associations: Paradigms and Situations," in C. N. Cofer and B. S. Musgrave (eds.), *Verbal Behavior and Learning.* New York: McGraw-Hill.

Jensen, Arthur R., 1969. "How much Can We Boost I.Q. and Scholastic Achievement?" *Harvard Educational Review,* 39, Winter.

Jensen, Arthur R., 1973a. *Educability and Group Differences.* New York: Harper & Row.

Jensen, Arthur R., 1973b. *Genetics and Education.* New York: Harper & Row.

Jersild, Arthur, 1952. *In Search of Self.* New York: Teachers College, Columbia University.

Jersild, Arthur, 1955. *When Teachers Face Themselves.* New York: Teachers College, Columbia University.

Jersild, Arthur, 1963. "What Teachers Say about Psychotherapy," *Phi Delta Kappan,* 44:313–317.

Jersild, Arthur, 1968. *Child Psychology,* 6th ed. Englewood Cliffs, N. J.: Prentice-Hall.

Jersild, Arthur, Eve Allina Lazar, and Adele M. Brodkin, 1962. *The Meaning of Psychotherapy in the Teacher's Life and Work.* New York: Teachers College, Columbia University.

Johnson, E. W., 1959. *How to Live through Junior High School.* Philadelphia: Lippincott.

Johnson, G. O., 1950. "A Study of the Social Position of Mentally Handicapped Children in the Regular Grades," *American Journal of Mental Deficiency,* 55:60–89.

Johnson, Sheila K., 1972. "A Woman Anthropologist Offers a Solution to the Woman Problem," *The New York Times Magazine,* August 27, 1972, pp. 7–39.

Jones, Reginald, (ed.), 1972. *Black Psychology.* New York: Harper and Row.

Jones, Richard M., 1968. *Fantasy and Feeling in Education.* New York: New York University Press.

José, Jean, and John J. Cody, 1971. "Teacher-Pupil Interaction as it Relates to Attempted Changes in Teacher Expectancy of Academic Ability and Achievement," *American Educational Research Journal,* 8(1):39–49.

Jourard, Sidney M., 1964. *The Transparent Self.* Princeton, N.J.: Van Nostrand.

Kagan, Jerome, 1964a. *Developmental Studies of Reflection and Analysis.* Cambridge, Mass.: Harvard University Press.

Kagan, Jerome, 1964b. "Impulsive and Reflective Children," in J. D. Krumbolz (ed.), *Learning and the Educational Process.* Chicago: Rand McNally.

Kagan, Jerome, 1966. "Motivational and Attitudinal Factors in Receptivity to Learning," in Jerome S. Bruner (ed.), *Learning about Learning.* Washington: U.S. Department of Health, Education, and Welfare, Office of Education.

Kagan, Jerome, 1973. "Kagan Counters Freud, Piaget Theories on Early Childhood Education Effects," *APA Monitor,* 4(2):1–7.

Kamii, Constance, and L. Dermon, 1972. "The Engelmann Approach to Teaching Logical Thinking: Findings from the Administration of Some Piagetian Tasks." In D. R. Green, M. P. Ford, and G. Flamer (eds.), *Piaget and Measurement.* New York: McGraw-Hill.

Karabel, Jerome, 1972. "Open Admissions: Toward Meritocracy or Democracy," *Change,* 4(4):38–43.

Kaufman, Bel, 1964. *Up the Down Staircase.* New York: Avon Books.

Keller, Fred S., 1968. "Good-Bye Teacher . . .," *Journal of Applied Behavior Analysis,* 1:79–88.

Kelley, G. A., 1955. *The Psychology of Personal Constructs,* Vol. I. New York: Norton.

Keniston, Kenneth, 1965. *The Uncommitted.* New York: Harcourt, Brace & World.

Keniston, Kenneth, 1968. *Young Radicals.* New York: Harcourt, Brace & World.

Kerlinger, Fred N. (ed.), 1973. *Review of Research in Education.* Itasca, Ill.: F. E. Peacock.

Kersh, Bert Y., 1963. "The Motivating Effect of Learning by Directed Discovery," in John P. DeCecco (ed.), *Human Learning in the School,* pp. 277–287. New York: Holt, Rinehart and Winston.

Kimble, Gregory A., and Norman Garmezy, 1963. *Principles of General Psychology,* 2nd ed. New York: Ronald Press.

Kinkade, Kathleen, 1973a. "A Walden-Two Experiment," *Psychology Today,* 6(8):35–93.

Kinkade, Kathleen, 1973b. *A Walden Two Experiment: The First Five Years of Twin Oaks Community.* New York: Morrow.

Kinsey, A. C., W. B. Pomeroy, and C. E. Martin, 1948. *Sexual Behavior in the Human Male.* Philadelphia: Saunders.

Kirk, Samuel A., 1948. "An Evaluation of the Study of Bernardine G. Schmidt, entitled: 'Changes in Personal, Social, and Intellectual Behavior of Children Originally Classified as Feebleminded'," *Psychological Bulletin,* 45:321–33.

Kirk, Samuel A., 1958. *Early Education of the Mentally Retarded.* Urbana: University of Illinois Press.

Kirk, Samuel A., 1972. *Educating Exceptional Children* (2nd ed.). Boston: Houghton Mifflin.

Kirk, Samuel A., and G. Johnson, 1951. *Educating the Retarded Child.* Boston: Houghton Mifflin.

Klausmeier, Herbert J., and Richard E. Ripple, 1971. *Learning and Human Abilities: Educational Psychology,* 3rd ed. New York: Harper & Row.

Klein, G. S., 1954. "Need and Regulation." In M. R. Jones (ed.), *Nebraska Symposium on Motivation,* pp. 225–274. Lincoln, Nebr.: University of Nebraska Press.

Klein, G. S., and others, 1962. "Tolerance for Unrealistic Experiences: A Study of the Generalizability of Cognitive Control," *British Journal of Psychology,* 53:41–55.

Kogan, N., and M. A. Wallach, 1964. *Risk Taking.* New York: Holt, Rinehart, & Winston.

Kohl, Herbert, 1967. *36 Children.* New York: New American Library.

Kohl, Herbert, 1969. *The Open Classroom.* New York: Vintage.

Kohlberg, Lawrence, 1966. "Moral Education in the Schools: A Developmental View," *School Review,* 74:1–30.

Köhler, Wolfgang, 1925. *The Mentality of Apes.* New York: Harcourt, Brace and World.

Kolb, David A., 1965. "Achievement Motivation Training for Underachieving Boys," *Journal of Personality and Social Psychology,* 2:783–792.

Kolstoe, Oliver P., 1970. *Teaching Educable Mentally Retarded Children.* New York: Holt, Rinehart, & Winston.

Kolstoe, Oliver P., 1972. *Mental Retardation: An Educational Viewpoint.* New York: Holt, Rinehart, & Winston.

Kough, Jack, and Robert F. DeHaan, 1955. *Identifying Children with Special Needs.* Chicago: Science Research Associates.

Kozol, Jonathan, 1967. *Death at an Early Age.* Boston: Houghton Mifflin.

Kozol, Jonathan, 1972. *Free Schools.* Boston: Houghton Mifflin.

Krathwohl, David R., Benjamin S. Bloom, and Bertram B. Masia, 1964. *Taxonomy of Educational Objectives. Handbook II: Affective Domain.* New York: McKay.

Krogman, W. W., 1962. "How Your Children Grow," *Saturday Evening Post,* July 14–21.

Kumar, V. K., 1971. "The Structure of Human Memory and Some Educational Implications," *Review of Educational Research,* 41(5):379–417.

LaNoue, George R. (ed.), 1972. *Educational Vouchers: Concepts and Controversies.* New York: Teachers College Press.

Lavatelli, Celia Stendler, 1970. *Piaget's Theory Applied to an Early Childhood Curriculum.* Boston: American Science & Engineering, Inc.

Lavatelli, Celia Stendler, 1971. *Teacher's Guide* to accompany *Early Childhood Curriculum—A Piaget Program.* Boston: American Science & Engineering, Inc.

Leacock, Eleanor Burke, 1969. *Teaching and Learning in City Schools.* New York: Basic Books.

Leonard, George, 1969. *Education and Ecstasy.* New York: Dell.

Levy, Leon H., 1969. "Reflections on Replications and the Experimenter Bias Effect," *Journal of Consulting and Clinical Psychology,* 33:15–17.

Lewin, Kurt, 1951. *Field Theory in Social Science.* New York: Harper & Row.

Lewin, Kurt, 1954. "Behavior and Development as a Function of the Total Situation," in Leonard Carmichael (ed.), *Manual of Child Psychology,* 2nd ed., pp. 918–970. New York: Wiley.

Lewis, W. Arthur, 1969. "The Road to the Top Is through Higher Education—Not Black Studies," *New York Times Magazine,* May 11, pp. 34–54.

Lieberman, Morton A., Irvin D. Yalom, and Matthew B. Miles, 1973. *Encounter Groups: First Facts.* New York: Basic Books.

Lieberman, Myron, 1960. *The Future of Public Education.* Chicago: University of Chicago Press.

Liebert, Robert M., and Rita W. Poulos, 1972. "TV for Kiddies, Truth, Goodness, Beauty—and a Little Bit of Brainwash," *Psychology Today,* 6(6):122–128.

Lillard, Paula, 1972. *Montessori: A Modern Approach.* New York: Schocken Books.

Lindsley, O. R., 1960. "Characterization of the Behavior of Chronic Psychotics as Revealed by Free Operant Conditioning Methods," *Diseases of the Nervous System,* Monograph Supplement, 21:66–78.

Lindvall, C. M., 1967. *Measuring Pupil Achievement and Aptitude.* New York: Harcourt Brace.

Linkletter, Art, 1962. *Kids Sure Rite Funny.* New York: Crest Books.

Linkletter, Art, 1965. *A Child's Garden of Misinformation.* New York: Crest Books.

Lipe, Dewey, and Steven M. Jung, 1971. "Manipulating Incentives to Enhance School Learning," *Review of Educational Research,* 41(4):249–280.

Lipinski, Beatrice, and Edwin Lipinski, 1967. "Motivational Factors in Psychedelic Drug Use by Male College Students," *Journal of the American College Health Association,* 16:145–149.

Lippitt, R., and R. K. White, 1958. "An Experimental Study of Leadership and Group Life," in E. E. Maccoby, T. M. Newcomb, and E. E. Hartley (eds.), *Readings in Social Psychology,* pp. 446–511. New York: Holt, Rinehart and Winston.

Lopata, Helena Z., 1971. *Occupation: Housewife.* New York: Oxford University Press.

Lorenz, Konrad, 1952. *King Solomon's Ring.* New York: Thomas Y. Crowell.

Lorenz, Konrad, 1957. "Companionship in Bird Life," in C. H. Schiller (ed.), *Instinctive Behavior.* New York: International Universities Press.

Lorenz, Konrad, 1966. *On Aggression.* New York: Harcourt, Brace and World.

Louttit, C. M., 1947. *Clinical Psychology.* New York: Harper.

Luchins, A. S., 1942. "Mechanization in Problem Solving: The Effect of *Einstellung,*" *Psychological Monographs,* 54(248).

Lynd, Albert, 1953. *Quackery in the Public*

Schools. Boston: Little, Brown.

Lysaught, Jerome P., and Clarence M. Williams, 1963. *A Guide to Programed Instruction.* New York: Wiley.

Maccoby, Eleanor E., and Miriam Zellner, 1970. *Experiments in Primary Education: Aspects of Project Follow-Through.* New York: Harcourt Brace.

Maccoby, Michael, 1972. "A Psychoanalytic View of Learning," *Change,* 3(8):32–38.

MacMillan, Donald L., 1973. *Behavior Modification in Education.* New York: Macmillan.

Mager, Robert F., 1962. *Preparing Instructional Objectives.* Palo Alto, Calif.: Fearon.

Mager, Robert F., 1968. *Developing Attitude toward Learning.* Palo Alto, Calif.: Fearon.

Mager, Robert F., 1972. *Goal Analysis.* Belmont, Cal.: Fearon.

Mahan, Harry C., 1967. "The Use of Socratic Type Programmed Instruction in College Courses in Psychology." Paper read at Western Psychological Association Convention, San Francisco, May, 1967.

Markle, Susan Meyer, 1964. *Good Frames and Bad: A Grammar of Frame Writing.* New York: Wiley.

Marrow, Alfred J., 1969. *The Practical Theorist: The Life and Work of Kurt Lewin.* New York: Basic Books.

Maslow, Abraham H., 1943. "A Theory of Human Motivation," *Psychological Review,* 50:370–396.

Maslow, Abraham H., 1954. *Motivation and Personality.* New York: Harper.

Maslow, Abraham H., 1968. *Toward a Psychology of Being,* 2nd ed. Princeton, N.J.: Van Nostrand.

Maslow, Abraham H., 1971. *The Farther Reaches of Human Nature.* New York: Viking.

May, Rollo, 1950. *Man's Search for Himself.* New York: Norton.

May, Rollo, 1969. *Love and Will.* New York: Norton.

McClelland, David C., 1961. *The Achieving Society.* Princeton, N.J.: Van Nostrand.

McClelland, David C., 1965. "Toward a Theory of Motive Acquisition," *American Psychologist,* 20:321–333.

McClelland, David C., J. W. Atkinson, and R. A. Clark, 1953. *The Achievement Motive.* New York: Appleton-Century-Crofts.

McGeoch, J. A., and A. L. Irion, 1952. *The Psychology of Human Learning,* 2nd ed. New York: Longmans, Green.

McIntosh, D. M., 1963. *Statistics for the Teacher.* New York: Pergamon Press.

McLaughlin, J. W., and J. T. Shea, 1960. "California Teachers' Job Dissatisfaction," *California Journal of Educational Research,* 11:216–224.

McNemar, Quinn, 1942. *The Revision of the Stanford-Binet Scale.* Boston: Houghton Mifflin.

McNemar, Quinn, 1962. *Psychological Statistics,* 3rd ed. New York: Wiley.

Meacham, Merle E., and Allen E. Wiesen, 1969. *Changing Classroom Behavior: A Manual for Precision Teaching.* New York: International Textbook Co.

Mecklenburger, J. A., J. A. Wilson, and R. W. Hostrop, 1972. *Learning C.O.D.— Can the Schools Buy Success?* Hamden, Conn.: Shoestring Press.

Medley, D. M., and H. E. Mitzel, 1963. "Measuring Classroom Behavior by Systematic Observation." In N. L. Gage (ed.), *Handbook of Research on Teaching.* Chicago: Rand McNally.

Meichenbaum, D. H., K. S. Bowers, and R. R. Ross, 1969. "A Behavioral Analysis of Teacher Expectancy Effect," *Journal of Personality and Social Psychology,* 13:306–316.

Mensh, I. N., M. B. Kantor, H. R. Domke, M. C. Gildea, and J. C. Glidwell, 1959. "Children's Behavior Symptoms and Their Relationship to School Adjustment, Sex, and Social Class," *Journal of Social Issues,* 15(1):8–15.

Mercer, Jane R., 1972. "IQ: The Lethal Label," *Psychology Today,* 6(4):44–97.

Merrill, Barbara, 1946. "A Measurement of Mother–Child Interaction," *Journal of Abnormal and Social Psychology,* 41:37–49.

Messick, Samuel, 1970. "The Criterion

Problem in the Evaluation of Instruction: Assessing Possible, Not Just Intended, Outcomes." In M. C. Wittrock and David E. Wiley (eds.), *The Evaluation of Instruction*, pp. 183–202. New York: Holt, Rinehart, & Winston.

Messick, Samuel, and N. Kogan, 1963. "Differentiation and Compartmentalization in Object-Sorting Measures of Categorizing Style," *Perceptual and Motor Skills*, 16:47–51.

Milhollan, Frank, and Bill E. Forisha, 1972. *From Skinner to Rogers—Contrasting Approaches to Education*. Lincoln, Nebr.: Professional Education Publications.

Miller, P. E., 1966. "The Effects of Age and Training on Children's Ability to Understand Certain Basic Concepts." Unpublished Ph.D. dissertation, Teachers College, Columbia University.

Money, John, and Anke A. Ehrhardt, 1973. *Man and Woman, Boy and Girl*. Baltimore: The Johns Hopkins University Press.

Montessori, Maria, 1912. *The Montessori Method*. New York: Stokes.

Montessori, Maria, 1949. *The Absorbent Mind*. New York: Dell.

Montessori, Maria, 1965. *Dr. Montessori's Own Handbook*. New York: Schocken Books.

Montessori, Maria, 1966. *Spontaneous Activity in Education*. New York: Schocken Books.

Moore, Omar Khayyam, 1966. "Autotelic Responsive Environments and Exceptional Children," in O. J. Harvey (ed.), *Experience, Structure, and Adaptability*, pp. 169–216. New York: Springer.

Morrison, H. C., 1926. *The Practice of Teaching in the Secondary School*. Chicago: University of Chicago Press.

Mosston, Muska, 1966. *Teaching Physical Education*. Columbus, Ohio: Merrill.

Mosteller, Frederick, and Daniel P. Moynihan (eds.), 1972. *On Equality of Educational Opportunity*. New York: Vintage.

Moustakas, Clark, 1956. *The Self*. New York: Harper & Row.

Moustakas, Clark, 1966. *The Authentic Teacher*. Cambridge, Mass.: Howard A. Doyle.

Moustakas, Clark E. (ed.), 1966. *The Child's Discovery of Himself*. New York: Ballantine.

Murchison, Carl (ed.), 1932. *A History of Psychology in Autobiography*, Vol. II. New York: Russell & Russell.

Murray, Henry A., and others, 1938. *Explorations in Personality*. New York: Oxford University Press.

Murray, Henry A., and Clyde Kluckhohn, 1948. *Personality in Nature, Society and Culture*. New York: Knopf.

Murrow, Casey, and Liza Murrow, 1971. *Children Come First*. New York: McGraw-Hill.

Mussen, Paul H. (ed.), 1972. *Carmichael's Manual of Child Psychology*, Vols. I & II. New York: Wiley.

Mussen, P. H., J. J. Conger, and J. Kagan, 1969. *Child Development and Personality* (3rd ed.). New York: Harper & Row.

Neill, A. S., 1960. *Summerhill*. New York: Hart.

Neill, A. S., 1966. *Freedom—Not License!* New York: Hart.

Neill, A. S., 1972. *Neill! Neill! Orange Peel!* New York: Hart.

Newman, Fred M., and Donald W. Oliver, 1967. "Education and Community," *Harvard Educational Review*, 37(1):61–106.

Newman, S. E., 1957. "Student vs. Instructor Design of Study Methods," *Journal of Educational Psychology*, 48:328–333.

Nixon, Robert E., 1962. *The Art of Growing*. New York: Random House.

Northway, M. L., 1940. "A Method for Depicting Social Relationships Obtained by Sociometric Testing," *Sociometry*, 3:144–150.

Nyquist, Ewald B., and Gene R. Hawes (eds.), 1972. *Open Education: A Sourcebook for Parents and Teachers*. New York: Bantam.

Office of Economic Opportunity, 1972. *An Experiment in Performance Contracting: Summary of Preliminary Results*.

OEO Pamphlet 3400–5. Washington, D. C.

Ojemann, Ralph H., 1968. "Should Educational Objectives Be Stated in Behavioral Terms?" *Elementary School Journal,* 68(5):223–231.

Ojemann, Ralph H., and Karen Pritchett, 1963. "Piaget and the Role of Guided Experience in Human Development," *Perceptual and Motor Skills,* 17:927–40.

O'Kane, James M., 1972. "Skidding and Making it," *Change,* 4(1):6–23.

Olson, W. C., and B. O. Hughes, 1950. *Manual for the Description of Growth in Age Units.* Ann Arbor: University of Michigan Elementary School.

Olton, Robert M., and Richard S. Crutchfield, 1969. "Developing the Skills of Productive Thinking," in Paul H. Mussen, Jonas Langer, and Martin Covington (eds.), *Trends and Issues in Developmental Psychology.* New York: Holt, Rinehart and Winston.

Ortego, Philip D., 1971a. *Montezuma's Children.* El Paso, Texas: Chicano Research Institute.

Ortego, Philip D., 1971b. "Schools for Mexican-Americans: Between Two Cultures," *Saturday Review,* April 17, 1971, pp. 62–81.

Orwell, George, 1946. *Animal Farm.* New York: Harcourt, Brace, & World.

Orwell, George, 1949. *1984.* New York: Harcourt, Brace, & World.

Ozmon, Howard, and Sam Craver, 1972. *Busing: A Moral Issue.* Bloomington, Indiana: Phi Delta Kappa Educational Foundation.

Page, Ellis B., 1972. "Miracle in Milwaukee: Raising the IQ," *Educational Researcher,* 1(10):8–16.

Passow, A. Harry, ed., 1967. *Reaching the Disadvantaged Learner.* New York: Teachers College Press.

Pavlov, Ivan, 1960. *Conditioned Reflexes.* Translated by Anrep. New York: Dover Press.

Peddiwell, J. Abner, 1939. *The Saber-Tooth Curriculum.* New York: McGraw-Hill.

Perrone, Vito, 1972. *Open Education: Promise and Problems.* Bloomington, Indiana: Phi Delta Kappa.

Pestalozzi, Johann, 1969. *The Education of Man.* New York: Greenwood Press.

Peters, Charles C., and Walter R. Van Voorhis, 1940. *Statistical Procedures and Their Mathematical Bases.* New York: McGraw-Hill.

Peters, William, 1971. *A Class Divided.* Garden City, N. Y.: Doubleday.

Pettigrew, T. F., 1958. "The Measurement and Correlates of Category Width as a Cognitive Variable," *Journal of Personality,* 26:532–544.

Phillips, John L., Jr., 1969. *The Origins of Intellect: Piaget's Theory.* San Francisco: Freeman.

Piaget, Jean, 1950. *The Psychology of Intelligence.* London: Routledge and Kegan Paul.

Piaget, Jean, 1952. *The Language and Thought of the Child.* London: Routledge and Kegan Paul.

Piaget, Jean, 1952. *The Origins of Intelligence in Children.* New York: International Universities Press.

Piaget, Jean, 1953. "How Children Form Mathematical Concepts," *Scientific American,* 189:74–79.

Piaget, Jean, 1963. *Origins of Intelligence in Children.* New York: Norton.

Piaget, Jean, 1970. *Science of Education and the Psychology of the Child.* New York: Grossman.

Piaget, Jean, and Barbel Inhelder, 1969. *The Psychology of the Child.* New York: Basic Books.

Pines, Maya, 1967. *Revolution in Learning.* New York: Harper & Row.

Pines, Maya, 1969, "Why Some Three-year-olds Get A's—and Some Get C's," *New York Times Magazine,* July 6, pp. 4–17.

Pipe, Peter, 1966. *Practical Programming.* New York: Holt, Rinehart and Winston.

Pistor, F., 1940. "How Time Concepts Are Acquired by Children," *Educational Method,* 20:107–112.

Pittenger, Owen E., and C. Thomas Gooding, 1971. *Learning Theories in Educational Practice.* New York: Wiley.

Pitts, Carl E. (ed.), 1971. *Operant Conditioning in the Classroom.* New York: Crowell.

Plowden, Lady B., et al., 1967. *Children and Their Primary Schools: A Report of the Central Advisory Council for Education*. London: Her Majesty's Stationery Office.

Polya, G., 1954. *How to Solve It*. Princeton, N. J.: Princeton University Press.

Postlethwait, S. N., and J. D. Novak, 1967. "The Use of 8-mm Loop Films in Individualized Instruction," *Annals of the New York Academy of Science*, 142:464–470.

Postman, Neil, and Charles Weingartner, 1969. *Teaching as a Subversive Activity*. New York: Delacorte Press.

Postman, Neil, and Charles Weingartner, 1971. *The Soft Revolution*. New York: Delacorte Press.

Poteet, James A., 1973. *Behavior Modification: A Practical Guide for Teachers*. Minneapolis: Burgess.

"The Power of Competency-Based Teacher Education," 1972. Report of the U.S. Office of Education, Task Force '72. Committee on National Program Priorities in Teacher Education. Washington, D. C.

Premack, David, 1965. "Reinforcement Theory," in D. Levine (ed.), *Nebraska Symposium on Motivation, 1965*, pp. 123–188. Lincoln, Nebr.: University of Nebraska Press.

Pronko, N. H., 1969. "On Learning to Play the Violin at the Age of Four without Tears," *Psychology Today*, 2(12):52–66.

Pulaski, Mary A., 1971. *Understanding Piaget: An Introduction to Children's Cognitive Development*. New York: Harper & Row.

Putnam, Tracy J., 1958. *Epilepsy: What It Is and What to Do about It*. Philadelphia: Lippincott.

Radke, Marian J., 1946. *The Relation of Parental Authority to Children's Behavior and Attitudes*. Minneapolis: University of Minnesota Press.

Rambusch, Nancy M., 1962. *Learning How to Learn: An American Approach to Montessori*. Baltimore: Helicon Press.

Rasberry, Salli, and Robert Greenway, 1970. *Rasberry Exercises*. Sebastopol, Cal.: Freestone Publishing Co.

Raths, Louis, Merrill Harmin, and Sidney B. Simon, 1966. *Values and Teaching*. Columbus, Ohio: Merrill.

Read, K. H., 1945. "Parents' Expressed Attitudes and Children's Behavior," *Journal of Consulting Psychology*, 9:95–100.

Redl, Fritz, and William W. Wattenberg, 1959. *Mental Hygiene in Teaching*, 2nd ed. New York: Harcourt, Brace and World.

Reich, Charles A., 1970. *The Greening of America*. New York: Random House.

Repo, Satu, ed., 1970. *This Book Is About Schools*. New York: Random House.

Report of the National Advisory Commission on Civil Disorders, 1968. New York: Bantam Books.

Rheingold, H. L., 1956. *The Modification of Social Responsiveness in Institutional Babies*. Monographs of the Society for Research on Child Development, 21, No. 2. Lafayette, Ind.: Child Development Publications.

Rheingold, H. L., and N. Bayley, 1959. "The Later Effects of an Experimental Modification of Mothering," *Child Development*, 30(3):363–372.

Ribble, Margaret, 1943. *The Rights of Infants*. New York: Columbia University Press.

Riesen, A. H., 1958. "Plasticity of Behavior: Psychological Aspects," in H. F. Harlow and C. H. Woolsey (eds.), *Biological and Biochemical Bases of Behavior*, pp. 425–450. Madison: University of Wisconsin Press.

Riessman, Frank, 1962. *The Culturally Deprived Child*. New York: Harper & Row.

Riessman, Frank, and Hermine L. Popper, 1968. *Up from Poverty*. New York: Harper & Row.

Robbins, Melvyn P., 1966. "A Study of the Validity of Delacato's Theory of Neurological Organization," *Exceptional Children*, 32:517–523.

Robinson, Francis P., 1961. *Effective Study*. New York: Harper & Row.

Robinson, Halbert B., and Nancy M.

Robinson, 1965. *The Mentally Retarded Child.* New York: McGraw-Hill.

Roe, A., 1960. *Automated Teaching Methods Using Linear Programs.* Report No. 60–105. Los Angeles: Department of Engineering, University of California.

Roethlisberger, F. J., and W. J. Dickson, 1939. *Management and the Worker.* Cambridge, Mass.: Harvard University Press.

Rogers, Carl R., 1951. *Client-Centered Therapy.* Boston: Houghton Mifflin.

Rogers, Carl R., 1961. *On Becoming a Person.* Boston: Houghton Mifflin.

Rogers, Carl R., 1963. "Learning to Be Free," in S. Farber and R. Wilson (eds.), *Conflict and Creativity: Control of the Mind.* New York: McGraw-Hill.

Rogers, Carl R., 1964. "What Psychology Has to Offer Teacher Education." Paper prepared for Conference on Educational Foundations, Cornell University, April 27–28, 1964.

Rogers, Carl R., 1969. *Freedom to Learn.* Columbus, Ohio: Merrill.

Rogers, Carl R., 1972. *Carl Rogers on Encounter Groups.* New York: Harper & Row.

Rogers, Carl R., and Barry Stevens, 1967. *Person to Person: The Problem of Being Human.* Lafayette, Calif.: Real People Press.

Rosenthal, Robert, 1966. *Experimenter Bias Effects in Behavioral Research.* New York: Appleton-Century-Crofts.

Rosenthal, Robert, 1969. "On Not So Replicated Experiments and Not So Null Results," *Journal of Consulting and Clinical Psychology,* 33:7–10.

Rosenthal, Robert, and Lenore Jacobson, 1968. *Pygmalion in the Classroom.* New York: Holt, Rinehart and Winston.

Ross, Leonard Q., 1938. *The Education of H°Y°M°A°N K°A°P°L°A°N.* New York: Harper.

Rossi, Alice S., 1969. "Equality between the Sexes: An Immodest Proposal," in Rose Laub Coser (ed.), *Life Cycle and Achievement in America.* New York: Harper & Row.

Rosten, Leo, 1959. *The Return of H°Y°M°A°N K°A°P°L°A°N.* New York: Harper.

Rothbart, Myron, Susan Dalfen, and Robert Barrett, 1971. "Effects of Teacher's Expectancy on Student-Teacher Interaction," *Journal of Educational Psychology,* 62(1):49–54.

Rothkopf, E. Z., 1970. "The Concept of Mathemagenic Activities," *Review of Educational Research,* 40:325–336.

Rothman, Esther, 1971. *The Angel Inside Went Sour.* New York: McKay.

Rubin, David, 1972. *The Rights of Teachers.* New York: Avon.

Rubovits, Pamela C., and Martin L. Maehr, 1971. "Pygmalion Analyzed: Toward an Explanation of the Rosenthal-Jacobson Findings," *Journal of Personality and Social Psychology,* 19(2):197–203.

Sanders, Norris M., 1966. *Classroom Questions: What Kinds?* New York: Harper & Row.

Sarason, Irwin G., and others (eds.), 1971. *Reinforcing Productive Classroom Behavior: A Teacher's Guide to Behavior Modification.* New York: Behavioral Publications.

Schlesinger, H. J., 1959. "Cognitive Attitudes in Relation to Susceptibility to Interference," *Journal of Personality,* 22:354–374.

Schmidt, Bernardine G., 1946. "Changes in Personal, Social, and Intellectual Behavior of Children Originally Classified as Feebleminded," *Psychological Monographs,* No. 5, p. 60.

Schmidt, Gilbert W., and Roger E. Ulrich, 1969. "Effects of Group Contingent Events upon Classroom Noise," *Journal of Applied Behavior Analysis,* 2:171–179.

Schoer, Lowell A., 1970. *Test Construction: A Programmed Guide.* Boston: Allyn & Bacon.

Scott, John Paul, 1968. *Early Experience and the Organization of Behavior.* Belmont, Calif.: Brooks/Cole.

Scott, W. A., 1963. "Conceptualizing and Measuring Structural Properties of Cognition." In O. J. Harvey (ed.), *Motivation and Social Interaction.* New York: Ronald Press.

Scriven, Michael, 1967. "The Methodology of Evaluation." In Ralph W. Tyler and others (eds.), *Perspectives of Curriculum Evaluation,* pp. 39–83. Chicago: Rand McNally.

Seagoe, May V., 1970. *The Learning Process and School Practice.* Scranton, Pa.: Chandler.

Sears, Pauline S., 1940. "Levels of Aspiration in Academically Successful and Unsuccessful Children," *Journal of Abnormal and Social Psychology,* 35:498–536.

Sears, Pauline S., and Ernest R. Hilgard, 1964. "The Teacher's Role in the Motivation of the Learner," in Ernest R. Hilgard (ed.), *Theories of Learning and Instruction,* 63rd Yearbook, Part I, National Society for the Study of Education. Chicago: University of Chicago Press.

Segal, Rebecca, 1972. *Got No Time to Fool Around.* Philadelphia: Westminster Press.

Sellar, W. C., and R. J. Yeatman, 1931. *1066 and All That.* New York: Dutton.

Sexton, Patricia, 1969. *The Feminized Male.* New York: Random House.

Sexton, Patricia, 1970. "How the American Boy is Feminized," *Psychology Today,* 3(8):23–67.

Shaffer, Laurence, and Edward Shoben, Jr., 1956. *The Psychology of Adjustment,* 2nd ed. Boston: Houghton Mifflin.

Shaw, Alfred L., 1969. "Confirmation of Expectancy and Change in Teacher's Evaluations of Student Behavior," *Dissertation Abstracts International,* 30(5-A):1878–79.

Shockley, William, 1971. "Negro IQ Deficit: Failure of a 'Malicious Coincidence' Model Warrants New Research Proposals," *Review of Educational Research,* 41(3):227–248.

Shuey, Audrey M., 1966. *The Testing of Negro Intelligence* (2nd ed.). New York: Social Science Press.

Shulman, Lee S., and Evan R. Keislar (eds.), 1966. *Learning by Discovery.* Chicago: Rand McNally.

Shuttleworth, F. K., 1939. "The Physical and Mental Growth of Girls and Boys Age Six to Nineteen in Relation to Age at Maximum Growth," *Monographs of the Society for Research in Child Development.* 46(210).

Sidman, M., and L. T. Stoddard, 1966. "Programming Perception and Learning for Retarded Children," *International Review of Research on Mental Retardation,* 2:151–208.

Silberman, Charles E., 1970. *Crisis in the Classroom.* New York: Random House.

Simon, Sidney B., Leland W. Howe, and Howard Kirschenbaum, 1972. *Values Clarification: A Handbook of Practical Strategies for Teachers and Students.* New York: Hart.

Skeels, H. M., R. Updegraff, B. L. Wellman, and H. M. Williams, 1938. *A Study of Environmental Stimulation: An Orphanage Preschool Project.* University of Iowa Studies in Child Welfare, 16(1).

Skinner, B. F., 1938. *The Behavior of Organisms.* New York: Appleton-Century-Crofts.

Skinner, B. F., 1948. *Walden Two.* New York: Macmillan.

Skinner, B. F., 1951. "How to Teach Animals," *Scientific American,* 185(6):26–29.

Skinner, B. F., 1953. *Science and Human Behavior.* New York: Macmillan.

Skinner, B. F., 1957. *Verbal Behavior.* New York: Appleton-Century-Crofts.

Skinner, B. F., 1968. *The Technology of Teaching.* New York: Appleton-Century-Crofts.

Skinner, B. F., 1971. *Beyond Freedom and Dignity.* New York: Knopf.

Skinner, B. F., and Sue Ann Krakower, 1968. *Handwriting with Write and See.* Chicago: Lyons & Carnahan.

Smedslund, J. 1961. "The Acquisition of Conservation of Substance and Weight in Children," *Scandinavian Journal of Psychology,* 2:11–20, 71–84, 85–87, 153–155, 156–160, 203–210.

Smith, G. M., 1962. *A Simplified Guide to Statistics for Psychology and Education.* New York: Holt, Rinehart and Winston.

Smith, H. Allen, 1956. *Write Me a Poem,*

Baby. Boston: Little, Brown.

Smith, H. Allen, 1959. *Don't Get Perconel with a Chicken.* Boston: Little, Brown.

Smith, Mortimer, 1954. *The Diminished Mind.* Chicago: Regnery.

Snitzer, Herb, 1968. *Living at Summerhill.* New York: Collier Books.

Snow, Richard E., 1969. "Unfinished Pygmalion," *Contemporary Psychology,* 14:197–199.

Sorensen, J. S., E. A. Schwenn, and Herbert J. Klausmeier, 1969. "The Individual Conference: A Motivational Device for Increasing Independent Reading in the Elementary Grades." Practical Paper No. 8. Madison, Wis.: Wisconsin Research and Development Center for Cognitive Learning.

Sorensen, J. S., E. A. Schwenn, and J. Bavry, 1970. "The Use of Individual and Group Goal-Setting Conferences as a Motivational Device to Improve Student Conduct and Increase Student Self-Direction: A Preliminary Study." Technical Report No. 123. Madison, Wis.: Wisconsin Research and Development Center for Cognitive Learning.

Spearman, Charles, 1927. *The Abilities of Man: Their Nature and Measurement.* New York: Macmillan.

Spiro, Melford E., 1963. *Kibbutz: Venture in Utopia.* New York: Schocken.

Spiro, Melford E., 1965. *Children of the Kibbutz.* New York: Schocken.

Spitz, René, and K. M. Wolf, 1946. "Anaclitic Depression; an Inquiry into the Genesis of Psychiatric Conditions in Early Childhood, II," in A. Freud et al. (eds.), *The Psychoanalytic Study of the Child,* Vol. II. New York: International Universities Press.

Standing, E. M., 1966. *The Montessori Revolution.* New York: Schocken Books.

Stennett, R. G., 1966. "Emotional Handicap in the Elementary Years: Phase or Disease?" *American Journal of Orthopsychiatry,* 34:444–449.

Stephens, J. M., 1956. *Educational Psychology.* 2nd ed. New York: Holt.

Stephens, J. M., 1965. *The Psychology of Classroom Learning.* New York: Holt, Rinehart and Winston.

Stephens, J. M., 1967. *The Process of Schooling.* New York: Holt, Rinehart and Winston.

Stone, L. Joseph, and Joseph Church, 1972. *Childhood and Adolescence* (3rd ed.). New York: Random House.

Suchman, J. Richard, 1961. "Inquiry Training: Building Skills for Autonomous Discovery," *Merrill-Palmer Quarterly,* 7(3):147–171.

Sullivan, Harry Stack, 1953. *The Interpersonal Theory of Psychiatry.* New York: Norton.

Taba, Hilda, and Deborah Elkins, 1966. *Teaching Strategies for the Culturally Disadvantaged.* Chicago: Rand McNally.

Taber, J. I., R. Glaser, and H. H. Schaefer, 1965. *Learning and Programmed Instruction.* Reading, Mass.: Addison-Wesley.

Tanner, Daniel, 1972. *Using Behavioral Objectives in the Classroom.* New York: Macmillan.

Tanner, J. M., 1963. "The Regulation of Human Growth," *Child Development,* 34(4):817–847.

Tanner, J. M., 1968. "Earlier Maturation in Man," *Scientific American,* 218:21–28.

Taylor, Calvin W., and Frank Barron, 1963. *Scientific Creativity.* New York: Wiley.

Taylor, D. W., P. C. Berry, and C. H. Black, 1958. "Does Group Participation When Using Brainstorming Facilitate or Inhibit Creative Thinking?" *Administrative Science Quarterly,* 3:23–47.

Terman, Lewis M., 1916. *The Measurement of Intelligence.* Boston: Houghton Mifflin.

Terman, Lewis M., and Maud A. Merrill, 1937. *Measuring Intelligence.* Boston: Houghton Mifflin.

Terman, Lewis, and Maud A. Merrill, 1960. *Stanford-Binet Intelligence Scale: Manual for the Third Revision, Form L-M.* Boston: Houghton Mifflin.

Terman, Lewis, and Melita Oden, 1925.

Genetic Studies of Genius: Mental and Physical Traits of a Thousand Gifted Children. Stanford, Calif.: Stanford University Press.

Terman, Lewis, and Melita Oden, 1954. *Genetic Studies of Genius: The Gifted Group at Mid-Life. Thirty-five Years' Follow-up of the Superior Child.* Stanford, Calif.: Stanford University Press.

Thelen, Herbert A., 1960. *Education and the Human Quest.* New York: Wiley.

Thelen, Herbert A., 1967. *Classroom Grouping for Teachability.* New York: Wiley.

Thomas, Don R., Wesley C. Becker, and Marianne Armstrong, 1968. "Production and Elimination of Disruptive Classroom Behavior by Systematically Varying Teacher's Behavior," *Journal of Applied Behavior Analysis,* 1:35–45.

Thompson, W. R., and W. Heron, 1954. "The Effects of Restricting Early Experience on the Problem-solving Capacity of Dogs," *Canadian Journal of Psychology,* 8:17–31.

Thorndike, Edward L., 1898. "Animal Intelligence: An Experimental Study of the Associative Processes in Animals," *Psychological Monographs,* 2(4).

Thorndike, Edward L., 1924. "Mental Discipline in High School Studies," *Journal of Educational Psychology,* 15:1–22, 83–98.

Thorndike, Edward L., 1932. *The Fundamentals of Learning.* New York: Teachers College, Columbia University.

Thorndike, Robert L., 1963. "The Measurement of Creativity," *Teachers College Record,* 64:422–424.

Thorndike, Robert L., 1968. "Review of *Pygmalion in the Classroom,*" *Educational Research Journal,* 5:709–711.

Thorndike, Robert L., and Elizabeth Hagen, 1969. *Measurement and Evaluation in Psychology and Education* (3rd ed.). New York: Wiley.

Thurstone, L. L., and Thelma G. Thurstone, 1941. *Factorial Studies of Intelligence.* Chicago: University of Chicago Press.

Tiger, Lionel, and Robin Fox, 1971. *The Imperial Animal.* New York: Holt, Rinehart, & Winston.

Toffler, Alvin, 1970. *Future Shock.* New York: Random House.

Tolor, Alexander, William L. Scarpetti, and Paul A. Lane, 1967. "Teachers' Attitudes Toward Children's Behavior Revisited," *Journal of Educational Psychology,* 58:175–180.

Tolstoy, Leo, 1967. *Tolstoy on Education.* Translated by Leo Wiener. Chicago: University of Chicago Press.

Torrance, Ellis Paul, 1960. *Status of Knowledge Concerning Education and Creative Scientific Talent.* Minneapolis: University of Minnesota Press.

Torrance, Ellis Paul, 1962a. "Developing Creative Thinking through School Experiences," in S. Parnes and G. Harding (eds.), *A Source Book for Creative Thinking.* New York: Scribner.

Torrance, Ellis Paul, 1962b. *Guiding Creative Talent.* Englewood Cliffs, N. J.: Prentice-Hall.

Torrance, Ellis Paul, 1965. *Gifted Children in the Classroom.* New York: Macmillan.

Torrance, Ellis Paul, 1966. *Torrance Tests of Creative Thinking. Norms-Technical Manual.* Princeton, N. J.: Personnel Press.

Townsend, E. A., and P. J. Burke, 1963. *Statistics for the Classroom Teacher, a Self-teaching Unit.* New York: Macmillan.

Travers, R. W. M., (ed.), 1972. *Handbook of Research on Teaching,* 2nd ed. Chicago: Rand McNally.

Troost, Cornelius J., (ed.), 1973. *Radical School Reform: Critique and Alternatives.* Boston: Little, Brown.

Trowbridge, M. H., and Cason, H., 1932. "An Experimental Study of Thorndike's Theory of Learning," *Journal of General Psychology,* 7:245–258.

Trubowitz, Sidney, 1968. *A Handbook for Teaching in the Ghetto School.* Chicago: Quadrangle Books.

Trump, J. Lloyd, 1959. *Images of the*

Future. Washington: National Association of Secondary School Principals.

Trump, J. Lloyd, and Delmas F. Miller, 1968. *Secondary School Curriculum Improvement: Proposals and Procedures.* Boston: Allyn & Bacon.

Tyler, F. T., 1964. "Issues Related to Readiness to Learn," in Ernest R. Hilgard (ed.), *Theories of Learning and Instruction,* 63rd Yearbook, Part I, National Society for the Study of Education. Chicago: University of Chicago Press.

Tyler, Leona E. (ed.), 1969. *Intelligence: Some Recurring Issues: An Enduring Problem in Psychology.* New York: Van Nostrand-Reinhold.

Tyler, Ralph W., 1934. "Some Findings from Studies in the Field of College Biology," *Science,* 18:133–142.

Tyler, Ralph W., 1964. "Some Persistent Questions on the Defining of Objectives," in C. M. Lindvall (ed.), *Defining Educational Objectives.* Pittsburgh: University of Pittsburgh Press.

Tyler, Ralph W., 1966. "The Objectives and Plans for National Assessment of Educational Progress," *Journal of Educational Measurement,* 3:1–4.

Ulich, Robert S., 1954. *Three Thousand Years of Educational Wisdom.* Cambridge, Mass.: Harvard University Press.

Ullman, C. E., 1952. *Identification of Maladjusted School Children.* Public Health Monograph No. 7. Washington, D. C.: U. S. Government Printing Office.

Underwood, Benton J., 1964. "Laboratory Studies of Verbal Learning," in Ernest R. Hilgard (ed.), *Theories of Learning and Instruction,* 63rd Yearbook, Part I, National Society for the Study of Education. Chicago: University of Chicago Press.

Valett, Robert E., 1967. *The Remediation of Learning Disabilities.* Palo Alto, Cal.: Fearon.

Valett, Robert E., 1968. *The Psychoeducational Inventory of Basic Learning Abilities.* Palo Alto, Cal.: Fearon.

Valett, Robert E., 1969. *Programming Learning Disabilities.* Palo Alto, Cal.: Fearon.

Vasquez, Richard, 1970. *Chicano.* New York: Doubleday.

Vilar, Esther, 1973. *The Manipulated Man.* New York: Farrar, Straus, & Giroux.

Voeks, Virginia, 1970. *On Becoming an Educated Person* (3rd ed.). Philadelphia: Saunders.

Vygotsky, L., 1962. "The Development of Scientific Concepts in Childhood," in E. Hanfmann and G. Vokar (eds. and trans.), *Thought and Language,* pp. 82–118. New York: Wiley.

Walberg, Herbert J., and Susan Christie Thomas, 1972. "Open Education: A Classroom Validation in Great Britain and the United States," *American Educational Research Journal,* 9(2):197–208.

Wallas, G., 1921. *The Art of Thought.* New York: Harcourt, Brace and World.

Washburne, Carleton W., 1922. "Educational Measurements as A Key to Individualizing Instruction and Promotions," *Journal of Educational Research,* 5:195–206.

Watson, John B., 1924. *Psychology from the Standpoint of a Behaviorist.* Philadelphia: Lippincott.

Watson, John B., 1925. *Behaviorism.* New York: Norton.

Watson, John B., 1928. *Psychological Care of Infant and Child.* New York: Norton.

Watson, John B., and R. Rayner, 1920. "Conditioned Emotional Reactions," *Journal of Experimental Psychology,* 3:1–14.

Watson, Peter, 1972. "IQ: The Racial Gap," *Psychology Today,* 6(4):48–99.

Weber, Lillian, 1971. *The English Infant School and Informal Education.* Englewood Cliffs, N. J.: Prentice-Hall.

Webster, Staten W. (ed.), 1966. *The Disadvantaged Learner.* San Francisco: Chandler.

Wechsler, David, 1944. *The Measurement of Adult Intelligence.* Baltimore: Williams & Wilkins.

Wechsler, David, 1949. *Wechsler Intelligence Scale for Children.* New York: Psychological Corporation.

Wechsler, David, 1955. *The Wechsler Adult Intelligence Scale Manual.* New York: Psychological Corporation.

Welch, Elizabeth A., 1967. "The Effects of Segregated and Partially Integrated School Programs on Self-Concept and Academic Achievement of Educable Mentally Retarded Children," *Exceptional Children,*34:93–100.

White, Burton L., Jean Carew Watts, and others, 1973. *Experience and Environment: Major Influences on the Development of the Young Child,* Vol. I. Englewood Cliffs, N. J.: Prentice-Hall.

White, Robert W., 1959. "Motivation Reconsidered: The Concept of Competence," *Psychological Review,* 66:297–333.

White, Robert W., 1966. *Lives in Progress,* 2nd ed. New York: Holt, Rinehart and Winston.

Whiting, J. W. M., and I. L. Child, 1953. *Child Training and Personality: A Cross-Cultural Study.* New Haven, Conn.: Yale University Press.

Whyte, William H., Jr., 1956. *The Organization Man.* Garden City, N.Y.: Doubleday.

Wickman, E. K., 1928. *Children's Behavior and Teacher's Attitudes.* New York: Commonwealth Fund, Division of Publications.

Wilson, S. R., and D. T. Tosti, 1972. *Learning is Getting Easier.* San Rafael, Cal.: Individual Learning Systems.

Winder, Alvin, and David Angus (eds.), 1968. *Adolescence: Contemporary Studies.* New York: American Book Co.

Witkin, H. A., and others, 1962. *Psychological Differentiation.* New York: Wiley.

Wittrock, M. C., 1966. "The Learning by Discovery Hypothesis," in Lee S. Shulman and Evan R. Keislar (eds.), *Learning by Discovery.* Chicago: Rand McNally.

Wittrock, M. C., and David E. Wiley, (eds.), 1970. *The Evaluation of Instruction.* New York: Holt, Rinehart, & Winston.

Wohlwill, J. F., 1959. "Un Essai d'Apprentissage dans le Domaine du Nombre," in J. Piaget (ed.), *Etudes d'Epistémologie Génétique,* Vol. 9. Paris: Presses Universitaires de France, 1959.

Woodring, Paul, 1953. *Let's Talk Sense about Our Schools.* New York: McGraw-Hill.

Woodring, Paul, 1957. *A Fourth of a Nation.* New York: McGraw-Hill.

Woodring, Paul, 1957b. *New Directions in Teacher Education.* New York: Fund for the Advancement of Education.

Woodring, Paul, 1965. *Introduction to American Education.* New York: Harcourt, Brace and World.

Woodring, Paul, 1968. *The Higher Learning in America: A Reassessment.* New York: McGraw-Hill.

Woodworth, R. S., 1938. *Experimental Psychology.* New York: Holt.

Wright, A. Richard, 1945. *Black Boy.* New York: Harper.

Yarrow, L. J., 1961. "Maternal Deprivation: Toward an Empirical and Conceptual Reevaluation," *Psychological Bulletin,* 58(6):459–490.

Young, Michael, 1959. *The Rise of the Meritocracy.* New York: Random House.

Zeigarnik, B., 1927. Uber das Behalten von erledigten und unerledigten Handlungen, *Psychologische Forschung,* 9:1–85.

INDEX